THE STATE OF THE EUROPEAN UNION

VOLUME 7

A project of the European Union Studies Association

PREVIOUS TITLES IN THE SERIES

VOLUME 6: Law, Politics, and Society
Edited by Tanja A. Börzel and Rachel A. Cichowski

VOLUME 5: Risks, Reform, Resistance, and Revival
Edited by Maria Green Cowles and Michael Smith

VOLUME 4: Deepening and Widening
Edited by Pierre-Henri Laurent and Marc Maresceau

VOLUME 3: Building a European Polity?
Edited by Carolyn Rhodes and Sonia Mazey

VOLUME 2: The Maastricht Debates and Beyond
Edited by Alan W. Cafruny and Glenda G. Rosenthal

VOLUME 1: Policies, Institutions, Debates in the Transition Years
Edited by Leon Hurwitz and Christian Lequesne

The State of the European Union

With US or Against US? European Trends in American Perspective

VOLUME 7

edited by

NICOLAS JABKO and CRAIG PARSONS

OXFORD
UNIVERSITY PRESS

This book has been printed digitally and produced in a standard specification in order to ensure its continuing availability

OXFORD
UNIVERSITY PRESS

Great Clarendon Street, Oxford OX2 6DP

Oxford University Press is a department of the University of Oxford.
It furthers the University's objective of excellence in research, scholarship,
and education by publishing worldwide in

Oxford New York

Auckland Cape Town Dar es Salaam Hong Kong Karachi
Kuala Lumpur Madrid Melbourne Mexico City Nairobi
New Delhi Shanghai Taipei Toronto
With offices in
Argentina Austria Brazil Chile Czech Republic France Greece
Guatemala Hungary Italy Japan South Korea Poland Portugal
Singapore Switzerland Thailand Turkey Ukraine Vietnam

Oxford is a registered trade mark of Oxford University Press
in the UK and in certain other countries

Published in the United States
by Oxford University Press Inc., New York

Reprinted 2007

ISBN 978-0-19-928395-8

PREFACE

The State of the European Union: With US or Against US? European Trends in American Perspective is Volume 7 in a series sponsored by the European Union Studies Association (EUSA) and published by Oxford University Press. EUSA is a large, international, and lively organization of scholars interested in the construction of Europe housed at the University of Pittsburgh (USA). EUSA's annual volume has become a landmark in the field, with each edition sharply focused on an important and timely topic treated by a team of prominent and well-informed specialists. Volume 7, put together by Nicolas Jabko and Craig Parsons, may be the best yet.

Observers of European integration are well aware that Europe has developed "Atlantically." From the 1940s until today, the creation of what is now the European Union (EU) has been conditioned by the power and purposes of the USA, most often as key European leaders sought ways to maximize their choice and autonomy in a broader order largely shaped by Americans. The Coal and Steel Community (ECSC) came out of complicated European maneuverings around American determination to rearm Germany in the early stages of Cold War. The Rome Treaties were in part an economic response to the seeming permanence of Cold War and confirmed American strategic dominance over Western Europe. The EEC's crises in the 1970s were a response to American monetary policy changes, in particular the closing of the Bretton Woods "gold window." The European Monetary System (EMS) which emerged, was meant as a way of stabilizing European exchange rates to save the "Common Market." Subsequently the vicissitudes of the EMS, almost always prompted by international shifts related to US monetary policies, led eventually to, Economic and Monetary Union (EMU) and the Euro. The renewal of European integration in the 1980s around the Single Market Program and EMU were designed to confront dramatic US-led international market changes signaling the emergence of globalization. In general, transatlantic trade and security issues have been central on both sides of the great Ocean, through the GATT, WTO and NATO. Seasoned sailors know that the Atlantic flows in unpredictable ways. The development of EU Europe has consistently confirmed their wisdom, as will this volume.

The end of Cold War after 1989 brought unforeseen consequences for both the US and EU Europe. Europe's collective security blanket abruptly had a different texture, shown by sad events in Yugoslavia, endless defense reviews, St. Malo, and the European Security and Defenses Policy (ESDP), such as it has turned out to be. It has been hard for the EU and its member states to reconsider their place in the world. Their small northwestern corner of the European continent had its comforts and the brave new post-Cold War world was full of new problems, sometimes even with the US, as Iraq showed. Europe's noble democratizing mission, honed on Greece, Spain, and Portugal, had to be rethought to greet ex-Communist countries on the other side of what had once been an Iron Curtain. Enlargement to the East, fundamental to Central and Eastern European transitions to democracy, nonetheless threatened institutional, economic, and political balances that the Cold War EU had earlier struck. In the trade realm, where transatlantic realities had been paramount, European economies were challenged by competitive goods, services, and ways of doing things from a rapidly globalizing environment, despite the Single Market, EMU and the Euro. These challenges, often originating across the Atlantic, threatened what has been called the "European model of society." And if the US remained the economic superpower that Europeans know, former Cold War adversaries and neutrals, like China and India, emerged to create a world that Europeans have been at pains to understand. To cope, the EU had to change its institutions to enhance their efficiency and accountability, hence the unending Intergovernmental Conferences, Treaties and Constitutions which have consumed immense amounts of energy but seem never to resolve things. Europe is becoming a quasi-federal something, but what? Answering this has led to new reflections on how other such federal somethings, including the US, came into being. Finally, EU member states, large and small, have had to rethink their positions on integration, with the US trying to influence them in the process. At the same time European peoples have become ever more perplexed, even skeptical, about where it all may lead.

The State of the European Union: With US or Against US? European Trends in American Perspective is perfectly timed to consider these issues. Jabko and Parsons have assembled a stellar team of specialists and assigned them to consider the full range of matters on transatlantic tables. What kinds of foreign economic and security policies is EU Europe moving toward, and how do they fit with those the US seems so intent on promoting? What institutional balance between the local, national and transnational has Europe been creating? The EU has worked intensively since the mid-1980s to build an economic order that can stand up to new competition and globalization, but is this work paying off? Are European identities and "belongingness" advancing or retreating? How have Americans—leaders and ordinary citizens—responded to the challenges of European change? For answers to many of these central questions, plus a very large number of important insights, EUSA invites you to read the remarkable pages that follow.

George Ross, Chair, EUSA, Morris Hillquit Professor in Labor and Social Thought (Sociology and Politics), Brandeis University, and Senior Faculty Associate, Minda de Gunzburg Center for European Studies, Harvard University.

ACKNOWLEDGEMENTS

This project would not have taken place without the support of the Maxwell European Union Center at the Maxwell School of Syracuse University, which is itself supported by generous funding from the European Commission. The editors are also grateful to the directors and staff of the Centre d'Études et de Recherches Internationales (CERI) and Sciences-Po in Paris, which hosted and helped organize the two meetings of our contributors in 2003 and 2004. We also thank the European Union Studies Association for selecting our project for placement in the prestigious "State of the EU" series, which is the best venue for this research we could have imagined.

Nicolas Jabko and Craig Parsons
Paris and Eugene, Oregon

CONTENTS

LIST OF FIGURES

LIST OF TABLES

LIST OF BOXES

LIST OF ABBREVIATIONS

AARP	American Association of Retired People
AIM	Alternative Investment Market
ASH	Action on Smoking and Health
BEPGs	Broad Economic Policy Guidelines
BSE	Bovine Spongiform Encephalopathy
CDU	Christian Democratic Union
CEE	Central and Eastern Europe
CEEP	European Centre of Enterprises with Public Participation and of Enterprises of General Economic Interest
CESR	Committee of European Securities Regulators
CFSP	Common Foreign and Security Policy
CJD	Creutzfelt-Jacob Disease
CJS	Council General Secretariat
CJTFs	Combined Joint Task Forces
CNCT	Comité National Contre le Tabagisme
CPCO	Centre de Planification et de Conduite des Opérations
CPVO	Community Plant Variety Rights Office
EASA	European Aviation Safety Agency
EBA	Everything But Arms
EC	European Community
ECB	European Central Bank
ECJ	European Court of Justice
ECRE	European Council on Refugees and Exiles
ECSC	European Coal and Steel Community
EDA	European Defence Agency
EEA	European Environment Agency
EEG	European Employment Guidelines
EES	European Employment Strategy
EFSA	European Food Safety Authority
EMEA	European Agency for the Evaluation of Medicinal Products
EMU	Economic and Monetary Union
EP	European Parliament
EPC	Economic Policy Committee
EPP	European People's Party
ERA	European Railway Agency

ERT	European Round Table
ESDI	European Security and Defence Identity
ESDP	European Security and Defence Policy
ESP	European Social Policy
ESS	The European Security Strategy
ETUC	The European Trade Union Confederation
EU	European Union
EUMC	European Union Military Committee
EUMS	EU Military Staff
EUPM	European Union Police Mission
FAC	Foreign Affairs Council
FDA	Food and Drug Administration
FSAP	Financial Services Action Plan
FYROM	Former Yugoslav Republic of Macedonia
GAS	General Affairs Council
GATS	General Agreement on Trade in Services
GDP	Gross Domestic Product
GM	Genetically Modified
GMO	Genetically Modified Organism
HG	Headline Goal
HHG	Helsinki Headline Goal
IAS	International Accounting Standards
IFOR	Implementation Force
IFRS	International Financial Reporting Standards
IGC	Intergovernmental Conference
ILO	International Labor Organization
IMF	International Monetary Fund
INS	Immigration and Naturalization Service
JHA	Justice and Home Affairs
LSE	London Stock Exchange
MC	Military Committee
MFA	Ministry of Foreign Affairs
MS	Military Staff
NAACP	National Association for the Advancement of Colored People
NAFTA	North American Free Trade Agreement
NAPsincl	National Action Plans for social inclusion
NGO	Nongovernmental Organization
OHIM	Office for Harmonization in the Internal Market
OMC	Open Method of Coordination
PSC	Political and Security Committee
PU	Policy Unit

QMV	Qualified Majority Voting
RPR	Rassemblement pour la République
R&T	Research and Technology
SCIFA	Strategic Committee on Immigration, Frontiers and Asylum
SEA	Single European Act
SFOR	Stabilization Force
SIS	Schengen Information System
SPC	Social Protection Committee
SVC	Scientific Veterinary Committee
TABD	Transatlantic Business Dialogue
TACD	Transatlantic Consumer Dialogue
TAED	Transatlantic Environmental Dialogue
TALD	Transatlantic Labour Dialogue
TEU	Treaty on European Union
UMFA	Union Minister for Foreign Affairs
UNICE	Union of Industrial and Employers' Federations of Europe
UNSC	United Nations Security Council
UNPROFOR	UN Protection Force
USGAAP	US Generally Accepted Accounting Principles
USM	Unlisted Securities Market

LIST OF CONTRIBUTORS

CHRISTOPHER ANSELL is Associate Professor of Political Science at the University of California, Berkeley.

REBECCA CHEN is a Ph.D. candidate in political science at the University of California, Berkeley.

RENAUD DEHOUSSE is University Professor at the Institut d'Études Politiques, Paris.

JUSTIN GREENWOOD is Professor of European Public Policy at the Robert Gordon University, Aberdeen.

VIRGINIE GUIRAUDON is Marie-Curie Professor of Politics and Social Sciences at the European University Institute, Florence.

C. RANDALL HENNING is Associate Professor at the School of International Service, American University, and Visiting Fellow at the Institute for International Economics.

JOLYON HOWORTH is Jean Monnet Professor of European Politics at the University of Bath and Visiting Professor of Political Science at Yale University.

NICOLAS JABKO is FNSP Research Fellow at Sciences Po, Paris.

R. DANIEL KELEMEN is University Lecturer in Comparative European Politics at Lincoln College, Oxford University.

ROGAN KERSH is Associate Professor of Political Science and Public Administration at the Maxwell School of Syracuse University.

PAULETTE KURZER is Professor of Political Science at the University of Arizona.

JEFFREY LEWIS is Assistant Professor of Political Science at Cleveland State University.

SOPHIE MEUNIER is Research Associate at the Center for International Studies, Princeton University.

JAMES MORONE is Professor of Political Science at Brown University.

BRUNO PALIER is a Researcher at the Centre de Recherches Politiques (CEVIPOF) in Paris.

CRAIG PARSONS is Assistant Professor of Political Science at the University of Oregon.

PHILIPPE POCHET is a Researcher at the Institute of European Studies, Université Libre de Bruxelles, and Director of the Observatoire social européen (OSE) in Brussels.

ELLIOT POSNER is Assistant Professor of Political Science and International Affairs at the George Washington University.

BRIAN RATHBUN is Assistant Professor of Political Science at McGill University in Montreal.

JOHN A. SCHERPEREEL is Adjunct Assistant Professor of Political Science at the University of Wisconsin–Milwaukee.

VIVIEN A. SCHMIDT is the Jean Monnet Professor of European Integration in the Department of International Relations at Boston University.

MICHAEL SHACKLETON is Head of the Conciliations and Co-decision Unit of the European Parliament Secretariat.

MARTIN SHAPIRO is the James W. and Isabel Coffroth Professor of Law at the UC Berkeley School of Law.

JONATHAN STORY is the Shell Fellow of Economic Transformation and Professor of International Political Economy at INSEAD.

ALASDAIR R. YOUNG is Lecturer in Politics at the University of Glasgow.

1

Why Another Book on Europe—And Why In Reference To the United States?

NICOLAS JABKO AND CRAIG PARSONS

A few decades hence we will probably perceive the first decade of the twenty first century as a turning point for modern Europe. Europeans are suddenly confronting some new choices about their place in the world, especially relative to the USA. The most immediate, headline-grabbing tensions reflect European conflict with the US administration of George W. Bush. For more than fifty years the transatlantic alliance was the immovable keystone of European and American relations with the world. But in the Iraqi intervention that Bush portrayed as part of a post-9/11 'war on terror', the US president explicitly posed a blunt general question to the world—'Are you with us or against us?'—and much of Europe chose the latter. This division is not an isolated incident: it followed a few years of increasingly strident transatlantic friction on the environment, ballistic missile defense, international law, domestic tariffs, and various regional crises. The widespread European shock at Bush's 2004 reelection crystallized the split in both directions. Most Europeans no longer see a partner when they look across the Atlantic. The White House does not seem to care.

As cooler heads on both sides remind us, recent tensions can look less significant in broader perspective. The US–EU bond remains the most extensive peaceful relationship in international politics (Hamilton and Quinlan 2004). In many ways the European Union (EU) is closer to the USA than it ever was. The globalization (or Americanization?) of cultures and economies has generated a growing number of shared or parallel experiences and reference points. Moreover, transatlantic quarrels are nothing new. Regional interventions have regularly been the object of US–European disagreement, and differences of opinion on environmental policies or international law are not purely the invention of America's forty-third president. Still, the recent changes in US global strategy and tone make Europe's choices sharper, and the trade-offs steeper, than they have been for five decades. Europeans have been pushed quite explicitly to question their established worldviews.

The impression of a major European turning point becomes all the more compelling when we set these external challenges alongside internal developments. The fifty-year project of the EU is entering a new phase. The completion of the Single Market program and the inauguration of the euro realized some of the most ambitious visions of the EU's founding fathers. Beyond this point of economic and monetary union, however, most thinking about European integration has been exceedingly vague. The generation of leaders who forged their careers in the early postwar period is passing from the scene. Younger generations tend to accept the EU more easily, but may also feel less of a need to develop the EU further. The coincidence of this transition with the massive EU enlargement to the east (and beyond, as now seems inevitable, to Turkey) creates opportunities to reopen some of the fundamental bargains and principles of the EU.

The external and internal choices facing Europeans—how to relate to the USA and how to shape their continent—are tightly linked. They reflect a single complex historical crossroads more than distinct sets of options that can be freely mixed and matched. An EU that continues on a federal track, centralizing new tasks, will obviously relate differently to the USA and to the world than one that opts for a more decentralized and heterogeneous future. Some routes of integration and centralization may make the EU more of a partner for the USA; others may leave the EU better able and inclined to react against the USA. Hints of some of the potential paradoxes along the way have been visible in the overlap of the Iraqi crisis with the EU's 'constitutional' process, with Europeans simultaneously fascinated by the experience of US federalism and increasingly critical of US policies.

Perhaps most shockingly for observers and even many practitioners of EU politics, these external and internal choices are also intensely political. The EU polity and the scholarly literature about it are both dominated by a technocratic, bureaucratic focus on collective problem-solving in an interdependent world. Distributional fights are a constant and well-acknowledged part of the EU arena, but real challenges to the EU project—like those from Charles de Gaulle, Margaret Thatcher, recent Polish maneuvering on voting rules, or some challenges to Turkey's EU candidacy—often seem to be treated by European leaders and EU scholars as 'exogenous shocks' that reach atavistically from beyond the grave of old Europe. Not entirely coincidentally, such attitudes serve to obscure the meaningful politics that drive the EU project forward. Both the Bush presidency and the end of the EU's road map remind us that there is no escape from politics. The tone and substance of shifts in US policies have shattered the tacit twenty first century views that politicians are all the same and that modern governments naturally veer to the center. The absence of grand European projects and pervasive worries about an EU 'democratic deficit' also seem likely to bring deep political agendas to the fore. Europe may certainly muddle through this historic transition, refusing to deliberate consciously and collectively on a deep political level, but that too would be a political choice with far-reaching consequences.

With this historic turning point as backdrop, this book proposes to help students and scholars sort through the many trends of change in contemporary Europe. Our goal is to highlight the politics of the trends that have brought Europeans to their current juncture, and to play out how current trends may carry them in certain directions in the future. Two things are fairly novel about the way we propose to do so. First, most scholarship on the changing European landscape either tries to boil down change to one grand theory or implies that European politics is so complex that a broad mapping of change is very difficult. We are sympathetic to the more complex characterizations of the European arena, but argue that we can both capture and break down much of that complexity with a middle-ground approach. Our basic strategy is to spell out not just one but several distinct causal mechanisms that we see interacting in the European arena, and to trace them across various policy areas and institutional settings. Rather than trying to stretch one core story across as much of the European landscape as possible, we tell several stories that sketch each other's bounds. We hope the result is an unusually accessible treatment of complex political change. With the same goal in mind we avoid academic jargon wherever possible, setting out our mechanisms and their effects in relatively simple language.

Second, at a more substantive level, we frame our analysis in a set of questions about how the EU is becoming more or like the USA in various domains. Our undertaking is not evenly comparative: our contributors are interested in how much *Europe* is changing and why. But we use questions about whether the EU is converging on American policy positions or institutional patterns to help map out our answers. We believe our theme of 'with us or against us' generates some interesting insights. It is especially useful to make European trends comprehensible and relevant to US audience. But it is also revealing for non-specialist Europeans who have little patience for EU jargon and want to understand how EU politics really works. Finally, we hope the book will also make some aspects of US politics more transparent to European readers.

This introduction sets out why we think this approach will be particularly useful for people who want to understand where Europe is coming from and going to. First, we make a practical case for our basic approach to charting change in contemporary Europe. Second, we set out the mechanisms of change that our contributors will trace. Third, we discuss the benefits of framing such a study in references to the USA. Last, we summarize the chapters into a broad chart of European trends in US perspective.

1. Thinking About Political Change in Europe

Most thinking about trends of political change in Europe (and elsewhere) falls into two broad approaches. Many scholars try to formulate a grand theory that captures the irreducible essence of political dynamics in some arena. Others imply that political arenas tend to be too complex to have a single core story, and so offer either narrower focuses on *a* (but not necessarily *the*) core story or broader focuses that feature a variety of intermingling factors rather than a stylized causal logic. Our substantive sympathies lean toward the latter view: we think today's Europe (like the world around it) is a place where several different processes of change interact in complex ways. But precisely because we suspect there are several irreducible forces at work in today's Europe, we think it crucial to preserve the clarity and drive of stylized causal logics. If lots of things matter, any coherent argument depends on drawing out particular mechanisms and highlighting their distinct importance as much as possible. Thus, this section argues for a middle ground approach to the study of political change in Europe. We retain the 'core story' method of setting out relatively simple causal logics and pitting them against each other to explain political patterns. Rather than seeking to proclaim an overall winner, however, we try to use several contrasting logics to help define each other's boundaries.

1.1. How Scholars Have Thought About European Change

As a first step in characterizing our approach, it is helpful to glance back across the main analyses of political change in Europe since World War II. Until recently (and still to a large degree today), this subject has been dominated by two clashes of grand theories. One major battle has been fought at the European level, where scholars have debated what kind of broad theory best accounts for the changes represented in the process of 'European integration' and the emergence of the EU. Some explain the EU as a straightforward reaction to deep structural conditions of interdependence. Others see the core EU story as one of dynamic institutions, in which the postwar innovation of 'supranational' agents gradually carried Europeans forward to more integration. The second major battle has focused on issues of change in Europe's national political economies, and especially whether or not they are becoming more similar to each other. Some see general trends of convergence as European societies respond to the structural imperatives of globalizing markets and post-industrial economies. Others cast the central dynamic as institutional, with differences in national institutions sustaining major national differences over time.

The first battle, between structural and institutional theories of European integration, has raged for forty years.[1] The structural view explains the EU as a set of bargains between sovereign states who were pushed to cooperate by underlying interdependence. Geopolitical pressures of the Cold War encouraged west European states to collaborate more intensively. The midsized European countries also faced strong economic incentives to build a larger market together. These economic concerns became increasingly dominant over geopolitics as the threats of the early Cold War receded and economic integration accelerated. National governments were pushed by interest groups to respond to these incentives, especially in moving to liberalize foreign trade and to lessen state intervention in the domestic economy. At the same time, governments were careful to maintain control over the integration process (Moravcsik 1998). Capturing the benefits of cooperation meant delegating some power to new European institutions, but states retained effective oversight through the EU Council of Ministers and other mechanisms. From this view, then, even today's elaborately institutionalized EU can still be understood as a series of international bargains between distinct national interests. The core trends of change in Europe continue to be national responses to structural pressures for free-market-style cooperation (with some geopolitical elements). These responses sometimes come together in international bargaining to make further changes to the EU institutions, and will continue to do so in the future as a function of international conditions.

The institutional view of European integration challenges the notion that Europe changes in direct response to clear structural imperatives. Instead it suggests that the main direction and pace of change in postwar Europe has turned on institutional factors. What may appear as a market modernization process is actually best understood as an incremental development trajectory. Initial postwar European cooperation may have responded to fairly clear structural incentives, but once substantial power was delegated to new European institutions in the 1950s these new agents 'fed back' to alter European politics. The new technocrats at the European Commission became entrepreneurial leaders who crafted clever new proposals for more integration and persuaded national actors to support them. The new judges at the European Court of Justice (ECJ) moved actively to interpret European law in integrative directions, and were protected from opponents by the apolitical veil of the legal arena. The creation of a European arena of policymaking created

[1] A full survey of this rich early literature would be well beyond the scope of this chapter. For our purposes, it is sufficient to say that the terms of the debate were largely set by two early students of European integration, namely Ernst Haas on the institutionalist side and Stanley Hoffmann for the structuralist interpretation. See especially Haas 1958; Hoffmann 1995.

opportunities for national actors who wanted to challenge national regulations. What began as a narrow sectoral experiment in the European Coal and Steel Community (ECSC) transformed itself incrementally into the quasi-federal government of the EU. Presumably, such centralizing, integrative dynamics will continue in the future (Haas 1958; Lindberg 1963; Pierson 1996; Sandholtz and Stone Sweet 1998).[2] In this view, the entire process of European integration is fueled by the unintended, self-propelling consequences of early institutional choices.

The first several decades of integration studies largely featured an all-or-nothing debate between variants of these two perspectives. Some critics did point out, reasonably enough, that both dynamics seemed to be taking place to some degree across EU history. In some important episodes of change, national leaders seemed to formulate their own agendas in response to concrete policy problems and struck an intergovernmental deal; in others Europe's institutional agents seemed to provide the frame or impetus to movement. In one of the most famous versions of this observation, Donald Puchala (1972). described this literature as several blind men feeling different parts of an elephant. Still, even Puchala's metaphor suggested that scholars should be looking for some sort of single, coherent core story in analyzing European trends. There was *an* elephant behind it all. Similarly, the self-critique in the 1970s by the leading institutionalist theorist, Ernst Haas (1975), suggested mainly that some sort of still-more-grand synthetic theory was necessary to explain why institutional dynamics sometimes failed to operate. In general, these early criticisms did not dispel the notion that we should be looking for some sort of single core mechanism to understand European integration. They suggested that this mechanism might involve a synthesis of elements previously seen as separate, but tended to overlook the possibility that the integration process might be the end result of several irreducible and even conflicting mechanisms.

Meanwhile, the second major battle over change in Europe featured similar kinds of debates at the national level. Across a variety of policy areas, scholars argued as of the 1970s that major structural trends were pushing Europe's diverse national polities to change in similar ways. One group of such arguments pointed to external economic pressures and crises as drivers to change. International trade increased incentives to alter trade policies, and shifted domestic political power to international trading sectors

[2] Pierson (1996: 139) describes European integration as a process that follows 'a consistent direction over time': 'As the density of EC policymaking increases, such interaction effects become more prevalent, unintended consequences multiply, and the prospects of gaps in member states controls multiply.' Sandholtz and Stone Sweet (1998: 4–5) argue that institutional dynamics will 'gradually, but inevitably, reduce the capacity of the [EU] member states to control outcomes'.

and away from those oriented to home markets (Gourevitch 1986; Frieden 1991; Garrett 1992). Rising international competition from Asia and the USA in high-value-added production and from new Third World producers in low-end production empowered European business to argue that it could ill afford high wages and benefits, undercutting the domestic bargaining power of labor. Mushrooming international capital flows deprived national finance ministries and central banks of the power to ration access to funds in their home markets, weakening government oversight of business and creating pressure for regulatory reform. Other scholars argued that European capitalism had reached a 'second industrial divide' in the 1960s or 1970s (Piore and Sabel 1984). Shifts from classic mass-production manufacturing to services and more specialized 'post-Fordist' manufacturing made the workforce more heterogeneous, broke down class structures, and altered citizens' political preferences. These changes further weakened class-based mobilization (above all labor), and brought a shift in public opinion to 'postmaterialist' values that realigned political party systems to new issues like environmentalism. Though often presented with a relatively specific focus, all these arguments tended toward similar conclusions. In a changing structural landscape, European countries with diverse histories were converging, each in its own way, on a less labor-friendly, more free-market style of governance.

Against this array of structural arguments about national convergence arose a large number of institutional arguments about continued divergence. Their core story was that the inclination and ability of European countries to change depended on the institutional legacies of the past. For many reasons European countries had developed nationally distinct arrangements between economic actors over time: between employers and workers, between finance ministries and banks, between unions and left-wing parties, and so on. Thus when new internal or external pressures arose—when new technology increased international capital flows or altered manufacturing practices, or new international competition reconfigured markets—how each European country reacted and changed depended on how its preexisting institutions blocked or enabled certain responses (Shonfield 1969; Katzenstein 1978; Zysman 1983; Hall 1986; Hall and Soskice 2001). These arguments about national political economy tended to be less grand-theoretical than the institutional arguments about European integration. They often focused on particular national cases and were less theoretically explicit.[3] They also departed somewhat from a zero-sum battle of theories in guardedly integrating some of the logic of their structural competitors. They accepted that

[3] Many of these authors coalesced into the school of 'historical institutionalism', which is defined partly by theoretical eclecticism (Hall and Taylor 1996).

structural-economic incentives and constraints drove most change in Europe, but added that institutions strongly shaped the direction and extent of change. Still, in response to the general structural theories they challenged, they focused on capturing as much explanatory territory as possible for institutional factors—and so effectively defined the core of scholarship on European political economy as a clash between these two core stories. Similar debates arose across the study of national-level change in European finance, industrial relations, welfare-state reforms, and other areas: were European countries converging for structural reasons, or diverging for institutional ones?

In broad conceptual terms, these two great battles about political change in postwar Europe were overlapping skirmishes in one theoretical war between structural and institutional approaches to politics. Whether focused at the European or national level, the vast majority of studies of change in Europe sought to reduce whatever changes they observed either to particular structural imperatives or to a particular institutional inheritance. Yet for professional reasons, the two battles remained quite separate into the 1990s. What came to be known as EU studies began as a study of international cooperation and so was claimed by theorists of international relations. National-level political economy, meanwhile, remained the preserve of theorists of comparative politics. Even though the two groups fought over the same basic intellectual positions and sought to explain related processes of change—and even though all these scholars portrayed their work as a search for the core story of change in the same arena—they went to two different sets of conferences, tended to write for two different sets of journals, and expressed themselves in two different vocabularies.

This parallel-but-bifurcated approach to the study of change in Europe began to lose its dominance in the 1990s. This was not because the grand battles between structural and institutional approaches went away. In fact, some of their most forceful formulations appeared at the end of the 1990s (at the EU level, Moravcsik 1998; Sandholtz and Stone Sweet 1998; at the national level, Berger and Dore 1996; Kitschelt *et al.* 1998; Hall and Soskice 2001). But alongside the older battles arose new work that was quite different in substantive focus and theoretical approach. In reaction above all to the major expansion of EU authority around the 'Single Market project' of the late 1980s and early 1990s, scholars from a variety of backgrounds began to reach across European and national levels, and also moved away from grand theory debates. They coalesced loosely into three new bodies of literature.

The largest of the new literatures emerged as specialists in comparative politics began to find that they could no longer discuss change in national politics and economies without becoming expert on EU affairs. Some also pointed out that the EU as a system of governance was increasingly worth comparing to federal states. These observations gave birth to a literature that looked at Europe as an arena of 'multilevel government', largely through the lens of comparative federalism (Sbragia 1992; Marks *et al.* 1996; Hooghe and Marks 2001; Nicolaidis and Howse 2001; Kelemen 2003). They argued that the rules of the European game had changed since the 1980s, and that we needed to better understand the complex interactions of European, national, and subnational institutions before we could go much further. While they traced a variety of stories of particular changes in institutional relationships, their focus was on characterizing the current operation of the European arena rather than what drove its evolution over time. Instead of presenting a new core story of change, they suggested we should first elaborate a broader and more nuanced view of what Europe had changed into.

At the same time specialists in EU affairs began to see EU regulations and policies producing more effects on the ground in domestic arenas, and created a new research focus on 'Europeanization' of national polities (Ladrech 1994; Schmidt 1999, 2002; Cowles *et al.* 2001; Featherstone and Radaelli 2003; Dyson and Goetz 2003). This literature was more specific and causal than the related work on multilevel government, concentrating on one pattern of change within a quasi-federal system. But its creators also did not aspire to a new core story of European change. They more modestly portrayed Europeanization as one interesting process in a newly complex system of governance. They were particularly interested in the dynamics of institutional 'fit'. EU regulations and policies created pressures or incentives for national institutions to act in certain ways, and particular national institutional legacies made some countries (or institutions and groups within countries) better able than others to respond effectively. German subnational governments and groups, for example, seemed to be well prepared for EU-level action by their experiences in a federal system at home. Similar actors in centralized Britain or France found the EU context less comfortable, and so 'Europeanization' generated more pressure for change in their domestic institutions. This contributed to a modest shift in power to French and British subnational government.

The third new focus of European studies concerned how the rise of 'multilevel government' and the broader context of globalization affected democracy. This literature tried to combine analysis of political possibilities with normative discussions of how a changing Europe *should* be organized in light of democratic theory. One of the main emphases was the model of 'deliberative democracy' advanced by the German social theorist Jürgen Habermas, who saw broad public discussion and debate as more important to meaningful democracy than the traditional mechanisms of elections and parliamentary representation (Cohen 1991; Held 1995; Habermas 1996; Erikson and Fossum 2000). Some saw (and continue to see) Europe-wide deliberation as the savior of democracy in a context where the EU institutions had stretched and complicated the ability of voters to dictate policy choices through elections. While this body of work clearly aimed at analyzing change in Europe, it did so in a very eclectic way—pointing to a variety of sources of challenges to democracy, and often operating in a mostly normative mode of criticism of current practices or advocacy of new proposals.

Each of these three new literatures had a well-justified focus within their picture of a complex Europe, but the overall story of European change they hinted at was something of a cautionary tale. They tended to criticize earlier grand theory-style work for its narrowness, and argued that we could not understand what was happening without closer attention to a wider range of interacting dynamics. Multilevel government theorists characterized the new European arena as one of 'mutual dependence, complementary functions, and overlapping competencies' (Marks *et al.* 1996). Scholars working on Europeanization agreed that the overall picture was one of 'continuous interaction and linkages between national and European levels' driven by a variety of forces (Cowles *et al.* 2001). These literatures and the work in democratic theory came up with a wide range of new labels to emphasize the complexity of the new European system: the EU was a 'postmodern state', a space of 'neomedievalism', an example of 'network governance', or simply a 'confusion of powers' (Ruggie 1993; Kohler-Koch 1996; Cerny 1999; Schmidt 1999). But these labels, and the arguments underlying them, were mainly negative concepts. Their common point was that contemporary Europe had become so complex that it could *not* be analyzed through traditional state models or grand theories. Many of these scholars themselves lamented the fact that they had yet to develop more positive characterizations of the evolving European scene—and that Europe only seemed to be getting more complex (Marks *et al.* 1996). As John Peterson and Elizabeth Bomberg (2001) wrote in one relatively recent survey of European change, 'We do our best . . . but concede (a bit wearily) that the multilevel polity we began to understand in the 1990s seems to be transmuting into what, effectively, are multiple and different polities.'

1.2. A Middle-Ground Approach to European Change

This brings us to where the study of political change in Europe stands today—and to our own agenda. We propose a pragmatic 'third way' between the grand-theory debates and more eclectic views of a complex landscape. This is not because we see any of these literatures as misguided; they simply have goals that are different from ours in this book. We want to map out salient trends of change in a way that will be legible to a fairly broad audience. Grand theorists, by contrast, are engaged in deep scholarly battles to highlight the most fundamental aspects of politics. This often means straining out complicating factors that would be important to a more comprehensive view of the European arena. Studies of comparative federalism, 'multilevel government', Europeanization, or democracy pay more attention to such factors. But their overall emphasis on the complexity of the EU can make it especially difficult for laymen to understand the politics of integration. In addition, with a partial exception for the 'Europeanization' literature, their primary focus is how the current system of European governance operates (or should operate), rather than in how it changes. Despite the sea of ink spilled over the 'new Europe' in the past fifteen years, then, this book targets a fairly empty niche.

Thus it is mainly in terms of ambitions that we occupy a 'middle ground' between general theorists and complex thinkers, rather than in a deep substantive or methodological sense. In the interest of bringing broad swaths of the European terrain into fairly sharp relief for a nonexpert audience, we want to be a bit bolder than most complexity thinkers and a bit more nuanced than most general theorists. We pitch our discussions at a level of abstraction below that of general theories of 'intergovernmentalism', 'neofunctionalism', and the like, but still try to point to political dynamics that appear to manifest themselves in fairly distinct mechanisms. Though we have mentioned our relative sympathy for more complexity-based approaches, we do not mean to claim that more abstract and general theoretical approaches could not synthesize and systematize much of what our authors argue. We simply suggest that in a collective volume with broad teaching aspirations, it makes sense to aim for a coherent, theoretically grounded, composite breakdown of political change in Europe, without attempting something more grandiose.

To sum up what we have argued so far, we see a market niche and strong pragmatic rationale for a middle ground, compound study of multiple mechanisms of political change in contemporary Europe. The next sections spell out what the study will look like.

2. Six Mechanisms of Change in Contemporary Europe

The suggestion that multiple causal forces are at work in Europe does not mean that everything matters. On the contrary, any attempt to sort through European complexities in a relatively coherent way depends on reducing the picture to a fairly small set of trends. We have identified our mechanisms mainly by culling what we see as the most plausible, widely accepted arguments from the diverse literatures mentioned above. We think that all well-informed observers of contemporary Europe, whatever their theoretical commitments, would agree that these six mechanisms are operating in Europe to some extent. Of course theorists would quickly begin to debate their relative importance, and that is exactly what we propose to do amongst ourselves. These mechanisms do not all matter equally or evenly across the European arena, and our main goal is to suggest when and where they matter, and how often they interact. But again, our somewhat original point of departure is the expectation that all of these mechanisms will be important. Readers will not find any of what academics call 'straw man' arguments here: flimsy hypotheses set up to be knocked down to showcase the cleverness of other arguments.

Each mechanism offers a stylized answer to the question, 'What is driving change in Europe?' For each we first set out its core dynamic and then suggest in general terms what we would look for to see its impact. The mechanisms are relatively broad, each containing several possible variants, but they reflect distinct basic ways of thinking about what is going on.

1. **External threats to the European status quo**: All European countries are modest-sized polities that are unusually open to the outside world. The EU project has made them even more permeable to external pressures in many ways (though in some ways it has enhanced Europeans' abilities to control their own destiny). Europeans thus regularly feel compelled by external threats to adapt their institutions and policies simply to defend their relatively comfortable status quo. These threats come in many forms, from terrorism to migration, to volatile financial markets, to increasing economic competition, to the spread of the English language and US culture. But it makes sense to group arguments about such threats under a single mechanism because they tend to share a common core story. Europeans have an array of institutions and policies that are intended to sustain certain social, economic, or political outcomes; new developments outside of Europe directly threaten these arrangements, and Europeans are pushed to react accordingly.

This kind of thinking implies that European changes we observe should trace fairly directly and reasonably to measurable changes in real external threats. To see how far this mechanism can carry us, we would look for evidence of widely shared perceptions of certain threats, a logic dictating particular changes in policies or institutions as the most reasonable response to those threats, and (ideally) rhetorical evidence where political actors explicitly say or write that certain changes were necessary to cope with new external developments.

2. **Aspirations to global leadership**: Beyond the external pressures Europeans defend their status quo, and set high goals for themselves. The EU increasingly claims a role of global political as well as economic leadership, with Europeans seeking to increase their influence and status even without any

clear threats that require such initiatives. In economic affairs, EU leaders declared in March 2000 in Lisbon that Europe should become 'the most competitive and dynamic economy in the world' by 2010. In political and security affairs, the Saint-Malo summit of 1998 launched the initiative to create a 'European Security and Defense Policy'. In both cases the extent of the need for major new European initiatives to preserve the European status quo is debatable—but the desire of many Europeans to obtain these goals is not. The notion that Europe can, and should lead the world in economic dynamism and political vision generates a mechanism of change in its own right.

This mechanism locates the source of European changes on the 'supply side' of positive visions rather than on the 'demand side' of clear needs to protect established benefits. It is often difficult to tell the difference, of course, since political actors often claim (and believe) that their positive projects are desperately needed. Drawing a distinction requires us to look at how widely perceived is the 'need' for a given change, and the extent to which its justification focuses on particular threats to the status quo or ambitions for some version of 'progress'.

3. **Internal demographic and technical change**: Distinct from external pressures or global ambitions, European institutions and policies are built on certain internal foundations that are dynamic and can compel political change. Among the most concrete examples are demographic patterns, such as fertility rates or the age profile of a society, and technological innovation. These are to some degree structural facts over which governments have little control, providing a distinct source of pressure for political change. When aging populations raise the cost of health-care policies, or when waves of young people swell or shrink the ranks of schoolage children, new demands are made on established policies. The same can be true when new telecommunication technologies make possible faster and more decentralized interactions in financial markets, when technical change in manufacturing or service provision alter how certain workers relate to employers, or as evolutions in agricultural productivity cut jobs and drive people out of the countryside.

The key issue in attributing causal importance to this mechanism is to establish how much apparently 'structural' changes genuinely dictate change in particular directions. Often evolutions that appear to bubble up out of social patterns or innovation are in fact shaped strongly by politics and institutions. Policies on childcare or other social services can affect reproductive choices and fertility rates; funding for research or the shape of financial market institutions can effectively select for certain kinds of innovation. Even once we establish that certain demographic or technical changes are spontaneous dynamics of their own, it is also often ambiguous how much they really require particular kinds of political responses. We need to pay careful attention to the origins of internal evolutions and to their logical linkages to particular demands for change to disentangle this mechanism from others—most notably the institutional legacies noted below.

4. **National jockeying for advantage**: Our first three mechanisms suggest core stories in which Europeans as a group try to cope with problems and exert collective influence. The acuteness of pressure from external threats, global ambitions, and internal structural evolutions will of course vary across Europe—some countries have lower fertility rates, some Europeans are more likely to be targets of terrorism, some will be more vulnerable to turmoil in financial markets, and so on—but if those mechanisms were strong we would expect them to affect Europe quite broadly. A different kind of mechanism departs from the observation that the EU is an assortment of distinct polities with long histories of nation- and state-building. Much of their interaction is driven not by shared problems or aspirations but by bargaining between very separate national agendas. EU spending on regional development policy in the 'Structural Funds', for example, emerged historically when the British insisted on an urban-focused subsidy to offset some of their payments to the Common Agricultural Policy. The Structural Funds later expanded mainly because the Spanish government made more 'cohesion' money a condition of its support for further steps in market integration. Changes in national governments can thus create new demands (or new impasses) to the European agenda for reasons that are quite distinct from the preceding mechanisms. Even more common is that changes that do trace partly to those mechanisms are partly refracted and reoriented by idiosyncratic national concerns.

This mechanism traces European change to the ebb and flow of each country's disposition to fight for its immediate material advantage and distinct cultural agenda. It operates to the extent that national strategies are difficult to explain as responses to a country's position vis-à-vis broad external threats or internal structural evolutions—instead focusing simply on getting more of the European pie, or on imposing distinct national preferences for a particular kind of pie. In the latter category are positions like the French focus on cultural policy, Swedish neutrality, or British attachment to sovereignty. Each country's disposition to insist on these national priorities varies a good deal for idiosyncratic reasons of domestic politics, most obviously when more nationalist leaders win elections. When a de Gaulle or Thatcher takes power, the possibilities for European bargaining change.

5. **The impact of institutional legacies**: Our literature review underscored that the unintended impact of institutions has featured prominently in thinking

about European change since 1945.[4] Europeans may have set up certain institutions or policies as reasonable responses to problems in the past, but the legacies of these choices have often constrained later options in unforeseen ways. For example, the CAP was set up long before anyone imagined the accession of East European countries, but it has greatly complicated their negotiations for membership. Institutional legacies may even actually compel new initiatives, especially where earlier institutional projects involved delegating power to new organizations; organs like the European Commission or ECJ that are ostensibly created to facilitate today's policy cooperation may lobby for or even force policy change down the line.

This mechanism focuses on change that Europeans undertake as the unintended result of having set up certain institutions in the past. In its strong variant it generates direct pressure for change itself, when organizations created in the past become relatively autonomous and push policies in new directions. Famous (if contested) examples are the ECJ's creation of 'mutual recognition' in regulatory harmonization, or the Commission's crafting of the 'Single Market 1992' program. The subtler but probably more pervasive variant is when new external threats or internal evolutions create direct pressure for change but people find their options strongly shaped by their institutional inheritance—and so the latter effectively steers change in a particular direction.

6. **The defense or extension of democracy**: One given of the European landscape is that citizens want to be—or at least feel—involved. Deep democratic norms make most policies or institutions subject to attack if they are perceived as unresponsive to the public. Some Europeans even portray the main goal of the EU as the rescue of national democracy from the wider world, mitigating global challenges by extending democratically controlled policies to a larger level. Others see the EU itself (or some aspect of it, like the European Central Bank) as the main threat to national democracy. Either kind of thinking can generate a mechanism of change distinct from those discussed above. Models of democracy are fundamentally views of legitimate process, independent to some degree from substantive concerns. They lead to debates about institutions as ends in themselves—desirable or undesirable separate from their capacity to counter tangible threats, empower global action, or secure national advantage.

To see the distinct effects of efforts to defend certain democratic principles, we should look for arguments that appeal to democratic legitimacy but which are at least partly separable from tangible motivations. The impact of democratic models would be most distinct where these arguments actually

[4] A massive tradition in scholarship on the USA makes the same point, suggesting that complex polities evolve in unpredictable directions due to accidents and unintended consequences of earlier choices (perhaps most famously in Skowronek 1982).

go against more tangible interests—when, for example, small-country EU governments advocate powers for the European Parliament (EP), which effectively dilutes their overrepresentation in other EU institutions like the Council of Ministers. Another pattern to look for is where arguments about democratic legitimacy trace to national experiences with particular institutions more than any clear substantive concerns. Thus the British or French may tend to question the compatibility of democracy and federalism more than Germans.

Once again, our emphasis on the distinctiveness of these mechanisms does not mean that any of them ever operates entirely on its own. Many EU initiatives contain both responses to tangible threats and new aspirations for further influence; institutional legacies often shape the implications of demographic or technical change; debates often combine clashes of national priorities and of different notions of legitimate processes; and so on. This does not prevent our authors from sorting carefully through the evidence to see how much any given development in Europe reflects each dynamic. These mechanisms tell distinct enough core stories that our chapters' characterizations of change will play out quite differently depending on how much relative importance each mechanism receives. Others who see a particular development differently will be able to point to where we are wrong and offer a contrasting story.

A final introductory point is that despite the open-ended structure of our approach—designed mainly to follow where the evidence takes us—it offers a nontrivial prediction for the broad future of European politics. Even before we begin to map out the relative impact of these six mechanisms, we arrive at a general expectation that is quite different from the main predictions for change that emerge from our literature review.

The three most grand theoretic views of European change discussed above each hint at a different broad future for the continent. If we play out their logic, most structural thinkers expect fairly continuous movement toward liberalization and international cooperation (though they tend to expect that national governments will retain political control and so limit the emergence of a truly federal EU). Most institutionalists who focus on the national level expect continued national divergence and less liberalization, and so implicitly expect relatively limited development of a federal-style EU as well. Most institutionalists who focus on the European level, however, expect more liberalization in parallel with further centralization and federalization.

While our emphasis on an arena of complex interactions makes us reluctant to predict the effects of any particular mechanism—such speculation can only be part of our empirical conclusions—this picture of many cross-cutting processes of change leads us to expect that the unusual, quasi-federal format of today's Europe will be more stable than most scholars suggest. The particular mixes of liberalization and regulation or national and supranational control in specific areas will be very dynamic, but the arena overall is unlikely to become something other than a relatively weak federation in the foreseeable future. Our thinking here is much like 'pluralist' theories of domestic politics, which suggest that constant crosscutting competition between interest groups makes for broadly stable polities. The multiple mechanisms of change we see in contemporary Europe are likely to prevent any single movement from dominating. Though the previous fifty years arguably reflect a core wave of change—with the world wars and intensified international independence initially encouraging centralization in the EU—we see no such overarching trend today. Many contrasting currents will make European seas particularly choppy in coming decades, but they may also prevent any massive waves from building.[5]

3. Why Look at Europe Through Reference to the US?

We have now developed a somewhat novel way of posing questions about change in Europe and, at a general level, the mechanisms of change we propose to trace. The other novelty of our project is to frame our map of European change in references to the USA. References to the USA are unavoidable for any study of Europe, of course; no one could discuss developments in EU foreign and security policy, Europe's ambitions in economic liberalization, or the initiative for a European constitution without bringing up Europe's major ally, main competitor, and oft-mentioned rhetorical model. The US will naturally come up in almost all of our chapters as an actor or source of pressure and as a model (or occasionally an antimodel) for European aspirations. But our use of US references extends beyond the direct role that the USA plays as part of Europe's world. Our larger theme of 'with us or against us' shapes the book in two ways.

First, all the chapters make a special effort to play out how the trends they describe may impact transatlantic relations. This is an obvious focus given recent US–European conflicts, but we extend it unusually far across the European landscape—beyond discussions of foreign policy or commercial relations and into more internal issues that may affect transatlantic relations in the long run. How might changing relationships between the EU's Council of Ministers, Commission, and Parliament affect the strength of US–EU partnership? Does the progress (or lack thereof) toward a European social

[5] For a more specific version of this argument in the context of the Structural Funds, see Ansell, Parsons, and Darden 1997.

policy have implications for how Europeans and Americans will see each other in the future? Such indirect connections are arguably no less important to transatlantic ties than more immediate interactions. Some of the strongest commonalities and enduring differences between Americans and Europeans are located in institutions and attitudes that form the quiet backdrop to diplomatic or trade relations.

Second, as noted at the outset, we use comparison to the USA to chart our maps of European change. Obviously we claim no novelty with the basic notion of transatlantic comparison, which is an old and growing scholarly tradition. But as with our approach to change, we have different goals from most work that has used US comparisons to help understand Europe. The basic challenge for any such study is the sheer size and complexity of the European and US arenas; even book-length projects have difficulty in analyzing both in depth and breadth. One body of scholarship resolves this problem by focusing on relatively narrow comparisons. Working in the classic comparative tradition of national cases, it contrasts slices of European and US polities in areas like industrial relations, welfare states, regulation, and so on (e.g., Steinmo 1993; Hattam 1993; Vogel 1996; Blyth 2002). The other major solution—featured in the work on comparative federalism mentioned above—is to zoom out to a broad survey of similarities and differences between the EU and the US system (Nicolaidis and Howse 2001). Neither solution works well for our attempt to explore multiple mechanisms of European change in some detail. In one book, we cannot realistically trace several contrasting dynamics of change across the European landscape, aggregate them into a broader map, and do anything similar on the American side.

Our alternative is to use the USA as a systematic and explicit 'shadow case.' We do not try to capture the dynamics of two giant arenas; again, this is a book on Europe. Instead our chapters set out the relevant US institutions or policies in just enough detail to offer a useful point of contrast for European patterns. We think this strategy has small risks and substantial payoffs. The risk is that our American points of comparison could be too simplistic or static. Several of our contributors are experts on the USA as well, however, and throughout the project we have invited commentary from US specialists to keep us honest.[6] This small risk is counterbalanced by three kinds of payoffs. First, our American shadow case gives us a fixed reference point that focuses our discussion of European change. By combining our primary question, 'what has changed relative to Europe's recent past?', with

[6] Our Americanist contributors Rogan Kersh and James Morone were originally invited to participate simply in this role of keeping Europeanists honest in their US references. They went beyond the call to provide the excellent concluding chapter.

the additional question, 'what has changed relative to the USA?', we create a fairly sharply defined space for our arguments to fill in. Second, as the concluding chapter elaborates, we have found that a series of intriguing points arise from combining questions about the quality of transatlantic agreements or disagreements with comparative questions about the ways in which Europe is becoming like or unlike the USA as a polity. The relationship between the two often turns out to be paradoxical, with 'polity convergence' often encouraging policy divergence, or vice versa.

Third—and most important for the broad value of the book—a presentation of Europe 'in American perspective' makes our analysis particularly accessible to an American audience, and more generally to any non-specialist audience who has a hard time understanding the EU on its own terms. Using a technique that will be familiar to anyone who has ever taught politics, we take a US system that is more familiar to many readers and use it to help organize discussions of a less familiar arena. Of course some pieces of the European puzzle display neither convergence nor divergence with the USA; Europeans are forging their own path in the world to a substantial degree. Yet even these areas of distinctiveness are easier to locate and present (especially to Americans, but also more generally) in contrast to the other big, diverse, industrialized, democratic federation across the pond. Placing a rich European map over an outline of US governance will make areas of convergence, divergence, and uniqueness stand out.

4. Charting European Trends in American Perspective

The book is organized in five parts, each sharing both a theme and relative emphasis on a subset of the mechanisms summarized above.

Section 1 addresses the EU's external political and economic policies. Unsurprisingly, these chapters feature consistent emphasis on trends flowing from external threats and European aspirations for global leadership—though they also invoke other mechanisms to varying degrees. Jolyon Howorth's chapter argues against the conventional wisdom that EU divisions on Iraq killed any idea of a European defense and foreign policy. In fact, the Europeans have continued to move steadily in the direction of a meaningful European Security and Defense Policy (ESDP) for two reasons. First, the Europeans have to cope with an external challenge. The end of the Cold War has diminished the geopolitical importance of Europe for the USA. Second, the renewal of European integration in the 1980s and 1990s has boosted European hopes for a global leadership role. The member states may be divided on what to do, but nobody really questions the idea that Europe should play a greater role on the world stage.

Brian Rathbun's chapter, like Howorth's, singles out the challenge of post-Cold War threats and the Europeans' aspirations for a leadership role. He argues that these aspirations are not uniform, however. In his view, the recent degradation of transatlantic relations is the temporary result of divergent partisan worldviews on the two sides of the ocean. Most Europeans are no peaceniks, but most are to the political left of the Bush administration, and Rathbun argues that this strongly contributed to their disagreements with the worldview that prompted the US war on Iraq. Recent developments in Iraq and European divisions on this topic may have undermined the long-term prospect of a coherent European foreign policy, but in the short term they have strengthened the prospects for a European defense policy. The Europeans have come to recognize that the build up of a common defense is a more realistic first step than a common foreign policy.

Randall Henning and Sophie Meunier assess progress toward unified EU trade and financial policies. In economic relations, the EU clearly has the capacity to exercise a global role on par with the USA. Yet the EU is not always able to effectively defend its interests. While the EU has firmly established its role as a global player in trade, it has faced difficulties in acquiring such a role in money and finance. Henning and Meunier argue that institutional legacies provide the explanation for this uneven progress. Trade policymaking is centralized, whereas centralization is incomplete in the area of money and finance. Power struggles among the various EU bodies and member states hamper effectiveness.

Section 2 delves into the internal evolution of EU institutions. Despite all the hype about the novelty of Europe's constitutional treaty, these chapters suggest that institutional legacies are very resilient, both at the EU and at the national level, and will largely determine the further trajectory of institutional change. Renaud Dehousse's chapter on Europe's constitutional process highlights the challenges of defending and extending democracy in a widening Europe, but focuses above all on institutional and cultural factors. The new treaty is an incremental improvement over previous ones, not a major revolutionary change. The title of his chapter ('We, the States') underscores the reluctance of member states to delegate power to Brussels, and their tendency to jockey for what they each perceive to be their national advantage. Yet he also points out that more intergovernmentalism is not the inevitable long-term outcome of the new constitution. Over time, this last bout of institution-building could turn out to have significant unintended consequences.

Michael Shackleton's piece on the EP provides a thought-provoking counterpoise to the increasingly widespread notion that the EU is moving toward parliamentary government. In order to allay concerns about the EU's 'democratic deficit', the member states have granted the Parliament ever more powers since the 1980s. In the fall of 2004, the EP was even able to force a change in the composition of the Commission. But Shackleton argues that the logic of institutional development points in a different direction than parliamentarism. Over time, the EP has increasingly played the autonomous lawmaking role of a 'bargaining body'—much like the Congress vis-à-vis the executive branch in the USA. By the same token, the EP's weak organic relationship with EU executive bodies means that its members do not feel bound by the policies of the executive toward the United States. The growing strength of the EP may thus make the EU increasingly like the USA institutionally, but on many policies a stronger EP probably augments the potential for substantive divergence.

Jeffrey Lewis similarly stresses the role of institutional legacies in the evolution of the Council of Ministers. The Council increasingly resembles an upper house of legislature in a bicameral system more than any international organization. But the EU still gives far more power to territorially based interests at the Council level than do federal systems in the USA or Germany, and the Council also blurs legislative and executive powers in a unique way. Lewis emphasizes that it is by no means a static body, tracing the rise of a deliberative style of decision-making, the sharing of the Council's legislative powers with the EP, and the creation of new foreign policy prerogatives. If some of these changes can be explained by new concerns—like the perceived need to react to USA's 'empire' in the world—Lewis points above all to the internal deepening of the Council's tradition as a consensus-oriented diplomatic body.

Daniel Kelemen's chapter analyzes the remarkable development of autonomous agencies at the EU level in recent years. He argues that the EU's adoption of a 'hub and spoke' model of bureaucracy, with independent agencies appended to the central Brussels administration, is not just about the pursuit of efficient governance in a thinly stretched 'regulatory state'. Institutional legacies and national concerns about the evolution of the EU have played a much more important role than economic or administrative concerns in this development. Thus if the hub-and-spoke model can be analyzed as the extension of an already complex set of administrative and functional instruments of day-to-day policymaking and regulation at the EU level, it is also a consequence of the member states' increasing reluctance to build state capacity in Brussels.

Section 3 turns to the politics of the EU's economy, and introduces a slightly more bottom-up view of change. Most of the chapters depict a complex interplay of causal mechanisms, with actors adapting to external economic pressures but also pursuing their own goals and interests within specific institutional settings. Elliot Posner explores the emergence of small capitalization markets like the US Nasdaq in Europe, as part of a broad but uneven process of financial reforms. He finds that financial globalization and market forces were not nearly so decisive in shaping these reforms as the common wisdom suggests. Rather, the key factor was supranational entrepreneurship, itself motivated by an EU bid for global leadership in this area. The relative freedom enjoyed by EU bureaucrats in Brussels, who were relatively immune from national-level political infighting, helps explain the success of this operation. In turn, intergovernmental competition explains the flurry of national stock market initiatives, as governments tried to preempt an EU-level replacement of national markets.

Jonathan Story's chapter highlights a tension between the still fairly distinct logics of national financial systems across the EU, and an overarching monetary union that acts as a 'neoliberal engine'. Since the advent of the euro, EU member states have been moving into a world of increasingly unified global financial markets. Yet they have not completely discarded their old nationally based financial systems. Among big EU member states, only the UK has played the game of globalization wholeheartedly—and the paradox is that it is not a member of the eurozone.

Bruno Palier and Philippe Pochet's chapter takes a very different view. They point out that the Europeans are trying to come up with new policies to face common challenges as a result of internal demographic and technical change as well as market pressures. This is especially clear in the area of labor market reform, unemployment, and welfare state reform. The EU choice has been to establish a new policy instrument, the Open Method of Coordination, in order to facilitate the exchange of ideas. So far the substance of these ideas is decidedly 'liberal, or at least supply-side oriented'. But there is also an effort to delineate a viable European social model, in order to avoid convergence on the US-style model of market-centered capitalism.

In their chapter, Justin Greenwood and Alasdair Young deal with the institutional setting for interest intermediation at the EU level. They address the puzzle of the apparently apolitical nature of EU lobbying. As the EU becomes more democratic, we would normally expect a push for a stronger representation of interests at the EU level and, therefore, a convergence on the US model of interest group pluralism. Yet there are limits to how far the EU will converge on that model. This is because of specifically European institutional legacies that play a countervailing role—the EU's focus on regulatory rather than openly redistributive issues, its consensus-oriented style of policymaking, the habits of interest group mobilization at the national rather than at the EU level, and the limited scope for EU-level litigation.

Section 4 looks at the interplay between culture and policymaking in the evolution of the EU. This is an area where institutional legacies often play a crucial role in shaping cultural perceptions and policy developments.

Paulette Kurzer's chapter emphasizes the role of historically formed institutional legacies in EU risk perception and policymaking on health and environmental issues. The EU and the US worry about very different public health and environmental risks. While tobacco has been the focus of increasingly aggressive public interest campaigns and policies in the USA, only Genetically Modified Organism (GMOs) have caused a comparable stir on the public health front in Europe. Kurzer demonstrates the impact of evolving cultural values and preferences on these two hot topics. She also shows that institutional arrangements matter. In the aftermath of the mad cow scandal, the EU's multilevel structure of decision-making has empowered a small group of member states and determined Nongovernmental Organization (NGOs) to win the battle against GMOs.

Virginie Guiraudon's chapter documents the evolution of EU immigration policies. On the one hand, member states are motivated to respond to global economic and security challenges. In the 1980s and 1990s, policymakers' main concern was to adapt the EU to a more unified labor market. Increasingly since 9/11, they have attempted to address the global challenge of terrorism. On the other hand, they remain sensitive to immigration as a key issue of national sovereignty (and electoral politics). Even though it would arguably make more economic and political sense to centralize immigration policies to some extent, the European citizens and national elites are not ready for it. Thus the delegation of powers to the EU level remains limited.

John Scherpereel looks at the changing politics of EU enlargement. He argues that both interests and identity have always entered into the EU's enlargement decisions. Of course, geopolitical and economic considerations are always present, both in the EU and in the candidate member states. Yet in the EU—as in the expanding USA in the nineteenth century—enlargement decisions have involved increasingly important normative and cultural considerations over time. As Scherpereel puts it, 'who belongs?' and 'to whom are we obliged?' have become critical questions. Bargaining dynamics usually prevail, however, during the negotiation phase. Once the decision to enlarge has been made, normative considerations tend to fade and institutional considerations become increasingly important. In the end, how acceding states adapt is key to the success or failure of enlargement processes.

Section 5, lastly, deals with the evolution of the EU as a polity in the broadest sense. This is an area where concerns about the defense and extension of democracy are paramount, although by no means exclusive of other mechanisms. Martin Shapiro's chapter argues that the emergence of constitutional judicial review is the result of an extension of democracy but also of institutional legacies and institution-building over time. He offers a convergence story on constitutional judicial review in the EU and the USA. In both cases, there has been a movement from free trade review to individual rights review. But Shapiro's account is not a simple convergence story, since the Europeans also retained significant elements of their national ('Kelsenian') tradition of specialized constitutional courts. Rather, he sees the European evolution as part of a 'global fascination with human rights'. In addition, the new European emphasis on individual rights was also a way for the courts to reinforce not just individual rights but also federalism and a way for the member states to fudge their differences with vague but uplifting promises.

Chris Ansell and Rebecca Chen's chapter deals with the political structure of the EU as an amalgam of different logics: intergovernmental, confederal, or federal. They argue that past institutional legacies and the extension of democracy have the greatest impact on the evolving balance between these different logics. Institutional legacies could take the EU either toward the preservation of state sovereignty, or toward a more overtly federal model. Given these legacies, the Europeans face a dilemma between two solutions for democratizing the EU. One solution is to restore democratic sovereignty by reasserting the sovereignty of the member states—but this would not really make the EU more democratic. The other is to strengthen democracy at the EU level by making EU institutions themselves more democratic—yet this would require giving them more power and would therefore heighten concerns about sovereignty.

Vivien Schmidt investigates how regional integration at the EU level has changed the exercise of power and authority and the practice of democracy at the national level. National political institutions and cultures are resilient, but the EU has had an impact on patterns of power and authority everywhere. This is especially clear in 'simple' polities like Britain and France, which were less prepared for the EU model of multilevel governance than less centralized or 'compound' polities like Germany and Italy. In both cases, however, there have been very few attempts to change the national discourse on democracy. The disconnection between practice and discourse feeds into the perception of a 'democratic deficit' at the EU level.

In the concluding chapter, Rogan Kersh and James Morone, two scholars of US political development, look at the EU through an US prism. Recent transatlantic tensions stem not only from aggressive US diplomacy of the second Bush administration, but also from a bifurcation of Europe away from the US economic and political model. At the same time, the European capacity to stand up to American power is limited. Kersh and Morone find especially striking the EU's focus on administrative issues and its 'great silence' on politics. While the EU has apparently managed to avoid nasty political polarization, the lack of political passions also prevents the emergence of a true European nation. In the foreseeable future, the EU will remain at most a federal state, but certainly not a nation. What this entails for the transatlantic relationship remains to be seen.

References

Ansell, C., Parsons, C., and Darden, K. (1997). 'Dual Networks in European Regional Development Policy', *Journal of Common Market Studies,* 35/3: 347–75.

Berger, S. and Dore, R. (eds.) (1996). *Global Capitalism and National Diversity*. Ithaca, NY: Cornell University Press.

Blyth, M. (2002). *Great Transformations*. New York: Cambridge University Press.

Cerny, P. (1999). 'Globalization and the Erosion of Democracy', *European Journal of Political Research*, 36/1: 1–26.

Cohen, J. (1991). 'Deliberation and Democratic Legitimacy', in A. Hamlin and P. Pettit (eds.), *The Good Polity*. Oxford: Basil Blackwell.

Cowles, M. G., Caporaso, J., and Risse, T. (eds.) (2001). *Transforming Europe: Europeanization and Domestic Change*. Ithaca, NY: Cornell University Press.

Dyson, K. and Goetz, K. H. (eds.) (2003). *Germany, Europe, and the Politics of Constraint*. Oxford: Oxford University Press.

Eriksen, E. O. and Fossum, J. E. (eds.) (2000). *Democracy in the European Union: Integration through Deliberation?* New York: Routledge.

Featherstone, K. and Radaelli, C. M. (eds.) (2003). *The Politics of Europeanization*. Oxford: Oxford University Press.

Frieden, J. (1991). 'Invested Interests: The Politics of National Economic Policy in a World of Global Finance', *International Organization,* 45.

Garrett, G. (1992). 'International Cooperation and Institutional Choice: The European Community's Internal Market', *International Organization*, 46/2: 533–60.

Gourevitch, P. M. (1986). *Politics in Hard Times: Comparative Responses to International Economic Crises*. Ithaca, NY: Cornell University Press.

Haas, E. B. (1958). *The Uniting of Europe: Political, Social, and Economic Forces, 1950–1957*. Stanford, CA: Stanford University Press.

—— (1975). *The Obsolescence of Regional Integration Theory*. Berkeley, CA: Institute of International Studies.

Hall, P. A. (1986). *Governing the Economy*. New York: Oxford University Press.

—— and Soskice, D. (eds.) (2001). *Varieties of Capitalism: The Institutional Foundations of Comparative Advantage*. Oxford: Oxford University Press.

Habermas, J. (1996). *Between Facts and Norms: Contributions to a Discourse Theory of Law and Democracy*. Cambridge, MA: MIT Press.

Hamilton, D. and Quinlan, J. (2004). *Partners in Prosperity: The Changing Geography of the Transatlantic Economy*. Washington, DC: Center for Transatlantic Relations and Johns Hopkins University Press.

Hattam, V. (1993). *Labor Visions and State Power*. Princeton, NJ: Princeton University Press.

Held, D. (1995). *Democracy and the Global Order*. Cambridge: Polity Press.

Hoffmann, S. (1995). *The European Sisyphus: Essays on Europe, 1964–94*. Boulder, CO: Westview Press.

Hooghe, L. and Marks, G. (2001). *Multi-Level Governance and European Integration*. New York: Rowman & Littlefield.

Katzenstein, P. J. (ed.) (1978). *Between Power and Plenty: Foreign Economic Policies of Advanced Industrial States*. Madison, WI: University of Wisconsin Press.

Kelemen, R. D. (2003). *The Rules of Federalism*. Cambridge, MA: Harvard University Press.

Kitschelt, H., Lange, P., Marks, G., and Stephens, J. (eds.) (1998). *Continuity and Change in Contemporary Capitalism*. New York: Cambridge University Press.

Kohler-Koch, B. (1996). 'Catching Up with Change: The Transformation of Governance in the European Union', *Journal of European Public Policy*, 3/3: 359–80.

Ladrech, R. (1994). 'The Europeanization of Domestic Politics and Institutions: The Case of France', *Journal of Common Market Studies*, 32/1: 69–88.

Lindberg, L. (1963). *The Political Dynamics of European Economic Integration*. Stanford, CA: Stanford University Press.

Marks, G., Hooghe, L., and Blank, K. (1996). 'European Integration from the 1980s: State-Centric vs. Multi-level Governance', *Journal of Common Market Studies*, 34/3: 341–78.

Moravcsik, A. (1998). *The Choice for Europe*. Ithaca, NY: Cornell University Press.

Nicolaidis, K. and Howse, R. (eds.) (2001). *The Federal Vision*. Oxford: Oxford University Press.

Peterson, J. and Bomberg, E. (2001). 'The European Union After the 1990s: Explaining Continuity and Change', in M. G. Cowles and M. Smith (eds.), *The State of the European Union*, Vol. 5: *Risks, Reform, Resistance, and Revival*. New York: Oxford University Press, pp. 19–41.

Pierson, P. (1996). 'The Path to European Integration: A Historical Institutionalist Analysis', *Comparative Political Studies*, 29/2: 123–63.

Piore, M. and Sabel, C. (1984). *The Second Industrial Divide*. New York: Basic Books.

Puchala, D. J. (1972). 'Of Blind Men, Elephants and International Integration', *Journal of Common Market Studies*, 10: 267–84.

Ruggie, J. G. (1993). 'Territoriality and Beyond : Problematizing Modernity in International Relations', *International Organization*, 47/1: 139–74.

Sandholtz, W. and Stone-Sweet, A. (eds.) (1998). *European Integration and Supranational Governance*. New York: Oxford University Press.

Sbragia, A. (ed.) (1992). *Euro-Politics: Institutions and Policymaking in the 'New' European Community*. Washington: Brookings Institution.

Schmidt, V. A. (1999). 'National Patterns of Governance under Siege: The Impact of European Integration', in B. Kohler-Koch and R. Eising (eds.), *The Transformation of Governance in the European Union*. London: Routledge.

—— (2002). *The Future of European Capitalism*. Oxford: Oxford University Press.

Shonfield, A. (1969). *Modern Capitalism: The Changing Balance of Public and Private Power*. Oxford: Oxford University Press, 1969.

Skowronek, S. (1982). *Building a New American State: The Expansion of National Administrative Capacities, 1877–1920*. New York: Cambridge University Press.

Steinmo, S. (1993). *Taxation and Democracy*. New Haven, CT: Yale University Press.

Vogel, S. K. (1996). *Freer Markets, More Rules: Regulatory Reform in Advanced Industrialized Countries*. Ithaca, NY: Cornell University Press.

Zysman, J. (1983). *Governments, Markets and Growth*. Ithaca, NY: Cornell University Press.

I

External Foreign, Security, and Economic Policies

2

A European Union with Teeth?

JOLYON HOWORTH

In spring 2003, as the war in Iraq appeared to ride roughshod over any coordinated European security and defence policy (ESDP), it became known wisdom within the security community that the European defense project launched in December 1998 at the Franco–British summit in Saint-Malo had been delivered a major body blow. Tony Blair's suggestion that Jacques Chirac was to blame for the fact that British soldiers were dying in Basra constituted the nadir of the Saint-Malo process.[1] On April 29, 2003, the mini-summit between France, Germany, Belgium and Luxembourg appeared to threaten a new future and a new direction for ESDP—one from which the UK would be excluded. Yet paradoxically, 2003 proved to be a turning point for the European defense project.

Two unprecedented police operations—European Union Police Mission (EUPM) in Bosnia and *Proxima* in Macedonia—and the EU's first ever military operations (*Concordia* in Macedonia, *Artemis* in Congo, and, above all, from December 2004, *Althea* in Bosnia[2]) demonstrated that the EU—despite the skepticism of many pundits—was capable of engaging in coordinated coercive missions. 'Berlin Plus,' that mysterious magic wand allowing the EU to borrow military assets, including operational planning, from the USA, appeared actually to be workable.[3] EU–NATO relations were

[1] Blair interview in *The Sun*, April 18, 2003: 'Interviewed for the first time since the start of the war, Mr Blair talked about ... his anger at treacherous French President Jacques Chirac. Mr Blair admitted he had been furious with Mr Chirac of France for putting British troops at risk by sabotaging UN action against Iraq. "I was very upset how it played out at the United Nations, he said. If the UN had given a strong and unified ultimatum to Saddam it is possible we could have avoided conflict." ' For the Saint-Malo Declaration, see Rutten 2001, 8–9.

[2] The details of all past and current EU operations can be accessed at the EU Council website.

[3] The 'Berlin Plus' arrangements allowed the EU to enjoy 'assured access to NATO planning,' 'presumed access to NATO assets and capabilities' and a predesignated Europeans-only chain of command. The arrangements were agreed in principle at a NATO summit in Berlin in June 1996. The devil proved to be in the detail and it took six years of hard bargaining (the 'Berlin Plus negotiations') to nail down the details. This was finally achieved in December 2002. See Haine 2003, 178–80.

slipping into gear. If anybody had predicted, on the morrow of Saint-Malo, that five years later the Europeans would be poised to engage in military operations under an EU flag, they would have been laughed out of court. On the planning and procurement front, the decision taken at Thessaloniki in June 2003 to establish a European Defence Agency represented a significant step forward toward a more rational planning process, a step which was rapidly complemented by Franco–British agreement to cooperate on the construction of aircraft carriers. On the institutional front, the proposals formulated in the Treaty Establishing a Constitution for Europe—to create a Union Minister of Foreign Affairs (UMFA) and a President of the Council, to introduce 'structured cooperation' and some sort of 'solidarity clause' as well as many other stimuli to integrated action—were moving ahead.[4] Moreover, Iraq, far from leading to exacerbated tensions between Paris, London and Berlin, appeared in an indirect way to have helped generate a working and constructive brand of 'trilateralism' (Menon 2004). Finally, arrangements for EU strategic capacity in terms of operational planning, intelligence and a new 'Headline Goal' for 2010, including a new 'battle-groups' concept, all seemed to have broken through conceptual, political and practical hurdles. The adoption in December 2003 of the Solana *Security Strategy* document (European Council 2003), with all its shortcomings and limitations, finally gave the EU a much-needed framework within which to flesh out its broader strategic ambitions. The EU, it seemed, had suddenly come a very long way in a very short time.

1. From Foreign Policy Coordination to a European Security and Defense Policy

The EU's emergence as a security and defense actor happened very fast. Attempts to coordinate foreign policy, mainly via European Political Cooperation (Nuttall 1992), had been going on since the early 1970s and had been given a boost by the institutional and political implications of the Single Market project in the late 1980s. These developments in turn were galvanized by the end of the Cold War and the Maastricht proposals for a Common Foreign and Security Policy (CFSP) (Regelsberger *et al.* 1997; Peterson & Sjursen 1998). But the *security* component remained controversial throughout the 1990s, with most 'Atlanticist' EU member states, led by the UK, continuing to insist that NATO was the only competent body for this policy area. Attempts to create a European Security and Defence Identity (ESDI)

[4] On these constitutional developments with specific reference to ESDP see Howorth 2004*a*.

from inside NATO proved problematic and unsatisfactory (Howorth & Keeler 2003: 7–10). By the turn of the century, the EU had transcended its own previous diffidence. No longer content with the quest for ESDI, the Union itself now sought a European Security and Defence Policy (ESDP), which in the Saint-Malo Declaration of December 1998 explicitly called for the 'capacity for autonomous action, backed up by credible military forces'. The story of how the EU got to this point has been told repeatedly (Howorth 2000; Hunter 2002; Quinlan 2001). But some milestones in the shift from ESDI to ESDP need to be reviewed.

Two powerful forces combined to act as midwife to ESDP. The first—exogenous—derives from the shifting tectonic plates of the international system in the aftermath of the Cold War. This process corresponds closely to the first of the six 'mechanisms of change' which inform this volume: external threats to the European status quo. When the Berlin Wall fell on November 9, 1989 (11/9), it brought down with it a Eurocentric reading of international relations which had been unquestioned since the Treaty of Westphalia in 1648. Europe had been the fulcrum of world history since the sixteenth century as its internal wars and external expansion dictated the fates of countries and peoples around the globe. All of that came to an end in 1989. For the USA and for much of the rest of the world, the 'dawn of peace in Europe' (Mandelbaum 1996) shifted the continent to the margins of the international radar screen. The focus of policymakers and military planners in Washington DC switched to Asia, to the Gulf, to the Middle East. Europe (with the irritating but hardly strategically significant exception of the Balkans) was simply no longer a problem. US disengagement was already, in November 1989, a foregone conclusion. The security of the European continent should henceforth be delivered through Europe's own efforts and resources. Why was this problematic? The biggest difference between US forces and European forces as they emerged from the Cold War derived from geography. The Europeans, perched on the front line of the Iron Curtain, were configured for static line defenses, based on mass mobilization of conscripts, artillery and tanks. The Americans, coming from across the ocean, were configured for distant force projection involving strategic transport facilities, rapid mobility and sophisticated 'standoff' weaponry. It was these assets that were now required to engage in the crisis management missions of the twenty first century. The US possessed them; the Europeans did not. Europe, in short, suffered from a 'capabilities gap'. While the Europeans discussed ways to *transform* their lumbering militaries into useful—and usable—instruments, it seemed sensible that they should seek access, through NATO, to US assets which would allow them—temporarily—to plug the capabilities gaps between their past and their future. This would take the pressure off US forces which were more urgently needed elsewhere, and would allow EU forces, pending their professionalization and modernization, to take over peacekeeping missions in areas such as the Balkans where the USA had no identifiable interests. The drive to force European militaries to take responsibility for their own backyard began unequivocally in Washington, DC.

The second major force behind ESDP stems from the dynamic processes unleashed within the EU itself by the developments of the late 1980s and early 1990s. This is an expression of the second mechanism for change informing this volume: aspirations to global leadership. Although the community's embrace of 'actorness' was long in gestation, there was never any doubt that the European project was a *political* project. Its fundamental objective was the resolution of a double conundrum: how to bind together the fates of Europe's core nations in a way which would both render intra-European war unthinkable and maximize European influence in the outside world. The notion that the European nations might increasingly look to their own interests—in contradistinction to those of the USA—already predated the fall of the Berlin Wall as nervous European leaders pondered the security dilemmas posed by an unpredictably unilateralist US president. But as European integration gathered speed in the late 1980s, impelled by the Single Market project, by the prospect of a single currency and by the Schengen process, the internal forces behind *foreign* policy convergence meshed with those suggesting the need for greater *security* policy autonomy. These dynamics were intensified after 11/9 by the growing awareness of the strategic challenges faced by the EU as a consequence of enlargement to the countries of Central and Eastern Europe (CEE). Widening presupposed deepening—itself charged with political dynamics.

As a result of these two main impulses, the EU faced a twofold security challenge by the mid-1990s. First, at the level of politics and institutions, there was the problem of identifying the most appropriate mechanism for decision-taking in matters of security and defense. As the North Atlantic Treaty Organization (NATO)'s very survival came increasingly into question, and as the WEU proved to be both too weak and too diverse in membership to be effective, pressures mounted to cross yet another Rubicon and open up the EU itself to defense and security policy areas—a course which the UK in particular still strenuously resisted. At the military level, it involved the development of a serious EU military capacity which would allow the Union to assume responsibility for crisis management tasks. At a meeting at Petersberg, close to Bonn, in June 1992, the WEU had defined three such tasks: 'humanitarian and rescue tasks; peacekeeping tasks; tasks of combat forces in crisis management, including peacemaking.'[5] The latter might even include high intensity war-fighting such as the Kosovo operation

[5] The latter is a roundabout euphemistic way of saying 'war-fighting,' an expression which was considered unacceptable by the German delegation at Petersberg.

of 1999. This implied radical transformation of the EU's predominantly conscript-based, line-defense forces into deployable, professional intervention forces geared to 'out of area' crisis management. Such a transformational process would clearly take time. But crises—in the Balkans and elsewhere—would not wait. As a stopgap measure, the procedures known as Berlin Plus were devised to allow the EU to plug the capabilities gap by borrowing assets from the USA. EU-only units could be put together from inside NATO by generating European Combined Joint Task Forces (CJTFs; see Terriff 2003). In short, a ESDI was to be forged, 'separable but not separate' from NATO and coordinated by the WEU. In the event, these rather awkward procedures proved unsatisfactory (Howorth & Keeler 2003). By the time Tony Blair, whose first year in office was dominated by domestic politics, was ready to look seriously into defense issues, a group of senior officials in Whitehall, liaising with their opposite numbers in Paris, had come up with an alternative. Since the inadequacies of WEU were clearly a large part of the problem, the organization, whose fifty-year treaty base was up for renewal in 1998, should, it was suggested, be scrapped. The EU should take on for itself—directly—the political responsibility for deciding on and overseeing military operations. And, in the hypothesis (which the experience of Kosovo rendered increasingly likely) of an EU-only operation which the USA wanted no part of, it should develop *autonomous* forces in order to escape dependence on complex borrowing arrangements such as Berlin Plus. That was the Rubicon crossed by Tony Blair at the historic meeting with Jacques Chirac in Saint-Malo in December 1998 (Howorth 2004). No longer content with a security and defense *identity*, the EU now embarked on the altogether more ambitious project of developing a ESDP.

Saint-Malo raised a range of major problems which the EU collectively and the member states individually have been grappling with ever since. The institutional implications were rapidly resolved and the EU successfully implanted in Brussels a raft of new bodies—the High Representative for the CFSP (HR-CFSP—Javier Solana) and his advisory Policy Unit (PU); the Political and Security Committee (COPS from the French acronym) comprising ambassadors from each member state; the European Union Military Committee (EUMC) formally made up of the Chiefs of the Defence Staff of the member states; and the EU Military Staff (EUMS) comprising some one hundred and fifty senior officers from across the Union. This institutional nexus has already demonstrated its ability to work and to work well. It is set to be fine-tuned by the institutional innovations of the EU Constitution (Duke 2003).

More problematic was the resolution of the EU's working relationship with NATO. This involved two interlocking issues. The first was the implementation of the 'Berlin Plus' arrangements for transfer to and from the EU of NATO military assets. The second was the involvement in ESDP of non-EU NATO members such as Turkey and Norway. The latter problem dominated the headlines, while the former was tackled from behind closed doors. Turkey was particularly disturbed by the ESDP project for three reasons. First, while as an associate member of the WEU from 1992 onwards, Turkey had been fully involved in intra-European security discussions, ESDP offered no such facility. The six non-EU European member states of NATO[6] not only found themselves excluded from the EU's COPS, but watched from the sidelines as four former neutral countries (Austria, Finland, Ireland, and Sweden) took up full seats on that committee. Second, Turkey feared that it was witnessing a process whereby the USA (in which Ankara had enormous faith) progressively transferred responsibility for European security to the EU (in which Ankara had very little faith). Third, this was all the more unacceptable for the Turks in that most scenarios for armed conflict and crisis management in the European theatre seemed to be situated in the southeastern parts of the continent, an area which Turkey regarded as its own 'backyard'. In particular, Turkey feared the use of ESDP military assets to intervene in Cyprus on behalf of an EU member state, Greece. Ankara therefore decided, in spring 2000, to block the Berlin Plus process by threatening to veto the transfer to the EU of those indispensable NATO assets without which the EU could hardly embark on military operations. The challenge of securing the EU's own 'near-abroad' involved not only a new relationship with NATO and with the USA, not only a radical reconfiguration of available EU military assets but also a new deal with the EU's immediate neighbors.

It took almost three years of high level negotiations, led mainly by the UK and the USA, to reach an agreement acceptable both to Ankara and to Athens (Tofte 2003). On December 16, 2002, the EU and NATO issued a 'Declaration on ESDP,' announcing the strategic partnership between them, and asserting that, while the EU would ensure 'the fullest possible involvement of non-EU European members of NATO within ESDP', NATO, for its part would guarantee the EU 'assured access to NATO's planning capabilities'. The Declaration also announced 'arrangements to ensure the coherent, transparent and mutually reinforcing development of the capability requirements common to the two organizations' (Haine 2003: 178–9). On paper, at any rate, the EU had finally solved the conundrum of its complex relationship with NATO. However, the fine print of the EU–NATO relationship remains highly classified and the specific details of the Berlin Plus arrangements have never been made public. Many analysts believe that, in the event

[6] Turkey, Norway and Iceland—joined in April 1999 by the Czech Republic, Hungary and Poland.

of two crises arising in the world simultaneously, one vital to the USA and one vital to the EU, the likelihood of the latter being able to count on the availability of key military assets belonging to the former is slim. Such a situation also stimulates the European drive for real autonomy in the area of military capacity. This remained the fundamental challenge as the EU entered the twenty first century.

2. European Military Capacity: How Much and What For?

In 2003 the EU-15 spent almost $200 billion on defense, almost half the US defense budget for that year—$404 billion (Annexe Table 2.1). That is more than three times the defense budget of the second biggest military spender on earth (Russia at $65,200 billion) and more than that of the *five* next biggest spenders put together (Russia, China, Japan, Saudi Arabia, India—$198,238 billion). It is an enormous amount of money. And yet the Union collectively gets very little bang for its euros. Out of that $200 billion, the EU-15 attempts to fund fifteen separate armies, fourteen air forces and thirteen navies. If one includes in the equation the ten 2004 accession countries, the total EU expenditure rises to $208 billion, equivalent to the *six* next biggest military spenders. But that sum funds twenty-five armies, twenty-one air forces, and eighteen navies. For what? The only one of the new accession states with any significant military clout is Poland, which ranks (at $4,095 million) in ninth place out of the EU-25, ahead of Belgium, Denmark, Portugal, Austria, Finland, Ireland and Luxembourg among the existing member states. Of the armed forces of the EU-25, only seven are fully professionalized. The others still rely to varying extents on conscripts, even if the trend is clearly towards the abolition of the draft. Furthermore, just three countries in the EU (France, the UK and Germany) together spend 62 percent of the combined EU-15 expenditure (60 percent of the EU-25). If Italy is added to the trio, the four nations contribute almost 75 percent of the EU-25 defense expenditure. The average expenditure of the lowest-spending twenty-one states comes to just $2,705 million. That is less than the defense budget of Vietnam. For as long as this situation exists, return on investment will be suboptimal. A major rationalization of the EU's defense spending is overdue. It is not necessarily greater spending that is required, as is so often asserted. Wiser spending would certainly help. But only once the EU has clearly established what it hopes to achieve, with what force levels and with what state of equipment, can it have any clear idea about *how much* money is needed. An initial attempt to create a 'ballpark' target for EU military forces came in December 1999.

The Helsinki Headline Goal (HHG), established at the European Council in Helsinki in December 1999, was conceived as a broad 'force catalogue' from which would be drawn appropriate resources for a range of hypothetical European missions, including the three levels of 'Petersberg Tasks' (humanitarian aid, peacekeeping and peacemaking). The main force catalogue was to comprise 60,000 troops, 100 ships and 400 aircraft, deployable within sixty days and sustainable for one year. However, there were several major problems with the HHG.

The first problem was the methodology. Voluntary bottom-up contributions might (just) secure the raw numbers. They do not guarantee the delivery, still less the mobilization, of a coherent fighting force. The key concept is *usability*. In 2004 there were almost 1.7 million troops in uniform in Europe. Of that number, only about 10 percent (170,000) were adequately trained even for serious *peacekeeping* operations, let alone for war-fighting. Of those, probably a maximum of 50,000 could be used for the type of *peacemaking* operation needed in a conflict such as that of Iraq. Factoring in the requirements of rotation, then the number falls to 15,000 to 20,000 troops genuinely *usable* in serious military missions (Venusberg 2004: 27). Quantities are not sufficient. What is required is far greater quality.

The second problem with the HHG has to do with the procurement of *strategic systems*. If the EU is to engage seriously in (potentially distant) crisis management operations, it needs the tools of modern force projection. The Union has identified the main areas of strategic deficiency—currently ten (Missiroli 2003: 94).[7] But in order to generate an effective EU capacity in the area of unmanned aerial vehicles, or strategic transport, or air-to-air refuelling, it is not enough to rely on voluntary efforts, or even to appoint a lead nation to chair a working group. There has to be collective political agreement to drive the process forward towards agreed targets. That means top-down, pooling and specialization. Such processes touch on sensitive issues of 'sovereignty.' The EU is moving towards the recognition of 'coordination responsibility' for key procurement projects.[8] This approach needs considerable systematization.

The third—and potentially biggest—problem with the HHG process was the absence of clear debate about the nature of the military operations the EU aims to mount. The original thinking behind the Helsinki Headline Goal derived from Kosovo. What the EU had in mind—especially in the context of the use, in the Saint-Malo Declaration, of the notion of *autonomous* forces—was the ability to carry out a Kosovo-type operation with minimal reliance

[7] Air-to-air refuelling; combat search and rescue; headquarters; nuclear, biological, and chemical defences; Special operations forces; Theatre ballistic missile defense; strategic air mobility; space; unmanned aerial vehicle/surveillance and target acquisition units; interoperability.

[8] Germany: strategic air lift; Spain: air-to-air refuelling; UK: headquarters; Netherlands: PGMs for delivery by EU F-16s.

on US inputs. This could be done in two ways. A Kosovo operation could have been mounted in 1999 with the EU's existing military assets. But it would have been very different from the US-led operation, involving ground troops and potentially many casualties. On the other hand, the EU could aim to develop a US-style capacity to fight high-level network-centric warfare (Arquilla & Ronfeldt 2001).[9] This would require even heavier defense spending. Would the price be politically acceptable? If not, would something less than a fully integrated system—what has been called a 'network-enabled' capacity—be affordable? Would it work? Answers remain elusive. To confuse capabilities planning even further, the EU decided in 2004 that it will engage in the 'global war on terrorism'. Article III-309 of the proposed Constitution extended the Petersberg tasks[10] and added the need to 'contribute to the fight against terrorism'. Yet the war on terrorism requires different instruments from those involved in driving the Serbian army out of Kosovo. Can Europe afford both when currently it seems unable to afford either? These internal contradictions at the heart of the HHG process required urgent attention. Some initial progress was made in 2004 with the announcement of a new 'Headline Goal'.

At the European Council meeting on June 17, 2004, Headline Goal 2010 (HG 2010) was adopted. Building on the HHG, the HG 2010 commits the Union 'to be able by 2010 to respond to a crisis with rapid and decisive action applying a fully coherent approach to the whole spectrum of crisis management operations covered by the Treaty on the European Union.' Interoperability, deployability and sustainability are at the heart of the project and the member states have identified an indicative list of specific milestones within the 2010 horizon, including the establishment of the European Defence Agency (EDA) by the end of 2004; the implementation of an EU strategic lift joint coordination by 2005; the ability by 2007 to deploy force packages at high readiness broadly based on the EU 'battle-groups' concept; the availability of an EU aircraft carrier by 2008; and 'appropriate compatibility and network linkage of all communications equipment and assets' by 2010. By focusing on small, rapidly deployable units capable of high intensity warfare,

[9] 'Network-centric warfare enables the military to leverage extensive information to their advantage in an effort to dramatically increase combat effectiveness and efficiency through self-synchronization across the host of entities operating on the network. ... The network-centric warfare system of the future will completely integrate every aspect of logistics and communications right down to the individual soldier ... The real time theater wide battlefield management system coupled with intelligent collaborative scenario planning systems will create the ability to retask units or division in seconds.' (Coleman 2004) See <*http://www.iwar.org.uk/index.htm*> for full details on information warfare.

[10] To include 'joint disarmament operations, *humanitarian and rescue tasks*, military advice and assistance tasks, conflict prevention and *peacekeeping tasks, tasks of combat forces undertaken for crisis management, including peacemaking* and postconflict stabilization'. The italics list the original Petersberg tasks.

HG 2010 shifted the objective from quantity to quality. It also resolved (at least partially) the contradiction between a Kosovo-style capability and the requirements of the 'war on terrorism'. The newly created battle-groups, of which up to thirteen are projected for 2007, can be used for both types of operation.[11] By the end of 2004, the EU was beginning to look like an increasingly credible potential military actor. The battle-groups model was inspired by the first ever experiences of the EU in armed combat, which took place in 2003.

On March 31, 2003, the EU launched its first military operation—a peacekeeping mission in the Former Yugoslav Republic of Macedonia (FYROM), taking over from a NATO force. Operation *Concordia* used NATO planning under the 'Berlin Plus' procedures. It deployed 357 troops (from all EU states except Ireland and Denmark, and from fourteen additional nations—an average of thirteen troops per participating member state) into a small mountainous country, successfully keeping the peace between bands of lightly armed irregulars and the Macedonian 'army' which boasts a defense budget less than half that of Luxembourg. This was an operation high in political symbolism and modest in terms of military footprint. By the end of the mission, it was clear that the biggest problem in Macedonia was no longer armed conflict but criminality—hence *Concordia* was succeeded on December 15, 2003 by an EU police operation, *Proxima.*[12] *Concordia*'s primary value was that it allowed the EU to test its recently agreed procedures covering every aspect of the mounting of a military operation—however modest—from command and control through use of force policy, to issues such as logistics, financing and legal arrangements and memoranda of understanding with host nations (Messervy-Whiting 2003).

From June to September 2003, the EU launched its first ever *autonomous* operation outside of the NATO framework. Operation *Artemis*, in the Democratic Republic of Congo offers even richer lessons about EU capabilities than *Concordia* (Cornish 2004). The initial assessment suggests that the mission, which involved rapid force projection to a distance of 6,500 kilometres into unknown and hostile terrain, was a success. France was the

[11] Battle-groups are units of 1,500 troops for combat in jungle, desert or mountain conditions, deployable within fifteen days and sustainable in the field for up to thirty days. At a meeting of the Council of Defence Ministers on November 21, 2004, it was announced that the following battle-groups were being established. France, UK, Italy and Spain will each form a 'national' BG. Others will be formed through the following combinations: France/Germany/Belgium/Luxembourg/Spain; France/Belgium; Germany/Netherlands/Finland; Germany/Czech Republic/Austria; Italy/Hungary/Slovenia; Italy/Spain/Greece/Portugal; Poland/Germany/Slovakia/Latvia/Lithuania; Sweden/Finland/Norway; UK/Netherlands.

[12] A previous police operation had been launched in Bosnia on January 1, 2003—the EUPM in Bosnia'.

'framework nation,' supplying 1,785 of the 2,200 troops deployed. Sixteen other 'troop contributing nations' (TCNs) were involved.[13] Operational planning was conducted from the French Centre de Planification et de Conduite des Opérations (CPCO) at Creil, to which were seconded officers from thirteen other countries, thus demonstrating the potential for multinationalization of a national HQ. The operation was exemplified by rapid deployment (seven days after UNSC Resolution 1484 on May 30), a single command structure, appropriately trained forces, clear rules of engagement, good incorporation of multinational elements, excellent interservice cooperation, and adequate communications. NATO procedures were used throughout. *Artemis* demonstrated conclusively that the EU can undertake a peacekeeping operation, and on a significant scale, even at some distance from Europe.

The transfer (from NATO to the EU) of responsibility for the Stabilization Force (SFOR) in Bosnia-Herzegovina (BiH) (Implementation Force—IFOR—December 1995), in December 2004 (Operation *Althea*), represented an even greater test of the EU's military muscle. The initial NATO force deployed in BiH Implementation Force (IFOR, December 1995) involved some 60,000 troops. This was scaled down constantly to a January 2003 total of 12,000. Projections for 2004 foresaw a further reduction to about 7,000 troops centred on ten battle-groups of around 750 soldiers each. Over 80 percent of the troops in NATO's SFOR were already from EU member states. Operation *Althea* was the EU's most ambitious military mission to date. It was preceded by a range of indispensable strategic and political developments.

3. Political Developments and Ongoing Dilemmas

The European Security Strategy (ESS), approved by the European Council on December 12, 2003 (European Council 2003), aims to harmonize the different views of the current and future member states without falling into lowest common denominator rhetoric. The paper inevitably constitutes something of a compromise between different cultures and approaches among the EU's member states. The first section deals with the global security environment and gives recognition to the mixed perceptions of globalization that exist. It pays greater attention to the root causes of poverty and global suffering than its US equivalent ([US National Security Strategy] 2002). It identifies five key threats: terrorism, weapons of mass destruction (WMD), failed states, organized crime, and regional conflicts. The document

[13] These provided strategic air lift (Germany, Greece, UK, Brazil and Canada), engineers (UK), helicopters (South Africa), and special forces (Sweden).

has been criticized in some quarters for its alleged alignment, via this focus on threats, with US security policy. The EU document is nevertheless more nuanced than its US equivalent, stressing the 'complex' causes behind contemporary international terrorism and recalling the destabilizing effects of regional conflicts such as Kashmir, the Great Lakes and the Korean peninsula, all of which feed into the cycle of terrorism, WMD, state failure and even international criminality. Nonetheless, it is unequivocal in stating that the EU faces the same challenges as the USA.

The second section outlines the EU's 'strategic objectives'. Two features are stressed: that 'the first line of defense will often be abroad' – via conflict prevention; and that none of the new threats is 'purely military' or manageable through purely military means. The strategic objectives rest on two main pillars: building security in the European region, and creating a viable new international order. The former is absent from US policy, the latter only fleetingly entertained. The EU document is strong in its assertion of a commitment to upholding and developing international law and in recognizing the UN as the main source of international legitimacy. However, the most innovative aspect of this section is the new emphasis on using the EU's powerful trade and development policies in a conditional and targeted way. The final section addresses the policy implications for the EU. The EU needs to be 'more active, more capable and more coherent.' One of the boldest statements of the document (which guaranteed applause in the USA) is the need to develop a strategic culture that fosters 'early, rapid and, where necessary, robust intervention'. The Strategy, it is claimed, will contribute 'to an effective multilateral system leading to a fairer, safer and more united world'.[14] However, the ESS was only the first statement of European strategic intent. It called for a wider-ranging approach coupling means and ends in a credible way.

Such a concept was put forward in May 2004 by the 'Venusberg Group'—a research team from the Bertelsmann Foundation (Venusberg 2004). The new proposals call for the EU to develop 'a holistic, strategic civil military vision that combines achievable means and ends'. The EU, it argues, must be able to carry out 'a far broader range of missions than currently envisaged, over far greater distance, at potentially higher levels of conflict intensity and for longer periods'. New institutions such as an EU Security Council, an EU Security Minister, and an EU Homeland Security Agency are envisaged. The EU, it is argued, should not seek to close the capabilities gap with the USA, but to bridge the gap between the EU's own strategic environment and its real military capabilities. This will require intensive cooperation with NATO

[14] Three good analytical critiques of the Solana document are Haine 2003*a*, Biscop and Coolsaet 2003 and Toje 2005.

and with the USA but also robustly autonomous EU facilities such as operational planning, including an EU Permanent Combined Joint Headquarters, as well as satellite-based intelligence, jointly trained special forces, and the development of a 10,000-strong European *Gendarmerie* to bridge the gap between combat soldiering and policing.[15] It also takes on board the entire range of procurement projects currently prioritized under the HHG process. It calls for a EU Joint Intelligence Committee as well as a European Security and Defence College, a common research and technology budget coordinated through a strong European Defence Agency and even a 'Buy European First' strategy for procurement. Impulsion would come from an Anglo-Franco-German 'Trirectoire' (a highly contentious proposal), a 2 percent of GDP benchmark for defense budgets and rationalization of existing spending through a Defence Business Affairs Programme. These ambitious and comprehensive proposals are likely to constitute a major sounding board for the debate on European security and defense developments over the next ten to fifteen years. They indicated considerable dynamism in the project as Europe stood on the brink of becoming a credible military actor.

4. The European Constitution and its Defense and Security Implications

The Constitutional Treaty of August 2004 (Art. III-311) called for the creation of a European Defence Agency subject to the authority of the Council. Armaments cooperation has hitherto taken place rigorously outside the EU framework. Two main reasons lie behind this belated decision to change tack. The first is the relative failure of previous attempts to coordinate procurement and armaments cooperation. The second is the accelerating reality of ESDP and the concurrent perceived need to link capabilities to armaments production. The urgency of these drivers was reflected in the fact that, at the Thessaloniki Council in June 2003, it was agreed not to await ratification of the Treaty in order to launch the EDA. The agency was to be created immediately. In early 2004, an Agency Establishment Team set about clarifying its objectives and role and narrowed down four basic purposes: To work for a more comprehensive and systematic approach to defining and meeting ESDP's *capability* needs: to promote *equipment collaboration*, both to contribute to defense capabilities and to

[15] This was taken further in September 2004 when France, Italy, Spain, Portugal, and the Netherlands agreed to mount such a Gendarmerie—which will be open for other to join in the future. The force will be 3,000 strong, and is expected to be available for deployment from 2005.

foster further restructuring of European defense industries; to encourage the widening and deepening of regulatory approaches and the achievement of a European defense *equipment market*; and to promote defense-relevant *research and technology* (R&T), 'pursuing collaborative use of national defense R&T funds' and 'leveraging other funding sources, including those for dual use or security-related research'.[16]

The EDA will be guided by a Steering Board meeting at the level of Defense Ministers, nominally headed by the HR-CFSP (later Union Minister for Foreign Affairs) and managed by a chief executive.[17] It offers the first real opportunity for the EU to bring its defense planning, military capability objectives and armaments coordination in line with the urgent tasks it is facing on the ground. It will have to be 'pragmatic and practical, focusing on areas where the agency can make a visible difference, thereby establishing credibility that could foster greater ambitions for the future' (IISS 2004). The EU governments are poised to take a major step forward towards more rational armaments and defense planning. The dynamics of ESDP suggest that they will progressively situate their national plans within a European framework. This would be the first step on a potentially very long road. But even the longest journey has to start with the first step.

Another breakthrough came in 2003 in the field of operational planning. This was a contentious issue which had, for several years, pitted the UK against France. Operational planning is the sine qua non of any military mission. Paris had always been keen to develop *autonomous* EU operational planning capabilities, but London had resisted, arguing that this was an expensive duplication of an already existing NATO capability. The UK insisted that, in the event of an 'EU-only' operation (i.e. without reference to NATO and without the support of NATO planning via Berlin Plus), such missions should have recourse to the *national* operational planning facilities which existed in the UK (Northwood), France (Creil) and, to a lesser extent, in Germany, Italy and Greece. However, at the controversial defense summit between France, Germany, Belgium and Luxembourg on April 29 2003, at the height of the Iraq crisis, the summiteers decided to forge ahead and create an 'EU' operational planning cell at a Belgian army base in Tervuren, a suburb of Brussels. This provoked outrage in Washington and London and, for a moment, seemed destined to derail the entire ESDP project (IISS 2003). However, later that summer as Tony Blair sought to mend fences with his European partners, a compromise was arrived at involving three distinct

[16] Private policy paper by Burkard Schmitt, Deputy Director of the EU Institute for Security Studies. I am grateful to Dr Schmitt for sending me this paper, on which I have drawn in the following paragraphs. For an earlier paper by Schmitt, see 'Progress towards the European Defence Agency', *Analyses* (Paris: EU-ISS), Winter 2004.

[17] After a fierce battle between France and the UK, the Chief Executive was named as Nick Witney, the former head of the UK MOD's International Security Policy Division.

operational planning facilities. For EU operations under Berlin Plus, a dedicated EU unit has been attached to NATO at SHAPE. For most 'EU-only' operations, including most battle-group missions, an appropriate national HQ will be multinationalized. But for certain EU-only operations, particularly those involving combined civil and military dimensions, a dedicated (and autonomous) EU planning cell is being developed at ESDP headquarters in the rue Cortenberg in Brussels. Thus face was saved on all sides and the EU's capabilities considerably enhanced.

Another potential breakthrough in 2004 came in the field of *intelligence gathering*. The agreement between the EU and the USA for the coordination of the former's Galileo satellite navigation system with the US GPS system potentially constitutes a major step forward on the road to EU autonomy in intelligence gathering (Lindstrom 2003). Galileo is a civilian program. Although it has considerable military potential, the political decision to develop that potential has yet to be taken. For the EU collectively to forge an integrated intelligence capacity several major hurdles would have to be cleared—not the least of which is the intimate relationship between the UK and the US intelligence services. However, a recent report suggests that much can be done vastly to improve the current level of intelligence coordination, including expansion of the existing EU Situation Centre, extending the competencies of Europol and establishing a European network of National High Authorities of Intelligence and improving cross-agency cooperation at national level (Muller-Wille 2004).

It should be borne in mind that ESDP is but a subset of the EU's CFSP. In recent years, partly because events in the former have developed at breakneck speed, the attention of commentators and analysts has tended to focus on ESDP. Yet *foreign policy* emerged from the constitutional debates considerably strengthened. In particular, the new Union Minister for Foreign Affairs (UMFA) has the potential to become an immensely powerful figure. The post-holder will combine the current responsibilities of both the HR-CFSP and the Commissioner for External Relations, thus having one foot in the Council and one (as Vice President) in the Commission. This will allow him or her to coordinate the two main thrusts of the EU's external policy: security and overseas aid. The UMFA will also contribute both to the preparation of and to the implementation of CFSP/ESDP and will chair the new Foreign Affairs Council. He or she[18] will represent the Union in international organizations and at international conferences, and will 'conduct political dialogue' on the Union's behalf. The post-holder, elected for a five-year term, will replace the previous semestrial rotating Presidency, thus accumulating

[18] In fact, the first post-holder was appointed in June 2004, even before the post itself existed. Javier Solana will be the first UMFA.

even more authority. Moreover, the UMFA will preside over a 'European External Action Service,' which is intended to be introduced within one year after entry into force of the Treaty (Duke 2002). The creation of this position had, by 2003, become a standard proposal in think tank papers on the future of CFSP. Somewhat paradoxically, it was promoted hardest by the larger member states, whose propensity to perpetuate *national* foreign policy preferences is strongest. The explanation is to be sought not only in their assumption that the post-holder will be drawn from among *their* senior politicians (one reason why the post was resisted by some smaller states) but more significantly in the growing embrace, on the part of those larger states, of the notion of a common foreign policy as a 'power maximizer'. The stage is clearly set for a trial of strength between some national capitals and the new UMFA. But all the signs are that foreign policy will increasingly be Europeanized. In today's complex world, lone European voices command less and less attention. Divided European voices have minimal impact.

Two further challenges were raised in the constitutional debates: how to maximize the political coordination of military capacity, and whether to move towards some statement of European collective defense. A new instrument which emerged from the Convention and the Intergovernmental Conference that followed it was 'structured cooperation.' This involved an attempt, promoted by France and Germany, to go beyond 'enhanced cooperation' as provided for in the TEU and to allow a small number of militarily well-endowed states to drive forward ESDP in the name of the entire Union. The Draft Constitution specifies (Art. I-41(6) and III-312) that 'those member states whose military capabilities fulfil higher criteria and which have made more binding commitments to one another in this area with a view to the most demanding missions shall establish structured cooperation within the Union framework.' While this would allow the more 'muscular' member states to forge ahead with coordinated EU military capacity and even to form coalitions with a view to mounting EU missions, the procedure was seen by many member states, including the UK, to carry two main dangers. The first was that membership of 'structured cooperation' would be restricted to a small band of self-selected countries and would be overtly 'exclusivist'. The second was that it would be seen as an alternative to NATO. As a consequence of Britain's desire to mend fences with its European allies after Iraq, a trade-off was reached in September 2003 between France, Germany and the UK whereby the latter dropped its objections to structured cooperation in exchange for explicit commitments by the former two countries that the scheme would be as *inclusive* as possible and that it would work in harmony with NATO. The capabilities required for membership were identified as either a specialist 'niche' contribution or participation in one of the battle-groups currently being planned under the new *Headline*

Goal 2010. Most EU member states, given the political will, should be able to find a way of joining. Structured cooperation, in short, is all about *capacity*. What use the EU makes of that capacity is entirely up to the Council, acting unanimously. No member state will be forced to do anything. But the potential to act—in the name and under the flag of the EU—is considerable. This was a minor revolution in EU affairs.

It was complemented to some extent by another innovation: the introduction into the Constitutional Draft of a 'mutual assistance' clause stating, 'If a Member state is the victim of armed aggression on its territory, the other member states shall have towards it an obligation of aid and assistance by all the means in their power, in accordance with Article 51 of the United Nations Charter.' This was a highly sensitive issue. An early version of this arrangement had been vetoed by Tony Blair as his first act of security policy at the Amsterdam Council in June 1997. The Atlanticist states feared it would lead to a downgrading of the Alliance. The 'neutral' states feared they would be sucked into something they did not agree with. On the other hand, the Europeanist states had hoped for a much more robust statement. The final text was a largely common sense recognition that, in the event of attack against a member state, the others will do what they feel they can (or wish to) do to help out. It is a small step towards the recognition of common interests, rights and responsibilities. In the context of a constitution which has already enshrined structured cooperation, the very fact that a specific clause on mutual assistance is included in the text at all acquires real political significance. At the same time, a new 'solidarity clause' in the event of a terrorist attack or a natural or man-made disaster, was also introduced into the treaty (Art. III-329). The EU is explicitly attempting to pull ever more closely together, even in these areas which were once the last (and indeed the first) bastion of sovereignty.

5. Conclusions

I noted at the outset of this chapter that two powerful forces were projecting the EU towards some form of ESDP. The first was as a result of exogenous pressures from the USA and other parts of the world. Although US pressure was a major midwife of ESDP, US reactions to the new infant have been varied and contradictory (Sloan 2000). The initial (semiofficial) reaction was of the 'Yes, but . . . ' variety. ESDP would be acceptable to Washington if it proved to be what the Saint-Malo declaration said it intended to be: a contribution to a revitalized transatlantic alliance. For this to happen, certain conditions must be met, including Secretary of State Madeleine Albright's instant strictures against NATO 'decoupling, duplication and discrimination' (Albright 1998). This position has ebbed and flowed in the reactions of administration spokespersons with the regularity of the tides. It has alternated with the expression of serious opposition to the entire ESDP project. This has assumed two contradictory forms. The opposition is motivated either by a belief that ESDP will in fact emerge as a rival to NATO,[19] or that it will prove to be such an incompetent force that it will merely aggravate alliance tensions.[20] As ESDP began to emerge as a viable military actor in 2003–4, the latter fears were silenced and the 'debate' on ESDP featured the two former attitudes. Official Pentagon and State Department spokespersons, faced with a US military which was vastly overstretched in late 2004, began reiterating the initial ESDP mantras: European military capacity was to be welcomed because, if EU–US political tensions could be resolved, the European force could relieve the US armed forces. However, other conservative commentators, scrutinizing some of the debates within the Convention, were forced to the conclusion that the 'political integration of the EU presents the greatest challenge to continuing US influence in Europe since World War II, and US policy must begin to adapt accordingly' (Cimbalo 2004; see also Hulsman 2004).[21] The US administration is faced with an 'agonizing reappraisal' of its entire attitude towards European unity. At the time of writing (December 2004), it was unclear which route it would take. Meanwhile, however, ESDP continued to thrive.

Endogenously, the internal developments of the European integration process have had a marked effect on this new policy area. Much has been accomplished very rapidly in a period of five short years. Yet any overall evaluation of European military capacity has to be set within a very clear timeframe. Over the next five years (the short term), the EU will need to absorb the lessons of *Concordia*, *Artemis*, *Althea* and other such operations, concentrate on plugging the gaps in strategic assets, develop genuinely integrated operational capacity and perfect command, logistics and communications procedures. This will limit actual operations to the type and style of those we have already witnessed and are about to witness. During this period also, however, the EU will need to plan procurement projects for the medium term

[19] When Tony Blair first visited President Bush after the latter's election, in February 2001, he was first given a grilling by Vice President Cheney who expressed his clear opposition to ESDP. See Stephens 2004: 190.

[20] This was implicit in the remarks of State Department official Richard Boucher who contemptuously dismissed the four-nation summit in Brussels in April 2003 as the 'chocolate-makers' summit'.

[21] The author went on to argue that the US administration 'must condemn the terms [of the EU Constitution] as absolutely unacceptable because they are impossible to square with effective NATO membership'. Unfortunately, the author was reading the wrong text, having confused the Convention draft with the actual Constitution.

(the following fifteen years). This will necessitate tough political decisions about the ultimate size, scale and style of EU military ambitions. How far down the road towards US-style network centric warfare will the Union wish to go? How many new generation platforms and other strategic systems will it require—for what purposes? How far afield does it anticipate intervening? In parallel, the Union will have to develop a holistic *Strategic Concept* along the lines of the proposals discussed above. Without clear guidelines as to its ultimate objectives and purpose, progress will be stalled. In the longer term, only two factors prevent the EU from developing genuinely autonomous and seriously credible military muscle: its ability to cooperate and to integrate and the political will to implement its decisions and to act robustly in support of the values and interests outlined in its evolving security strategy. That is the internal challenge facing the next generation of Europeans.

Annexe

TABLE 2.1. *EU Member States Defence Expenditure (2003)*

Country	US$m	US$ per capita	% of GDP	Forces (000)*
USA	404,920	1,391	3.7	1,427
1. France	45,695	765 (1)	2.6 (2)	259.0
2. UK	42,782	722 (2)	2.4 (3)	212.6
3. Germany	35,145	426 (10)	1.5 (18)	284.5
4. Italy	27,751	481 (8)	1.9 (10=)	200.0
5. Spain	9,944	242 (15)	1.2 (22)	150.7
6. Netherlands	8,256	509 (7)	1.6 (16=)	53.1
7. Greece	7,169	671 (3)	4.1 (1)	177.6
8. Sweden	5,532	618 (5)	1.8 (14=)	27.6
9. Poland	4,095	107 (22)	2.0 (8=)	163.0
10. Belgium	3,923	379 (11)	1.3 (21)	40.8
11. Denmark	3,334	619 (4)	1.6 (16=)	22.8
12. Portugal	3,173	311 (13)	2.1 (6)	44.9
13. Austria	2,488	309 (14)	1.0 (23)	34.6
14. Finland	2,300	441 (9)	1.4 (19=)	27.0
15. Czech Rep	1,871	183 (19)	2.2 (5)	57.0
16. Hungary	1,589	157 (20)	1.9 (10=)	33.4
17. Ireland	803	204 (17)	0.5 (25)	10.4
18. Slovakia	627	117 (22)	1.9 (10=)	22.0
19. Slovenia	378	192 (18)	1.4 (19=)	6.5
20. Lithuania	342	99 (24)	1.8 (14=)	12.7
21. Cyprus	294	382 (12)	2.3 (4)	10.0
23. Luxemb'g	233	520 (6)	0.9 (24)	0.9
22. Latvia	194	84 (25)	1.9 (10=)	4.9
24. Estonia	172	127 (21)	2.0 (8=)	5.5
25. Malta	95	237 (16)	2.1 (6=)	2.1
[** Romania]	[1,313 (17)]	[59 (26)]	[2.3 (4=)]	[97.2]
EU-15 Totals	198,528 m			1,605,900
EU-25 Totals	208.185 m			1,863,600
EU-15 Av	13,235	485	1.91	
EU-25 Av	8,327	361	2.2	

Source: The Military Balance 2004–2005, pp. 353–8.
*Forces figures are 2002.

TABLE 2.2. *European Armed Forces (2002/3)*

Country	Prof/Consc	Army	Navy	Air Force	Total
Austria	**Conscript**	**34,600**	*****	**6,850***	**34,600**
Belgium	**Professional**	**24,800**	**2,450**	**10,250**	**39,200**
Cyprus	Conscript	10,000	*****	*****	10,000
Czechy	Conscript	39,850	*****	13,100	49,400
Denmark	**Conscript**	**14,700**	**4,000**	**3,500**	**22,700**
Estonia	Conscript	2,550	440	220	5,000
Finland	**Conscript**	**19,200**	**5,000**	**2,800**	**31,800**
France	**Professional**	**137,000**	**44,250**	**64,000**	**260,000**
Germany	**Conscript**	**191,350**	**25,650**	**67,500**	**296,000**
Greece	**Conscript**	**114,000**	**19,000**	**33,000**	**177,000**
Hungary	Conscript	**23,600**	*****	**7,700**	**33,000**
Ireland	**Professional**	**8,500**	**1,100**	**860**	**10,500**
Italy	**Conscript**	**116,000**	**36,000**	**48,000**	**216,000**
Latvia	Conscript	4,000	620	250	5,500
Lithuania	Conscript	7,950	650	1,150	13,500
Luxembourg	**Professional**	**900**	*****	*****	**900**
Malta	Professional	2,140	2,140**	2,140**	2,140
Netherlands	**Professional**	**23,150**	**12,130**	**11,050**	**49,600**
Poland	Conscript	104,050	14,300	36,450	163,000
Portugal	**Conscript**	**26,700**	**10,950**	**7,250**	**43,600**
Slovakia	Conscript	13,700	*****	7,000	26,000
Slovenia	Conscript	6,500	*****	530	9,000
Spain	**Professional**	**95,600**	**22,900**	**22,750**	**177,900**
Sweden	**Conscript**	**13,800**	**7,900**	**5,900**	**33,000**
UK	**Professional**	**116,670**	**42,370**	**53,620**	**210,400**
Norway	Conscript	14,700	6,100	5,000	26,600
Turkey	Conscript	402,000	52,750	60,100	514,850

*Austrian air service is part of the army.
**Maltese armed forces cover all three services.
Of **EU-15,** Austria and Luxembourg have no navy and Luxembourg has no air force.
Of **EU-15,** eight still field conscript armies (although Italy is phasing it out).
All EU Accession states (except Malta) have conscript armed forces.

TABLE 2.3. *World Military Expenditure (2003)*

Milit Spend '03	Expend.$millions	$ per capita	% of GDP
1. USA	404,920	1,391	3.7 ↑
2. Russia	65,200	455	4.9 ↑
3. China	55,948	37	4.1 ↑
4. France	45,695	765	2.6 ↑
5. Japan	42,835	337	1.0 -
6. UK	42,782	722	2.4 -
7. Germany	35,145	426	1.5 ↓
8. Italy	27,751	481	1.9 -
9. Saudi Arabia	18,747	832	8.9 ↓
10. India	15,508	15	2.6 ↓
11. South Korea	14,632	305	2.8 -
12. Turkey	11,649	165	4.9 -
13. Australia	11,758	591	2.3 ↑
14. Israel	10,325	1,544	9.5 -
15. Spain	9,944	242	1.2 -
16. Brazil	9,274	53	1.8 ↓
17. Netherlands	8,256	509	1.6 -
18. Taiwan	7,479	336	2.7 ↓
NATO	626,033	773	2.8 ↑
[NATO Europe]	[221,113]	[426]	[1.9] ↑

TABLE 2.3. (*Continued*)

Milit Spend '03	Expend.$millions	$ per capita	% of GDP
[EU 25]	[208,185]	[365]	[1.9] ↑
ME & N Africa	54,148	165	6.0 ↓
C & S Asia	24,388	16	2.6 -
E Asia + Austral	164,379	79	2.1 -
Carib + C/S Am	25,145	47	1.4 ↓
Sub-Sah Africa	7,716	11v	1.9 ↑

US expenditure ($405 bn) =.
The next *fourteen* combined (Russia to Spain = $408 billion).
'Axis of Evil' states + Russia + China + Japan + NATO Europe (= $395 bn).
The rest of the entire world (minus NATO Europe) (= $371 bn).
NB: US expenditure in 2007 = $470bn.
Source: The Military Balance 2004–2005, pp. 353–8.
↑ or ↓ = budget rise or fall as % GDP (2002–2003).

References

Albright, M. (1998). 'The Right Balance Will Secure NATO's Future', *Financial Times*, 7 December.

Arquilla, J. and Ronfeldt, D. (2001). *Networks and Netwars: The Future of Terror, Crime, and Militancy*. Santa Monica, CA: RAND.

Biscop, S. and Coolsaet, R. (2003). *The World is the Stage—A Global Security Strategy for the European Union*, Policy Paper No. 8, *Notre Europe*, Paris. accessed at <*www.notre-europe.asso.fr*>.

Cimbalo, J. (2004). 'Saving NATO from Europe', *Foreign Affairs*, 83/6.

Coleman, K. (2004). 'Network Centric Warfare', *Directions Magazine*, May 14.

Cornish, P. (2004). *Artemis and Coral: British Perspectives on European Union Crisis Management Operations in the Democratic Republic of Congo, 2003*. Unpublished report, Kings College, London.

Duke, S. (2002). 'Preparing for European Diplomacy?' *Journal of Common Market Studies*, 40/5.

—— (2003). *The Convention, the Draft Constitution and External Relations: Effects and Implications for the EU and its International Role*. Maastricht: EIPA.

European Council. (2003). *A Secure Europe in a Better World (Solana Strategy Paper)*. Brussels, December 12, accessible at <*http://ue.eu.int/uedocs/cmsUpload/78367.pdf*>.

Haine, J.-Y. (ed.) (2003). *From Laeken to Copenhagen. European Defence: Core Documents 3*. EU-ISS Chaillot Paper No. 57, available at <*www.iss-eu.org*>.

—— (2003*a*). 'European Strategy: First Steps', *EU-ISS Newsletter*, No.7 (July) available at <*www.iss-eu.org*>.

Howorth, J. (2000). *European Integration and Defence: The Ultimate Challenge?* WEU-ISS Chaillot Paper No. 43, available at <*www.iss-eu.org*>.

—— and Keeler, J. (eds.) (2003). *Defending Europe: The EU, NATO and the Quest for European Autonomy*. New York: Palgrave.

Howorth, J. (2004). 'Discourse, Ideas and Epistemic Communities in European Security and Defence Policy', in *West European Politics*, 27/1: pp. 29–52.

—— (2004*a*). 'The European Draft Constitutional Treaty and the Future of the European Defence Initiative: A Question of Flexibility?', *European Foreign Affairs Review*, 9/4.

Hulsman, J. (2004). 'A Conservative Vision for US Policy Towards Europe', *Heritage Foundation Backgrounder*, No. 1803.

Hunter, R. E. (2002). *The European Security and Defense Policy: NATO's Companion—or Competitor?* Monterrey, CA: RAND.

IISS (International Institute for Strategic Studies) (2003). 'EU Operational Planning', *Strategic Comments*, 9/10.

—— (2004). 'The European Defence Agency', *Strategic Comments*, 10/5.

Lindstrom, G. (2003). *The Galileo Satellite System and its Security Implications.* EU-ISS Occasional Paper No. 44.

Mandelbaum, M. (1996). *The Dawn of Peace in Europe.* New York: Twentieth Century Fund.

Menon, A. (2004). 'From Crisis to Catharsis' ESDP After Iraq', *International Affairs*, 80/4.

Messervy-Whiting, G. (2003). 'The Politico-Military Structure in Brussels: Capabilities and Limits', Discussion paper for the Geneva Centre for Security Policy Workshop on *The EU and Peace Operations*, 22–23 September.

Missiroli, A. (ed.) (2003). *From Copenhagen to Brussels. European Defence: Core Documents 4.* EU-ISS No. Chaillot Paper No. 67, available at <*www.iss-eu.org*>.

Muller-Wille, B. (2004). *For Our Eyes Only? Shaping an Intelligence Community within the EU.* Paris EU-ISS Occasional Paper No. 50.

Nuttall, S. (1992). *European Political Cooperation.* Oxford: Clarendon Press.

Peterson, J. and Sjursen, H. (1998). *A Common Foreign Policy for Europe. Competing Visions of the CFSP.* London: Routledge.

Quinlan, M. (2001). *European Defence Cooperation: Asset or Threat to NATO?* Washington DC: Woodrow Wilson Center Press.

Regelsberger, E., de Schoutheete, P., and Wessels, W. (1997). *Foreign Policy of the European Union. From EPC to CFSP and Beyond.* Boulder, CO: Lynne Rienner.

Rutten, M. (ed.) (2001). *From Saint-Malo to Nice. European Defence: Core Documents.* WEU-ISS Chaillot Paper No. 47, available at <*www.iss-eu.org*>.

—— (ed.) (2002). *From Nice to Laeken. European Defence: Core Documents 2.* EU-ISS Chaillot Paper No. 51, available at <*www.iss-eu.org*>.

Schmitt, B. (2000). *From Cooperation to Integration: Defence and Aerospace Industries in Europe.* WEU-ISS Chaillot Paper No. 40, available at <*www.iss-eu.org*>.

—— (2003). *The European Union and Armaments: Getting a Bigger Bang for the Euro.* EU-ISS Chaillot Paper No. 63, available at <*www.iss-eu.org*>.

Sloan, S. (2000). *The United States and European Defence.* WEU-ISS Chaillot Paper No. 39, available at <*www.iss-eu.org*>.

Stephens, P. (2004). *Tony Blair: The Making of a World Leader.* London: Penguin.

Terriff, T. (2003). 'The CJTF Concept and the Limits of European Autonomy', in J. Howorth and J. Keeler (eds.), *Defending Europe: The EU, NATO and the Quest for European Autonomy.* New York: Palgrave, pp. 39–60.

Tofte, S. (2003). 'Non-EU NATO Members and the Issue of Discrimination', in J. Howorth and J. Keeler (eds.), *Defending Europe: the EU, NATO and the Quest for European Autonomy.* New York: Palgrave, pp. 135–56.

Toje, A. (2005). 'The 2003 European Union Security Strategy: A Critical Appraisal', *European Foreign Affairs Review*, 10/1.

US National Security Strategy (2002). *The National Security Strategy of the United States.* Available at <*http://www.whitehouse.gov/nsc/nss.html*>.

Venusberg Group (2004). *A European Defence Strategy.* Bonn: Gütersloh, Bertelsmann.

3

Continental Divide? The Transience of Transatlantic Troubles

BRIAN RATHBUN*

> The United States and Europe are fundamentally different today. [U.S. Secretary of State Colin] Powell and [U.S. Secretary of Defense Donald] Rumsfeld have more in common than do Powell and [former French foreign minister] Hubert Védrine or even [British foreign minister] Jack Straw. When it comes to the use of force, mainstream American Democrats have more in common with Republicans than they do with most European Socialists and Social Democrats. During the 1990s even American liberals were more willing to resort to force... than most of their European counterparts. Whether [European governments] would have bombed even Belgrade in 1999, had the U.S. not forced their hand, is an interesting question.
>
> Robert Kagan, 'Power and Weakness,' *Policy Review* (June 2002)

Kagan is right. Powell and Rumsfeld do have more in common on foreign affairs than Powell and Straw or Védrine. However, the reason is the exact one that he denigrates in one of the most widely read statements on transatlantic relations in recent decades (Kagan 2003). The left and right in the USA and its major European allies conceive of the national interest and the means of achieving it in fundamentally different ways. Powell and Rumsfeld are Republicans, not social democrats like Straw and Védrine. By underestimating the importance of party ideology, Kagan misdiagnoses the current uneasy state of transatlantic relations as 'systemic' and 'incurable'. Here he is wrong.

This chapter offers a conjuctural argument about the much-lamented state of transatlantic relations. Its condition at any time is largely the result of the partisan character of governments and coalitions in North America and Europe. Transatlantic convergence depends on domestic convergence as well. The combination also largely determines whether more or less of an US presence in Europe and beyond is desirable to Europeans. Current tensions are due to the combination of a Republican administration in the USA

* Parts of this chapter are reprinted from *Partisan Interventions: European Party Politics and Peace Enforcement in the Balkans*, by Brian Rathbun. © 2004 Cornell University. Used by permission of the publisher, Cornell University Press.

on the one hand and a Gaullist government in France and a Red-Green coalition in Germany on the other. I trace the ups and downs of US-European relations since the end of the Cold War with a focus on debates about the use of force in the Balkans and Iraq. During the wars in Bosnia and Kosovo, there was often more disagreement *within* the USA, France, Germany, and Britain than *between* these countries, and international differences generally reflected the ideological incompatibility of different national governments. I offer a conceptualization of ideological differences on foreign policy and an explanation of where particular parties locate themselves on those continua.

I argue that leftist parties are more inclusive and antimilitarist than their rightist counterparts. By inclusive I mean both humanitarian and multilateralist. Leftist parties will fight humanitarian wars with more passion than rightist parties, provided they can overcome their antimilitarist objections, which most European leftists did (although at various speeds). Rightist parties have a more restricted sense of the national interest that generally does not include the promotion of welfare abroad. When Kagan writes that *even* US liberals wanted to bomb Milosevic, he should write the left *especially* supported the use of force. This was true in Europe as well with just a few exceptions. Much of the transatlantic tension during Bosnia owed to the presence of conservatives in the British and French governments and their disputes with the Democratic administration in the USA. Much of the transatlantic unity during Kosovo owed to the presence of leftist parties in the US, French, and British governments and the Gaullists in France, whose arguments tend to resonate with leftists although for ultimately more instrumental purposes. Contrary to Kagan's hypothesis, it was the Clinton administration, fearing a Republican uprising in the Congress at home, that was reluctant to pull the trigger in Kosovo. The Europeans, particularly the Labour government, helped the Democrats remain resolute.

Although the Republicans campaigned in 2001 on an isolationist platform against nation-building, humanitarian intervention and other international involvements, the world came to the USA in September 2001. The USA responded to a new strategic threat aggressively. Nevertheless, given the ideological fundamentals of rightist parties, a Republican administration could have been expected to behave in such a manner. While the European left endorsed the US invasion of Afghanistan as a legitimate act of self-defense, it objected to the US war in Iraq on the grounds that mark its approach to international politics. The forceful projection of American interests, at least as they were defined by the right, can be considered an exogenous shock, one of the mechanisms for change identified by the editors. Leftist parties by and large, as well as Gaullists, doubted the humanitarian rationale, believed that diplomacy was not given enough time and resented the unwillingness of the USA to accept international constraints on its behavior.

This has had some paradoxical effects on the development of EU institutions. It has strengthened the movement toward a European Security and Defense Policy but weakened the coherence of the Common Foreign and Security Policy. The former is a process of institutional creation to allow the projection of military force but does not specify any particular operation. The conjunctural factors that explain its origins emerged from the Iraq war unscathed. The latter, however, requires agreement on policy, which is not currently present due to transatlantic disturbances. However, the boost that the Iraq conflict has given ESDP might ultimately undermine it as it has led to the reemergence of traditional resentments of US power that date from the Cold War. The fading of these concerns in France in the early post-Cold War period were a precondition for ESDP success. The state of transatlantic relations, in large part a result of domestic politics in powerful EU member states, therefore has implications for EU's efforts to establish itself as a global leader—another powerful mechanism for change at work in this story.

1. A Hobbesian Right and a Kantian Left?

Kagan argues that Europe and the USA live in different worlds. The former is 'entering a posthistorical paradise of peace' foreseen by the liberal idealist philosopher Immanuel Kant, where conflicts are solved with diplomacy through the framework of international institutions that govern behavior and constrain states. The USA, in contrast, continues to inhabit an environment resembling one described by another great philosopher, an 'anarchic Hobbesian world where international laws and rules are unreliable and where true security and the defense and promotion of a liberal order still depend on the possession and use of military might.' Some might call this a 'realist' world, although this is an inappropriate term as realists do not eschew all international agreements when they serve useful purposes. Nor do they necessarily believe that in the use of force convinces others of resolve and helps countries realize their future interests peacefully. The concepts of the security dilemma and the balance of power, central to realist thought, remind states that violence or the threat of it often begets more of the same.

Nevertheless, Kagan does pinpoint central concepts that divide not so much continents, but nations themselves—multilateralism and antimilitarism. I argue that these notions are part of two fundamental cleavages distinguishing left from right in foreign policy (Rathbun 2004). Leftists fight the battles of the weak against the strong. This stress on realizing *equality*, whether it be defined economically or socially, marks a broader notion of community at home (Lipset 1954; Putnam 1973; Gerring 1998). These parties aim at integrating the underprivileged more fully into society.

The parallel internationally is what I call an 'inclusive' conception of the national interest. The clearest analogue is the left's stronger support for foreign aid, the international equivalent of domestic welfare programs (Lumsdaine 1993).

More broadly an inclusive conception of the national interest manifests itself at two levels, that of the individual and the nation. In terms of the former, leftists demonstrate their inclusiveness by their concern for promoting universal human rights, the principle that all mankind is equal and should enjoy certain freedoms. As regards the latter, leftists are more genuine believers in an international community and are consequently more comfortable with using multilateral organizations as frameworks for resolving differences as they embody this cosmopolitanism (Chittick and Freyberg-Inan 2001). This is not to say that leftists build international organizations for their own sake, but have few qualms when they support their purpose. In contrast, rightists exhibit what I call a more exclusive conception of the national interest, one that focuses on the tangible consequences of world events for their own nation, and as a result finds international organizations less legitimate. Rightists prefer instead maintaining a free hand to defend their own interests. They resist relinquishing of sovereignty, sometimes even in a symbolic sense. There are, however, some notable exceptions to this tendency, particularly among the French right. The uniqueness of Gaullism has been the wedding of universalist principles, originally the province of the revolutionary left in France, to a particular conception of how to promote France's more exclusive national interests. France, as the embodiment of the values of human rights and democracy, deserves a place at the table of great powers. The inclusive concern, I have argued elsewhere, is nevertheless largely instrumental, certainly in comparison with the French left (Rathbun 2004: ch. 5). It serves the promotion of French grandeur.

The left is also more antimilitarist than the right, both due to its egalitarianism and libertarianism. While in the economic sphere, leftists endorse state power so as to fulfill a redistributive agenda, in the social and political spheres, the left fights against coercive state or religious authority in favor of individual freedom. Both equality and liberty contribute to antimilitarism. The use of force to resolve conflicts is an imposition of right and wrong rather than an agreement on the basis of dialogue or law. In addition, its end result is the subordination of one party under another, the creation of an unequal hierarchy of weak and strong. Leftists object to both the ineffectiveness and the immorality of war. The right, on the other hand, is more inclined to believe in the effectiveness and the necessity of force.

Antimilitarism, or dovishness, manifests itself in the language and strategy of what is called the 'spiral' model of international politics. Under this logic, force, or the threat of violence, only exacerbates conflict and prohibits compromise by hardening positions. Concessions, on the other hand, create trust and help parties reach mutually beneficial agreements. Hawkishness is marked by the opposite logic, sometimes called the deterrence/compellence model. It is evident in strategies of standing firm, so as to indicate resolve and thereby induce capitulation on the other side. Not doing so will invite provocation and attempts to take advantage (Jervis 1976: ch. 3; Snyder and Diesing 1977).

Use of deterrence/compellence or spiral language to justify a position, cannot, however, always be taken as a sign of an ideological preference along the hawk-dove continuum. It is also a marker of willingness to intervene that might reflect preferences along the inclusive/exclusive dimension. Those who support humanitarian intervention are likely to claim that the only way to prevent human rights abuses is to use the only language that dictators and ethnic cleansers understand—force. In the left's case, this is indicative that it has resolved the value conflict posed by humanitarian intervention in favor of the ends as opposed to means. Some leftists, however, resolved the conflict in favor of a pure and consistent pacifism in which force is never to be used regardless of the goal.

2. European Party Debates Over Humanitarian Intervention in the Balkans

These are broad strokes and the actual policymaking process is more complicated, yet there were significant differences between parties within each country over humanitarian intervention in the Balkans along these dimensions. In Britain, the Conservative government under Prime Minister John Major sent 1800 troops to Bosnia in 1992 to protect convoys delivering humanitarian aid, but insisted throughout that the UN Protection Force, or UNPROFOR, had a purely peacekeeping and not an enforcement mandate. Tory MPs rarely argued explicitly that Britain had no interest in trying to right humanitarian wrongs in Bosnia, but expressed their displeasure in other ways, claiming that the conflict was an intractable, civil war, in which all sides were morally culpable and no worse than others in the world. An adviser to Foreign Secretary Douglas Hurd said later, 'To see it as a civil war made it much more acceptable that one should be seeking to play an honest-broker role rather than taking anyone head on' (Interview with the author, July 2, 2001). Unwilling to get involved further, the British insisted that the wording of the UN resolution creating safe areas for Bosnian Muslims in 1993 state that UNPROFOR's mandate was to 'deter against attacks' on the peacekeepers themselves rather than to 'defend' the safe areas, the formulation that the French preferred. Although the British were certainly not singularly responsible, their behavior send a demonstrative signal to the Bosnian Serbs of their lack of commitment to resolving the conflict and contributed to the latter's seizure of UN hostages in May 1995 and the fall of the safe areas in July 1995. However much its response to the former—to organize a rapid reaction force of troops with heavy weapons—seemed to indicate a new determination, the government undermined that impression by declaring publicly that the force was not there to fight for the safe areas and that Britain was even contemplating withdrawal (Rathbun 2004: ch. 3)

In stark contrast, the humanitarian aspects of the operations in the Balkans appealed greatly to Labour as they resonated with their leftist emphasis on creating equality within domestic society (Labour Party 1996). The party was highly critical of Tory threats to withdraw from Bosnia, and pleaded that the UN honor its commitments to protect the safe areas, not just the peacekeepers. Ironically, because it concerned the promotion of human rights and not narrower, selfish interests, the most strident supporters of more robust military action in Bosnia were drawn from the far left of the party, most of whom had supported unilateral disarmament during the 1980s. Labour brought the same approach into office during the Kosovo crisis. Unlike the Conservative government in Bosnia, it escalated in the face of failure with the complete support of a parliamentary party ideologically committed to peace enforcement. The Labour government responded to Milosevic's massive ethnic cleansing operation following the onset of NATO airstrikes with a keynote speech on a new 'doctrine of international community' that articulated a general obligation to intervene in the internal affairs of states in cases of gross violations of human rights, making the war about more than just the Kosovars (Blair 1999). Privately the government pledged half of Britain's standing army to a land operation at a secret meeting of NATO defense ministers in May 1999. The planning and increasingly public discussion of the ground campaign, instigated by Britain, is regarded as one of the most important factors in NATO's victory.

The German debate over Bosnia was the exact opposite of that in Britain, but this does not mean that the same partisan cleavages in Britain do not exist in Germany. The rightist Christian Democratic Union (CDU) did not reject participation in the Bosnian operation as immaterial for Germany's vital interests like the right in Britain because instability in the Balkans had much more tangible consequences for Germany. More importantly, intervention there provided an opportunity to overcome constitutional restrictions and societal objections to deploying the military overseas. By gradually escalating the scale of participation in UN operations, particularly in Yugoslavia, it deliberately set out to change the German public's attitude on the use of force and create legal precedents that would expand the radius of military intervention. Germany would thereby gain a degree of military sovereignty lost following the Second World War. An adviser to CDU defense minister Volker Rühe admitted, 'That was a strategy. We had to create facts on the ground. So we participated in the enforcement of the embargo in the Adriatic. We made great efforts to make sure that it was not portrayed as an intervention. That was the rhetorical and political trickery. Of course it was an intervention' (interview with the author, February 2, 2001).

The German left resolved the value conflict posed by peace enforcement in a very different way than the British left, due to the tragic consequences of German's militarist past. Pacifism was still the dominant factor in left's considerations. In fact, for the Greens and Social Democrats, there was no contradiction since Germany's historical experience had shown the use of force was incapable of promoting human rights. This sentiment was captured in their slogan, 'Never Again War! Never Again Auschwitz!' Bosnia, however, was a sobering experience and increasing numbers of leftist politicians, beginning with the centrists and foreign and defense policy experts, abandoned a complete pacifism for a more differentiated approach in which force could be used for humanitarian but not strategic purposes. This gradual transformation was accelerated by those events in Bosnia that seemed to expose a value trade-off, such as the Srebrenica massacre, as well as the left's entry into government in 1998, which made the Red–Green coalition directly responsible for the fate of the Kosovar Albanians. By the turn of the millennium, as in Britain, it was the Social Democrats and Greens who advocated deploying German forces worldwide for humanitarian operations, while the CDU complained under their breath that interventions in places such as East Timor could more easily be done by other countries (Rathbun 2004: ch. 4). Germany is now second only to the USA in the number of forces deployed in UN and NATO missions out-of-area.

France, at first glance, appears to make the strongest case for uniqueness in foreign affairs. The Socialists and Gaullists point to an overarching agreement on the basic principles of France's role in international affairs as a source of pride. Bosnia and Kosovo showed, however, that it is often superficial. The French were unique in that their Gaullist center-right party, then known as the Rassemblement pour la Republique (RPR), was more committed than its counterparts in the USA, Britain and Germany to intervene with force if necessary in the Balkans. Only the far right National Front argued explicitly that these operations were not in the national interest. Following its crushing defeat of the Socialists in the 1993 parliamentary elections, the RPR assumed most of the day-to-day control over foreign policy and pushed through two of the most important initiatives of the Bosnian War. Foreign Minister Alain Juppé was responsible for the creation of the safe areas in 1993, and with the USA capitalized on the outrage following the Bosnian Serb bombing of the Sarajevo marketplace in 1994 to force through a NATO ultimatum that broke the siege of Sarajevo.

As was the case in Germany, however, the right's motivation was to a large degree instrumental. Its activist diplomacy served to preserve France's standing as a major player in world affairs in a new security environment. The end of the Cold War devalued France's traditional emblems of prestige, its nuclear weapons, and participation in UN operations served as a means to the long-standing Gaullist end of asserting France's global importance for resolving the most significant political crises of the day. Rightist support for these types of missions, however, was shallower than the left's, which was more genuinely committed to human rights protection. While the Gaullist government played its very public diplomatic role, it was more quietly withdrawing French peacekeepers from Bosnia, removing over a third in 1994. An adviser to French defense minister François Léotard explained, 'From the beginning, there was the feeling in the right-wing government, especially on the part of the Prime Minister and Minister of Defense, that UNPROFOR was really a trap, and the way to get out of the trap was to reduce the size of the contingent' (interview with the author, March 13, 2001). As in Britain, the French Socialists claimed this would undermine European commitment to peace in Bosnia. Only the strong leadership of Jacques Chirac prevented a complete pullout and his response was more the result of indignation at Bosnian Serb provocations of the hostage and safe area crises than humanitarianism. The President refused to allow the humiliation of French soldiers by the Bosnian Serbs, which in a chain of events had the effect of bringing peace to Bosnia.

Partisan differences were identical in Kosovo, but again initially obscured by the somewhat unique position of the French Gaullists, who supported the air campaign against Milosevic. The Socialists, now the lead party in the parliamentary coalition, were more reserved than in Bosnia. However, this was due to the necessity of holding together a cabinet that also included Communists fiercely opposed to the war on pacifist grounds. Privately the Socialist government expressed support and were actively planning for a ground war, although Prime Minister Lionel Jospin disowned this position publicly. Interestingly, no major figure in the Gaullist party ever publicly endorsed a possible land invasion. The most vehement advocate of a ground campaign were the French Greens, who responded to Jospin's admonition to keep a 'cool head' by responding that a refusal to intervene with ground forces showed a 'cold heart' (Les Verts 1999).

3. The American Party Debate Over Intervention in the Balkans

The partisan debates over intervention in the Balkans therefore demonstrated increasing convergence, but not in the sense of the left and right taking similar positions within countries. Rather it was a convergence of the positions of the European left on the one hand and the European right on the other. Most important for the former was the reorientation of the German left. The latter is more difficult to see at first glance given the instrumentalization of the Gaullists and Christian Democrats, but no less important. The question remains, however, as to whether the US debate mirrors that of Europe, and how the policies of European governments of a particular partisan flavor interacted with those of US administrations and the consequences for transatlantic relations.

During the Congressional debates over how and whether to intervene in the Balkans, the Democrats, like the European left, also conceived of the national interest more broadly and inclusively. Ron Dellums, the former chair of the House Armed Services Committee, argued during a Bosnia debate against 'the notion of narrowly construed vital national interests' and claimed a responsibility to risk US lives to save others in Bosnia (*Congressional Record*, November 17, 1995:13244 (emphasis added)). The Democrats broader conception of community was also evident in comments by Senator Barbara Boxer: 'If it is not in the national interest to stop the most god-awful ethnic cleansing since Hitler.... I do not know what is. We are human beings first and foremost' (*Congressional* Record, May 3, 1995: 4531). As in Britain, many others identified upholding human rights as an explicit part of the national interest. In Bosnia, 45 of 46 senators and 179 of 197 representatives voted to deploy 20,000 American peacekeepers to guarantee the Dayton Accords in December 1995. In Kosovo, 43 of 45 party senators and 181 of 211 representatives voted to support the air campaign.

Although Republicans utilized numerous other arguments against participation identical to the Tories about the practicality, legality, and morality of intervention, almost every single Republican speaker in both houses during the debates over Bosnia and Kosovo objected to the lack of tangible US concerns in the region. In this rhetorical sense, the US right was unique. Phil Gramm, a Republican candidate for President, derided President Clinton for running 'our nation's foreign policy as if it were social work,' recognizing the left's link between domestic and foreign policy and dismissing both (*Congressional Record*, December 13, 1995: 18455). Republicans frequently stated that they could not justify the loss of US lives to save Bosnians. Only interests like stability and access to oil in the Gulf signified threats critical enough to use force.

When the right gained control of Congress in 1994, it attacked the Clinton administration with a vengeance. Not only did the House of Republicans vote against deploying peacekeepers to Bosnia, they passed a resolution preventing the use of Defense Department funding for such an operation. During Kosovo, the overwhelming number of House of Republicans refused a resolution supporting the campaign even well after it had started. Another resolution to withhold funding for any possible ground invasion after the onset of hostilities found almost unanimous Republican backing.

These Congressional differences were also evident in the distinct approaches of the Republican administration under President Bush and its successor under President Clinton. The Republican Bush administration showed no interest in sending troops to Bosnia, even peacekeepers, and couched their objection in terms familiar for the right. Former national security adviser Brent Scowcroft explained that engagement in Bosnia was not justified for an administration that was 'heavily national interest-oriented' (Power 2002: 288). Secretary of State James Baker put this exclusivist opposition more colorfully when he declared that the USA 'does not have a dog in this fight (Drew 1994: 193). This introduced an asymmetry in the exposure of US and European soldiers to risk that was perhaps the primary obstacle for the Clinton administration in defining a common transatlantic position for the next three years.

Bill Clinton seized on the Bosnia issue in a presidential campaign otherwise dominated by domestic matters. He framed the debate as an inclusive left fighting for human rights and democracy against a disinterested, exclusive right. The governor advocated bombing Bosnian Serb units that were sieging Sarajevo and using force to facilitate the delivery of humanitarian aid and opening camps to inspection. However, by the time of his inauguration in January 1993, the situation was much different on the ground, and interventionists' hopes for a decisive new policy were disappointed. The Bosnian Serbs controlled almost three-quarters of the territory in Bosnia-Herzegovina by the time Clinton took office and the staggering difficulties for the outgunned blue helmet mission were already clear. The window of opportunity for an US ground presence had effectively closed during the Republican presidency, putting the Americans and Europeans in very different structural positions.

4. The Old Problem: Too Little America

The new Democratic administration still wanted to take some action, and proposed a strategy of 'lift and strike,' by which the UN would lift the arms embargo so as to allow the outgunned Bosnian Muslims a more even hand

and simultaneously strike Bosnian Serb positions from the air. The Europeans resisted as it would endanger their troops while the Americans remained safely above. They wanted US troops on the ground. The differences created a transatlantic crisis. Multilateralist fears of endangering the transatlantic relationship led the Democrats to drop the idea.

With the election of the Gaullist parliamentary majority in 1993, Franco–American relations improved, if not transatlantic relations as a whole. As argued above, the Gaullists were eager to take a greater diplomatic role in the conflict and welcomed US engagement so as to ease the burden on what was a declining French troop presence. It was a coalition of the USA and France that pushed through the safe area initiative as well as the Sarajevo ultimatum, which first involved NATO airstrikes as a punitive measure for Bosnian Serb noncompliance with UN resolutions. The Conservative British government was highly opposed to both but went along grudgingly.

France and the USA remained the primary drivers of the military action in Bosnia. Outraged by Bosnian Serb audacity, Chirac reacted to the fall of the safe areas by proposing to contribute 1,000 troops using US helicopters to the besieged city of Gorazde, where 300 British peacekeepers were struggling to keep the Bosnian Serbs at bay. The proposal was a key factor in involving the Americans deeper in the resolution of the war as it forced the USA to respond. Clinton had felt increasingly upstaged by Chirac, who derided the USA's lack of leadership. The Americans thought that a bombing campaign to destroy Serb air defenses would have to be the first step before reinforcing Gorazde by helicopter anyway, and used that idea as an alternative to the French plan, again over British objections. The US idea became the basis for the ultimatum made to the Bosnian Serbs not to menace any of the remaining enclaves, a violation of which triggered the military operation of late August 1995 that contributed to the end of the war.

Another factor pushing for an increased commitment in Bosnia was growing Congressional support for the unilateral lifting of the arms embargo on the Bosnian Muslims and the effects it would have on European troop commitments. Republican leaders Dole and Gingrich were looking for a cost-free alternative that would not involve US air or ground troops (Power 2002: 426; Holbrooke 1999: 71). The Europeans made known they would withdraw if more weapons flowed into the region, which would have triggered the deployment of 25,000 US forces to extricate them, a commitment that a multilateralist Democratic administration had every intention of honoring. By summer 1995, the balance of power in both chambers had shifted to the Republicans and Dole pushed his bill through the House and Senate in July. Clinton vetoed the measure, but with a veto-proof, two-thirds majority, the threat of a Congressional override was credible. This undoubtedly motivated the Americans to find a diplomatic resolution to the war.

Since it was on the hook for over 20,000 troops, it made sense that they be peacekeepers and not evacuators.

Without the asymmetry of commitment from the outset and the presence of a Labour government in power in Britain and France, US policy under the second Clinton administration was much more in line with the Europeans during the Kosovo crisis. The French left (and of course the right) complained about lack of US consultation on bombing targets, but this as much for public consumption as anything. The French, for all of their public rhetoric, were more concerned about a lack of US commitment to a possible ground war than US dominance of military planning. The problem again was too little US involvement. The Labour government played a key role in bolstering US resolve on planning for ground troops when the initial airstrikes were ineffective. The shadow of the US Congress led the President to rule out ground troops at the beginning of the conflict according to national security adviser Sandy Berger, and US hesitance persisted throughout the campaign (Daalder and O'Hanlon 2000: 97). As reviewed above, the administration had good reason to be concerned about Republican opposition. Again, there was more disagreement within countries than between them, more transatlantic than US convergence.

5. The New Problem: Too Much America

Kagan (2002) writes that, 'Today's transatlantic problem, in short, is not a George Bush problem. It is a power problem'. His argument is that gross disparities in power, and the threats it attracts, have led to very different foreign policy cultures in the USA and Europe. Here he is again right and wrong. The problem with transatlantic relations is not a George Bush problem, but rather the combination of his administration and those who think most differently in Europe.

The Iraq war itself was another partisan intervention. In a very different security environment, Governor Bush campaigned in 2000 against 'nation-building,' claiming that the purpose of the military was to fight and win wars, not to put countries back together following ethnic strife and humanitarian disasters. This was completely consistent with the exclusive policy of his party in Congress throughout the 1990s. Yet the administration's interventionist policies after the terrorist attacks in September 2001 were as well. Three principles have marked President Bush's foreign policy, each of which corresponds to the two ideological dimensions that I identify as organizing partisan conflict. Every one of them was foreseeable. The Democrats and the left in Europe have defined their opposition along these three lines.

The first characteristic is that it is driven primarily by self-interested motivations, what I call an exclusive foreign policy. Although a strong humanitarian case could have been made against Saddam Hussein, the President and his advisers unabashedly stressed his possession of weapons of mass destruction and links to terrorist organizations intent on harming the USA, at least before the war. Neoconservatives in the government might genuinely believe in the benefits of and chances for democracy promotion in the Middle East, but Republicans tend to support such action only in areas of vital strategic interest. Their halfhearted response to the crisis in Liberia illustrates the point. This focus on strategic interest has created particular problems for the administration given the difficulty it has had in finding evidence of those weapons. Obvious attempts to reframe the war as primarily humanitarian have been met with skepticism. Rice (2000: 47), in distinguishing the Republican presidential challengers from the Clinton administration, complained already in 2000 that 'the "national interest" is replaced with "humanitarian interests" or the interests of "the international community" '. The belief that the USA is exercising power legitimately only when it is doing so on behalf of someone or something else was deeply rooted in Wilsonian thought, and there are strong echoes of it in the Clinton administration. To be sure, there is nothing wrong with doing something that benefits all humanity, but that is, in a sense, 'a second-order effect'.

The second critique that Democrats have made is that the Bush administration is too quick to pull the trigger, not allowing enough time, for instance, for the weapons inspectors in Iraq to report on the status of its programs. The administration is too hawkish. The Republicans clearly believe in the efficacy of force and that using it demonstrates US resolve to others, particularly other adversaries in the Middle East. Nor is it shy in announcing its willingness, as evident in the President's doctrine of preemption. This tendency has created particular problems for the administration in the controversy over how it used somewhat ambiguous intelligence in making the case for war. Information was selectively used to justify a war that the Bush administration wanted, regardless of the facts, goes the critique.

The third critique of Republican foreign policy is perhaps the most commonly repeated, that it is unilateral. Many cited the President's willingness to bring in the UN in September 2001 as a major concession to multilateralism, but the administration's message was invariant: if the UN would not act, the USA would. The USA would welcome the UN and others if they would like to come along, but it would not grant any international organization or state any ability to supercede US interests. This focus on sovereignty can also be seen in the administration's withdrawal of President Clinton's signature from the International Criminal Court. The move should be seen as a way of ensuring that the Senate cannot take up the ratification of the treaty creating the Court in the future, however unlikely that might be. Under international law, 'unsigning' the treaty also permits the USA to actively work against its purposes, for instance, by tying military aid to bilateral agreements that countries will not surrender US soldiers to the ICC. Again, Rice gave fair warning in the same article, claiming already in 2000 that it would be a mistake to ask the UN to sanction the use of US military power in its vital interest. She castigated the Clinton administration of treating multilateral agreements and institutions as 'ends in themselves' (*ibid.*).

Whereas during the Clinton years, the Europeans by and large complained that there was not enough US leadership, the tables turned with the Bush administration. The German left seems to have taken the Republicans at their word, that the war's primary motive was to disarm Saddam Hussein, not to liberate the Iraqi people. The Social Democrats and Greens have come around to humanitarian intervention, but only in cases in which there was no clear self-interested rationale, particularly when it involves a preemptive war, as opposed to one of self-defense. In such a case, even a mandate from the Security Council would be insufficient, as the Chancellor clearly stated. In interviews with the author several years ago before the new security environment had evolved, politicians of both leftist parties always stated that support for another war against Iraq would be unthinkable for Germany. They were right. Some have argued, and President Bush is thought to believe, that Schröder's position was determined by his precarious electoral position in the summer of 2002. The Chancellor might have played on public opposition to win an election, but his coalition's position was determined long before. There is nothing in an ideological explanation that argues that leaders will not take electoral advantage of policies to which their parties and supporters are genuinely committed.

Many have since mistaken the Red–Green coalition's strong stance against a war in Iraq as a return to an innate German pacifism. However, governing coalition leaders took great pains to stress the deployment of thousands of troops in other theaters abroad, noting that Germany was second only to the USA in this regard. As is always the case when politicians oppose wars, they stressed how the conflict could spiral, creating instability in a volatile region including in Palestine, and serving as a lightning rod for terrorist recruiting efforts.[1] Yet Germany's history was barely mentioned. The left's objection

[1] On Germany's contributions to other military operations, see comments in the *Plenarprotokoll* by Gerhard Schröder, 15/25 (February 13, 2003): 1874–5; Peter Struck, 15/25 (February 13, 2003): 1894; Ursula Mogg, 15/24 (February 12, 2003): 1856. On the possible destabilizing effects of war, see comments by Gerhard Schröder, 15/25 (February 13, 2003): 1875; Ludger Volmer, 15/25 (February 13, 2003), 1900; Uta Zapf, 15/24 (February 12, 2003): 1854.

was to the exclusivist goals of the USA, not antimilitarism per se. Somewhat counterintuitively, the war showed how far the left has evolved in Germany.

The war in Iraq put the Christian Democrats in the uncomfortable position of supporting a policy of solidarity with the USA that the overwhelming majority of the German public did not believe in during an election year. However, the compellence/deterrence logic that marks their thinking on strategic and exclusive matters enabled them to criticize a Red–Green policy they did not support without an explicit endorsement of German participation in the war. All leading CDU politicians stressed that the credible threat of war was actually the only path to peace, as only the likelihood of armed conflict would induce Iraq to come clean about its weapons programs. For this reason, they focused ire on the Chancellor's statement that Germany would support no military action regardless of the circumstances, since it removed any incentive to comply with UN resolutions. The very presence of UN inspectors in Iraq, the CDU argued, was due to US policy.[2] This was classic hawkish thinking about the efficacy of force, which distinguished the right from the left in Germany, while allowing them to duck charges of warmongering. After the election, however, the CDU did introduce a resolution in parliament that called for Germany to provide numerous measures of military support to the USA in case of war.[3]

The German election was therefore arguably the most important event for transatlantic relations in recent years. If Stoiber's Christian Democrats had defeated Schroeder's Social Democrats, there is little likelihood that Germany would have appeared alongside France and Russia in press conferences objecting to US policy. Without Germany, France would have been out of step with most of the other west European governments, save Belgium. The Netherlands, Spain, Denmark, and Italy, all with right-leaning governments, offered moral and even material support to the war and the operation in its aftermath. Having only Russia at its side would have undermined the French self-conception as the guarantor of international law and undermined its moral authority.

The diplomatic alliance of France and Germany did more to reinforce the impression of a solid European bloc against the war than any other factor. Public opinion was also overwhelming, although an equally plausible explanation is that they were intentionally leading public opinion on an issue they believed in and thought was a political winner. Yet French policy was driven by seemingly contradictory motivations that were very different from

[2] In *Plenarprotokoll*, see comments by defense experts Glos and Schmidt and party leader Merkel: Michael Glos, 15/25 (February 13, 2003): 1893; Angela Merkel, 15/25 (February 13, 2003), 1880–1; Christian Schmidt, 15/24 (February 12, 2003), 1854.

[3] *Bundestag Drucksache* 15/434 (February 13, 2003). See also *Bundestag Drucksache* 15/421 (February 11, 2003).

Germany's,—the desire to promote French stature and influence by checking US power while at the same time leaving the door open to being a part of any military operation. The French right took back the parliament and reelected President Chirac in 2002, and therefore enjoyed complete preeminence in foreign affairs. He sounded the same familiar themes of international law and the UN's monopoly on decisions regarding the use of force that Germany did, but there is substantial reason to believe that this was not a genuine conversion to multilateralism. The French right discovered the utility of the UN only in the 1990s when it suited traditional Gaullist interests. Pushing major issues through the Security Council enhanced France's stature and influence. Iraq was no different. The inspectors were so important to the French right because they served as impartial arbiters of whether Saddam Hussein had weapons of mass destruction. They served as a check on US power. The Americans would not be the ones to determine whether Iraq was a threat to international security.

Just as importantly, if they verified the weapons programs existed, they also offered a way for France to fight alongside in the war without appearing like US lackeys. The French right would want to be involved in the most significant action in international affairs in a decade. Ultimately this did not come to pass, but we should not infer from the course of events that it was not possible. Chirac was very careful not to rule out French participation in a military action and explicitly contrasted the French position with that of Germany, to the chagrin of the French left, more ideologically opposed to the war.[4] The French–German axis would have been even more passionately antiwar had the French Socialists been in power. The French government's opposition became more implacable as it became clearer in the early months of 2003 that the Americans would not allow the inspectors to be the ultimate judges about Iraq's intentions. The French right needed that sanction.

Perhaps the most puzzling aspect of the European response to the war in Iraq was the solid support of Prime Minister Tony Blair. Some of this should be attributed to the fact that the party had undergone a substantial ideological reorientation during the early 1990s. This was New Labour, a more centrist party with a more exclusive conception of the national interest than the old left. It was certainly more right-leaning than its counterparts in Europe. In Bosnia and Kosovo, this had not been a factor, as the moderates and left wingers within Labour were in broad agreement. Predictably, however, the Prime Minister lost many of his most ardently interventionist colleagues from the Kosovo War during the conflict with Iraq. It also appears that Britain under Labour was pursuing a conscious strategy of

[4] 'French Leader Offers America Both Friendship and Criticism', *New York Times* (September 9, 2002).

moderating US policy privately with influence gained by showing public support.[5] Nevertheless, despite this and the centrist cast of his party, much causal weight must be placed on the personal commitment of the Prime Minister to risk a war without the solid support of his party.

Due to the particular institutional parameters in which Blair was working, he paid a heavy price. Here the partisan argument is vindicated. Unlike in presidential systems, parliamentary governments cannot buck their parliamentarians without serious consequences. Antiwar Labour backbenchers proposed a resolution stating that the case for war had not yet been proven. In one of the most significant backbench revolts in British parliamentary history, it garnered 139 Labour votes. Although Blair's tenure has been marked by reform of many cherished and previously untouchable leftist policies, the war has been by far his greatest challenge and the closest he has come to losing power. Only a fraction of the rebels were Labour's traditional pacifists. Many, including one of the junior ministers who resigned in protest, made an explicit point to allude to their support of the Bosnia and Kosovo interventions.[6] Again the primary point of opposition was the lack of a solid inclusive rationale.

The government's policy was only possible with the support of the right, which heartily endorsed the war. Generally opposed to humanitarian intervention, the Conservatives embraced a military action that advanced Britain's vital interests. Tory party leader, Ian Duncan-Smith, noted that Hussein had a terrible human rights record and was in breach of UN resolutions, but explicitly contrasted those facts with the primary Conservative rationale for the war: '[T]he main reason why we will be voting for the motion is that it is in the British national interest. Saddam Hussein has the means, the mentality and the motive to pose a direct threat to our national security.'[7] Recently ousted party leader William Hague made almost identical remarks: '[A]lthough there are legal arguments on either side, we are not morally obliged to take action—if we were, we would have to take action against many other countries.... We should take action because it is in the national interest'.[8]

The war in Iraq was therefore a mirror image of Bosnia, where Labour support had been critical for maintaining the British peacekeeping presence in Bosnia in the face of right wing pressure to withdraw, even while Labour wanted to do more. The Liberal Democrats also backed the government in

[5] The Prime Minister and Foreign Secretary claimed to have such an intent. See comments in *Hansard*: Tony Blair (March 18, 2003): col. 770–1; Jack Straw (March 18, 2003): col. 896.

[6] See comments in *Hansard* by John Denham (March 18, 2003): col. 798.

[7] *Hansard* (March 18, 2003): col. 775.

[8] Ibid: col. 792.

this case. During Iraq, the leftist Liberal Democrats joined with the Labour rebels. The Conservatives avoided any temptation to weaken the Blair government, instead pledging total support to Blair for an exclusive pursuit they could rally behind.

6. ESDP Without CFSP: Transatlantic Relations and European Union Progress

What if anything, does this mean for the creation of a Common Foreign and Security Policy (CFSP) and a European Security and Defense Policy (ESDP)? How does the state of transatlantic relations, largely I argue a function of the domestic politics of Britain, France, Germany and the USA, affect broader EU institutional processes? The creation of the ESDP was, like European policies in Bosnia and Kosovo, also profoundly affected by partisan developments within these four countries (Rathbun 2004: ch. 6). Labour under Blair was keen to engage Britain with Europe after its election in 1997. While it had come out against European defense cooperation previously, this was mostly due to reluctance to expose itself politically to a Eurosceptic electorate and a lack of any true knowledge of the subject after over a decade in the political wilderness. The party rejected the Conservative Party's nationalist appeals about the loss of British sovereignty. It had a more inclusive approach that enabled it to think pragmatically, rather than ideologically about ESDP. Its reversal of British policy broke the logjam on a common defense policy. None of this would have been possible, however, without the French rapprochement with NATO in the mid-1990s, pursued by the Gaullists as a way of reestablishing French *rang* in a markedly different geopolitical environment. Only by returning to its seat at the table of the most important military organization could France have its say on the crisis management operations that were at the time the most pressing issues of foreign affairs. The French right interpreted sovereignty not so much as decision-making autonomy, as the British right did, but as influence.

The Iraq war was widely predicted to mean a sizeable setback, if not the end, to the process of European Security and Defense Policy given the rift that developed between Britain and France, the two most prominent security players without whose agreement cooperation goes nowhere. The Iraq war did profoundly damage the prospects of a Common Foreign and Security Policy in the medium term. CFSP is the embodiment of a European bid for global leadership. Yet the Europeans could not organize a common response on the most prominent question of the day. Given the emergence of a profound cleavage over the role of US power in the world, it is extremely unlikely that this predominantly intergovernmental forum will be made any more supranational by significant extension of Qualified Majority Voting. Forsaking the veto is most likely when states do not believe they will disagree. Differences over transatlantic relations color everything. The pro-American credentials of candidates for the head of the European Commission, who has no real authority in CFSP, were even a major issue. Intra-European relations on foreign policy are far too politicized for institutional changes in CFSP. Yet as Jolyon Howorth reviews in his contribution to this volume, ESDP has moved steadily ahead. How can this be?

The players are the same since before and after the Iraq war. Blair continues to want to keep Britain engaged in Europe. Military cooperation is the best way for them to show their enthusiasm. In the CFSP, Britain has to make its interests consistent with other members. But the ESDP is about a process, an institutional arrangement for the prosecution of military operations not yet defined, that are prospective in nature. Here Britain can remain pro-European. And ironically, it might be because of those divisions that progress has been made. If they can't agree on common policies under the CFSP, then more attention is dedicated to ESDP as a conciliatory gesture. It is likely that the creation of a new EU military planning cell, which the Labour government had previously opposed as too supranational and threatening to NATO, was a concession in this direction. The British were interested in CFSP when they first took office. A primary rationale for building ESDP was to add the credible threat of force to the CFSP, making it carry more weight. But it is now likely too controversial to touch.

Yet there is internal contradiction in the current relationship between CFSP and ESDP that will likely come to the surface and might undermine ESDP if European relations with the USA do not begin to markedly improve. The French are increasingly interested again in an autonomous Europe and CFSP because of the forceful projection of US interests that reminds them of the Cold War. The problem is again too much America, as opposed to not enough, which was the case in the immediate Cold War period. French acceptance of a European presence in the USA was a necessary condition for progress in ESDP. But this conviction will inevitably suffer as a result of the Iraq war and the reelection of President Bush. ESDP will serve the agenda of a more autonomous foreign policy for Europe, as embodied in the CFSP. This might undermine the original Franco–British bargain over ESDP if the Gaullists return to their more instinctive distrust of US hegemony.

The same phenomenon will likely emerge in Germany as well. Even before the Republicans won the White House in 2000, the Greens and Social Democrats were increasingly talking like Gaullists, having been chastened by the experience of not being consulted significantly during the Kosovo War because of their paltry military contributions. The Greens had long opposed ESDP as the militarization of what should be a civilian-based EU. But even they came to embrace it, partially as a way of strengthening CFSP as a balance to US predominance. Aachim Schmillen, the Green head of policy planning, said, 'Without an ESDP and the military means, everything is determined by the Pentagon and the White House' (Interview with the author, May 11, 2001). On the left of the Greens the opinion was the same. 'If the EU really wants to be able to act within the CFSP, that does not work with military capabilities', said Nachtwei. 'Without this capacity for military conflict resolution there will be no real partnership with the USA (Interview with the author, February 15, 2001). Social Democratic and Green opposition to US policy is, as argued, very different from the Gaullists, based more on principle rather than self-interest, but the result is the same: support for ESDP as a counterweight to US power, a sentiment that can only have increased in the wake of the Iraq war. The ESDP for the German left will be a vehicle for a more forceful and autonomous Europe vis-à-vis the USA. If this is the case, British enthusiasm for ESDP will likely wane.

7. Conclusion

Although transatlantic relations are in worse shape than they have been in years, if not decades, it should nevertheless be remembered that it could have been worse. For instance if Tony Blair had not risked his premiership during the Iraq war in the face of a Labour Party revolt, there would have been even more of an appearance of a monolithic European antiwar bloc. Although the Gaullists are no fans of US tendency to throw (either intentionally or accidentally) its weight around, their opposition was due more to a resentment of US power than what the USA did with it. The Socialists led a more passionate and principled antiwar opposition. Had they won the 2002 elections, Franco–American relations might have soured even further. The reelection of President Bush, however, makes it unlikely that the USA will change what it is doing with its power. Relations are likely to remain strained between the USA and France and Germany.

As argued above, this will create problems for the ESDP as it changes some of the motivations behind the project. The pessimistic prospects for CFSP and ESDP could change, however, particularly if Blair moves aside for a Labour Party leader more in tune with the wishes of the party. This would have the effect of defusing the salience of the transatlantic issue and have a positive impact on CFSP, as Labour as a whole is more in line with the German left and the French right than Blair. There is clearly a strong basis of public opinion on which to draw. The war in Iraq has unified the European left at the grassroots level against the USA in a way not seen since NATO's 1980s decisions over nuclear deployments to the continent. And many of those in Europe who did not object to the war initially have turned against it in the wake of the poor postwar planning and the failure to find weapons of mass destruction, that is on the basis of incompetence rather than principle. Even British Conservatives, who supported the war and could not therefore question Blair's decision to participate, can question the integrity of the Labour government without undermining their own arguments in favor of the war. They had the right idea; they were just misled. These mixed motivations, in addition to the shaping of public opinion by antiwar governments, explains the very solid basis of anti-US public opinion.

This is highly ironic for Kagan. His hypothesis about stark differences between US and European worldviews, which he argues are the function of starkly different levels of power, is widely accepted in the Bush administration, particularly after the experience of the run-up to war. Feckless Europeans cannot be counted on to make the tough decisions to maintain peace and stability in the world. This misread the differing reasons for dissent in Europe and overestimated the extent of consensus. Yet proceeding as if the Kagan hypothesis were valid is one of the few ways to galvanize European sentiment in such a way as to make it true. If the Bush administration continues down this path, party differences might come under duress. Only then can Kagan claim to be right.

References

Blair, T. (1999). 'Doctrine of the International Community', Speech to the Economic Club of Chicago, April 27.

Chittick, W. O. and Freyberg-Inan, A. (2001). 'The Impact of Basic Motivations on Foreign Policy Opinions Concerning the Use of Force: A Three-Dimensional Framework', in P. Everts and P. Isernia (eds.), *Public Opinion and the International Use of Force*. New York: Routledge, pp. 33–56.

Daalder, I. and O'Hanlon, M. (2000). *Winning Ugly: NATO's War to Save Kosovo*. Washington: Brookings Institution Press.

Drew, E. (1994). *On the Edge: The Clinton Presidency*. New York: Simon and Schuster.

Gerring, J. (1998). *Party Ideologies in America, 1828–1996*. Cambridge: Cambridge University Press.

Holbrooke, R. (1999). *To End a War*. New York: Modern Library.

Jervis, R. (1976). *Perception and Misperception in International Politics*. Princeton, NJ: Princeton University Press.

Kagan, R. (2002). 'Power and Weakness', *Policy Review*, 113 (June–July 2002): 3–28.

—— (2003). *Of Paradise and Power: America and Europe in the New World Order*. New York: Knopf.

Labour Party (1996). *Road to the Manifesto: Labour's Strategy for Britain in the Modern World.*

Lipset, S. M. (1954). 'The Psychology of Voting: An Analysis of Political Behavior', in *Handbook of Social Psychology*. Cambridge: Addison-Wesley.

Lumsdaine, D. (1993). *Moral Vision in International Politics: The Foreign Aid Regime, 1949–1989*. Princeton, NJ: Princeton University Press.

Power, S. (2002). *'A Problem from Hell': America and the Age of Genocide*. New York: Harper Collins.

Putnam, R. (1973). *The Beliefs of Politicians*. New Haven, CT: Yale University Press.

Rathbun, B. (2004). *Partisan Interventions: European Party Politics and Peace Enforcement in the Balkans*. Ithaca, NY: Cornell University Press.

Rice, C. (2000). 'Promoting the National Interest', *Foreign Affairs,* 79/1: 45–63.

Snyder, G. H. and Diesing, P. (1977). *Conflict among Nations*. Princeton, NJ: Princeton University Press.

Les Verts (1999). 'Guerre au Kosovo: "Tête froide," cœur froid?', March 28.

4

United Against the United States? The EU's Role in Global Trade and Finance*

C. RANDALL HENNING AND SOPHIE MEUNIER

Trade and money lie at the heart of the European Union (EU) as a polity. Fostering trade among its members and promoting unity vis-à-vis the USA and other trading partners were original *raisons d'être* of the European Economic Community. From its very beginning in 1957, the Community has been a single actor in legal terms in international trade policy and thus a global player in trade relations. In 1999, the introduction of the single currency made the euro area a single actor formally in monetary and exchange rate policy as well. Long since a global player in international trade, the EU is now emerging as a global player in money and finance.

As decision-making processes in economic policy become increasingly federal, the EU acquires greater weight on the world stage. The EU and the USA are now quite similar, as illustrated by a few basic indicators presented in Table 4.1. Their Gross Domestic Products (GDP) are roughly comparable. In 2003, the GDP of the euro area was three-quarters that of the USA, while that of the EU-15 was slightly below, and that of the EU-25 slightly above that of the USA. The GDP of Japan, the next largest single economy, was roughly 40 percent of that of the EU. The euro-area and US populations are also roughly comparable (309 million and 291 million, respectively), while the population of the EU-15 (382 million) and the EU-25 (456 million) greatly exceed that of the USA. The total exports and imports of the EU-15 (about $3 trillion) substantially exceeded those of the USA ($2.6 trillion). In 2003, the EU-15 ran a trade surplus of about $160 billion, while the USA ran a trade deficit of about $490 billion. Finally, the international reserves of the euro area ($223 billion, excluding gold) also greatly exceed those of the USA ($75 billion), though were less than one-third those of Japan. European integration thus gathers under one political entity formidable economic clout, shifting the structure of global economic relations.

* The authors would like to acknowledge the excellent research assistance of Youliana Ivanova and the helpful comments of Benjamin J. Cohen, Andreas Falke, Jeffrey J. Schott and the editors of this volume, Nicolas Jabko and Craig Parsons.

TABLE 4.1. *Comparison of Europe, United States, and Japan, 2003*

	EU-25	EU-15	Euro-12	US	Japan
Population (million)	457	382	309	291	127
GDP (billion $)	10,936	10,444	8,148	10,854	4,278
GDP per capita (thousand $)	24.0	27.3	26.4	37.3	33.6
Exports of goods and services (billion $)	n/a	1,477	1,530	1,042	505
Imports of goods and services (billion $)	n/a	1,562	1,389	1,530	436
International reserves minus gold (billion $)	425	321	223	75	663
Stock market valuation (trillion $)	7.9	7.8	4.9	14.3	4.9
Bond market valuation (trillion $)*	13.1	12.8	10.2	19.1	6.9
Outstanding bank loans (trillion $)*,†	18.0	17.7	12.8	5.9	6.2

Notes: GDP data for all countries, exports and imports data for EU 15, US and Japan converted into dollars at a rate of 1.12 dollars per euro (average for 2003); exports and imports data for EU 15 excludes intra-group trade and assumes that services trade is distributed in the same proportion as merchandise trade; exports and imports data for EU 12 excludes intra-group trade and is converted into dollars at a rate of 1.12 dollars per euro.

*2002 Data.

†Assets of commercial banks.

Source: International Monetary Fund, IFS (May 2004) for international reserves; International Monetary Fund, Global Finance Stability Report (April 2004) for bond market valuation and outstanding bank loans; The European Economy Statistical Annexe (Spring 2004) for population, GDP, exports and imports for EU 15, US and Japan; World Federation of Exchanges World Wide Web site for stock market valuation; ECB Statistics Pocketbook (May 2004) for EU-12 exports and imports data.

As the EU's global role strengthens, it becomes increasingly important as a partner for the USA, both in conflict and well as cooperation. Whether the EU is inclined to challenge or cooperate with the USA depends in turn on how its preferences compare to those of its main transatlantic partner. While broad structural similarities might contribute to convergence, institutions and internal politics also bear on preference aggregation and can potentially cause preferences to diverge. Transatlantic convergence may be greater than in the past, but it is far from complete.

The status of the EU as a heavyweight in trade, however, has not been fully matched by its status in money and finance, where its role has emerged more gradually. Europeans had hoped to replicate in the financial sphere the EU's success in the trade sphere when creating the single currency. They believed that the euro, among other purposes, could empower Europe on the international stage and raise its stature in global economic diplomacy generally. While this remains a prospect, it is fair to say that the monetary union has so far fallen short of the role the common market plays in international trade politics. We argue that institutions provide the primary explanation for the difference.

This chapter compares the EU's performance in trade to that in monetary and financial affairs. The discussion below begins by examining how the EU became an international actor in the field of trade and is now becoming one in the field of finance. These two sections review the institutions by which policy is set and address the pressures for change coming from enlargement and institutional reform, including the prospective European constitution. The discussion then explores the sources of the difference between the EU's success in trade and its more limited success in international finance. The chapter concludes by examining the convergence between EU and US policymaking institutions and the prospects for transatlantic cooperation and conflict.

1. The EU As a Political Heavyweight in Trade

If there is any area in which the EU has unquestionably become a leading power in the international system, it is clearly in the field of trade. The Founding Fathers of Europe might have envisioned long-term political prospects for the European Community, but they conceived it primarily as a common trading area with external borders. The objective of the 1957 Rome Treaty was indeed to create among the original six members a customs union in which there would be no barriers to trade and a common external tariff would be applied to imports from third countries. From its very beginning, then, the Community became a single actor in international trade policy and almost immediately started talking on an equal legal footing with the USA in commercial negotiations. With sustained economic growth and successive enlargements from six to twenty-five countries, the influence of the EU in international trade politics and negotiations strengthened over the decades.

1.1. Institutions and Processes of EU Trade Policy

The common commercial policy is based on three main principles: (*a*) a common external tariff, (*b*) common trade agreements with the rest of the world, and (*c*) the uniform application of trade instruments across member states. The EU competence over trade policy covers various roles. In addition to participating in multilateral trade negotiations, the EU concludes and monitors commercial agreements with many countries (such as free trade agreements with the European Economic Area and preferential agreements with Mediterranean countries and African-Caribbean-Pacific countries under the Lomé, and later Cotonou Conventions). The EU is also in charge of protecting its member states against unfair trade practices, mainly through the use of policy instruments to deal with dumping and subsidies. The common commercial policy also covers key aspects of intellectual property, investment and competition.

The common commercial policy is the most prominent EU policy to have been under supranational competence from the very beginning. Although member states might occasionally depart from common positions on selected issues, formally and legally Europe 'speaks with one voice' in bilateral, regional and multilateral negotiations. Trade policy in the EU involves two levels of delegation.[1] First, the Rome Treaty formally transferred the competence to negotiate and conclude international agreements on trade from the individual member states to the collective entity—this is often referred to as 'exclusive competence,' 'community competence,' or 'supranational competence.'

The second level of delegation is the practical transfer of competence from the Council of Ministers to the Commission—the two main institutions involved in external trade policymaking. Schematically, the concrete mechanisms for making trade policy are as follows. The Commission elaborates proposals for the initiation and content of international trade negotiations. The key policy discussions then take place in a special advisory committee, the 'Committee 133,' named after Article 133 on trade policy. Once the Committee has amended Commission proposals, they are transmitted to COREPER (the Committee of Permanent Representatives, which prepares most of the work of the Council of Ministers), which then transmits the negotiating proposal to the Council of Ministers. Deciding according to qualified majority in most cases, the Council sets objectives for trade negotiations (known as the 'negotiating mandate'), which it then hands out to the Commission. The actual conduct of international trade negotiations for the EU is carried out by members of the Commission, acting under the authority

[1] For more on the complexities of EU trade policy and in particular the cumbersome sharing of trade competences, see for instance Meunier and Nicolaidis 1999; Meunier 2000, 2005.

of the Trade Commissioner. Once the negotiations are over, the final agreement must be ratified by the Council (sometimes by the individual member states as well), according to qualified majority in most cases and unanimity in areas involving trade in particular services.

This complex system, carefully crafted over more than four decades of participation by the EU as a central actor in international trade policy, has turned the European edifice into one of the world's two trade superpowers. The very idea that nation states could give up such a key area of their external affairs was, and continues to be, revolutionary. The granting of competence over trade to the supranational authority has not always been without political controversy, and member states have fought hard to conserve some of their competence over trade, especially in the multiple sectors of services (Meunier and Nicolaidis 1999). Nevertheless, trade is overall the policy area in which the EU has presented the most united front to the rest of the world throughout the years in a variety of fora, as described below.

1.2. The EU as an International Trade Actor

In its initial decades of existence, the EU was a passive actor in international trade negotiations, more preoccupied by building its own internal policies and defending them against assaults by the outside world, than by initiating international policy changes. As a result, it exerted a more protectionist pressure on the world political economy, especially given the definition of the Community's bargaining position at the lowest common denominator of its members (Meunier 2000). Since the early 1990s, however, the EU has been initiating international policy changes, rather than reacting to them. This transformation was driven in part by external threats from perceived US unilateralism, by aspirations to global leadership, and by the changing nature of trade. As a result, the EU is now a very active—and proactive—member in a variety of international trade fora.

1.2.1. Multilateralism in the World Trade Organization

The EU and its twenty-five member states all belong to the World Trade Organization. It is, however, the EU who speaks on behalf of its members in the vast majority of WTO negotiations, with a common position coordinated in Brussels and/or Geneva according to the procedures presented earlier. This is true for the negotiation of broad multilateral trade agreements, as well as for the management of trade disputes (even though there are exceptions and ongoing conflicts over issues of competence).

The first multilateral trade agreement to be conducted under the auspices of the World Trade Organization is the Doha Round, which was launched in 2001. The Doha Round is about negotiating away trade barriers with the goal of improving general economic welfare, in particular for the developing countries. Agriculture is the key variable in this round, with developed countries being asked to reduce their trade-distorting subsidies for farmers and the tariffs, quotas, and nontariff barriers that they use to protect their domestic agriculture. Among the other central issues were originally the so-called 'Singapore issues'—investment, competition policy, government procurement, and trade facilitation—pushed by the EU and strongly resisted by most developing countries. By August 2003, the EU and the USA had reached a common proposal on reform of the protection of their agriculture. This was not enough, however. The 2003 Cancun meeting collapsed, mainly due to differences over agricultural reform among the USA, the EU and a group of developing countries led by Brazil and India (called the G-22). The abrupt end of the meeting left a big uncertainty on how to proceed next with talks on agriculture, industrial goods, and the Singapore issues, especially during an electoral year in the USA.

In spring 2004, the EU revised its position in at least three important respects in order to remove obstacles to the multilateral talks. Most importantly, the EU put on the table all agricultural export subsidies, with the proviso that the others do the same and that the final agreement offer an overall balanced package on agriculture. Because the issue of agricultural export subsidies had been a sticking point in multilateral trade negotiations for decades, this proposal is potentially very significant indeed. Secondly, the EU indicated more flexibility on the so-called Singapore issues, which probably means abandoning them for the duration of the round, since most countries are not ready to launch multilateral negotiations on investment, competition and public procurement. Finally, the EU proposed a special deal for the ninety poorest countries in the world, which could benefit from freer access to world markets while not opening up further their own markets.

The EU also participates in the multilateral trade regime through its involvement in the formal settlement of trade disputes in the WTO. A cornerstone of the WTO since its inception in 1995 and an innovation over the previous GATT regime, the Dispute Settlement Mechanism enables WTO members to enforce existing trade agreements. Members can ask for the constitution of panels, which adjudicate between plaintiffs and defendants. When members refuse to comply with the judges' recommendations on bringing their national practices in line with WTO rules, then the winning party is allowed to compensate for lost trade through retaliatory sanctions, often in the form of duty increases.

The EU has been an active participant in this process. In 2004, the EU was actively involved in twenty-nine WTO disputes as both a plaintiff (sixteen cases) and a defendant (thirteen cases) with eight of its trading partners (Argentina, Australia, Brazil, Canada, India, Korea, Thailand and the

USA) (European Commission 2004). In almost half of these cases (fourteen out of twenty-nine), the EU was paired against the USA—eleven times with the EU as the plaintiff (e.g. US Antidumping Act and Foreign Sales Corporation) and only three times with the EU as the defendant (GMOs, hormones, and trademark/geographical indications). This institutionalized mechanism for resolving trade disputes has enabled the EU to curb occasional unilateralist tendencies of US trade policy—even if the first two cases (on bananas and beef hormones) settled in favor of the US position.

1.2.2. Bilateralism and Regional Agreements

The EU has also become a major player in negotiating regional trade agreements, expanding the number of such agreements over the decades. At the outset, the EU concluded trade agreements primarily with its immediate neighbors (mainly to the East) and the former colonies with which it shared historical ties, mainly through the successive Lomé (later Cotonou) conventions. Since the end of the Uruguay Round, which coincided with the entry into force of the North American Free Trade Agreement (NAFTA) in 1994, the EU has pursued a web of regional agreements with a variety of additional countries (Sbragia 2004). This activity was prompted in part by the distinct US shift toward regionalism as well as the increasingly global aspirations of Europe. As a result, the EU now has preferential trade agreements of various types with a wide variety of countries and regional entities—including the Euro-Mediterranean Agreement (covering Algeria, Egypt, Israel, Lebanon, Morocco, Palestine, Syria and Tunisia), an agreement with South Africa, agreements with many countries in Latin America (Mexico, Chile, and prospectively Mercosur), and agreements with countries and regional organizations in Asia (Vietnam, ASEAN).

1.3. Challenges and Opportunities

The reasons for the EU's formidable successes in trade policy are multiple, ranging from structural to institutional. Yet the complex trade policymaking apparatus that has enabled the EU to emerge as one of the world's two trade superpowers is currently being challenged on two fronts, and pressure for change is coming from several mechanisms simultaneously. How will the recent enlargement as well as the proposed Constitution, both of which are happening in conjunction with the Doha Round, affect the status of the EU as an international powerhouse in trade policy?

1.3.1. Enlargement

The recent enlargement of the EU to ten new countries increased the single market: it augmented the geographical size of the EU by 34 percent and boosted the total population by 75 million to a total of 457 million. It did not trigger any immediate disruption of trade within Europe, however, since the transition had been prepared for a decade. Indeed, on the eve of enlargement, over 95 percent of the trade of the EU-15 with the new entrants was already free and the trade impacts of EU enlargement had already taken place.

Nevertheless, these structural transformations may challenge established institutions and compel political change. Structurally, enlargement will make the EU stronger in relation to its trade negotiating partners, because a larger single market is both more attractive to outside economic players and the threat of being cut out more costly. By joining the EU, however, the new entrants are bringing in a wealth of different histories and cultures, which also means a wealth of distinct economic interests and capabilities. These will have to be included and amalgamated in the definition of a common European position on trade.

This increased diversity poses a challenge to the current institutional mechanisms, not adequately equipped to accommodate ten additional different viewpoints. Diversity could incapacitate the EU to make decisions and bog down multilateral trade liberalization. It could also lead to common positions that tend to be the lowest common denominator and, therefore, to a protectionist bias of the EU in international trade negotiations. On the other hand, some analysts have argued that enlargement could make the internal EU negotiations more difficult to control for trade ministers, and thus could further concentrate trade policymaking power in the hands of the Commission, which has a historical and functionalist interest in promoting trade liberalization.

The new entrants started to apply the EU's Common External Tariff on the day of their accession. In most cases, third countries will benefit from a drop in custom duties as a result of enlargement. Official EU calculations predict that enlargement will lead, overall, to a reduction in average tariffs from 9 percent to 4 percent. In some highly visible cases, however, the current custom duties of the new entrants are lower (when not null) than those of the EU—which presumably will lead to trade frictions, in particular with the USA (in a similar way to the 'chicken war' of 1963).

From a political perspective, one could expect the new entrants to pursue a general policy line more favorable to the USA, as was suggested by the 'old Europe, new Europe' incident on Iraq. The US administration can certainly be expected to pursue its strategy of 'divide and rule'—although this may seem less successful than two years ago. However, the expansion of qualified majority voting should limit the incidences when such tactics can work. Moreover, on some issues, the new entrants will likely have trade interests contrary to those of the USA. Analysts expect Poland and several other new entrants to become strong supporters of antidumping measures for basic industrial goods such as steel, chemicals and textiles. Moreover, since the sector of services is still relatively undeveloped in these countries, this may weaken internal EU support for greater services liberalization in the WTO. Finally, the countries that stand to benefit from the generous EU agricultural provisions may not be inclined to make concessions on that issue. It seems, however, that enlargement will not change the way the EU behaves on agricultural trade as much as was originally expected (and feared), in large part because the benefits of the CAP will be extended fully to the new entrants only after a phase in period of ten years, by which time one can expect a reform and adaptation of Eastern European agriculture to have taken place.

Finally, enlargement makes Russia one of the EU's main trade partners: the EU now buys 41 percent of its imported gas and 21 percent of its oil in Russia. The EU is Russia's main trading partner, accounting for above 50 percent of its overall trade. On the other hand, Russia is the EU's fifth trading partner, behind the USA, Switzerland, China and Japan, and accounts for around 5 percent of the EU's overall trade. The EU is openly supporting Russia's membership in the WTO and seems to be competing with the USA to secure favorable trade relations with that country.

1.3.2. Institutional Reform

The institutions for making trade policy in the EU—in particular the rules for competence and external representation—are being challenged by enlargement. How will twenty-five, if not more, countries be able to reach a single voice on matters of trade and abide by the results of international agreements negotiated on their behalf, even when doing so might sometimes contravene their particular interests? In order to keep an efficient decision-making system in an enlarged Europe, the Constitutional Convention in charge of drafting a constitution for Europe introduced rules to simplify the complex policymaking apparatus in trade. The proposed Constitution clarifies that trade policy is an exclusive supranational competence, whether in goods, services, intellectual property and foreign direct investment (Art. I-13)—going further toward supranationality than the 2000 Nice Treaty. Moreover, the use of qualified majority voting within the Council would be broadened—with only a few exceptions remaining in matters of trade in cultural and audiovisual services (Art. III-315, para. 1), at the insistence of France, supported by a majority of member states, including Belgium, Germany and Poland.

EU institutions are also subject to complaints about the lack of democratic legitimacy of the policymaking process in trade—in particular demands for a greater role for the EP. These demands have increased as the reach of trade policy expanded to politically sensitive issues that used to be the exclusive domain of domestic regulation, such as food safety and culture. The Commission also pushed strongly for a greater role for the parliament in trade policy. Indeed, former Trade Commissioner Pascal Lamy had already voluntarily started to involve the EP in the process on trade-related issues such as GMOs (Lamy 2002).

The proposed Constitution, accordingly, would introduce several institutional changes that could open broad avenues for parliamentary influence over trade policy and agreements. Trade-related legislation, such as antidumping rules, would be adopted jointly by the Council and the Parliament under the so-called 'co-decision procedure.'[2] Once trade negotiations are launched, the Parliament would be kept informed of the progress of the talks on a formal basis. Importantly, the Parliament would have to approve the conclusion of trade agreements struck within the WTO or bilaterally. Overall, should it be ratified, the Constitution would mean more equal power of the Council and the Parliament over trade policy, with a role for Parliament closer to that of the US Congress under fast-track procedures.

In brief, the challenges facing EU trade policy in the years ahead should not diminish its central role as one of the world's two foremost trade powers. Its high degree of centralization, in spite of the increasing heterogeneity of national preferences as a result of enlargement, should still ensure the EU's global influence in the world political economy. Having a single voice in trade, which can make the EU a stronger bargainer and thus stronger actor on the world stage, could potentially serve as a template for other sectors in which the EU is integrating. Money and finance is an obvious area where lessons could be learned from the EU's long experience in trade policy.

2. The EU as a Nascent Power in Money and Finance

European monetary integration was motivated in substantial measure by a desire to shield member states from the consequences of international monetary instability, spawned in part by US policies. Economic integration and an interest in realigning control over monetary policy, among other factors, also contributed to European monetary integration. But the desire to deflect systemic instability and establish a counterweight to the USA was fundamental to the creation of the euro area (Henning 1998). The size and importance of the euro area in international trade and finance makes the monetary union a natural potential rival for the USA and the euro a natural competitor for the dollar over the long term. The slow pace of development of euro-area

[2] The Commission remains in charge of the implementation of antidumping rules.

institutions for external policy, however, has constrained the role of the euro area as an international monetary leader and the role of the euro as an international currency.

2.1. Institutions and Processes of External Monetary Policy

The common external monetary policy derives from the single monetary policy of the euro area. Just as they accept an unqualified obligation to adhere to the euro area's monetary policy and participate in its institutions, member states also accept an obligation to abide by a single external policy and speak with unity on external matters relating to the monetary union. The institutional machinery of external monetary relations is not nearly as developed as that for external trade policy, however, and remains a work in progress. One salient manifestation of the incomplete development of the former is the periodic tendency of officials—prime ministers, finance ministers, European Commissioners and ECB board members—to speak publicly about the exchange rate with little or no internal coordination.[3]

The Council, ECB and Commission are the main institutions associated with external monetary policymaking. Under the Maastricht Treaty, the Council has the authority to determine the exchange rate regime of the euro—that is, for example, whether the currency will be fixed or floating against those of major partners. Once that strategic choice has been made, the ECB has broad discretion in implementing the policy. Under either choice, the Council and the ECB are enjoined to reach a consensus on a policy that is consistent with price stability within the euro area—the highest objective assigned to the ECB by the treaty. Under the present floating regime, the Council may issue 'general orientations' to the ECB with respect to exchange rate policy. To date, no such orientations have been formally issued and the ECB retains broad latitude, with discretion over the level, timing and size of foreign exchange interventions, for example. Officials of the Commission participate in meetings of the Council and ECB and share the right of initiative on matters relating to the exchange rate regime and external negotiating arrangements.[4]

Because not all of the members of the EU participate in the euro area, of course, the main deliberations about external monetary policy gravitate to the Eurogroup, in the case of the Council, and the Executive Board and Governing Council, in the case of the ECB. Both finance ministry and central

[3] For details regarding the key provisions of the Maastricht Treaty, their interpretation and application, see, among others, Henning 1997; McNamara 1998; Everts 1999; Henning and Padoan 2000; McNamara and Meunier 2002.

[4] The European Parliament reviews exchange rate matters as part of its oversight hearings on monetary policy. Discussed in Jabko 2003.

bank officials are represented in the Economic and Financial Committee (EFC)—the successor to the pre-euro Monetary Committee—and its euro-area working parties that prepare the work of the Eurogroup. The Commission helps to organize these meetings and participates in them.

The disjuncture between centralization of competence on monetary policy and decentralization on many financial policies and fiscal policy compounds the complexity of external monetary policymaking. This is particularly the case when fiscal and financial policies spillover into exchange rate and external monetary policy, and in international bodies where both sets of issues are treated (Campanella 2000). Because institutional prerogatives differ across issue areas, moreover, the legal determination of boundaries between such areas is a key decision. International financial issues arising within the International Monetary Fund (IMF), for example, have been deemed to fall outside the treaty requirement to adhere strictly to a common position. In contrast to bilateral exchange rate negotiations with the USA, European member states have instead subjected such deliberations to 'common understandings' among the European executive directors at the Fund.

External monetary policymaking thus differs from external trade policymaking in several ways. First, the monetary union introduced a new European institutional actor, the ECB, and conferred strong and independent authority upon it. The presence of the ECB has required reconfiguring the roles of the Commission and Council. Second, differences that inhere in the substantive policy challenges also bear on policymaking in the two areas: lack of discipline among European officials can have an immediate effect on foreign exchange markets but a negligible one in goods markets. Finally, being much younger, the monetary union has not yet been forced by circumstances to develop a sustained, coherent position and bargain with multiple actors in international negotiations. The one partial exception, joint intervention in the foreign exchange market in autumn 2000, had mixed results. Because EU authorities have confronted successive rounds of GATT/WTO negotiations, the roles of the member states and institutions in trade have been relatively well defined.

2.2. The Euro Area in International Forums and Organizations

The arrangements for representing the euro area in international financial institutions are complex, representing a balance between the need to convey a common position and the prerogatives of member states. Complexity is enhanced by the fact that the issues addressed in these forums and institutions vary with respect to where competence lies in the EU. In this respect, the distinction between money and finance is particularly important.

Consider three levels: bilateral relations, particularly with the USA; the finance G-7; and the IMF.

2.2.1. Bilateral Relations

In bilateral relations with the USA, the euro area's counterparts are the Treasury department and the Federal Reserve. On central banking matters and monetary policy, the ECB is empowered to consult and cooperate with the Federal Reserve. On matters in which Ecofin and political authorities have an important role, such as the choice of exchange rate regime, issuance of general orientations regarding exchange policy, and foreign exchange intervention, however, the euro-area counterpart to the Treasury is complex. The finance ministers in the Eurogroup have collective political responsibility and relate to US authorities through their chairman and, on more operational matters, through the chairman of the deputy-level EFC. Once consensus among political authorities is reached, on foreign exchange intervention for example, the ECB might coordinate operations directly with the US Treasury—abandoning a long-established norm against such 'cross-talk.' The one case of intensified coordination and joint intervention, as of this writing, occurred near the euro's record lows in September 2000.

2.2.2. Finance G-7

Differentiated competence within the EU has contributed to an elaborate choreography of officials within finance G-7 meetings. Composed of the finance ministers and central bank governors of the USA, Japan, Germany, France, Britain, Italy and Canada, that body includes three members of the euro zone and one member of the EU that is not a member of the euro zone. The president of the ECB is empowered to speak to questions of monetary and exchange rate policy, but shares authority with the Eurogroup on exchange rate matters, has little authority on financial regulation, and no authority on fiscal matters. Euro-area finance ministers have authority over national fiscal policy, but are under no strict obligation to coordinate in that area nor to defer to the Eurogroup chairman on a number of other issues that come before the G-7. At G-7 meetings, therefore, the ECB president attends in the morning session on multilateral surveillance and exchange rate questions, but usually leaves and is replaced by the three national central bank governors within the euro area in the afternoon session on financial and regulatory matters. The political side of the euro area is represented by the chairman of the Eurogroup, who remains throughout the full meeting, as do the three euro area finance ministers and, of course, the finance ministers and central bank governors of the three non-European countries and those of the UK. The choreography is further complicated by the inclusion in some sessions of the European Commissioner for Economic and Financial Affairs and Russian finance minister.

2.2.3. International Monetary Fund

It is fair to say that European countries hold a very strong position within the IMF. Seven of the twenty-four Executive Directors are nationals of EU member states. European governments play a strong role in electing three additional Executive Directors. The EU-25 collectively control more than 32 percent of total votes within the Fund and, through the constituency system, potentially control an additional 12.5 percent (Truman 2004). By convention, to top it off, the Managing Director has always been a European (Kahler 2001).

The USA, however, is often regarded as having greater influence over the policies of the IMF and is sometimes resented by Europeans. Why would this be? One answer may be that a unified actor is more influential than a complex, nuanced and differentiated one. Member states' policies within the IMF, as has been noted above, have generally been interpreted as not falling under a strict EU treaty obligation to adhere to a common policy. (The Fund's Article IV surveillance review of monetary policy in the euro area is an exception.) The European EDs, the ECB representative to the IMF, and the Commission financial attaché in Washington meet regularly to establish 'common understandings' on IMF issues. Their work is supported by the Brussels-based external relations working party of the EFC. Common understandings fall short of common position, though, and members have taken different positions on some important issues before the Fund, such as lending to Argentina.

The structure of representation of members of the IMF within the Executive Board, the 'constituency system,' brings formidable centrifugal pressure to bear on any common position of the governments of the euro area. The twelve members of the monetary union sit in eight constituencies. Belgium, Austria, and Luxembourg share a constituency with seven other countries. The Netherlands leads a constituency of nine non-EU European countries plus Israel. Spain sits in a constituency dominated by Latin America. Ireland sits in a constituency composed of Caribbean countries plus Canada and represented by a Canadian executive director. Presenting a coordinated EU position while balancing constituency interests is a difficult task indeed.

Over the long run, it would be desirable from the standpoint of European interests, those of the non-European members, and the health of the IMF as an institution to consolidate the European presence in the IMF into a single seat (Henning 1997; Polak 1997; Thygesen 1997; Eichengreen and Ghironi 1997). The long-term future of the Fund rests on better aligning voting strength with the overall economic importance of members and regions.

A consolidation would coincide with a reduction in the overall size of the European quota—because intra-European transactions would be eliminated from the calculation of quota share, among other reasons—which would redress the overrepresentation of Europe relative to East Asia and other emerging economies (Kenen *et al.* 2004). The zero-sum nature of redistribution of quota and voting shares, however, makes reform of the governance structure exceedingly difficult. Securing the accession of a number of smaller European countries, among others, to reductions in shares is the crux of the problem. This is only likely to be feasible in the context of a broad, cross-issue agreement brokered by the USA and leading European members.

Over the short- to medium-term, a number of intermediate steps to aggregate European representation could be considered. The constituency system could be reconfigured by grouping EU countries together, requiring non-EU countries to find other constituencies. EU members that are not in the monetary union might be grouped separately from euro-area countries. The UK, which appoints its own ED, would continue to do so. But France and Germany, which also appoint their own EDs, have expressed an interest in consolidating their two seats—although doing so might require changes to the Fund's Articles of Agreement (Coeuré and Pisani-Ferry 2003; Truman 2004; Bini-Smaghi 2004; Bénassy-Quéré and Bowles 2002; Trésor 2002). One could expect changes such as these to reduce the centrifugal forces on European EDs and enhance Europe's influence in the institution.

2.3. The International Role of the Euro

So far, the euro has not become a true rival to the dollar as an international currency. Tables 4.2 and 4.3 display the relative roles of international currencies during and after the inception of the monetary union. As measured by the share of currencies in official reserves, the respective roles of currencies appears very stable. The US dollar comprises roughly 65 percent while the euro comprises roughly thirteen to fourteen percent, about the same as the combined share of its predecessor currencies. As measured by shares in external bank assets and bond issues, the roles of both the dollar and euro appear to have increased somewhat since 1999, at the expense of the Japanese yen, with the dollar continuing to play a significantly larger role in both categories. As measured by eurocurrency deposits, the euro's role has shrunk compared to the roles of predecessor currencies while the dollar's dominance has increased.

Trends such as these lead Cohen, for example, to argue that the prospects for the euro's international role are 'dim' (Cohen 2003). Inertia in international financial markets is compounded, in Cohen's analysis, by higher transaction costs in euros compared to dollars, an apparent deflationary bias

TABLE 4.2. *Share of national currencies in total official holdings of foreign exchange reserves, end of year (in percent)*

Currency	1988	1989	1990	1991	1992	1993	1994	1995	1996	1997	1998	1999	2000	2001	2002
Dollar*	64.0	60.0	57.5	58.5	63.1	63.3	62.8	62.4	65.0	66.4	66.5	68.4	68.1	68.3	64.8
Japanese yen	6.9	7.2	7.9	8.4	7.6	7.7	7.9	6.8	6.0	5.2	5.4	5.5	5.2	4.9	4.5
Pound sterling	2.3	2.3	2.8	3.2	3.1	3.0	3.3	3.2	3.4	3.7	3.9	4.0	3.9	4.0	4.4
Swiss franc	1.8	1.4	1.3	1.2	1.0	1.1	0.9	0.8	0.8	0.7	0.7	0.7	0.7	0.7	0.7
Euro	—	—	—	—	—	—	—	—	—	—	—	12.7‡	13‡	13‡	14.6‡
Deutsche mark	14.2	17.8	17.0	15.6	13.3	13.7	14.2	13.7	13.1	12.9	12.2	—	—	—	—
French franc	1.0	1.4	2.3	2.8	2.7	2.3	2.4	2.3	1.9	1.4	1.4	—	—	—	—
Netherlands guilder	1.0	1.1	1.0	1.0	0.7	0.7	0.5	0.4	0.3	0.4	0.4	—	—	—	—
Unspecified†	6.6	6.6	8.2	7.0	6.5	6.6	6.4	8.9	8.3	8.4	9.3	8.8	9.1	9.0	11.0

* ECUs issued against dollars are treated as dollars.

† The residual is equal to the difference between total foreign exchange reserves of IMF member countries and the sum of the reserves held in the currencies listed in the table.

‡ Excludes the euros received by euro area members when their previous holdings of other euro area members' legacy currencies were converted into euros in January 1, 1999.

Source: IMF Annual Report (1998, 2002).

TABLE 4.3. *Currency shares of private external assets, 1995–2002*

Asset type and currency	1995	1996	1997	1998	1999	2000	2001	2002
Shares of external bank assets								
Dollar	31.9	32.6	35.2	34.3	39.5	43.3	45.2	41.8
Deutsche mark	11.7	12.3	10.6	11.3	—	—	—	—
Other pre-euro currencies	8.6	9.3	10.8	13.0	—	—	—	—
ECU	1.8	1.4	1.0	1.4	—	—	—	—
Euro	—	—	—	—	27.6	27.8	28.5	33.4
Pound sterling	2.9	3.5	4.0	4.2	4.2	4.3	4.4	4.3
Swiss franc	3.0	2.6	2.6	2.6	2.4	2.2	2.1	2.0
Japanese yen	10.9	9.9	9.9	10.1	9.0	8.2	6.1	5.5
Other	29.0	28.3	25.9	23.1	17.3	14.2	13.6	12.9
Denomination of external bond issues								
Dollar	34.1	37.6	42.0	45.2	47.1	48.7	50.8	46.2
Deutsche mark	12.2	11.1	10.1	10.3	—	—	—	—
Other pre-euro currencies	7.7	13.9	13.4	13.7	—	—	—	—
ECU	3.6	2.3	1.9	3.7	—	—	—	—
Euro	—	—	—	—	28.8	30.0	32.2	37.5
Pound sterling	7.0	7.5	8.2	8.0	7.7	7.7	7.1	7.1
Swiss franc	8.0	5.1	4.3	3.8	2.7	2.2	1.7	1.8
Japanese yen	15.8	16.7	14.4	11.7	10.4	8.6	5.8	5.0
Other	11.6	5.9	5.8	3.6	3.3	2.8	2.3	2.4
Denomination of eurocurrency deposits								
Dollar	44.3	45.9	48.9	47.3	64.3	66.4	67.9	63.2
Deutsche mark	16.6	14.9	12.9	12.4	—	—	—	—
Other pre-euro currencies	10.1	10.9	10.0	11.7	—	—	—	—
ECU	3.4	2.7	2.1	3.3	—	—	—	—
Euro	—	—	—	—	12.1	11.4	13.3	16.7
Pound sterling	3.2	3.8	4.4	4.9	5.5	4.9	4.9	5.2
Swiss franc	4.3	4.1	3.5	3.5	3.1	2.9	3.2	3.2
Japanese yen	5.9	6.0	6.6	6.8	7.9	7.5	5.1	5.2
Other	12.2	11.7	11.7	10.0	7.1	6.8	5.5	6.4

Source: BIS Quarterly Review (various issues)

of the monetary union, and the fragmented governance structure of the euro area.[5] These factors are formidable constraints on the role of the euro and we concur in particular on the importance of governance.

Two countervailing considerations nonetheless raise serious questions about the reliability of the past as a guide to the future. First, the EU is gradually integrating its capital markets (though the Posner and Story con-

[5] For more optimistic assessments, see Bergsten 1997, 2002; Mundell 1998; Portes and Rey 1998; European Central Bank 2002. See also Andrews, Henning and Pauly 2002.

tributions to this volume highlight persistent sources of fragmentation). While the euro-area stock and bond markets are smaller than those of the USA (Table 4.1), they are substantially larger than those of Japan and could well grow more quickly with further liberalization. Even if the European capital market does not become fully comparable to that in the USA, continued progress would make the euro more attractive and weaken the network effects that underpin inertia in the use of currencies. Structural reforms that raised the European growth rate would further increase the attractiveness of the euro.

Second, the USA is committing a substantial fiscal error by running large deficits when a shift toward surplus is needed. As a result, the USA is running an unprecedentedly large current account deficit and rapidly accumulating external debt. The role of the dollar did not suffer substantially from macroeconomic policy mistakes in the 1970s and 1980s, for example. But the formation of the monetary union and consolidation of its capital market provides alternatives to the dollar that did not exist in previous decades. The resilience of the dollar in the face of US policy mistakes will thus now be tested in a new international monetary environment.

2.4. Less Success in Money Compared to Trade

The reasons for the euro area's lack of political success in international monetary affairs relative to trade affairs revolve around economic structure and institutions, considered in that order below.

While the EU speaks for the full membership on trade matters, first of all, it speaks only for only those that have adopted the euro on monetary matters, a twelve-country minority of EU member states. The UK conducts its monetary and financial relations with the USA, Japan, and the international monetary community separately, as do the remaining 'outs.' Economic underperformance has also limited the attractiveness of the euro area as a destination for investment and location for financial intermediation and has limited the appeal of the euro as an international currency. Moreover, the euro area is relatively young and international roles of currencies exhibit considerable inertia. To the extent that the role of the currency is important to political success at the global level—and this should not be exaggerated—that inertia limits the pace at which the EU can begin to assert itself in this arena.

Turning to institutional explanations, differentiated competence of the Community across issue areas that are functionally linked to monetary and exchange rate policy—including fiscal, financial, regulatory, tax, development assistance, debt relief, and trade policy—limits the unity and coherence of the Union as a monetary actor. Importantly, institutional coherence within the external monetary sector is limited by weak discipline, leadership rotation, and absence of mandate. European officials, while under a formal obligation to speak with a common voice in external monetary relations, have nonetheless sometimes made numerous and conflicting pronouncements on, for example, exchange rates. Until recently, the six-month rotation of the EU presidency undercut continuity in euro-area political representation. In September 2004, anticipating a provision of the proposed constitution, the Eurogroup elected a chairman for two years. Significantly, however, the group left his role on external matters unspecified. When attending G-7 meetings, officials representing the euro area might present a common position, but still rarely (if ever) hold a mandate to negotiate and strike agreements with US, Japanese, and British counterparts. The absence of mandate might stem in part from the relative infrequency of explicit exchange rate agreements; but it also stems from reliance on consensus as the effective decision rule within the Eurogoup and the difficulty in securing agreement there. By contrast, the European Commissioner for External Trade holds office for five years and is granted an explicit mandate for multilateral trade negotiations by the Council.

2.5. Challenges and Opportunities

Enlargement of the EU from fifteen to twenty-five members in May 2004 and consideration of the proposed constitution raise a number of challenges and opportunities that bear on Europe's external monetary and financial relations.

2.5.1. Enlargement

Although most of the ten new members are eager to join the monetary union, many also face daunting convergence challenges and will have to wait at least until late in this decade for a decision on suitability for inclusion. The size of the new economies is small compared to that of the euro area. (The status of the UK is considerably more important to the future of the monetary union in economic and financial terms.) The inclusion of the new EU members would have political, symbolic and governance implications for the euro area greater than their economic size alone might imply.

To provide for reasonably expeditious decision-making after any Eastward expansion of the monetary union, institutional modifications have been made within both the ECB and the Council. The ECB has instituted a system of rotating voting rights on the Governing Council in which the national central bank governors of larger countries will vote more frequently than those from smaller countries. On the political side, the Eurogroup will continue to be the relevant configuration of finance ministers for the euro area. Its size will naturally increase as new countries adopt the euro. The EFC and its working parties have been reduced in size, in part by excluding national central bank deputies from some meetings, with an eye to accommodating new members. These changes take effect irrespective of the fate of the proposed constitution.

2.5.2. Prospective European Constitution

External representation of the monetary union, like that of the EU in general, was largely overlooked by the European Convention of 2002–2003, the Intergovernmental Conference that followed, and the negotiations under the Irish and Dutch presidencies that produced the proposed EU constitution. If the constitution were ratified by the twenty-five member states, at least three provisions could affect external representation and policymaking in the monetary and financial area: those regarding the president of the European Council, the chairman of the Eurogroup, and the voting procedure for establishing representation. Although the constitution will probably not be ratified soon, a quick review of these provisions identifies, with respect to the EU's external monetary and financial character, the (a) stakes in the constitutional debate and (b) limits of external reform under consideration.

The constitution creates the office of president of the European Council, which gathers the heads of government of the member states. The president of the Council is elected for two and a half years, renewable once, to prepare and chair quarterly meetings, facilitate cohesion of the Council and represent the collective views of member governments (Art. I-22). Would the president choose to make pronouncements on exchange rates and exchange rate policy? Would she actively promote the Council in exchange rate policymaking? Would he seek to develop consensus within the Council on external monetary matters, the appropriate level of the exchange rate, and the limits of fluctuation beyond which pronouncements and action might be appropriate? As this official will have responsibility across the full scope of substantive matters concerning the Council, and because he or she might well compete with the president of the Commmission among other officials for policy leadership, these questions are germane.

The constitution provides for the formal establishment of a chairman of the Eurogroup, the group of finance ministers from the euro area (Protocol on the Euro Group, Art. 2). Until September 2004, when this provision was implemented by the group without ratification of the constitution, the chairman of this informal group usually rotated on a six-month basis, as has the chairman of the more inclusive Ecofin. (When the Ecofin chairman was not from a euro area country, the Eurogroup chairman was the finance minister from the next euro-area country in the rotation.) The Eurogroup now elects a chairman for two-and-a-half years. This procedure will have a basis in the constitution, provided that document is fully ratified. The change is potentially important because the new chairman can be selected on the basis of expertise and consensus-building skill and his or her continuity could strengthen the working relationship with members of the group, the ECB, the US Treasury, and the other members of the finance G-7.

Finally, the constitution would alter the decision rule by which external representation of the EU and euro area in international organizations is determined. Under present procedures, external representation in monetary negotiations is decided by the Council by qualified majority and in international financial negotiations by unanimity (Art. 111). Under the constitution, representation in both areas would be decided by the standard double majority that applies to all majority decision-making—a 55 percent majority of member states in the Council representing 65 percent of the population. Those decisions are for the euro-area member states alone (Art. III-196). Single countries or small groups of countries would not be able to block the proposal of a large majority under these provisions as they are presently able to do. This would apply to decisions, for example, to consolidate the representation of EU countries in the International Monetary Fund.

3. Transatlantic Convergence in Trade and Finance?

As a world-class heavyweight in trade and an emerging global player in finance, the EU might be expected to go head-to-head with the USA on a variety of issues. However, the broad economic structure of the EU increasingly resembles that of the USA. EU institutions, while distinct, are also becoming somewhat more similar to US institutions in the two issue areas. Does broad structural convergence mean a parallel convergence of preferences and policies? Does greater coherence of the EU's actions in the international political economy necessarily mean an easier transatlantic partnership?

3.1. Convergence and Tensions in Trade

Ask any American or European official about the state of the transatlantic trade relationship, and they will usually start with a reassuring claim that 98 percent of the trade that occurs between them is uncontroversial. As Pascal Lamy, the former EU Trade commissioner, puts it: 'If you look from the moon, things don't look so bad' (Emling 2003). And it is true that even in a tense geopolitical environment, most European and American traders and investors conduct 'business as usual.' During the first half of 2003, in spite of the transatlantic rift over Iraq, US corporations invested $40 billion into

Europe, a 15 percent increase from 2002, and European companies invested $36 billion into the USA. Moreover, when frictions arise, they can now be mediated and solved within the framework of the World Trade Organization dispute settlement procedure. Indeed, of the thirty-five WTO cases involving the EU in the period 1999–2004, thirteen were EU–US disputes (Lamy 2004). Several of the famous bilateral disputes have been settled recently—such as bananas, beef hormones, and even steel. The potential sources of transatlantic conflict are still multiple, however, ranging from WTO disputes to the growing role of the EU as an alternative to the USA in the global political economy.

3.1.1. Transatlantic Trade Disputes

Transatlantic commercial relations are revealing two regions deeply intertwined. The EU and the USA are each other's main trading partners, exchange about $1 billion in goods and services daily, and account for around one fifth of each other's total trade. The investment relationship is even stronger than the trade relationship, with the EU and the USA being each other's largest investor, making these two economic powerhouses highly interdependent (Hamilton and Quinlan 2004). If these constant trade interactions foster convergence, they also create tensions, now resolved within the multilateral framework (Petersmann and Pollack 2003). The annual volume of bilateral EU–US litigation in trade increased substantially after 1995, when the WTO implemented its dispute settlement mechanism. Since 1995, disputes between the EU and the USA have accounted for 20 percent of all WTO disputes, whereas bilateral EU–US trade accounts for only 10 percent of world trade (Sapir 2002; Hufbauer and Neumann 2002). The most difficult EU–US disputes to resolve are those resulting not from sheer protectionism but from regulatory differences—such as beef hormones and Genetically Modified Organisms. They reveal that despite convergence on many points, there are substantial differences between the EU and the USA on the regulation of risk and progress in society (Vogel 1997; Pollack and Schaffer 2001). These disputes are harder to resolve than disputes based on the protection of narrow, special interests (such as steel) because they challenge democratic legitimacy: why, in the name of free trade, should European citizens be forced to face risks which they have legitimately agreed to prevent through precaution and patience?

3.1.2. The EU as a Multilateral Power

Another source of potential transatlantic trade tensions is the growing political use by the EU of its trade power. The formidable power of the EU in trade results partly from its central role in the multilateral trade system. The EU has always argued that its single market is a building block for multilateralism and often posits itself as champion of multilateralism—by contrast to the USA. Since the mid-1990s, the EU has positioned itself as a leader in multilateral trade negotiations. Before the end of the Uruguay Round in 1994, the roles were quite reversed: the USA had then managed to isolate the EU by building up a coalition of GATT members against the CAP. Today, the EU is mobilizing WTO members against perceived US unilateralism on issues such as steel, taxation, and antidumping. Although it retreated on the Singapore issues, the EU offered constructive proposals to help break the post-Cancun deadlock in the multilateral trade negotiations.

Moreover, the EU's active pursuit of regionalism through bilateral agreements further reinforces its global power. In part a reaction to US move in the 1990s, the emphasis on regional agreements has increased EU power by restoring a level playing field for European companies competing in Mexico and Chile, for instance. Regionalism has also enhanced the EU's normative power. In a way, the EU has acted as a 'globalizer' with Latin America, exporting its cultural and political dimensions along with its economic agreements.

The EU is also very active with developing countries through its trade policy. In 2001, just before the launch of the Doha Round, the EU launched the 'Everything but Arms' initiative (EBA), designed to offer preferential market access to the exports of the 48 least developed countries in the world. This initiative enabled the EU to change its image in the WTO by holding the high moral ground and by, perhaps, ensuring future support for its positions in multilateral trade negotiations.

3.2. (Non)convergence and EU (non)Leadership in Finance

The formation of the monetary union and creation of the ECB marked a dramatic convergence of the euro area with the USA. Since 1999, the EU has had a common currency governed by a central bank that is similar though not identical to the Federal Reserve System. Institutional convergence was less dramatic on the political side of the monetary union, where the Ecofin Council and Eurogroup contrast with the relative centralization of the US Treasury and other agencies of the executive. Owing to the independence of both central banks, the difference in the composition of the political authorities is less important in domestic monetary policymaking than in external policy.

The relative dominance of the US Treasury and its relationship to the Federal Reserve on international monetary matters are often noted in EU deliberations over the institutions of bilateral, plurilateral and multilateral relations. Ecofin reinforced coordination on IMF matters in 2002 with the specific aim, for example, of developing a working relationship with the

Managing Director and Fund staff similar to that of the Treasury (Trésor 2002). The monetary union has developed consultation mechanisms that compensate for the multiplicity of officials involved in external monetary and financial relations. On the one hand, these mechanisms appear to provide a workable basis for managing problems such as the extreme weakness of the euro in 2000. On the other hand, they do not approach the relative coherence of the US model (or national models within Europe before the monetary union), have not been tested by severe crises, and are not likely to underpin a strong leadership role on the part of the euro area in international monetary affairs.

Implementation of the constitutional provision establishing a two-and-a-half year chairman of the Eurogroup goes some distance toward creating a genuine 'Mr./Ms. Euro' (Henning 1997; Everts 1999; McNamara and Meunier 2002). This step remains incomplete, however, until the Eurogroup also grants an effective mandate to the chairman to speak in international meetings (beyond simply reading a prepared text) and negotiate with some flexibility with counterparts, in close consultation with ECB officials. Creating the office and conferring a mandate is a significant step toward greater institutional coherence; but the Eurogroup process, and the tilt in the balance of initiative toward the ECB on intervention, for example, will continue to distinguish the euro area from the USA's institutionally.

With respect to preferences regarding the content of policy, as distinct from institutions, the euro area and USA exhibit more convergence. The two large monetary areas have adopted similar targets for inflation. While both pay lip service to fiscal sustainability, the USA has embarked on a new era of fiscal deficits while France, Germany, and Italy, among others, have broken the rules of the Stability and Growth Pact. The greatest apparent difference in macroeconomic preferences is the lower tolerance for unemployment in the USA compared to the euro area. On the exchange rate regime, the question of most direct relevance to the external concerns of the monetary union, the euro area and USA clearly prefer flexibility. The compatibility of their preferences for the level of the exchange rate is being tested in the present cycle of adjustment of global current account imbalances, during which the dollar has fallen considerably against the euro.

US current account deficits and the problem they pose for global adjustment in the mid-2000s is a useful lens through which to measure the institutional maturity of the euro area. The adjustment process will almost certainly involve conflicts over which states must change policy, accept currency (ap) depreciation, and by how much. During the Plaza-Louvre period, the USA confronted a disparate group of European states tied only loosely through the European Monetary System. Now, however, the USA confronts a full-fledged monetary union in Europe that is three-quarters its economic size.

Will this structural change affect the management of the adjustment process and the distribution of the costs of adjustment? Our tentative answer is that the effect over the medium term, while significant, is likely to be partial rather than a quantum transformation. The complexity and fragmentation of euro-area decision-making and representation constrains its ability to assert itself strongly vis-à-vis the USA. To act as a full-fledged 'counterweight' to the USA in monetary affairs, as some proponents of the euro had hoped, the EU will probably have to proceed further toward a federal institutional structure.

4. Conclusion

The EU is becoming a more assertive actor in both international trade and money, but its international leadership is further developed in the trade than in the monetary sphere. Institutional arrangements for designing policy and making decisions with respect to these external matters are a substantial part of the explanation for the difference. Further evolution of the EU as a polity will affect the EU's global role in both areas.

The power of the EU in the world political economy can be expected to grow as the EU uses economic instruments in lieu of foreign policy. On the trade side, indeed, the EU's power transcends the requirements for defending its own interests in international commercial negotiations. Its trade power influences the adoption of EU regulatory practices in much of the rest of the world and promotes other values and policies—from the environment to human rights. Whether a US rival or an ally, the EU is an alternative to the USA for countries seeking a powerful and prosperous partner. The disputes over beef hormones, GMOs and data privacy are evidence of the EU's ambitions to shape the global rules of the game.

Convergence between the EU and USA varies according to issue area and institutional and substantive questions. Institutional convergence in both trade and finance depends in large measure on the fate of the proposed European Constitution. Even with substantial reforms, however, the roles of the Council and Eurogroup will continue to differentiate the EU from the USA. With enlargement, the role of member states in external economic policymaking and the efficiency of Council decision-making will remain fundamentally important. Substantive convergence on trade and finance is likely to continue. But that convergence will vary across specific issues such as, on the trade side, market access; linkages to labor standards, environment and competition; dispute resolution; and regional trade arrangements. On the financial side, the degree of convergence will vary across macroeconomic objectives, exchange rates, payments adjustment and financial rescues. Convergence on substantive preferences, more fundamentally, does not necessarily reduce transatlantic conflict. While similar preferences can ameliorate conflict on some issues—such as macroeconomic coordination and exchange rate regimes—convergence can be a source of tensions in others, such as current account surpluses, exchange rate levels, and competitiveness in specific sectors.

Convergence of the respective roles of the EU and US legislatures in trade policymaking could be especially important. Any grant of greater authority to the EP to ratify international agreements, as envisioned in the proposed Constitution, or to define the negotiating mandate would shift the EU in the direction of the USA and other national models. Granting such authority to the EP would not necessarily augur well for transatlantic cooperation, however. While it would give greater internal legitimacy to trade policy, the EP could also give greater entrée to policymaking to particularistic interests. As the Council would retain a strong role, moreover, granting co-decision powers to the EP would add another veto point. Under the Nice framework the EP's role in approving any result of the Doha Round could be limited to consultation. Under the proposed Constitution, it could block an agreement entirely.

References

Andrews, D., Henning, C. R., and Pauly, L. W. (eds.) (2002). *Governing the World's Money*. Ithaca, NY: Cornell University Press.

Bénassy-Quéré, A. and Bowles, C. (2002). 'A European Voice for the IMF', *CEPII Newsletter*, No. 216.

Bergsten, C. F. (1997). 'The Impact of the Euro on Exchange Rates and International Policy Cooperation', in P. Masson, T. H. Krueger, and B. G. Turtelboom (eds.), *EMU and the International Monetary System*. Washington, DC: International Monetary Fund, pp. 17–48.

—— (2002). 'The Euro Versus the Dollar: Will There Be a Struggle for Dominance?' Paper presented at the Annual Meeting of the American Economic Association, Atlanta, January 4.

Bini-Smaghi, L. (2004). 'A Single EU Seat in the IMF?', *Journal of Common Market Studies*, 42: 229–48.

Campanella, M. I. (2000). 'The Battle between ECOFIN-11 and the European Central Bank: A Strategic Interaction Perspective', in M. G. Cowles and M. Smith (eds.), *The State of the European Union*, Vol. 5: *Risks, Reform, Resistance, and Revival*. New York: Oxford University Press.

Cœuré, B. and Pisani-Ferry, J. (2003). 'One Market, One Voice? European Arrangements in International Economic Relations'. Paper prepared for the conference on 'New Institutions for a New Europe', Vienna, October 10–11.

Cohen, B. J. (2003). 'Can the Euro Ever Challenge the Dollar?' *Journal of Common Market Studies*, 41: 575–95.

Eichengreen, B. and Ghironi, F. (1997). 'European Unification and International Monetary Cooperation', in B. Eichengreen (ed.), *Transatlantic Economic Relations in the Post-Cold War Era*. New York: Council on Foreign Relations.

Emling, S. (2003). 'US, European Union toe-to-toe over trade issues', *The Atlanta Journal-Constitution*, November 2.

European Central Bank (2002). *Review of the International Role of the Euro*. Frankfurt am Main: ECB.

European Commission (2004). *General overview of active WTO dispute settlement cases involving the EC as complainant or defendant*. Brussels: European Commission, April 7.

Everts, S. (1999). *The Impact of the Euro on Transatlantic Relations*. London: Centre for European Reform.

Hamilton, D. and Quinlan, J. (2004). *Partners in Prosperity: The Changing Geography of the Transatlantic Economy*. Washington, DC: Center for Transatlantic Relations and Johns Hopkins University Press.

Henning, C. R. (1997). *Cooperating with Europe's Monetary Union*. Policy Analyses in International Economics No. 49. Washington, DC: Institute for International Economics.

—— (1998). 'Systemic Conflict and Regional Monetary Integration: The Case of Europe', *International Organization*, 52: 537–73.

—— and Padoan, P. C. (2000). *Transatlantic Perspectives on the Euro*. Washington, DC: The Brookings Institution.

Hufbauer, G. and Neumann, F. (2002). 'US-EU Convergence, Conflict and Cooperation', paper presented to the conference, 'Transatlantic Perspectives on the US and European Economies,' Harvard University, April 11–12.

Jabko, N. (2003). 'Democracy in the Age of the Euro', *Journal of European Public Policy*, 10/5: 710–39.

Kahler, M. (2001). *Leadership Selection in the Major Multilaterals*. Washington, DC: Institute for International Economics.

Kenen, P., Shafer, J. R., Wicks, N., and Wyplosz, C. (2004). *International Economic and Financial Cooperation: New Issues, New Actors, New Responses*. London: Centre for Economic Policy Research.

Lamy, P. (2002). 'La Politique Commerciale et la Convention', statement to the European Convention, Brussels.

—— (2004). 'Trade Policy in the Prodi Commission 1999–2004: An Assessment', European Commission, November 19.

McNamara, K. R. (1998). 'European Monetary Union and International Economic Cooperation'. Report on a workshop organized by the International Finance Section, Princeton University (April 3).

McNamara, K. R. (1998). and Meunier, S. (2002). 'Between National Sovereignty and International Power: The External Voice of the Euro', *International Affairs*, 78: 849–68.

Meunier, S. (2000). 'What single voice? European institutions and EU-US trade negotiations', *International Organization*, 54(1).

—— (2005). *Trading Voices: The European Union in International Commercial Negotiations*. Princeton, NJ: Princeton University Press.

—— and K. Nicolaïdis (1999). 'Who speaks for Europe? The delegation of trade authority in the EU', *Journal of Common Market Studies*, 37/3: 477–501.

Mundell, R. (1998). 'The Case for the Euro – I and II', *Wall Street Journal*, March 24–25.

Petersmann, E-U. and Pollack, M. A. (2003). *Transatlantic Economic Disputes: the EU, the US, and the WTO*. Oxford and New York: Oxford University Press.

Polak, J. J. (1997). 'The IMF and Its EMU Members', in P. Masson, T. Krueger, and B. Turtelboom (eds.), *EMU and the International Monetary System*. Washington, DC: International Monetary Fund, pp. 491–511.

Pollack, M. A. and Shaffer, G. C. (2001) *Transatlantic Governance in the Global Economy*. Lanham, MD and Oxford: Rowman & Littlefield.

Portes, R. and Rey, H. (1998). 'The Emergence of the Euro as an International Currency', *Economic Policy*, 26 (April): 305–32.

Sapir, A. (2002). 'Old and New Issues in EC-US Trade disputes'. Paper prepared for the conference, 'Transatlantic Perspectives on US-EU Economic Relations', Harvard University, April 11–12.

Sbragia, A. (2004). 'The European Union, the United States, and Globalization'. Paper presented at the Conference of Europeanists, March 11–13, Chicago.

Thygesen, N. (1997). 'Relations among the IMF, the ECB, and the IMF's EMU Members', in P. Masson, T. Krueger, and B. Turtelboom (eds.), *EMU and the International Monetary System*. Washington, DC: International Monetary Fund, pp. 512–30.

Trésor [Direction du Trésor, French Ministry of Finance] (2002). 'La governance du Fonds monétaire international: état des lieux et pistes de réforme', in P. Jacquet, J. Pisani-Ferry and L. Tubiana (eds.), *Gouvernance mondiale*. Report of the Conseil d'analyse économique No. 37.

Truman, E. M. (2004). 'The Euro and Prospects for Policy Coordination'. Paper presented to the conference, 'The Euro at Five: Ready for a Global Role?' Institute for International Economics, Washington, DC, February 26.

Vogel, D. and European Community Studies Association (1997). *Barriers or Benefits?: Regulation in Transatlantic Trade*. Washington, DC: Brookings Institution Press.

II

Institutional Evolutions

5

'We the States': Why the Anti-Federalists Won

RENAUD DEHOUSSE

In the documents put forward by the European Parliament (EP) to 'sell' the draft constitutional treaty, one image keeps reappearing: that of an open book, draped in the colors of the European flag, on which is written, 'We, the peoples of Europe, have decided . . . '. The symbolic constitutional reference is obvious. It tries to accredit the idea that the European Convention marked a great 'constitutional moment' (Ackerman 1991) at the end of which the representatives of the European peoples have defined the way that they will be governed.

Indeed, constitutional rhetoric flourished throughout the work of the convention. References to the Philadelphia Convention and the birth of the American Constitution were frequent. The Convention delegates often regarded the Philadelphia debates as a model to guide their own work. Valéry Giscard d' Estaing affirmed it in a speech at the Library of Congress in February 2003. On the occasion of a transatlantic summit, Romano Prodi travelled to Philadelphia to present the 'Constitution' which had just been adopted. As one US observer remarked in the aftermath of the Iraqi crisis, not without some mischievousness, it is somewhat ironic to see the Europeans, generally inclined to criticize the USA, so impassioned for its constitutional history and calling on the spirit of the *Federalist Papers* (Dinan 2003).

Obviously, the reality is much more complex. Through these multiple references to the spirit of Philadelphia, the Europeans hoped, above all, to exorcize the ghosts of Nice—the tug of war between national representatives that had marked the previous intergovernmental conference (IGC) that concluded in Nice in December 2000. The message was clear: bargaining dominated by exclusive concern for national interests would not lead to outcomes that would meet the expectations of Europeans. This rejection of the traditional model of intergovernmental conferences was decisive in the choice of a seemingly new method—the convention method—to tackle the question of institutional reform (Magnette 2004). When it came to substantive choices, by contrast—the kind of powers should European institutions be vested with, and the controls they should be subjected to—the US constitution was the object of a general rejection in that it allowed for the development of a political system which was considered too centralized for present-day Europe. Hence *inter alia* the rejection of the old formula of a 'United States of Europe,' which had rallied the support of European federalists in the early postwar period.

Nevertheless, US constitutional history provides many reference points which allow us to better understand the choices made by the European Convention and in the ensuing IGC. Section 1 of the chapter notes that when one looks at the dynamics that prompted a quest for institutional change, the similarities are striking. Section 2 considers the equally striking differences regarding the outcome of the two conventions. The main thesis of this chapter is that in the European case, the supporters of 'states' rights' have had the upper hand. In section 3, I try to explain why, in spite of the novelties it introduced, the conventional method led to such a 'conventional' outcome. Drawing on this, section 4 highlights a few lessons that can be drawn from the Convention's experience as regards the dynamics of political change in Europe.

1. Why Reform?

It may appear pointless to compare two processes of reform that are separated by a distance of more than two centuries. What can there be in common between the agricultural economies of the original thirteen colonies of the USA and the large, mainly postindustrial markets of Europe? Many technological innovations, interspersed with bloody wars stand between them. These changes were also accompanied by profound transformations in the nature of the relationship between citizens, as well as in democratic theory. Yet, in spite of these numerous differences, one can find similarities between the dynamics that gave rise to the two convention processes.

In both instances, dissatisfaction with existing institutional structures was the main catalyst for change. In postrevolutionary USA, the Articles of Confederation were repeatedly criticized because of the restrictions they placed on the powers of the Continental Congress, which proved incapable of dealing with small landholder agitation and attacks on private property, or ensuring free trade among the former colonies. The fear of foreign—that is to say, European—interference within the domestic affairs of the new nation was also very strong (Lacorne 1991).

On the European front, the difficult ratification of the Maastricht Treaty revealed that the 'permissive consensus', which had marked the first decades of European construction, had not carried into the 1980s. The Union was thus increasingly criticized for its alleged lack of democracy. Moreover, as the prospect of enlargement drew near, it became more and more apparent that the institutional architecture was going to be put under strain—some said definitively paralyzed—by the accession of ten new members. It had been conceived for a union of six countries and was already showing signs of weakness with fifteen member states. Although the problem had already been addressed at the intergovernmental conferences of Amsterdam (1997) and Nice (2000), no clear solution emerged. The Nice Treaty was eventually agreed upon after negotiations that reached a level of animosity unprecedented in the history of European integration. It left open a great many questions: the distribution of power between the Union and member states, the role of national parliaments, the status of the Charter for Fundamental Rights, etc. The scars left by Nice prompted a number of governments to support the idea of reopening the discussion even before the treaty had been ratified by all.

The notion of a 'European Convention' as a way to move forward was prompted by two distinct but related considerations. On a substantive plane, many political leaders argued that the reforms agreed upon in the previous intergovernmental conferences were insufficient to enable the Union to operate efficiently once central and eastern European countries joined. On a procedural plane, they argued that the Nice IGC had eloquently demonstrated that the classical, diplomatic model of treaty revision, according to which changes were to be negotiated by national representatives and unanimously agreed, was no longer adapted to the necessity of our time. As Spanish Prime Minister José Maria Aznar emphasized in the inaugural session of the convention, 'Nice is the reason we are here' (Aznar 2002). The precedent of the little-known first European Convention, organized in 1999–2000 to streamline the protection of fundamental rights at the European level, was seen as a promising route (it had smoothly delivered the new Charter of Fundamental Rights), and was heralded by the reform camp as a sound alternative. A more open assembly, comprising European and national parliamentarians in addition to government representatives and operating in public, could more easily overcome the conflicts between national interests that had plagued the previous attempts at institutional reform, and facilitate a convergence around solutions acceptable to all (Magnette 2004).

The first months of the Convention confirmed the existence of two opposing camps. On the one hand, the reform camp, like the American Federalists in 1787, advocated a substantial institutional overhaul. This group comprised a series of actors who had misgivings about the previous reform attempts: the Commission and the EP, who are deprived of formal powers in intergovernmental conferences, and the governments of a number of smaller member states. The latter, some of which had been bruised in Nice, feared that the large countries' insistence on a redistribution of power in the Union would end up weakening their own position in the EU—hence their strong support for the so-called 'community method,' in which states' influence is compensated by the role of supranational actors. This view was frequently heard in long-standing members of the Union, such as Benelux countries, generally supported by Finland, Greece, and (initially) Portugal, but rarer among the new member countries, who proved generally more reluctant to endorse transfers of sovereignty (Dauvergne 2004; Norman 2003).

The Convention included only a handful of openly Eurosceptic delegates, hostile in principle to any form of integration, and they were largely isolated, which led them ultimately to present their own, alternative project. But, many Conventioneers, as they were called, favored some kind of status quo. While the representatives of larger countries were mostly concerned with preventing a dilution of their influence in an enlarged Union, they were not particularly favorable to major institutional changes. The reforms they supported therefore, primarily aimed at consolidating the EU system without further transfers of sovereignty, for example through the establishment of a stable Presidency of the Union (in lieu of the current system of six-monthly rotation), or of a Foreign Minister, who would be in charge of the whole EU foreign policy, but accountable to the member states rather than to the EP.

As these countries were rather lukewarm about institutional reform, they had insisted on a number of safeguards. First, in contrast to the precedent established by the lower-profile convention that had produced the Charter of Fundamental Rights, they took care to appoint themselves the persons who would pilot the work of the Convention. The former President of France, Valéry Giscard d'Estaing, who was to chair the meeting, was flanked by two vice presidents, themselves former prime ministers: Belgium's Jean-Luc Dehaene and Italy's Giuliano Amato. Moreover, a presidium, composed of representatives of the various 'components' of the Convention, but in which all large countries were represented in one form or another, was to assist them in their steering work. Second, it was agreed that the Convention's results would be screened later on by an intergovernmental conference. As the latter was to follow the standard procedure for treaty reform, unanimity would be required for any change (Magnette 2004). Successive developments were to demonstrate the importance of this element.

2. A Treaty Or a Constitution?

In Europe as in the USA, the rejection of the status quo quickly convinced the Conventioneers that they had to go beyond their original mandates. When recommending to the Continental Congress the convocation of representatives from the thirteen founding states, the Annapolis Convention had mentioned only one issue, that of interstate trade. By accepting this suggestion, the Congress had taken care to specify that the 'only task explicitly conferred' upon the Philadelphia convention was 'to revise the Articles of Confederation,' and that the result of its work should be ratified by every state. Likewise, the Laeken declaration of 2001, whereby the European Council convened the Convention on the Future of Europe, specified that the latter's role would be limited to tackling a list, albeit a long one, of questions and to drawing up 'a final document that would include and explain the various options, specify their support, or make recommendations in the event of a consensus'. The possibility of a constitution was indeed contemplated, but only as a long-term option: the Convention was merely invited to consider its potential advantages and disadvantages.

As is known, in spite of the above precautions, both conventions were adjourned with the solemn adoption of a constitutional text. However, the similarities end there, for the status of the two texts is fundamentally different. Three things need to be recalled here concerning the document adopted in Philadelphia.

First, it was adopted in the name of the people of the USA, to which the first words of the text refer: 'We the people of the United States of America....' Reference to the states' representatives disappeared in the last stages of drafting. In addition, not all were represented in Philadelphia: Rhode Island was opposed to the idea of the convention and refused to send delegates. Two New York representatives who disagreed with the direction the convention was taking left during the summer of 1787. It was therefore on a purely personal capacity that the third New York delegate, Alexander Hamilton, in conflict with the authorities of his state, signed the constitution (Bowen 1966). The conditions in which the constitution came into force confirm the birth of a new body politic. In accordance with what had been envisaged, the constitution came into force as soon as nine states had ratified it. The decisive ratification, that of New Hampshire, occurred while the debate (which led to the publication of *The Federalists Papers*) still raged in New York and Virginia—states that then accounted for a fifth of the Union's inhabitants. Could one imagine today the acceptance of the European constitution without the backing of, say, Germany and Italy? Admittedly, New York and Virginia ended up approving the constitution by a narrow majority. However, their approval, although politically important, was deprived of legal strength: the voice of the American people had surpassed that of the states.[1]

[1] This of course does not mean the latter ceased *ipso facto* to assert its authority. The question of the primacy of the Union was eventually settled by a bloody civil war.

Second, the new constitution gave rise to a national government much more powerful than the confederate institutions that had preceded it. This was the principal subject of the Convention and the thorniest issue of its debates. Many delegates—beginning with those of Virginia—desired the establishment of a strong central power (Beer 1993). Even if the final compromise was not entirely satisfactory from their standpoint, it nevertheless took several significant steps in their direction. The new government's legitimacy was no longer based on the will of the states alone. To be sure, they could still influence federal decisions through the Senate, whose members were elected by their legislative assemblies. However, the citizens of the Union (or at least those who had the right to vote) were directly represented in the House of Representatives. Just as important was the fact that Union decisions were directly applicable, without having to first be ratified by the state assemblies. The direct links between the citizen and the new institutions were therefore numerous.

Lastly—hardly necessary to recall—the Philadelphia convention saw important innovations. On the political level, its most important achievement was without a doubt the invention of federalism, *tertium genus* between unitary structures and the relatively loose confederate arrangements that were the subject of abundant discussion in the literature of the time (Beer 1993). The basis of this qualitative jump was an agreement on a bicameral Parliament. This was the fruit of a 'great compromise' between the advocates of a strong national government (who desired a distribution of seats in the legislature according to state population) and those adherents to a more traditional balance (who defended the principle of sovereign equality between states). As is known, in the end, both principles found their place in the constitution: the first in the creation of the House of Representatives, and the second in the provisions relating to the Senate. The innovations were not limited to the sole field of constitutional engineering, since the compromise was defended in the name of a new vision of democracy and legitimacy. Even today, James Madison's comments on the necessity of preventing the 'capture' of public institutions by 'factions' representing private interests (Madison 1982 [1787–8]) is a point of reference for the pluralist model of democracy, which is at times indicated as a model for the EU (Majone 1998).

These three elements underline all that separates the Philadelphia convention from its European counterpart. The most striking difference is the legal status of the document adopted by each body. Although the text drafted by the European Convention makes abundant use of constitutional language, it is essentially a consolidated and amended version of former treaties. In accordance with the Laeken Declaration of December 2001, the text has been examined by a traditional intergovernmental conference and will come into effect only if it is ratified by every member state, in accordance with its own constitutional rules (Art. IV: 447). In the future, any revision will also require unanimous agreement (Art. IV: 444 and 445). In other words, the reference to a constitution, which suggests that the people determine how they will be governed, is misleading. In the final analysis, here the will of the member states, and not that of a would-be European people, will prove decisive.

Next come the differences in the content of both draft constitutions. Whereas Philadelphia had seen the birth of a national government (opening the door to its considerable reinforcement thereafter), the European Convention was largely dominated by member states' fear of seeing their influence within the European political system diluted. The nature of these fears varied according to the country. The large countries (with the notable exception of Germany) shared a desire to contain the influence of supranational institutions, whereas the lesser-populated countries worried about the possible emergence of a 'directoire' of big countries.

These two fears surface in the institutional structures defined by the Convention. Somewhat paradoxically, it is in referring to what it intended to avoid that one can best understand the draft constitutional treaty. Evidently, the emergence of a strong power at the European level, relying directly on the will of the people, was not desired. The debate over the appointment of the European Commission clearly proves that point. Member governments indicated that they intended to keep control of the choice of the Commission's president, and they won their case. Although the necessity to take into consideration the result of the European elections and the principle of election by the EP were explicitly proclaimed, the Parliament will merely be given the right to vote on a candidate nominated by the European Council. Despite the subtly phrased wording of Article 27, this solution has all the appearances of a status quo.[2] True, even in the present system, the Parliament has acquired over the last decade a significant role in the appointment of the Commission (Dehousse 2000; Costa 2004). The difficulties met by the Barroso Commission have demonstrated that when it uses its powers, it can veto the appointment of individual Commissioners, or a reshuffling of portfolios within the executive. But it cannot alter the political balance of the executive, which depends mostly on the situation at national level. MEPs, whose election depends on their respective national political formations, will not lightly take the risk of a clash with the political

[2] The first paragraph provides: 'Taking into account the elections in the European Parliament, and after appropriate consultation, the European Council, ruling with a qualified majority, will propose to the European Parliament a candidate for commission president. This candidate is to be elected by parliamentary majority. If this candidate does not receive a majority, the European Council will propose, within one month, a new candidate to the European Parliament, and the same procedure will follow.'

leaders represented in the European Council (see Hix 1997). It is unlikely that the entry into force of the constitution will change this.

The eagerness to protect states' rights appears as one of the main threads of the draft Constitution. The political leadership of the European Council has been reaffirmed, and it has been extended to the whole of EU external relations (Art. III: 293)—an inconceivable result only a few years ago. The large member states, who wished to improve its effectiveness, insisted on the creation of a permanent presidency, while reaffirming the role of the Commission in policy initiation, coordination and control of EU policies. To compensate for what appeared to many as a victory for the 'large countries,' equality between member states was the watchword with regard to Commission reform. Although the principle of a reduction in the size of the Commission was accepted, with the aim of preserving its effectiveness, a system of 'equal rotation' among states has been foreseen. The products of antagonistic fears, this shaky compromise will prevent large member states from nominating a Commissioner in each Commission. One could thus have a Commission where, say, Latvia, Cyprus and Slovenia would each be represented, but France and England would not! It is doubtful that the authority of the Commission would thereby be reinforced, which explains the forceful opposition of the Prodi Commission to this formula (European Commission 2003).

The same concern for member states' interests can be found in the provisions relating to foreign policy. The draft constitution essentially institutionalizes foreign policy competition between three centres of power: the new foreign minister, in charge of development and execution of common foreign and security policies (Art. 28: para. 2), the president of the European Council, in charge of representing the EU abroad (Art. 22: para. 2), and the Commission itself, which will retain responsibility for a whole range of 'soft policy' instruments like international trade and developmental aid (Art. 28: para. 1) as well as the right to represent the EU in these fields. The first debates over the status of a future EU diplomatic service suggest that the workings of this curious *ménage à trois* will not be easy. Moreover, several member states have indicated that they intended to preserve their autonomy as regards foreign policy—hence *inter alia* the refusal to shift to qualified majority voting for most of the decisions to be taken in that area. Considering these elements, it is difficult to imagine how a common EU foreign policy could go beyond the predominantly verbal diplomacy in which Europe is currently engaged.

At all these levels, thus, in front of the uncertainties linked to what was then the forthcoming enlargement, member states' individual and short term concerns appear to have prevailed over the interest of all in devising an efficient system of government.

By no means does this mean, however, that the draft constitution is devoid of interest, nor that it did nothing to strengthen central EU institutions. But in a somewhat unexpected way, it can be observed that the principal elements of consolidation, such as the extension of the legislative co-decision and of qualified majority, are similar to those of the last intergovernmental conferences. On these two points, the progress made in Maastricht, Amsterdam, and even Nice, which was presented throughout the Convention as a counter-model, were far from insignificant. As for the 'innovations' introduced by the Convention, they were hardly new ideas, but rather inspired by earlier suggestions. The idea of an EU President had been proposed ten years ago by Valéry Giscard d'Estaing himself. The adoption of a hierarchy for community legal instruments was among Commission proposals in Maastricht (European Commission 1991). The dismantling of the infamous 'pillars' structure had begun in Amsterdam. As for the work on treaty simplification, which the Prodi Commission greatly insisted on since its appointment, it had been the subject of many preparatory studies (EUI 2002*a*, 2002*b*). To prolong the enumeration would be tiresome, but it is easy to see that the Convention experience, which was praised for its originality, tends to confirm previous constructivist analyses of institutional reform at the European level, according to which pure innovations are relatively rare during 'great institutional moments' (Falkner 2002).

The debates within the Convention confirmed the existence of two poles. On one side were the federalists, who militated in favor of executive reinforcement (in particular through the election of the Commission President by the EP, or even by universal suffrage). On the opposite side were those who favored a more traditional intergovernmental system with overall legitimacy remaining in the hands of national governments. Several months of intense discussions did not produce any synthesis of, or compromise between, these two visions. Despite the innovative language of the draft constitution, the elements of continuity largely prevailed and there were no true qualitative leaps toward further integration. To the extent that changes were introduced, they were primarily motivated by the desire to prevent the emergence of stronger central government. Using US constitutional terminology, one could say that the 'anti-federalists'—the defenders of American 'states' rights'—had the upper hand.

3. Why Have the Anti-Federalists Prevailed?

The analysis of a process as complex as the constitutional Convention defies monocausal explanations. Obviously, the final result is tied to a whole host of factors. First of all, it is clear that the modest results of the Convention's main objectives for institutional reform were considerably influenced by a climate which can at best be described as unfavorable to further transfers of power to the European level. Since the Delors Commission (1985–95), national governments have learned that European integration could reduce their margin of maneuver—sometimes considerably, as testified by the present difficulties of those countries struggling to respect the Stability Pact connected to monetary union. Protecting national autonomy against encroachments by European institutions has become a leitmotif in many capitals. The candidate countries, which only recovered their sovereignty ten years before, moved in the same direction. Anything remotely related to the idea of centralization is viewed with general mistrust. Many of the innovations of the last decade—whether institutional or policy related—were inspired by this same 'antifederalist' climate, which the general tone of the Laeken Declaration reflected extremely well. Just to mention two examples, when an attempt was made to give EU foreign policy more muscle, the result was a High Representative—outside the Commission—being entrusted with the task; similarly, the great program relating to Europe's economic and social competitiveness launched in Lisbon in March 2000, was deliberately conceived as an alternative to the supranational, top-down 'community method' (Wallace 2000; Dehousse 2004). Clearly, since Maastricht there has been in Europe an 'anti-Brussels' climate, much like the 'anti-Washington' sentiment often seen in the USA.

As indicated earlier, this climate also influenced the way in which the Convention's mandate was defined in Laeken. Several governments (including France, Great Britain and Spain) could not accept giving up the familiar framework of intergovernmental conferences in favor of a body within which they formed but one rather heterogeneous-'component'. Hence their insistence that the Convention be confined to a preparatory role. As a consequence, the shadow of the IGC, which had the final say, hung over the assembly throughout its work. The views expressed by government delegates were the subject of particular attention as it was known that their country would enjoy a right of veto at the IGC.

This 'privileged position' of the governmental actors considerably influenced the work of the assembly. Valéry Giscard d' Estaing was often criticized for lending a more attentive ear to the member state governments, especially those of the 'large' countries, than to his fellow Conventioneers. Yet, the procedures designed in Laeken left him little choice if he wanted the Convention's work to be accepted by the IGC (Kerr 2003). In addition, when it was recognized that the Convention had become a theatre of interesting dynamics, several governments changed their delegate, usually to appoint their foreign affairs minister, thereby contributing to the 'intergovernmentalization' of the debates. As in all intergovernmental conferences, France sought shared positions with Germany, arousing anger in many capitals, which were alarmed at the prospect of a hegemonic leadership. Governments gave ample evidence of a strong *esprit de corps*, placing first priority on agreement among themselves. The joint proposal tabled in January 2002 by the French and German governments was, of course, emblematic in this respect, but one could add that when tabling amendments to the drafts submitted by the Praesidium, government delegates usually tried to rally support among their peers, rather than from representatives of other institutions.

Toward the end of the Convention, the principal challenge was no longer to find the most adequate response to any substantive or institutional problem, but instead to find the necessary concessions to appease one government or another. Negotiation had indeed supplanted the deliberative spirit that had characterized the first debates within the Convention (Magnette 2003; Duhamel 2003). Unsurprisingly, member states' influence was quite strong on issues on which they had strong preferences. To mention but a few examples, the *exception culturelle* dear to the French government's heart was maintained, the word 'federal' was withdrawn at the British government's request, and several national governments, including Germany, successfully opposed the extension of majority voting in the social field.

The third reason that explains the success of the 'anti-federalists' is linked to the way in which the debates unfolded within the Convention. Although the discussion began with a rather vast overview of European issues, followed by a period of listening to the public, no convergence really emerged with respect to the potential ambitions of an enlarged Union. However, historically, European integration has been built and has evolved on the basis of discrete political projects. This is true for a simple reason: it is easier to reach an agreement on concrete proposals, whose costs and benefits can be evaluated in a more or less precise way, than to agree on an abstract vision of public good and on the institutional arrangements that are necessary to see them through. Visions of justice are manifold, and the more heterogeneous and broad the discussion group, the more difficult it will be for a consensus to emerge. This is why steps forward always took the form of clearly identified projects: the coal and steel community, the single market, the single currency, and so on. If the transfers of powers required by such initiatives were accepted, it is because they appeared as means to achieve a fairly clearly identified goal. Majority voting was portrayed as necessary to eliminate trade barriers, whereas the establishment of an independent central bank was ostensibly essential to guarantee the credibility of the single currency. On the other hand, when the debate remains confined to questions of an institutional nature, the latter become an end in themselves. National suspicions awaken and the negotiation takes the forms of a zero-sum game, making agreement uncertain. Such was the case in Amsterdam, and even more so in Nice (Dehousse 2001).

In the absence of a common project, the debates within the Convention quickly became tense as soon as institutional questions were addressed. The artificial divide between 'large' and 'small' states, which had been largely absent in past decades, as noted by the Convention's tri-presidency, became a central problem (Amato *et al.* 2003) On institutional issues, the Conventioneers' positions were strongly influenced by their political culture or their institutional interests. For example, the French and the British were sensitive to the need for a strong leadership (as exists in their respective national regimes), the Germans insisted on the idea of a catalogue of respective EU and member state powers (as in the German Basic Law), while the MEPs were naturally inclined to praise the merits of parliamentary democracy. The compromises between these various models were made all the more difficult by the political symbolism carried by the EU institutions themselves. The distribution of Council votes, for example, is perceived as an indicator of each nation's importance, despite having far less real importance than is usually believed. A government that 'lost' in the Council tally might bear political costs on the domestic plane. Abstract concepts were also a source of incomprehension: the reference to federalism in the preamble provoked a sharp reaction from the British, for whom the word is invariably synonymous with centralization—an ahistorical reading, certainly, but now so deeply ingrained in British culture that it has became a factor to be taken into account.

4. The Dynamics of Political Change

On the basis of this account, one could be tempted to conclude that even within the Convention the traditional logic of interstate bargaining remained intact: national interests shaped the eventual outcome, interstate bargains proved decisive on major issues, and decisions tended to reflect the preferences of the larger states (Moravcsik 2004). Nonetheless, several elements do not fit with this view.

First, as regards institutional issues, it is easy to overestimate the influence of the Franco–German axis. As one might expect from their very different national political cultures, the two governments' starting positions were fairly far apart. Germany favored a federal-type solution and promoted a strengthening of the Commission, whereas France remained faithful to its traditional intergovernmentalism. Eager to present a common position, the two heads of the executive finally agreed on a text that was made public during the fortieth anniversary celebration of the Franco-German Elysée

Treaty. The Franco–German document included both countries' favorite solution, with little concern for coherence. It called for a president of the European Council (to satisfy the intergovernmental camp) and for the Parliament to elect the president of the Commission (an important goal of the federalists). No wonder, then, that this compromise 'inspired' the final agreement, for it incorporated antagonistic solutions. This is precisely one of the key strengths of past Franco–German proposals: they often strike a balance between distinctly opposite preferences, such that other governments can get something out of them as well. To speak of dominant leadership in such a case would be excessive, though, since the proposal's success appeared to depend on its ability to elicit support from other governments. Indeed, at the very moment when the institutional debate heated up in the Convention, the crisis triggered by the US intervention in Iraq demonstrated that a Franco-German agreement is not sufficient to carry the day if it does not reflect the preferences of a large number of national governments.

Second, acknowledging the central part played by national governments during the Convention does not entail a complete adhesion to traditional 'realist' analyses, which stress the role of domestic interests in the formation of national preferences. The importance of this latter factor, brightly illustrated by Spain and Poland's rejection of the Constitution in order to preserve their weighted votes within the Council, cannot be denied. Nonetheless, one should not overlook the importance of ideas in the process of institutional reform (Christiansen *et al.* 2002). As was mentioned earlier, a state's traditional position is often inspired by its politico-institutional culture. Whereas the French and British visions of the common good emphasize the need for leadership, the Germans generally favor a federal system similar to their own, and the Swedes favor the principle of transparency that is enshrined in their constitution. Obviously, it can be difficult to establish a clear causal link between ideas and the positions upheld by a government, since ideas and interests can coincide. Germany's defense of an increased role for the Parliament could as easily be a means to promote its own interests, since it has the greatest number of MEPs. At the same time, however, there is no shortage of counterexamples to make the 'ideational' argument plausible. The federal government's proparliament attitude does not date back to the treaties of Maastricht and Nice, which improved Germany's parliamentary representation; rather it corresponds to a traditional position held by German diplomats since the Single European Act. In contrast, a purely interest-based logic would see larger states pleading in the Parliament's favor—where they are better represented than in the Council—with resistance from the smaller states, conforming to a cleavage common to all federal systems. Yet, the UK and France are not among the Parliament's allies, whereas the small Benelux countries are. In other words, the position of a government can be influenced by 'worldviews' or perceptions of legitimacy which do not necessarily correspond to its interests (Rittberger 2003).

Third, institutions have contributed to shape the final result. The word is used here in the broadest sense of rules constraining the behavior of political actors, rather than as a mere reference to the organs set up by the EU treaties. Clearly, the working methods of the Convention have designed a setting in which deliberation was encouraged and even regarded as a social norm by Conventioneers. This was further reinforced by several factors. The decision not to vote, but rather to seek the broadest possible consensus in order to enhance the Convention's authority vis-à-vis national governments, incited delegates to look for compromises, while the public nature of the debates encouraged them to adopt an argumentative style. While it is likely that those elements had more influence on the rhetorical debates than on the eventual outcome, they appear to have facilitated convergence on a number of points, such as the simplification of the treaties, the erasure of the 'pillars structure' inherited from the Maastricht Treaty, or the conferral of a legal personality to the Union—all items on which the UK had been unwilling to compromise in the past (Magnette 2003). Moreover, the division of labor between the Convention and the IGC operated as a two-way process: on the one hand, Conventioneers were forced to pay attention to the views expressed by governments; but on the other, having declared their support for the Convention's efforts and hailed its draft as an historic achievement, national governments could not easily take the risk to derail it. They therefore had to concentrate their objections on a number of points, both during the Convention and in the ensuing IGC. Thus, France ended up accepting the idea of a double majority (a majority of states representing a majority of the population) which it had rejected three years earlier in Nice. It also endorsed a greater role for the EP as regards agricultural expenses, an issue that is often regarded as a key national interest by French governments and on which French officials had announced they were prepared to fight (Jabko 2004; author's interview, French Foreign Ministry, spring 2003). In other words, although they did not radically transform the nature of the reform process, the new rules of the game designed in Laeken did bear on the final results.

5. Conclusion

While references to Philadelphia and the US constitutional experience have flourished during and after the European Convention, the draft constitution does not represent a watershed in the history of European integration, either in terms of substance or in terms of process.

As regards the former, the constitution has codified more than it has innovated. Many of the reforms it has introduced (more majority voting and more rights to the Parliament) are extensions of changes decided in earlier treaty modifications. Moreover, most of the 'pure' innovations it contains seem to be inspired by a concern to 'contain' the Commission and preserve the power of states in the European architecture. The constitution appears equally conservative as regards the process of political change, since unanimity remains required for any modification. As a result, it is difficult to regard it as a milestone marking the creation a new body politic.

Such an outcome is hardly surprising given the way the Convention's mandate was defined. As its decisions were to be scrutinized in an old style IGC in which member states would retain their veto power, one could have expected that the final product would be strongly influenced by national governments' preferences. This, however, leaves open the question of how such preferences were formed. National interests (or rather the governments' interpretation of those interests) obviously played a role, but one can also see the mark of ideational elements, such as visions of democracy and legitimacy, as well as of institutional constraints. As suggested in the introduction to this volume, no grand theory can on its own make sense of such a complex event; the final outcome has been influenced by a multiplicity of causal factors. Among these, the influence of national governments largely remains the most decisive (though not the only) independent variable, which explains the many 'anti-federalist' undertones of the draft constitution.

This does not rule out the possibility, however, that this document will one day be regarded as an important step in the history of European integration. History has taught us to be modest when evaluating the results of institutional reforms. The Single European Act, which is now assigned a critical role in the revival of European integration in the mid-1980s, was described by Margaret Thatcher as a 'modest step,' and was subjected to fierce criticism by a number of scholars who deemed it too conservative. Related references to the US experience can be enlightening. Many scholars of US politics would argue that the federal potential of the constitution was not exploited right away, and that it took more than a century to build the American state and the body politic referred to in the text drafted in Philadelphia. In the same fashion, some elements in the draft constitution may unexpectedly cause new dynamics to emerge. The sheer reference to a 'constitution' has already given rise to debates that were much more open than in the past. Several countries, including some in which this was not formally required, have already indicated they consider a referendum necessary before ratification. Granting a legal status to the Charter of Fundamental Rights might lead some actors to exploit this new legal channel to further their interests. The Court of Justice might find there a fertile ground for a revival of judicial activism. In other words, chances are good that, even if it was largely controlled by the governments, the reform process will have unexpected consequences.

References

Ackerman, B. (1991). *We the People: Foundations.* Cambridge, MA: Harvard University Press.

Amato, G., Dehaene, J. L., and Giscard d'Estaing, V. (2003). 'L'Europe de demain: la fausse querelle entre "petits" et "grands" ', *Le Monde*, 14 November.

Aznar, J. M. (2002). Speech at the inaugural session of the Convention (CONV 4/02).

Beer, S. H. (1993). *To Make a Nation.* Cambridge, MA: Harvard University Press.

Bowen, D. (1966). *Miracle at Philadelphia: The Story of the Constitutional Convention, May to September 1787.* Boston, MA: Little, Brown.

Christiansen, T., Falkner, G., and Jørgensen, K. E. (2002). 'Theorizing EU Treaty Reform: Beyond Diplomacy and Bargaining', *Journal of European Public Policy*, 9/1, 12–32.

Costa, O. (2004). 'Le parlementarisme au-delà de l'Etat: le cas de l'Union européenne', in O. Costa, E. Kerrouche, and P. Magnette (eds.), *Vers un renouveau du parlementarisme en Europe*. Brussels: Editions de l'ULB, pp. 271–94.

Dauvergne, A. (2004). *L'Europe en otage? Histoire secrète de la Convention.* Paris: Saint-Simon.

Dehousse, R. (ed.) (2004). *L'Europe sans Bruxelles? Une analyse de la méthode ouverte de coordination.* Paris: L'Harmattan.

—— (2001). 'Rediscovering Functionalism', in C. Joerges, Y. Mény, and J. Weiler (eds.), *Which Constitution for Which Kind of Polity?* Florence: European University Institute.

—— (2000). '1999, an I du parlementarisme européen?', *Pouvoirs,* 93 (Spring): 197–207.

Dinan, D. (2003). 'The Draft Constitution: American Interest', *EUSA Review*, 16/4, 3–5.

Duhamel, O. (2003). *Pour l'Europe: le texte intégral de la constitution expliqué et commenté.* Paris: Seuil.

EUI (European University Institute) (2002*a*). *A Fundamental Treaty for the EU.* Florence: EUI, May 15.

—— (2002*b*). *Reforming Treaty Revision Procedure.* Florence: EUI, July 31.

European Commission (1991). *Intergovernmental Conferences: Commission Contributions*, Supplement 2/91 in the *Bulletin des Communautés européennes*, 119–21.

—— (2003). *A Constitution for the Union.* Brussels: European Commission, September 17 , COM (2003) 548 Final.

Hix, S. (1997). 'Executive Selection in the European Union: Does the Commission President Investiture Procedure Reduce the Democratic Deficit? *EIOP working paper,* 1/21.

Kerr, J. (2003). 'Europe's treaty and the art of the possible', *Financial Times,* 26 November.

Jabko, N. (2004). 'The importance of being Nice: An institutionalist analysis of French Preferences on the future of Europe', *Cahiers européens de Sciences Po*, 2: 1–23.

Lacorne, D. (1991). *L'invention de la république : le modèle Americain*. Paris: Hachette.

Madison, J. (1982 [1787–88]). *The Federalist Papers*. New York: Bantam Books.

Magnette, P. (2004). 'La Convention européenne: argumenter et négocier dans une assemblée constituante multinationale', *Revue française de science politique*, 54/1: 5–42.

—— (2003). 'Coping with Constitutional Incompatibilities: Bargains and Rhetoric in the Convention on the Future of Europe', *NYU Law School Jean Monnet Working Paper Series*, 14/03.

Majone, G. (1998). 'Europe's Democratic Deficit: The Question of Standards', *European Law Journal*, 4/1: 5–28.

Moravcsik, A. (2004). 'What Can We Learn from a Constitutional "Decade of Deliberation" in Europe? A Social Scientific Approach'. Paper presented at the conference 'Altneuland: the Constitution of Europe in an American perspective', Princeton, NJ, April.

Norman, P. (2003). *The Accidental Constitution: The Story of the European Convention*. Brussels: EuroComment.

Rittberger, B. (2003). 'The Creation and Empowerment of the European Parliament', *Journal of Common Market Studies*, 41/2: 203–25.

Wallace, H. (2000). 'The Institutional Setting: Five Variations on a Theme', in H. Wallace and W. Wallace (eds.), *Policy-Making in the European Union*. Oxford: Oxford University Press, pp. 3–37.

6

Parliamentary Government or Division of Powers: Is the Destination Still Unknown?

MICHAEL SHACKLETON[1]

On October 27, 2004 Commission President Barroso was obliged to tell the plenary of the European Parliament (EP) in Strasbourg that he needed more time before presenting his new Commissioners for approval. He recognized that as a result of the hearings held in the Parliament earlier in the month, his team was unlikely to win the vote of approval required by the treaties. Even if it did, the vote in favor would be too narrow for him to launch its work successfully. Within ten days he presented a reshuffled Commission, with the original Italian and Latvian nominees replaced and the Hungarian candidate given a new portfolio. The Parliament gave its approval to the new team by a large majority on November 18.

These events were widely interpreted as marking a turning point in the life of the European Union (EU). Josep Borrell, President of the Parliament, argued that the parliamentary hearings had 'breathed life into our Europe which is more often than not seen as a monolithic bureaucracy, remote from everyday people and excessively consensual.'[2] Others, including the leader of the British Conservative Party, Michael Howard, argued that it was a dangerous precedent for the nominees of sovereign governments to be overturned by a Parliament for which less than 50 percent of the European electorate had turned out to vote at the elections held in June 2004.

The struggle over the composition of the Commission thus brought to the fore the issue of the democratic character of the European Union (EU). No one wished to claim that the European project could be advanced by stealth by the political elites far from the gaze of the electorate; all were obliged to confront and debate the character of the Parliament's contribution to the democratization of the Union. Did the enforced change in the composition of

[1] The views expressed in this article are strictly personal and do not represent the official position of the European Parliament. The author would particularly like to thank Amie Kreppel and Renaud Dehousse for encouraging him to pursue the ideas found here, and his colleagues Stephen Clark and Ian Vollbracht for their thoughtful comments.

[2] *The Guardian*, November 13, 2004.

the Commission, something not provided for in the treaties, inject a much-needed dose of parliamentarism into the EU? Or did it reflect a dysfunction in the workings of the EU, an ongoing crisis in the institutional structure? The simple fact that such questions were posed underlined the contested nature of democracy in the Union.

This chapter takes as its starting point that the argument over the composition of the Commission has to be understood in the context of the kind of institution the EP is becoming. It will suggest there are two different kinds of parliamentary role that the Parliament has pursued throughout its history and particularly since it was directly elected for the first time in 1979. On the one hand, the Parliament has sought to reinforce its control over the Commission, with a view to making this executive body responsible to a parliamentary majority; on the other, it has pressed to improve its position in the legislative procedure, aiming to achieve a greater degree of parity with the Council of Ministers. The desire to make the Commission accountable to a parliamentary majority derives directly from the European tradition where legislatures are the ultimate arbiters of the fate of executives, where there is a fusion of powers between these two branches of government. By contrast, the search to strengthen the EP as a legislature is based on a different logic, one much more akin to the US idea of a separation of powers.

The changes made to the Barroso Commission in the autumn of 2004 might appear to suggest that it is the first of these roles that is assuming greater importance. However, such a claim runs counter to the institutional legacy of the last twenty-five years. The kind of powers the Parliament has acquired, combined with the way in which the EU is structured, make the Parliament much more likely to develop into an institution comparable to the House of Representatives in the USA than it is to become like a national parliament on the European model. Moreover, there are good reasons for believing it will not become a hybrid body fulfilling both roles. If this is right, we could also expect the Parliament to have the potential to become a source of distinct policy positions from those pursued by the executive, whether in the Commission, the Council of Ministers or the European Council.

In other words, the EU is at one and the same time creating a type of parliamentary institution that converges on a pattern familiar to US observers as well as one that could be the source of policy options that conflict with US preferences, precisely because it enjoys autonomy and remains separate from the other sources of power in the EU system. Polity convergence is combining with the potential for policy divergence in a way that makes the institution of more than academic interest for the US observer.

To present this argument, the chapter will first recall the growth in the powers of the Parliament, noting that the development of its legislative role has been matched by a growing say over executive appointment. The second section will consider the obstacles to the establishment of a full parliamentary regime, with a government dependent on retaining a majority in the Parliament. The third section will suggest why it is easier to envisage the reinforcement of the independence of the Parliament as a legislature, with its members not required to support the party line of the executive. The fourth section will point to the difficulty of imagining a hybrid regime where the Parliament plays both roles. Finally, some comments will be offered on the impact that the emergence of such a Parliament may have on transatlantic relations.

1. Acquiring a Wider Armoury of Powers

The powers that the Parliament exercises today are the product of decisions taken throughout the history of the EU. There was no obligation to create a parliamentary assembly at European level: such an assembly already existed within the framework of the Council of Europe. Nor was it necessary to envisage that its rights could evolve over time. Yet already in 1958 the Rome Treaty included the provision that the Parliament might be directly elected, rather than composed of national parliamentarians, even though its powers were limited to consultation on most legislation and the right to censure the Commission.

The expansion of the Parliament's powers is also unique. No other Union institution has seen its initial prerogatives so completely transformed over time. Member states have been willing to agree to significant improvements in the Parliament's position virtually every time that the Treaties were revised from 1958 onwards. At least part of the explanation should be sought in the existence and strength of the democratic idea, the belief in government deriving its legitimacy from the people, and the reluctance of any national government to be seen overtly to resist its development at European level (Costa and Magnette 2003). Hence we should not be surprised, for example, that governments found it hard to resist indefinitely the implementation of the provision in the Rome Treaty for the holding of direct elections at some future date.

Within the institution the initial lack of powers constituted an agenda for reform that has consistently guided it over the subsequent half century as MEPs sought determinedly to escape the accusation that they were part of a 'talking shop,' with no effective influence on the shape of European policies. This pressure to alter the status quo established in 1958 grew particularly strong after the first direct elections that the member states eventually agreed should take place in 1979.[3] A new breed of full-time members came to the

[3] The one major change in the Parliament's position prior to direct elections was its acquisition of budgetary rights in 1970 and 1975 (see Corbett *et al.* 2003: 212 ff.). These powers have remained essentially unchanged in the intervening decades (with the prospect of a further extension under the Constitution) but have always constituted an important symbol of the Parliament's emergence from relative obscurity.

Parliament, committed to altering the institution's weak position in relation to the Commission and the Council. The first fruits of their efforts came with the Single European Act (SEA) in 1987. The commitment of the member states to the establishment of a single market and their willingness to contemplate a broader use of qualified majority voting led the way to a change in the way in which laws were to be agreed at European level. The SEA introduced two readings for a limited range of legislative acts and made it possible for the Parliament to have its amendments adopted, provided they obtained the support of the Commission and unless the Council could find unanimity to reject them (Corbett *et al.* 2003: 182–3).

However, it was the Maastricht and Amsterdam treaties that brought about the most significant changes in the position of the Parliament, changes that have to be seen in the context of the wider debate that emerged in the early 1990s about the idea of a 'democratic deficit' at the European level. The difficulties in ratifying the Maastricht Treaty, with Denmark first voting no and then yes and France only approving the text by a very small margin, prompted a major debate about whether the legitimation of the EU by indirect means was sufficient. Nearly all protagonists agreed that it was not and that the democratic idea needed to find fuller expression in the structures of the EU than it had done hitherto. Much less accord existed on what was needed to 'solve' the problem. There was, for example, a major surge of interest in the development of the role of national parliaments, with some arguing for an alliance of all parliaments, European and national, against executives, others calling for a new parliamentary chamber of national parliamentarians and all seeming to agree that a modification of the existing pattern of relations could help to reduce the gap between the institutions and the European citizen.

Nevertheless, the most significant changes were those that reinforced the Parliament's role, suggesting that member states felt unable to offer a better alternative to overcoming the 'democratic deficit.' The Maastricht Treaty that entered into force in November 1993 complemented the existing consultation and cooperation procedures for legislation with a new procedure, known as co-decision. Under this procedure, if the Council cannot accept the amendments proposed by the Parliament at its second reading, a Conciliation Committee, with an equal number of members from each institution, is convened with a view to reconciling their differences within a maximum period of eight weeks.[4] This legislative reinforcement of the position of the

[4] The Conciliation Committee can be compared—with care and caution—to Conference Committees in the United States Congress and the *Vermittlungsausschuss* that brings together representatives of the Bundestag and the Bundesrat in Germany. All three seek to overcome differences between two bodies whose agreement is required before legislation can enter into force.

Parliament was matched by a provision whereby governments agreed to consult the EP before nominating by common accord the President of the Commission, thereby giving the Parliament a say in the formation of the Commission and not simply in its dismissal. They also synchronized the Commission's term of office with that of the Parliament, so that now the appointment of a new Commission President and of the whole new Commission coincides with the arrival of a new Parliament.

In addition, the Parliament was accorded the right under the Treaties to set up committees of inquiry to examine 'alleged contraventions or maladministration in the implementation of Community law.' The detailed rules governing these committees do not give the Parliament a general power of summons but do provide a mechanism for it to invite national as well as Community officials to appear before it, thereby increasing its potential influence over executive decisions beyond the Brussels world (Shackleton 1998).

Further changes took place under the Amsterdam Treaty (signed in 1997 and ratified in 1999) that served to strengthen the Parliament's role. As far as executive appointment is concerned, it was agreed that the nomination of the governments of the member states for President of the Commission has to be *approved* by the Parliament. In other words, the President of the Commission needs the support of a parliamentary majority, in accordance with the classic tenets of parliamentary government in Europe. At the same time, the co-decision procedure was substantially extended from fifteen to thirty-eight areas covered by the Treaty and was also made to reflect more clearly the principle of parity between Council and Parliament. Agreement on legislation can now be reached in first reading on the basis of the Parliament's position without the Council having formally to adopt a common position. Once in conciliation, failure to reach agreement within the eight weeks provided for definitively ends the legislative procedure: the Council is no longer able to retable its own position to the Parliament for consideration as a potential solution.

Once again the question has to be asked: why were governments willing to grant such a major increase in powers to a majoritarian body that was not under their control? Simon Hix has argued convincingly that contrary to governmental expectations, the Parliament exercised important discretion in interpreting the provisions of the Maastricht Treaty, that these interpretations became de facto rules, and that in the Amsterdam Intergovernmental Conference (IGC) governments decided to incorporate these rules into the Treaty because they did not see them as fundamentally altering the balance of power between the institutions (Hix 2002). However, perhaps even more important is his conclusion that the changes represent major advances for parliamentary government that cannot be reversed. 'Once democracy is established, there is no going back within the bounds of the existing constitutional norms' (Hix 2002: 280). We have a Parliament with a major role in the EU, a role that the European Constitution serves to anchor even more firmly into the decision-making system.

The question now is what kind of future can be envisaged for the institution. So much time and energy has been expended on the search for new powers that the existence of alternative models for the future has been largely overlooked. And yet it is clear from the range of powers that have been acquired that there are essentially two possible directions. The first would involve creating a parliamentary system with a *fusion* of executive and legislative power, with both deriving their authority from the same set of elections and the executive resigning in the event of its losing majority support in the legislature. This is the vision that coincides with the model that Europeans tend to have in their minds when they think of a Parliament. The second supposes a clear *separation* of powers with holders of executive power elected separately from the legislature and not forming part of the legislative body. Such a view is much less familiar in Europe and reflects more obviously the federal arrangements of the USA.

2. Towards a Parliamentary Regime?

The accumulation of powers described in the last section can be regarded as the equivalent at Union level of the development of the kind of parliamentarism that is found in European nation states. From this perspective, MEPs have fought to strengthen their position against an overpowerful executive and are slowly succeeding in asserting their position as part of the move towards a more democratic structure in the EU. Certainly this is the kind of imagery that is used in parliamentary debate and that has served as an important driving force in the pressure for change. As Hix has suggested, the standard version of the 'democratic deficit' thesis posits that the 'EU will only be democratic if European elections are fought by cohesive Euro-parties which present rival agendas for EU policy action, the winning parties form the executive and the parties act cohesively to ensure that their officeholders implement their electoral programme' (Hix 1998: 20).

Are the structures and processes of the Community such as to enable the democratic deficit to be filled in this way? There are good reasons for believing that a development of this kind remains relatively unlikely. The powers of dismissal and appointment that the Parliament have acquired as well as the overall role of the Commission as an executive body are all exercised in such a way as to militate against the recreation at European level of the classical parliamentary model seen in the member states.

At first sight, the power of dismissal of the Commission—the earliest power that the Parliament acquired—looks like the mechanism by which the confidence of an executive can be tested to see if it still enjoys broad political backing. In fact, as Simon Hix has pointed out, the right of censure is 'more similar to the power of the US Congress to impeach the US President than to the power of a parliamentary majority to withdraw the support of the government' (Hix 1998: 25–6). This was confirmed in 1999 by the circumstances under which the Commission resigned in anticipation of a vote of censure by the Parliament. It did so not because of differences over policy direction, but rather as a result of charges of incompetence and maladministration.

Moreover the rules of decision-making in the EU make it most unlikely that this will change in the future. A motion of censure requires a two-thirds majority of the votes cast, representing a majority of the members of the Parliament. Such a high hurdle effectively excludes a move by one of the major parties in the EP to employ a political sanction against the Commission. There has to be a broad consensus, which is itself unlikely to be forthcoming on a question of policy, above all when it is overlaid with national differences. Indeed it is one reason for remaining a little sceptical about whether the Parliament would have had a sufficient majority in 1999 to censure the Commission if the latter had not decided to anticipate such a vote and resign.

Similar obstacles make it difficult to see how a party logic can apply to the appointment of the Commission President. At first sight, the arrangements foreseen under the Constitution offer a clear way of linking the political process of the European elections much more directly with the selection of the Commission President. Two former MEPs have pointed to the way in which they thought the system could be adapted to remedy its present top-down character and to instil more life into European elections. 'If each European political family were to declare its candidate for President of the European Commission in time for the next European elections, that could inject new life and vigor into the electoral process and strengthen the identity and cohesiveness of political groups' (Clegg and van Hulten 2003: 26). Voting in European elections could then be seen as having direct consequences at European level rather than serving essentially as a comment on national political life.

However, such an arrangement faces formidable obstacles before it could become a reality. In the first place, it assumes that the national political party structures would be willing to accept such nominations. There would be likely to be strong resistance to such a move that could only serve to weaken the position of national structures at the expense of the European party groups. In a EU where the member states enjoy so strong a role in determining the structure of the system, such a change would run very much against the grain. Furthermore, the proposal overlooks the inevitable tension between candidates nominated by European party groups and candidates proposed by the European Council. The system, even in the form proposed in the Constitution, does not reduce the European Council to a body that simply registers decisions made elsewhere. It retains the right to make its own decision, even if it has to take account of the election results and to consult with the Parliament.

The Parliament has the formal right to turn down any candidate proposed by the European Council but the question is whether it would be willing to do so. In 2004 the EPP-ED, representing the center-right in the Parliament, argued that their success in the European elections should be reflected in the choice of Commission President. The eventual choice of Mr Barroso, whose party is in the EPP, was as much influenced by the fact that the majority of the twenty-five governments were of the center-right as by any threat of the Parliament to withhold its support from a candidate of another party. In fact, on the only occasion where a large fraction of the Parliament was unhappy with the candidate proposed (Santer in 1994), pressure exercised by national governments on their MEPs succeeded in ensuring that the choice of the European Council was confirmed. European party groups can display a considerable level of cohesion on legislative issues but such cohesion is much less easy to assure when the exercise of executive authority is at stake. Even a negative vote would not enable the Parliament to *impose* its choice on European governments.

A further contrast with the European parliamentary model can be found in the texture of the general relationship that exists between Parliament and Commission. The struggle that surrounded the resignation of the Santer Commission in 1999 and the often difficult relations between the two institutions in the intervening years have obscured the fact that there is an ongoing tradition of seeing the Commission as the ally of the Parliament in its struggles with the Council. The Parliament has continued to want the Commission to commit itself to the Parliament's side in an institutional rather than a political sense, a position reciprocated by the Commission.

At the same time, the Commission has maintained that it is a nonpartisan body, a view that the Parliament has not wanted to contradict. This somewhat apolitical approach has been reinforced by the way in which prospective members of the Commission have been cross-examined in the hearings organized by the Parliament. These hearings have normally been rather technical in character, with the members of individual parliamentary committees seeking to establish the general suitability of each candidate for specific, sectoral portfolios rather than examining their political position.

The argument over the nomination of Rocco Buttiglione, the initial Italian candidate for the Barroso Commission, might appear to contradict this argument as it pitted the center-left against the center-right in the Parliament in a fierce struggle, easily understandable to the general public. Nevertheless, the decision of the Civil Liberties Committee to reject Mr Buttiglione was primarily determined by a judgement as to his suitability for a particular post rather than an evaluation of his political affiliation. A majority felt that given his views on homosexuality and the family, he was not suitable to be Commissioner responsible for Justice and Home Affairs; for any other post he would almost certainly have met with minimal objections.

The Parliament has also wanted to maintain the Commission as a separate institution, enjoying autonomy in its relations with the other institutions rather than becoming a subordinate body. Very few members of the Parliament have supported the idea that the Commission should lose its monopoly of the right of legislative initiative. Traditionally parliaments in Europe do enjoy a right of initiative but in the European context, the EP has accepted the more limited provisions of Article 192, which enable it to invite the Commission to produce a legislative proposal. To go further would be to open up the possibility that member states would also argue for such a right of initiative, complementing what they already have in the Justice and Home Affairs arena. In fact, the Convention accepted the traditional Parliament position and the Constitution states in Article I–26 that 'Union legislative acts may be adopted only on the basis of a Commission proposal, except where the Constitution provides otherwise.'

Similarly, the Parliament wanted to uphold other roles for the Commission that are not compatible with the role of a traditional executive. In the conciliation procedure provided for under Article 251 of the existing Treaty, the Commission is given the task of *mediating* between Council and Parliament with a view to facilitating an agreement. It is a task the Commission assumes very seriously and one that it is reminded of if it tends to favor one or other of the legislative bodies too overtly. Such a task would be very difficult if the Commission reflected the political majority of the Parliament: it could not be easily accepted as evenhanded in the negotiations. Council could claim that the Commission would necessarily favor the concerns of the majority in the Parliament where its support came from.

Such practices have made it very difficult for the kind of political legitimation of an executive seen in a national European context to emerge. A potentially tighter link with the Commission has also to be set against the significant changes being proposed in the Constitution for the European Council with the creation of a post of President. Whatever her or his mandate, whatever the relationship with the Commission President, this post reinforces the split in executive functions between European institutions and makes it even more difficult to imagine the creation of the traditional mechanisms of parliamentary control and accountability. Parliament could only hope to have a very partial control over the executive at European level.

Magnette has argued that 'The Commission is not subordinate to a parliamentary majority that can *sanction* it, but rather scrutinized by MEPs who can only try to *influence* it. The pyramidal and hierarchic structure of the parliamentary state is replaced, here, by horizontal relations of mutual control' (Magnette 2001: 308). In fact, these horizontal relations extend further to the Council, thereby making it still more difficult to envisage the emergence of a classic parliamentary regime with a government enjoying the backing of a majority. Rather we can see something that reflects a continuing separation of powers.

3. Towards the Parliament as a Legislature?

What we are witnessing is the slow emergence of a bicameral legislature, where the Parliament serves as one branch of the legislative authority, representing the peoples of Europe, with the Council operating as the other branch, representing the member states. In particular, the arrival of co-decision in 1993 and its considerable extension in 1999 completely transformed the position of the Parliament. As we have seen, again, this was an institution that had no legislative role under the initial ECSC Treaty and only consultative rights during the first thirty years of the Rome Treaty.

The notion of a bicameral legislature is much contested outside Parliament and inside academia. It is obvious that the Council exercises tasks other than that of a legislature—hence the impossibility of agreeing on a legislative formation of the Council in the Convention and the IGC that followed it. And yet the very special character of the Council cannot conceal the nature of the political process that is emerging as a result of the changes in the legislative powers acquired by the Parliament over the last fifteen years. It is not simply that the Parliament exercises more influence than it did before it acquired greater legislative prerogatives. There is every reason to accept the suggestion that the EP is a parliament with strong policymaking power (Judge and Earnshaw 2003). More important from the perspective of this chapter is the fact that the Parliament (and indeed the Council) now behaves very differently.

First, the Parliament has become a 'bargaining' body that negotiates with other institutions—above all the Council—in the search for agreed solutions. Such a development was not predetermined. The power of co-decision did not necessarily entail detailed face-to-face negotiations. The Vedel report (Vedel 1972), a document prepared by a group of experts at the request of the

Commission to consider the powers of the EP, speaks of co-decision but never imagined a Parliament amending texts in the way it does now. Rather it supposed the institution would say 'Yes' or 'No' to a text devised by the Council, somewhat in the way that Parliament now exercises a power of assent over, for example, prospective new members of the EU. Such a power gives some room for negotiation but the scope is much less than when specific amendments are the subject of a compulsory interinstitutional debate.

The formal provisions providing for face-to-face deliberations between two institutions that had rarely had very much to do with each other in the previous forty years have played a vital role in creating a new legislative culture (Shackleton & Raunio 2003). Parliament and Council have been willing to act together to develop informal mechanisms to find solutions. Most famously, the two institutions recognized that negotiations could not be successfully conducted in Conciliation Committees attended by over 100 people and agreed to institute smaller meetings, known as trialogues, where only twenty to twenty-five people are present. These smaller meetings have played an essential part in developing trust between the two institutions and enabling the most intractable of differences to be addressed and solved in a way that both parties could accept, without feeling that they have had to surrender (Shackleton 2000).

In addition, there has been dramatic growth in the search for agreements in advance of second reading with a view to avoid conciliation. This has been particularly evident since Amsterdam, which opened up the way for agreements on legislation to be reached without the Council having to come to a common position. The result has been the growth of contacts between all three institutions at every level, with rapporteurs, committee chairs and officials drawn into a thick network of relations on virtually every one of the co-decision files under discussion (which averaged eighty per year between 1999 and 2004). We are witnessing the closure of nearly 80 percent of co-decision files without conciliation and often on issues of considerable political salience, as for example, the arrangements for European political parties agreed at first reading in June 2003 and the regime for GMOs settled at second reading the following month. (European Parliament 2004).

These changes are ones that the Council has been willing to adapt to and accept, despite the challenge to its long monopoly as a legislator. Indeed its own ways of working have not stood still. The Conclusions of the Seville European Council in the spring of 2002 provided for Council to meet publicly when acting in a legislative capacity, thereby counteracting disparaging comments about its level of transparency as compared with the Parliament. The extent of Council openness can be debated but the direction of change is clear. In an interinstitutional agreement reached in June 2003 on 'Better Lawmaking,' the Council went so far as to indicate that it would make its best efforts to ensure that it was represented at the appropriate level at committee meetings to be able to take the floor to explain the institution's position. For several years the Council had always resisted such calls to present its opinion in committee, not wishing to commit itself as an institution in front of the Parliament and fearing it might be isolated in such a parliamentary debate. The change agreed represents a willingness on the part of the Council to countenance a measure of 'parliamentarization' of its work—a change prompted first and foremost by the arrival of co-decision.

Second, the bargaining between the institutions and inside the institution has witnessed a high level of bipartisanship and cross-party agreement. Compromise has become a central feature of the work of the institution. In part this can be explained by the voting requirements in the Parliament. Whereas in first reading only simple majorities of those present are required to pass amendments, in second reading amendments require the support of an absolute majority of all members of the Parliament, that is half plus one (367 in the post-enlargement Parliament of 732 members). Such majorities cannot be carried by one group in the Parliament; negotiations are needed between the groups to enable them to find joint agreement. Without such negotiation, the Council's common position stands and the Parliament can exercise no influence. Hence there is a strong incentive to overcome differing ideological perspectives.

Hix (2002) has argued that the level of cohesion within groups and the degree of left-right competition in the EP have increased substantially, thereby making the EP more like other parliaments in Europe. He shows convincingly that party allegiance is much more important than nationality in determining how members vote and that members vote the party line more often than legislators in the USA. At the same time, the degree of cooperation across party lines remains strong. This need not mean a Socialist-European People's Party (EPP) coalition: winning coalitions are fluid, with the Liberals, for example, having played a major role in the fifth legislature (1999–2004) in determining whether or not an absolute majority was achieved for legislative acts requiring an absolute majority. As Kreppel (2003) has noted, the extent of these coalitions is much more reminiscent of the USA than of European legislatures. She points to clear opposition between Republicans and Democrats of on average 54 percent between 1980 and 1998 and a figure of around 45 percent for clear opposition between Socialists and EPP between 1980 and 1996. Even if this latter figure is now increasing, as Hix suggests, it remains much smaller than equivalent figures for national European legislatures.

The Hix study is based on an evaluation of roll call votes, and one of the difficulties of the new bargaining culture of the Parliament is that it conceals much of the discussion within and between the groups. Many issues are not debated on the floor of the house but rather compromises are worked out in advance without roll call votes being called for. Clegg and van Hulten put the point as follows when speaking about agreements reached at second reading: 'political argument is usually displaced by detailed horse-trading to secure the widest possible cross-party support for a given position or set of amendments' (Clegg and van Hulten 2003: 14). At the July 2003 session in Strasbourg, for example, a whole series of votes at second reading, including the legislation on GMOs mentioned above, took place where the texts had already been prenegotiated with the Council and there was very wide support for these compromises within and between groups. Under these circumstances, no roll call votes were called as no group had a strong interest in revealing how others had voted. Hence the figures used by Hix tend to understate the degree of cross party voting and bipartisanship that takes place.

Third, the new powers give even greater power and influence to parliamentary committees and the rapporteurs working within them. The Parliament was always a parliament of committees where all debate begins in committee before moving onto the floor of the house. The system of rapporteurs, with one MEP responsible for a draft proposal from its transmission to the Parliament by the Commission to the conclusion of the procedure, has heavily influenced the level of specialization with members often acquiring over time very high levels of knowledge of issues under discussion and thereby being heavily courted by Community officials and outside interests in a way that national parliamentarians in Europe can hardly imagine.

The arrival of co-decision has served to enhance still further the role of committees, as they become the place where the legislative stance of the institution is essentially determined. The result is often fierce argument between committees as to who should be responsible for a proposal. Opinion-giving committees are not able to table any amendments in plenary that are defeated in discussion in the responsible committee and are obliged to seek support for their position in political groups or as thirty-seven individual members—a path that rarely leads to success. And within committees the role of rapporteurs has also been enhanced. The desire of the Council to find agreements earlier in the legislative procedure and to avoid the heavy constraints of conciliation has encouraged it to engage in extensive contacts with rapporteurs and shadow-rapporteurs (the latter appointed by groups other than that of the rapporteur in recognition of the importance of that individual) in often very informal surroundings. It has proved very effective as a way of finding solutions, but has also generated a challenge to the tradition of open debate in committee, with members not involved in the negotiations obliged to ratify compromises devised elsewhere.

Some claim that these arrangements are unhealthy and give too much influence to individual members at the expense of a coherent political group position. Clegg and van Hulten (2003) have argued that there should be more party political discipline with greater emphasis on politics than on technical lawmaking. And yet arguably it is the structure of the legislative process itself that produces the kind of lawmaking we have in the EU. It certainly contrasts with the roles of parliamentarians in national parliaments in Europe, but looks very familiar to students of US politics.

Perhaps claims about the excessive influence of individuals would be more likely to win support if the end results of the legislative process had been widely seen as unsuccessful. In fact, not only has Parliament acquired new powers, it has exercised them in a way that has strengthened its claim for their further extension. It has proved able to assume its role as an independent institution, bargaining towards mutually agreed outcomes on a wide range of legislative issues. Not all—not least interlocutors in the Council—imagined it would be able to fulfil such a role. The success of the institution was well illustrated by the debates in the Convention on the Future of Europe. Virtually every speaker, regardless of their institution of origin at European or national level, spoke of co-decision in a highly supportive manner, as the normal way legislation should be approved. By contrast, the competing procedures (notably consultation and cooperation) were treated as inadequate, if not illegitimate. The result was that the final text of the Constitution makes minimal changes to the nature of the procedure itself as it exists today but incorporates two major modifications. First, the word 'co-decision' is suppressed and replaced by the term 'the ordinary legislative procedure'—a remarkable transformation of the exceptional into the normal. Second, the procedure is to apply to around ninety legal bases, including important parts of agricultural and fisheries policy, long seen as beyond the reach of the Parliament.

As a result of these changes the Parliament has been placed on a trajectory that will reinforce the various features of its work described in this section. It will bargain even more with Council throughout the legislative procedure, it will be forced to find agreements across party lines on a wider set of issues, and more of its committees and rapporteurs will acquire the experience of aggregating opinion within the institution in the search for compromise. In short, we will have a Parliament that will look much more like a legislature than a chamber for debate, thus prompting comparison with the US Congress but offering a clear contrast with its national counterparts in Europe.

4. Is a Hybrid System Possible?

Is the distinction offered up to now too stark? Is it not possible to imagine a hybrid system, with the Parliament continuing to reinforce its legislative role as well as strengthening its control over the executive in the way it has done in the last fifteen to twenty years?

Certainly the EP will not become a simple legislative machine. The arrangements proposed in the Constitution provide ample space for the Parliament to develop new ways of exerting influence over the composition and behavior of the executive bodies of the Union, including the Commission and its President. MEPs are strongly influenced by European parliamentary traditions and recognize the strength of the argument that elections should provide an opportunity to change the direction of government. 'Throw the rascals out' remains a central tenet of democratic politics. Hence the constant desire to introduce a stronger partisan logic into the choice of executive positions, such as the President of the Commission. Nevertheless, the logic of the EU institutions provides strong arguments for supposing that the two directions discussed here are not ultimately reconcilable and that whatever the rhetoric, one is much more likely to prevail than the other.

In the first place, the institutions are structured in such a way that none can directly control the other. There is a constant attempt by each to influence the other but they remain separate. The appointment of the Commission by other institutions, the European Council and the Parliament, does not contradict this separateness because of the balance that is maintained in the roles of each of the appointing bodies. To have ended that balance by giving the effective right of appointment to the Parliament alone would not only have reinforced the partisan nature of the Commission and made it dependent on the support of a majority in the Parliament, it would also have opened the Parliament up to a challenge to its autonomy. A number of members of the Convention argued that a corollary of the Parliament appointing the Commission would be the possibility for the Commission or Council to be able to dissolve the Parliament. Such a suggestion was met with little enthusiasm in the Parliament, but it underlines the contradiction in calls for parliamentary government at European level. Within such systems executives are normally much more able to control parliaments and thereby to reduce their influence as legislators. In fact, the rejection of the option of dissolution and of the suggestion that Parliament has the prime say in the election of the Commission President can be seen as a confirmation of the strength of the existing logic of the institutions based on a separation, not fusion of powers. In the words of Federalist Paper 51, 'the several constituent parts' have 'by their mutual relations, the means of keeping each other in their proper places.'

A second reason for being sceptical about the hybrid option is that it overlooks a significant feature of the Union, namely that it provides for an extremely delicate balance between an extraordinarily wide range of interests, with all able to identify with one or other part of a divided system of government. The introduction of a logic of partisanship, based on the decisions of a political majority within a parliamentary government, would provide a very severe test for that balance. Arguments of the lack of a 'demos' at European level reflect the fact that there is no wider sense of belonging in the EU, nor sufficient trust amongst the participants, that would serve to legitimize majority decisions based on one political family being able to put through its programme. This strong resistance to majoritarian mechanisms is reflected in the constant struggle of all the institutions constantly to balance competing interests, to avoid the sense that 'losers' are only on one side of the argument. In this sense, the European system does bear a close relationship to the American one, with reluctance on both sides of the Atlantic to countenance a centralization of power. It is a tendency that enlargement seems certain to reinforce.

This is not to claim that the EU is explicitly seeking to copy the US model, still less that the Parliament will become like one of the branches of the US Congress. Even with all the powers foreseen in the Constitution, the legislature at EU level will continue to operate within a much narrower sphere than the Congress. The kind of political issues that traditionally predominate in the minds of European citizens, such as education, healthcare and pensions, are all ones that will continue to be decided at national level. MEPs will not obtain the kind of powers that congressmen have in influencing the location of investment and government funds in their own states. European legislation does not spread anything like as far as that decided at federal level in the USA. It remains more regulatory in nature, with only limited distributive or redistributive functions.

Rather the suggestion here is that the dispersion of power within the EU provides greater scope for the EP to develop its role as a legislature than it does for it to become a chamber for debate where governments stand and fall on the basis of majority vote. Europeans are faced with problems similar to Americans in finding a way to legitimize the exercise of power amongst very diverse interests. It is difficult to imagine that it can be done other than by ensuring a consistently high level of bargaining and compromise between autonomous institutions rather than by allowing any institution preeminence.

5. A Potential Scenario

If the Parliament is more likely to become a separate legislative body, thereby converging on an institutional form found in the USA, what can we expect the impact of such a body to be on the policies of the EU towards the USA? A parliament sustaining a majority in the executive enjoys a very different status from one that is seen as an independent institution with powers to influence the shape of legislation. It is freer to criticize the executive without endangering the latter's continuance in office—a tendency that one could expect to be even greater when the political color of the majority in the Parliament, elected at a different moment from most national governments, does not match that of the Council of Ministers. Convergence in institutional form could therefore very well be accompanied by divergence in policy preferences.

Criticism of the executive by the legislature was well illustrated in the spring of 2004 when the Parliament voted against the agreement reached between the Commission, acting on behalf of the member states, and the USA on the provision of data about air passengers flying to the USA. A majority in the Parliament felt that the amount of information to be supplied was excessive and that it was to be kept for more time than was necessary. Moreover, it was felt that the agreement contradicted the existing EU legislation on the protection of data. The agreement was signed nonetheless, provoking the Parliament to decide to go to the European Court of Justice. The case is not designed to illustrate the influence of the Parliament—its challenge may not be successful—but rather to show how an independent Parliament can feel free to attack an executive decision, something that it would be most unlikely to do if the executive operated on the basis of a partisan majority.

At the same time, the development of autonomy of this kind can be seen to be having its effect on the way in which others treat the Parliament, even in an area where the Parliament's role is very restricted. For example, its role in international agreements is strictly limited. In most cases there is no right of assent, no possibility to say no. Yet this has not stopped Pascal Lamy, the Commissioner for External Trade from 1999 to 2004, acting as if the Parliament did have such rights. He specifically decided to involve MEPs in trade negotiations and expanded the delegations of the EU at Seattle and Doha to include a larger number of parliamentarians (Lamy 2002). It would be naïve to imagine that the presence of MEPs would by itself influence outcomes but it points in the direction of Parliament as a body strengthening the bargaining position of the Commission. Pat Cox, President of the Parliament from 2002 to 2004, has argued explicitly that the EP should be able to serve the same kind of role as that of the Congress in the World Trade Organization:

> In the final phase of negotiations, imagine Robert Zoellick, the United States Trade Representative, turning to Pascal Lamy for the EU and saying: 'you have a better case than I have but I cannot give in because of the Congressional monkey on my back.' We should put a parliamentary monkey on Pascal Lamy's back if we want to protect European interests in this increasingly globalized market place. (Cox 2003)

Indeed, such a monkey may have already have been placed there as a result of legislative decisions that the Parliament has been directly involved in. The agreement reached in co-decision in July 2003 on the labelling of GMO products as part of a package to end the moratorium on GMO imports brings together member states and the EP around a position which is likely to be defended robustly in any case brought before the World Trade Organization. The Council and Parliament are bound to defend together the results of the legislative process in this case outside the EU, just as they do when faced by a challenge inside its borders.

6. Conclusion

It is now over thirty years since Andrew Shonfield wrote of Europe journeying to an unknown destination (Shonfield 1973). For much of that same period a similar claim could be made about the development of the EP. It was by no means clear what kind of institution the EP would become as it struggled, with remarkable success, to achieve a more prominent role.

Over this period the Parliament has moved forward on a trajectory heavily influenced by previous decisions, with member states reluctant to deny its claims for greater powers and unable to put forward a coherent alternative structure for ensuring democracy at European level. At the same time, the existing structure of the Union has shaped that trajectory, making it increasingly easy to imagine a reinforced separation of powers between the executive and legislative branch rather than a fusion of powers of the kind familiar to Europeans.

As a result, those who consider that the legitimacy of the EU depends on the creation of parliamentary government are likely to be disappointed. The Parliament will remain a specialist, rather than a generalist legislative body, reflecting and integrating the ever more diverse interests of the Union and acting autonomously from the many and various executive bodies of the Union. Such a direction may make the circumstances surrounding the establishment of the Barroso Commission less significant than they appeared at the time, but provides powerful grounds for a greater US interest in the fortunes of the Parliament, an institution that has otherwise seemed subsidiary to the transatlantic debate.

References

Clegg, N. and van Hulten, M. (2003). *Reforming the European Parliament*. Brussels: Foreign Policy Centre.

Corbett, R., Jacobs, F., and Shackleton, M. (2003). *The European Parliament*, 5th edn. London: John Harper.

Costa, O. and Magnette, P. (2003). 'Idéologies et changement institutionnel dans l'Union Européenne. Pourquoi les Gouvernements ont-ils constamment renforcé le Parlement européen', *Politique européenne*, 9 (Winter): 49–75.

Cox, P. (2003). 'Filling the Democratic Gap', in J. Weiler, I. Begg, and J. Peterson (eds.), *Expanding the European Union: Reassessing the Fundamentals*. Oxford: Oxford University Press.

European Parliament (2004). *Activity Report 1May 1999 to 30 April 2004 of the delegations to the Conciliation Committee*. Strasbourg: European Parliament, PE 287.644.

Hix, S. (1998). 'Elections, Parties and Institutional Design: A Comparative Perspective on European Union Democracy', *West European Politics*, 21/3: 19–52.

—— (2002). 'Constitutional Agenda-Setting Through Discretion in Rule Interpretation: Why the European Parliament Won at Amsterdam', *British Journal of Political Science*, 32: 259–80.

Judge, D. and Earnshaw, D. (2003). *The European Parliament*. Basingstoke: Palgrave Macmillan.

Kreppel, A. (2003). 'The Environmental Determinants of Legislative Structure: A Comparison of the US House of Representatives and the European Parliament', Paper prepared for the 8th Biennial European Union Studies Association Conference, Nashville, TN, March.

Lamy, P. (2002). *L'Europe en première ligne*. Paris: Seuil.

Magnette, P. (2001). 'Appointing and Censuring the European Commission: The Adaptation of Parliamentary Institutions to the Community Context', *European Law Journal*, 7/3: 292–310.

Shackleton, M. (1998). 'The European Parliament's New Committees of Inquiry: Tiger or Paper Tiger?', *Journal of Common Market Studies*, 36/1: 115–30.

—— (2000). 'The Politics of Co-decision', *Journal of Common Market Studies*, 38/2: 325–42.

—— and Raunio, T. (2003). 'Co-decision since Amsterdam: A Laboratory for Institutional Innovation and Change', *Journal of European Public Policy*, 10/2: 171–87.

Shonfield, A. (1973). *Europe: Journey to an Unknown Destination*. Harmondsworth: Penguin.

Vedel, G. (1972). *Report of the Working Party Examining the Problem of the Enlargement of the Powers of the European Parliament*. Brussels: European Communities.

7

Is the Council Becoming an Upper House?

JEFFREY LEWIS

1. Introduction: The Council and the EU polity[1]

The Council of the European Union (EU) is a leading example of a composite institutional construction in modern international relations. It is also one of the most arcane. Even among EU scholars who make a living at studying the institutional complexities of the EU polity, the Council system remains the most enigmatic, least accessible, and difficult to describe with conventional terminology. Helen Wallace (2002), who has studied the Council since the 1960s, has dubbed it the 'chameleon' of EU institutions. The reason, simply summarized but with far-reaching implications, is that the Council is part-intergovernmental, part-supranational, instrumentalist and collectivist, club-like and competitive, and wields legislative and executive powers. In short, the Council defies the standard grammar of international organizations and intergovernmental negotiation. Nor, as this chapter will argue, does the Council fit neatly into the categories of domestic institutions used by comparativists.

What you see also depends on where you look. Inside the Council, we find a highly variegated structure which currently includes over 200 working groups of national policy specialists, two high-powered diplomatic committees of continuous negotiation (known jointly as the Committee of Permanent Representatives, or Coreper),[2] nine issue-specific ministerial Councils, and quarterly summits among the heads of state and government. Assuming ratification, the new Constitution will add to the mix an appointed president

[1] I thank the project participants and especially the editors for comments on earlier versions of this chapter. Interviews with Council officials used in this project were facilitated by financial support from the Max-Planck Institute for the Study of Societies and the American Political Science Association's Small Grant Program.

[2] The 'permanent representatives' of Coreper II are known as the EU ambassadors and in Coreper I as the deputies.

of the European Council and an EU foreign minister with a supranational ministry of foreign affairs (MFA) to provide centralized diplomatic services.

After more than fifty years of operation, the Council remains an institution that is exceedingly difficult to pin down and categorize—not simply because of the multilayered complexity of the institution—but because it has remained in a relatively fluid state. Some argue that the Council system is a *permanent* experiment in collective decision making (Wallace 2002; de Schoutheete 2002: 31). And, to state the obvious, EU federalism does not yet represent a stable equilibrium or a fixed, immutable division of powers. Despite Giscard's proclamation that the Constitutional Convention would be Europe's '1787,' few observers believe the results are anything near definitive. When viewed in the historical timeframe of US, German, or Swiss federalism, which developed over hundreds of years of organic evolution, wars, and crises, EU federalism is obviously still in its infancy.

That said, over the last ten years the EU's decision-making institutions have evolved considerably and toward a federal-like arrangement which has a clearer separation-of-powers design. This chapter finds that much like the US Senate and other upper chambers in bicameral federal systems, the Council represents one chamber of the legislature in a separation-of-powers system. Although belying simple classification, the Council has also enhanced executive functions critical to the overall operation of the EU, especially in areas of external relations and 'history making' decisions by the heads of state and government in the European Council.

This chapter offers an analysis of what the Council is becoming and how this relates to US-EU relations. After a brief survey of how the Council fits into the broader EU system, I assess how the Council's role now resembles an upper house in a bicameral federal-type polity. I argue that while there is good reason to view the EU system as one of 'authentic' bicameralism, with the Council sharing analogous representational functions as the Bundesrat (upper house) in the German federal system and roughly equivalent legislative authority as the US Senate model, a number of important differences remain. Comparison to the Bundesrat and US Senate approximates but still understates the degree to which the EU institutionally protects territorially based interests. The image of the Council as upper house also obfuscates the crucial design feature which endows it with legislative *and* executive functions. Section 2 shifts focus to a set of change processes within the Council and examines the implications of these changes for the EU's ability to govern internally and negotiate externally in international affairs. Specifically, the three patterns are the institutionalization of deliberative methods of negotiation, legitimation of the EP as a 'co-equal' legislator, and new 'federalizing' efforts in Justice and Home Affairs and Foreign Policy with internal restructuring to speak with a single voice in international affairs. Section 3 examines how these changes in the Council may affect transatlantic relations, and whether new institutional innovations can resolve the timeworn question of who Americans should call if they wish to talk to Europe. In a final concluding section, I find that, paradoxically, as the Council becomes more institutionally hybrid (blurring legislative and executive functions) the EU may become a more visible external actor and a more effective negotiator with the USA.

1.1. The Council's Legislative and Executive Functions in the EU

If there remains a great deal of imprecision as to what *kind* of institution the Council represents, there is much less confusion over what role the Council plays in the EU system. Simply put, the Council is the heart of EU decision-making. While developments such as the growth of independent agencies (including the ECB), the Commission's comitology networks, and especially the ascendance of the EP complicate the legislative 'balance' considerably, they do not alter this underlying foundation. The legislative function of the Council is an essential design feature in the EU going back to the original Coal and Steel Community blueprint; member state representatives operating in the Council would act as gatekeepers for the adoption of new laws proposed by the Commission.

But the Council also plays an executive function in the EU. The endowment of executive roles in the Council system was an intentional design feature by EU framers and derives from multiple sources. First, different member states serve as natural policy leaders in certain areas (e.g. the environment for the Nordics, fisheries for Spain, financial services for the British, transport for the Dutch.). Second, the Council General Secretariat (CGS) provides an increasingly important executive role in finding solutions as an 'honest broker' and behind-the-scenes compromise-building (Beach 2004; Hamlet 2004). Third, the juridical chairmanship of meetings at each and every level of the system is provided by a rotating presidency which turns over every six months. The rotating presidency, which survived the 2004 'constitutional' IGC but was emasculated from chairing European Council meetings and the new Foreign Affairs Council, is a key source of executive leadership in the EU.[3] The legitimacy of the rotating presidency to supply

[3] Article I-24 confirms that the presidency (save foreign affairs and the European Council) will continue on the basis of equal rotation. However, included as a declaration to the Final Act of the 2004 IGC, the European Council will develop new groupings of three member states who will run the presidency for eighteen months. Within each presidency grouping, each member will have a six month rotation to chair all meetings of the Council. Thus, it appears that the presidency will formalize the long-standing 'troika' custom.

EU leadership derives from the principle of equality: Luxembourg has the same rights and obligations to run the Council as France, Britain, or Germany. The weight of obligations to run an effective presidency has historically meant that member states are self-conscious of acting in generalized European interests and avoiding the perception of pushing nationalistic positions or agendas.[4] The presidency has also served as a powerful socializing agent to educate or reeducate national officials to EU collective decision-making (Sbragia 1994: 74; Lewis 1998: 487–8). Fourth, the European Council acts as a 'collective head of state' for the EU. Its remit has no bounds: 'it deals with whatever problem it wants to deal with, in the manner it judges most appropriate' (de Schoutheete 2002: 31). As such, the European Council is an exemplar of 'cartelized executive control over international (and hence domestic) agendas' (Moravcsik 1994: 17). Finally, some draw attention to the executive leadership that can be provided at critical junctures by the 'Franco-German engine' and can act as an impetus to further integration (Webber 1998; Calleo and Staal 1998).

Taking into account these executive roles, equating the Council as an upper chamber can seem overly simplistic. The analogy misses the design features that give the Council both legislative and executive functions. The basic point here is that EU federalism involves a nontraditional 'separation of powers.' Schmidt (2001: 339) has aptly called the EU's horizontal division of authority a 'dynamic confusion of powers' which 'involves not only the lack of traditional separation among the various EU institutions but also the mixing up of their very roles' (see below for an example of the new Union foreign minister). Some might be tempted to impose more clarity on the EU's 'dynamic confusion' by drawing a hard distinction between the European Council and the Council of Ministers (i.e. the European Council is executive in function while the Council of Ministers is legislative). This would be a mistake, however, since the European Council and Council of Ministers are so tightly coupled in practice. While legally speaking the European Council is a separate institution, it permeates every aspect of the Council system.

The blurring of legislative and executive functions in the Council's work is a pattern amplified by changes in the Constitutional Treaty. A striking example is the new Union foreign minister, who will be in charge of CFSP, chair the Foreign Affairs Council, *and* be Vice President of the Commission with responsibility for coordinating the Commission's competencies in

[4] Symbolically, the duties of the EU presidency are well captured in the practice of maintaining a separate national delegation at all Council meetings. This underscores the executive priorities of the presidency to find collective European solutions. For example, Danish Prime Minister Rasmussen projected that 90 percent of his time would be spent finalizing Eastern Enlargement negotiations during the six months of Denmark's 2002 EU presidency (*Financial Times*, July 2, 2002).

external relations. Never before has a high profile position been created which explicitly straddles the institutional divide between the Council and Commission and further blurs the distinction between the executive and legislative 'branches'.

In all of its individual parts and richly nuanced methods for conducting business the Council is impossible to neatly summarize. As a collective creature, it is quite easy, for few would disagree that the Council system is designed to represent the member governments and as such it has evolved into the legislative nucleus of EU policymaking. The next section assesses whether different national models offer any guidance as to where EU federalism may be heading and what institutional role the Council will occupy.

1.2. The Council as the EU's Upper House

Leaving aside the hybrid nature of the Council and the 'dynamic confusion of powers' that blur legislative and executive authority for a moment, the question remains whether we can develop broader generalizations about the Council's institutional evolution from a comparative federalism perspective. The fact that the framers of EU federalism have consistently and explicitly rejected federalist models (and even the 'f' word) does not make such comparison any easier.[5] But there are many in the field of EU studies who hold that such comparative analyses can and should be done. In the 1997 *ECSA Review* forum 'Does the European Union Represent an *n* of 1?,' Gary Marks argues, 'Comparison is entirely feasible even assuming that the EU is unique. What matters is second order similarity, that is, the existence of underlying dimensions on which one may play the EU alongside other cases' (Caporaso *et al.* 1997: 2). There is in fact a growing body of research utilizing comparative federalism to gain insight into the EU (Hay 1966; Capelletti *et al.* 1986; Scharpf 1988, 1994; Sbragia 1992; Hesse and Wright 1996; Nicolaidis and Howse 2001). There are fewer attempts to directly compare EU institutions to comparative counterparts in other federal contexts.[6]

Institutional developments over the last decade allow us to characterize the EU as a bicameral legislative system. As Michael Shackleton documents in his chapter in this volume, the catalyst was the introduction of co-decision (in the Maastricht Treaty of 1992) and its steady extension to new issue-areas following subsequent treaty reforms. The Council, in effect, acts as an upper chamber representing territorial member state interests and the EP is the

[5] The word federalism was deleted from the draft Constitutional Treaty at the insistence of the British.

[6] See Kreppel (2002) for a detailed comparison between the US House of Representatives and the EP. See also Tsebelis and Money (1997) and Shackleton (this volume).

lower house representing 'the people'.[7] This characterization fits the typical pattern of federal-based bicameral systems (e.g. USA, Germany, Switzerland). In the EU, ultimately, 'the people' select both sets of representatives (via direct elections of MEPs and, more indirectly, by national elections that result in ministers representing coalition governments); however, much like the US federal design, the two houses represent 'different manifestations of 'the people's' will' (Tsebelis and Money 1997: 27). The EU's legislative 'branch' now matches the federal conception of the US model, where 'the lower house reflected a popular dimension, while the upper house reflected a territorial dimension' (ibid.).

In a fundamental way, as a second order comparison, the Council is analogous to an upper house in a federal polity because of the way the Council enshrines the representation of territorially based interests. In representational terms, the Council is most similar to the German Bundesrat model. In a detailed comparison between the EU and German case, Sbragia (1992: 288) argues that 'the Bundesrat offers an example of an institution wielding general power in which the interests of territorial governments (defined as executives rather than legislatures) are protected by those very governments'. Thus the 'institutionalization of the territorial dimension' (ibid.: 287) in the Bundesrat is identical in function as the Council is in the EU system. One could push this point further, since as a chamber of states the EU conceptualization of the Council is even more protective of territorial claims than the Bundesrat. In the German case, state participation in national decision making carries a price, as Scharpf (1996: 365–6) explains:

> In Germany . . . joint decision-making has in no way helped to protect the autonomy of the *Länder*. Rather, West Germany has long been described as a 'unitary federal state' in which the goal of uniform living conditions has taken precedence over other concerns. In constitutional theory, German federalism is justified as an additional (and most effective) set of checks and balances restraining the exercise of central government power, rather than as an effective protection of regional identities, diversity, and autonomy. In political terms, it is fair to say that *Länder* governments have traded their autonomy for political influence at the federal level.

EU federalism gives the constituent units (member states) a similar policy-making voice in the 'center,' but in a way that enshrines the protection (rather than subsumption) of individual identities and diverse administrative,

[7] An active proposal during the Constitutional Convention, ultimately rejected, to better tie national parliaments into the EU involved creating a new second chamber made up of national parliamentarians. Arguably, this design would have been 'bolder and closer to federalist conceptions' but also problematic in generating 'multiple mandates' (Quermonne 2002: 27). It is interesting to note here that Germany's federal design of 'interlocking politics' (*Politikverflectung*) also is criticized for short circuiting the input of the Länder parliaments (*Landtage*) in the policymaking process (Hüttman 2002: 104).

political, and cultural traditions. Recent research has confirmed that EU policymaking has not led to a convergence of domestic structures or policy coordination systems and that a diversity of models exist (Kassim *et al.* 2001; Knill 2001).

The process of appointing representatives in the Council is strikingly similar to the process found in the Bundesrat. The electoral mechanism is indirect in both cases. Hüttmann (2002: 106) points out that the Bundesrat 'is in constitutional terms an "eternal organ," renewed only gradually through the effects of Land elections and thus through the changed political composition of the Land governments.' The makeup of the Council, especially at the juridical decision-making level of the ministers, is the same. As Hayes-Renshaw (2002: 65) summarizes: 'The Council as a body has permanent tenure, although the individuals who make it up may (and frequently do) change in the wake of elections or cabinet reshuffles in their national capitals.' Thus the representational functions and selection methods of the Council and the German Bundesrat are closely compatible.

In terms of legislative authority, the US Senate offers a more appropriate second order comparison. The reason is that the EU's design is *unlike* the German pattern and unlike *most* bicameral legislatures where the upper chamber is subordinate to the lower chamber (Patterson and Mughan 1999: 12). In the EU's legislative order, the upper chamber is not limited to a 'revisory role' typical to most other federal-based senates (ibid.). In Brussels we see the reverse: the 'popular' chamber has revise and review authority. The German Bundesrat, while it protects the territorial interests of the constituent states, is more limited in power than the Council because it must exercise authority through veto rights. What is more, veto rights of the Bundesrat (*zustimmungsbedürftige Gesetze*) only apply to about 60 percent of federal legislation. The Bundesrat model was based on a compromise for Germany's 'second chamber', where unlike the US Senate, the Bundesrat would allow the 'Länder only to "participate" (*Mitwirkung*) in the legislative process, and not to be engaged equally (*gleichberechtigt*) like a genuine "second chamber" ' (Hüttman 2002: 106).

Thus, comparing legislative authority, the Council as upper house is most compatible with the power found in the US Senate. And like the US Senate, the EU Council system is highly insulated from fundamental reform. While the Council may lack procedural legitimacy in the eyes of European publics—in terms of *how* decisions are made—as the legitimate protector of states' rights and identities, the Council draws few detractors. Mughan and Patterson (1999: 340) draw a parallel observation that the US Senate stands out among upper chambers as 'unusually immune' from political reform 'because of its exalted constitutional status in a system of separated powers.' A very similar institutional evolution marks the Council's role in the EU system—a trend highlighted by the Constitutional Treaty's provisions on the Council and especially the European Council.

Voting power and the equality of representation is an amalgam of models found elsewhere. The complexity of voting power in the Council is a reflection of the political sensitivities of making binding EU laws under conditions where a sovereign state (big or small) might be outvoted under supermajoritarian rules.[8] In Germany, representation in the Bundesrat is based on population size, a concept anathema to the Council. In comparative terms, the EU is more similar to the US Senate (or Swiss Ständerat) where there is equal representation regardless of the state (or canton) population. Representation in the EU Council system is fundamentally based on a concept of parity, where 'equal representation is provided to unequal territories' (Patterson and Mughan 1999: 15). But equal representation in the Council is balanced by the system of weighted votes in legislative matters where qualified majority voting applies. This weighting can be crudely compared to the Bundesrat's allocation of seats (see Table 7.1).

Reform of the 'unrepresentativess' of voting weights (especially after the controversial small state-big state divide which emerged during the Nice Treaty negotiations) was addressed at the Constitutional Convention, leading to a new system of double majority voting after 2009 (see Exhibit 7.1).

The Convention's recommendation to scrap the complicated and opaque triple majority voting system devised at Nice proved to be the single most contentious issue to resolve at the 2004 IGC. The resulting double majority system (which removes weighted voting requirements) creates a very federal-like supermajoritarian voting system that blends the 'unrepresentativeness' of the US Senate model (equal votes by state regardless of population) with the weighted representation found in the Bundesrat design (see Table 7.2).

Another second order similarity between the Council and upper chambers found elsewhere is the degree of elitism found in its representatives. This is not propertied or hereditary elitism (à la the British House of Lords) but a technocratic elitism of functionally organized policy communities. Especially dominant are foreign ministry officials who are typically *primus inter pares* in domestic policy coordination of national positions on EU issues. And within the Council's informal hierarchy, while the General Affairs and External Relations Council is no longer the uncontested hegemon (witness the ascendance of the Ecofin and Eurogroup Councils), the EU foreign ministers are still very influential.[9]

[8] It is interesting to note that between 1996 and 2000, 45 percent of all losing 'no' votes were cast by the 'Big 4' (Germany, Britain, France, Italy) (Hayes-Renshaw 2002: 64, Table 3.6; author's calculations).

[9] The dysfunctions of General Affairs were recognized by Constitutional Treaty revisions, which created a new General Affairs and External Relations Council (GAERC) responsible for overall coordination of EU affairs and follow-up to European Council summits and an External Relations designed to focus specifically on CFSP issues and chaired by the EU foreign minister.

TABLE 7.1. *Voting weights in the German Bundesrat*

Länder	Number of Votes in the Bundesrat	% of Total German Population	% of Total Votes in the Bundesrat
North Rhine-Westphalia	6	21.9	8.7
Bavaria	6	14.7	8.7
Baden-Württemberg	6	12.6	8.7
Lower Saxony	6	9.5	8.7
Hesse	5	7.3	7.2
Saxony	4	5.6	5.8
Rhineland-Palatinate	4	4.9	5.8
Berlin	4	4.2	5.8
Saxony-Anhalt	4	3.3	5.8
Schleswig-Holstein	4	3.3	5.8
Brandenburg	4	3.1	5.8
Thuringia	4	3.1	5.8
Mecklenburg-W.Pomerania	3	2.2	4.3
Hamburg	3	2.1	4.3
Saarland	3	1.3	4.3
Bremen	3	0.8	4.3

Source: Patzelt (1999: 68, Table 3.1). Population figures are from 1995.

Box 7.1. **The new system of qualified majority voting (Art. I-25 Constitutional Treaty)**

The 'old' system of weighted voting will be phased out on November 1, 2009 (coinciding with the inauguration of the next European Commission following the 2009 European elections). The new system is based on two criteria:

- A majority of member-states, totally at least 55 percent of them (i.e. at least 15 member states)
- Representing at least 65 percent of the total EU population

In addition, a blocking minority must comprise at least four member states. This clause was added as a safeguard to make it more difficult for a hypothetical coalition of big states to form a blocking minority (three of the four big states – Germany, France, Britain, Italy – represent more than 35 percent of the EU population).

In general, an important design implication of the Council system is the 'extraordinary centralization of domestic power in the hands of national executives' who have 'exploited foreign policy prerogatives to centralize and consolidate control over representation in the Council of Ministers'

TABLE 7.2. *2009 EU voting weight projections based on 2003 total population statistics*

	(1000)	% of EU-25	% of total votes needed for 65% threshold
EU-25	453,685.0		
Germany	82,536.7	18.19	27.98
France	59,630.1	13.14	20.22
United Kingdom	59,328.9	13.08	20.12
Italy	57,321.1	12.63	19.43
Spain	40,683.0	8.96	13.79
Poland	38,218.5	8.42	12.95
Netherlands	16,192.6	3.57	5.49
Greece	11,018.4	2.43	3.74
Portugal	10,407.5	2.29	3.52
Belgium	10,355.8	2.28	3.51
Czech Republic	10,203.3	2.24	3.45
Hungary	10,142.4	2.23	3.43
Sweden	8,940.8	1.97	3.03
Austria	8,067.3	1.78	2.74
Denmark	5,383.4	1.19	1.83
Slovak Republic	5,379.2	1.19	1.83
Finland	5,206.3	1.15	1.77
Ireland	3,963.6	.87	1.34
Lithuania	3,462.6	.76	1.17
Latvia	2,331.5	.51	0.79
Slovenia	1,995.0	.43	0.66
Estonia	1,356.0	.29	0.45
Cyprus	715.1	.15	0.23
Luxembourg	448.3	.09	0.14
Malta	397.3	.08	0.12

Source: Eurostat. Theme 3: Population and Social Conditions. Population Statistics (2004 edn.: 55).

(Moravcsik 1994: 15, 16–7). But the EU's technocratic elitism can be found across the gamut of functional policy areas, from the central bank and finance ministry officials who make up the eurozone policy network to the newer military and defense staffs who are entrusted with developing the ESDP. The broader implication here is how the Council becomes a vehicle for domestic actors to insulate policymaking at the collective European level via technocratic expertise. To mention just a few examples, the foreign ministries have done this with proprietary claims to Coreper II (the senior committee to prepare ministers' meetings) and the post of EU ambassador, central bankers and finance officials have upgraded macroeconomic authority in the eurozone, and the interior ministries have centralized their policy hold over JHA matters (on the latter, see Guiraudon in this volume).

The technocratic elitism of the Council has important implications for discourse in the EU legislative process as well. As Schmidt (2001: 346) notes, 'in the Council it is generally the politics of national interest rather than party or money per se. And the arguments themselves are more often than not couched in technical terms, even if they serve as a cover for more political motivations.' Unlike other upper chambers, partisanship is much less determinative of legislative outcomes. In the case of Germany, for example, 'state governments do not always place highest priority on representing state interests in the Bundesrat. Instead, they choose to take a party position . . . ' (Patzelt 1999: 67). In contrast to this, the Council has institutionalized a deliberative negotiating environment (see section 2 later) with discourse engineered to 'depoliticize conflict' (Meyer 1999: 617).

There are two final areas where second order comparison shows major differences between the Council and national analogues. First, EU bicameralism is asymmetrical, and likely to remain so for some time.[10] The reason for this is that EU federalism is clearly evolving as a version of 'segmented federalism' which Sbragia (1992: 262) has described as 'treaty-based federal arrangements in certain policy areas.' Segmented federalism creates a differential role for the parliament in different policy areas. In some policy areas—foreign, security, and defense policy, or taxation to name a few—the EP remains the Council's junior partner. In general the EP does not have 'co-equal' rights in the EU's more heavily 'intergovernmental' policy areas (though see the next section for where this is changing). But unlike traditional national models of asymmetrical bicameralism where the upper house is weaker, here the opposite is the case and power relations are reversed. Second, one must carefully footnote where EU federalism simply does not look like national analogues at all. Both German and American federalism have several key ingredients that the EU experiment lacks: large fiscal resources, a common political culture and public opinion, interparty competition, and (relative to an EU of 25+) high levels of economic and cultural homogeneity (Scharpf 1994: 222; Schmidt 2001: 338).

2. Major Patterns of Change in the Council's Institutional Evolution

In this section, I focus on three processes of change which have restructured how the Council works: the rise of deliberative negotiation, the sharing of

[10] See Lijphart (1984) for the classic typology of 'symmetry' among bicameral legislatures.

legislative authority with the EP, and new policy federalization with the centralization of executive authority. Taken together, they clearly illustrate how the Council system has become less like a classical intergovernmental bargaining table and more like an upper chamber in a federal polity.

2.1. *The Informal Institutionalization of Deliberative Negotiation*

In the standard textbook account, the Council is the main 'intergovernmental' element in the EU and the institution designed to represent member state interests and carefully control the integration process. There is a conventional wisdom that the Council has grown more intergovernmental in character over time: the addition of the European Council, the proliferation of working groups, the decisional authority of the EU permanent representatives, the preservation of unanimity voting in key policy areas, the insulation of certain policy-areas from the Commission, EP, and ECJ, and so on. As a result, many implicitly assume that the EU scores very low in what Weiler (1981) has called 'decisional supranationalism' (as opposed to very high marks in 'normative supranationalism,' viz. the EU legal order).

But there is solid empirical evidence to cast doubt on this reading. Helen Wallace (2002: 327) notes that 'both the practitioners' debate and the scholarly discussion have become trapped by a series of conventional wisdoms about the character of the Council' which are 'not always well-founded in evidence'. Newer research shows that the Council is an altogether more enigmatic construct than the conventional view holds (Wessels 1991; Westlake 1995; Van Schendelen 1996; Hayes-Renshaw and Wallace 1997; Beyers and Dierickx 1998; Lewis 1998, 2003*b*; Egeberg *et al.* 2003; Egeberg 1999; Trondal 2000; Trondal and Veggeland 2003). Consider the paradoxical example of the European Council which is both an intergovernmental body at the highest political level and a grouping that has significantly increased the supranational characteristics of the EU over the last three decades (de Schoutheete and H. Wallace 2002: 5). There is thus a need to develop more nuanced imagery of the Council to take into account its diverse display of intergovernmental and supranational traits. In particular, the conventional wisdom seriously underestimates the importance of the deliberative element to how the Council operates.

The deliberative side of Council negotiations is often overlooked because most accounts implicitly hold that it can matter only in the rarest of circumstances in contrast to the norm of typical interstate bargaining under the shadow of the vote or veto. But standard bargaining theory misses a wide range of behaviorial patterns and negotiation outcomes in the Council. Standard bargaining theory cannot explain why, for example, delegations practice self-restraint in dropping demands or requesting concessions that the group fails to accept, even under conditions where the formal decision rule of unanimity applies and the recourse to the veto exists.[11] To understand why, we must look more closely at the role of discourse and deliberative interaction.

Discourse theorists have begun to develop sophisticated arguments to account for the EU's deliberative environment (Joerges and Neyer 1997; Joerges 1999; Puetter 2003). Neyer (2003: 698) explains that as a 'mode of interaction' deliberation is more effective than bargaining. The reason, he explains, is that 'under conditions of deliberation, any individual preference can be assessed in terms of its coherence with the permissible basic norms (such as reciprocity, the principle of nondiscrimination, or the precautionary principle), and all preferences which fail to withstand the test are eliminated from the sample of possible solutions . . . deliberative procedures provide a filter which at least narrows the set of possible solutions and thus makes political compromise more likely.' The difficulty of maintaining this deliberative environment is both that it is 'politically more costly than bargaining' (ibid.) and requires a tremendous amount of upkeep to maintain the social capital, thick trust, and mutual responsiveness that undergirds the process.

But like many federal legislatures where the 'real' work is done in committee, the Council system has developed an extensive committee network designed for continuous negotiation. To take one example, the operational similarities between the internal workings of the Council and the Bundesrat are striking. According to Patzelt (1999: 74–5) Bundesrat committee meetings operate in an 'atmosphere of open-mindedness and mutual trust' with a strong tradition of 'meticulous preparation' to the point where the '"real" plenary debate has become a thing of the past'. He goes on to add:

> Indeed given the chamber's heavily crowded agenda, for things to be otherwise would be impossible. Consequently, plenary sessions are formally required but necessarily highly staged events. In the final analysis, their purpose is not to provide a forum for debate but to pass a multitude of bills and administrative ordinances and to provide a stage for the last explanation and justification of policy proposals that are about to pass into law. This time pressure and premium on results makes for plenary sessions that are characterized by an orientation toward facts, by a pervasive lack of political passion, and by a concentration on the issues at hand. (ibid.)

This description could easily be confused for a session of the Council of Ministers! It is the deliberative element of the Council's work which really sets it apart from other intergovernmental forums. The second order similarity to national polities is intriguing. As Hüttmann (2002: 104) finds in the case of Germany's 'interlocking politics', the most distinguishing design trait

[11] See Lewis (2005) for examples.

is that 'the institutional structure represents a consensus-inducing mechanism: 'it is the process that fashions the consensus, rather than the latter necessarily being present beforehand'. The Council has evolved a similar set of governance machinery. A senior 1990s era EU ambassador claimed: 'The Council ... is a consensus-seeking system. This penetrates, in my mind, everything we do.'[12] The Council has institutionalized a dense normative context for collective decision making which places great value on maintaining reputational concerns and what negotiation theorists call 'process interests' or 'intrinsic interests in the character of the negotiation process itself' (Lax and Sebenius 1986: 72). The Council's institutional environment is also based on a certain element of collusion to 'cut slack' and reshape domestic 'win sets' (which is linked to the technocratic elitism mentioned above).

Because the Council is first and foremost a consensus-building institution, even isolated delegations can assume obligatory norms of accommodation will kick in rather than simply being outvoted. This even applies to member states in policy areas where they have earned a reputation for obstinacy, such as the British in all things related to social policy (see Lewis 2003 for examples). In general, everyday Council negotiations seem less about finding majority thresholds or weighing the costs or benefits of veto threats than finding compromise solutions that everyone can live with. Justifying arguments with explanations and yielding to their collective legitimation or rejection is standard fare in the Council. There are also similarities here to internal bargaining in the US Senate. In the Senate, as Sinclair (1999: 48) explains:

> Because ... a filibuster is always a possibility, a bill's supporters must think in terms of building a supermajority coalition .... Consequently, the bargaining power of minorities is much enhanced. The legislative process in the Senate is frequently characterized by bargaining to accommodate small groups and even individuals.

A similar logic operates in the Council. Council negotiators are well aware that everyone is in a difficult position sometime, and will need the 'friendly ear of a colleague' for special understanding or a concession. There are very few winner-take-all outcomes or debates which drive isolated delegations into a corner. The unwritten convention is that as long as a delegation shows an openness to compromise they will not be outvoted, regardless of whether a majority or blocking minority exists. To receive understanding, delegates are obligated to explain their situation and justification for help or concession. Under these circumstances, pushing for a vote is considered inappropriate. The deliberative dynamic goes a long way toward explaining the lack of

[12] Interview, Brussels, March 18, 1997.

widespread cost–benefit calculations and instrumentalism in the Council and the consistent use of voting as a last resort (Lewis 2005).

In the Council, the power of a good argument can be as compelling as a blocking minority or the shadow of the veto. This is especially true when it comes to norms of mutual responsiveness and trying to help out a delegation who has 'special problems' with some form of derogation, safeguard, or flexibility clause. In general, the possibility for persuasion acts as a great equalizer in Council negotiations. As a result, smaller member states who articulate clear, sound arguments can often influence discussion much more than the number of votes they hold. A financial counselor from a large member state drew the following contrast: 'Sweden, who is always taking part in the debate, has influence far beyond their votes. Germany is the opposite; they have less influence than votes.'[13]

Much of this institutional environment—moderating demands, conforming to informal rules, showing empathy, and so on—can be captured within a rationalist bargaining framework. However, the standard rationalist interpretation of bargaining misses or downplays the deliberative element of Council decision-making because these behaviors are not being guided only or even primarily by a logic of consequences. There is an irreducible element of collective community standards which operate according to a noninstrumental appropriateness logic.[14] Council officials do not practice these behaviors only because they expect future payoffs (e.g. 'I'll help because I may need special consideration next week'), but because they are seen as the 'right thing to do' and the normal way of conducting business in this institutional setting. Capturing this angle of the story requires a 'soft' constructivist interpretation of institutional environments and norm-guided behavior (Lewis 2003).

Discursive resources can be used rhetorically. 'Some are better at using nice European words and advancing interests,' one ambassador claimed, 'The Finns are wonderful—always talking about Europe.... [Or], always good for Europe is what is good for French national interests.'[15] And Peterson and Jones (1999: 34) argue, new members to Coreper 'must learn to use the language (even rhetoric) of appeals to the "European project."' However, participants claim to be able, in general, to differentiate when someone is using 'the language of Europe' instrumentally, and such actions can be subject to group reproach or even laughter.

[13] Interview, Brussels, May 17, 2000.

[14] See March and Olsen (1998) for a discussion of the logics of consequences and appropriateness.

[15] Interview, by telephone to national capital, April 22, 2003.

Why would sovereign nation-states create such a bargaining environment? Member governments might *intentionally* create a deliberative style of negotiation to cope with a legislative agenda as intensive and far-reaching as the EU (Neyer 2003). Certainly, the systematic increase in Permanent Representatives' de facto decisional authority during the era of 'eurosclerosis' in the 1970s and early 1980s, when researchers began to label Coreper 'a Council of Ministers in permanent session' (Busch and Puchala 1976: 240), is no mere coincidence. Indeed, there is convincing empirical evidence of states sometimes deliberately choosing insulated, in-camera settings and shunning transparency so as to avoid posturing effects, which can cause 'uncompromising positions . . . greater polarization of debate, and more frequent breakdowns in bargaining' (Stasavage 2004: 679). It may thus be wholly within rationalist explanations to predict why such an interaction context is formed. But many rationalists, particularly those who stress a thick consequentialist and interest-maximization logic, would have difficulty accounting for the deliberative element of Council negotiations. The Council's negotiating environment is a very durable site of international negotiation where a 'less self-centered' conceptualization of rationality is practiced (Kahler's phrase citing Sen 1998: 935, fn. 56).

While highly durable, this deliberative environment is almost exclusively an informally institutionalized part of the Council's culture. As such, the Council's collective culture is subject to change, both incrementally and through (less frequent) transformational change. Examples of incremental adaptation include the growth of the working groups structures (as the EU deepened), the steady rise of A-points (or Agreed points which are passed pro forma by the ministers en bloc at the start of a meeting) which empowered 'lower levels' of the Council as de facto decision-makers, and the development of a powerful CGS and Secretary-General to name a few. Transformational change includes the addition of the European Council in the early 1970s and the resurrection of QMV in the late 1980s. While the former is well documented (Bulmer and Wessels 1987; Werts 1992) the latter is not. The transformative effects of the Single European Act (SEA) were not the increased use of voting; in fact, there is ample evidence that voting under QMV is relatively rare. Out of 260 directives in the 1992 Project that were subject to QMV, roughly 220 were adopted by consensus without any vote at all (de Schoutheete 2000: 9). The transformation lies in the way deliberation became more deeply embedded in the Council's institutional environment following the technical ability to call for a vote. As Sbragia (1993: 31) puts it, 'the real breakthrough in the SEA had to do with how national governments dealt with one another.' While more contentious, many anticipate transformational change in the Council following Eastern enlargement. Essentially, the argument is that CEEC enlargement crosses a threshold in EU governance capacities and will have transformational effects on how the Council operates.[16] The next section documents another transformational change in the Council, the empowerment of the EP as a genuine co-legislator and the legitimation of co-decision as the EU's ordinary legislature procedure.

2.2. The Rise of the EP and the Emergence of 'Authentic' Bicameralism

For the first forty years, the EU had essentially a unicameral legislature, the Council. With few exceptions (such as approving the budget), the EP was a token in the legislative mix. Since the early 1990s, we have witnessed a transformational change in the EU legislative process. In federal terms, the Treaty on European Union (TEU) was a 'big bang' moment where the EP was granted real legislative authority with co-decision. Co-decision originally applied to fifteen areas of EU affairs, mostly related to the Single Market and 'Community pillar' policy areas such as the Environment. The 1997 Amsterdam Treaty more than doubled the reach of co-decision to thirty-eight policy areas; and the Nice Treaty extended this further to forty-three. Amsterdam also revamped the co-decision procedure to give the Council and EP the opportunity to conclude agreement during the first reading, a process that greatly enhanced the efficiency of interchamber negotiations. The Constitutional Treaty refers to co-decision as the EU's 'ordinary legislative procedure' which will apply to about eighty policy areas. In short, the Council has moved from being a 'sole legislator' to a 'true co-legislator' (European Parliament Activity Report 2004: 9).

The interinstitutional dynamic between the Council and the EP has become a key part of EU policymaking and the intensity of the links between the two institutions has increased significantly. There now exists a common legislative culture between the two institutions, facilitated by close contacts between senior officials in the CGS and the EP Secretariat. The biggest innovation is the 'trialogue' which was originally designed as a way for the Council, EP, and Commission to negotiate in a more intimate setting (of twenty to twenty-five people) and stave off full conciliation meetings where there are usually 100 or more people involved.[17] In the smaller trialogue

[16] There are both quantitative/logistical arguments (i.e.—that a Council of 25+ simply cannot continue to function the same) and qualitative/cultural arguments (i.e.—the heterogeneity of the new members). For a sample of such arguments, see Ungerer (1993) and Peterson and Jones (1999).

[17] The EU conciliation committee is functionally similar to the USA and German (*Vermittlungsausschuss*) conference committee (see later). The Council side is represented by the EU deputy permanent representatives (Coreper I) and the EP is represented by equal numbers of MEPs from the relevant EP committee. The Council's use of the deputies makes it similar to the German model where the conference committee is a standing committee with the state delegates usually represented by the minister presidents of the Länder (Tsebelis and Money 1997: 180).

format, only the key principals take the floor (especially the committee chair and rapporteur from the EP, and the Coreper I deputy representing the presidency) for a frank and open exchange of views. The trialogue methodology has been central to the development of a new legislative culture with a strong track record for finding joint compromises (Shackleton 2000) (see Table 7.3).[18] The shadow of conciliation has dramatically increased the informal contacts between Council and EP officials during the first and second reading stages. It is estimated that the deputy permanent representatives in Coreper I now spend 50 percent of their time either preparing for or trying to avoid formal conciliation (Bostock 2002: 223). Council actors now even 'lobby' the EP directly; a development that would have been seen as beneath them ten years ago. One deputy permanent representative claimed, 'I now go to Strasbourg at least two times per year for conciliations where we have a special interest to see a rappoteur or chair directly.'[19]

Perhaps the most intense set of interactions, directly comparable to dispute settlement in other bicameral polities, can be seen when the EP and Council cannot agree on a joint text at the first or second reading and a conciliation committee is formed. In the early to mid-1990s, conciliation interactions between the Council and EP were awkward and relations were strained. According to a member of the CGS legal service, 'I remember the first conciliation and it was very difficult. There were two different cultures: a diplomatic culture and a parliamentarian culture. The parliamentarian culture was to speak at length about a problem; this was clashing with the diplomatic culture carried by the Coreper people. It took two years to change things. Now there is a common conciliation culture.'[20]

A key background condition for the development of the EP–Council culture has been the degree of insulation and confidentiality of conciliation negotiations. Similar to the German *Vermittlungsausschuss* and US conference committees, the meetings take place in camera, with little publicity and virtually no outside scrutiny. The impact of secrecy on bargaining outcomes is highly significant in this context. As Stasavage (2004) argues, insulation allows negotiators to avoid posturing which can lead to bargaining breakdowns. EU conciliation practices show second order similarity to the early evolution of norms and custom in the US Congress' conference committees. In her authoritative historical account, McCown (1967: 72) concludes, 'The leaders [of Congress] learned that there might be more chance for agreement if the details of legislation were left to a small group from each House, who,

[18] Though it should be noted that the new 'shared legislative culture' between the EP and Council may come at the expense of the Commission. Shackleton (2000: 336) notes that in trialogues, 'the Commission sometimes feels in a clear position of inferiority, whereas the other two institutions enjoy an increased sense of solidarity.'

[19] Interview, Brussels, May 27, 2003. [20] Interview, Brussels, June 1, 2003.

in various ways, might be induced to agree.' In addition, like their American and German counterparts, EU conciliators have a relatively high degree of autonomy to reach compromise because they operate under a 'closed rule' setting which prevents the parent chambers from amending any agreement. In this sense, EU conciliation committees are identical in functional role as their US conference committee counterparts. According to Tsebelis and Money (1997: 63), 'the conference committee acts as a unicameral mini-parliament under majority rule, which then proposes a compromise to the parent bodies under closed rule (without accepting amendments).' Confirming this design, Bostock (2002: 222) tells us, 'if all EU negotiation is a dark mystery, legislative co-decision is a blacker shade of dark.' Ostensibly introduced to address the EU's democratic deficit, the emergence of a legislative culture based on such norms of closed-door negotiation is not without irony. But the reliance on insulated, in camera negotiations is keeping with the much older and established legislative culture founded within the Council. It remains to be seen whether the EU conciliation committee will become the equivalent of the 'third house' of the EU legislature in way the conference committee has evolved in the USA (Vogler 1971).

There are still a few areas where co-decision will frequently go to full conciliation, such as environmental legislation and budgetary issues, but overall the ability to reach a joint agreement at the first or second reading is steadily improving. The Commission estimates that since Amsterdam and the 217 cases of co-decision between May 1999 and November 2002, only 13 percent went to full conciliation (compared to 40 percent of all files between Maastricht and Amsterdam) (see Table 7.3).[21] The learning curves may have been sharp at first (CGS and Permrep officials recall the first interactions as 'painful' and 'hostile') but the aggregate data show that the Council and EP actively seek to compromise, facilitated by a number of informal procedures, such as the trialogue method to front-load EP–Council compromise. We now see as many files concluded at first reading as we saw stretching out to full conciliation in the pre-Amsterdam era. In short, we have witnessed the development of a new legislative paradigm in EU politics and in all areas where co-decision now applies a genuine version of bicameralism. According to EP figures, out of eighty-six conciliation procedures completed between 1994–2004, the parliament proposed a total of 1344 amendments, of which 809, or 60 percent, were accepted in conciliation following a compromise with the Council (EP Activity Report 2004: 14).

[21] Another 12 percent were formally settled at conciliation as 'A' points on the very first meeting (European Commission Secretariat-General, 'Co-decision: November 1993 to November 2002: An Analysis.' October 24, 2002).

TABLE 7.3. *Co-decision outcomes since 1994*

	Total Co-decisions	% concluded at 1st Reading	% concluded at 2nd Reading	% concluded at Conciliation
1994–99	30		60	40
1999–00	68	19	57	28
2000–01	67	28	42	30
2001–02	76	24	49	28
2002–03	87	28	55	17
2003–04	105	39	46	15

Source: European Parliament Activity Report, May 1, 1999 to April 30, 2004, PE 287. 644: 13.

The highly networked relations between Council and EP officials who deal with co-decision and conciliation have helped produce a more consensual legislative model than found in many other national settings. While early MEPs saw their appropriate counterparts from the Council to be ministerial level officials rather than civil servants from Coreper, they gradually learned that the deputy permanent representatives had a very flexible mandate to negotiate. On the Council side, there are some who view the MEPs as somewhat unreliable, sometimes not showing up for conciliation meetings or dragging a meeting out far into the night. But relative to the US context, it appears that EU intercameral relations are very collegial and healthy. In the case of US conference committees, Sinclair (1999: 51) reports:

> For years, House members have derided senators as media-obsessed prima donnas, as showhorses rather than workhorses. They have complained that the senators they deal with in conference lack in-depth expertise, depend too much on staff, and often do not even show up and yet hog more than their share of the media attention and credit.

But others who study US conference committees emphasize the impact of long-term, repeated interactions among delegates which work to build relations of trust and a willingness to compromise (Longley and Oleszek 1989). Here the second order similiarity to EP–Council conciliation, while barely a decade old, is quite apparent. In summary, co-decision has created a new legislative paradigm in the EU, one which looks quite like other federal-based bicameral polities. EP–Council relations are now geared towards extensive interactions to front-load compromise at the first or second reading stage, facilitated by the 'trialogue' method and interpersonal relations between actors who regularly participate in co-decision proceedings. We move now to consider a third area of change in the Council's operation, the growing federalization of EU policy in foreign and internal affairs.

2.3. *'Federalizing' CFSP and JHA: No Longer Taboo*

The third major change sequence, and the most recent, is the deepening of Common Foreign and Security Policy (CFSP) and Justice and Home Affairs (JHA) competencies at the EU level. The EU is currently federalizing two broad policy areas that as recently as Maastricht were considered by most governments as off limits for Brussels (seen vividly in the creation of the fire walled 'pillar' system). Since other chapters in the volume deal with these subjects in greater detail (see the chapters by Howorth and Guiraudon), the focus here will be the impact on the Council's internal structure and the centralization of authority to speak with a single voice.

The deepening of CFSP has primarily focused on the 'S' portion, now known in eurospeak as European Security and Defense Policy (ESDP). The showcase of ESDP is the development of small, mobile 'battle groups' that can be dispatched independently of NATO. As Howorth documents in his chapter (this volume), the EU has launched police and/or military operations since 2003 in Macedonia, the Congo, and Bosnia. Perhaps more significant institutionally, is the momentum behind efforts for a new centralized military headquarters and a supranational EU foreign ministry.[22] This would build upon the 1999 Helsinki summit decision to create three new Council preparatory structures for ESDP: the permanent Political and Security Committee (PSC) composed of ambassador-level diplomats, the Military Committee (MC) of chiefs of defense, and the Military Staff (MS) who are involved in early warning, situation assessment, and crisis management operations. All told, the EU now has the institutional machinery in place (and enabled by the new 'enhanced cooperation' clause) to develop much more coherent Union policies on security and defense issues. Of course, the EU is still light-years away from having the equivalent of a federally-funded foreign policy, a limitation which Europe's current budget politics translate into an immutable fact.

Justice and Home Affairs has also developed significantly since Maastricht. While far from 'federal,' the JHA field is federalizing in directions few in the Council would have predicted from the early post-Maastricht encounters between national officials in this field. Since then, new EU competencies and legislation dealing with cross-border crime, immigration and asylum track with a neofunctionalist spillover logic, especially the burst of new legislation following the political green light provided by the 1999 Tampere European Council. A major turning point was the agreement on a European

[22] The initiative for a new military headquarters comes from a controversial defense summit between four EU member states (France, Germany, Belgium, and Luxembourg) in April 2003. The initiative for a new Union foreign ministry comes out of the Constitutional Convention and was endorsed at the June 2003 Thessaloniki European Council summit.

arrest warrant in December 2001, which followed in the wake of the 9/11 attacks and was subject to intensive negotiations in the Council in the late fall. The EU arrest warrant covers extremely sensitive political issues of extradition and the surrender of nationals/residents and applies to a wide range of criminal offenses (e.g. terrorism, cross border crimes such as trafficking in drugs, weapons, or human beings). But the major breakthrough of the agreement came with the application of the concept of mutual recognition to different national definitions of crime in order to promote judicial cooperation. As one EU ambassador explained, 'We knew we had to apply mutual recognition here to get judicial cooperation across the board, but this was very controversial and is based on trust—something that is still lacking among these officials.'[23] While political momentum behind the EU arrest warrant was driven by the exogenous shock of 9/11, other JHA advances are being pushed by the expansion of EU borders into the 'porous' regions of Central and Eastern Europe. Numerous European Council summits have produced presidency conclusions that call for updating the Schengen border controls (the new 10 are expected to join Schengen in 2007–08). And at the 2003 Thessaloniki European Council summit, EU called for 'new institutional mechanisms . . . for the management of external borders,' which may eventually include the creation of a new independent EU border guard agency (Financial Times, June 22, 2003).

In short, both foreign and interior policies show real signs of (partial) federalization at the EU level and these policy areas are currently among the biggest 'growth industries' in the Council's business. It is not yet clear how the two change sequences discussed above—deliberative negotiation and the coequal input of the EP—will or will not eventually apply to these policy fields. One point that does seem clear is that these federalization efforts, especially in foreign policy, are being coordinated with upgrades in the Council's executive capacity. The 'mode' of policymaking that is developing in these fields is one where the European Council closely gatekeeps, the CGS serves as 'honest broker,' and the Commission and EP remain on the sidelines.[24] The new Union foreign minister and European Council president are likely to reinforce this pattern while at the same time stir up the EU's 'dynamic confusion of power.' Paradoxically, as the next section will suggest, this may have the long-term consequence of enabling the EU to become a more coherent international actor.

[23] Interview, Brussels, May 27, 2003.

[24] This pattern fits broadly with what Wallace (2000: 33–4) calls an 'intensive transgovernmentalism mode.'

3. How Will the Evolving Council Affect Transatlantic Relations?

Ideas that would have been taboo to the French, British, and Germans at Maastricht—such as the creation of a European foreign minister and a supranational foreign ministry—are now seen as a way to cement the EU as a coherent international actor. A key development was the 1999 decision to upgrade the posting of Council Secretary-General to also include the position of High Representative in foreign affairs. An argument could be made that the EU's decision to create a Union foreign minister—a 'European Colin Powell' as it was referred to by Council insiders—represents a clear case of institutional isomorphism.[25] In this view, American unilateralism is goading the EU to define its own identity in international affairs. One former EU ambassador, discussing the Council's foreign policy upgrades, referred several times to Europe's need to counterbalance the US 'empire' and 'the new Rome.'[26] Desire to speak with a single voice, while not new (going back at least to Kissinger's famous quip in the 1960s about whom he should call to speak to Europe) is now a showcase of European Council summits. The European Council itself is in one sense an example of institutional mimicry, where member states have recreated a 'collective head of state' at the transnational level to gain greater international influence. de Schoutheete (2002: 36–7), a longtime participant in Council politics, has argued that raising the EU's 'external visibility' has long been a key objective; it is natural, as he puts it, 'that member governments should try to make use of high-level meetings to deliver political messages to the outside world'.

Institutional mimicry helps account for the decision to create a permanent European Council president. Although many small states still fear the potential this has for institutionalizing a directoire of large states, this explanation offers some plausibility for their grudging endorsement. There is a similar change process taking place in eurozone policymaking, with proposals to create a Union finance minister to chair the eurogroup Council. One apparent difference from the foreign secretary post is the Union finance minister would be chosen from among the twelve current eurozone finance ministers and would not have the additional executive functions performed by the foreign minister 'double-hatting' as a Vice President of the Commission. Part of the momentum behind this proposal is the desire to reassert leadership in the enforcement of budget deficit rules following the demise of the stability and growth pact.[27] But from statements by Giscard and his praesidium during the European Convention, it is also motivated by a desire

[25] See DiMaggio and Powell (1991) for more on institutional isomorphic change.

[26] Interview, by telephone to national capital, April 22, 2003.

[27] Here there is also already the precedent of a permanent chair for the EFC (and formerly the Monetary Committee).

to make the international representation of the eurozone (at the IMF, the G-8, etc.) more coherent.[28]

Thus current efforts to create a new single face in EU foreign policy, the eurozone, and at the level of 'blockbuster' politics with the European Council president, could have dramatic long-term effects on US–EU relations. At a minimum, the concept of the transatlantic partnership would benefit from having clearer defined and stable interlocutors on the European side in key areas for international cooperation.[29] This of course assumes the Constitutional Treaty survives ratification in its current form and that the appointments of these new positions are not controversial. The net effect of this, while adding to the EU's 'dynamic confusion of powers' (Schmidt's phrase) will likely be a more visible role in international affairs which could help recast the US–EU 'partnership' on more equal footing.

4. Conclusion

This chapter has argued that the Council is closer to an upper chamber in a federal polity than an 'ordinary' international organization. In support of this argument, we found second order similarity to other federal systems in several key respects. First, the Council institutionally resembles a second chamber in the EU as a result of the firm entrenchment of co-decision as the EU's 'ordinary legislative procedure.' Participants in the Council and EP now speak of a new legislative culture in the EU (Shackleton 2000; Bostock 2002). Second, EU bicameralism, like most other federal versions found at the national level, relies heavily on informal institutionalized mechanisms to resolve intercameral disputes over the content of new laws. The EU conciliation committee is functionally the same and operationally alike to both the German and American versions of conference committees. All three rely heavily on in camera negotiations to produce legislative compromise. The EU's invention of the 'trialogue' method can be seen largely as an extension of the Council's venerable tradition of a legislative process built on consensus-inducing mechanisms. Third, the Council functionally resembles a federal-like upper chamber designed to represent territorial claims. The closest national analogue, in representational terms, is the German Bundesrat. Both

[28] This will also be facilitated by the new Constitutional Treaty's provision which gives the EU formal 'legal personality' to sign international agreements and have a seat at international organizations.

[29] The template for this already exists in the area of EU trade policy although the EU is represented here by the Trade Commissioner. It is clear that US–EU trade relations (especially dispute settlement) benefit from the tightly coupled networking between Robert Zoellick and Pascal Lamy.

the Council and Bundesrat protect the territorial interests of their constituent states. Yet this chapter also found functional similarity to the US Senate, especially in terms of overall legislative power and the 'unequalness' of representation to even out differences between big and small. Much like the compromise that US framers were forced to make which gave each state two seats in the Senate regardless of population, EU framers have designed controls such as the rotating presidency and a reliance on deliberative negotiation to even out relative power and size disparities.

These comparisons required considerable care and caveats, however, because the EU's bicameral order is asymmetrical in favor of the Council in a number of exempt policy areas such as taxation and most of foreign policy (including the common commercial policy). This reverses the power relations usually found between upper and lower houses in a federal polity. In addition, comparison to other upper houses fails to capture the Council's significant executive roles in EU governance. Comparative analysis thus spotlights the hybrid nature of the Council's role, a pattern likely to be amplified by revisions in the Constitutional Treaty which extend the Council's executive functions further, specifically in foreign policy and generally in the 'history making' role of the European Council under a centralized president.

Compared to even a decade ago, the EU has a much more federal conception of its institutional decision-making structure and has reinforced the already healthy 'creative tension' between the branches. The Council and its blend of legislative and executive functions is an exemplar of this tension. While the EU system is now clearly an example of authentic bicameralism, the Council's institutional trajectory and collective expression of national sovereignty lends support to the view that it most closely approximates a 'post modern' form of political organization. On this reading—as Ansell and Chen argue in this volume—comparing EU federalism to national analogues may miss deeper implications for how the Council reorders basic relations between sovereign states (Ruggie 1993; Sbragia 1994; Schmitter 1996). Ultimately, explaining EU federalism may require what Nicolaïdis (2001: 464) calls thinking 'outside the state-centric paradigm' and 'the traditional Weberian hierarchy of the state.' In the meantime, recognition of the EU polity's uniqueness in modern international relations does not rule out comparison and generalization to a broader universe of cases and interinstitutional relations within bicameral federal polities. As the contributors to the 1997 *ECSA Review* on this subject all seemed to agree, the '$n = 1$' problem is hardly insurmountable (Caporaso *et al.* 1997). This chapter has attempted to push that conversation in a positive direction by drawing more finely-grained comparisons between the Council's evolving institutional role in the EU's legislative system and other national models of bicameral federalism.

References

Beach, D. (2004). 'The Unseen Hand in Treaty Reform Negotiations: The Role and Influence of the Council Secretariat'. Unpublished manuscript.

Beyers, J. and Dierickx, G. (1998). 'The Working Groups of the Council of the European Union: Supranational or Intergovernmental Negotiations?', *Journal of Common Market Studies*, 36: 289–317.

Bostock, D. (2002). 'Coreper Revisited', *Journal of Common Market Studies*, 40/2, 215–34.

Bulmer, S. and Wessels, W. (1987). *The European Council: Decision-Making in the European Community*. London: Macmillan.

Busch, P. and Puchala, D. (1976). 'Interests, Influence, and Integration: Political Structure in the European Communities', *Comparative Political Studies*, 9/3, 235–54.

Calleo, D. and Staal, E. (eds.) (1998). *Europe's Franco-German Engine*. Washington, DC: Brookings.

Caporaso, J., Marks, G., Moravcsik, A., and Pollack, M. (1997). 'Does the European Union Represent an N of 1?', *ECSA Review*, 10/3: 1–5.

Cappelletti, M., Seccombe, M., and Weiler, J. (eds.) (1986). *Integration Through Law: Europe and the American Federal Experience*. New York: de Gruyter.

DiMaggio, P. and Powell, W. (1991). 'The Iron Cage Revisited: Institutional Isomorphism and Collective Rationality in Organizational Fields', in W. Powell and P. DiMaggio (eds.), *The New Institutionalism in Organizational Analysis*. Chicago: University of Chicago Press, pp. 63–82.

Egeberg, M. (1999). 'Transcending Intergovernmentalism? Identity and Role Perceptions of National Officials in EU Decision-Making', *Journal of European Public Policy*, 6: 456–74.

—— Schaefer, G., and Trondal, J. (2003). 'The Many Faces of EU Committee Governance', ARENA Working Paper No. 03/2. Oslo: Norway.

European Parliament Activity Report of the Delegations to the Conciliation Committee. 1 May 1999 to 30 April 2004. PE 287.644.

Hamlet, L. (2004). 'Reconsidering Supranational Entrepreneurship in the European Union: The Case of the Council Secretariat'. Unpublished.

Hay, P. (1966). *Federalism and Supranational Organizations: Patterns for New Legal Structures*. Urbana, IL: University of Illinois Press.

Hayes-Renshaw, F. (2002). 'The Council of Ministers', in J. Peterson and M. Shackleton (eds.), *The Institutions of the European Union*. Oxford: Oxford University Press, pp. 47–70.

—— and Wallace, H. (1997). *The Council of Ministers*. New York: St Martin's Press.

Hesse, J. J. and Wright, V. (eds.) (1996). *Federalizing Europe: The Costs, Benefits, and Preconditions of Federal Political Systems*. New York: Oxford University Press.

Hüttman, M. (2002). 'The Practice of Federalism in Germany', in J. Rose and J. Traut (eds.), *Federalism and Decentralization: Perspectives for the Transformation Process in Eastern and Central Europe*. New York: Palgrave, pp. 97–123.

Joerges, C. and Neyer, J. (1997). 'Transforming Strategic Interaction Into Deliberative Problem-Solving: European Comitology in the Foodstuffs Sector', *Journal of European Public Policy*, 4/4, 609–25.

—— (1999). ' "Good Governance" Through Comitology?', in C. Joerges and E. Vos (eds.), *EU Committees: Social Regulation, Law, and Politics*. Oxford: Hart Publishing.

Kahler, M. (1998). 'Rationality in International Relations', *International Organization*, 52/4: 919–41.

Kassim, H. *et al.* (eds.) (2001). *The National Co-ordination of EU Policy: The European Level*. Oxford: Oxford University Press.

Knill, C. (2001). *The Europeanization of National Administrations: Patterns of Institutional Change and Persistence*. Cambridge: Cambridge University Press.

Kreppel, A. (2002). 'The Environmental Determinants of Legislative Structure: A Comparison of the US House of Representatives and the European Parliament'. Paper prepared for the conference, 'Exporting Congress? The Influence of the US Congress on World Legislatures', Miami, FL, December 6–7.

Lax, D. A. and Sebenius, J. K. (1986). *The Manager as Negotiator: Bargaining for Cooperation and Competitive Gain*. New York: Free Press.

Lewis, J. (1998). 'Is the "Hard Bargaining" Image of the Council Misleading? The Committee of Permanent Representatives and the Local Elections Directive', *Journal of Common Market Studies*, 36/4: 479–504.

—— (2003). 'Institutional Environments and Everyday EU Decision-Making: Rationalist or Constructivist?', *Comparative Political Studies*, 36/1: 97–12.

—— (2003*b*). 'Informal Integration and Supranational Construction of the Council', *Journal of European Public Policy*, 10/6: 99–109.

—— (2005). 'The Janus Face of Brussels: Socialization and Everyday Decision-Making in the European Union', *International Organization*, 59/4.

Lijphart, A. (1984). *Democracies: Patterns of Majoritarian and Consensus Government in Twenty-One Countries*. New Haven, CT: Yale University Press.

Longley, L. and Oleszek, W. (1989). *Bicameral Politics: Conference Committees in Congress*. New Haven, CT: Yale University Press.

March, J. and Olsen, J. (1998). 'The Institutional Dynamics of International Political Orders', *International Organization*, 52/4: 943–69.

McCown, A. (1967). *The Congressional Conference Committee*. New York: AMS Press.

Meyer, C. (1999). 'Political Legitimacy and the Invisibility of Politics: Exploring the European Union's Communication Deficit', *Journal of Common Market Studies*, 37/4: 617–39.

Moravcsik, A. (1994). 'Why the European Community Strengthens the State: Domestic Politics and International Cooperation', Harvard University, Center for European Studies Working Paper Series No. 52.

Mughan, A. and Patterson, S. (1999). 'Senates: A Comparative Perspective', in Patterson, S. and Mughan, A. (eds.), *Senates: Bicameralism in the Contemporary World*. Columbus, OH: Ohio State University Press, 333–49.

Neyer, J. (2003). 'Discourse and Order in the EU: A Deliberative Approach to Multi-Level Governance', *Journal of Common Market Studies*, 41/4: 687–706.

Nicolaïdis, K. (2001). 'Conclusion: The Federal Vision beyond the Federal State', in K. Nicolaïdis and R. Howse (eds.), *The Federal Vision: Legitimacy and Levels of Governance in the United States and the European Union.* New York: Oxford University Press, pp. 439–81.

—— and Howse, R. (eds.) (2001). *The Federal Vision: Legitimacy and Levels of Governance in the United States and the European Union.* New York: Oxford University Press.

Patterson, S. and Mughan, A. (1999). 'Senates and the Theory of Bicameralism', in S. Patterson and A. Mughan (eds.), *Senates: Bicameralism in the Contemporary World.* Columbus, OH: Ohio State University Press, pp. 1–31.

Patzelt, W. (1999). 'The Very Federal House: The German Bundesrat', in S. Patterson and A. Mughan (eds.), *Senates: Bicameralism in the Contemporary World.* Columbus, OH: Ohio State University Press, pp. 59–92.

Peterson, J. and Jones, E. (1999). 'Decision Making in an Enlarging European Union', in J. Sperling (ed.), *Two Tiers or Two Speeds? The European Security Order and the Enlargement of the European Union and NATO.* Manchester: Manchester University Press, pp. 25–45.

Puetter, U. (2003). 'Informal Circles of Ministers: A Way Out of the EU's Institutional Dilemmas?' *European Law Journal*, 9/1: 109–24.

Quermonne, J. L. (2002). 'The Question of a European Government', *Notre Europe. Groupement d'Études et de Recherches*, Research and European Issues No. 20.

Ruggie, J. (1993). 'Territoriality and Beyond: Problematizing Modernity in International Relations', *International Organization*, 47/1: 139–74.

Sbragia, A. (1992). 'Thinking About the European Future: The Uses of Comparison', in A. Sbragia (ed.), *Euro-Politics: Institutions and Policymaking in the 'New' European Community.* Washington, DC: Brookings, pp. 257–91.

—— (1993). 'The European Community: A Balancing Act', *Publius*, 23 (Summer): 23–38.

—— (1994). 'From "Nation-State" to "Member State": The Evolution of the European Community', in P. Lützeler (ed.), *Europe After Maastricht: American and European Perspectives.* Providence, RI: Berghahn Books, pp. 69–87.

Scharpf, F. (1988). 'The Joint-Decision Trap: Lessons from German Federalism and European Integration', *Public Administration*, 66: 229–78.

—— (1994) 'Community and Autonomy: Multi-Level Policy-Making in the European Union', *Journal of European Public Policy*, 1/2: 219–42.

—— (1996) 'Can There Be a Stable Federal Balance in Europe?', in J. J. Hesse and V. Wright (eds.), *Federalizing Europe: The Costs, Benefits, and Preconditions of Federal Political Systems.* New York: Oxford University Press, pp. 361–73.

Schmidt, V. (2001). 'Federalism and State Governance in the European Union and the United States: An Institutional Perspective', in K. Nicolaïdis and R. Howse (eds.), *The Federal Vision: Legitimacy and Levels of Governance in the United States and the European Union.* New York: Oxford University Press, pp. 335–54.

Schmitter, P. (1996). 'Imagining the Future of the Euro-Polity with the Help of New Concepts', in G. Marks *et al.* (eds.), *Governance in the European Union.* London: Sage, pp. 121–50.

de Schoutheete, P. (2000). *The Case for Europe: Unity, Diversity, and Democracy in the European Union*. Boulder, CO: Lynne Rienner.

—— (2002). 'The European Council', in J. Peterson and M. Shackleton (eds.), *The Institutions of the European Union*. Oxford: Oxford University Press, pp. 21–46.

—— and Wallace, H. (2002). 'The European Council', *Notre Europe. Groupement d'Études et de Recherches*. Research and European Issues No. 19.

Van Schendelen, M. P. C. M. (1996). ' "The Council Decides": Does the Council Decide?' *Journal of Common Market Studies*, 34/4 (December): 531–48.

Shackleton, M. (2000). 'The Politics of Co-decision', *Journal of Common Market Studies*, 38/2: 325–42.

Sinclair, B. (1999). 'Coequal Partner: The US Senate', in S. Patterson and A. Mughan (eds.), *Senates: Bicameralism in the Contemporary World*. Columbus, OH: Ohio State University Press, pp. 32–58.

Stasavage, D. (2004). 'Open-Door or Closed Door? Transparency in Domestic and International Bargaining', *International Organization*, 58/2: 667–703.

Trondal, J. (2000). *Administrative Integration Across Levels of Governance: Integration Through Participation in EU Committees*. Unpublished PhD thesis, University of Oslo.

—— Veggeland, F. (2003). 'Access, Voice, and Loyalty: The Representation of Domestic Civil Servants in EU Committees', *Journal of European Public Policy*, 10: 59–77.

Tsebelis, G. and Money, J. (1997). *Bicameralism*. New York: Cambridge University Press.

Ungerer, W. (1993). 'Institutional Consequences of Broadening and Deepening the Community: The Consequences for the Decision-Making Process', *Common Market Law Review*, 30/1: 71–83.

Vogler, D. (1971). *The Third House: Conference Committees in the United States Congress*. Evanston, IL: Northwestern University Press.

Wallace, H. (2000). 'The Institutional Setting: Five Variations on a Theme', in H. Wallace and W. Wallace (eds.), *Policy-Making in the European Union*. 4th edn. New York: Oxford University Press, pp. 3–37.

—— (2002). 'The Council: An Institutional Chameleon?' *Governance*, 15/3 (July): 325–44.

Webber, D. (1998). 'The Hard Core: The Franco-German Relationship and Agricultural Crisis Politics in the European Union', European University Institute Working Paper RSC No. 98/46.

Weiler, J. (1981). 'The Community System: The Dual Character of Supranationalism', *Yearbook of European Law*, 1: 268–306.

Werts, J. (1992). *The European Council*. Amsterdam: Elsevier.

Wessels, W. (1991). 'The EC Council: The Community's Decisionmaking Center', in R. Keohane and S. Hoffmann (eds.), *The New European Community: Decisionmaking and Institutional Change*. Boulder, CO: Westview Press, 133–54.

Westlake, M. (1995). *The Council of the European Union*. London: Cartermill.

8

The Politics of Eurocracy: Building a New European State?

R. DANIEL KELEMEN[1]

How can an executive with a staff of less than 25,000 regulate a modern polity with a population of 450 million? The answer is that it cannot. In the long term, the European Commission—with a staff the size of the administration of a typical midsized European city—cannot hope to implement and enforce the massive body of accumulated Community law (the *acquis communautaire*) across twenty-five countries comprising nearly half a billion people, to develop new policies and to shepherd them through the European Union's (EU's) legislative process. While some early Europhiles may have dreamt of erecting a massive Eurocracy in Brussels, and while many Eurosceptics still fear that this is occurring (Siedentop 2001), today this collective dream or nightmare can only be viewed as a flight of fancy. Quite simply, the member states would not permit it, and the European Parliament (EP) and Commission do not seek it.

But to say that the EU will never build a massive Weberian state bureaucracy in Brussels is not to say that it will not build a novel state-like organization. In his seminal study of American state building, Skowronek (1982: 8) describes the nineteenth-century American state as 'a governmental order that failed to evoke the sense of a state.' Skowronek points out that leading nineteenth century scholars including Tocqueville and Hegel did not consider America a 'real state' in that it lacked many of the formal institutional arrangements associated with the classical European state model. Yet, Skowronek emphasizes, the 'peculiar genius' of the early American state lay precisely in this 'apparent, but ultimately illusory, statelessness.' To say that the contemporary EU fails to evoke 'a sense of state' is a gross understatement. Yet despite this apparent statelessness, the EU is developing an increasingly powerful 'governmental order.' The EU's regulatory capacity is expanding along two fronts: one judicial and one bureaucratic. First, because

[1] The author would like to thank officials, from the European Commission for their help with this research; the Department of Politics and International Relations at the University of Oxford and the Zikha Fund at Lincoln College, Oxford for their financial support and Leonid Peisakhin for his research assistance.

the EU cannot rely on a massive state bureaucracy, it is encouraging the judicialization of policy processes. As a growing literature on EU legal integration demonstrates, the EU actively enlists national courts and private litigants to act as decentralized enforcers of EU law (Mattli and Slaughter 1998; Stone Sweet and Caporaso 1998; Fligstein and Stone Sweet 2001; Alter 2001; Cichowski 2001; Kelemen 2003). Second, the EU has moved to expand its executive capacity through the establishment of specialized, decentralized European agencies outside the structure of the Commission.

This chapter focuses on this second dimension of the growth of the EU's regulatory state. The construction of EU agencies has hardly grabbed the headlines. Yet, quietly the EU has established twenty-three such agencies with a combined budget of over €900 million and staff of approximately 2,500. A handful of other agencies are currently in the pipeline and the trend appears likely to accelerate.

The creation of European agencies is puzzling in important respects. The early rhetoric supporting the European agencies emphasized the benefits of delegating the technical aspects of regulation to these purportedly 'independent' bodies. It was far from clear, however, of which political actors these agencies were supposed to be independent (Kelemen 2002: 94). Independent of the member states? As we will see below, this was certainly not the case. Independent of the Commission? Perhaps, but at the time the Commission itself was viewed by many as an 'independent' regulator. Why then were new European agencies created when additional resources and authority could simply have been delegated to the Commission?

This chapter examines the politics behind the establishment of European agencies. Many accounts of the European agencies have emphasized the functional motivations behind their creation (Everson 1995; Everson *et al.* 1999; Kreher 1997; Majone 1997, 2000, 2002).[2] The Commission's stated rationale for agencies hinges on the need for technical expertise, independence and credibility in the regulatory process. As the Commission (2002: 5) explained in its Communication on agencies, 'The main advantage of using the agencies is that their decisions are based on purely technical evaluations of very high quality and are not influenced by political or contingent considerations.' Majone, the most prominent academic analyst of the EU agencies, echoes this functionalist approach to EU agencies. Majone's approach to the EU agencies has been primarily normative. He argues that the agencies *should be* insulated from politics such that they can perform their tasks based on apolitical, technocratic judgments and can thus ensure the credibility of EU policymaking. In particular, he argues that, 'the growing politicisation of the Commission ... is possibly the strongest argument in favor of an in-

[2] But see Shapiro 1997, Dehousse 1997, and Flinders 2004, Kelemen 2002 for more consciously political accounts of agency creation.

creased recourse to nonmajoritarian institutions of regulatory policymaking at the European level' (Everson *et al.* 1999: 21; Majone 2002: 330). Majone's normative analysis seems to spill over into his positive analysis. His explanations of why agencies actually are established reflect the same functional arguments for why they should be established. However, this functional, efficiency based understanding ignores much of the actual political struggle over the creation of European agencies.

This chapter seeks to reinject a dose of politics into these excessively functionalist accounts of agency creation. The chapter examines how political conflict and compromise between the Commission, the Parliament and the Council of Ministers have influenced the design of European agencies. The chapter draws on the literature on the politics of agency design in the USA and identifies insights applicable to the European agencies. While the US literature does shed light on how principal-agent concerns influenced the design of EU agencies, the institutional terrain and the politics of agency design has differed in significant ways. As Skowronek (1982) demonstrated in his study of the expansion of federal administrative capacities in the USA, the builders of an administrative state must contend with the defenders of preexisting institutions. In the EU, where European level agencies have been established, they have in most cases been built on policy terrain already occupied by powerful national bodies. This, along with other systematic limits on EU resources, helps explain salient features of the European agencies, such as the 'network model' that underpins most of them.

The chapter is divided into five sections. Section 1 clarifies the precise definition of a European agency and surveys the landscape of existing agencies. Section 2 examines the politics of Eurocracy in general terms, highlighting the positions of key actors and the causal mechanisms behind the creation of European agencies. Section 3 details the development of the first wave of European agencies in the early 1990s. Section 4 discusses the second, ongoing wave of agency creation. Section 5 concludes.

1. What Is a European Agency?

Given the proliferation of institutions, bodies, authorities, centres, foundations, offices, and agencies in the EU and the variations in their functions and legal statuses, it is important to clarify precisely what we mean when we speak of a European agency. European agencies (regardless of the label attached to them) can be defined as EU level public authorities with a legal personality and a certain degree of organizational and financial autonomy that are created by acts of secondary legislation in order to perform clearly specified tasks (Commission 2002: 3, 1996). This definition distinguishes European agencies from other independent bodies established in the Treaties, such as the European Central Bank, the European Monetary Institute or Europol.

The agencies differ significantly in their structures, functions and resources. They perform a variety of tasks ranging from gathering information and providing scientific advice, to conducting compliance inspections, to making binding regulatory decisions, to coordinating networks of national administrators, to administering Community spending programs. Broadly, they can be divided into two categories, (*a*) executive agencies that perform managerial tasks on behalf of the Commission and (*b*) regulatory agencies that provide information and advice, make regulatory decisions and coordinate regulatory networks. Though the vast majority of these agencies have been established under the EU's first pillar (the EC Treaty), more recently agencies have been established under the second and third pillars of the EU. Table 8.1 lists the name, location, year of founding, and primary functions of existing European agencies and those in final stages of the legislative process.

2. The Politics of Eurocracy

European agencies were created first as a political response to a set of functional pressures associated with the 1992 single market programme. As the Commission and analysts such as Majone suggest, the growing regulatory burden (in terms of data gathering, monitoring, rule-making, licensing) associated with the completion of the single market programme served as an important motivation behind the creation of European agencies. However, these functional pressures[3] did not press inexorably for European agencies as a solution and certainly did not dictate the shape that agencies eventually took. Indeed, the most straightforward means by which to meet the regulatory demands associated with the single market programme would have been to expand the Commission's staff and resources. Moreover, functional pressures alone cannot explain the ongoing disagreements between the Commission, Council and Parliament over the design of European agencies.

To explain the creation of European agencies we must understand how strategic interactions between the Council, the Commission and, in some cases, the EP shaped their design (Kelemen 2002: 95). The European agencies are bureaucratic agents of the EU's political principals. Clearly the member states in the Council are powerful principals in the EU context (Pollack 1997; Franchino 2000). With its growing power in the 1990s, the EP also emerged

[3] The impact of the functional pressures associated with complex regulation on a pan-European scale parallels in important respects the causal mechanism Jabko and Parsons term 'technical change'.

TABLE 8.1. *European Union Agencies*

Name	Location	Year	Primary Function
Cedefop—European Centre for the Development of Vocational Training	Thessaloniki	1975	Dialogue/ information
Eurofound—European Foundation for the Improvement of Living and Working Conditions	Dublin	1975	Dialogue/ information
EEA—European Environment Agency	Copenhagen	1990	Information
ETF—European Training Foundation	Torino	1990	Executive
EMCDDA—The European Monitoring Centre for Drugs and Drug Addiction	Lisbon	1993	Information
EMEA—The European Agency for the Evaluation of Medicinal Products	London	1993	Regulation
OHIM—Office for Harmonization in the Internal Market	Alicante	1993	Regulation
EU OSHA—European Agency for Safety and Health at Work	Bilbao	1994	Dialogue/ information
CPVO—Community Plant Variety Office	Angers	1994	Regulation
CdT—Translation Centre for the Bodies of the European Union	Luxembourg	1994	Executive
EUMC—European Monitoring Centre on Racism and Xenophobia[4]	Vienna	1997	Information
EAR—European Agency for Reconstruction	Thessaloniki	2000	Executive
European Union Institute for Security Studies	Paris	2001	Pillar II/ Information
European Union Satellite Centre	Torrejón de Ardoz	2001	Pillar II/ Information
EFSA—European Food Safety Authority	Parma	2002	Regulation/Risk Assessment

[4] In 2003, the Council agreed to extend the mandate of the Centre and transform it into a Fundamental Rights Agency. The Commission plans to propose a regulation for the new agency in 2005.

TABLE 8.1. (*Continued*)

Name	Location	Year	Primary Function
Eurojust—European Body for the Enhancement of Judicial Cooperation[5]	The Hague	2002	Pillar III/ Coordination
EMSA—European Maritime Safety Agency	Lisbon	2002	Regulation/ Inspection
EASA—European Aviation Safety Agency	Cologne	2002	Regulation
ENISA: European Network and Information Security Agency	Heraklion	2004	Information/ Coordination
ERA: European Railway Agency	Lille/Valenciennes	2004	Regulation
European Centre for Disease Prevention and Control	Stockholm	2004	Information
European Defense Agency	Brussels	2004	Pillar III/ Coordination
European Agency for the Management of Operational Cooperation at the External Borders	Brussels (temporary location)	2004	Pillar II/ Coordination
Community Fisheries Control Agency (proposed)	Vigo	2006	Monitoring/ Inspection
European Chemicals Agency (proposed)	Helsinki	?	Regulation

as a powerful political principal exerting control over the European agencies. Finally, the European Commission, itself an agent of the Council and Parliament, has used its agenda setting power in the EU's legislative process to shape the design of European agencies.

The interinstitutional politics behind the creation of European agencies has been conditioned by two of the causal mechanisms that Jabko and Parsons highlight in their introduction to this volume—the impact of institutional legacies and efforts to defend or extend democracy. Institutional legacies influenced the politics of agency design in two important respects. First, Commission officials seeking ways to expand the EU's regulatory capacity confronted the fact that European agencies would have to be established on terrain already occupied by national regulatory authorities.

[5] The Constitutional Treaty (Art. III-274(1) calls for transformation of Eurojust into European Public Prosecutors Office charged with investigating and prosecuting cross-border crime.

As discussed below, the need to accommodate existing national regulators helps explain the emergence of a 'network model' for European agencies. Second, institutional legacies in the form of legal requirements concerning the EU's 'institutional balance' limited the scope of delegation to agencies.

Efforts to address the EU's purported democratic deficit and the widespread recognition among European elites of the need to enhance the transparency and accountability of the EU's policy processes have also influenced the politics of agency design. First, pressure to democratize the EU undermined the legitimacy of the opaque, unaccountable comitology system that long underpinned the Commission's regulatory policymaking. European agencies were designed as a more democratically palatable alternative. In contrast to their comitology forbears, European agencies were designed to be more visible, subject to greater transparency requirements and parliamentary and judicial scrutiny.

Building on the principal-agent framework and recognizing the import of the causal mechanisms described above, one can summarize the politics of agency design as follows: Given the Council's (and to a lesser extent the Parliament's) opposition to expanding the Commission, the Commission proposed the establishment of 'autonomous' European agencies as an alternative means by which to expand the EU's regulatory capacity. Though the delegation of routine technical duties to agencies led to a loss of bureaucratic 'turf' for the Commission in some cases, this delegation benefited the Commission insofar as it allowed the Commission to concentrate its resources on its core tasks—policy initiation and policy enforcement (Kelemen 2002; Wilson 1989: 182–83). In its approach to European agencies, the Council of Ministers sought to defend the prerogatives of national regulatory bodies and to limit both growth and potential political or bureaucratic 'drift' (McCubbins *et al.*, 1999) of supranational regulatory bodies. Also, the Council recognized that its existing mechanisms for oversight of EU regulatory processes—the notoriously opaque and unaccountable comitology committees—could not withstand the democratic deficit critique in the long term. These preferences led the Council to support the creation of European level regulatory agencies subject to the requirements that (*a*) they be controlled by management boards dominated by member state representatives, and (*b*) they be designed along a hub and spoke model that integrated national regulatory authorities into their operations. Finally, since the EP became an active player in the politics of agency design in the mid-1990s, it has taken a different approach to bureaucratic oversight than the Council, demanding the establishment of bureaucratic structures and administrative procedures that enhance the transparency and facilitate 'fire-alarm' oversight (McCubbins and Schwartz 1984; Pollack 1997; Franchino 2000: 76; Kelemen 2002: 97). Unlike the resource-rich member states that could oversee the agencies directly through their positions on agency management boards and scientific advisory panels, the Parliament preferred to conduct oversight by enhancing ('fire-alarm') opportunities for actors in civil society to detect and challenge agency malfeasance. These conflicting demands from the EU's political principals have shaped the design of European agencies in terms of the resources they are granted, the administrative procedures they must follow, the judicial scrutiny to which they are subject and the limitations placed on their authority.

3. The First Wave of European Agencies: 1990–94

The 1992 single market programme presented the Commission with a regulatory conundrum. Commission President Delors and other Commission leaders recognized that with its small staff and budget, the Commission was ill equipped to handle the dramatic increase in regulatory tasks associated with the single market initiative. However, the most obvious route to enhancing the EU's regulatory capacity, expanding the Commission, was foreclosed by politics. There was widespread political opposition across the member states to any major expansion of the Commission bureaucracy, and even the EP was apprehensive about significant personnel growth. With attacks on the emerging superstate in Brussels a staple of Eurosceptic rhetoric, the Commission itself was reluctant to be seen as a burgeoning bureaucracy. In this context, the Commission sought novel avenues through which to expand the EU's regulatory capacity and turned to the idea of 'independent' European agencies. The popularity of independent regulatory agencies was growing across EU member states in the late 1980s, and the Commission suggested adopting the agency model at the EU level.[6]

Commission President Delors set the ball rolling in January 1989 by proposing the establishment of a European Environment Agency (EEA). After the success of the EEA proposal, proposals for a variety of agencies emerged from the Commission bureaucracy, and the Commission Secretariat General quickly stepped in to coordinate the process of agency design (Kelemen 2002: 102). Six new European agencies were established between 1990 and 1994.

This 'first wave' resulted from a political compromise between the Commission and the member states in the Council. The first agencies were designed under decision-making procedures that limited the role of the EP to consultation. The Parliament generally supported the Commission's pref-

[6] The idiocyncratic European agencies had been established in 1975 (see Table 8.1), but these did not provide the model for the new wave of agency creation.

erences regarding agencies, but remained a rather passive player in the early stages of agency creation. Beginning with the debates over the EEA, there was ongoing disagreement between the Commission and Council as to what powers should be delegated to the European agencies and what mechanisms for political oversight and control should be put in place. As the price for allowing the Commission to expand the capacity of the EU's regulatory state, the Council demanded firm intergovernmental control of the agencies and narrowly circumscribed their mandates. While the precise outcome varied across agencies, all agencies were subject to the control of management boards composed overwhelmingly of member state representatives. In this sense, the agencies were anything but independent. Rather, as the Commission noted later in the debates concerning the European Food Safety Authority, where responsibilities previously performed by the Commission were transferred to a European agency controlled by an intergovernmental management board, this arguably reduced regulatory independence (Commission 1998). As for their mandates, most agencies were restricted to information-gathering roles, while the Office for Harmonization in the Internal Market (OHIM—Trademarks and Design), the Community Plant Variety Rights Office (CPVO) and the European Agency for the Evaluation of Medicinal Products (EMEA) were given limited regulatory powers (Kreher 1997). While some proponents of the EEA had initially called for the agency to be granted extensive rule-making and inspection powers, neither the EEA nor any of the other first wave agencies were granted such extensive powers. Opposition to such far-reaching delegation of powers came both from member states who opposed excessive centralization of power and from the Commission legal service itself, which emphasized that EU law, in the form of the *Meroni* doctrine, limited the scope for delegation. In short, Meroni prohibited the delegation of broad discretionary powers to bodies not foreseen in the treaties as this could threaten to alter the 'institutional balance' between the primary Community institutions.[7]

The network model at the heart of the design of the new agencies (Dehousse 1997) also reflected the bargain between the Commission and the Council. In essence, the network model served to minimize the natural tension between a growing supranational bureaucracy and existing national bureaucracies by melding the latter into the former. In this model, the European agencies would serve as hubs of regulatory networks with the national authorities their spokes. The European agencies would rely on existing national administrative capacities, in some cases even delegating tasks to national administrations on a rotating basis. At the same time, the

[7] See the discussion of the *Meroni* doctrine below.

European agencies could use their position at the hub of these networks to gradually pressure national administrations to conform to common European norms and practices. As a result, national administrations would not see European agencies as a threat to their existence and in some cases might even see their like-minded European counterparts as allies in domestic struggles.

Finally, the 'decentralization' of EU agencies to locations across the EU member states also served to make the agencies more palatable to member state governments. Not only would the agencies coordinate networks of existing national authorities, they would do so from locations outside Brussels. For the member states, such decentralization presented attractive opportunities for pork barrel politics. Indeed, at the Laeken summit in 2001, heads of state have battled over the locations of a series of new agencies. While such decentralization created some logistical problems for the Commission, this was a small price to pay for the significant expansion of EU regulatory capacities that the agencies could deliver.

The European Agency for the Evaluation of Medicinal Products (EMEA) was among the most significant agencies established in the early 1990s. The EMEA was designed to accelerate the process of assessment and authorization of pharmaceutical products and thus to facilitate the completion of the internal market in pharmaceuticals (Kelemen 2004: 144–9). The Commission overcame the concerns of national drug testing authorities by proposing a network structure that preserved an integral role for these national authorities. Essentially, the EMEA would coordinate a regulatory network in which national authorities would take turns assessing and authorizing pharmaceuticals for the European market, following central guidelines. Finally, the Commission dealt with the legal limitations imposed by the European Court of Justice (ECJ's) *Meroni* doctrine and the institutional balance principle by retaining ultimate responsibility for any drug authorizations. The outcome of the entire EMEA drug assessment process would not be a legally binding approval, but rather a recommendation to the Commission, which would then take responsibility for the legally binding authorization.

4. The Second Wave of European Agencies: 2001—present

European agencies, which first appeared as ad hoc experiments in institutional design, are becoming central elements in the EU's model of governance. The 2001 White Paper on European Governance (Commission 2001) acknowledged the development of European agencies and suggested that the creation and greater empowerment of more such agencies might be a way to improve EU regulation. The White Paper also called for the establishment of a formal framework for the creation, operation and supervision of such agencies. In 2003, the Council adopted a framework (Council of Ministers (EC) No 58/2003) for the creation of the relatively uncontroversial category of 'executive agencies' that perform managerial tasks on behalf of the Commission. As for the more controversial 'regulatory agencies,' in a 2002 Communication (Commission 2002) the Commission proposed a set of guidelines for such a framework and the Commission proposed a draft interinstitutional agreement in 2005 on the basis of this Communication (European Commission, December 2005). Meanwhile, the creation of new agencies has continued apace, with eleven new agencies being created since 2001. The agency model has extended to the EU's second and third pillars with agencies being established in areas such as defence procurement (European Defence Agency) and border control (European Agency for the Management of Operational Cooperation at the External Borders).

The politics of agency design has changed in significant respects in recent years. The central conflicts still concern what the agencies should do, and who should control them. However, the EP has become an increasingly significant player in agency design and oversight. With the growing involvement of the Parliament and heightened profile of existing agencies, questions concerning the transparency and accountability of European agencies have become ever more prominent.

A central bone of contention between the Commission, Parliament and Council remains the design of management boards that oversee the agencies. No uniform model for the composition of these management boards has emerged. Indeed, in a recent report on regulatory agencies, the European Parliament (2004) identified at least ten variants in the structure of boards of existing agencies. The Commission continues to push for structures that would insulate the agencies from traditional intergovernmental politics. In its communication on agencies, the Commission (2002: 9) emphasized that the administrative boards of existing agencies 'fail to take sufficient account of the Community dimension,' which is Eurospeak for saying that the boards serve as fora in which national representatives pursue national interests. Instead the Commission proposed a model where management boards would have fifteen members, with six appointed by the Commission, six by the council and three nonvoting members representing stakeholders. The Parliament acknowledged this as an acceptable model, but expressed a preference for a model in which the Commission would draw up a list of candidates to be submitted to the Parliament for scrutiny and to the Council for final approval (European Parliament 2004). Also, the Parliament has backed away from its earlier demands for direct representation on agency management boards, now preferring to clearly separate itself from agency operations and maintain an outside oversight role. The Council has yet to take a unified stance on the appropriate model for agency management boards (Council 2004). While member state governments agree that member state representatives should constitute the overwhelming majority of board members, the notion that the member states might have to give up on the principle of each state being represented is gaining ground in the Council (Interview, European Commission, December 2004).

Along with the growth of its legislative power, the EP has sought to exert itself as a watchdog of the EU executive, including European agencies. Since the mid-1990s the EP has used its budgetary powers in order to impose accountability requirements on European agencies. Agency budgets fall under the 'noncompulsory' part of EC budget, which enables the EP to hold agency budgets on reserve and discharge funds on a partial, ongoing basis. The use, or even the threat, of this reserve procedure, has enabled the Parliament to impose a variety of accountability requirements on European agencies (Dehousse 1997; Kelemen 2002: 105; Flinders 2004: 536).

The Parliament has also demanded that the agencies adopt formal, transparent and judicially enforceable administrative procedures. Such procedures create opportunities for the Parliament's interest group allies to challenge agency actions and thus to engage in the sort of 'fire-alarm' oversight favored by Congress in the US context (McCubbins and Schwartz 1984). The Parliament first succeeded in pressing such transparency demands in the case of the European Food Safety Authority (EFSA), the founding regulation of which required EFSA to hold public meetings and to specify and publish its internal procedures (Regulation 178/2002, Art. 38).

The founding regulations for the recently established European Aviation Safety Agency (EASA) and the proposed European Railway Agency (ERA) also reflect such transparency and accountability requirements. EASA has been given the authority to issue airworthiness codes and to issue (or suspend or revoke) individual airworthiness and environmental certifications for aircraft products. These decisions are legally binding and clearly have significant impacts on the producers and users of such products. The regulation (Reg. 1592/2002) establishing the EASA requires the agency to establish 'transparent procedures' for issuing certification specifications and demands that the agency 'consults widely' with interested parties according to a fixed timetable and that it 'make a written response to the consultation process' (Art. 43). Similarly, in taking individual decisions on aircraft parts the agency *shall* ensure that the party concerned and any other party with a direct and individual concern be granted a hearing and that the decision state the agency's reasons (Art. 44). Such requirements effectively establish a 'giving reasons requirement' (Shapiro 2002; 2001) and provide the legal basis for interested parties to challenge agency decisions on both substantive and procedural grounds.

Similarly, the founding directive of the proposed European Railway Agency (ERA) requires the agency to consult with prescribed representatives of 'the social partners' (Art. 4) and of organizations representing customers and passengers (Art. 5). The regulation requires the Agency to take 'due account' of these consultations. As in the case of the EASA, it seems likely that the question of whether or not an agency has given such consultations 'due account' may eventually be subject to judicial scrutiny.

Indeed, the founding regulations of European agencies increasingly foresee the likelihood of such legal challenges and make provisions for it. Where early agencies sometimes contained no explicit provisions concerning judicial scrutiny, recently established agencies, such as the EASA, establish rigorous systems of judicial oversight. Private parties that want to challenge EASA decisions will bring cases, in the first instance, to EASA's internal Board of Appeal, whose decisions can then be appealed at to the ECJ.

The second wave of agency creation shows no signs of abating. The mismatch between the Commission's extensive regulatory responsibilities and its inadequate resources remains. Indeed, with the expansion of the EU's policy mandate and the continued political resistance to any substantial growth in the size of the Commission, this mismatch has grown. The growing politicisation of the Commission is likely to encourage even more delegation to European agencies. The Parliamentary censure of the Santer Commission and most recently the forced reshuffle of the proposed Barroso Commission under pressure from the Parliament seem to herald a new era in EU politics. The days when the Commission could be viewed as an independent, technocratic 'superagency' dedicated to the completion of the common market are gone (Majone 2002: 330). The growing politicization of the Commission lends weight to supporters of European agencies, such as Majone, that the independence and credibility of Community regulation can no longer be assured in the context of the Commission. Moreover, the Commission's enforcement of Community law is subject to ever closer Parliamentary scrutiny, and the Commission's monopoly of initiative on new EU policies has been undermined to an extent by the advent of the co-decision procedure. As a result, the Commission leadership has great incentives to focus its limited resources on these core competences and thus is likely to prove more willing to delegate day-to-day regulatory tasks to agencies.

One long-standing legal obstacle to greater delegation is showing signs of giving way. Article 4 of the Rome Treaty as interpreted by the ECJ in *Meroni*[8] establishes a strict nondelegation principle. Scholars of Community

[8] Case 9/56 Meroni & Co. S.p.A. *v*. High Authority of the ECSC [1957–58] ECR 133 for an even more restrictive ruling concerning delegation to bodies not foreseen in the treaties, see Case 98/80 Romano *v*. Institut National d'Assurance Maladie Invalidité [1981] ECR 1241. Also see Everson 1995.

law and the Commission Legal Service itself have long held that *Meroni* limits the delegation of broad, discretionary powers to bodies not foreseen in the treaties. Such delegation threatens to upset the 'institutional balance' between the EU's three primary institutions, and thus can only be allowed through treaty revision. Majone (2002) points out that while the Commission Legal Service continues to adhere to this strict interpretation of *Meroni*, a growing faction within the Commission advocates a looser interpretation of *Meroni* that would allow a broader delegation of discretionary powers to agencies. Strikingly, despite the voluminous academic literature on the *Meroni* doctrine and the great emphasis observers place on it, the ECJ has never relied on *Meroni* to settle subsequent disputes of delegation of powers (Bergström and Rotkirch 2003: 27). In any event, it is difficult to imagine the ECJ severely limiting the remit of an agency that had won the support of the Commission, Council and Parliament (Kelemen 2002: 99). Arguably, *Meroni* has served as a convenient legal justification that helped the Commission retain all rule-making powers while delegating only the more mundane co-ordination and information gathering tasks to agencies. As the Commission's political willingness to delegate rule-making powers increases, its emphasis on *Meroni* is likely to decrease. Indeed, we already see signs of this in the mandate of the recently established EASA, whose rule-making powers make it the most powerful European agency to date (also see Commission 2002:8).

5. Conclusions: Building a New European State?

The growth of European agencies has been one of the most significant developments in the EU's institutional development over the past decade. The European agencies, and the networks of national officials that they coordinate, are emerging as a vital element of the EU's governmental order. The agencies have made virtue of political necessity: they are reliant on national administrations, but they are using their tight coupling with networks of national regulators as a means through which to spread common administrative practices. It is tempting to view the empowerment of European agencies as a diminution of the Commission's control over the EU executive. And indeed, some information gathering, monitoring and decision-making functions that might otherwise have been performed by the Commission were delegated to European agencies. However, for the most part, the resources and responsibilities granted to European agencies were not taken away from the Commission in any sense. Rather, many of the tasks delegated to agencies would otherwise have been performed by obscure comitology committees (Dehousse 1997: 258; Krapohl 2004). In many respects, the first wave of European agencies represented a dramatic upgrading and formalization of the committee system that had long underpinned EU regulatory policymaking.

More recently, with the advent of second and third pillar agencies and the establishment of regulatory agencies with greater rule-making powers, it seems that European agencies have entered a new phase. European agencies have become an accepted part of the EU's institutional architecture. While delegation to agencies raises serious concerns over accountability, a variety of oversight structures and judicial safeguards have been put in place and the EU's primary institutions—the Commission, Parliament and Council—seem willing to grant the agencies even greater responsibilities. With the growing transformation of the Commission from independent regulator to political executive, European agencies may one day be viewed as the true Eurocracy.

References

Alter, K. (2001). *Establishing the Supremacy of European Law: The Making of an International Rule of Law in Europe*. Oxford: Oxford University Press.

Bergström, C. F. and Rotkirch, M. (2003). *Decentralized Agencies and the IGC: A Question of Accountability*. Stockholm: Swedish Institute for European Policy Studies Report No. 14.

Chiti, E. (2004). 'Decentralisation and Integration into the Community Administrations: A New Perspective on European Agencies', *European Law Journal,* 10/4: 402–38.

Cichowski, R. A. (2001). 'Judicial Rulemaking and the Institutionalization of European Union Sex Equality Policy', in A. Stone Sweet, W. Sandholtz and N. Fligstein (eds.), *The Institutionalization of Europe*. Oxford: Oxford University Press, pp. 113–36.

Commission of the European Communities (1998). *Communication on Food, Veterinary and Plant Health Control and Inspection*. COM (98) 32 final, 28 January, 1998.

—— (2001). *European Governance: A White Paper*. COM (2001) 428 final.

—— (2002). *The Operating Framework for the European Regulatory Agencies*. COM(2002) 718 final.

Council of Ministers. (2003). *Council Regulation (EC) No 58/2003 of 19 December 2002 Laying Down the Statute for Executive Agencies to be Entrusted with Certain Tasks in the Management of Community Programmes*. Official Journal L 011, 16/01/2003 P. 0001–0008.

Council of Ministers (2004). *Council Conclusions on the Commission Communication on 'The operating framework for European Regulatory Agencies'*. Press Release 10746/04 (Presse 203), 28 June.

Dehousse, R. (1997). 'Regulation by Networks in the European Community: The Role of European Agencies', *Journal of European Public Policy,* 4/2: 246–61.

European Parliament (2004). *European Parliament Resolution on the Communication from the Commission: 'The operating framework for the European Regulatory Agencies'*. Document P – TA (2004)0015.

Everson, M. (1995). 'Independent Agencies: Hierarchy Beaters?' the *European Law Journal,*' 1/2: 180–204.

—— Majone, G., Metcalfe, L., and Schout, A. (1999). *The Role of Specialized Agencies in Decentralizing EU Governance*. Brussels: European Commission.

Fligstein, N. and Stone Sweet, A. (2001). 'Institutionalizing the Treaty of Rome', in A. Stone Sweet, W. Sandholtz and N. Fligstein (eds.), *The Institutionalization of Europe*. Oxford: Oxford University Press, pp. 29–55.

Flinders, M. (2004). 'Distributed Public Governance in the European Union', *Journal of European Public Policy*, 11/3: 520–44.

Franchino, F. (2000). 'Control of the Commission's Executive Functions: Uncertainty, Conflict and Decision Rules', *European Union Politics,* 1/1: 63–92.

Kelemen, R. D. (2002). 'The Politics of "Eurocratic" Structure and the New European Agencies', *West European Politics* 25/4: 93–118.

—— (2003). 'The EU Rights Revolution: Adversarial Legalism and European Integration', in Tanja Börzel and Rachel Cichowski (eds.), *The State of the European Union*, Vol. 6: *Law Politics and Society*. Oxford: Oxford University Press.

—— (2004). *The Rules of Federalism: Institutions and Regulatory Politics in the EU and Beyond.* Cambridge, MA: Harvard University Press.

Krapohl, S. (2004). 'Credible Commitment in Non-Independent Regulatory Agencies: A Comparative Analysis of the European Agencies for Pharmaceuticals and Foodstuffs', *European Law Journal,* 10/5.

Kreher, A. (1997). 'Agencies in the European Community—A Step Towards Administrative Integration in Europe', *Journal of European Public Policy,* 4/2: 225–45.

Majone, G. (1997). 'The New European Agencies: Regulation by Information', *Journal of European Public Policy,* 4/2: 262–75.

—— (2000). 'The Credibility Crisis of Community Regulation', *Journal of Common Market Studies,* 38/2: 273–302.

—— (2002). 'Delegation of Regulatory Powers in a Mixed Polity', *European Law Journal,* 8/3: 319–39.

Mattli, W. and Slaughter, A-M. (1998). 'Revisiting the European Court of Justice', *International Organization*, 51/1: 177–209.

McCubbins, M., Noll, R., and Weingast, B. (1999). 'The Political Origins of the Administrative Procedures Act', *Journal of Law, Economics and Organization,* 15/1: 180–217.

McCubbins, M. and Schwartz, T. (1984). 'Congressional Oversight Overlooked: Police Patrols Versus Fire Alarms', *American Journal of Political Science*, 28: 165–179.

Pollack, M. (1997). 'Delegation, Agency and Agenda-Setting in the European Community', *International Organization,* 51/1: 99–134.

Siedentop, L. (2001). *Democracy in Europe*. New York: Columbia University Press.

Shapiro, M. (1997). 'The Problems of Independent Agencies in the United States and the European Union', *Journal of European Public Policy,* 4/2: 276–91.

—— (2001). 'The Institutionalization of European Administrative Space', in A. Stone Sweet, W. Sandholtz, and N. Fligstein (eds.), *The Institutionalization of Europe*. Oxford: Oxford University Press.

—— (2002). 'The Giving Reasons Requirement', in M. Shapiro and A. Stone Sweet (eds.), *On Law, Politics and Judicialization*. Oxford: Oxford University Press.

Skowronek, S. (1982). *Building a New American State: The Expansion of National Administrative Capacities 1877–1920*. Cambridge: Cambridge University Press.

Stone Sweet, A. and Caporaso, J. (1998). 'From Free Trade to Supranational Polity: The European Court and Integration', in W. Sandholtz and A. Stone Sweet (eds.), *European Integration and Supranational Governance*. Oxford: Oxford University Press.

Wilson, J. Q. (1989). *Bureaucracy: What Government Agencies Do and Why They Do It*. New York: Basic Books.

III

Europe's Political Economy

9

Stock Exchange Competition and the Nasdaq Bargain in Europe

ELLIOT POSNER*

One of the most important contemporary developments in global capital markets is the emerging European Union (EU) financial regulatory regime. Progress toward a single financial market in Europe that would lower the costs of capital for governments and corporations has followed an uneven and slow path. Yet in the aftermath of the euro's inauguration in 1999, there has been a substantial push to integrate securities, banking and insurance regulation of member countries, coordinate implementation and enforcement of common rules and create a regional zone of cross-border competition in the financial sectors. These are the immediate aims of the Financial Services Action Plan (FSAP) of March 2000 and the Lamfalussy Process of February 2002, the two high-profile and formal initiatives to shift regulation from the national to the supranational levels (Commission 1999; Lamfalussy 2001). Their effects can already be felt inside the EU and across the Atlantic (Posner 2004*b*).

This chapter, however, explores a prior, less well-known development in the emerging European financial system: a frenzied cross-border battle to imitate a US institution, the Nasdaq Stock Market. Beginning in 1996, the stock exchanges[1] across Europe created new stock markets for smaller companies. Most were deliberately modeled on the US-based market, and several, like the Alternative Investment Market (AIM) in London, the Nouveau Marché in Paris and the now-defunct Neuer Markt in Frankfurt, became household names during the turn-of-the-century boom in international stock prices. To explain financial change in the EU, observers

* In addition to Nicolas Jabko, Craig Parsons, James Morone and the other participants of this volume, I thank Kathleen McNamara, AnnaLee Saxenian, Steven Weber and John Zysman for their comments. I am grateful for the financial support of the UC Berkeley's Institute of European Studies (IES) and Center for German and European Studies (CGES), the Institute on Global Conflict and Cooperation (IGCC) and the MacArthur Foundation.

[1] Stock *exchanges* are organizations. In Europe, until the mid-1990s, they were mutually owned by national financial insiders (brokers, market makers, specialists, banks and other financial intermediaries). Since then, many have demutualized. Stock exchanges supply stock *markets*, sets of rules that provide a regulated arena for the buying and selling of ownership shares in companies (also known as stocks and equities).

today tend to focus almost exclusively on the FSAP, the Lamfalussy Process and other official and formal developments. I show that a narrow emphasis on formal laws and procedures provides an incomplete explanation for changing arrangements and is likely to miss the pivotal role of European supranational political entrepreneurs and informal processes in spurring and shaping outcomes. The burst of institutional copying demonstrates how the politics of regional integration may penetrate ongoing domestic battles over the direction of regulatory change. It illustrates how easily the pressures of cross-border competition within the EU, once sparked, may lead to the speedy adoption of US financial forms. This happened in the new market story despite profound distributive and moral implications and in the absence of serious public debate.

By 'copying the Nasdaq', I mean that the exchanges mimicked the US market's underlying principle, a social bargain about who is allowed to obtain capital from corporate capital markets: Relatively untested young companies, if willing to reveal high levels of financial information, may seek financing from giant pools of investment capital. In Europe, the new bargain opened a source of capital on relatively favorable terms to a class of firms with historically few financing options. Approximately €50 billion flowed into the nearly 1,600 newly listed companies between 1996 and 2003.[2] Having started from a nearly zero base, these figures, even if only modest by US standards, represent a significant reallocation of financial resources.[3]

The introduction of the Nasdaq principle also marks a curious turn in European finance. Stock markets, like other mechanisms that allocate capital, are political institutions, which benefit and harm social groups and economic sectors in different ways. The incentives embodied in the original Nasdaq encourage risk-taking behaviors, which have become defining elements of contemporary US capitalism. Venture capitalists and others invest millions in start-up companies (some cobbled together in garages by recent college graduates), in large part because the Nasdaq rules permit them to sell shares at a later date to the public and amass huge personal fortunes for entrepreneurs and themselves. These market rules, in short, affect the risks US citizens must bear, how they save for retirement, where they work, their job security and ability to buy homes, and the disparity between rich and poor.

European financial systems, even in the UK, have historically provided a different set of incentives, and this is why the introduction of the US-style

[2] These calculations are based on publicly available statistics on the exchanges' websites. My estimates are almost identical to those of Bottazzi and Da Rin (2002). The only significant difference is my inclusion of London's Alternative Investment Market (AIM). While not a Nasdaq copy, its origins stem from the same process discussed below.

[3] Based on statistics from the World Federation of Exchanges, the amount of new capital raised through the US Nasdaq during the same period was approximately US $400 billion.

markets is surprising and important. The high-risks, high-rewards world of the US market is antithetical to post-World War II social compromises that led European governments to protect citizens from the extremes of capitalism. The new markets undermine these social bargains, exposing Europeans to the wild swings of global financial markets by introducing a novel asset, shares in dicey untested companies. When prices were rapidly increasing, households in the UK, France and Germany were among the biggest beneficiaries. But following the March 2000 international market crash, they paid dearly.[4]

The Nasdaq copies also triggered an inflow of internationally mobile capital into funds managed by European venture capitalists. Until then, venture capitalism, at least in its US variety, hardly existed in Europe. With the new markets, venture capitalists began to believe they could make profits by investing in start-ups, just like their US counterparts.[5] The markets

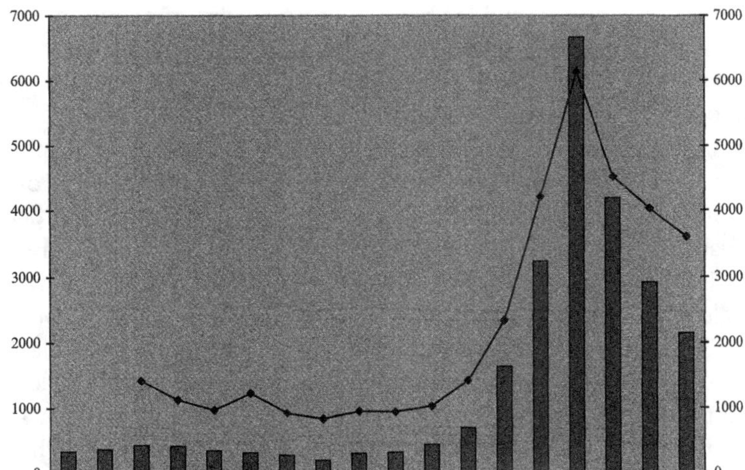

	1986	1987	1988	1989	1990	1991	1992	1993	1994	1995	1996	1997	1998	1999	2000	2001	2002	2003
Millions of Euros	336	373	432	422	351	319	278	201	310	321	444	711	1638	3240	6664	4184	2919	2139
Number of Financings			1427	1130	974	1231	930	843	958	939	1031	1424	2332	4202	6130	4516	4026	3606

GRAPH 9.1. Venture capital investments in early stage companies, Europe.
Source: EVCA.

[4] Based on percentages of institutional versus household buyers, I estimate the following: German households lost approximately sixty-five billion euros, as share prices on the Neuer Markt fell between April 2000 and May 2001. French households lost approximately twenty billion euros on the Nouveau Marché during the same period. Interviews with executives of Parisbourse (Paris, May 18, 2000) and Deutsche Boerse (Frankfurt, May 16, 2000).

[5] Venture capitalists make profits by divesting from their risky investments in smaller companies at a higher price than they paid. Selling shares of those companies to the public through a stock market is the preferred mechanism to do so. This is why the new markets changed venture capitalists' expectations about taking high risks in Europe. Interviews with EVCA executive (Zaventem, April 26, 2000) and prominent European venture capitalist (Leuven, April 26, 2000).

thus opened Europe to one of the riskiest forms of capitalism. Anticipating that 70–90 percent of investments in young companies will fail and lead to closures, job losses and social dislocation, the venture capital business plan challenges the values underpinning European welfare states.

These potentially far-reaching effects on European societies are not the only reason the new markets are interesting. Their origins involved a sudden policy switch on the part of the empowered financial elites who had traditionally controlled the production of new markets. Until 1994, national stock exchanges that created the new stock markets had vehemently opposed adopting the Nasdaq form in Europe and, as jealously protected national organizations, faced little foreign competition, especially in the smaller company sector. In fact, they had used government-delegated authorities to supply stock markets of their choosing. Only under the pressure of cross-border competition did the exchanges adopt the Nasdaq form.

What explains this sudden burst of cross-border competition in a financial domain historically characterized by protected national markets? Financial globalization, the leading explanation for increased competition, does a poor job of accounting for the rivalry that ended in Europe's Nasdaq copies. The timing simply does not correspond to rising levels of capital mobility, and economic forces were not enough to shape the preferences of or empower financiers. To the contrary, the markets emerged from a political context infused with concerns about Europe's international competitiveness vis-à-vis the USA and the process of integrating national financial systems into a single regional market. The rivalry among the new markets, however, did not arise from the type of politics or the policy tools that EU scholars typically expect. The bulk of the literature focuses on formal legislation, legal appeals and officially delegated powers. But new EC legislation did not spark competition by lowering barriers to trade and foreign firms, harmonizing regulations or introducing the principle of mutual recognition; nor did the European Commission receive newly delegated powers or launch formal legal cases against alleged anticompetitive behavior of firms and governments, adjudicated by supranational judges.

The new markets are instead the offspring of political entrepreneurs who sparked competition with a different policy instrument, a new market entrant. Behind the scenes, supranational bureaucrats backed a pan-European Nasdaq copy called Easdaq, whose potential success promised to create a region-wide sector of entrepreneurial finance and challenge the national monopolies of established stock exchanges. The possibility of losing out to a pan-European upstart rival prompted the exchanges to create Nasdaq copies of their own and drew them into a contest across borders. They did so despite the many good reasons for believing that the Europe of the 1990s lacked regulatory and social foundations necessary for US-style markets.

This episode of competition via informal supranational entrepreneurship provides evidence in support of three of the five mechanisms this book's introductory chapter identified as drivers of institutional change. First, the Commission intervention in Easdaq was in part a deliberate bid for EU political and economic global leadership. The Brussels officials had since the early 1980s wanted to encourage venture capitalism as a means for bolstering Europe's international competitiveness in high technology sectors and preventing the exodus of EU engineers, technology and capital to the USA. They believed the creation of a region-wide stock market, such as Easdaq, would attract venture capitalist activity.

Second, the intergovernmental political process was a necessary condition for the intervention to draw the exchanges into competition, but its impact did not follow a linear cause-and-effect trajectory of bargaining between preestablished national positions. The history of the Nasdaq copies illustrates how in a complex polity like the EU, intergovernmental compromises foster high levels of uncertainty for market participants, opportunities for political entrepreneurs and unanticipated outcomes (Stone Sweet and Sandholtz 1998; Stone Sweet *et al.* 2001). EC legislation that introduced mutual recognition as a principle for integrating the financial services industry left open as many questions as it resolved, especially concerning the degree to which stock exchanges would be able to compete across borders. By liberally interpreting the possibilities for pan-European markets, motivated commission officials fueled uncertainty among the incumbent exchanges. They reacted by creating their own new domestic markets, rather than risk the migration of a new entrepreneurial financial sector to an alternative regional marketplace or to one of the other national exchanges. The Commission officials thus only achieved half of what they wanted. With competing national markets, the EU became a more attractive location for venture capitalist investment, though without the pan-European infrastructure that Commission officials had envisioned. The exchanges, for their part, undermined the Easdaq project but supplied new markets that they would not have created in the absence of the Commission-initiated competition.

Finally, EU institutional idiosyncrasies played a role. Financiers and finance ministries did not in the early 1990s consider Brussels bureaucrats appropriate actors in the capital market policymaking. Nor did the EU civil servants have considerable formal powers in the sector. They were, however, able to take advantage of several EU particularities to enhance their influence. For example, they used the complex organization of their supranational bureaucracy as a resource. The officials who intervened in Easdaq did not have to report to finance ministers and were relatively shielded from the powerful domestic finance–government coalitions that had blocked similar types of innovations in the past. They were also able to reshape the political landscape in ways more favorable to their agenda (Fligstein and Mara-Drita 1996; Barnett and Finnemore 1999; Jabko 1999; Heritier 2001; Mazey and Richardson 2001; Stone Sweet, *et al.* 2001). They mobilized venture capitalists into a European-level interest group in the 1980s, behind which the Brussels officials could pursue their agenda in the 1990s. The commission officials also framed the Easdaq market as a solution to a highly salient political problem: structural unemployment. They did as much as anyone to promote a political discourse that associated the US Nasdaq form with job creation in the USA. The decision by Commission officials to back a proposed market based on the Nasdaq principle, rather than one of many alternative forms, largely reflects this strategic calculation about the best way to overcome opposition to a pan-European market. With Easdaq framed as an answer to Europe's unemployment crisis, the exchanges and their government supporters could not easily oppose the adoption of the American form—which is why they created domestic Nasdaq copies of their own.

I thus trace the cross-border competition that gave rise to the adoption of a US principle for allocating capital to supranational political entrepreneurship. Seeking to integrate a financial sector and improve EU's relative economic competitiveness, Commission officials acted strategically to improve their influence within a highly complex polity.

New financial interests, borne from the Nasdaq copies, are today pressing for another public intervention to overcome fragmentation and create a single, Europe-wide Nasdaq-like market (EVCA 2004). Will policymakers, under pressure to match American economic performance, take a further step towards US-style high-risk finance? This chapter explains why and how Europeans, known for their aversion to the extremes of US capitalism, arrived at this astonishing question, and what the answer tells us about the direction of EU finance and societies.

1. The Background

Selling shares is one of several possible means by which companies acquire capital. Unlike bank lending, stock market financing involves large numbers of dispersed investors. In contrast to corporate bond markets, it requires companies to exchange ownership (or equity) for capital. In the post-World War II decades, national arrangements for allocating capital were relatively sealed off from one another and developed in strikingly different ways. Varying reliance on markets and public and private bank lending affected the ability of governments to control the distribution of capital and therefore the types of companies receiving it (Zysman 1983). The French state-dominated system, for instance, which placed significant discretion in the hand of government officials, was distinct from the credit-based German system built around cartels of private and public banks. Both of these systems depended heavily on bank intermediation, however, as opposed to British arrangements that let large numbers of market participants distribute financial resources to big corporations through stock markets but left smaller companies to rely on banks.

Scholars debate the effects of financial globalization (primarily high levels of capital mobility) on national financial systems, disagreeing over the degree to which markets have replaced bank and government financing (Vogel 1996; Deeg and Perez 2000; Laurence 2001; Verdier 2003). In the Europe of the 1980s and early 1990s, reforms to national financial systems occurred at different times and unevenly. Established firms and exchanges had developed vested interests in their own systems and slowed change processes or redirected it in ways that perpetuated protectionist arrangements. One striking consequence was the dearth of cross-border competition in most areas of finance (Story and Walter 1997).

1.1. The Stock Market Solution: Improving Smaller Company Financing

Despite a history of efforts in Europe to improve financing options for smaller companies, the above pattern took on an exaggerated form in this sector, where national banks, government programs and networks of friends and family were the main sources of external capital. During the economic crises of the 1970s, politicians and policymakers focused the political spotlight on smaller companies and their difficulty in obtaining capital. They saw these firms, especially entrepreneurial ones in high-technology sectors, as seedbeds of innovation, job creation, economic growth and enhanced international competitiveness. Pressuring their stock exchanges to improve financing options for young companies by creating new stock markets was one national government response.

Instead of copying the Nasdaq, which was launched in 1971 and already becoming a sensation on the continent, the exchanges and their governments experimented with alternative forms that did not require young firms to reveal high levels of information about their internal finances. Although these national markets looked very different from one another, they all reflected, to a large extent, the protectionist nature of their respective stock exchanges. Low levels of financial information, reported according to domestic accounting standards, ensured that only locals were willing to invest in listed firms. The exchanges also made sure that the best young companies on the 1980s markets would feed upward to replenish the pool of stocks traded on the main national markets, which is why they were dubbed ‘feeder markets'. This feeder process and the relatively small investor base undermined these early experiments and limited their ability to improve conditions for young firms. But they also ensured that financing of smaller companies would remain the preserve of domestic banks, brokers, accountants and other service providers.

With the failure of the feeders in the aftermath of the 1987 international stock market crash, the national exchanges and governments again returned to the question of smaller company markets. Once again, the exchanges rejected the Nasdaq principle, continuing a decade-long pattern of blocking the US form's adoption in Europe. They perceived the Nasdaq model as a threat and believed it naïve to think it would work in a place with very different regulatory traditions. The brokers and banks that owned the exchanges did not have the expertise or the available capital to benefit from the US form and worried its adoption would favor foreign and especially US companies and leave most locals at a disadvantage on their own turf. Governments, for their part, increasingly saw the financial services industry as a strategic sector that combined international prestige, relatively inexpensive capital, high-paying jobs and a potential tool for industrial policy. Concern about the place of their countries' financial services industries in an anticipated single European financial system led them to back their exchanges, even if it undermined other goals, such as promoting smaller companies.

Despite a common theme of opposition to the Nasdaq form, the various domestic debates about what to do in response to the failed feeders produced dissimilar outcomes. In April 1994, for example, the London Stock Exchange (LSE) announced the closure of its 1980s market, the Unlisted Securities Market (USM), with implicit support from the UK Treasury.[6] In February 1993 the Paris Exchange,[7] following a study by the French securities regulator, implemented a series of incremental reforms to its 1980s market, the Second Marché. With little widespread perception of a smaller company financing problem in Germany, the Frankfurt Exchange left its 1980s smaller company markets largely unchanged.

Within months of these domestic-level deliberations, the exchanges abruptly shifted course, announcing the creation of new national markets, most modeled on the Nasdaq principle. They were reacting to the perceived threat of a new competitor, Easdaq, a pan-European Nasdaq copy, proposed in June 1994 and created by a group of venture capitalists, supported by the Commission. The exchanges feared that Easdaq would capture a future entrepreneurial financial sector. The LSE reacted first with a competitive

[6] Letters between Chancellor of the Exchequer and CISCO leader, March 1993. Available in CISCO (now Quoted Company Alliance) archives in London.

[7] The Paris stock exchange was the SBF, then the Paris bourse and now, after its merger with the Amsterdam, Lisbon, and Brussels exchanges, Euronext.

response, announcing the creation of AIM in September 1994, just five months after deciding to end their experimentation in smaller company stock markets. The Paris exchange moved next, in February 1995, with the announcement of plans for the Nouveau Marché. Within a few years, nearly every national exchange in Europe had entered the cross-border competition over which would supply the future Nasdaq of Europe.

Table 9.1 illustrates the twenty-five year pattern from feeders to Nasdaq copies. Traditional stock markets required companies in search of capital to be large and have relatively long histories and profit records. The 1980s feeder markets reduced these barriers that prevented smaller companies from listing. Unlike in the case of the feeders, however, the guiding principle of the Nasdaq copies demands companies reveal high levels of information. In most cases (Frankfurt, Paris, Brussels, Amsterdam, and London), the exchanges devised new informational requirements that went well beyond the minimum national regulatory standards, though the degree to which the exchanges lived up to and enforced them varied.[8]

Frankfurt's Deutsche Boerse went the furthest, requiring companies on the Neuer Markt to provide all public information in English, supply quarterly reports, and accounts in the US Generally Accepted Accounting Principles (USGAAP), International Accounting Standards (IAS) or national standards with reconciliation. At the time, not even the most established companies listed on the main stock markets had to follow such high standards (Fuhrmans 2000; Johnson 2000). When stock prices on the Neuer Markt collapsed due largely to scandals rooted in poor compliance with the new rules, the exchange at first redoubled its enforcement efforts. Unable to restore the Neuer Markt's reputation, however, the Frankfurt Exchange in 2003 created Prime Standard, its second market in ten years underpinned by the Nasdaq bargain. This one had even stronger rules that more closely mirrored those governing the original US market.[9] Rigorous informational standards also became the pattern on those new markets originally more Nasdaq-like in principle than in practice. The Paris bourse and LSE both reacted to early problems with their new markets by tightening standards. Both exchanges subsequently added a second market that more closely conformed to the Nasdaq rules.[10]

[8] For details, see Posner 2002; 2004*a*.

[9] See *www.deutscheboerse.de* and Barber 2001; Benoit 2001*a*, *b* and Burghof and Hunger 2004.

[10] After first making AIM's rules more rigorous, the LSE in 1999 created Techmark in reaction to the Neuer Markt's apparent success and AIM's apparent inability to compete (Mandell 1997: 8–10). In 1996, the Paris exchange brought the Nouveau Marche's rules more in line with Nasdaq's. In 2001, Euronext created NextEconomy, which requires much more stringent informational standards than did the Nouveau Marché (Financial Times 1996; Euronext 2001).

TABLE 9.1. *Proposals for smaller company stock markets in Europe, 1977–2003*

Year	Name of Market and Owner	Status	Principle
1977	Compartiment Spécial, Fr Exchange	Closed	French Feeder
1978	Mercato Ristretto/Expandi, It Exchange	Operating	Italian Feeder
1980	Unlisted Securities Market, Br Exchange	Closed	British Feeder
1982	Bors 3, De Exchange	Closed	Danish Feeder
1982	Officiele Parallel Markt, Ne Exchange	Closed	Dutch Feeder
1982	Segundo Mercado, Barcelona Exchange	Closed	Spanish Feeder
1982	Swedish OTC Market, Swe Exchange	Closed	Swedish Feeder
1983	Second Marché I, Fr Exchange	Reformed	French Feeder
1984	Stock Exchange II, Bors II, Nor Exchange	Closed	Norwegian Feeder
1984	Second Marché, Be Exchange	Reformed	Belgian Feeder
1985	ECU–EASD, Private Actors	Never Opened	Pan-European Nasdaq
1986	Segundo Mercado, Balbao Exchange	Operating	Spanish Feeder
1986	Segundo Mercado, Madrid Exchange	Operating	Spanish Feeder
1986	Segundo Mercado, Valencia Exchange	Never Opened	Spanish Feeder
1987	Geregelter Markt, Ge Exchange	Closed	German Feeder
1987	Third Market, Br Exchange	Closed	British Feeder
1989	EASDAQ I, UK (Scotland), Private Actors	Never Opened	National Nasdaq
1989	European OTC Market, Private Actors	Never Opened	Pan-European Nasdaq
1989	Eur. Securities Market, Private Actors	Never Opened	Pan-European Nasdaq
1992	Dutch Participation Exchange, Ne Exchange	Closed	Dutch Alternative
1992	Eur. Priv. Equity Exchange, Br Private Actors	Never Opened	British Alternative
1992	Mercato Locale Del Nord Ovest, Turin Exch.	Never Opened	Italian Alternative
1993	EASDAQ–UK, Private Actors	Never Opened	National Nasdaq
1993	ECASE, Br Private Actors	Never Opened	National Nasdaq
1993	The Enterprise Market, Br Exchange/Private	Never Opened	National Nasdaq
1993	The National Market, Br Exchange/Private	Never Opened	British Alternative
1993	Second Marché II, Fr Exchange	Operating	French Feeder
1994	MESEC, Fr Exchange	Never Opened	Pan-European Nasdaq
1994	Mercato Telematico delle Imprese, It Exchange	Never Opened	Italian Feeder

TABLE 9.1. (*Continued*)

Year	Name of Market and Owner	Status	Principle
1995	Alternative Investment Market, Br Exchange	Operating	British Alternative
1995	Electronic Share Interchange, Private Actors	Never Opened	British Alternative
1995	Mittelstandmarkt Bremen, Ge Exchange	Never Opened	National Nasdaq
1996	EASDAQ, Private Actors	Closed	Pan-European Nasdaq
1996	Nouveau Marché, Fr Exchange	Operating	National Nasdaq
1997	Euro.NM Belgium, Be Exchange	Operating	National Nasdaq
1997	Euro.NM Amsterdam, Ne Exchange	Operating	National Nasdaq
1997	Neuer Markt, Ge Exchange	Closed	National Nasdaq
1999	SWX New Market, Swz Exchange	Closed	National Nasdaq
1999	NM-List, Fi Exchange	Operating	Finnish Alternative
1999	Techmark, Br Exchange	Operating	National Nasdaq
1999	Nuovo Mercato, It Exchange	Operating	National Nasdaq
1999	SMAX, Ge Exchange	Closed	National Nasdaq
1999	Austrian Growth Market, Au Exchange	Closed	National Nasdaq
2000	Nuevo Mercado, Sp Exchange	Operating	National Nasdaq
2000	ITEQ, Ir Exchange	Operating	National Nasdaq
2000	iX-Nasdaq Merger, Br-Ge Exchanges	Never Opened	Binational Nasdaq
2001	Nasdaq Europe, US Exchange	Closed	Pan-European Nasdaq
2002	NextEconomy/NextPrime, Euronext	Operating	Multinational Nasdaq
2003	Prime Standard, Ge Exchange	Operating	National Nasdaq

2. The Origins of Competition and the New Markets[11]

The cross-border contest that pressured stock exchanges to produce Europe's new markets did not emerge from increases in capital mobility, formal Commission laws or ECJ legal decisions. Its origins instead lie in the political entrepreneurship of EC officials who fostered and then took advantage of conditions that made regional-level competition likely. This section uses the historical record to describe the Commission's motivations and strategies and to explain the intended and unintended consequences of their actions.

[11] For a more detailed version of this section, see Posner 2002; 2004*a*. On the origins of Easdaq, see Weber and Posner 2000.

2.1. Motivations and Strategies of the European Commission Officials

National government officials were not alone in advocating smaller company stock markets. Career civil servants from two subdivisions of the European Commission were also ardent promoters.[12] In the late 1970s, a small group endorsed the idea of venture capital as a solution to the widely perceived problem that Europe lagged behind the USA in the area of technological innovation, causing economic problems such as unemployment, slow growth and a lack of international competitiveness.[13] Perceiving US-style venture capitalism as a source of innovation, they set out to make Europe's regulatory and financial arrangements more conducive to venture capital investment. Since venture capitalists rely on stock markets to make profits, the Brussels officials adopted the goal of promoting smaller company stock markets.

The domestic politicians and officials behind the 1980s feeder markets had all sought to promote *national* solutions. The Commission's efforts, by contrast, championed *European* solutions. This preference meant very little in the 1980s, as Brussels exerted only modest influence over financial policy-making. In 1994, however, the Commission's predilection for European solutions, reflected in the Easdaq proposal, proved critically important, as the new market's pan-European scope was a main reason the exchanges perceived the market as a competitive threat.

Brussels officials favored regional-level policies because of their constitutive role as supranational bureaucrats overseeing the European integration process. As an abundance of empirical scholarship demonstrates, Commission civil servants are inclined to interpret problems in terms of fragmented national economies unable to compete with large US markets and see solutions in further integration.[14] Two decades of reports, studies, proposals, policies and interviews substantiate this pattern in the case of the commission officials involved in smaller company stock market issues (Commission 1978; 1984; 1985; 1990; 1993*b*; 1994*b*; 1995*b*; von Moltke 1996).[15] The officials believed the biggest obstacle to venture capitalism in Europe and the benefits it promised was the absence of a regionally integrated financial market. Without it, they feared Europe's entrepreneurs, engineers, capital and tech-

[12] The subdivisions that promoted the Nasdaq form were Innovation, formerly DG13, and Small-and-Medium-Sized Enterprises (SMEs), formerly DG23.

[13] Commission 1978; 1984; 1985. Interview with European Commission official, DG Enterprise, Innovation Policy (Luxembourg, May 5, 2000).

[14] For a recent discussion of the commonly held assumption that Commission officials are competence-maximizers, see Pollack 2003: 35.

[15] Telephone interview with former DG13 official (May 4, 2000). Interviews with official from the former DG13 (Luxembourg, May 5, 2000), official from the former DG2 (Luxembourg, June 7, 1999) and officials from the former DG23 (Brussels, June 1997). Written correspondence with DG Enterprise official (May 8, 2001).

nology would migrate to the US. Even those officials opposed to the Easdaq scheme favored regional markets in principle.[16] Their opposition was based on arguments about the feasibility of such markets given that regulation remained at the national level.[17]

2.2. Five Proposals, One Intervention

On at least four occasions before their 1994 intervention, commission officials considered proposals for a pan-European stock market.[18] They came close to intervening with subsidies in 1989. In the wake of the Single European Act and the run-up to a single European market, the idea of a pan-European smaller company market was taken up by an interdivisional group, organized to explore ways to push along the regional integration project and overseen by the Commission's Secretariat General's office.[19]

The proposals failed to win Commission support despite a growing internal coalition, largely because at the end of the day prointervention officials did not believe they could overcome opposition from the national government–stock exchange coalition.[20] Resistance within the Commission came primarily from those with closest relations to finance ministries and exchanges.[21] Their subdivision had been transformed in 1980 into the service charged with the highly politicized task of facilitating financial integration. They were against the pan-European stock market, in part, because of the opposition from their constituents. Reflecting the views of their 'negotiating partners'—especially the German universal banks who owned the Frankfurt Exchange[22]—the officials argued that if a pan-European market for entrepreneurial firms were economically viable, the exchanges and other financial actors would have created one. These civil servants also had pragmatic concerns about the lack of an official regulatory foundation in Europe for US-style entrepreneurial activity.

[16] Others have found a wider range of views in their studies of the European Commission. See Cram 1994; Hooghe 2001.

[17] Interview with an official from the former DG15 (Brussels, June 8, 2004).

[18] They were ECU–EASD (1985), EASDAQ I (1989), EOTC (1989) and ESM (1989). See Table 9.1.

[19] Six DGs participated in addition to the Secretariat General's office: DG2 (Economic Affairs), DG13 (Information and Innovation), DG15 (Financial Institutions and Company Law), DG16 (Regional Policy), DG28 (Credit and Investment), and DG23 (SMEs, Enterprise).

[20] DG13's new allies were DG16 and, especially, the newly created DG23 (SFE 1989).

[21] These officials worked primarily in DG15.

[22] Interview with Schulman and Sundberg of the ECU–EASD proposal (Geneva, May 8, 2000).

2.3. *Three New Conditions of the European Commission's Making*

Commission officials finally intervened in support of Easdaq in 1994. Three developments, largely of their own making, gave them confidence that an intervention might have broad repercussions and withstand the expected confrontation with the stock exchanges and their supporters inside the commission and national governments. First, there was now in place a core group of European venture capitalists, organized under the European Venture Capital Association (EVCA), ready to take advantage of any support the commission was willing to give. The creation of EVCA was the Brussels officials' first important action to promote European venture capitalism. In 1983, they helped forge a European-level political voice for venture capitalists by instigating the creation of and then supporting EVCA (Commission 1981; 1982; 1983). In 1994, EVCA became the vehicle through which the officials could pursue their goals.

There was a consensus among European venture capitalists in the early 1990s that their industry faced a crisis, which they dubbed the 'exits problem'. They wanted new stock markets that would allow them to divest (i.e. exit) from their investments in risky companies. From the perspective of European venture capitalists, an appropriate stock market was one that attracted numerous buyers, especially international institutional investors, managers of giant pools of mobile capital, whose participation was expected to create strong demand (and high valuations) for the risky shares.

Nevertheless, even the venture capitalists were deeply divided over which institutional form would best attract these market participants and thereby solve the exits problem.[23] Some thought a new market was unnecessary because in the age of mobile capital European companies could list on the US Nasdaq itself. Most, however, thought this would limit stock market financing to a small group of European companies and argued for new Europe-based markets. Still, intense conflicts over the appropriate institutional form for new European markets remained. Some venture capitalists wanted to avoid confrontation with national financial elites by leaving control to the national exchanges. Others believed the exchanges would never create markets to meet their needs and argued for independent Nasdaq copies. Even those advocating the US institutional form were split over whether the markets should be national or pan-European. Ultimately, by backing a faction of EVCA venture capitalists promoting Easdaq, the Commission officials tipped the balance in favor of the pan-European Nasdaq form.[24]

[23] Anslow 1993*a*, *b*; Cohen 1994; EVCA 1994*c*; Peeters 1994. Telephone interview with former Secretary General of EVCA (April 27, 2000).

[24] As early as February 1993, independent reports from EVCA's Business Seminar in Venice show that Commission officials were welcoming proposals for a Nasdaq-like project. 'Visit to the European Commission,' August 8, 1993, CISCO Archives. Interview

The proposal for Easdaq first surfaced in an EVCA working group headed by Jos Peeters, a leading Belgian venture capitalist. Peeters represented the faction among EVCA's members who believed the only solution to their 'exits crisis,' was a pan-European Nasdaq-like market independent of national stock exchanges, despite the conflicts it might foster with the national financial establishments. For Commission officials, encouraging Europe's companies and financiers to use the US-based Nasdaq undermined their objective of creating rival financial markets in Europe. They thought Easdaq's pan-European design, by melding nationally fragmented markets, would promote this goal and, for reasons explained below, believed that the Nasdaq form would help overcome expected opposition.

The role of political entrepreneurs in shaping the preferences of venture capitalists runs counter to leading ideas about how firms develop public policy agendas. Many scholars argue that investors, receiving clear price signals and feeling competitive pressures from the international economy, know what they want in domestic arrangements and then demand that regulators and politicians adopt their preferred institutional forms (Frieden and Rogowski 1996; Laurence 2001). European venture capitalists, as we have seen, did not have clear preferences. Rather, political actors in the end played the central role in shaping EVCA's proposals for stock markets. In the 1980s, the usual political entrepreneurs taking on this type of role came from national ministries or regulators who sought to adjust national financial systems to a changing global economy. The Nasdaq copy story shows how in the EU of the early 1990s supranational actors, Commission officials, even without formally delegated authorities could influence institutional change processes.

A second reason Brussels officials believed Easdaq might withstand the expected resistance was the presence of a political discourse in Europe about job-creation and the Nasdaq Stock Market in the USA. Structural unemployment by the early 1990s had become a highly salient political issue across Europe. The civil servants first exploited the aura surrounding the US market by promoting the argument that a Nasdaq in Europe would have the same job-creation effects as the original had in the USA (Schmidt 1984; EVCA 1985; Commission 1990; Bannock 1994; Commission 1994; EVCA 1994*a*, *b*; Hayter 1994; Commission 1995; Coopers and Lybrand 1995. Also, see Weber and Posner 2001). They then framed Easdaq as a solution to Europe's unemployment problem. It was primarily for this strategic reason that the commission officials preferred the Nasdaq form and backed the

with former DG13 official (Luxembourg, July 5, 2000). European Commission officials in attendance represented DGs 13, 16, 18 and 23 (EVCA 1993). Also see, Commission 1994*a*.

Easdaq proposal among the many alternatives.[25] Their objective was to make it difficult for national stock exchanges and their respective governments to oppose the pan-European market. With the benefit of hindsight, we see that the strategy was only partially successful. The exchanges felt pressure to embrace the Nasdaq form, but not the pan-European scope of Easdaq, about which the Commission officials cared most. The resulting competing national Nasdaq imitations, while improving the landscape for venture capitalist investment and smaller company finance in Europe, fell short of establishing the envisioned region-wide market.

Finally, the Commission officials liberally interpreted new EC legislation to strengthen the legitimacy of the intervention. The long-awaited passage of the 1993 Investment Services Directive (ISD) extended the principle of mutual recognition, a form of shared sovereignty, to European stock exchanges. At least in principle, an exchange regulated in one EU country could operate in another via electronic networks and computer terminals (Steil 1998).

The importance of the ISD for smaller company finance, however, did not lie only or primarily in the content of the actual text (there was no mention of a pan-European stock market, let alone the Nasdaq institutional form) or the precise intentions of the member governments. Rather, its importance, like that of so many other pieces of EC legislation, stemmed largely from the opportunities it offered political entrepreneurs. No one, especially not the national stock exchanges, knew what the implications of a European 'passport' in the financial services would mean. The Commission officials interpreted these unknowns and uncertainties as an opportunity, leading them to believe that an intervention in Easdaq would foster a sense of new possibility and thereby gather support and increase its chances of survival.

2.4. An Intervention

The immediate intervention took the form of financial support for two preliminary studies, followed by subsidies for the early months of operations.[26] Funds for Easdaq's venture capitalists came from two spending programs, the second phase of the Strategic Programme for Innovation and Technology Transfer 1989–93 (SPRINT) and a multiannual program

[25] Telephone interview with Commission official, formerly with DG13 (May 4, 2000). Interview with Commission official, DG23 (Brussels, June 1997).

[26] Because it was privately owned, commission officials were prohibited from giving financial resources directly to Easdaq. They instead funded the European Association of Securities Dealers (EASD), a non-profit organization, set up in 1994 for this purpose. Interview with former EVCA official (London, April 1999) and DG2 official (Luxembourg, June 7, 1999). Written communication from DG Enterprise official (May 8, 2001).

approved by the government representatives for small and medium-sized enterprises that ran from 1993 to 1996.[27]

For a short period the Paris Exchange also flirted with the idea of supporting the venture capitalists. But once it pulled out and Commission support became public, an angry backlash broke out. Ministers of Finance supported their respective stock exchanges' vehement opposition to the Commission's 'interference' in creating Easdaq, claiming it was an illegitimate actor in the financial realm. In the UK, the Treasury maintained its position that private market actors alone should determine the supply of new markets.[28] In France, the Trésor and the stock exchange together rallied to oppose the Easdaq project and enlisted in the battle Edith Cresson, one of France's two Commissioners and former Prime Minister.[29]

The officials received cover against the onslaught from other Commissioners, the politically appointed leaders of the Commission. Those in charge of enterprise policy staunchly supported DG23's top official and the Easdaq project. They gave Director General Dr Heinrich von Moltke and his staff the green light to carry out actions in support of Easdaq, rejected the complaints of fellow Commissioners at the College level and showed very little contrition for doing so. Speaking at an Easdaq conference in June 1996, von Moltke conveyed the sentiment of his officials and the Commissioners:

> We at the Commission, and particularly in Directorate General 23, the enterprise policy DG which I head, are very happy to see Easdaq being launched, because it will fill a very real gap in the financing of European Small and Medium-sized Enterprises, or SMEs. It represents one of the fruits of the Commission's policy in this area, and I hope you will forgive me a small touch of pride when I say that had it not been for the Commission's original initiative, we might not all be here today. The proposal would have got off the ground, because it satisfies a market need, but much much later, and with greater uncertainty. (von Moltke 1996)

2.5. Consequences of the Intervention

Until the 1994 Commission-backed Easdaq initiative, the national stock exchanges had not perceived the many proposals for new markets as credible competitive threats. They believed either that a new stock market could not create cross-border competition, that the proposal would crumble on its own

[27] Council Decisions 93/379/EEC, 89/286/EEC and 94/5/EC. See Commission 1989; 1993a.

[28] Letters between Chancellor of the Exchequer and CISCO leader, March 1993. Available in CISCO archives in London.

[29] Interview with Trésor official in the Bureau du Marché Financier (Paris June 1999) and DG13 official (Luxembourg, May 5, 2000). DG15's and the Stock Exchanges' opposition to the Easdaq initiative came out in the open during a FIBV conference in Milan on 6–7 July 1995 6. See especially the comments of Jose Fombellida, DG15, (FIBV 1995).

accord from lack of support, or that their formidable political and financial resources would ensure its failure. Yet the 1994 initiative was different from its predecessors in the ways discussed above: the presence of an organized private sector interest group, an available political discourse about the need for a European Nasdaq copy, new uncertainties generated by the ISD, and at the center, a set of Brussels bureaucrats anxious to exploit all three in pursuit of an independent agenda. In short, because of fifteen years of Commission activism, the EU policy area of smaller company finance had become significantly more institutionalized, making cross-border competition a real possibility.

Brussels' support for the 1994 venture capitalist initiative unleashed a host of new uncertainties for Europe's stock exchanges with three immediate consequences. First, national exchanges felt pressured to react with competitive responses. Was Easdaq to be an alternative market for listing new national firms and attracting national investors and financial service providers? Would the other exchanges support Easdaq or create Nasdaq copies of their own? Uncertain answers to these questions drew each of the exchanges into the contest over who would supply Europe's future Nasdaq copy.

Second, the exchanges imitated the Nasdaq's underlying principle and, to various degrees, its rules.[30] Two reasons explain why they did so rather than adopting one of the alternatives. First, they did not want to be seen as opposing what was perceived by many as a possible solution to Europe's unemployment problem. Second, they sought to attract institutional investors who were familiar with the Nasdaq form and tended to perceive it as a highly efficient institution. To be competitive, the exchanges believed they had to supply a Nasdaq copy or the institutional investors would invest in shares listed on a rival market that better mirrored the US form.

This rapid shift in behavior is more evidence against leading theories about the role of global capital. The timing of events makes clear that new levels of capital mobility were not the trigger that empowered the venture capitalists to threaten the exchanges. By 1994, cross-border capital mobility in Europe had been a fact of life for several years.[31] Excluded from national financial policymaking networks, Europe's venture capitalists had regularly lost in battles against the stock exchanges. Only in the immediate aftermath of the Commission intervention, when there was a possibility that venture capitalists would have access to an alternative marketplace, did the exchanges pay attention to the needs of venture capitalists.

[30] The exception was the LSE's first of two new markets, AIM.

[31] EC Directive on Capital Movements (Council Directive 88/361/EEC of June 1988).

Nor was the stock exchange competition a direct effect of new EU legislation. Some scholars argue that new competition emerges primarily from formal rules and laws that reflect the intentions of policymakers. Rather than a determining factor, however, the 1993 ISD put in place what Stone Sweet and Sandholtz call a 'density of supranational rules' that opens opportunities for political entrepreneurs (Stone Sweet and Sandholtz 1998: 5; Stone Sweet, Fligstein *et al.* 2001). While Commission officials found pockets of support for a pan-European Nasdaq market in national governments, the domestic officials charged with financial market policy remained steadfast against Commission interventions and never intended the ISD to contribute to these further developments.

Finally, the terms of the new cross-border rivalries quickly took on a familiar European character, as the governments and exchanges sought to tame and manage what had been unbridled competition. Even though an early effort to create a formalized cartel-like network of Nasdaq copies proved unstable,[32] non-European and upstart European entrants nonetheless faced insurmountable obstacles as the largest exchanges quickly dominated the new cross-border competition. Even the US Nasdaq itself, after its 2001 purchase of the failing Easdaq, was unable to compete.

Had the LSE, the Paris bourse, and the other established European exchanges known that the terms of competition would be so favorable, they might have reacted more slowly, taking a wait-and-see approach. After all, Easdaq's failure has shown that the support of a supranational bureaucracy hardly ensures success in overcoming formidable obstacles to creating new stock markets. Indeed, markets are institutions that rest on a web of relations between financial intermediaries, investors, companies seeking capital and service providers. In hindsight, the Easdaq project seems naïve. But under the new conditions of EU finance, fostered by supranational entrepreneurs, the mere possibility of success mattered most. Perceptions and uncertainties, not a reasoned feasibility assessment, stoked fears of competition and quickly brought a reaction and institutional innovation to smaller company finance.

Several of the other original new markets, in addition to Easdaq, have now closed as well, due to some combination of cutthroat competition, insufficient regulation and poor enforcement of existing rules.[33] While the rivalry and institutional experimentation continues, the new market that today

[32] The Paris, Frankfurt, Brussels and Amsterdam exchanges set up Euro.NM, a loose network connecting the new Nasdaq copies, to limit cross-border competition. Interview with DG2 official (Luxembourg, June 7, 1999). Telephone interview with Easdaq official and former Euro.NM official (May 24, 1999).

[33] For economic analyses of the new markets, see the chapters in (Giudici and Roosenboom 2004*a*).

appears to have the best chance of becoming Europe's answer to Nasdaq is London's AIM, which has become the core financial institution to a thriving international biotechnology sector, boasts over 1000 companies and ended 2004 with a market capitalization of 31.8 billion pounds (FT 2004; Firn 2005).[34] The twist of the story is that AIM, while originating from the same Commission-initiated competition, is the least Nasdaq-like of the bunch. Reacting to Easdaq before the full contours of the new competition were clear, the LSE gave AIM a homegrown form that weathered the recent boom and bust better than its American lookalikes. Its success has come as a surprise even to the LSE, which launched Techmark in 1999 in large part because AIM looked to be failing in comparison to Frankfurt's Neuer Markt. It also suggests that more than one institutional form may support the high-risk economic activities sought by Commission officials and others.

The LSE's rivals, still very concerned about their relative position in a quickly integrating European financial system, have taken note (Euronext 2001; 2004). They continue to replace failed markets with new ones, but are now hedging their bets about what constitutes success by offering two options for smaller companies: Markets and rules that mirror the Nasdaq principle and those that copy AIM's model of lighter and less costly regulation. Whichever form ultimately wins out, to be a competitive financial center in Europe now means catering to smaller companies in addition to larger ones.

3. Conclusion

Europe's smaller stock markets offer useful clues for understanding the larger and still-unfolding process of regional integration of national financial systems. First, the episode of cross-border mimicry illustrates that supranational political entrepreneurship in the EU is possible even in an issue area where national officials jealously guard their policymaking sovereignty. Brussels civil servants, for example, played a significant informal role in the post-euro acceleration of the financial integration process. In a classic example of policy spillover, commission officials successfully argued that Europe would not benefit fully from the new currency's advent until all obstacles to a single financial market were removed.[35]

[34] In comparison, the Neuer Markt, at its peak, had 342 firms of a much larger average size and a market capitalization of 234 billion euros (Burghof and Hunger 2004). For AIM statistics, see <*www.londonstockexchange.com*>.

[35] Interview with Delegation of the European Commission official in Washington, DC (May 4, 2004).

The FSAP, proposed by the Commission in May 1999 and endorsed by the European Council in March 2000, provides the formal EU legislation deemed necessary to integrate national financial services industries as well as an ambitious timetable. As of May 2004, EU policymakers had almost completed the original list of forty-two measures, which included legislation covering company statutes, money laundering, UCITS (mutual funds), accounting standards, market abuse, occupational pensions and prospectuses. Policymakers, regulators and financiers have now turned to the Lamfalussy Process (approved by the European Parliament in February 2002), the new formal, supranational decision-making procedures for expediting the production of EU legislation for insurance, banking and investment services and coordinating implementation and enforcement. The new process created European-level bodies like the Committee of European Securities Regulators (CESR) and places Commission representatives at all levels of a complex decision-making procedure.

A truly integrated financial services industry—a 'single European financial market'—still lags far behind these Commission-instigated regulatory developments. Yet in putting in place one set of rules for all financial services companies operating in the EU's twenty-five member states, the FSAP and Lamfalussy process are sending waves across the Atlantic, recasting European-US relations in financial services. Large US-based securities firms make approximately twenty percent of their net revenues from the fifteen original EU markets, close to double the number from Asia.[36] By creating a single regulatory regime with which US financial services companies operating in Europe will have to comply, the EU has simultaneously enhanced its relative market power vis-à-vis US regulators who now show a new openness to cooperative management of conflicts (Posner 2004*b*).

Second, the adoption of the Nasdaq principle highlights key conditions under which Europeans are likely to borrow US standards. Policymakers are often of two minds about setting standards in the financial integration process. On the one hand, financial firms on both sides of the Atlantic rely heavily on one another's markets, providing strong incentives for policymakers devising new Europe-wide rules and standards to coordinate with their American counterparts. On the other hand, the goal to create a rival financial system to keep European firms, capital and brains from migrating across the Atlantic and the desire to preserve control over the allocation of capital and the production of new rules and standards sometimes drive policymakers to select homegrown or non-US standards, a scenario that raises costs for firms operating in both the USA and Europe.

[36] See SIA's policies positions toward EU capital markets at <*www.sia.com*>.

Unlike much scholarship that points to the role of global forces in determining the selection of standards, the smaller company stock market story underscores the importance of political context. In the 1980s, looking at national politics was sufficient for understanding decisions to adopt traditional domestic standards. By the 1990s, however, focusing on national politics alone would not have offered answers for why the exchanges adopted a US form. Supranational officials were the political actors primarily responsible for choosing the US principle that was later copied by the exchanges. They selected it, moreover, for reasons inextricably linked to their role and relative powers within the EU political system.

EU politics will not always lead to the adoption of US models, and in several critical recent cases it has not. In harmonizing accounting standards for public companies listed in the EU, for instance, policymakers deliberately avoided the USGAAP, even though it would have removed a major obstacle to deeper transatlantic financial integration, and instead selected International Accounting Standards/International Financial Reporting Standards (IAS/IFRS). European finance ministers, accepting the Commission's arguments, did not want to cede control over the production of new standards to their largest global rival (Commission 1995*a*). The example cautions against expectations of a fully compatible EU–US financial regulatory regime based on American standards, and illustrates the significance of political context within which decisions are made.

Finally, the process by which Europeans adopted US-style markets reveals a gap between the potential social impact of rules governing the allocation of capital and the often limited and narrow decision-making processes that determine what those rules will be. A paradox of Europe's new markets is that the aspect of change with the potential for bringing the greatest effects, the introduction of the Nasdaq principle, was more a by-product of political maneuver than a decision derived from deliberation over the possible impact.

It is still too soon to know the future of the US financial model in Europe. As the recent success of London's AIM shows, the particular institutional form may matter less than the cross-border competition that is driving Europe's exchanges to find ways to support US-style high-risk finance. There are renewed demands, moreover, from venture capitalists and others with interests in entrepreneurial finance for another public initiative to create a pan-European Nasdaq copy (EVCA 2004; Giudici and Roosenboom 2004*b*). Will Europe's elites give them the market they want? Whatever the ultimate answer, it is extraordinary that Europe has arrived at this juncture and even more so given that Brussels bureaucrats ushered them to it.

References

Anslow, M. (1993*a*). ' "EPEE", "PAREX", "NASDAQ" or "EASDAQ"?' *European Venture Capital Journal*, 26: 1.

—— (1993*b*). 'Two Ideas For A Private Equity Exchange', *European Venture Capital Journal*, 26: 14–7.

Bannock, G. (1994). *European Second-Tier Markets for NTBFs*. London: Graham Bannock and Partners.

Barber, T. (2001). 'Germany's Investors Dig in for the Long Term', *Financial Times*, March 15: 3.

Barnett, M. N. and Finnemore, M. (1999). 'The Politics, Power and Pathologies of International Organizations', *International Organization*, 53/4: 698.

Benoit, B. (2001*a*). 'Analysts to Face Toughest Set of Rules Yet', *Financial Times*, May 21: 21.

—— (2001*b*). 'Bourse Tightens Rules on Market', *Financial Times*, July 23: 16.

Bottazzi, L. and Da Rin, M. (2002). 'Europe's "New" Stock Markets', *CEPR Discussion Papers*, 3521.

Burghof, H. and Hunger, A. (2004). 'The Neuer Markt: An (Overly) Risky Asset of Germany's Financial System' in G. Giudici and P. Roosenboom (eds.), *The Rise and Fall of Europe's New Stock Markets*. Amsterdam: Elsevier, pp. 295–328.

Cohen, R. (1994). 'Special care for young companies', *Financial Times*, March, 8: 20.

Coopers and Lybrand (1995). *Corporate Finance: EASDAQ - A New Opportunity?* London: Coopers and Lybrand.

Cram, L. (1994). 'The European Commission as a Multi-Organization: Social Policy and IT Policy in the EU', *Journal of European Public Policy*, 1/2: 195–217.

Deeg, R., and Perez, S. (2000). 'International Capital Mobility and Domestic Institutions: Corporate Finance and Governance in Four European Cases', *Governance: An International Journal of Policy and Administration*, 13/2: 119–54.

Euronext (2001). 'Euronext launches NextEconomy and NextPrime Segments', Amsterdam, Brussels, Paris, Euronext Press Release, December 18.

—— (2004). 'New Euronext List Gears up for Launch', Amsterdam, Brussels, Paris, Euronext Press Release, November 2.

European Commission (EC) (1978). *The Community and Industrial Innovation*. Brussels: Commission of the European Communities.

—— (1981). European Commission Bulletin of the European Union/European Community. France, Bull EC 12-1981, 2.1.18.

—— (1982). European Commission Bulletin of the European Union/European Community. France, Bull EC 11-1982, 2.1.24.

—— (1983). European Commission Bulletin of the European Union/European Community. France, Bull EC 6-1983, 2.1.46.

—— (1984). European venture capital pilot scheme. Brussels: Commission of the European Communities, Directorate General Information and Innovation, EUR 9082 EN-FR final.

European Commission (EC) (1985). Improving venture capital opportunities in Europe (Eur 9756 EN/DE/FR). Proceedings of the symposium, October 3–5, 1984. Luxembourg: Commission of the European Communities.

—— (1989). European Commission Bulletin of the European Union/European Community. France, 2.1.69.

European Commission (EC) (1990). Fiscal Environment of, and Corporate Vehicles for, venture capital in the European Communities (EUR 11527 EN), Authored by Deloitte Haskins & Sell (Reference Date: December 31, 1987). Brussels, Commission of the European Communities/Directorate-General Telecommunications, Information and Innovation.

European Commission (1993*a*). European Commission Bulletin of the European Union/European Community. France, 1.2.144.

—— (1993*b*). Financial Problems of SMEs. Brussels, Commission of the European Union, COM (93) 528, November 10.

—— (1994*a*). Meeting with the Press: Background Note for Press (DG23, Direction B, Unit 3, June 21). Brussels.

—— (1994*b*). Prospects for the creation of a European-level capital market for entrepreneurial companies. Brussels: European Commission, Directorate General XXIII, Meeting with the Press (in preparation for June 21).

—— (1995*a*). Accounting Harmonisation: A New Strategy vis-à-vis International Harmonisation. Brussels: Commission of the European Union, COM 95 (508) EN.

—— (1995*b*). Reporting on the feasibility of the creation of a European capital market for smaller entrepreneurial managed growing companies. Brussels: Commission of the European Union, COM (95) 498 final, October 25.

—— (1999). Financial Services Action Plan. Brussels: Commission of the European Union, COM (1999) 232.

European Venture Capital Association (EVCA) (1985). 'New survey shows need for European over-the-counter securities market', *Information Bulletin*, December 23. Brussels: EVCA.

—— (1993). 'Programme: EVCA's Business Seminar', February 12. Venice, Italy: European Venture Capital Association.

—— (1994*a*). *Expert Meeting, European Capital Markets for Entrepreneurial Companies, April 18, 1994: List of Attendees*. Zaventem, Belgium: EVCA Archives.

—— (1994*b*). *Program and Summary of European Capital Markets for Entrepreneurial Companies, 2nd Meeting, 28–9 June 1994*. Paris: Coordinated by EVCA with the support of the European Commission.

—— (1994*c*). *Venture Capital Special Paper: Capital Markets for Entrepreneurial Companies—A European Opportunity for Growth*. Zaventem, Belgium: EVCA.

—— (2004). 'European Stock Market Financing for High-Growth Companies: An Analysis of the European "New Markets" Experience', *EVCA Research Paper*. Zaventem, Belgium: EVCA.

FIBV (Fédération internationale des bourses et valeurs) (1995). *Workshop: Financing Small and Medium-Sized Businesses for Future Growth. Proceedings*. July 6–7. Milan: Federation of International Stock Exchanges.

Financial Times (1996). 'Nouveau Marché rule change'. *Financial Times*, October 29: 29.

Firn, D. (2005). 'London the Laboratory for Biotechnology Launches', *Financial Times*, 6 January: 18.

Fligstein, N., and Mara-Drita, I. (1996). 'How to Make a Market: Reflections on the Attempt to Create a Single Market in the European Union', *American Journal of Sociology,* 102/1: 1–33.

Frieden, J. A. and Rogowski, R. (1996). 'The Impact of the International Economy on National Policies: An Analytical Overview', in R. Keohane and H. Milner (eds.), *The Internationalization of National Economies*. Cambridge: Cambridge University Press, pp. 25–47.

FT (2004). 'AIM High: London's Junior Stock Market Has Outlasted European Rivals.' *Financial Times*, October 6: 16.

Fuhrmans, V. (2000). 'Playing by the Rules: How Neuer Markt Gets Respect', *Wall Street Journal*, August 21: 1.

Giudici, G and Roosenboom, P. (2004*a*). *The Rise and Fall of Europe's New Stock Markets*. Amsterdam: Elsevier.

—— —— (2004*b*). 'Venture Capital and the New Stock Markets in Europe', in G. Giudici and P. Roosenboom (eds.), *The Rise and Fall of Europe's New Stock Markets*. Amsterdam: Elsevier, pp. 1–24.

Hayter, G. (1994). *EASDAQ: A Concept Paper*. London: EVCA, EASDAQ–UK, Nasdaq, SBF-Bourse de Paris.

Heritier, A. (2001). 'Overt and Covert Institutionalization in Europe', in A. Stone Sweet, W. Sandholtz, and N. Fligstein (eds.), *The Institutionalization of Europe*. Oxford: Oxford University Press, pp. 56–70.

Hooghe, L. (2001). *The European Commission and the Integration of Europe: Images of Governance*. Cambridge: Cambridge University Press.

Jabko, N. (1999). 'In the Name of the Market', *Journal of European Public Policy,* 6/3: 475–98.

Johnson, S. (2000). 'Which Rules Matter? Evidence from Germany's Neuer Markt'. Unpublished paper.

Lamfalussy, A. C. (2001). *Final Report of the Committee of Wise Men on the Regulation of European Securities Markets*. Brussels: European Union's Economic and Finance Ministers (ECOFIN).

Laurence, H. (2001). *Money Rules: The New Politics of Finance in Britain and Japan*. Ithaca, NY: Cornell University Press.

Mandell, D. (1997). 'Alternative Investment Mood', *CISCO Voice*, December: 8–10.

Mazey, S. and Richardson, J. (2001). 'Institutionalizing Promiscuity: Commission-Interest Group Relations in the EU', in A. Stone Sweet, W. Sandholtz and N. Fligstein (eds.), *The Institutionalization of Europe*. Oxford: Oxford University Press, pp. 71–93.

Peeters, J. B. (1994). 'A European Market for Entrepreneurial Companies', in W. D. Bygrave, M. Hay, and J. B. Peeters (eds.), *Realizing Investment Value*. London: Financial Times/Pitman Publishing.

Pollack, M. A. (2003). *Engines of European Integration: Delegation, Agency, and Agenda Setting in the EU*. Oxford: Oxford University Press.

Posner, E. (2002). 'Financial Change and European Union Politics: The Origins of Europe's Market of "Nasdaq Markets" ', Political Science, Ph.D. dissertation. Berkeley, UC Berkeley.

Posner, E. (2004*a*). 'Copying the Nasdaq Stock Market in Europe: Supranational Entrepreneurship in an Age of Global Finance', *PEIF Working Paper (UC Berkeley's Institute for European Studies), <http://ies.berkeley.edu/pubs/workingpapers/peif.html/>*.

—— (2004*b*). 'Market Power without Single Market: The New Transatlantic Relations in Financial Services'. Unpublished paper.

Schmidt, H. (1984). *Special Stock Market Segments for Small Company Shares: Capital Raising Mechanism and Exit Route for Investors in New Technology-Based Firms*. Brussels: Commission of the European Communities, DG Information Market and Innovation (EUR 9235 EN).

SFE (Scottish Financial Enterprise) (1989). 'Notes from meeting between Sundberg, Schulman, SFE and the Commission's Inter-DG Working Group', October 11. Brussels.

Steil, B. (1998). *Regional Financial Market Integration: Learning From the European Experience*. London: Royal Institute of International Affairs.

Stone Sweet, A., Fligstein N., and Sandholtz, W. (2001). 'The Institutionalization of European Space', in A. Stone Sweet, N. Fligstein and W. Sandholtz (eds.), *The Institutionalization of European Space*. Oxford: Oxford University Press, pp. 1–28.

Stone Sweet, A., and Sandholtz, W., (1998). 'Integration, Supranational Governance, and the Institutionalization of the European Polity', in W. Sandholtz and A. Stone Sweet (eds.), *European Integration and Supranational Governance*. Oxford: Oxford University Press, pp. 1–26.

Story, J., and Walter, I. (1997). *Political Economy of Financial Integration in Europe: The Battle of the Systems*. Cambridge, MA: MIT Press.

Verdier, D. (2003). *Moving Money: Banking and Finance in the Industrialized World*. Cambridge: Cambridge University Press.

Vogel, S. K. (1996). *Freer Markets, More Rules: Regulatory Reform in Advanced Industrial Countries*. Ithaca, NY: Cornell University Press.

Von Moltke, H. (1996). *The role of DG XXIII with regard to EASDAQ. EASDAQ—The European Stock Market for Growing Companies*. June 26, Brussels.

Weber, S. and Posner, E. (2000). 'Creating a Pan-European Equity Market: The Origins of EASDAQ', *Review of International Political Economy,* 7/4 Winter: 529–73.

Zysman, J. (1983). *Governments, Markets, and Growth: Financial Systems and the Politics of Industrial Change*. Ithaca, NY: Cornell University Press.

10

Financial Restructuring in the Age of the Euro: Still a Battle of Systems?

JONATHAN STORY

In January, 2002, eleven countries in the European Union (EU) adopted euro-notes and coins for retail use, thereby taking the EU a step closer to business conditions in the USA. Yet implementing corporate strategies across Europe is still heavily conditioned by different national jurisdictions and their distinct institutional configurations. These configurations represent bundles of norms—freedom, efficiency, justice or security—and their distinctness resides in which of these principles predominates: in the USA, liberty; in the UK, utility; in France, justice, or in Germany, security. The particular mix of liberty, efficiency, justice or security arrived at over a lengthy period in any one jurisdiction also produces unintended consequences. According to a powerful tradition in scholarship and much of the rhetoric surrounding the EU, these different mixes, with their intended and unintended consequences, were supposed to fade away due to market competition between them or EU and global regulation over them. This has not occurred. Underlying differences between jurisdictions have not been eliminated, and competition in market and political arenas between corporations rooted in different member state jurisdictions remains a defining characteristic of Europe. The 'battle of the systems' within the EU is as lively as it ever was, if not livelier.

This does not mean that there has been no transatlantic convergence in economic institutions and policies since the advent of the euro. Some has indeed occurred. I will argue, however, that this convergence is taking place for political reasons rather than in straightforward response to global competition or common economic conditions. Moreoever, I will argue that one of the prime reasons for recent divergence in the style of transatlantic relations from the past—notably not just over Iraq, but over the litany of differences regarding the environment, intellectual property rights, export subsidies, or GM foods—is exactly this implicit convergence in policy priorities across the Atlantic resulting from the intra-European politics leading to European Monetary Union (EMU), and the successful launch of the euro.

National calculations drove the EU to a single currency and a single capital market, and national calculations continue to prevail in the market for corporate assets after the euro's introduction. Europe is not converging on a single capitalism, but the many forms it takes are all subject to similar forces. There is convergence in the processes at work in the world and in Europe—the complex processes often summarized as 'globalization'—but there is continued divergence in the national structures which endure, restructure and shape them.

Far from being a simple response to a broadly 'globalizing' context, the euro is an eminently political creation—an act of will by the participant states using Europe's more traditional and also newer instruments of diplomatic statecraft. However much the euro may have made Europe more similar to the USA, its interstate diplomatic nature makes its causes and effects quite different from the politics of monetary policy or financial markets in the USA. In the US polity, class or religious distinctions form the sociological bedrock of pluralist politics in a federal system, much as they do in the domestic politics of European states. In the European polity, by contrast, the salient feature is diplomacy between nation-states—of which the EU is essentially an updated version. Monetary union resulted when two prime sets of national motivations combined in EU diplomacy. One was to stabilize the interdependent European economy operating in a multicurrency system, where the dollar and the Deutschmark called the shots into the 1990s. The other was to prevent the emergence of a united Germany as the unequivocal potential leader of Europe.

More domestic-style class politics certainly relate to the euro project and have been altered by it, but the connection has been indirect. Before monetary union, class politics was played out in the highly developed welfare institutions of the European member states, interacting one with another through the price mechanism whose central components were interest and exchange rates. Germany ruled the roost, so that German macroeconomic preferences, being closely tailored to Germany's microeconomic arrangements, took precedence over those of most other states in the EU and beyond. After monetary union, national politics continue to operate, but in a new setting. Achieving near full employment in the euro-area requires creating Europe-wide labor, product and service markets. National welfare states and a single currency and capital market are not necessarily antagonistic, but they are not comfortable bedfellows. Thus if the euro was the product mainly of interstate concerns and strategizing, it is exerting considerable pressure on national-level class politics as well.

Using Neil Fligstein's terminology (Fligstein 2001, 190) efficiency is socially constructed rather than constructed by markets, and monetary union—as a formidable promoter of efficiency in euro-land markets—is eminently a social construct. The central argument here is that the French policy of embracing Germany in the EU that drove the euro project has led to an impasse due to the coexistence of distinct and highly mercantilistic national-level policies; thus EMU can only be consummated through the adoption of policies heavily biased in a neoliberal direction at the level of the Union. This impasse, maturing from the late 1960s, essentially resulted in the Europe-wide hegemony of the Deutschmark and the Bundesbank, effectively making the latter the Federal Reserve's counterpart within the EU. It was sustained by Germany's powerfully integrated business system.[1] As of 1989, the prime protagonists of monetary union-Chancellor Kohl, President Mitterrand, and Commission President Delors feared that German unity would consolidate German primacy, and the solution they reached—the creation of a European Central Bank along Bundesbank lines—definitely addressed their shared concern.[2] The Deutschmark is no more, and Germany is far from dominant in the EU. But this eminently political act to establish a single currency, and with it, a capital market denominated in euros, creates a structure of incentives which points to an unravelling of significant features of national business systems—notably, national cross-shareholdings, clubby corporate governance arrangements, patient bank finance, or protectionist national labor market practices.

Monetary union thus reinforces competitive pressures running through global markets, while reducing the EU's collective vulnerability to global exchange rate shifts. By the same token, monetary union deprives member states of interest and exchange rate tools, and in addition, substitutes a national capital market for a European capital market. France or Germany are that much more like Texas or California in the USA. But, like other member states, they also carry long national legacies. The interplay between national legacies and the new monetary and capital market regime is what 'the battle of the systems' in updated form (Story and Walter 1997) is all about. But first some brief definitions.

[1] The term 'national business system' has been coined by Richard Whitley to describe specific patterns of economic coordination and control in market economies (Whitley 1999).

[2] There is a large literature on the theme of monetary union. Authors place different weight on contributing factors from the impact of global financial markets on intra-European exchange rates; domestic politics; interdependence within Europe; and Germany's place in postwar Europe. My take on the story—that all these perspectives point to the pivotal role of Germany—is spelt out in De Cecco and Story 1993. See also Tsoukalis 1977; Ludlow 1982; Simonian 1985; Balkhausen 1992; Baun 1996; Aeschimann and Riché 1996; Connolly 1996; Dyson and Featherstone 1999; Moravcsik 1998.

1. National Financial Systems, Corporate Governance, and Models of Capitalism

There are at least two stories which may be told about how national financial systems change over time. One points to convergence over time on a standard, and the other to continued divergence. While proponents of the first story allow that financial arrangements obviously start historically in response to differing situations, over time they expect convergence to occur through market competition and institutional mimicry. The way that the capital-allocation process is configured reflects the interests of protagonists, but it also affects national economic performance as well as international and financial relationships. The capital market process occurs through the process of control over corporations and organizations. All financial systems are active intermediaries between political and social structures and relationships, and corporations or organizations operating in some form of market arrangement. Corporate strategy is understood here as the link between the external capital market, populated by shareholders and financial institutions, and the internal allocation of corporate resources (Porter 1992). Convergence from different national starting points then ostensibly works through the market pressures on countries or corporations to adopt in a new standard the best practices observed in different situations. For corporations, the argument goes, it is the mix of European-type sensitivity to local conditions, together with Japanese national efficiency and US corporate capabilities to leverage the transfer of corporate know-how to international markets, that will make the new composite standard for global champions (Bartlett and Ghoshal 1989).

The divergent story holds that institutional arrangements start in response to differing situations, and carry on doing so. They are 'path-dependent,' since their protagonists, even allowing for a changing composition over time, always have to make policy in an inherited situation. As institutionalist economists point out, how the markets are structured, what values are embedded in the prevailing rules and which organizations develop within the range of prevailing incentives, makes all the difference to outcomes (North *et al.* 1991, 109). Market structures have their own discrete histories, are permeated by the values which have been agreed or legislated on in particular political contexts, and yield different specializations and efficiencies. The diversity of states is duplicated in the diversity of corporate strategies issuing from different local conditions as they permeate international or global markets. Given the nature of oligopolistic competition among few corporations in a particular branch and the variety of states in world markets, such differing conditions provide diverse incentives affecting the strategies of firms (Prahalad and Doz 1987). Firms may go international, or even aspire to become citizens of the world. But their activities amount to the international operations of national firms (Yao 1992; Pauly and Reich 1997).

In Europe, these two perspectives are less distinct than may appear in that they offer overlapping expectations about where European capitalism is heading. In the convergent story, the emphasis is more on market emulation and institutional mimicry among member states and with the USA. The emphasis in the divergence story is more on EU aspirations to federal statehood overriding the individual states, to create a 'United States of Europe'; on EU efforts to legislate a European financial area, similar to prevailing conditions in the USA; and on different national positions and structures. The 'United States of Europe' at the end of the EU federal line may or may not resemble the USA, but whether it is different or similar it will assuredly differ from one or many of the existing national positions. These national positions and structures remain divergent, most evidently in the way that distinct national capitalisms relate to human capital: not just the detailed mechanisms of the labor market, but also to training, labor participation, or social security systems. Labor market institutions are prime differentiators among member states.

With the adoption of the single currency and capital market, which of the national systems will prevail in the EU, or which mix of them will emerge predominant is one, if not *the* most controversial issue in European and national politics. Opinion polls regularly indicate very low confidence in large corporate managements, express fears that globalization gives even more power to corporate managers, and record that the number one concern for EU publics is unemployment. The message is clear enough: capitalism, particularly of the 'Anglo-Saxon' variety, has next to no support. But that is the direction indicated by the processes of 'globalization,' significantly strengthened by monetary union, the EU's most significant policy to date. The next section starts by presenting the evolution of some central features of the Anglo-American shareholder and labor market system, because this is the dominant context within which the French state-centred financial and labor system, and the German bank-corporate consensual system have to adapt.

2. The Atlantic Alliance and the EU Member States

The permanent context of repeated European efforts to fix currencies or to establish monetary union has been provided since the 1940s by the USA as the world's banker. Equally permanent has been London's ambition to reestablish a preeminent position in international finance. Growing financial interdependence between New York and London provided the medium through which ever more volatile funds in dollars and other currencies were switched across the Atlantic, helping to undermine the postwar-system of stable exchange rates. When oil producing states sought to recuperate the value of their dollar reserves by raising oil prices in 1974, surplus revenues from the Gulf states flowed into the London interbank markets, where banks borrowed from each other in dollars and lent on to developing countries, notably in Latin America. Funds available for recycling also found there way on to the London and New York markets from the trade surplus countries of continental Europe and Asia-Pacific. Buoyed by North Sea oil production, the UK resumed its role as an exporter of capital when controls were raised in October 1979. Successive conservative governments thereafter shifted assets from public sector control to private ownership and the discipline of the capital markets, such that when by 1997 Prime Minister Blair entered 10 Downing Street, UK companies in public ownership accounted for 2 percent of gross domestic product (GDP) as against 12 percent in 1979.

Regulatory competition between London, New York and Tokyo spurred financial market reforms in the 1980s, opened the doors wide to foreign financial institutions, and spurred development of traded securities, futures and equities. In October 1986, the 'Big Bang' in the London markets ended the separation of brokers and jobbers that had been in place since the 1920s. Brokers had represented their private clients for a commission and recommended the purchase of bonds or equities. Jobbers had kept an inventory of stock, for which they held a monopoly on trading. This privilege derived from the 1920 Finance Act, whereby jobbers paid stamp duty on purchases of stock. Separation of function between brokers and jobbers provided an incentive for the broker to serve the client's interest rather than to unload stock, which was in the hands of the jobber. The stamp duty underpinned the jobber's monopoly. A compensation fund existed to protect the investor from the failure of a firm, and fixed commissions were charged on services rendered in order to preserve this single-capacity grouping of functions and to feed the compensation fund. The price of the cartel reflected in higher transaction costs of government bonds and shares. But the arrangement proved relatively free of scandals, and served to protect the shareholders from fraud. Its abolition marked the triumph of efficiency norms in UK financial policy over those of security.

The 'Big Bang' opened the markets to full participation by US or Japanese investment banks and European universal banks. Equity ownership became much more widely diffused. By 2002, the UK had a ratio of market capitalization to GDP of 115 percent. This was several times that of other large European countries (such as Germany's 35 percent, and France's 67 percent) and second only to the USA (combining New York and Nasdaq) with 136 percent. The major innovations of the Blair government were to complete conservative financial market reforms first by announcing the independence of the Bank of England, and then in 2001 by introducing a single all-powerful regulator over all financial markets in the UK. In the EU, up to forty different authorities sought to cover the same field of activities. Denmark and Sweden, two 'Eurosceptic' countries, went the UK way.

Successive conservative governments also introduced statutory law to labor markets for the first time, strengthened management powers to hire and fire and reinforced labor market institutions. Corporate profits improved, and nonresidential investment took off. London became the EU's prime city of capital, and the 'third leg' in the triad of world financial centres, together with New York, with Tokyo being seriously challenged by Hong Kong, which returned to China in 1997. London became the major market for world foreign exchange transactions, and the prime capital market for the EU, with 65 percent of world foreign equity turnover and 95 percent of EU equity turnover taking place in London. European institutions dominated equity trading, loan business and currency markets there. Other European financial centres, such as Frankfurt, Paris and Milan, have a similar relationship to London as cities such as Boston, San Francisco and Chicago have to New York—the difference being that Europe's financial hub in London is located outside the euro area. London as the capital for many of Europe's most important wholesale financial markets is increasing its importance as a global financial centre.

The London markets are notably different from Paris and Frankfurt. Whereas London remained the central market for the sterling area into the 1970s, in Germany, and then in France, financial systems were hitched more closely to state industrial policy. The banking acts of 1934 and 1941 in both countries served as the foundation for legislation in the postwar decades that protected national financial markets, allowed for bank financing of reconstruction, and later of corporate expansion. Insurance markets were even more protected, with both French and German law making it a criminal offense for insurance policies to be sourced abroad until these measures were reversed by the EU's Court of Justice (ECJ) in 1986. Both German and French financial market structures were domestic, primarily funding national corporations. In London, the dominant markets were (and are) wholesale, servicing businesses from all over the world. In the USA as in the UK, managerial hierarchies came to run large, publicly quoted and diversified corporations, taking their sources of external financing from the capital market, which in turn obliged chief executive officers to pay paramount attention to shareholder interests as represented by the managers of financial institutions. British corporations were obliged to earn high rates of return in order to retain the loyalty of investors on whom they remained dependent for future capital. Maintaining the corporations' share price was the main aim, for fear that a reduced dividend could have serious consequences in terms of a lower share price and a predatory takeover. That encouraged global corporate investment strategies so that share prices could be sustained, despite downturns in one or other market. By 2003, the UK's outward stock of foreign direct investment was near equivalent to the outward stock of Germany and France combined.[3]

The spread of shareholder capitalism in both the UK and the USA drew on a legal tradition that regards a company as a private entity, set up by investors for their own benefit, who in turn hire managers to conduct business. Managers keep constant track of input costs, such as labor, raw materials or capital, and seek the most efficient use of state-of-the-art technologies or organizational practices to produce goods or services that provide value for the consumer at attractive prices. Government's major task is to provide the regulatory and legal structure within which open capital markets may function, and to supply a safety net for the unemployed, the infirm or the old. Consumer and shareholder interests are assumed to be paramount. Domestic markets are deliberately kept open to foreign competitors and to inward investors. Government policy is predicated less on giving political advantage to national producers than on satisfying the demands of national shareholders and consumers. What the nationality of the shareholders may be is less important than the performance of the corporation. As mentioned, corporate performance is best assured by diversifying the locations of its businesses so as to avoid downturns in any single national market. Both US and UK corporations have worldwide reach.

There are manifold advantages in such a division of tasks between corporate managers and government officials. If financial agents consider that corporate managers are asleep at the switch, they may sell shares on shareholders' behalf, making the corporation vulnerable to takeover as predators bid to buy shares, sometimes with advice from investment banks, at a premium to the market. This market for corporate assets facilitates corporate mergers and restructurings, and is legitimated on the grounds of providing the most efficient set of incentives for all participants in the market to maximize wealth. Labor market legislation in particular has to be supportive, so that labor forces may be shrunk or shifted in task or location with the minimum of friction. The model also assumes that the government will not prove a light touch for corporate lobbies seeking to avoid restructuring or takeover through access to the public purse, as a less demanding source of funds. A shareholder-driven corporate economy, underpinned by a share-

[3] Following are the 2003 outward foreign direct investment stocks in millions of dollars US-2, 069,013; UK—1,128,584; Germany—622,499; France—643,398 (United Nations 2004).

holder democracy, has the voting public participate in the performance of corporations and in the rewards.

Not surprisingly, the British government championed free financial services in the EU, with a careful eye to consolidating London's status. It found allies in London-based financial institutions, the Commission, the ECJ jurisprudence, and—initially—the Dutch, Luxemburg and German governments. Together with the Commission and the ECJ, the UK government helped to elaborate a policy doctrine which aimed 'to secure acceptance of the equivalence of national legislations rather than their replacement by European law.'[4] This 'home country principle' holds that business conducted in any one of the member states should be subject to home country regulations whatever national regulations are applied by the regulatory authorities of the host country.

The major breakthrough toward creating the internal market came with the EU decision to move to freedom of capital movement. The EU directive was adopted in June 1988, to be followed by directives on banking, insurance, and investment services. This latter proved most controversial of all, given the many national sensitivities involved. Disputes spilled over into policies covering mergers and acquisitions, competition law and social policy. As the EU legislative train slowed after 1993, however, it became apparent that key features of national financial systems remained in place.[5] Over a decade later, Commissioner Bolkestein, in charge of the Financial Services Action Plan to open up financial service markets launched at the Lisbon EU summit in March 2000, called on member states to implement and enforce the rules—including the thirty-nine detailed directives of the FSAP—which they had struggled to agree upon.[6] The UK's position ran on similar lines (HM Treasury 2004). Legislating 'at the EU level' meant little if member states kept to their old ways.

One persistent source of national differentiation lay in labor market policy, as evidenced in the graph showing quite divergent productivity and participation rates. These different rates are the expression of distinct labor market structures, policies and cultures (Figure 10.1).

[4] Statement of Robin Hutton, director of banking, insurance and financial institutions in the Commission, quoted in *Financial Times*, December 5, 1977.

[5] According to Secretary General of the Banking Federation, Umberto Burani, the home country principle—supposedly the centrepiece of the financial services programme—'has been introduced in no legislation.' 'Interview avec Umberto Burani', *Europolitique*, No. 1958, May 12, 1993.

[6] Mr Frits Bolkestein, Member of the European Commission in charge of the Internal Market, Taxation and Customs Future Directions for European Financial Integration. Opening remarks at the conference on European Financial Integration: Progress and Prospects, Palais d'Egmont, Brussels, June 22, 2004 Europa Press Releases <*http://europa.eu.int/rapid/press*>.

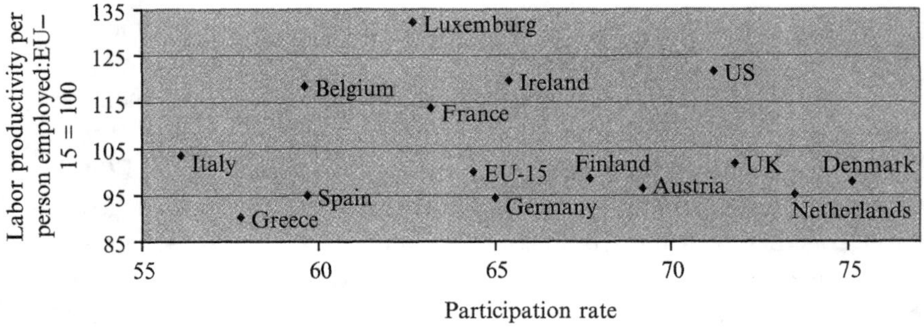

FIGURE 10.1. Participation rate in labor market and labor productivity per person in EU member states and in the USA.

Source: Eurostat.

Consistent with the thrust of its domestic policy, Prime Minister Thatcher's government championed a market-friendly social policy for the EU, presented in the proposal for an Action Programme for Employment and Growth (Brewster and Teague 1989, 94–9).[7] The Programme, with Irish and Italian backing, stood in stark contrast to the Commission's preferences for social protection. It was promptly scotched by an alliance between Commission President Delors and the early 1987 Belgium Presidency, which proposed a 'plinth' of fundamental social rights to accompany the move to the internal market. The matter then meandered through the EU institutions, becoming strongly impregnated with the preferences of the German and French Labour Ministries and trade unions. A general Social Charter was adopted by the European Council at Strasbourg in December 1989, and written into the Maastricht Treaty in a separate protocol where eleven states other than Britain agreed to adopt the EU's Action Programme of 1989[8] by qualified majority voting on social policy. This program served as the template of future EU legislation on social policy, adumbrated in the Maastricht Treaty of 1992, in the Employment Chapter of the Amsterdam Treaty of 1997, and in subsequent agreements and initiatives. In 1997, the incoming Labour government agreed to sign up to EU social policy in order to differentiate from the preceding Tory governments. But the honeymoon over labor policy did not last long.[9] By 2004, the UK's Minister for Europe,

[7] Résolution du Conseil du 22 décembre 1986 concernant un programme d'action pour la croissance de l'emploi (86/C 340/02).

[8] *Europolitique* No.1553, January 10, 1990. These measures dealt with 'atypical work,' with a view to limiting labor market competition; working hours; work contracts; and an EC instrument for information, consultation and participation of workers in multinational corporations.

[9] At the Lisbon March 2000 summit, Blair berated his EU colleagues for holding to 'the old social model,' rooted in the social legislation and welfare of the 1960s and 1970s. *The Economist*, December 2, 2000.

Denis MacShane, would interpret continental intentions as sinister in intent. 'There is a concerted effort by key players in Brussels—in the Commission, in the Council of Ministers and the EP—to take Britain in the direction of rigid labor markets.' The minister accused the EU of seeking to 'punish' the UK for having a flexible labor market.[10]

Another source of differentiation was corporate governance structures. Anglo-American capital markets posed a threat through emulation and mimicry to continental institutions of national capitalism, but also opened tempting opportunities to facilitate corporate internationalization strategies. In terms of legislative activity, continental member states in the late 1980s and early 1990s had little problem in fostering EU directives in financial services which held shareholder capitalism at bay. They justified regulation that tended to favor managerial prerogatives in terms of their ostensible contribution to national welfare. EU directives on banking and insurance, for instance, allowed bank–insurance tie-ups, opening the way in EU legislation to recognize national financial conglomerates. These conglomerates could access global capital markets, but—it was hoped—their managements would maintain control over French or German corporations. Yet the advantage of the Anglo-American financial market system of corporate governance is that it places competition between corporations before competition between states. Shareholders reward or punish corporations, and are indifferent to whether the reward or punishment is meted out to workers and managers in one country or another. As its opponents repeatedly pointed out, the distinctive feature of shareholder capitalism is that it is a-national.

3. Germany's Voyage From Primacy to Province

The bank-based system of corporate control is associated with Germany, where the rules of the game have traditionally enabled banks to take deposits, extend loans to firms and issue securities on capital markets in a tight relationship to clients. After unification in 1870, following Prussia's military victory over France in the war of 1870, German economic policy was oriented toward protection against foreign competition, and to state promotion of cartels. In the 1920s, war reparations, inflation, and reconstruction kept German banking fragile, and interest rates high. National Socialism derived much of its ferocity from the promise to deliver Germany from the tyranny of 'cosmopolitan' finance, symbolized in Berlin as Germany's financial metropolis. These echoes persisted into the 1990s. As Mr. Kopper, the

[10] 'EU 'punishing' UK over labor market,' *Financial Times*, November 30, 2004.

speaker for the Board of the Deutsche Bank, said in 1994, both communism and national socialism saw the interest rate as a source of exploitation: 'The systems collapse and the prejudices survive.'[11]

Germany's banking system has been highly decentralized. The 'big three' German private sector banks—Deutsche, Dresdner and Commerz, joined more recently by the HypoVereinsBank—only have 4.5 percent of nationwide savings deposits. Savings and communal banks, which lend to local businesses and governments, account for over four-fifths of banking activity, and provide commercial bank, consultancy and market support for Germany's small and medium-sized businesses. They benefit by local patronage and subsidy. Pensions are split between the pay-as-you-go public system and tax deductible employer pension funds that are available as a source of capital for corporate management (O'Sullivan 2000, 262–3) Given the strong reliance for finance of Germany's small, medium and large companies on internally generated sources of funds (mainly earnings) and on borrowings, the equity market has remained narrow. Pension reserves amount to around 50 percent of all company capital of German firms. Not surprisingly, the German system flourished best when pension payouts were relatively small, and when inflation and interest rates were low. From 1973 on, low interest rates were best assured through a freely floating exchange rate and with a trade sector in solid surplus. There was thus a very close association indeed in Germany between the macroeconomic management of the currency and the microeconomic management of firms.

If the bank system is decentralized, ownership in Germany is concentrated, as displayed in Table 10.1:

The main private banks hold or manage shares—along with the major insurance firm Allianz—of the 100 big firms, which accounted for up to 50 percent of the huge trade surplus which Germany accumulated over the DM's lifespan. The 'big' banks, in other words, were—and are—part of a nexus of banks, insurance companies and industrial corporations which own each others' shares and share each others supervisory board seats. At the heart of this nexus lie Allianz and Munich Reinsurance, the two Munich insurance and reinsurance giants.[12] This cross-holding of shares is a principal feature of German corporate governance, and is aimed at cementing long-term relationships between firms. It is also enduring: in the years following German unity in 1990, despite increased German dependence on global financial markets, the concentration of share management and ownership

[11] 'Kopper gesteht Arroganz,' *Handelsblatt*, June 15, 1994.

[12] As Wolfgang Schieren, the head of Germany's leading insurance firm, admitted, 'Allianz is today a holding company, whose objective is to hold participations.' Interview with Wolfgang Schieren, *Die Zeit*, September 12, 1991.

TABLE 10.1. *Comparative concentration of share ownership*

Proportion of Stock owned	Germany	France	CH	NL	USA	UK
0–4.9	9.5	37.3	17.8	23.7	95.0	48.6
5–9.9	7.8	14.2	17.6	30.0	3.5	31.0
10–24.9	17.8	15.1	17.9	9.6	1.4	10.5
25–49.9	13.9	9.4	15.6	10.1	0.1	2.6
50–74.9	12.9	8.1	8.0	6.8	–	2.4
75+	38.1	15.8	23.1	19.7	–	4.9
$N = 100$	821.0	1224	614.0	603.0	5925	1859.0

Source: Ulrich Jürgens, Joachim Rupp, The German System of Corporate Governance: Characteristics and Changes, Berlin, May 2002, WZB.
N: Shareholdings (= proportion of stock)
Germany: 650 largest firms (1993), $N = 821$ shareholding
France: 500 largest firms (1997), $N = 1224$ shareholdings
CH: 300 largest firms (1995), $N = 157$ shareholdings
NL: 300 largest firms (1995), $N = 244$ shareholdings
US: 250 largest firms (1997), $N = 5925$ shareholdings
UK: 520 largest firms (1995), $N = 1859$ shareholdings

remained largely unchanged. In 2000, the 5 percent largest companies listed on the Deutsche Börse, centered in Frankfurt—forty-two in number—accounted for 73.5 percent of total market capitalization. The narrow role played by equity markets is illustrated by the fact that the number of foreign listed stock corporations are about four times higher than the 750 German publicly traded companies.

Three prime advantages are often cited in favor of this nexus of 'bank power'—a recurrent theme in the politics of the Federal Republic. One is to protect Germany's listed corporations from foreign takeover. The argument was most clearly laid out by Alfred Herrhausen, speaker for the Board of the Deutsche Bank (a few days before his assassination), in an address to the *prominenz* of German politics and business in October 1989. It would be inadvisable, he declared, for legislation to oblige banks to sell their stakes. 'I can anticipate excited protests if banks sell our stakes in important German firms to foreigners on the grounds of the continuing and in principle welcome trend to the internationalization and globalization of the economy.'[13]

A second advantage is that the banks' role in corporate governance helps to provide stable long-term finance for German firms—large, medium, and small. Private limited companies in particular have expanded in number from 70,000 in 1970 to close to 400,000 by 2000. These family-owned firms form the bedrock of German business, being highly specialized on world export

[13] 'Es Riecht nach Komplott und Konspiration,' *Die Welt*, October 27, 1989.

markets, tied in often as subcontractors to the large corporations, and financed largely through retained earnings or borrowing from banks when the occasion requires. They are notably averse to public listing on the German stock exchange, for fear of diluting their owners' control over the business. In particular, they are embedded in local policy networks, where local banks play a key mediating role between local politicians, firms, trade unions and trade associations. Their battlefield resides in competition on product markets, as the national economy remains open to foreign suppliers. Because they have to satisfy the demands of their stakeholder constituency of workers, suppliers, clients and the local community, there is an incentive for firms to invite shareholders to patience and to reduce dependence on banks through strategies aimed at conquering market shares. The language of corporate conquest evinces mixed responses when heard by other Europeans.

A third advantage, it has often been argued, has been the role played by bankers as co-guardians of a stable, property-holding democracy which co-opted labor unions through their representatives' acquired positions on works councils and on corporate supervisory boards. Yet in each recession, supervisory boards were charged with incompetence. Managers bore the brunt of German firms' growing dependence on more volatile, and less predictable world markets. In the case of AEG in 1982, of Metallgesellschaft in the winter of 1993, and of the Schneider construction group in April 1994, the impending disaster had not been monitored. The banks were seen as ready to lend to large groups, regardless or unaware of the risk, and supervisory boards were accused of operating as closed shops. There was also a marked propensity for senior managers to defend the status quo, and to lay the blame for failures not on the financial system of corporate governance, but on personalities.

The disadvantages of 'bank power' became evident to the 'big banks' in the deep recession of 1979–82. When the Bundesbank raised interest rates to counter inflationary conditions, firms with high debt exposures died like ninepins. As a result, the Bundesbank launched its programme in 1982 for 'Finanzplatz Deutschland,' which proceeded at the lethargic pace permitted by Germany's federal system, where stakeholders have multiple sources of access to participate in public policy. The result has been a stream of laws to promote financial markets in 1989, 1996, and 1998, during which the German Stock Exchange was set up, along with a an efficient settlements system and a US-type Securities and Exchange Commission, while market opening arrangements agreed internationally and in the EU were introduced. Despite the boom in technology equities in the second half of the 1990s, and a novel public interest in shareholding, equity markets remained narrow. The shadow capital pool of corporate pension funds was also shrinking as payouts rose.

Furthermore, there was an inherent contradiction between the bank-industrial cross-holding system, which required open markets for exports and for corporate assets in other countries, while at the same time curtailing foreign market access and ownership at home. The home market served as a launch pad for the conquest of foreign markets, and the domestic market was protected by all manner of corporate practices. As a result, the financial system as a whole had to deal with the consequences of large trade surpluses, which flowed from joint corporate interest in market shares. Domestic inflationary pressures had to be kept down through rapid recycling of funds earned from exports. This entailed a build up of portfolio investments in other markets around the world, revaluations of the currency, and foreign direct investments to avoid the high costs of domestic production. This was national mercantilism's Achilles heel. Corporations became detached from banks as their external sources of funds on world markets grew, while regulatory segmentation within the financial system began to break down as financial institutions competed across boundaries for new clients. Over time, and despite national legislation passed in 1975 to curtail share acquisitions in listed German corporations from falling into the hands of foreign (Mideastern) owners, German corporate shares leaked out onto global markets.

One policy that would have cured the German economy of its propensity to run trade surpluses was a market-oriented reform of the German financial system, and the development of a highly liquid, transactions-based capital market in the manner of London. A starting point would have been for the Bundesbank to have met the commercial banks' demands and repatriate the euro-Deutschmark bond market (to which the banks' surplus funds were recycled) by ending the tax disadvantages weighing on domestic bond business. This would have promoted a liquid secondary market, flanked by a short term money market. Dearer credit would encourage firms to move away from bank borrowing as the primary source of external funding, to the new issue of equities. An enlarged primary issue market for equities would in turn foster a demand for a secondary market for equities. National ownership would be diluted. Germany would become a major source of international capital, and move to a regular deficit on trade account. European integration would be accelerated.

As long as the Deutschmark ruled, financial market reforms fell shy of such radical change (Story 1996). A constant theme of the Bundesbank was its hostility to fast money markets and new financial instruments. Indeed, during the internal market negotiations of 1988 to 1993, the German delegation insisted on legislation to protect monetary policy by keeping a firewall between the domestic monetary market and short-term capital flows.[14] This preference for stable domestic monetary and financial conditions helped to underwrite Germany's growing structural predominance registered in the trade surpluses. The surpluses in turn became a perennial subject of European diplomacy from the mid-1960s on. Europe's 'great affair'—how to create an exchange rate or monetary system for a highly interdependent region of separate states—may be dated from then, lasting through to German unity, the Maastricht Treaty in 1992 and finally the achievement of a single currency in 1999.

By stating an 'irreversible commitment' to substitute a European currency and central bank for the Deutschmark and the Bundesbank, the Maastricht Treaty circumvented German inhibitions about abandoning the Deutschmark. In effect, German policy over the 1990s dithered with diminishing vigor between the federal orientation for the EU, and a national inflection of looking after German interests first. The dithering changed to inflection in late summer of 1993. More volatile exchange rate conditions in 1992–3 seemed to promise a new independence for the Bundesbank from international constraints. Corporate Germany was uncomfortable about relying on foreign investors as marginal suppliers of external funds. In September 1993, Chancellor Kohl launched his government 'Report on Securing Germany's Economic Future,' aiming to cut costs and expand exports. The clear objective was to return to trade surplus and corporate financial independence. These steps coincided with the Constitutional Court's judgement that the Maastricht Treaty created a 'confederation, which is sustained by the states.' But then in 1995, the Deutschmark revalued sharply in response to the outflow of dollars from the Mexico financial crash and from the yen after the Kobe earthquake disaster which hit Japan. The Deutschmark spike prompted shouts of anguish from corporate managers, their workforces and their financial backers. Better to have the protection of a stable financial area within an European monetary union, the message of German business ran, than the constant volatility of the Deutschmark fully exposed to global financial markets. This was the moment when Kohl in effect won his battle for the hearts and minds of corporate Germany to go ahead with the Maastricht plan to introduce the euro in the years 1999–2002. The single currency swept aside rearguard actions in Frankfurt to block the development of a money market, and German corporate equities and bonds—as for other member countries—were converted into euro-denominated assets,

[14] This condition found expression in the Central Bank Governors' deliberations on liberalization of capital movements, and on the insider trading directive. *Europolitique*, No. 1401, April 30, 1988, and *Journal Officiel*, No. L 334/30 18.11.1989.

exchangeable across a much wider territory than before and without incurring foreign exchange risk.

The process called 'globalization' in Europe was unleashed largely by German unity. Much of 'globalization' more broadly was similarly inaugurated by the end of the Cold War structure of two Germanies, two Europes and two great powers. The immediate impact was to incorporate within one interdependent global system all of the countries previously embedded in or attached to the communist system. The collapse of the Soviet Union transformed the Eurasian continent and accelerated the entry of China and India to global markets. Most importantly, the world labor market was in effect widened to incorporate three billion potential workers, with unit labor costs anything up to 60–100 times lower than those prevailing in Europe, the USA and Japan. Monetary union, which EU member states agreed in their majority had to accompany the move to liberalize capital movements, was part of this process. With all OECD countries adopting free capital movements, the global capital market took off, with a sharp rise in foreign direct and portfolio investments to 'emerging' markets. German outward investment, rising from a low rate, rose sharply, particularly to central-eastern Europe where wage rates were much lower, similar productivity rates could be achieved as in Germany, and profit contributions to capital enhanced. Failure to fundamentally alter labor market structures meant that jobs were lost in manufacturing, but the losses were not compensated by an expansion of the services sector or an adequate shift to high-value added activities (Figure 10.2).

There were other forces at work undermining the inherited German national business system. Wealthier and older German savers joined in the

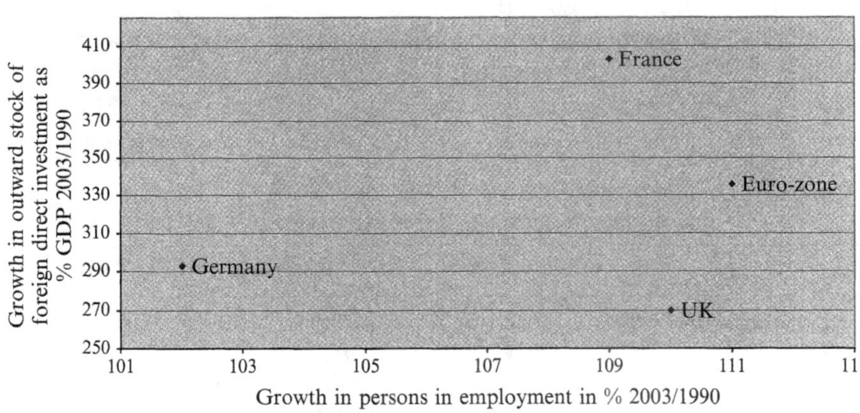

FIGURE 10.2. Growth in employment relative to outward direct investment: 2003/1990.
Source: UN, Eurostat.

boom for hi-tech stocks, equated with the Deutsche Börse's opening in 1997 of the Neuer Market, fashioned on the US technology stock exchange Nasdaq (see Elliot Posner's chapter in this volume). Legislation was also passed to encourage private funded pensions, with the funds managed by the banks. But when boom turned to bust in 2001 and Deutsche Telecom stocks plummeted, the equity market turned sour. With investors learning time and again that they had been taken for a ride, the market was closed. Meanwhile, Germany's big private banks had long since seen domestic business as a declining proportion of their activities. As their global investment banking arms grew, they developed a sharper shareholder-friendly policy with regard to the major listed corporations whose shares they continued to manage, and whose boards they continued to frequent. This externalization of Germany's leading banks went along with the increased reliance on global funding to finance the cost of German unification, and with a sharp rise in equity funding as a proportion of corporate external borrowing (Table 10.2).

When in 1999–2000 Vodafone, an upstart UK-based service provider, launched its successful hostile takeover bid of Mannesmann, 60 percent of Mannesmann's shares were circulating outside national territory. The battle symbolized the 'battle of systems.' Here was a 109-year-old, blue-chip German company being taken over by an upstart Anglo-Saxon company that had only been in existence for fifteen years. Only a handful of hostile takeovers had been launched in Germany in the 1990s, and the last transnational bid (Pirelli's grab in 1990 for German tire maker Continental) had failed. But the Vodafone bid showed up some of the discrete changes underway in Germany's business system. Vodafone's bid involved a straight share swap, giving unprecedented leverage to smaller shareholders; the bid took place with the concurrence of the IG Metall union; and Deutsche Bank—traditionally Mannesmann's prime banker ('hausbank')—did not play a lead role, nor did the government mobilize a constituency to oppose the bid, despite that fact that Vodafone was targeting only 10 percent of Mannesmann's business and announced its intention to sell off the rest. Not least,

TABLE 10.2. *Comparative corporate sector liabilities/total: 1980 and 2000*

	UK		Germany		France	
Money market instruments	0.3	0.9	0.4	0.4	0.0	1.3
Loans	26.5	22.5	68.5	42.8	44.6	16.1
Bonds	2.3	6.5	2.8	1.3	5.2	3.4
Equities	48.4	70.2	28.3	55.4	50.2	79

Source: Data from national balance sheets.

Vodafone's capital market valuation surpassed German corporate champions, like Siemens, by a wide margin.

Vodafone's successful bid evoked much heart searching among the *prominenz* of Deutschland AG—Germany 'incorporated.' There were two diametrically opposed ways forward: one was to enforce shareholder-value principles, with high share prices as the main line of defense against takeover; the other was to reduce the exposure of companies to the share price through share buyback schemes. Before the bid, business and government had supported the EU Commission's draft Thirteenth Directive on Company Law Concerning Takeover Bids put forward in 1996, and German corporations had started to introduce shareholder-value concepts in their divisional reports. Following the Vodafone bid, the German government changed direction and successfully mobilized support in the EP against the directive. The German government then passed a law granting managers the right to fend off a hostile approach without consulting shareholders. Yet the government also introduced tax reforms, which came into practice in 2002, lowering the high taxes hitherto charged on the sale of share packages.

In October 2004, the EU introduced the European Company Statute, whereby companies operating in more than one member state had the option to choose under which country's corporate law they could operate.[15] The draft had meandered by fits and starts through the EU's complex institutional processes, but had been stalled by the politics of different national labor laws, particularly with regard to the presence of trade union representatives on boards. This 'codetermination' law had come onto the German statute book in 1976, against the wish of German business leaders. Subsequently German management went along with the law, not least because it made trade union leaders de facto allies against foreign hostile takeovers. The Vodafone-Mannesman takeover showed that this condition no longer held, while German private banks had espoused many components of shareholder-value ideas. The 2004 EU Company Statute thus met a more favorable response: it opened the option for German corporations to establish themselves in UK law, thereby sidetracking the codetermination rules and two-tier corporate board of German law and practice.

Thus it is that global markets and EU legislation, with the support of German government and of some German business, are slowly unravelling Germany's national cross-shareholding nexus. What stretches ahead is a prolonged list of rearguard actions and last-ditch fights. In the new Europe, Germany would be a province in a Union, not a hegemonic power in a Europe of states. The EU Commission has stated that regulation of takeover

[15] See Rudiger von Rosen, 'The storm gathering over corporate Germany', *Financial Times*, September 29, 2004.

bids is a key element in achieving an integrated capital market in the Union by 2005. Yet Germany, France and Sweden lined up against the Commission's proposal to ban multiple-voting rights that give holders of small stakes a disproportionate influence. And Germany bought UK support to block an EU takeover regime with a deal to block a separate proposal to extend the rights of temporary workers.

4. France's Voyage from State to Market

France is the classic reference point for the model of top-down development through a state-led financial market system (Zysman 1983; Schmidt 1996, 2003). In terms of historical precedence, though, the title should arguably be awarded to Italy or to Turkey. Typically, the state-led model of industrialization featured as a 'third way' between US capitalism and the Soviet system, and appealed to countries—like post-1945 France—whose agriculture was backward, where small business enterprises predominated, and larger corporations were few and far between. From the 1940s through to 1984–6, the French Ministry of Finance regulated the capital market directly. Surplus funds of deposit taking institutions were taken up by public-sector institutions which lent them to specific industries, such as housing, agriculture, nuclear energy, or regional investments. Large French firms did not tend to have a capital base, instead depending on financing through state channels.

The creation of a single currency requires the unravelling of national corporate structures and their transformation under the dual hammer of EU regulations and an EU-wide market. But the history of French debates about 'the German model' from the 1960s to the introduction of the euro indicated that the limits to French adaptability were traced by the changing contours of domestic politics. Indeed, the defining characteristic of this lengthy discussion about Germany through French eyes was its consistent framing in terms of national patterns of policy. Germany was to be imitated because thereby France could resist German competition better, or Germany was not to be imitated because France could only compete with Germany on markets by developing its own *sui generis* capitalism.

There have been two discernible 'German models' in French economic policy. One was centered on the banks, in putative imitation of German practice, and the other was centered on the state as the guarantor for national success. Finance Minister Debré's bank reforms of 1966 enabled two investment banks to form federations of companies, accounting in the aggregate for 48 percent of industrial value added and 60 percent of exports (Morin 1974, 1977; Bellon 1980). An alternative programme to this French version of the 'German model' had been forged with the signing in 1972 of a common program between the Communists and the revived Socialist Party.[16] Following his electoral victory of May 1981, the new President Mitterrand opted for a 100 percent nationalization of thirty-six private banks, two investment banks and eleven industrial conglomerates. This extended public sector accounted for one-third of sales, one-fifth of employment and over half of industrial investments. State banking encompassed 90 percent of banking activity and employed 200 thousand people. This state-led 'force de frappe'[17] was to foster investment, to promote new technologies; to reduce national dependence on foreign suppliers; and to encourage greater risk taking. State capital was to flow into a few publicly-owned groups, organized on Japanese keiretsu lines. But capital injections to industrial groups went on current expenditures. The state paid heavy indemnities to the owners. State corporations had to borrow from state banks. Corporations threatened closure unless funds were made available.

The crescendo to the French political battle over nationalization and privatization, and over national protection or freer trade within a wider European context, was reached in 1983, when Mitterrand decided to keep the existing exchange rate arrangement, tying the franc to the deutschmark. Financial market reforms, already in preparation, were accelerated. Unlike in Germany, the French state revolutionized its capital markets fast, introduced a Banking Act in July 1984 that provided a uniform set of prudential rules for all financial institutions. The Act centralized regulatory powers for all bank sectors and initiated a revolution for banking in France. Banks could no longer count on automatic rediscounting at the Banque de France, while tighter regulations forced banks to raise their own capital, and to pay more attention to profits. Finance Minister Bérégovoy also moved forcefully to constitute a unified capital market, and to push French corporate financing towards the model of Anglo-American financial markets (Zerah 1993). The reforms entailed wholesale importation of US methods to French conditions. In 1988, the six regional stock exchanges were merged with the Paris Bourse, and French law was adapted to accommodate mutual fund techniques developed by *les Anglo-Saxons*. But withdrawal of the Finance Ministry from refinancing banks meant that France's undercapitalized firms might fall into foreign ownership.

This did not prevent governments of both right and left from privatizing state assets in three waves in 1986–8, again in 1993, and especially in the years

[16] The new Socialist Secretary General told his party militants, in language redolent of the neosocialist fascists of the 1930s, that 'the dominant phenomenon of capitalist concentration, money, enters everywhere and devours those whom it is supposed to assist'. Quoted in Nay 1984, 322.

[17] 'French industrial policy,' *Financial Times*, January 8, 1982.

1997–2002, when the left government presided over even larger sales than its conservative predecessors. Market capitalization of equities rose from 5.5 percent GDP in 1982 to 37 percent by 1993, and 63 percent by 2002. One result is that France has come to resemble the UK, more than Germany, in terms of household sector assets, and in corporate sector liabilities. Indeed, French corporate external financing is more reliant on equities than the UK (see Table 10.2).

France is also much closer to the UK than to Germany in terms of the dispersion of equity ownership (see Table 10.1). If we add to that the original intent of the 1984–6 government to introduce New York-style capital markets to Paris, the creation of money market funds, or the opening in the 1990s of the Nouveau Marché for hi-tech stocks—also along Nasdaq lines—then the conclusion could well be drawn that, despite rhetoric to the contrary (or perhaps as an explanation of official rhetoric about *le capitalisme sauvage*) France is more 'Anglo-Saxon' than it would care to admit. Indeed, the internationalization of French enterprises over the 1990s grew from a much lower base than the UK to reach about half the value of the overseas stock of UK investment. As can be seen in Figure 10.1, what distinguished France from Germany was the speed with which French corporations internationalized, as well as the volume of jobs created by the French economy in the 1990s. If this foreign investment trend were to be sustained over the coming decade, it is not inconceivable that the French economy becomes as globalized as the UK, albeit in its own specific way. The outlier with regard to equity finance is Germany, not the UK; the major difference between France and the UK lies in labor markets, where—with a similar population of sixty million each—the UK employs five million more than France (see Table 10.3). France's un- and underemployment rate is just under 20 percent of the employable labor force.

Thus even though the deep French capital market reforms preceded those in London, France has not been able to maximize the benefits. Turnover in French shares moved to London, as did French financial institutions—not to Frankfurt. The main reason for this is the lack of locally supplied liquidity to the market for reasons similar to those in Germany. Unlike *'les Anglo-Saxons,'* France lacks major pension funds or institutional investors. Social security is provided on a pay-as-you-earn basis and the burden of financing additional welfare is allocated to employers and employees. Companies are not able to keep pension reserves as own funds, as in Germany. The reformers of 1984–8 had recognized the urgency of developing funded pensions. But they ran into resistance from managers, who disliked to lose existing prerogatives; trade unions which were opposed to losing their position as comanagers of social spending in the social security system; and political parties of left and right who, following Mitterrand, talked about equity

TABLE 10.3. *Growth of Persons in Employment (in '000s), 1990–2003*

	1992	1997	2003
Germany	37,878	37,208	38,248
France	22,742	23,215	24,104
Italy	22,920	22,215	24,286
UK	26,933	28,104	29,771

Source: Eurostat.

markets as 'Anglo-Saxon'. When in 1996 the conservative government tried to spring reform of social security on the public without consultation, it retreated in the face of massive strikes. The left government of 1997–2002 then took to consultation with a vengeance as the smoothest way to introduce extensive privatization, and to smuggle in reforms in the social security system. The resulting reforms lowered the strain on the public pension system by reducing the average pension and smuggling in the possibility of lengthening work lives. But they do not answer the need of the Paris market for a local supply of funds.

The shortfall is made up by US, Irish, Dutch or UK institutional investors, who have over 40 percent of Paris' market share. So when successive French governments privatized, they faced the prospect of previously nationally owned industries being 'dissolved in Europe'.[18] Here the 'German model' served a purpose, but the tools were distinctly French. French diplomacy in Brussels secured legislation in EU directives, allowing bank-insurance tie-ups to act as 'a powerful and organized financial heart' of corporate ownership (Banque de France 1993).[19] The savings banks—with 30 percent of total French deposits, led by the Caisse des Dépots et Consignations—were available as a source of funds at the disposal of the Finance Ministry. The nationalized insurers AGF, GAN and UAP were regrouped into holding companies and took advantage of new legislation to buy stakes in banks and industrial companies. The senior ranks of the French state and business were and are dominated by the state corps of engineers and financiers who have made their way to the pinnacles of both public and private sectors, making the retention of senior corporate positions on the career circuit of the *grand corps d'état* an ever-present consideration. Besides, the purpose of privatization was not to divest the state of all shares so much as to open up capital to the corporations to strengthen their chances as national champions that would be capable of

[18] The expression is that of Olivier Pastré, consultant to the Trésor: 'Pastré: le reveil des ZINvestisseurs,' *La Tribune de l'Expansion*, September 7, 1992.

[19] 'La logique du coeur financier,' *Le Monde*, October 8, 1991.

entering alliances with foreign corporations from a position of strength. Equally, state intervention was there when needed to keep French corporations like Crédit Lyonnais, the insurer GAN or Alstom on the French career circuit—and out of the hands of Deutsche Bank or Siemens.

Thus if France has been a market economy since the 1980s, it has retained some of the institutions and much of the spirit of Gallo-capitalism—the vision of France as a plucky *résistant* determined to retain independence. Yet joining the world but proclaiming the French exception is a difficult balance to achieve. Gallo-capitalism in its ancient 1940s format sought to allocate national resources for national purposes. But as markets open to foreign competition, government officials find themselves immersed in an ocean of corporate details about which they know next to nothing. Foreign investors seek entry and bring access to technologies, management skills and foreign markets. Inward investors compete with national producers on their home markets, and this prompts national producers to retaliate by entering international markets by both trade and investment. As state capitalism's corporations internationalize, their tendency is to seek to loosen the ties that bind them to their home state.

Such was the fate of Jean-Marie Messier, who turned the water utility Compagnie Générale des Eaux into a $51 billion global telecommunications and media giant, Vivendi. Messier went on a six-year, $17 billion buying spree to create a company that promised to be 'the world's preferred creator and provider of personalized information, entertainment and services to consumers anywhere'. Vivendi included the pay-TV company, Canal Plus, one of France's cultural powerhouses. This spree made Vivendi highly vulnerable to the meltdown in financial markets at the tail of the dotcom boom in March 2001, when Vivendi registered losses of €13.1 billion—the largest in French history. Messier's financial strategy was simple enough: the water business—based on de facto local monopolies—supplied cash to the fast growth telecoms and media business; and Vivendi borrowed funds on the back of its equity, 43 percent of which was held by investment institutions, including Calpers, the Californian Public Employees Retirement Pension fund. The Bronfman family, also a shareholder, tried to stage a board revolt in May 2002, and the board—dominated by French institutions—squelched it. But keeping 'Anglo-Saxon' investors happy with a sliding share price was not sustainable. Messier sought to identify Vivendi with global markets, made his primary residence in New York, and talked aloud, saying that France's *exception culturelle* was an outdated idea. This alienated the Parisian left-bank, nationalist cultural establishment. Without friends in Paris, his career fell into ruins with startling speed. France's 'cultural exception' policy remains well in place as the heart of French rationale for a French-led Europe to resist the US hyper-power.

5. The EU: No Longer a French Garden

Throughout the years from 1968 to 2001—from West German Finance Minister Strauss' famous 'Nein' to de Gaulle's request for a Deutschmark revaluation, recorded on the front page of the Bild Zeitung, through to the conversion of national currencies to euros on the retail markets in December 2001—the thrust of French diplomacy was to prevent Germany's emergence as Europe's prime power, the preferred partner of the USA in Europe, and managing a Deutschmark through the Bundesbank as the lead agent of Germany's financial and corporate power nexus. The motive behind successive French administrations was to dilute or to dissolve the Bundesbank within a new European monetary regime, run on lines more compatible with the exigencies of the French economy.

Those exigencies could be summarized in two concerns of French public policy: the high and rising rates of unemployment recorded since the mid-1970s, and disquiet at Germany's growing preponderance in Europe, since the Deutschmark began its ascent on the back of widening trade surpluses to replace sterling as the world's second reserve currency after the dollar. Domestic considerations of equity and of political prudence counselled against tampering too much with state welfare provisions, while concerns about efficiency pointed to the promotion of economic structures able to withstand competition on open European and world markets. The UK was the obvious ally in helping to contain Germany by promoting EU-wide legislation to dilute the German corporate nexus in the name of EU integration, but Germany was the ally against the UK to protect France's *acquis sociaux*.

The heart of the deal between France and Germany over monetary union was for Germany to agree to substitute the Deutschmark for the euro, under the aegis of a European Central Bank designed along Bundesbank lines, in return for French and German agreement to defend, and to extend, *les aquis sociaux,* into the domain of EU policy. Maintenance of western Europe's welfare policies was considered vital to ensure continued popular support for the internal market programme. These considerations flowed together as Germany moved to unity in the course of 1989, leading to the signing of the Maastricht Treaty in 1991–2. The Franco-German alliance was cemented on a more futuristic note, when on April 19, 1990 Kohl and Mitterrand issued their joint declaration on European monetary and political union. The declaration opened the way to the negotiations on EU that produced the Maastricht Treaty in winter 1991–2. That Maastricht was above all a political deal to dilute German unity in a broader EU is illustrated by Chancellor Kohl's acceptance of an 'irrevocable' commitment for monetary union by 1999. There was no going back.

Nonetheless, when monetary union was implemented in the years 1999–2002, its operations were fashioned by the difficulties which the Kohl governments in particular faced in selling an 'irrevocable' commitment to the Bundesbank and the German people.

First, the Bundesbank deployed its structural power over the Deutschmark in financial markets to eject first the pound sterling and the lira in August 1992 from the exchange rate mechanism, and then had to come to terms with the French government to widen the exchange rate fluctuation bands to 15 percent either side of the central rates. The pound sterling has remained outside the exchange rate mechanism and the UK is not a member of monetary union.

Second, German Finance Minister Waigel launched the idea of a 'stability pact,' with the clear intent of preventing Italy's reentry: the assumption was that Italy would not be sufficiently continent in fiscal matters to qualify for monetary union. Paradoxically, the greatest offenders against the stability pact since 2001 have been France and Germany.

Third, over the decade German business became converted to monetary union as continued dollar unpredictability on global exchange markets threatened to undercut German export price competitiveness. World financial markets voted for the Deutschmark, thereby bringing the Deutschmark into the euro about 20 percent over value, while France entered way below its purchasing power parity to the Deutschmark. This only added to the burden Germany inherited from Kohl's decision to export West German welfare provisions to eastern Germany, resulting in an indefinite transfer of resources from west to east amounting to 5–6 percent GDP per annum.

5.1. Monetary Union as a Neoliberal Engine

But the fundamental paradox of monetary union is that the EU of the first decade of the millennium is stuck with a currency and capital market, backed by ECJ jurisprudence and global product markets, that create a structure of continental-wide incentives for market agents to operate as if the trend was irreversibly set towards a US-type market and business system. Because monetary union is irreversible, the states within the Euro-zone face further structural changes to adapt to the reality which they have willed, not least because monetary union is an engine of European federalist aspirations. Monetary union has tilted European markets significantly away from a Europe of the states. At its most fundamental and obvious level, monetary union has eliminated national currencies and exchange rates among the participating countries. As a consequence, monetary union eliminates associated transaction costs, where payments are made between buyers and sellers in two or more currencies. This clearly reinforces the basic idea of a common market in goods and services and parallels the single market initiative to clean-up remaining market distortions. At least four far-reaching consequences follow that move Europe in a neoliberal (and American) direction—though for the moment each remains virtual for the same reason: the reality of the EU is of a diverse and interdependent set of states, each with their own legacies.

First, monetary union has integrated national bond markets, and has begun to do the same for equities. For European financial institutions, the potential for growth in equity markets is huge, given the corporate consolidations, privatizations and business transfers which lie ahead. No longer do companies issuing securities have to worry about various pockets of investors separated by foreign exchange risk, nor do investors have to worry about asset-allocations across currency-zones where they face not only the possibility of exchange rate changes but also different directions in economic policies and their subsequent impact on relative asset values. A unified capital market helps allocate capital more efficiently on an EU-wide basis, encourages savings and investment, and facilitates technological innovations, along with other determinants of economic growth. What investors in Euro-land do confront in their hunt for opportunities are inherited national impediments to an EU-wide 'level playing field.' As stated in the report on EU competitiveness chaired by former Dutch Prime Minister Wim Kok, one of the prime impediments to EU competitiveness is the low level of trade in services—representing only 20 percent of intra-EU trade, but 70 percent of economic activity (Kok 2004). The list of impediments is long, running from a cumbersome system for transfrontier settlement of commercial transactions, to national procurement policies, local insurance and pension markets, and different bankruptcy laws and accountancy practices.

Second, monetary union and the absence of national central banks means a single financial market in which all borrowers except the sovereign (the EU as a whole) compete on an even footing. The European Central Bank (ECB) can only purchase EU debt instruments in order to assure adequate growth of the money supply and, under such circumstances, only the EU as a whole can finance deficits by having its debt monetized (purchased and held by the central bank). Because the ECB is concerned solely with price stability, the ECB goal of a 2 percent ceiling for Euro-zone inflation represents a very high rate of interest for zero inflation rate Germany and a negative rate of interest for high growth, higher inflation Ireland. Combined with the post-2000 recession and the overvaluation of the Deutschmark at the time of entry to the euro—plus the continued burden on German taxpayers of integrating eastern Germany to their welfare system—Europe, and its largest economy, Germany, has fallen into a rigidity trap. The result has been to send fiscal imbalances in the big Euro-land member states way past the 3 percent GDP mark stipulated in the Stability and Growth Pact. National governments have had to accept that their debt issues are priced at market rates, rather than as sovereign instruments purchasable by a national central bank. Their growing debt cannot be inflated away. But the member states have found ways out of the Pact's straitjacket, from falsifying their accounts to effectively tearing up the Pact. The history of the Pact indicates that member states, especially France and Germany, continue to make or break rules agreed on in the EU when it suits them. The implication is that the ECB, a technical institution isolated from political interference by treaty, remains vulnerable to a political takeover by elected officials who are desperate to seek a way out of the monetary straitjacket which has been made for them.

Third, monetary union has significant implications for industrial and labor market policies. In terms of industrial policy, governments are constrained in their ability to sustain uncompetitive industries through budgetary transfers, without incurring rising debt levels and taxpayers hostility to the ratcheting up of tax levels. Monetary union has deprived them of the exchange rate tool. All this favors cutbacks in welfare provision, the promotion of privatization, and steps to promote a Europe-wide labor market to run alongside the Europe-wide currency, capital and products markets (Krueger 2000). The starting point, though, is that labor markets are national (again, see Figure 10.1): only 1.5 percent of the EU's total labor force is employed in another member state. Several factors account for low intra-EU labor mobility: cultural and language barriers; nontransportability of welfare-state programs; sizeable legal and financial impediments to establishing legal residency; difficult and expensive housing markets; and citizenship restrictions on public sector employment (Bertola 2000, 99–122). Furthermore, these institutional and cultural differences explain why the range of people in employment relative to the total employable population stretches from 56 percent in Italy to 75 percent in Denmark. The official EU objective is to achieve a 70 percent participation rate of the employable labor force by 2010: on that basis un-and under-employment in the Euro-zone in 2003 amounted to 18.5 percent.

Fourth, monetary union, complemented by effective competition policies to ensure that monopolies or oligopolies are not established on a European scale, would help denationalize corporate strategies—if everything else were equal. This was the lesson which *The Economist* proposed should be learnt from the total receipts in Europe of $675 billion from privatization between 1990 and 2002.[20] Privatization promised to create a broad shareholding public, with a stake in publicly listed corporations, regardless of nationality. This fosters competition between financial institutions for ever more

[20] 'Coming home to roost,' *The Economist*, June 27, 2002.

demanding investors: companies which wish to benefit by a single, transparent market will have to propose the very best projects; shareholders will not be inclined to buy shares unless returns on their investment are attractive; managers will want to accentuate the drive for efficiency; layoffs will accelerate. Clearly, none of this is readily compatible with the fragility of shareholder culture in Germany, with President Chirac's proposals favoring national champions, nor with the continued existence of national cross-shareholdings, trusts, poison pills or other vehicles designed to repel foreign invaders. Nor is it compatible with the perpetuation of national labor market protectionisms, the heart of which are the national welfare states.

One conclusion is that the EU model is not sustainable, and that the EU has no viable alternative in view (Pelkmans and Carey 2004). This is disputable for two reasons: the first is that monetary union was not primarily about economic considerations. Confusion over the complex motivations leading to the euro has led many observers to overemphasize the costs that would be incurred in creating a monetary union without intrastate labor mobility. It has led to expectations that monetary union would lead member states to speed up liberalization of their national markets in conformity with the thrust of EU policy. Monetary union would act as a neoliberal engine to break up national labor market protectionisms of all sorts. And it led to the conclusion that given the disparities in labor market institutions, monetary union amounted to a very high risk strategy (Dornbusch 1996; Feldstein 1997). Indeed it was. But the expected alternative, German hegemony, was rated an even higher risk by its prime protagonists. Monetary union was about preventing the emergence of Germany as the dominant power in Europe after the end of the cold war. It was an updating of the peace agreements between Germany and France, in particular, that have characterized their relations since 1945. Maastricht was a peace treaty, and 'irreversible.' The economic and social costs were the consequence.

Second, Maastricht put into place one money and capital market which only one of the four big states of the EU was prepared for. That country is the UK. Without a doubt, it features the most liberal of markets among major EU member states. Foreign companies, banks, personnel or products have ready access to a market where the rhetoric, and to a great extent the reality of policy is geared to benefiting the consumer. One reason for British public opinion being skeptical about the EU-project is that the British government in the 1980s implemented liberal market reforms without the aid of the EU institutions. Indeed, Prime Minister Thatcher's major concern was that the EU would be used to reintroduce the rigidities in the UK economic structure that her governments did so much to remove. Clearly, Thatcher's concern is shared in the Blair Labour government, despite or because of their signing on to the EU's social policy agenda. So the other reason why British public opinion is sceptical about Euro-land is that the major states are stuck on very high levels of un- and underemployment. They have not adapted their structures to the EU framework which Kohl, Mitterrand and Delors concocted to house Germany.

Monetary union represents a political revolution perpetrated by the EU's elites, who knew only too well that public aquiescence could not be won without pledging to preserve *les acquis sociaux*. The fundamental weakness at the heart of the package is that monetary union is sold to publics as designed to protect national welfare fabrics against the supposed depredations of 'Anglo-Saxon' capitalism. That means that the full implications of monetary union cannot be sold readily by successive French and German governments. They have to introduce reforms by stealth, through sleight of hand, and step-by-step. The resulting stresses and strains—evident in slow growth, budget imbalances, cheating on the statistics, noncompliance, unemployment and above all in the ever wider gap between the EU's language of 'solidarity' and the sad realities of social exclusion in the EU—ensure that the UK public remains skeptical to hostile about joining fully. Here is one more element of the 'battle of systems,' and an important one given that London has become the euro area's financial capital even as the UK remains outside the monetary union.

Where does this leave our story in the light of the editors' six mechanisms for change in the EU? Monetary union has addressed the French fear of Bundesbank hegemony as the Federal Reserve's main counterpart within the EU, but has strengthened Britain's position as the Euro-zone's centre for global finance. The euro, too, expresses an ambition, often voiced in France, for global leadership, as the alternative to the dollar, but it also strengthens already existing trends for corporations to widen their market horizons in order to defray the costs of technological innovations. It has stimulated the member states' dispositions to fight for their national priorities that they retain from their incompatible national legacies: the incompatibilities of the UK's established financial structure and labor market institutions with the national financial, corporate and labor market institutions of France and Germany, as well as the incompatibility of French and German national legacies with the neoliberal thrust of the euro and the accompanying capital market. The 'battle of the systems' continues in full swing, with each of the major states seeking to subvert the institutions of the other, either through market mechanisms or through EU legislation.

There is no evident way out of this condition. The major continental states feature low euro interest rates, bloated budgets, rigid labor markets in France, Germany and Italy and a high exchange rate. The UK's Labour government has presided over higher interest rates, a consumer boom, and a low unemployment economy outside the euro. It is a beneficiary of the labor market reforms introduced in the UK in the 1980s. Similar labor market reforms were notoriously not introduced in France, Germany or Italy. Here is the Euro's Achilles heel. The fundamental deficiency in implementing the Euro is that product, labor and financial markets have not been liberalized to the extent required for a monetary union, and for them to operate at optimum efficiency. They have not been liberalized because there is no consent for liberalization in the major countries. The euro was launched as a top-down project, with minimum democratic support; but it can only prosper if the ideological battle is won to ensure a bottom-up support for a liberal market society. That ideological battle has scarcely begun, especially in France and Germany—the two supposed leaders of the European project. So the immediate likelihood is not an early evolution to a liberal market society on the European continent, but an unstable and necessary temporary compromise between national social corporatism, generating major social tensions in France and Germany, and global markets, of which the euro, the Euro-capital market and the UK financial and corporate structures are active constituent parts. Perhaps unthinkingly or unwittingly, but probably irrevocably, the EU has entered uncharted waters.

6. References

Aeschimann, E. and Riché, P. (1996). *La Guerre de Sept Ans: Histoire secrète du franc fort, 1989–96*. Paris: Calmann-Levy.

Balkhausen, D. (1992). *Gutes Geld und schlechte Politik*. Düsseldorff: Capital.

Bartlett, C. and Ghoshal, S. (1989). *Managing Across Borders: The Transnational Solution*. Cambridge, MA: Harvard Business School Press.

Baun, M. (1996). 'The Maastricht Treaty as High Politics: Germany, France and European Integration', *Political Science Quarterly*, 110/4: 605–24.

Bellon, F. (1980). *Le Pouvoir Financier et l'Industrie en France*. Paris: Seuil.

Bertola, G. (2000). 'Labour markets in the European Union', *Ifo-Studien*, 46:1.

Brewster, C. and Teague, P. (1989). *European Community Social Policy: Its Impact on the UK*. London: Institute of Personnel Management.

Banque de France (1993). *Commission Bancaire Rapport 1993: La bancassurance en France*. Paris: Banque de France.

Connolly, B. (1996). *The Rotten Heart of Europe: The Dirty War for Europe's Money*. London: Farrar Straus & Giroux.

De Cecco, M., and Story, J. (1993). 'The Politics and Diplomacy of Monetary Union: 1985–1991', in J. Story (ed.), *The New Europe: Politics, Government and Economy since 1945*. Oxford: Blackwell.

Dornbusch, R. (1996). 'Euro Fantasies: Common Currency as Panacea', *Foreign Affairs*, 75/5: 110–24.

Dyson, K., and Featherstone, K. (1999). *The Road to Maastricht: Negotiating Economic and Monetary Union*. Oxford: Oxford University Press.

Feldstein, M. (1997). 'EMU and International Conflict', *Foreign Affairs,* 76/6: 60–73.

Fligstein, N. (2001). *The Architecture of Markets*. Princeton, NJ: Princeton University Press.

HM Treasury (2004). 'After the EU FSAP: UK Response to the Reports of the Four Independent Expert Groups', London: Crown Copyright.

Kok, Wim (2004). 'Facing the Challenge: The Lisbon Strategy for Growth and Employment', Report from the High Level Group chaired by Wim Kok. Luxemburg: Office for Official Publications of the European Communities.

Krueger, A. B. (2000). 'From Bismark to Maastricht: The March to European Union and the Labor Compact', NBER Working Paper No. 7456.

Ludlow, P. (1982). *The Making of the European Monetary System*. London: Butterworths.

Moravcsik, A. (1998). *The Choice for Europe: Social Purpose and State Power from Messina to Maastricht*. Ithaca, NY: Cornell University Press.

Morin, F. (1974). *La Structure Financière du Capitalisme Français*. Paris: Calmann-Lévy.

—— (1977). *La Banque et les Groupes Industriels à l'Heure des Nationalisations*. Paris: Calmann-Lévy.

Nay, C. (1984). *Le Rouge et le Noir, ou l'histoire d'une ambition*. Paris: Grasset.

North, D. C. *et al.* (1991). *Institutions, Institutional Change and Economic Performance*. New York: Cambridge University Press.

O'Sullivan, M. (2000). *Contests for Corporate Control: Corporate Governance and Economic Performance in the US and Germany*. Oxford: Oxford University Press.

Pauly, L. W. and Reich, S. (1997). 'National Structures and Multinational Corporate Behaviour: Enduring Differences in the Age of Globalizatrion', *International Organization,* 51/1: 1–30.

Pelkmans, J. and Carey, J-P. (2004). 'Can Europe Deliver Growth? The Sapir Report and Beyond', Centre for European Policy Studies Policy Brief No.45.

Porter, M. (1992). 'Capital Disadvantage: America's Failing Capital Investment System', *Harvard Business Review* VOL/NO (September–October): 65–83.

Prahalad, C. K. and Doz, Y. (1987). *The Multinational Mission: Balancing Local Demands and Global Vision*. New York: Free Press.

Schmidt, V. A. (1996). *From State to Market? The Transformation of French Business and Government*. New York: Cambridge University Press.

—— (2003). 'French Capitalism Transformed, Yet Still a Third Variety of Capitalism', *Economy and Society,* 32/4: 526–54.

Simonian, H. (1985). *The Privileged Partnership: Franco-German Relations in the European Community, 1969–84*. Oxford: Oxford University Press.

Story, J. (1996). 'Finanzplatz Deutschland: National or European Response to Internationalization?' *German Politics,* 5/3: 371–94.

Story, J. and Walter, I. (1997). *Political Economy of Financial Integration in Europe: The Battle of the Systems*. Cambridge, MA: MIT Press.

Tsoukalis, L. (1977). *The Politics and Economics of European Monetary Integration*. London: Allen and Unwin.

United Nations (2004). *World Investment Report 2004: The Shift Towards Services*. New York: United Nations.

Whitley, R. (1999). *Divergent Capitalisms: The Social Structuring and Change of Business Systems*. Oxford: Oxford University Press.

Yao, S. (1992). 'Global Corporations are National Firms with International Operations', *California Management Review*, 34/2: 107–26.

Zerah, D. (1993). *Le Système Financier Français: Dix Ans de Mutations*. Paris: La Documentation Française.

Zysman, J. (1983). *Governments, Markets and Growth: Financial Systems and Policies of Industrial Change*. Ithaca, NY: Cornell University Press.

11

Toward a European Social Policy—At Last?

BRUNO PALIER AND PHILIPPE POCHET

The achievements in European social policy (ESP) are generally considered weak at best. Most commentators have underlined the imbalance between extensive economic and monetary integration on the one hand and feeble social integration on the other. The difficulties in adopting a positive integration agenda—common regulation, as opposed to the simpler 'negative integration' of removing interstate barriers—are underlined in a context of increasing diversity in terms of national-level welfare state arrangements. Moreover, both the internal market and economic and monetary union (EMU) are usually seen as raising new barriers to social activism at the European level. Amy Verdun writes of EMU (1996: 80), 'Experts argued that they favored EMU exactly because it would lead to a process of harmonization through market forces. EMU would offer legitimacy for restructuring the expensive welfare states.' EMU, and particularly the conditions imposed to be part of the Eurozone, are generally considered to threaten earlier gains made by unions as well as the level of social spending, because they render demand-side responses impossible. As Fritz Scharpf recently put it (2002: 4), 'In short, compared to the repertoire of policy choices that was available two or three decades ago, European legal constraints have greatly reduced the capacity of national governments to influence growth and employment in the economies for whose performance they are politically accountable. In principle, the only options which remain freely available are supply-side strategies involving lower tax burdens, further deregulation, flexibilization, wage differentiation and welfare cutbacks to reduce the reservation wage.'

Theories of convergence have predicted that fiscal competition, social dumping and social tourism created by European economic integration (the single market and single currency) would imply a 'race to the bottom' in social policy, social protection systems being obliged to adapt through retrenchment and structural adjustment policies (Beck *et al.* 1997). It has also been argued that this detrimental impact could be accelerated by the European Court of Justice (ECJ). Its decisions are supposed to remove any obstacle to a free market such as monopoly or national rules which are obstructing free circulation of goods or services. In this perspective, the impact of European integration on national welfare programmes is analyzed in terms of 'negative integration' (Leibfried and Pierson 1995; Scharpf 2000). In a nutshell, the different steps in European integration have increased the liberal and supply-side bias and have negatively downgraded the national social models without enabling the creation of an European one. In the terms of the editors of this book, these trends would confirm the convergence towards the 'hegemonic American model'.

But scholarship since the mid-1990s has consistently shown that welfare states were not racing to the bottom. On the contrary, social expenditures were going up and appeared extremely difficult to control (Majone 1993). Moreover, since 1997, employment policies, and since 2000, social protection policies (especially policies dealing with pensions and social exclusion) have been formally included in European competencies under a specific procedure, now called the 'Open Method of Coordination' (often simply 'OMC' in Euro-speak). The arrival of employment and social policies on the European agenda and procedures can be understood as an unintended consequence (or 'spillover' effect) of European economic and monetary integration. While most of the literature which spoke of spillover effects of European economic integration on social policies foresaw a race to the bottom, very few predicted what has really happened: a competition over competence in the social field between different European organizations, leading to considerable innovation in European social policy orientation and practices.

In the field of employment policy, as well as in the field of social protection, 'economically oriented' actors (mainly Ministers of Finance and their supporting committees—the Economic and Financial Committee and the Economic Policy Committee) have tried to preempt the definition of policy orientation so that welfare reforms could conform to their own economic priorities. 'Socially oriented' actors (mainly social ministers, trade unionists and in a lesser extent NGOs) reacted by promoting alternative orientation for social policies. National governments, whose political orientation was more favorable to social policy by the mid-1990s, supported the launching of new European social strategies but with an intergovernmental (rather than supranational) form (Manow *et al.* 2004). Taking these recent developments into account, we argue that Europe might sustain both a distinct European economic and social model and novel forms of broader governance.

Taking now an US perspective, the US model has also undergone profound changes both in term of repartition of competencies and policies. Two leading scholars underlined that 'For American proponents of global justice, social Europe appears distant yet inspirational, with its weakness still a "vanguard" model for social regulation of global economy' (Compa and

Turner 2003: 14). There is ambiguity in such comparison. Should we compare the USA and the EU or NAFTA and the EU? By adopting the first approach we tend to consider EU as a federal political system, which is far from the actual reality. Taking the second perspective, we underline the intergovernmental nature of the EU integration. In this paper we will use the first approach, keeping in mind that this comparison could be biased by the difference of nature between the USA and the EU.

The aim of this chapter is to explore the internal and external dynamics which led the core of welfare state policy to be discussed at the European level. If measured by the number of directives adopted, the story of the ESP is more a story of failure than success. Nevertheless, since the beginning of postwar integration there have been at least five successful attempts to advance social priorities at the European level. The first section will briefly put in perspective these main developments of the four decades of ESP. The second section will present recent change in three different social policy fields: labor relations, employment and social security. The third and concluding section will argue that the distinctiveness of the new ESP is linked to a new approach of European integration, where the aim is less to construct a full-fledged federal entity than an innovative multilevel polity. Even if there is an evolution toward social policies in line with the new monetary regime—in other words, some signs of liberalization or 'Americanization' (Martin and Ross 2004)—we argue that there is still a specific European model of social capitalism opposed to the USA one.

1. A Rapid History of 'Social Europe'

'The European Communities, as a freshly established supranational organization, chose a fundamentally different path from the USA at crucial stages in the development of their respective social systems.... Contrary to the USA, the European Economic Community (EEC) chose in 1957 to leave the social policy to the national welfare states. This decision was taken on the basis of the Olhin report, which had been commissioned by the International Labor Organization, and which concluded that social policy differences between countries were sustainable, so harmonization of welfare states was not deemed necessary' (Cantillon 2004: 6). After this decision, different attempts were nevertheless made to develop the social dimension of the process of economic integration. The first step, in the early 1960s, was limited to the free movement of labor. This implied giving the same rights to Community and national workers in each member state and to provide the possibility of adding up benefits acquired in different places (pensions).

The domain of social protection was much more conflictual (Pakaslahti and Pochet 2003). In the 1970s the Community tried, in the words of the Rome Treaty, to define a way 'to promote improved working conditions and an improved standard of living for workers, so as to make possible their harmonization while the improvement is being maintained.' Several directives were adopted in a context of economic downturn and militant mobilization at the national level. Equality between men and women, health and safety in the workplace as well as certain elements of labor law (collective redundancy, transfer of undertakings, and insolvency of the employer) were concerned. These first European social programs were adopted in 1974, and can be considered as the social side of the simultaneous (if eventually aborted) Werner Plan for a monetary and political union in 1980 (Magnusson and Stråth 2001).

In the following decade, the Single European Act expanded the EC's social competencies and incorporated a provision on social dialogue into the treaties. But in the unfavorable political environment of the Thatcher and Reagan years it proved impossible to continue a process aiming a harmonizing national social policies. Thus, the end of the 1980s and the beginning of the 1990s were characterized by a strategy of defining minimum norms below which one should not descend, in a period of triumphant neoliberalism. This is the sense of the Community Charter of the Fundamental Social Rights of Workers (1989) and the action program which accompanies it. Its basic idea was to develop a set of minimum legal regulations at the European level. Nevertheless, the level of ambition was sometimes so low that the draft directives were even below the level of international conventions of the International Labour Organization (ILO).

In the same period, the development of social dialogue led to the signature of the first Social Agreement between the European social partners (the European Trade Union Confederation (ETUC) for labor, and the Union of Industrial and Employers' Federations of Europe (UNICE) and European Centre of Enterprises with Public Participation and of Enterprises of General Economic Interest (CEEP) for private and public employers respectively). This agreement was introduced only as a protocol to the Maastricht Treaty and not as a proper part of it, due to the opposition of the conservative British government. It empowers the European social partners to sign negotiated agreements which can then be adopted as directives by the Social Affairs Council. The strategic idea was to mirror the national-level arrangements in many member states wherein the social partners can regulate labor relations partly by themselves.

The fifth attempt for defining a European social dimension came when the Amsterdam Treaty of 1997 adopted an employment chapter and increased the use of Council majority voting in some social areas. The chapter was tentatively modelled on EMU procedures, and introduced the Open Method of Co-ordination (OMC). In a nutshell, OMC is a flexible means of working via national plans, which are assessed in accordance with common criteria (indicators), to follow guidelines decided jointly at European level by the Social Affairs Council. Without legal compulsion, peer pressures (and the force of public opinion) represent the means to ensure that national governments adhere to these European guidelines. It is an attempt to make official declarations at the European level morally 'binding' at national level, by the implementation of a set of complex procedures. Within this framework the EP and the ECJ play a minor role. OMC is already applied to economic coordination (the Broad Economic Policy Guidelines), to employment (the Luxembourg European Employment Strategy), poverty and social exclusion, and state pensions (for a general overview, see de la Porte and Pochet 2002*a*; Dehousse 2004). The European Employment Strategy has been presented as an example of 'multilevel governance'. The main objective is no longer to create a set of European rules distinct from the national regulations but to favor an interaction between different levels of power. The impact and interest of the OMC is to have mobilized the idea of diversity and balanced plurality (reached in particular institutional contexts with distinct configurations of actors) to achieve coordinated results. The process through which this should be achieved is 'learning', a change-inducing process through ideas, in which partners learn 'best practices' from each other in the absence of legally binding power.

But OMC is not the only innovation since the late 1990s. At the same time, the EU adopted in 2000 a Charter of Fundamental Rights, which covers civil as well as economic and social rights. As noted by Szyszczak (2001: 1129), 'The distinctive features of the substance of the new social policy paradigm reveal a shift away from earlier attempts at harmonization of social law towards creating a core of social rights in the employment field through a process of regulation, coordination and convergence.... Alongside these policies nestles a policy of coordinating Member states' economic, social protection and employment policies emphasizing the need to modernize, create flexibility and reduce public expenditure especially on passive labor market policies.'

Since the beginning, then, European social policy has been very inventive institutionally, using a wide variety of methods, including harmonization in progress, equal treatment between national and EU workers, minimal standards, negotiated legislation, a bill of fundamental rights, collective bargaining, policy coordination, soft law. Clearly, the substantive record shows more failures than successes in adopting European measures, but European social policy has to be understood in its historical dimension as a perpetual trial-and-error process. The extensive advocacy coalition for a social

Europe—composed by trade unionists, left parties and government, some key players in the Commission, and also academics or journalists—has very actively used the windows of opportunity offered by each revision of the treaties to insert social provisions (Jenson and Pochet 2005). In turn, the successive revisions of the treaties and the change (even modest) in the social provisions have had a positive impact on the legal resources of the actors. Nevertheless social democratic governments have never had a strategic vision toward a more social Europe, and even when a majority of them were in power at the national level (during the second half of the 1990s), they were unwilling to transfer much more competencies to the European level. To the contrary, it seems that governments have tried more and more to reduce the traditional 'community method' in favor of a intergovernmental one (most notably the OMC) and supporting the social dialogue and autonomous collective bargaining between European social partners. This two-level game could be compared with the difficulty in the USA for generalizing more progressive approaches adopted by some (Northern) states. In both cases (US and EU) the key elements explaining the difficulty to expand progressive policies from state to federal level are the opposition of poorer and rightist states to progressive federal policies and the fear from some wealthier ones that the federal level could pursue less ambitious policies than those they have already implemented.

2. Toward Which Social Europe?

In this section we will review recent developments in the different social domains: labor relations, employment, and social protection. The study of three contrasting fields allows us to have a more nuanced picture of overall patterns of change. Among the strategies defined and implemented at the European level, the European Employment Strategy (EES) is certainly the one which has progressed the most. In March 2003, it was decided to synchronize the Broad Economic Policy Guidelines (BEPGs) and the EES. For the first time in EU history, economic-policy actors and social-policy actors are interacting directly in shaping the future European model. By contrast, the hope placed in developing a complete framework for a European industrial relations system has faded. The social partners have taken steps in new directions in developing an autonomous social dialogue at the European level, but they are using very 'soft' instruments—mainly joint declarations instead of binding co-regulation. Concerning social protection, it is a new domain on the European agenda and the developments are so far uneven. Here, the method is even softer than in the case of the EES and the social dialogue.

2.1. Labor Market Policy

The European social partners (ETUC for labor, UNICE for private employers, CEEP for public employers) have so far succeeded in adopting three collective agreements which were turned into directives by the Council (Falkner 2000). They addressed parental leave in 1995, part-time employment in 1997 and temporary work in 1999. This is a relatively meagre achievement, though it is worth noting that the overall number of EU social directives has fallen quickly in the same period. On the other hand, it proved impossible during this period to conduct negotiations on proposals concerning works councils and information/consultation at national level. After this failure, the Commission proposed a draft directive which was adopted by the Council. More significantly, the last negotiations on temporary work which were considered as the third part of the regulation of atypical work contracts have come to nothing. This failure has broken the earlier rhythm of one European binding agreement every two years and dashed hopes for the smooth development of a binding European framework. In the most positive light, while many have seen these results as not very significant in terms of content, until recently the social partners did seem to gradually step up their negotiating capacity at the EU level, and have carved out at least a potential negotiating space.

Except when it has been under real threat of legislation, UNICE has shown virtually no interest in negotiating with the trade unions (Arcq *et al.* 2003; Branch and Greenwood 2001). It is also true that the employers have no interest in enhancing the role and place of the trade unions at the European level when at the same time they are trying to reduce union influence at the national level. During the 1990s this situation was partly hidden by the signature of national social pacts in various member states in order to reach EMU-related criteria (Fajertag and Pochet 1997). But once the countries were selected for EMU and the external pressure to qualify disappeared, most of the momentum for social partnership faded (most notably in Italy, Spain, Portugal or Greece; Pochet and Fajertag 2000). Trade unions, by contrast, are in favor of bargaining at the European level but have no means of forcing the employers to do so. The right to strike is still not recognized as a transnational right; even the wording of the Charter of Fundamental Rights is ambiguous on this point. Under these circumstances the employers retain veto power over any headway in respect of European collective agreements. On the other hand, some (uneven) progress has been made in the domain of sectoral agreements (Keller and Sörries 1998; Pochet *et al.* 2004).

In the European social dialogue, the Commission has played a crucial role but in a more self-effacing, less engaged and less supportive way. It intervenes indirectly, though still significantly, in the unequal balance of power between the social partners. The White (1993) and Green Papers (1994) of Commissioner Flynn opened debate around the scope of the social question which should be addressed at EU level, but did not carry a clear ambition to regulate social issues broadly at this level. Within this context the number of legislative proposals declined dramatically during the course of the 1990s (Pochet 2000). Hence a paradoxical situation has arisen in which the more powers the EU has gained in the social sphere, the fewer directives have been brought forward. This means that one cannot explain the weakness of the social dimension solely by the absence of a legal basis in the Treaty.

Ten years after the Maastricht agreement, the European social partners have assessed in a joint document (ETUC, UNICE and CEEP 2001) the main achievements of the last decade and what the next steps could be. They have identified three main challenges: the debate on Europe's future and governance, coping with enlargement, and completion of economic and monetary union and the associated development of coordination of economic, employment and social policies. These developments imply a repositioning of the social partners and a redefinition of their role. The most innovative part of their joint document is the willingness to reorganize and clarify the functions of European-level social dialogue, and to better articulate their action around the different aspects of the EU's Lisbon strategy and the annual European Spring Council. In the draft constitutional treaty, there is now a provision on a tripartite summit (social partners, Council) before the European Spring Council each year (Art. 48 §2). They ask for the development of an autonomous social dialogue based on a work program which would be built 'on a spectrum of diversified instruments (various types of European framework agreement, opinions, recommendations, statements, exchanges of experience, awareness-raising campaigns, open debates, etc.) and would comprise a balanced range of themes of common interest for employers and workers.' Their autonomous work programme adopted at the end of 2002 comprises twenty or so measures, including two proposals liable to be turned into a collective agreement (ETUC, UNICE/UEAPME and CEEP 2002; for more detail, see Degryse 2003).

The environment is completely different from the hopefulness in some quarters at the beginning of the 1990s. The number of legislative proposals in the 2001–2005 EU action programme is relatively small. The social dialogue at the European level is still searching for the best way for organizing itself. The new buzzwords at European level are 'soft law' and the OMC. Nevertheless, when compared with recent trends in social policy in the USA—mainly toward decentralization and reduce representation—the European achievements in this domain can be seen as fairly remarkable (Osterman 2000). It represents a relative success in creating federal actors (the European social partners peak organizations) which have the capacity and legitimacy to sign and to implement (directly or via a directive of the Council) European collective conventions. Certainly it has not led to the creation of 'Euro-corporatism' as predicted by Falkner (1998), and the initial idea to create a comprehensive and integrated set of European regulations has not materialized. Moreover, it should be stressed that this relative centralization contrasts with simultaneous decentralization in most member states. Perhaps the best description of the overall European pattern, with some decentralization of social partnership at national levels but a simultaneous elaboration of at least some European-level dialogue, is one of 'coordinated decentralization' (Traxler 1995).

2.2. *Employment Policy*

In the mid-1990s the EU member states decided, after considerable political bargaining, to engage in a concerted action to address the persistent problem of unemployment. Their concertation took the form of soft policy coordination, imitating the economic policy coordination procedure that led to the single currency. In addition to this imitation of the EMU coordination model, the two policies were explicitly linked. From the outset, the EES had to be in line with the policies set out in the economic policy area through an integrative approach (Pochet 1999).

The EES began to take form following the Essen European Council (1994), after the impulse launched by the Delors Commission in 1993 via the White Paper on *Growth, Competitiveness and Employment*. The proposal to add an employment facet to the European project was based on nonbinding conclusions of the European Councils, and lacked a legal base, a systematized methodology, a strong permanent structure, a long-term vision, or a control process. Member states were to proceed by simple intergovernmental cooperation. However, due to the counterpressure of several member states to limit the power of the EU in this area, the process did not at the time progress beyond the discursive level (Trubek and Mosher 2001: 8). Still, the White Paper was an important catalyst for raising the issue of employment on the European agenda.

This initial push eventually expanded into the introduction of an employment chapter into the Treaties due to the efforts of an advocacy coalition composed of trade unionists, leftist members of the EP, high civil servants in the Commission, and some national governments (van Riel and van der Meer 2002). Thanks to a new window of opportunity with the election of Tony Blair in the UK and Lionel Jospin in France, this loose coalition successfully incorporated the chapter into the Amsterdam Treaty. The Treaty states (Art. 109 o, para. 2), 'Member states . . . shall regard promoting employment as a matter of common concern' and that 'The Community shall contribute to a high level of employment by encouraging cooperation between Member states.' (Art. 109 p). The new provisions allowed for no additional financial support, however—only a reorganization of the expenses within the current EU budget. The process leading up to the EES was politically driven and based on consensual ideas at the political level. Rather than building the emerging strategy with efficient operational blocks, based on solid analyses, it was principally based on a new concept—'employability'—acting as a *leitmotif* for the process and legitimizing it among the member states. This notion meant that the focus of employment policies were to be on the competencies and willingness of job seekers rather than on macroeconomic conditions.

During the Luxembourg European Council in November 1997, the first set of nineteen European Employment Guidelines (EEG) was adopted, organized along four pillars: employability, the development of entrepreneurship, adaptability, and equal opportunities. Each pillar contained between three and seven guidelines. The EEG have been adapted during the yearly review process, becoming more detailed with time. Of the four pillars, it is especially the 'employability' pillar, related to the activation of the welfare state (i.e. its reorientation toward supporting employment rather than toward passive income replacement), that has from the outset proved to be the principal underlying political and paradigmatic block of the EES (Jacobsson 2001). During the conception of the EES, it was in particular the UK that insisted on the ambiguous concept of employability, which has without any doubt dominated the strategy to date (Kenner 1999).

When the EES was first launched, it was decided that it should be evaluated after a five-year period. The projected evaluation was organized around ten themes.[1] The political bargaining process dominated the actual revision of the EES, despite the substantial in-depth technical assessments. In January 2003, the Commission proposed restructuring the Strategy around three overarching objectives: achieving full employment by increasing the employment rate, raising quality and productivity at work; and promoting cohesion and inclusive labor markets (CEC 2003).

What is more, the EES timing was synchronized with that of the Broad Economic Policy Guidelines. Before that, most activity in the EES occurred between September and January, while the BEPGs occured from January to June. Some social actors argued in favor of keeping the asymmetry, on the grounds that the EES was still too fragile and might be totally overshadowed by the interests of the Economics and Finance Ministers and their advisory

[1] See <*http://www.europa.eu.int/comm/employment_social/news/2002/may/eval_en.html*>.

committees (the Economic Policy Committee and the Economic and Financial Committee).

The aim here was to achieve a more integrated approach between economic, employment and social policies. Fritz Scharpf (2002) has already concluded that, because of other European constraints, employment policies focussed on supply side strategies. Following Scharpf's argument, one can read the EES guidelines as a new orientation for the employment policies to render them 'Euro-compatible'—aligning social priorities on new economic policies. This could lead to conclude that the EES process will ultimately tend to produce the kind of employment policies that have already developed in the USA, from Reagan to the Clinton 1994 reform. We think that EES developments so far do not entirely support this expectation. Different European countries continue to implement different employment policies (Esping-Andersen and Regini 2000) and activation policies (Barbier 2004). Moreover, the EES process is one of interaction between considerations of economic policy and social policy—not just a story of the economic approach imposing its views on employment policies. Indeed, the integration of the two processes has changed EMU itself. Kenneth Dyson (2002: 101), has analyzed the dynamics of EMU in considerable detail, and argues, 'The ECB-centric euro-zone policy community had to absorb and accommodate the so-called Luxembourg 'process'—with its annual employment guidelines and national action plans—and the Cologne 'process'—the Employment Pact and the macroeconomic dialogue. These developments opened up the dialogue about EMU by transforming the definition of who was in the policy domain.' As he also points out (2002: 22), 'Since Maastricht in 1991, EMU has expanded in scope and its boundary with other policy sectors have become more permeable. Hence we are dealing with a variable—EMU—that has changed.'

However, compared to the USA, the link between monetary policy and employment policy is working in a very different way. Contrary to the US Federal Reserve Bank, the European Central Bank (ECB) is not committed to growth and employment creation. Its only fundamental obligation is to fight inflation. The interest rate policy followed by the ECB and the Federal Reserve clearly shows the difference in the approaches in the two sides of Atlantic: The JS Central bank did not hesitate to favor economic growth with low interest rates and a weak dollar when unemployment was high, while the ECB kept a more orthodox focus on inflation, even if it was at the expense of employment. On the other hand, it would be difficult to argue that training and lifelong learning are at the centre stage of US public policies.

2.3. Welfare State (Pensions, Social Exclusion, Healthcare)

In the USA, a central feature of recent welfare to work and healthcare reforms has been the devolution of broad discretionary authority over program design and implementation from federal government to states and localities. Europe, by contrast, has experimented with a double (though far from complete or even) shift of competences in social and employment policy, downwards from the national state to local and regional government, and upwards to the EU level. This upward trend was completely unexpected by most Europeanists. The general conclusion of experts in the mid-1990s was that European institutions influenced national social protection systems directly through the decisions of the ECJ or indirectly via single market decisions (e.g. Leibfried and Pierson 1995). The principle of subsidiarity consecrated at Maastricht—that government competencies in Europe should be located at the lowest functional level—seemed to push this issues even more to the margins. Nobody had predicted that issues such as poverty and social exclusion, pensions, and healthcare systems would be high on the EU's agenda for action by 2000. None of them fell within the treaty responsibilities of the EU.

However, at the same time, all national European governments seemed to recognize in the 1990s that welfare states needed reform to grapple with international competition. They should become 'employment friendly' in reducing their costs (especially nonwage costs) and in offering benefits that avoided disincentives to work and employment (activation, making work pay). Targeting spending on those who really need (and deserve) it also became part of the new norms, as did the notion that welfare should rely not only on public intervention, but also on all the other actors contributing to the welfare mix (family, NGOs, private firms) (Daniel and Palier 2001). One could argue that these new challenges are more due to the globalization process than to European integration per se. However, as Jonathan Story argues in his chapter, it is within the European single market that European firms and states have encountered the greatest increases in economic competition. It is also above all due to the Maastricht criteria that some of these countries have had to progressively change their traditional use of social policies. During the 1990s, the idea that the traditional welfare state had become ill-adapted to new economic and social environment developed in parallel with European integration. The search for new social solutions thus became part of the European agenda.

In July 1999 the Commission issued its Communication on *A Concerted Strategy for Modernizing Social Protection* (CEC 1999). The Communication was structured around four pillars (CEC 1999: 13–14): to make work pay and provide secure income; to make pensions safe and pension systems sustainable; to promote social inclusion; and to ensure high quality and sustainable healthcare. Late 1999 and early 2000 also brought a flurry of academic studies that began to identify a role for the EU in the transformation of social protection systems in the member states. For example, the Portuguese Presidency undertook what has been described by a key participant as 'a new kind of alliance between the intellectual community and the political community' (Rodrigues 2002: xi). Among them was the famous welfare-state scholar Gøsta Esping-Andersen, who sketched out in a positive fashion both a new way of thinking about social protection and a role for the Union (Esping-Andersen 2000). In these publications by Europe's leading social policy analysts,[2] it is possible to see an intellectual community emerging to propose an alternative to retrenchment—variously described as 'recasting welfare states' or seeking a 'new architecture for the welfare state'—as well as a role for European-level action.

In 2000, the Lisbon European Council decided to launch various processes under the umbrella of a new mode of action: the Open Method of Coordination. In the social domains, the first program was on poverty and social inclusion (de la Porte and Pochet 2002*b*). The Nice Council in December specified it in December 2000, identifying four general objectives, but no comprehensive guidelines or agreed indicators.[3] Not surprisingly, when the first National Action Plans for social inclusion ('NAPsincl') were submitted in June 2001, only one-third of the member states appeared to have taken the exercise seriously (de la Porte and Pochet 2002*b*: 42). They then were examined by the Commission and went to peer-review in July 2001. Forward movement started again under the Belgian Presidency. By the end of the Presidency, enough consensus had been created on eighteen indicators that they were accepted. Thereafter the process moved forward more steadily, with the next 'NAPsincl' presented in July 2003.

The second area of social protection was pensions. It was obvious that completion of the single market and then EMU would affect pension schemes in a major way. Within the single market, private insurance actors and bankers pushed pressure so that pension reforms would expand their market for pension funds, asking the Commission to produce directives allowing and regulating pension funds in Europe. Meanwhile, the EMU criteria lead government to look for solutions avoiding the increase in public

[2] See also Ferrera et al. 2000, commissioned by the Portuguese Presidency and then followed by the major conferences and papers organized during the Belgian Presidency (Atkinson *et al.* 2002; Esping-Andersen *et al.* 2002) and then the Greek Presidency (Amitsis *et al.* 2003).

[3] The four objectives are to promote participation by everyone in employment and access to resources, rights, goods and services, to prevent risk, to protect the most vulnerable, and to mobilize actors.

spending and taxes for pension, despite the fact that demographic trends would automatically lead to more spending for pension. In the EMU context, the only solution appears to diminish the level of future public pensions, thus again opening the field for complementary private pension funds. For several years discussion on pensions turned only on the issue of privatization. If free movement and the impact of EMU have shaped pension debates, this has happened until recently without the intervention of national ministers in charge of pensions within European institutions. Part of the reason is that there is no clear legal responsibility in the Treaty, and there is a wide diversity of national systems as well as of reforms already implemented or under way (Pochet and Natali, 2005). What has motivated the change of attitude of ministries responsible for pensions was the risk they would lose control of the issue. As Chassard (2001: 317) notes, 'It is important that the "social experts" should make their voices heard in this concert, so as not to leave the field open to those who view social protection from an exclusively financial angle.'

In 2000 a Social Protection Committee (SPC) was created to advise the Labour and Social Affairs Council. Around the SPC a network of experts, NGOs, and national civil servants specialized in social policy have since pushed for a more social and European analysis of social protection issues, but this network is significantly more heterogeneous than its homologue around the Economic Policy Committee (EPC, advisor to the Economic and Finance Council, Ecofin). Their difficulty in building solid arguments why this question should be dealt in social terms at the European level constitutes a clear weakness, if a purely economic and financial definition of the pension problem is to be avoided.

The European Council of Laeken (December 2001) approved a set of overall objectives[4] and the deployment of the OMC in this area. To give substance to the general principles, the EPC and the SPC were tasked with producing a joint paper, thereby signalling the tight connection between monetary and social policy when pensions are on the table. In carrying out their assignment, the Committees wrote a document that now frames thinking about pensions, describing it simultaneously as 'about' both economic and social policy, and as an exercise to be understood in light of the BEPGs. In the report, eleven objectives were endorsed. Even if the formulation of some is still vague and ambiguous, the hierarchy of objectives does place social considerations high. Macroeconomic issues about system

[4] These are: to maintain social cohesion and social solidarity; to safeguard the financial sustainability of pension systems, in particular by improving employment performance, by adapting the structure and the parameters of pensions systems, and by increasing the budgetary room for maneuver; and to adapt pension systems to a changing society and labor markets.

sustainability have, however, a very significant place also—five of the eleven objectives mention them. We observe, in other words, that the social dimension has become more important over time.

With this framing statement, further actions were undertaken. In September 2002 member states provided the first national strategy reports for pensions. These reports are quite explicit about the need to negotiate changes to pension systems, particularly with the trade unions. Several were drafted jointly by multiple national ministers, which will strengthen their legitimacy. In spring 2003, the Council and the Commission adopted a joint report to assess national pension strategies and identify good practice. In the meantime, the SPC and EPC have again been assigned a joint project, this time to develop indicators that can underpin the OMC (EPC and SPC 2002). The OMC on pensions is clearly 'softer' than the social inclusion procedure (Pochet 2004). There still are no indicators specifically formulated for the pensions OMC process, although quantitative analyses and benchmarks from other processes (that overlap with the aims of the OMC on pensions) are used in the process. However, there is a consensus on the need to further develop indicators to cover all aspects of the OMC on pensions. The next review of its progress is scheduled for 2006.

It is difficult to give definitive concluding remarks about the content and the impact of the OMC in social inclusion and in pensions. Both procedures are at a very preliminary stage, and the current goal is mostly to elaborate a common vision of what social exclusion is about, and how to fight it, and what should be done for pension in a social perspective at EU level. In a way we are still more in a phase of constructing a European discourse about social exclusion and pensions than in a phase of policymaking or implementation. Similarly, it is only in 2004 that the Commission started the OMC on healthcare. The process is only at the initial stage of defining very broad objectives: to guarantee equal access to healthcare to all, to guarantee the financial viability of healthcare systems, and the quality of care.

Through the OMC, the EU is accompanying national welfare states in a mutation which leads toward a more supply-side orientation to their social policies, which developed in a Keynesian context. The function of the OMC is to help national welfare states to leave the old Keynesian world, to find new principles, new function, a new architecture for social policies, so that social policies will be more in line with supply-side economic policies (Palier 2003*a*). The can be done in creating a European language and grammar which could increase the legitimacy of national reforms (in the sense that they could be presented as a European dynamic). Contrary to the US, however, the specificity of the European one is an explicit will to transform but not to dismantle its social model. This explains why the EC is simultaneously preoccupied with demonstrating the cost of not having social policies

(Fouarge 2003) and even with presenting welfare state spending as a productive factor in the economy.

3. Conclusion: To a Multilevel Social Polity?

In their introduction, the editors remind us of the varying shape and dynamics of European integration over issues, space, and time. In our area of focus, there has been a shift from subsidiarity to the OMC as the overarching principle of organization. The purpose of the subsidiarity principle, which was dominant in social policies until recently, was to bring decision-making closer to the citizens and to delegate to Europe only tasks which could not efficiently be carried out at a lower level. The notion of subsidiarity relies on fairly separate boundaries being created between the spheres to be handled at each level. A higher level will step in as a last resort so as to compensate for, correct or endorse policies pursued at a lower level (Bercusson *et al.* 1996: 65–6). The new OMC procedure is an attempt to intermingle the European and national levels on the basis of a new multilevel governance arrangement. This approach is based on the need to establish flexible coordination among the different levels in order to solve complex problems of governance in a globalized world. This form of regulation tends to look at problems in the round (and not one by one, as they are often tackled at specialized Councils of Ministers). As a new form of governance, it creates links between, for example, research, education and training policies and budgetary policy. Bringing back the European Council as a decision-making body of last resort indicates a willingness to address issues and options in a more open manner than before, when the Ecofin Council had a monopoly over expert opinion and decision-making. The OMC has a 'horizontal' and a 'vertical' face, like subsidiarity. But unlike subsidiarity, it tends not to separate out policies and levels, but rather, to address their complex interaction.

Compared with the subsidiarity process, which operates through the verification of competencies, agreement on divided responsibilities, and the implementation of them in proportionate action, the OMC puts another type of sequence in place. Any policy can be dealt with at the European level using the OMC. Depending on the precise policy involved, the cursor will focus on a point somewhere in the continuum ranging from simple cooperation to coordination (which can be considered as an appropriate form of proportionality). Once the process has been initiated, it is endless (or at least no end is explicitly envisaged). It is conceived as an iterative exercise. In social policy, then, the shift in the debate from the overarching principle of subsidiarity to that of the OMC has caused all the institutional actors to reposition themselves. Basically, subsidiarity implied a federal

Europe with centralized actors, while the OMC offers the perspective of multilevel governance with coordinated actors.

Within this new multilevel arrangement, the European bodies have created a new form of intervention which is less aimed at harmonizing institutions or legislation than at harmonizing ideas, visions, conceptions, knowledge and norms of action, in order to have policy goals converging towards 'a common political vision.' If one looks at the content of the new ideas promoted, what is clear is that a turn is proposed for social policies—generally a turn towards more supply-side oriented employment and social policies (Palier 2003*b*). While some consider that this new orientation is just a race to the US standard (which in many accounts is equivalent to the 'bottom'), we think that the OMC could actually help delineate a new European model. More and more European voices (some administrators, some experts, many social actors) are attempting, within the new framework built around supply-side economic policies, to find an enduringly European path for employment and social policies. This kind of thinking would seek more flexibility, competitiveness, cost-reduction but also new cohesion through new social priorities such as child poverty, the capacity for women to combine work and family life, the quality of work, the growth of employment rate (e.g. Esping-Andersen *et al.* 2002). Depending on the forces in presence, the OMC can either provide a channel for economically-oriented actors to impose basic liberal views on social policy, thus bringing Europe closer to the USA, or it can create a process through which various actors (from national and European level, economically and socially-oriented) find a way to create new perspectives for the old traditional European welfare model. We remain hopeful, therefore, that the content of European social policies is not clearly in the downwards direction. What we see so far, at least, is that the reaction of national member states and 'socially-oriented' actors have mobilized at multiple levels to maintain a balance with European social goals.

References

Arcq, E., Dufresne, A., and Pochet, P. (2003). 'The Employers: The Hidden Face of European Industrial Relations', *Transfer,* 9/2: 302–21.

Amitsis, G., Berghman, J., Hemerijck, A., Sakellaropoulos, T., Stergiou, A., and Stevens, Y. (2003), 'Connecting welfare diversity within the European social model'. Background report for the International Conference of the Hellenic Presidency of the Union, Ioanninna, 21–22 May, 2003.

Atkinson, T., Cantillon, B., Marlier, E., and Nolan, B. (2002), *Social Indicators—The EU and Social Inclusion.* Oxford: Oxford University Press.

Barbier, J-C. (2004). 'La stratégie européenne pour l'emploi: genèse, co-ordination communautaire et diversité nationale'. Research report for the DARES (French Ministry of Labor), Paris, January.

Beck, W., van der Maesen, L., and Walker, A. (1997). *The Social Quality of Europe*. The Hague: Kluwer Law International.

Bercusson, B., Deakin, S., Koistinen, P., Kravaritou, Y., Mückenberger, U., Supiot, A., and Veneziani, B. (1996). *A Manifesto for Social Europe*. Brussels: European Trade Union Institute.

Branch, A., and Greenwood, J. (2001), 'European Employers', in H. Compston and J. Greenwood (eds.), *Social Partnership in the European Union*. London: Palgrave, pp. 41–70.

Cantillon, B. (2004). 'European Subsidiarity versus American Social Federalism: Is Europe in Need of a Common Social Policy?'. Unpublished manuscript.

CEC (Commission of the European Communities) (1999). *Communication on a Concerted Strategy for Modernizing Social Protection*. Brussels, July, 14, COM (99) 347 final.

—— (2003). *Communication on the Future of the European Employment Strategy (EES)*. Brussels, January, 14, COM (03) 6 final.

Chassard, Y. (2001). 'European Integration and Social Protection: From the Spaak Report to the Open Method of Co-ordination', in D. G. Mayes, J. Berghman and R. Salais (eds.), *Social Exclusion and European Policy*. Cheltenham: Edward Elgar Publishing, pp. 291–321.

Compa, L. and Turner, L. (2003). 'Paths to Global Social Regulation: What can Americans Learn from the European Union?' in R. Hoffmann, O. Jacobi, B. Keller, and M. Weiss (eds.), *European Integration as a Social Experiment in a Globalized World*. Düsseldorf: Hans Böckler Stiftung, pp. 149–59.

Daniel, C. and Palier, B. (2001). *La protection sociale en Europe, Le temps des réformes*. Paris: La Documentation Française.

de la Porte, C. and Pochet, P. (2002*a*). *Building Social Europe through the Open Method of Co-ordination*. Brussels: P.I.E.-Peter Lang.

—— —— (2002*b*). 'Supple Coordination at EU Level and the Key Actors' Involvement', in C. de la Porte and P. Pochet (eds.), *Building Social Europe through the Open Method of Co-ordination*. Brussels: P.I.E.-Peter Lang, pp. 27–68.

Degryse, C. (2003). 'Cross-industry Social Dialogue in 2002: A Testing Year', in C. Degryse and P. Pochet (eds.), *Social Developments in the European Union 2002*. Brussels: European Trade Union Institute, Observatoire social européen and SALTSA, pp. 177–207.

Dehousse, R. (ed.) (2004). *L'Europe sans Bruxelles? Une analyse de la méthode ouverte de coordination*. Paris: L'Harmattan.

Dyson, K. (2002). 'EMU as Europeanization: Convergence, Diversity, and Contengency', in A. Verdun (ed.), *The Euro, European Integration Theory and Economic and Monetary Union*. Lanham, MD: Rowman & Littlefield, pp. 91–108.

EPC and SPC (Economic Policy Committee and Social Protection Committee) (2002). *Joint Draft for Council Report in Health Care and Care for the Elderly*. *<http://www.europa.eu.int/comm/economy_finance/epc/documents/epcspchealth_en.pdf>*.

Esping-Andersen, G. (2000). 'Challenges to the Welfare State in the 21st Century, Ageing Societies, Knowledge Based Economies, and the Sustainability of European Welfare States', Report for the Portuguese Presidency of the European Union. Brussels: European Commission.

—— Duncan, G., Hemelrijck, A., and Myles, J. (2002). *Why We Need a New Welfare State*. Oxford: Oxford University Press.

—— and Regini, M. (2000). *Why Deregulate Labour Markets?* Oxford: Oxford University Press.

ETUC, UNICE and CEEP (2001), Joint Contribution by the social partners to the Laeken European Council, Brussels, 7 December 2001.

ETUC, UNICE/UEAPME and CEEP (2002). *Work Programme of the European Social Partners 2003–2005*. Brussels, November, 28.

Fajertag, G. and Pochet, P. (1997). *Social Pacts in Europe*. Brussels: European Trade Union Institute and Observatoire social européen.

Falkner, G. (1998). *EU Social Policy in the 1990s: Toward a Corporatist Policy Community*. London: Routledge.

—— (2000). 'The Council or the Social Partners? EC Social Policy between Diplomacy and Collective Bargaining'. Paper presented at the XVIII World Congress of the International Political Science Association, Quebec, Canada, 1–6 August 2000.

Ferrera, M., Hemerijck, A., and Rhodes, M. (2000). *The Future of Social Europe: Recasting Work and Welfare in the New Economy*. Oeiras: Celta Editora.

Fouarge, D. (2003). 'Costs of Non-Social Policy: Toward an Economic Framework of Quality Social Policies'. Report for the European Commission, Employment and Social Affairs DG, Final Report.

Jacobsson, K. (2001). 'Employment and Social Policy Co-ordination: A New System of EU Governance'. Paper for the Scancor Workshop on Transnational Regulation and the Transformation of States, Stanford, CA: June 22–3.

Jenson, J. and Pochet, P. (2005). 'Employment and Social Policy since Maastricht: Standing Up to the European Monetary Union', in R. Fishman and A. Messina (eds.), *The Year of the Euro*. Notre Dame: The University of Notre Dame Press.

Keller, B., and Sörries, B. (1998). 'The Sectoral Social Dialogue and European Social Policy—More Fantasy, Fewer Facts', *European Journal of Industrial Relations*, 4/3: 331–47.

Kenner, J. (1999). 'The EC Employment Title and the 'Third Way': Making Soft Law Work?', *International Journal of Comparative Labour Law and Industrial Relations*, 15/1: 33–60.

Leibfried, S. and Pierson, P. (1995). *European Social Policy—Between Fragmentation and Integration*. Washington, DC: The Brookings Institution.

Magnusson, L. and Stråth, B. (eds.) (2001). *From the Werner Plan to the EMU: In Search of a Political Economy for Europe*. Brussels: P.I.E.-Peter Lang.

Majone, G. (1993). 'The European Community Between Social Policy and Social Regulation', *Journal of Common Market Studies,* 1/2: 153–70.

Manow, P., Schäfer, A., and Zorn, H. (2004). 'European Social Policy and Europe's Party-Political Center of Gravity 1957–2003', MPIfG Discussion Paper No.04/6, Max-Planck Institute for the Study of Societies, Cologne.

Martin, A. and Ross, G. (2004). *Euros and Europeans: Monetary Integration and the European Model of Society*. New York: Cambridge University Press.

Osterman, P. (2000). *Securing Prosperity: The American Labor Market: How It Has Changed and What to Do about It*. Princeton, NJ: Princeton University Press.

Pakaslahti, J. and Pochet, P. (2003). 'The social dimension of the changing European Union', SITRA publication series No. 256. Helsinki and Brussels: SITRA and Observatoire social européen.

Palier, B. (2003*a*). 'The Europeanization of Welfare Reforms', paper presented at the conference of Research Committee 19 of the International Sociological Association, Toronto, August 21–4.

—— (2003*b*). 'Social Protection Reforms in Europe: National Strategies for a New Social Model', Family Network Project F-82 working paper, Canadian Policy Research Network.

Pochet, P. (1999). *Monetary Union and Collective Bargaining in Europe*. Brussels: P.I.E.-Peter Lang.

—— (2000). 'Le nouvel agenda social européen'. *Revue belge de sécurité sociale*, 4:1059–74.

—— (2004). 'La MOC et la protection sociale: des développements ambigus', in R. Dehousse (ed.), *L'Europe sans Bruxelles? Une analyse de la méthode ouverte de coordination*. Paris: L'Harmattan, pp. 99–130.

—— and Fajertag, G. (2000). 'A New Era for Social Pacts in Europe', in G. Fajertag and P. Pochet (eds.), *Social Pacts in Europe—New Dynamics*. Brussels: European Trade Union Institute and Observatoire social européen, pp. 9–40.

—— Degryse, C., and Dufresne, A. (2004). 'Dialogue Social Sectoriel', Research Report for the European Commission, DG Employment and Social Affairs, Brussels.

—— and Natali, D. (2005). 'European Networks on Pensions: The Participation of Organised Interests to the EU Policy-making Process', *Belgian Review of Social Security*.

Rodrigues, M. J. (2002). *The New Knowledge Economy in Europe. A Strategy for International Competitiveness and Social Cohesion*. Cheltenham: Edward Elgar Publishing.

Scharpf, F. W. (2000). 'Globalization and the Welfare State: Constraints, Challenges and Vulnerabilities', Paper presented at the conference 'European Welfare States: Domestic And International Challenges', Cologne, October 5–6.

—— (2002). 'The European Social Model: Coping with the Challenges of Diversity,' *MPIfG Working Paper* No. 02/8, Max Planck Institute for the Study of Societies, Cologne.

Szyszczak, E. (2001). 'The New Paradigm for Social Policy: A Virtuous Circle?', *Common Market Law Review*, 38: 1125–70.

Traxler, F. (1995). 'Farewell to Labour Market Associations? Organized versus Disorganized Decentralization as a Map for Industrial Relations', in C. Crouch and F. Traxler (eds.), *Organized Industrial Relations in Europe: What Future?* Avebury: Aldershot, pp. 3–19.

Trubek, D., and Mosher, J. (2001). 'EU Governance, Employment Policy and the European Social Model', in *Symposium: Responses to the European Commission's White Paper on Governance*. New York University School of Law *<http://www.jeanmonnetprogram.org/papers/01/011501.html>*.

Turner, L. (1996). 'The Europeanization of Labor: Structure before Action', *European Journal of Industrial Relations,* 2/3: 325–44.

van Riel, B. and van der Meer, M. (2002). 'The Advocacy Coalition for European Employment Policy—The European Integration Process after EMU', in H. Hegmann and B. Neumaerker (eds.), *Die Europaische Union aus politökonomischer Perspective*. Marburg: Metropolis Verlag, pp. 309–28.

Verdun, A. (1996). 'An 'Asymmetrical' Economic and Monetary Union in the EU: Perceptions of Monetary Authorities and Social Partners', *Journal of European Integration/Revue d'Intégration Européenne*, 20/1: 59–81.

12

EU Interest Representation or US-Style Lobbying?

JUSTIN GREENWOOD AND ALASDAIR R. YOUNG

Particularly since the launch of the single European market programme in the mid-1980s, there has been an explosion of interest groups competing for influence at the European level. More recently, there have been explicit efforts to engage these interest groups in the policy process in an effort to bolster the democratic legitimacy of European Union (EU) rules. The policy process, however, is usually described as strikingly apolitical. Although there are winners and losers from the policy outputs, the policy process itself remains largely consensual, and thus its politics are often difficult to see.

This chapter charts and seeks to explain the development and character of EU interest group politics. It argues that the development of EU interest group politics has been shaped by the interaction of two key causal mechanisms for change: 'the impact of institutional legacies' and the 'defence and extension of democracy.' The initial surge in interest group participation was principally a consequence (legacy) of the transfer of authority to the EU and of greater policy activity in the wake of the single market programme. The subsequent efforts to integrate interest groups more fully into the policy process reflect an effort to extend democracy.

Institutional legacies, however, also limit the extent to which the efforts to extend European democracy will be successful. EU authority remains relatively restricted in scope, which means that, although the number and variety of interest groups present at the EU level have increased dramatically over the past twenty years, EU civil society is not nearly as developed as it is in the mature democracies of western Europe or in the USA. The importance of the policy areas that remain under member state control and the member states' role in the EU policy process further mean that the vast majority of interest groups will not transfer their focus entirely to the (federal) EU level.

Furthermore, four institutional legacies help to explain the apparently apolitical character of EU interest group engagement. One legacy is that the EU's primary business is regulation, which does not bring winners and losers into conflict as explicitly as do distributive politics. Although the costs (or benefits) of a regulation may be clear and significant to some actors, the benefits (or costs) tend to be opaque or diffuse for most actors. Moreover, regulations are often highly technical, which both makes them relatively inaccessible and privileges expertise and information. The second legacy is the tradition of diplomatic decision-making within a highly institutionalized framework, which means that compromise is highly prized. The third is the relatively weak tradition of pluralist politics within many of the member states. In member states with strong corporatist traditions, compromise is the language of politics. In those with statist traditions, interest groups are unused to wielding influence. The fourth institutional legacy, which may be changing, is that a particularly confrontational interest group tactic—litigation—has been restricted for EU interest groups. These four legacies reinforce each other and create the apparently apolitical character of EU interest group competition.

In order to cast the development of EU interest group politics into sharper relief, we examine them with reference to the development of interest group politics in the USA. There are two principal reasons for doing so. First, the USA is often held up as the archetypal interest group society—the pinnacle of pluralism as a source of democratic legitimacy. Second, the EU is often seen as more open to interest groups than most of its member states and thus, in this regard, as more similar to the USA. Although we think that this superficial similarity distracts from a number of important differences between the EU and the USA, it provides a useful foil for our analysis.

This chapter begins by sketching the proliferation of European interest groups since the 1980s and examining the impact of the institutional legacy of the single European market programme and of the efforts to extend democracy on this process. We shall also explore how other institutional legacies limit the extent to which the increase in the number and variety of interest groups can actually extend democracy. We then turn to our other puzzle—the strangely apolitical character of EU interest group politics. In addition, in the light of the preceding analysis, we will examine the character of transatlantic interest group relations. We conclude be reengaging with the prospects for extending democracy in the EU through interest group participation.

Before turning to the substance of our argument, it is worth noting that there is relatively little literature that has sought to compare interest group organization, mobilization and strategies in the EU and US. There are, in fact, relatively few studies that compare interest groups in different countries more generally.[1] The most relevant of these studies for our purposes is

[1] Some exceptions include Thomas (2001) on relations between groups and parties in liberal democracies; Baumgartner (1996), who compares public interest groups in France and the USA; and Schmitter and Streeck (1981) and Coleman and Montpetit (2000), who look at the organization of business interests.

Coleman and Montpetit's (2000) study of the organization of business interests in multitiered and centralized (national) systems. They argue that whether firms organize nationally or regionally (and then form national associations) depends on how they perceive their market. Firms that are focused on national or international markets are unlikely to organize at the level of smaller territorial subdivisions. Coleman and Montpetit argue that political and constitutional structures also affect how firms organize, but that these structures may be industry specific. Baumgartner's study (1996) of French and US public interest groups also stresses the importance of the political institutional context for explaining the organization and influence of interest groups. The argument advanced in this chapter is broadly consistent with these arguments.

1. Interest Representation in the European Union

Interest representation in the EU has recently undergone two significant developments. The first was a bottom-up increase in the number of interest groups operating at the EU level. The second has been a top-down effort to engage a variety of interest groups more extensively in EU policymaking. The first development is an institutional legacy of the single European market programme. The second is an attempt to extend democracy.

1.1. The 'Institutional Legacy' of the Single European Market

The increase in the importance of the European level of governance associated with the relaunch of the integration project attracted more groups to Brussels. This increase was a response not simply to the range and quantity of sectors and products affected by the single European market programme (Young and Wallace 2000*a*). The speed with which legislation was being developed created pressures for permanent representation in Brussels. Further, the reinvigoration of qualified majority voting meant that national interests could not rely on 'their' government to defend their interests, building alliances with likeminded firms, associations and governments became necessary, and being in Brussels made that easier.

This increase in interest group activity was most pronounced among business interests, which were most directly affected by the regulatory focus of the single European market (Coen 1997; Greenwood 1997; Schmidt 1999). Subsequently, however, non producer interests, particularly consumer and environmental groups, began to shift their activities to Brussels and/or restructure their activities in order to counter the perceived dominance of business interests and as the policy agendas—particularly environmental and consumer protection—'flanking' the single European market developed (Webster 1998; Young 1998).

In some respects, these developments parallel those in the USA. Both the New Deal and the surge of regulatory activity in the 1970s increased the importance of the Federal level, and encouraged the formation of national trade associations to inject business interests into the policy process (Berry 1984; Lowi and Ginsberg 2000). A significant difference from the EU experience, however, is that in the 1970s US business groups were responding to an upsurge in consumer and environmental regulation, rather than consumer and environmental groups responding to an increase in legislative changes perceived to be pro-business.

A second difference is that although the number of interest groups operating at the EU level has risen rapidly and has reached an impressive level, it is dwarfed by the number of interest groups operating in the USA (see Table 12.1).

TABLE 12.1. *Overview of interest representation in the EU and the USA (number of associations)*

Type of association	EU	US
EU/Federal interest groups	1450	est. 7,333[2]
Law firms/public affairs consultancies	268	5,536

Sources: Greenwood 2003; personal correspondence with the Public Records Office, US Senate, June 17, 2003 (figures as of September 30, 2002).

The reinvigoration of the European integration project may also be having an impact on the form, as well as the scale, of interest representation in Europe. Coleman and Montpetit (2000) suggest that as European integration progresses firms and other interests will begin to organize primarily at the EU level as they come to see it the principal locus for relevant policy. There are some limited signs of this. Around 16 percent of EU business associations are exclusively direct member associations of individual (large) companies (Greenwood 2002), in line with Coleman and Montpetit's expectation. In addition, 26 percent accept individual firms as members alongside the more traditional associational members (Greenwood 2002). Further, the 1990s saw an increase in direct lobbying of EU institutions by individual firms (Cowles 2001; Coen and Grant 2001). The development of business-EU relations has

[2] According to the 2000 edition of the *Encyclopaedia of Associations*, there were 22,000 nonprofit membership organizations that are national in scope. It is, however, estimated that only one-third of these devote resources to political activities (Grossman and Helpman 2001).

meant that national industry associations have had to adapt, changing their relationships with their national governments and strengthening their engagement in the EU policy process (Cowles 2001).

1.2. The Extension of Democracy: From the White Paper to the Constitutional Treaty

The second significant development in EU interest group politics has been the active promotion of civil society engagement in the EU policy process. In a quite conscious way, organized civil society players have been built in to the development of EU democratic mechanisms. The Commission has for some time deliberately built up the landscape of citizen interest groups so as to provide Madisonian style checks and balances in the EU political system, both upon EU political institutions and as mutual watchdogs among civil society organizations. The Commission channels around €1000 million of funding each year through civil society organizations (Commission 2000). Further, for the past decade, the EU's agenda has been preoccupied with the debate about a 'democratic deficit' of the EU, arising from lukewarm public endorsement (or rejection) of EU Treaties in member state referendums (see 'the defence and extension of democracy' discussion in the introductory chapter). This new 'policy frame' (Baumgartner and Jones 1993) is highly pervasive and has profoundly changed the nature of EU policymaking. Faultlines in EU representative democracy, such as the absence of majoritarian politics to bring 'politics to the people,' has laid emphasis upon supplementary participatory mechanisms of democratic development, some of which carry deliberative overtones.

The Commission, in particular, has good reasons for being accessible to all comers. In part this is because it needs policymaking partners as agents to carry its quest for more European integration to the member states. Interest groups provide invaluable technical support for policymaking. The Commission is a notoriously underresourced organization for the range and size of functions it undertakes, with around 6,000 policymaking officials. The Commission also actively solicits diverse interests in order to bolster the legitimacy of its policy proposals (Streeck and Schmitter 1991; Schmidt 1999). The Commission therefore has a determined policy not to erect barriers preventing access to it by interest organizations. It has thus consistently rejected the type of formal scheme of accrediting groups that can be found with other transnational organizations such as the Council of Europe and the UN. As a result, the Commission is a very open, increasingly transparent, policymaking institution. This transparency has been nurtured in a quite deliberate way by the Commission so as to equip interest groups with the ability to exercise accountability in the EU political system. Thus a document register on

Europa enables enquirers to obtain access to virtually any document (including third party documents) within fifteen days of requesting it, while open web-based consultations enable civil society players to see who is saying what to whom.

Initially business groups were the principal interlocutors because they could provide the information necessary for decision-making and the acquiescence that would facilitate implementation. Subsequently, however, there has been an unfolding agenda that promises to a broader range of civil society groups more participation in return for enhancements in their capacities and transparency. The driving concern behind these initiatives is to 'connect' with EU civil society, which is now the most predominant EU policy frame. These factors have resulted in a warm climate for public interests and their representative organizations to operate in, and resonate with the openness of access to policymaking found in the USA. Tony Long, Director of the Brussels European Policy Office of the WorldWide Fund for Nature since 1989, recently reflected that:

> all the talk in Brussels these days about the role of 'civil society' and the need to consult more widely is not just words . . . whatever the reason, civil society is becoming recognized as the missing element. (Davis 2003: 66)

Initiatives such as the 1995 'Citizens First!' campaign based around a public information drive were followed with major programs aimed at ensuring the transparency of EU policymaking and devices to interact directly with citizens. The turn of the millennium saw the White Paper on Governance, aimed directly at addressing the remoteness that many citizens feel from the EU. The agenda unfolding from the 2001 White Paper is changing the relationship between the EU institutions and interest groups in a number of ways that make it even harder for any one interest to routinely dominate the policy process. In particular, the White Paper encourages open consultations through documents placed on the internet. Voluntary accountability by the Commission in demonstrating how it responded to the input it receives also demonstrates the extent to which the Commission has pursued input (participatory) legitimacy.

The efforts to extend democracy through engaging civil society are also reflected in the Constitutional Treaty that was signed in October 2004. It contains provisions on representative (Art. I-46) and participatory democracy (Art. I-47), with the latter containing explicit recognition of the role of civil society organizations organized at the EU level, and a mechanism to enable individual citizens to participate directly in EU policymaking (see Box 12.1).

Outside the explicit agenda of extending democracy, a May 2002 decision by the European Court of First Instance may further open up the EU's policy process by agenda setting the ability of representative organizations to have

Box 12.1. **Article I-47: The principle of participatory democracy**

1. The institutions shall, by appropriate means, give citizens and representative associations the opportunity to make known and publicly exchange their views in all areas of Union action.
2. The institutions shall maintain an open, transparent and regular dialogue with representative associations and civil society.
3. The Commission shall carry out broad consultations with parties concerned in order to ensure that the Union's actions are coherent and transparent.
4. Not less than one million citizens who are nationals of a significant number of member states may take the initiative of inviting the Commission, within the framework of its powers, to submit any appropriate proposal on matters where citizens consider that a legal act of the Union is required for the purpose of implementing the Constitution. European laws shall determine the provisions for the procedures and conditions required for such a citizens' initiative, including the minimum number of member states from which such citizens must come.

the right to initiate litigation (Reid 2003). The present position is that only an entity directly affected by a particular measure, such as an individual or a company, may bring a complaint to the European courts, thus preventing interest groups taking up causes. Public interest groups seeking a change in the law therefore have to seek individual plaintiffs with a good case willing to let their name go forward (Harlow and Rawlings 1992). If interest groups become able to challenge legislation, as happened in the USA in the 1960s and 1970s, resorting to the courts is likely to become more common, as is the case in the USA.

The EU's emphasis on consulting civil society echoes, and in some cases surpasses, the steps taken by the US federal government to ensure that interest groups have access to administrative decision-making procedures (Berry 1984). Thus in both the EU and US organized civil society acts as a mechanism of participatory legitimacy in policymaking. In the EU, as in the US, 'lobbying' has become a major, legitimate channel of democratic politics (Berry 1984).

Without EU-wide political parties, the adversarial and majoritarian politics of presidential elections and elections that change 'government,' and an EU wide media, however, there are few other conveyor belts to take EU politics to its citizens. This places considerable pressure upon organized civil society to act as two way channels of communication and socialization. As elite organizations—mostly associations of national associations—however, they have severe limitations in undertaking this role, as we shall discuss below. Nonetheless, there are few alternatives, and in these circumstances the EU institutions have sought to work with them.

1.3 The Impact of EU Structures on interest Representation and Influence

Concerns about interest group politics as a source of participatory legitimacy focus on the danger that broader participation does not automatically guard against the undue influence of particular interests (Berry 1984). The EU's efforts to extend democracy, however, reinforce a number of characteristics of the EU's political system that work against particular interests routinely dominating the policy process. First and foremost, this is because of the fragmentation of EU decision-making between supranational institutions, and between supranational institutions and member states. As policymaking shifts venues, so new rules of the game apply. The technocratic nature of policymaking in the Commission, where policy is formulated, makes it a natural focus for interest groups. Yet even if a 'done deal' is reached in the technocratic Commission, most policymaking procedures channel measures through to EP, with its democratic credentials often making it lean towards public interests, and from there to the Council of Ministers. As the latter two institutions search interactively for a common agreement, the complexities of finding compromise increasingly exclude outside interests. These factors can be cleverly used by the Commission to insulate itself from pressure by pointing out to outside interests the need to propose something which stands a chance of finding agreement in other decision-making institutions (Grande 1996).

Furthermore, the pluralist character of the plethora of interests engaged in the EU policy process is augmented by the contending interests even within interest groups that stem from different national policy contexts (Young and Wallace 2000*b*). In combination with the Commission's openness, this means that the EU tends to be more open to 'outsider' interest groups than are the member state governments. The relationship between the Commission and interest groups, however, tends to be closer than in the USA. The Commission sponsors the core activities of a significant number of groups—some 60 percent of public interest groups in the mid-1990s (Aspinwall and Greenwood 1998). In addition, it has an extensive network of advisory committees with established interest group members (Streeck and Schmitter 1991; Webster 1998; Young 1998). In contrast, there is a much more pronounced separation between interest groups and government in the USA (Baumgartner 1996). This difference has complicated cooperation between EU and US public interest groups (see below).

Although the Commission is generally open to contending interests, there are 'islands of quasi-corporatism' in which particular Directorates General have particularly close and exclusive relationships (Greenwood *et al.* 1992). The relationship between the Directorate General for Employment and the European Trade Union Confederation is also extremely close, with some (Martin and Ross 2001) charging that the latter has become too dependent upon the former to achieve its goals.

While organized interests help to bring in resources such as expertise and information, these can overload the system together with the political demands they bring. For instance, a 2003 Commission proposal for a regulatory chemicals directive so as to place upon companies the burden of proof for product safety, resulted in some 6,500 separate responses to a consultation exercise. Both business and environmental lobbies were highly active but each has declared itself dissatisfied with the outcome, a feature that might be expected in highly pluralistic policy domains. Consequently, there is some concern that the search for input legitimacy might interfere with output (winning by results) legitimacy.

1.4 Forms of EU Interest Representation and Limits to the Extension of Democracy

There are two particularly striking characteristics of the approximately 1500 EU interest organizations, which have implications for the ability of an increase in EU level interest group activity to deliver a real extension of participatory democracy. First, EU interest groups tend to concentrate in relatively few policy areas and are often highly specialized, with quite technical concerns. Second, they tend to be associations of (national) associations.

The EU's most highly developed areas of policy authority are with regard to agriculture, trade and the single European market. This is a narrower policy remit that in traditional states. The EU has only a marginal role in key areas such as health care, welfare provision, moral issues (such as abortion), and national security. EU level interest groups, although beginning to branch out across the policy spectrum, naturally tend to reflect this policy focus. As a consequence, some of the largest and most influential lobbying groups in the USA, such as the AARP (formerly the American Association of Retired People) and the National Rifle Association, are concerned with issues that are outside the EU's policy purview. As the EU does not seem to deal extensively with issues that directly and consciously affect people's lives, EU interest groups do not attract broad, direct popular support.

In addition, the overwhelming regulatory focus of EU policy process tends to encourage highly specialized interest groups. As the most visible costs or benefits of regulations tend to affect only narrow groups of actors, there are a great many very highly specialized interest groups operating at the EU level. There are, for example, six separate trade associations representing aspects of the glass industry. The high degree of specialization in representation, therefore, may overstate the political significance of the number of EU interest groups, particularly that of business interests. Again, specialization works against engaging (even indirectly) broad publics in the EU's policy process.

Further, because the EU is a new political system built on top of existing national systems, interests in the EU tend to organize in associations of national associations. This has several implications for the potential of increasing engagement with EU interest groups to extend democracy. Although the framework of an association of associations provides for legitimacy through breadth, it also creates problems of effectiveness and representativeness. Such associations often have trouble reaching agreements among their members, which means they are unable to provide the Commission with the EU-wide perspective that it wants. In addition, such associations may be remote from their membership constituency. Some EU interest organizations—particularly public interest groups—have little interest in engaging their members in EU public affairs, and spend little time doing so (Warleigh 2001). They are elite players, sucked into the institutionalized world of Brussels politics, in which the transaction costs of mass membership activism are prohibitive. In response to this, the Commission's White Paper calls for European interest groups to improve their internal transparency and accountability:

> with better involvement comes greater responsibility . . . civil society organizations need to tighten up their internal structures, furnish guarantees of openness and representativity, and prove their capacity to relay information or lead debates in their member states. (Commission 2001: 15–17)

1.4.1. Examples of EU Interest Organizations

The preceding discussion is illustrated by the following brief overview of some of the major or illustrative interest groups active at the EU level.

The principal general EU business associations are: UNICE, a confederation of national employer and industry associations; the European Round Table of Industrialists (ERT), modelled on the US Business Round Table, a selective 'by invite only' organization comprising the CEOs of some of Europe's largest companies; the EU Committee of the American Chamber of Commerce (AMCHAM-EU), the 'voice of American business in Europe'; UEAPME, a confederation of national small business associations; and EUROCHAMBRES, representing national associations of Chambers of Commerce. These organizations have contrasting strengths and weaknesses. Breadth is a source of strength and weakness to the confederations, while

ERT and AMCHAM-EU enjoy the benefits and weaknesses of representing a selective constituency of, respectively, European and American large firms.

The high reputations of these latter two organizations principally derive from their novelty and impact at the time of their formation in the early 1980s, when the EU agenda was dominated by wealth creation questions and when a forward marching Commission was on the look out for key allies with fresh ideas. As with all organizations, this momentum has been difficult to sustain. Both continue to enjoy a reputation of bringing fresh thinking to policymaking, being quick off the mark, and helping to set agendas, but each has developed its own problems (see Greenwood 2003), and experienced a modest recent haemorrhaging of members.

AMCHAM-EU has been successful in curbing the worst excesses of brash and aggressive US lobbying which were evident from the late 1970s to the early 1990s over issues such as the Vredling Directive, the second Banking Directive (Cowles 1997), and the first Tobacco Advertising Directive. Around one third of the estimated 350 large firms visibly active in EU public affairs are American, and AMCHAM-EU has helped to socialize them in the ways of 'European lobbying.' This culture is substantially more low key, polite and subtle, as companies such as Philip Morris came to appreciate to their cost.

These general business associations are joined by almost 1,000 EU-level trade associations. As with all political systems, where there are shared interests between their members and common sectoral features, they work well. But there are a number of features about the EU environment which limit their influence, in addition to the structural factors discussed above. The EU is not a state, and therefore the Commission has a limited ability to 'licence' associations as monopoly policy partners to the extent that can be found in corporatist European countries. Without this source of coherence, associations have to turn to microspecialization as an organizing device. Whilst the effect in an individual association can be that of coherence, the overall system effect can be one of competing associations across the product chain. And the openness of the Commission to all-comers, together with the general fragmentation of EU decision-making, means that trade association members can and do bypass their representative associations in engaging directly with political decision-making. There is a substantial dialogue between the Commission and individual large companies, and in some parts of the Commission there is a preference for talking directly with large firms rather than trade associations, because of the grass roots experiences and fleetness of foot they bring to policymaking.

Further structural weaknesses affecting EU business associations include their specialization upon political representation. They either represent national associations or large firms, neither of whom require their European association to provide them with business services. This means that many of them have few resources and are highly dependent upon membership subscriptions, rather than their own income streams. They can be over controlled by their members and be restricted to articulating the short-term demands of their members, rather than having the ability to lead their members perceptions of what their interests are on particular issues.

Many public interest groups also take the form of associations. These groups tend not to have the same problems of conflicting interests, although priorities do differ. Some do face resource problems because of the relative poverty of their member associations, although some others have become substantial organizations in excess of twenty staff, in some cases with a high degree of Commission funding. Because they are not as specialized as the business associations they may have more member and therefore more absolute resources than some business associations, but they are responsible for covering a much broader range of policy.

Frequently the Commission 'pump primes' an activity that lies on the fringes of EU policy competencies by funding the foundation of public interest groups. The Commission then nurtures them through designation of official functions, such as 'observatory' status to supply it with information. This pattern is most clearly observed in the relationship between the Commission's Directorate General Employment and Social Affairs and public interests. Although not all relationships between Commission DGs and organized interests are this close, they all have features arising from mutual dependencies. Some relationships are mature, highly regulated, and driven by commitment at Commissioner level, such as those between development NGOs and DG Development. There is now a general tendency within the Commission for dialogue with 'families' of cognate public interest groups. Thus, the 'Contact Group of Civil Society' brings together cognate families of environmental groups (the 'G8'), human rights groups, world development groups, and the 'Social Platform,' thirty-nine leading organizations in the social policy field. These are evidence of maturity in the 'NGO' sector. Some analysts have seen in the external trade sector traces of deliberative democracy, with groups contributing significantly to policy frames and development through self managed and highly organized dialogue structures (Goehring 2002).

In some circumstances an interest group may even become a demand constituency for European integration. The European Women's Lobby, for example, has been credited with the EU's acquisition of new Treaty competencies (Helfferich and Kolb 2001) in ways foreseen by neofunctionalist theory. It also has involved its members in 'campaigns,' such as in the run-up to the Amsterdam Treaty, to explain to European women what was on offer from European integration. By undertaking these tasks, very strong relationships can arise between public interest groups, and the patron in the Commission. Where there are also funding dependencies, a few can become 'extensions' of the Commission.

2. The Apolitical Character of EU Interest Group Politics

Having examined the contours of EU interest group politics, we turn our attention to a puzzle that is particularly striking in contrast to the USA; the relatively apolitical charater of EU interest group competition. We contend that four institutional legacies account for this relatively apolitical form of politics.

The first institutional legacy is that the EU's business is overwhelmingly about regulation and the character of that activity tends to diffuse political competition. Although regulatory politics is usually understood to provoke interest group competition (Lowi 1964), a crucial issue in the mobilization of contending interest groups is the anticipated distribution of costs and benefits from the proposed legislation (Wilson 1980). If the benefits (or costs) of a proposal are diffuse or opaque, which is often the case with EU rules, support (or opposition) are likely to be weak. With only one side of the argument engaged the policy process appears apolitical.

Furthermore, even where there are engaged contending interests, the character of regulatory politics works against confrontation. Regulations tend to be highly technical and require specialist knowledge, which means that ideas and persuasion are the currencies of influence (Berry 1984). Influence comes from being a reliable and informative interlocutor that can provide expertise and deliver on commitments. The centrality of regulation in EU policy activity, therefore, contributes strongly to the apolitical character of EU interest group competition.

The second institutional legacy that works against confrontational politics is the diplomatic tradition upon which the EU is based. This has two implications for the character of interest group politics. The first is that there is a culture of consensual decision-making that emanates from the Council of Ministers on down (Wallace 2000). In diplomatic negotiations it is important to make sure that everybody is happy and efforts are made to avoid creating clear cut winners and losers. This tendency is reinforced by the highly institutionalized character of iterated cooperation in the EU (Keohane 1986; Hayes-Renshaw and Wallace 1997). Moreover, there is no 'EU government' and there is very little majoritarian politics.

The second implication is the relative weakness of the EP. Even though the Parliament's powers have been repeatedly augmented, they still fall far short of those of the US Congress. Most importantly, the EP does not have the authority to initiate legislation, as does the Congress. Differences in the locus of political authority between the EU and the USA affect not only where interest groups focus their attention, but also the tools at their disposal for seeking to influence policy. While interest groups in the EU must rely almost entirely on persuasion and expertise, interest groups in the USA have more coercive sources of influence. The most frequently used strategies in the USA, often used in combination, are lobbying, establishing access to key decision-makers, using the courts, going public and using electoral politics (Grossman and Helpman 2001; Lowi and Ginsberg 2000). Only the first two of these strategies are really available to EU interest groups, though the third might become a more viable option in the future. Thus the strategies available to EU interest groups are the less overtly political ones.

Thus the most striking difference between interest group politics in the EU and US concerns the impact of public opinion and electoral politics on the policy process. The importance of Congress in rule-making means that both money and voters are sources of influence in US interest group politics in ways that they are not in the EU. The much weaker party structure in the USA compared to Western Europe means that individual candidates must raise most of the funds for their campaigns. Further, the high cost of running for office means that Congresspeople need to be almost perpetually fundraising. Consequently, interest groups with money are at least likely to get a hearing. As noted above, the Commission plays a pivotal role in the policy process, but it is not elected. Candidates for the EP are supported by party funds and so there is no direct connection between contributors and legislators. These differences, combined with the Commission's dependence on external sources of expertise, explain why ideas, not money, are the currency of influence in the EU.

But money is only a means to an end—(re-)election. Consequently, US interest groups that are able to mobilize large numbers of voters, particularly in key constituencies, have enhanced clout. Such mobilization—so-called 'grass roots' or 'outsider' lobbying—can signal to legislators the electoral consequences of their actions (Goldstein 1999). The AARP, for instance, has thirty-five million members, including many members in the finely balanced state of Florida. It is a common (and increasingly so) strategy for US interest groups to mobilize their members to write to Congresspeople supporting a particular line of policy (Goldstein 1999). The unavailability in the EU of such tools of influence tends to make interest group politics less overtly political in the EU than in the USA.

The third institutional legacy that reinforces the relatively apolitical character of EU interest group politics is the lack of a tradition of pluralist politics in many of the member states (Schmidt 1999). In corporatist countries, such as Austria and Germany, consensus among supposedly rival interest groups is the norm. In the Scandinavian countries interest groups are thoroughly consulted, but are very much part of insider politics, and public disagreements are rare. A number of other member states, such as France, have statist polities, in which interest groups have little say in the policy process (Schmidt 1999). As EU associations are usually associations of national associations, these national traditions influence the behavior of EU interest groups.

The fourth institutional legacy is a product of the place of interest groups in the EU's legal system. The legal process by definition is conflictual, not consensual. Litigation is used much more extensively by interest groups in the USA, which may reflect the more confrontational nature of politics, but also reflects the important institutional legacies of the US court system. Analogous opportunities for EU interest groups to use litigation to advance their agendas are much more limited.

To start with, the Commission relatively rarely takes the kinds of decisions that might be challenged by firms on procedural grounds. Challenges to the Commission's decisions regarding antidumping duties and in competition policy, especially vetting mergers, are the exceptions rather than the norm. Firms are much more likely to seek to challenge national rules for not being compatible with EU rules.

Public interest groups in the USA have also used the courts to push change—sometimes of a profound nature (Baumgartner 1996). Perhaps the most striking example is the National Association for the Advancement of Coloured People's (NAACP) role in Brown *v.* Board of Education of Topeka, which opened the door to desegregation. Given the EU's treaties' emphasis on economic issues, even if public interest groups gain standing they will not be able to press such sweeping changes through the courts.[3] The most striking exception to this is with regard to gender equality, which has been enhanced in a number of member states, including the UK, as the result of legal action invoking the EU's treaties (Caporaso and Jupille 2001). Should the Constitutional Treaty be ratified, additional fundamental human rights will be incorporated into EU law. In the meantime, public interest groups, acting (in present circumstances) through affected individuals, can try to affect policy change through legal action, in limited but important policy areas, such as the environment. As outlined earlier, should groups be able to be litigants EU NGOs may begin using the courts in ways more similar to their US counterparts.

[3] Many of the rights that US public interest groups have successfully engaged through the courts in Europe fall under the European Convention on Human Rights, which is currently entirely separate from the EU.

3. Interest Groups in the Transatlantic Relationship

Given the differences in how US and EU interest groups are organized, in their relationships with their respective governments, and in the character of their politics, it is not a surprise that the transatlantic dialogues between interest groups in particular areas—business, labor, consumers and the environment—have, to differing degrees, struggled.

Even the Transatlantic Business Dialogue (TABD), which had long been regarded as a great success story, has recently had problems, though these are more external than internal. The TABD began in 1995 as a joint government initiative to provide a forum for transatlantic businesses to resolve their differences and to present joint policy proposals to the EU and US administrations. Like the ERT, its members are CEOs of firms, not firms themselves. Not surprisingly given their interests, much of the memberships of the ERT and AMCHAM-EU are engaged in the TABD. As the TABD is a direct member association engaging relatively similar members, it has not had the pronounced cultural clashes between EU and US members that have complicated the other dialogues (see below).

While the firm-engagement aspect of the process has worked quite well, there have been problems in getting business proposals converted into political action. As the TABD is 'results driven' (Coen and Grant 2001: 43), this has raised doubts about the long-term viability of the exercise. The April 28, 2003 'renewed commitment' by the Bush Administration and the European Commission to the TABD is an attempt to redress the problem posed by the limited impact of the TABD on policy to date.

The problems besetting the other dialogues are internal and more profound, and the political support has been weaker. The Transatlantic Environmental Dialogue (TAED) and the Transatlantic Labor Dialogue (TALD) and the Transatlantic Consumer Dialogue (TACD) all started in response to the TABD, and all three started as initiatives of the interest groups themselves, although they subsequently, in many cases reluctantly, received government support.

The TAED was initially funded by a foundation, but was subsequently funded by the EU and US, though only after US environmental groups' reservations about accepting government money were overcome. The TAED also wrestled (ultimately successfully) with whether non-membership organizations should be allowed to be full members and whether government officials should be able to participate, with the EU groups in favor of both and the US groups more reluctant (Bignami and Charnovitz 2001). Although the TAED was ultimately able to overcome its internal differences, it has since been wound up following the US government's withdrawal of funding.

The TACD, which is still active, has also experienced cultural differences related to the different relationships among consumer groups in the EU and the USA and between consumer groups and their respective governments. The European consumer groups were already used to cooperating with each other and with the Commission (Young 1998). The consumer movement in the USA, however, was less used to cooperating, was used to an arm's length relationship with government, and did not traditionally engage on international trade issues (Bignami and Charnovitz 2001). In addition, like US environmental groups, the US consumer groups distrusted the dialogue because it was government funded, and some, such as the Consumers' Union, are barred by their charters from accepting government money (Bignami and Charnovitz 2001). The US consumer groups also experienced more profound ideological differences than their EU counterparts, with some fearing that the TACD was simply a vehicle for legitimizing trade liberalization, rather than as a means of incorporating non-trade interests (Bignami and Charnovitz 2001). The TACD has largely managed to overcome these internal differences and has been remarkably successful at agreeing robust common positions (Bignami and Charnovitz 2001). It has also played an important role in educating consumer groups about concerns on the other side of the Atlantic, as the mobilization of US groups on the issue of genetically modified food after the first TACD meeting illustrates (Young 2003). The responsiveness of government, particularly on the US side, however, has proved disappointing (Bignami and Charnovitz 2001).

The TALD had fewer internal organizational problems than either the TACD or TAED. It was initiated as a joint project of the US and EU peak labor associations—the AFL–CIO and European Trade Union Confederation (ETUC), so questions of membership and coordination were rendered moot. Expectations were low, however, and neither organization seemed to take the dialogue very seriously (Knauss and Trubek 2001). There appear to be several reasons for this, including the nature of labor markets, the characters of the members and the focus of the transatlantic agenda (Knauss and Trubek 2001). First, there is not much in the way of labor issues to discuss, as labor markets and their associated regulations are local or national. Second, neither association has much control over its members and they are themselves very different. The ETUC is a confederation of national umbrella associations, many of which are used to engaging in collective bargaining at the national level. The AFL–CIO is a national umbrella association, which is used to being an 'outsider' group trying to get the government to listen to the voice of labor. Third, the transatlantic agenda is about market integration and there is little space in the formal agenda for labor issues. Not surprisingly, the TALD has been wound up.

4. Conclusion

Simply by bringing together twenty-five member states, the EU engages a greater variety of interests than does any individual member state, and so fosters the Madisonian principle of pluralism. Furthermore, as a pragmatic project to improve the quality of policies, the EU has tended to be more open to more interests than the governments of at least most of the member states.

The EU system of interest representation is not, however, nearly as pluralist as the USA. It retains some more European features. There are many fewer interests engaged in the EU and the dominance of producer over consumer interests can be greater, reflecting the economic focus of European integration. In addition, the EU system is more elite and institutionalized in nature, more remote from citizen mobilization and participation, and much more likely to formalize consultative arrangements with selected interest groups. The EU system of interest representation, therefore, seems to lie somewhere between the extremes of US pluralism and European corporatism and statism.

Some recent developments suggest the possibility of greater pluralism within the EU. The broadening of the EU policy agenda has engaged more numerous and more diverse interests in the EU policy process. The implementation of the Governance White Paper, which would be reinforced by the ratification of the Constitutional Treaty, commits the EU's institutions to consult with organized civil society. This will likely strengthen the hand of public interest groups, which have tended to be more excluded from the policy process, thus diluting further the dominance of producer interests. In addition, if interest groups do receive standing under EU law and are bolstered by the incorporation of the Charter of Fundamental Rights into the Constitutional Treaty, the door will be opened for public interest groups to pursue more sweeping policy change through litigation.

There are, however, important limits to the extension of democracy through increasing interest group participation. One is that the regulatory nature of EU policymaking tends to engage only relatively few, narrow interests. Although increasing consultation with specific groups on specific rules may enhance the legitimacy of particular pieces of legislation, it will not make many strides towards reducing the overall perception of the EU's democratic deficit. Further, most interest groups operating at the EU level are associations of national associations which creates problems of effectiveness and accountability within the very institutions to which the EU is looking to bolster its legitimacy.

Perhaps the most striking feature of the EU's pluralism is how consensual it is. This apparent blandness may contribute to the perception of the EU as a remote and secretive institution; disagreements occur only behind closed doors. This peculiarity, we have argued, is nonetheless easily comprehensible as a product of institutional legacies: the disguised redistributive qualities of regulations; the tradition of diplomatic decision-making and the accompanying weakness of electoral politics; different national traditions of interest group politics, many of which find competition alien; and the limited scope for EU interest groups to use the confrontational tool of litigation to advance their policy objectives.

Irrespective of this veneer of consensus, the EU's interest group politics are undergoing profound change, particularly in the direction of extending democracy. These changes have been encouraged by the institutional legacy of the single European market and its accompanying 'flanking' policies, as well as by attempts to broaden consultation in the policy process. There are, however, important institutional legacies that severely limit the extent to which bolstering interest group participation will redress the EU's democratic deficit. Interest group politics may be a necessary, but are not a sufficient, condition for democratic legitimacy in the evolving European polity.

References

Aspinwall, M. and Greenwood, J. (1998). 'Conceptualising Collective Action in the European Union,' in J. Greenwood and M. Aspinwall (eds.), *Collective Action in the European Union*. London: Routledge, pp. 1–30.

Baumgartner, F. R. (1996). 'Public Interest Groups in France and the United States', *Governance*, 9/1: 1–22.

—— and Jones, B. (1993). *Agendas and Instability in American Politics*. Chicago: University of Chicago Press.

Berry, J. M. (1984). *The Interest Group Society*. Boston, MA: Little, Brown & Co.

Bignami, F. and Charnovitz, S. (2001). 'Transatlantic Civil Society Dialogues', in M. A. Pollack and G. C. Shaffer (eds.), *Transatlantic Governance in the Global Economy*. Lanham, MD: Rowman & Littlefield, pp. 255–84.

Caporasso, J. and Jupille, J. (2001). 'The Europeanization of Gender Equality Policy and Domestic Structural Change', in M. G. Cowles, J. Caporaso, and T. Risse (eds.), *Transforming Europe: Europeanization and Domestic Change*. Ithaca, NY: Cornell University Press, pp. 21–43.

Coen, D. (1997). 'The Evolution of the Large Firm as a Political Actor in the European Union', *Journal of European Public Policy*, 4/1: 91–108.

—— and Grant, W. (2001). 'Corporate Political Strategy and Global Policy: A Case Study of the Transatlantic Business Dialogue', *European Business Journal*, 13/1: 37–44.

Coleman, W. D. and Montpetit, E. (2000). 'Multitiered Systems and the Organization of Business Interests', in J. Greenwood and H. Jacek (eds.), *Organized Business and the New Global Order*. London: Macmillan.

Commission (2001). *European Governance: A White Paper*. COM (2001) 428 final.

—— (2000). *The Commission and Non-Governmental Organizations: Building a Stronger Partnership*. COM (2000) 11 final, January 18.

Cowles, M. G. (1997). 'Organizing Industrial Coalitions: A Challenge for the Future?' in H. Wallace and A. R. Young (eds.), *Participation and Policy-Making in the European Union*. Oxford: Clarendon Press, pp. 116–40.

—— (2001). 'The Transatlantic Business Dialogue and Domestic Business-Government Relations', in M. G. Cowles, J. Caporaso, T. Risse (eds.), *Transforming Europe: Europeanization and Domestic Change*. Ithaca, NY: Cornell University Press, pp. 159–79.

Davis, J. (2003). 'This is My Life: Tony Long,' *E Sharp*, (April): 64–8.

Goehring, R. (2002). 'Interest Representation and Legitimacy in the European Union: The New Quest for Civil Society Formation', in A. Warleigh and J. Fairbrass (eds.), *Influence and Interests in the EU: The New Politics of Persuasion and Advocacy*. London: Europa, pp. 118–37.

Goldstein, K. M. (1999). *Interest Groups, Lobbying and Participation in America*. Cambridge: Cambridge University Press.

Grande, E. (1996). 'The State and Interest Groups in a Framework of Multi-Level Decision Making: The Case of the European Union', *Journal of European Public Policy*, 3/3: 318–38.

Greenwood, J. (1997). *Representing Interests in the European Union*. Basingstoke: Macmillan.

—— (2002). *Inside the EU Business Associations*. Basingstoke: Palgrave Macmillan.

—— (2003). *Interest Representation in the European Union*. Basingstoke: Palgrave Macmillan.

—— Grote, J., and Ronit, K. (1992). *Organized Interests and the European Community*. London: Sage.

Grossman, G. M. and Helpman, E. (2001). *Special Interest Politics*. Cambridge, MA: MIT Press.

Harlow, C. and Rawlings, R. (1992). *Pressure through Law*. London: Routledge.

Hayes-Renshaw, F. and Wallace, H. (1997). *The Council of Ministers of the European Union*. London: Macmillan.

Helfferich, B. and Kolb, F. (2001). 'Multilevel Action Coordination in European Contentious Politics: The Case of the European Women's Lobby', in D. Imig and S. Tarrow (eds.), *Contentious Europeans: Protest and Politics in an Integrating Europe*. Lanham, MD: Rowman & Littlefield.

Keohane, R. O. (1986). 'Reciprocity in International Relations', *International Organization*, 40/1: 1–27.

Knauss, J. and Trubek, D. (2001). 'The Transatlantic Labor Dialogue: Minimal Action in a Weak Structure', in M. A. Pollack and G. C. Shaffer (eds.), *Transatlantic Governance in the Global Economy*. Lanham, MD: Rowman & Littlefield, pp. 235–54.

Lowi, T. (1964). 'American Business, Public Policy, Case Studies and Political Theory,' *World Politics*, 16/4: 677–715.

Lowi, T. J. and Ginsberg, B. (2000). *American Government: Freedom and Power*, brief 6th edn., New York: W. W. Norton.

Martin, A. and Ross, G. (2001). 'Trade Union Organizing at the European Level', in D. Imig and S. Tarrow (eds.), *Contentious Europeans: Protest and Politics in an Integrating Europe*. Lanham, MD: Rowman & Littlefield, pp. 53–76.

Reid, A. (2003). 'EU Competition Law and Trade Associations,' in J. Greenwood (ed.), *The Challenge of Change in EU Business Associations*. Basingstoke: Palgrave Macmillan, pp. 74–92.

Schmidt, V. (1999). 'National Patterns of Governance under Siege: The Impact of European Integration', in B. Kohler-Koch and R. Eising (eds.), *The Transformation of Governance in the European Union*. London: Routledge, pp. 155–72.

Schmitter, P. C. and Streeck, W. (1981). 'The Organization of Business Interests: A Research Design to Study the Associative Action of Business in the Advanced Industrial Societies of Western Europe', Internationales Institut für Management und Verwaltung, Wissenschaftszentrum Berlin, Arbeitsmarktpolitik No. 13.

Streeck, W. and Schmitter, P. C. (1991). 'From National Corporatism to Transnational Pluralism: Organized Interests in the Single European Market', *Politics and Society*, 19/2: 133–64.

Thomas, C. S. (ed.) (2001). *Political Parties and Interest Groups: Shaping Democratic Governance*. Boulder, CO: Lynne Rienner.

Wallace, H. (2000). 'The Policy Process', in H. Wallace and W. Wallace (eds.), *Policy-Making in the European Union*, 4th edn., Oxford: Oxford University Press, 39–64.

Warleigh, A. (2001). 'Europeanizing Civil Society: NGOs as Agents of Political Socialization', *Journal of Common Market Studies*, 39/4: 619–39.

Webster, R. (1998). 'Environmental Collective Action: Stable Patterns of Cooperation and Issue Alliances at the European Level', in J. Greenwood and M. Aspinwall (eds.), *Collective Action in the European Union: Interests and the New Associability*. London: Routledge, pp. 176–95.

Wilson, J. Q. (1980). *The Politics of Regulation*. New York: Basic Books.

Young, A. R. (1998). 'European Consumer Groups: Multiple Levels of Governance and Multiple Logics of Collective Action', in J. Greenwood and M. Aspinwall (eds.), *Collective Action in the European Union: Interests and the New Associability*. London: Routledge, pp. 149–75.

—— and Wallace, H. (2000*a*). 'The Single Market: A New Approach to Policy,' in H. Wallace and W. Wallace (eds.), *The Politics of Policy-Making in the European Union*, 4th edn. Oxford: Oxford University Press.

—— and Wallace, H. (2000*b*). *The Politics of Regulation in the Enlarging European Union*. Manchester: Manchester University Press.

—— (2003). 'Political Transfer and Trading Up? Transatlantic Trade in Genetically Modified Food and US Policies', *World Politics*, 55/4: 457–84.

IV

Culture, Identity, and EU Decision-Making

13

Transatlantic Risk Perceptions, Public Health, and Environmental Concerns: Coming Together or Drifting Apart?

PAULETTE KURZER

This chapter begins from a puzzle. In the USA, social movements and civic interests poured considerable energies in fighting tobacco by pressing for a ban on smoking in public places, a steep tax, an end to teenage smoking, graphic warnings on cigarette packages, and for nicotine replacement treatments. The movement succeeded beyond expectation as many smokers have quit and cigarettes lost their glamour and appeal. By contrast, at around the same time, in the EU, smoking barely registered as a major health and environmental hazard and instead public opinion and a broad constellation of NGOs vilified genetically modified (GM) food and crops. In the USA, moral outrage validated the attacks on Big Tobacco while in the EU the same expressions of indignation guaranteed restrictive regulations of transgenic foods. In this chapter I will try to explain this contrast: why tobacco energized NGOs and policy entrepreneurs in the USA though not in the EU, while transgenic food provoked similar kinds of collective responses in the EU, though not in the USA. What does this contrast tell us about American and European approaches to and views of risk perceptions, environmental concerns, and public health scares?

To shed light on this question, I focus on two specific sets of variables to account for the apparent dissimilarities. First, the USA and EU-15 possess different 'cultural markers' in that they express different values/collective preferences. Second, institutional arrangements vary with the result that similar preferences and values will nonetheless produce different results. By the same token, it should be noted that the diffusion of knowledge about the health consequences of smoking has tainted tobacco in the EU as well. Presently, all European countries impose restrictions on smoking and cigarettes beyond and above what is the norm for a legal product. Likewise, European consumer opposition to transgenic food has convinced some of the largest US food companies to reconsider the reliance on genetically engineered ingredients with the result that here too we can say that the contrast has narrowed.

I proceed as follows. First I describe why the success of the US antismoking movement was not replicated in the EU-15. Next I repeat this exercise to understand why GMO turned into a major environmental health issue in the EU, not the USA. In the conclusion, I return to the differences in institutional arrangements and cultural markers to point out converging trends as the aura around tobacco has been tainted in most advanced industrialized countries and the potential risks of genetically modified plants and products are increasingly recognized in the USA.

1. The Fight Against Tobacco in the USA

Much has been published about the emergence of the US nonsmoking movement and US tobacco control (Glantz 1996; Studlar 2002; Feldman and Bayer 2004). To be sure, US society possesses some unusual cultural traits that can be regarded as conducive to tobacco control. First, Americans tend to worry about cancer. It is not totally clear why Americans are focused on the 'dreaded disease' but one possible explanation is that US risk analysis is narrowly focused on individual harms, and cancer usually strikes discrete individuals instead of an entire community or a collective (Proctor 1995). Accordingly, the US approach to public health is highly individualized. Early on, in 1937, the US Congress established a separate cancer institute (National Cancer Institute) to allocate resources into research at a time when coronary heart disease already killed twice as many people as cancer. After 1945, the 'war against cancer' dominated the popular medical debates.

Because of the 'war on cancer' fixation, the USA is one of the few OECD countries that evolved a separate body of risk assessment to regulate carcinogens in food, air, waterways, workplaces, and drinking water (Nathanson 1999, 2004; Vogel and Bensedrine 2002). The enactment of these laws could be understood as a response to the centrality accorded to individual risk assessment. Since individuals must make appropriate choices, it seems especially urgent to foster an environment in which people can make life plans without having to accept unreasonable risks due to possible deadly contaminants (Cranor 1993; Harrison and Hoberg 1994). In light of this apprehension, tobacco control activists could tap into genuine societal fears, for smoking is linked to numerous types of cancers (Petersen and Lupton 1996; Valverde 1998).

Aside from the cancer link, the antitobacco forces had another cultural advantage over similar kinds of movements in Europe. US society is tolerant, for want of a better term, of state paternalism and public moralizing.

Historically, the USA has had quite a few health-related social movements that aimed to alter individual behavior. Since the early 1970s, US health professionals have called on their compatriots to adopt a lifestyle of balanced nutrition, regular exercise, nonsmoking, moderate drinking, and safe sex. This preoccupation with balanced life styles fed into a new public health paradigm in which individuals are implored to take charge of their destiny.[1] Many observers would argue that the desire to tame the 'free will' is typically American and linked to the puritanical reforming impulse to fight against a huge variety of personal pleasures, which now includes eating high calorie foods (Clifford Engs 2000; Gusfield 1998; LeBesco 2004; Morone 2003). Such an odd tradition of classical liberalism, aligned with a Christian-oriented reform agenda, is more or less absent in Europe (Kersh and Morone 2002).

The moral-religious tone of the tobacco control campaign slowly made room for another debate that defended the rights of the nonsmoker to inhale clean air and accused smokers of harming 'innocent bystanders' (especially children and the unborn) (Bayer and Colgrove 2004). Tobacco control activists argued that the entitlements of the self-governing individual should never be at the expense of the health of others. Many European officials were slow to recognize the health implications of secondhand smoke and were not convinced of the need to issue a comprehensive ban on smoking in public spaces. They were therefore reluctant to restrain a self-regarding activity.

Finally, American tobacco interests are powerful. To be sure, the battle against Big Tobacco was long and drawn out and the Federal government and Congress throughout this period were receptive to the interests of cigarette companies. The anti-tobacco movement had to find alternate venues to pursue its policy agenda because federal legislation was blocked. The movement focused its resources on state governments and forged alliances with state officials staffing public health agencies and with local health voluntaries (American Lung Association, American Cancer Society, etc.) (Libby 1998; Wolfson 2001). Nevertheless, tobacco interests were deeply entrenched in the American political system and could call on influential actors. Eventually, tort litigation became the most potent antitobacco strategy (Derthick 2002).

In the USA, public interests relied on tort litigation to hold private companies accountable for harms caused by the use of their product. Gradually, by the 1990s, after trial lawyers adopted a new strategy based on aggregation of cases and began to file private class action tort and state healthcare reimbursement suits, courts ruled in favor of the plaintiffs. Of

[1] It is called *public* health because it is associated with governmental action and with healthcare delivery not provided by the private sector.

unexpected help was the release of damaging documents and shifts in public opinion (Parker-Pope 2001; Pertschuk 2001; Rabin 2001). But tort litigation is less common in the EU-15 because legal traditions are different. European antismoking groups have not had much luck suing cigarette manufacturers in court.

2. Views on Tobacco and Smoking in the EU

In the 1960s and 1970s the USA led the way in drafting restrictive and innovative environmental and health standards while Europe lagged behind (Harremoës *et al.* 2002). After 1990 the roles had been reversed and EU consumer and environmental regulations were now more precautionary than their US counterparts (Vogel 2003). Smoking, however, remained an exception. In the late 1980s the evidence of harm caused by environmental tobacco smoke was open to interpretation since US scientific studies had not fully documented that sidestream smoke could lead to lung cancer and other diseases in nonsmokers. Yet popular rejection of smoking had grown so much by this time that the antismoking activists could invoke the precautionary principle to sidestep the scientific uncertainty without much contestation. The absence of definitive data, they claimed, was no justification for inaction (Bayer and Colgrove 2004; Libby 1998).

Of course the EU advances exactly the same argument—the lack of positive proof of harm is no justification to assume that a product or technology is not harmful—to push for restrictive or protective standards beyond what the scientific evidence seems to suggest as necessary or advisable. Although 500,000 Europeans die annually prematurely due to tobacco-related causes, public opinion instead pushed European officials to apply this principle to restrict the commercialization of GM feed and food.

To be sure, some officials in the Commission lobbied for antitobacco measures to reduce smoking prevalence. For years, the Directorate General for health and consumer protection (and its predecessor) proposed measures to deal with the smoking epidemic but it was stymied by recalcitrant member states while encountering resistance inside the Commission itself. It failed to replicate the successes of the US tobacco control community because it could count on few allies both in and outside the EU institutions, and its proposals did not galvanize popular support. It was above all the absence of social or civic mobilization by NGOs and medical experts that thwarted the Commission's goal to curb the marketing freedoms of tobacco companies.

Why would tobacco control be received with indifference in Europe? Two different factors should be highlighted. In terms of cultural or value orientation, Europe in general (individual countries have slightly different stories) was not very sympathetic to the broader strategies of the antismoking movement. Second, institutional configurations were different and hindered an attack on an established economic sector. First, European public health norms or thinking differ from the USA. Broadly, Europeans prefer to delegate decisions on lifestyle choices to the individual and shun the imposition of an agenda that outlines 'appropriate' habits versus harmful activities. The European left regards the 'new' public health as intrusive because it relies on unacceptable intervention by the 'hygienic' state into individuals' most personal decisions. They accuse medical experts of invading the privacy of less sophisticated or capable citizens and find nothing laudatory and progressive about the call for balanced lifestyles. By comparison, the US left sees public health as one of the few instruments of positive intervention by the state that serves and protects the most vulnerable in society. Therefore, in many European countries, the idea of campaigning on behalf of tobacco control was often perceived as patronizing and 'unscientific' not only by civil society but also by medical specialists themselves. Of course the political right, whether in Europe or the USA, rejected tobacco control for financial and ideological reasons.

It follows that Europeans expressed greater sympathy for balancing the risks versus the pleasures of cigarettes in favor of the smoker and that European governments took a more nuanced position on the question of suppressing the right to light up a cigarette in public spaces. Even advocacy groups or nongovernmental organizations hesitated to propose measures to restrict individual freedoms, even on an issue of demonstrated individual and community public health risk (Hood *et al.* 2001; Sweeney 2004; Brandt 2004).

Finally, tobacco interests were also deeply ensconced in the decision-making structures of EU member states. In some countries, tobacco was a state monopoly and so brought public health advocates and their political allies in conflict with government ministries and with economic sectors dependent on tobacco sales (cf. Italy, France, Spain). In other countries (UK, Germany, the Netherlands), private tobacco companies cultivated close ties with government officials as well as assorted media outlets, sport organizations, cultural associations, retailers and so forth. In addition, the tobacco industry possessed considerable public relations skills. In the USA, the privileged position of tobacco forced activists to fall back on the judicial system to check its influence and marketing power. European activists could not easily resort to legal action. Tort litigation has been widely studied but the legal systems of EU member states are less amenable to liability suits (Derthick 2002; Studlar 2002). Although the US example inspired several

European lawsuits against cigarette companies, few former smokers or patients have actually won in court.[2]

However, three sets of countries fell under the spell of tobacco control more or less independently from the USA: France, the UK, and the Nordic countries, with the exception of Denmark. But none of them pushed the Commission to take Europe-wide steps.

French governments expressed little interest in public health until the 1970s and the ministry of health functioned as an 'administrative dwarf' (Kagan and Vogel 1993; Steffen 1999).[3] The public regarded public health advocacy as a government trick to save money on health care and intellectuals dismissed antismoking rhetoric as yet another indicator of how the state trampled civil liberties (Nathanson 2004). Yet by 1993, at least on paper, France had adopted a host of measures that were unparalleled in their breadth and scope to curb the consumption of cigarettes and alcohol.

What prompted this turnaround in France was a slew of studies showing that France had the highest consumption of pure alcohol per capita and the highest rate of alcohol-related deaths of fifteen European countries between 1966 and 1980. Responding to this distressing picture, French governments launched antidrinking campaigns. In the late 1970s health officials proposed advertising restrictions on alcoholic beverages and added tobacco to this bill to neutralize opposition. In 1976 the French Parliament passed the *Loi Veil* and the first comprehensive ban against alcohol and tobacco advertising and prohibited smoking in places of public accommodation. This law arrived years before anything comparable happened elsewhere (Craplet 2001).

In spite of the *Loi Veil*, patterns of consumption did not change much. By 1987 the cabinet of Prime Minister Chirac was again considering permission for alcohol advertising on TV. Outraged, five prominent medical doctors wrote an open letter to the government (and public) urging the government to withdraw its approval. Coincidently, a group of health experts had gathered in 1987 to publish a report on smoking faulting the government for showing little respect for its own laws because violations and noncompliance were rampant. Together, these experts convinced health minister Claude Evin (a Socialist who arrived in office after the reelection of President Mitterrand in 1988), to pass a comprehensive ban on alcohol and tobacco advertising. In 1991, the Socialist government produced one of the strictest laws in Europe on tobacco and alcohol advertising (*Loi Evin*).

[2] Philip Morris (Altria) entered into a settlement with the European Commission to pay $1 billion over twelve years to help in anticontraband and fraud efforts. This agreement concludes a long-running dispute over the smuggling of cigarettes, not smoking-related health costs.

[3] Grassroot organizations, such as the *Comité Nationale contre Le Tabacisme* (CNCT), were absent in the early phases, only to acquire some prominence in the 1990s.

This fresh interest in alcoholism and smoking did not spill over into the European arena, however, because French government representatives did not actively support the Commission when it sought to introduce a comprehensive ban on tobacco advertising after 1989 (Duina and Kurzer 2004). To a large extent French officials perceived the war against tobacco and excess drinking as a domestic issue with few implications outside France (Ugland 2003). Moreover, alcohol and tobacco control measures were an elite project directed from above without the active involvement of social groups. The original *Loi Veil* called for smoke free spaces in schools, hospitals, and in public transportation. But violations were rampant as most institutions failed to demarcate nonsmoking sections or ban smoking in its totality. The *Loi Evin* took matters more seriously and spelled out in greater detail how to create smoke free public spaces, but noncompliance or indifference remained widespread because the legal provisions were treated as hortatory, not as real laws.[4] Nonetheless, France instituted a comprehensive ban on direct and indirect cigarette and alcohol advertising at a time when few other European countries were contemplating such measures.

Somewhat more like the USA, British society has given rise to lifestyle movements, which poured substantial amount of energies in reforming the consumer habits of especially the lower classes. Also in conformity with the USA but unlike France, Britain established well-known schools of public health with prestigious training programs. But tobacco control stalled for years during the long reign of the Conservative party in spite of the fact that the first postwar study on smoking and lung cancer was published by two British physicians (Doll 1998).

Little happened in the 1960s, though in 1971 the lobbying group Action on Smoking and Health (ASH) was established. Its funding came from the government but it operated outside government channels in order to lobby for antismoking measures. At first, ASH singled out only cigarettes but by the late 1970s, ASH had reformulated its objectives and abstention emerged as the major aim. The tobacco industry became the enemy—rather than a collaborator in a shared agenda.

In the late 1970s, increased numbers of officials and experts adopted the new public health formulation and stressed the role of individual prevention and responsibility. The 'new public health' lobby pressed for more stringent action through an agenda focused on fiscal measures, the control of advertising, and the use of the mass media for health campaigns. But the governments of Margaret Thatcher and John Major preferred to highlight product

[4] In October 2004, French parliament decided to relax restrictions on wine advertisement to respond to the decrease in wine consumption and sales. John Thornhill, 'French attack on move to ease drink advert curbs', *Financial Times* (October 18, 2004), p. 2.

safety and voluntary regulations and relied on cooperation with industry to achieve these goals. The Conservative government had no interests in provoking the tobacco industry and in regulations to curb the availability of cigarettes. The argument it supplied for its reluctance to take measures against smoking consisted of the well-worn excuse, advanced by the tobacco industry and libertarians, that the risk of tobacco was voluntary. In the 1980s, ASH went on the offensive and aggressively publicized the effects of secondhand smoke. Repeating the mantra of the American nonsmoking movement, ASH declared that people had the right not to inhale smoke. In the mid-1980s, the British Medical Association also became more involved in public health issues and joined the antismoking campaign (Berridge 2004).

The election of Labour changed the climate for tobacco control. Labour's focus on exclusion and marginalization spilled over into a look at smoking whose prevalence rate was much higher in disadvantaged families (Berridge 1998). Also, parallel with US trends, British authorities and activists emphasized the addiction angle of smoking. In contrast to France, public campaigns by NGOs like ASH altered the discourse and persuaded many professionals to abstain from smoking.

Finland and Sweden also established strong antismoking measures. Scandinavians have always been concerned about the innate abilities of the average citizen to act sensibly (Kurzer 2001). Authorities coped with fewer scruples when they decided to reduce smoking prevalence and they could depend on scores of existing policy instruments to achieve their goals. Indeed, at present, both Sweden and Finland have the lowest rate of cancer of the respiratory tract in the EU thanks to the fact that they adopted antismoking measures ahead of other countries (Taylor 1984; Hara 2003).

In Finland, pressures to take government action dated from the early 1960s, when medical doctors and NGOs fought with the tobacco industry and ministries of finance and trade, both of which opposed smoking curbs on fiscal grounds. In early 1970s, public health studies showed that Finland scored high points for reducing infant mortality but had an extremely high death rate due to coronary heart disease and the second highest rate of cancer deaths in Europe. By the late 1970s Finnish governments had launched a comprehensive public health program that included information, legislation, and prevention. A total ban on tobacco advertising came into force in 1978 while all indoor areas aside from private homes and restaurants became smoke free areas.

The Swedish parliament passed a comprehensive tobacco control law in 1993, banning advertising and instituting age restrictions, health warnings, and smoke free public spaces and workplaces. While the National Board of Health and Welfare had contemplated antismoking measures much sooner, in the early 1970s, the tobacco industry and the ministry of finance objected strenuously. After these early attempts, health experts realized that tobacco control was a political matter because of the obstruction of the tobacco industry and finance ministry officials. In 1988, the Parliament approved the creation of a Commission on Tobacco Control, which issued a report in 1990. Although the central government ignored the conclusions in the report, local councils, and NGOs used its findings and proposals to campaign for further action. In the course of the following years, professional associations of doctors, dentists, psychologists, teachers, nurses, and pharmacists created antismoking lobbying groups and lobbied local authorities, members of parliaments, and national agencies.

Aside from this elite group of countries, others shunned tobacco control measures (e.g. Austria, Denmark, Germany, and the Netherlands) and smoking was not a hot topic in the EU until the late 1990s (Cooper and Kurzer 2003; Albaek 2004; Dubré 2004).

3. The European Commission and the War on Tobacco

In 1987 Commission officials launched the *Europe Against Cancer* program, targeting smoking as a way to bring down cancer mortality rates. In the following years, the Commission passed the 1989 directive outlawing tobacco advertising on television (89/552/EEC) and later directives regulating tobacco product labeling (89/622/EEC and 92/41/EEC), tar maximums for cigarettes (90/239/EEC), and minimum tax levels for tobacco products (92/78/EEC, 92/79/EEC, 92/80/EEC). Antitobacco measures had stalled by 1992 as the Commission sensed growing resistance against its legislative agenda and as the tobacco industry set up public relation firms in Brussels to help shape the deliberations and policy outcomes (Gilmore and McKee 2004).

A few years earlier in 1989, the Commission had proposed a comprehensive ban on direct and indirect tobacco advertising (Tobacco Advertising Directive—TAD1, 98/43/EC). Its aim was to ban tobacco advertising on the radio, Internet, print media, as well as cinema, posters, ashtrays, and so on. It also prohibited brand stretching and tobacco industry sponsorship of events in the EC (Bitton *et al.* 2002). The directive stalled until December 1997, however, because of a blocking minority of several member states. The Netherlands, UK, and Germany consistently opposed the directive while Denmark and Greece were lukewarm in their support. In all four countries (excluding Greece), private tobacco companies dominated the cigarette market and overall smoking rates were high because social norms had not (yet) turned against smoking. All four countries also shared a strong attachment to the concept of the self-governing individual, while state agencies spurned the role of a 'nanny' telling consumers which legal products to steer clear of.

In the same set of four countries—Denmark, Germany, the Netherlands, and the UK—industry self-regulation was the norm and tobacco companies signed 'gentlemen's agreements' promising to abstain from targeting minors, to issue health warnings, and to abide by existing marketing restrictions. Germany, the Netherlands, and the UK were also the main centers of tobacco manufacturing and exported to the rest of Europe. The combination of a liberal moral climate, industry self-regulation, and powerful international tobacco companies convinced national governments to oppose restrictions on the market freedom of tobacco companies.

Once Netherlands and the UK switched sides and three new member states came on board (Austria, Finland, and Sweden), the directive passed the Council of Ministers in December 1997 (Bouma 2001). When it came to the final vote, therefore, in December 1997 only Austria and Germany (with Denmark and Spain abstaining) opposed TAD1 (it garnered sixty-two out of eighty-seven votes).

As soon as the directive passed, the German Federal government (and four British tobacco companies) asked the ECJ to annul it. The German government claimed that TAD1 rested on no constitutional grounds and negated the freedom to advertise. Moreover, Germany argued that the TAD1 had public health as its primary goal while it did little to promote market integration. The ECJ agreed (C-376/98) and annulled the TAD1 in October 2000. It concluded that the Commission had overstepped its boundaries (Hervey 2001; Tridimas and Tridimas 2002).

Taking into account the objections of the ECJ, the Commission drafted a new directive. The TAD2 (COD 2001/0119) was published in May 2001 and differed from the TAD1 in one important way: it banned only direct tobacco advertising (Watson 2002).[5] In November 2002, the EP passed the watered-down TAD2 and the fifteen ministers of health reached an agreement on December 2, 2002 to have the TAD2 come into effect in the summer 2005. Again, two member states voted against the directive: Germany and, to the surprise of many, the UK.[6]

In this prolonged battle to protect and improve the health of EU citizens, the Commission eventually prevailed. But its victory was mainly due to the fact that opinions about smoking had shifted especially in countries, which earlier had not yet bought into the tobacco control paradigm. Smoking had declined in popularity regardless of whether tobacco control measures were pursued or not. While educated professionals increasingly quit smoking,

[5] Many member states had already banned advertisements in public entertainment places.

[6] The UK voted against it to protect its own agreement with Formula One racing industry.

public authorities were growing more alarmed about the public costs of treating tobacco-related diseases, which outweighed the earned income of tobacco taxes (Chaloupka *et al.* 2001). In the late 1990s, in short, awareness of the financial costs of smoking rose while tobacco consumption steadily declined or stabilized. Possibly, the 1998 Master Settlement Agreement reached between US state governments and tobacco companies lifted European reluctance to confront local tobacco companies, and in turn, made European tobacco companies more amenable to accept marketing restraints.[7] At this point, moreover, several pan-European antismoking NGOs emerged to provide support and information to the Commission and prestigious international organizations (World Health Organization and World Bank) had become involved in assessing the global costs of smoking and comparing national antismoking strategies.[8]

4. The EU and the Fight Against Green Biotechnology

Although half a million Europeans die each year of tobacco-related causes, this did not propel a frenzy of public health activity, at least until very recently. Rather, transgenic crops or products incited great concern and worries. Genetically modified or transgenic crops or products contain the DNA segment of another plant or animal or microbe to change its properties as a plant or plant product. Thus far, soybean, corn, cotton, and oilseed rape (canola) have undergone this process in order to make them resistant to herbicides (Roundup Ready soybeans) or insects (Bt-corn).

How can we begin to understand why transgenic crops and food provoke much anguish and regulatory activism in one region of the world but not in another? Why are Americans indifferent to genetic engineering of food crops while they greatly agonize about secondhand smoke, and vice versa?

As in tobacco control, a cluster of unique circumstances turned the European public against GMO. It seems indisputable that many of the questions surrounding GMO are driven by consumer anxiety. In turn, consumer fears are exploited by social movements, which link environmentalists, consumers, and small farmers together around issues of trade, corporate power, and scientific risk (Ansell *et al.* forthcoming). The anti-GMO forces built a

[7] US tobacco companies pledged to pay $205 billion to state governments to defray the costs of treating tobacco-related diseases.

[8] Several important antismoking NGOs are: European Network for Smoking Prevention <*http://www.ensp.org*> European Public Health Alliance <*http://www.epha.org*>. And the website linked to the International Cancer League <*www.globalink.org*>. See also, World Bank, *Tobacco control at a glance* (Washington, DC: World Bank, 2003). Available at <*http://www1.worldbank.org/tobacco*>.

presence at every level of decision-making—local, regional, national, and European—so that small volunteer groups are embedded in a larger national movement, which has ties to an international network of advocates in Brussels.

Consumer anxieties reflected a spate of food scandals that raised serious questions about the ability of national and European authorities to safeguard the food production system. By far the single largest crisis was mad cow disease, whose origins can be traced to the reliance on factory-like production methods to prepare cows for slaughter. The main elements of this story consisted of repeated dismissals by British officials when questions were raised about possible trans-species infection especially from cows to humans (Ratzan 1998; The BSE Inquiry 2003). Suddenly, in early 1996, the British government announced the discovery of new variant of Creutzfeldt-Jakob disease (vCJD) in young people and that it might have been caused by tainted beef, a revelation that thoroughly shocked the British and European public. The about face of the British government also drew attention to the role played by the Commission, which carried responsibility for the Community-wide beef market.[9]

The lack of oversight in the UK, the narrow commercial considerations taken by the Commission when dealing with the European beef market, and false scientific reassurances shook consumer confidence to its core. It fuelled doubts whether any pronouncement by an expert committee, public official, or politician could be trusted. Hence when policy officials reassured the public that Roundup Ready soybeans posed no health hazard, the public treated this announcement with a great deal of skepticism (Wynne 1995; Grant 1997; Poppe and Kjærnes 2003; Roth *et al.* 2003).

Although food scandals and BSE in particular turned the public against official declarations, green biotechnology evoked doubts from the beginning. In late 1996, Eurobarometer completed a survey on European attitudes towards agricultural and medical biotechnology. In that survey which coincided with the first wave of negative publicity surrounding GM soybeans, European respondents singled out genetically modified food as particularly risky (Bonny 2003; Eurobarometer 1996). From the beginning, GM food raised red flags in Europe.

Hostility to GM food illustrates two cultural attributes. European consumers reject the notion of tampering with nature for the sake of increased yields or some other vague benefit because Europeans prefer natural unadulterated 'simple' foods. Definitions of natural food go beyond taste, flavor,

[9] There was also an outbreak of e.coli, salmonella in eggs, and listeria. In 1999, a major public health scare emerged over dioxin contamination of food products produced in Belgium.

and texture to include the actual process of production. Environmental, ethical, and animal welfare considerations all play a role in evaluating how good or natural a product is.

The second cultural divergence is that Europeans hold different views on farming. In the USA, farming takes place in thinly populated regions and far from large metropolitan areas. The actual process of production carries few sentimental values; Americans mainly perceive farming as yet another industry. By comparison, in certain parts of Europe, farming is regarded as a special institution that is integrated in urban life and helps sustain disadvantaged regions and the environment. It is also seen as a link to the past and evokes much nostalgia. To be sure, the US popular imagination does not care much about preserving vestiges of rural life (Echols 1998).

Environmental NGOs and farming associations seized upon dormant misgivings to articulate an alternate viewpoint that mentioned the grave consequences of relying on genetic engineering to 'improve' the European food chain. In the USA, public interest groups lobbied for mandatory labeling but basically accepted green biotechnology in general. Some of the largest NGOs (Consumer Union and Environmental Defense Fund) were in agreement with US regulatory agencies and farming industry, believing that GM crops would help feed the world owing to increased yields. Even after the accidental contamination by the Aventis product Starlink corn led to an enormous and costly recall—it was approved for animal feed but landed in Kraft taco shells—the US public did not turn against green biotechnology (Bernauer 2003; Meins 2003). Americans continued to trust government regulations and 90 percent of consumers believed the US Department of Agriculture's statements on biotechnology. By comparison, only 12 percent of Europeans trusted their national regulators around the same time (Enriquez and Goldberg 2000).

There are also significant institutional differences. The complex decision-making structures in the EU foiled proponents of tobacco control because a small coalition of member states could block Commission proposals while the tobacco industry overwhelmed feebly organized public health associations and isolated antismoking activists. This same decision-making structure, however, abetted anti-GMO forces because this time a small group of member states and highly effective NGOs managed to raise the regulatory bar and approval procedures. Some public interest groups and national governments were willing to compromise by holding out for a rigoros approval process based on tracing and labeling of GMO. Nonetheless, to satisfy the anti-GMO position of a select group of member states, the Commission spent years on drafting amendments to existing directives to formulate a restrictive case-by-case authorization process. The objections of a minority group of member states forced the Commission to tighten and strengthen conditions for the marketing of GM product and for the release to the environment of GMO plants.

Compared to the US biotechnology industry, the European sector is relatively small and fragmented. Organizationally, it has been less successful in approaching key decision making centers to deflect negative publicity. Trade associations have struggled to design a European-wide campaign because public concerns range from the economic impact on farming, moral consequences of tampering with nature, the introduction of foreign species in existing habitats, potential health ramifications, and the imposition of US production methods. Many European firms have shed their green biotechnology divisions.

Multilevel decision-making structures and a large number of participants strengthened the bargaining position of GMO-averse forces. In the USA, decision-making has been centralized, the number or range of participants is limited, NGOs are less focused on GMO, and the public has faith in the regulatory process and is not agitating for higher standards, greater supervision, and an end to genetic engineering. Moreover, the US biotech industry has basically been able to set its own rules and enjoys cordial ties with the USDA (Meins 2003: 155).

Although Europeans are considerably more hostile to the idea of GMO than US consumers, resistance varies across the EU. On the one hand, we would expect northern European member states, which are distinguished by strong environmental activism and organic farming, to oppose GM foods/crops because of their potential to endanger biodiversity, purity of organic food, and human health. On the other, southern member states that possess vibrant 'traditional' or 'specialty' agriculture are heirs to a rich tradition of local food specialties and strong culinary identities and have their own objections against GMO (Kurzer and Cooper 2005). It follows that virtually all of the old EU-15 might be opposed to GMO.

In reality, the most durable and stubborn opposition came from countries where environmental groups forged a coalition with farming interests. In this group of countries, activists emphasized both the globalization angle since specialized farming and national culinary identity were at risk from GM technology and pushed as well for comprehensive labeling and tracing as possible solutions so that consumers can make an informed choice (Sassatelli and Scott 2001).

Austria, Italy, Denmark, France, Greece, and Luxemburg were the most critical and hostile. Belgium, Spain, Portugal, and Germany took more nuanced positions. The Commission, Finland, the Netherlands, Spain, Sweden, and the UK have tended to favor the careful development of GM products.

As can be seen from this list of countries, the public and government's reaction to GMO is unrelated to the approach to public health or smoking.

Denmark strenuously opposes GM food products yet it has been a laggard in tackling the smoking epidemic and Danish women record the highest mortality rate due to smoking-related lung cancer. Greece is another country with weak antismoking norms and has the highest prevalence rate of smoking in the EU (46 percent of the men smoke; see Sakellaris and Chatjouli 2001). Yet Greek public opinion overwhelmingly rejects GM foods. Austrian NGOs organized a people's referendum in 1997 to call for a ban on the import of GM foods and on patents on life, and for the release of GM food or animals (Torgersen and Seifert 2000). But as noted above, in 1997 the Austrian health minister voted along with Germany against the Commission-proposed ban on tobacco advertising.[10] In late 2004, Austria (and Luxemburg) had the distinction of having extremely modest antismoking measures and thus of recording lowest score in antitobacco control policies among twenty-eight European countries (EU-25 plus Iceland, Norway, and Switzerland) (Joossens 2004).

France is the only country that is consistent across both kinds of perceived health risks: it pioneered tobacco control at home and rejected GM products. However, tobacco was an elite project and the law was widely ignored, while GM food provoked mass mobilization and strong emotional reactions. Intensity of engagement and concern is inversed: smoking hazards are minimized while the harms caused by agricultural biotechnology are inflated (Boy and de Cheveigné 2001; Heller 2001; Joly and Marris 2003).

In Austria, Greece, Italy, and France, defense of traditional farming and culinary traditions shaped views on GM technology. However, it is important to note that trust or the lack of trust in regulatory institutions influenced opinions everywhere in Europe. In France, the blood scandal of the mid-1980s (in which health officials stifled evidence of the distribution by transfusion of HIV-contaminated blood) was still fresh and raised questions about the judgments of high level officials (Steffen 1999). In Greece, mistrust in public authorities, scientists and industry is pervasive and the public has no confidence that rules with regard to GMO will be enforced and implemented (Marouda *et al.* 1998). In Italy, trust in public agencies is generally low.

Another example of how concerns about smoking and GMO are fundamentally unrelated comes from Finland and Sweden. Both countries adopted early strategies to combat smoking-related diseases. Yet genetically engineered agriculture hardly produced waves of protest (Fjæstad *et al.* 2001; Rusanen *et al.* 2001). Of course, agriculture is peripheral in the northern latitudes and this part of the world is not known for growing local/regional

[10] In late 2004, the Austrian minister of health passed a law that all enclosed public spaces had to become smoke free. But violators who lit up would not be fined since the government did not want to start a campaign against smokers! 'Smoking ban—the Austrian way,' *Wiener Zeitung*, November 2, 2004.

specialties that require protection against the dominant influence of US-style mass production. Perhaps of equal importance, however, is relatively high trust in institutions partly owing to the absence of serious domestic food scandals.

In brief, the reaction to GMO differed across Europe and the debates often took national flavors (Torgersen *et al.* 2000). Environmental concerns topped the agenda in the UK, Germany, and the Netherlands. There, consumers and public interest organizations expect a wealth of information through labeling and tracing to make sure that they will not inadvertently digest food products containing GMO. In Southern Europe (and countries with large organic farming sector such as Austria), labeling and tracing also receive high priority, though of equal importance is the survival of distinct approaches to food production and preferences for fresh and organic food grown at local farms with ties to the community.

5. The Commission and the Fight About Framework Regulations for GMOs

Originally, the Commission saw its task as promoting the development of a new industry, but its focus was diverted to drafting regulations to satisfy consumer concerns. The Commission and Council produced numerous directives and regulations to address the complex dynamics of transgenic food products. The former DGXI (Environment and Consumer Policy) drafted the Contained Use Directive (90/219), which dealt with laboratory experiments and required the user to carry out prior risk assessment. The Commission also issued the Directive on Deliberate Release in 1990 (90/220), which required manipulated organisms intended for release in the environment to acquire official approval and undergo risk assessment studies before import, marketing, or release. The Council of Ministers of the Environment passed both directives, setting a floor of safety rules and allowed member states to administer higher standards as a concession to critics such as Denmark and Germany. At the end, the content of the directive was such that imports of GM seeds, field trails, commercial planting, and marketization of GM food and feed products were subject to the approval of each member state. Both directives provoked a storm of protest from industry, scientists, and the USA (Meins 2003; Patterson 2000).

In early 1996, the Commission approved Roundup Ready soybeans (manufactured by Monsanto) and later in the year approved Bt-corn (a Novartis product). In response, some member states declared a unilateral ban of both products (Austria, Denmark, France, Luxemburg) and the Commission declared a moratorium on all GM products in April 1998 to sort out the authorization process following the unilateral action of several member states to ban all GMO crops and products.

The Novel Foods Directive (97/258) dealt with food products that contain, consist of, or are produced from GMOs and introduced the idea of mandatory labeling. The directive prompted a heated discussion because it excluded additives and flavoring and it also did not apply to products already approved, namely Roundup Ready soybean and Bt-corn. Although the EP and Council adopted the directive in 1997, it was soon supplemented by the Novel Foods Regulation (1139/98) that proposed the need for a label if 'substantial' modification had taken place (Hunter 1999). The Council regulation included a provision to label food stuffs produced with modified soybeans or corn. The Council later amended the regulation to include additives and flavorings.

The earlier directive 90/220, which handled deliberate release of GMO, was originally less contested than its counterpart 90/119 because no deliberate release of GM crops took place in 1990. By 1996, GM crops were on the market and confusion and conflicting interpretations necessitated a revision of this directive as well. Its replacement was the directive on the deliberate release of GMO in the environment (2001/18/EC). The revised directive improves the strictness and transparency of the provisions, notably creating a more effective and efficient authorization procedure. According to the directive, authorization is on a case-by-case basis and national authorities must send the Commission and other member states a summary of the notification. The Commission must then immediately make the summary available to the public for comments. Directive 2001/18 EC also made an explicit reference to the precautionary principle and the need to take into account the indirect and long-term effects of the product in its assessment.

The EP, which since the 1997 Amsterdam Treaty has greater decision-making powers, has been insistent on comprehensive labeling requirements. In July 2003, after years of wrangling, the EP, Commission, and the Council were able to agree on the exact threshold at which point a product can be declared GM-free, namely if it contains less than 1 percent of GM matter.[11] The scientific and political dilemma was that consumers wanted firm guarantees that non-GM foods were totally free of any GM elements, something that is difficult to guarantee since many products will contain unintended presence of GM material as contamination or mixing can occur at many points in processing. In July 2003, the EP adopted two amendments to directive 2001/18 (deliberate release of GMO) and established guidelines

[11] Food products may still contain GM matter in the form of enzymes, food ingredients, and animal feed none of which is subject to mandatory labeling.

for labeling and tracing GMO from 'farm to fork.'[12] Its revisions set higher safety standards to protect the environment and human health and introduced a broader risk assessment approach and new concepts of traceability and monitoring which might help to identify and remedy adverse effects of GMOs at an earlier stage.

Whereas regulation 1830/2003 (passed July 2003) on labeling and traceability covers mandatory labeling of all food and feed containing or consisting of or produced from a GMO, national government officials have been sharply divided whether to approve the import of various GM food or feed varieties. In 2004, seven requests for approval were turned down by regulatory committees composed of representatives of national governments. Four member states have systemically rejected the Commission's requests (Austria, Denmark, Greece, and Luxemburg). Germany has withheld its vote because the coalition in Berlin is divided on whether to grant approval or not. Five countries side with the Commission: Finland, Ireland, Sweden, the Netherlands, and the UK (with the British voting six times in favor of approval and making an exception in one particular case).[13] Yet in spite of these votes, the Commission has proceeded to authorize the approval of GM products for sale in the EU. By January 2005, the Commission had approved seventeen types of GM corn for farming and genetically modified sweet corn in the absence of authorization by the Standing Committees or the Council of Ministers. The Commission's decision is based on the opinions of the European Food Safety Authority (EFSA), which subjects all GM products to testing and analysis. Brussels officials argue that the 'seal of approval' issued by EFSA indicates that the product is safe for consumption or alternatively safe to be released in the environment.

Five member states continue to invoke the safety clause because of ongoing doubts about the safety of GM crops and have refused to lift their ban on selected products. Germany, Austria, and Luxemburg continue to ban Bt176 corn from their markets due to its possible effect on nontarget insects and the potential for transfer of antibiotic resistance genes to humans and animals. France and Greece ban oilseed rape Topas 19/2 for similar kind of reasons. These products had already been approved by the EU before October 1998. In light of EFSA's approval, Brussels claims that it is illegal for member states to continue to ban these products. The USA, Canada,

[12] The directive sets out the principles for environmental risk assessment, postmarket monitoring requirements, mandatory information to the public with the requirement to ensure labeling and traceability at all stages of the placing on the market. 'Question and Answers on the regulation of GMOs in the EU,' *MEMO/04/85* (Brussels, April 15, 2004).

[13] UK officials voted down approval of GT73 oilseed rape, a product from Monsanto, and not meant for direct human consumption. Government officials fear contamination of conventional fields.

Argentina have complained to the WTO about the effective ban on GMO products in the EU.

In October 2004, as the threat of a negative WTO ruling hung over the Commission, Brussels urged the EU-25 to ask the holdouts to repeal their bans within twenty days. The proposal was defeated in the Regulatory Committee on the Deliberate Release of GMOs in the Environment by a sizable margin in late November 2004. This means that a group of member states under pressure from consumers and socioeconomic interests will continue to ban the sale of individual GM products in the near future.

6. With US or against US

It is too simplistic to conclude that the developments in the EU-15 constitute a straight challenge or rejection of US modes of thinking or operation. As public health has gained in salience, different societies address emerging issues differently. In the USA, a tradition of lifestyle movements and the litigation option contributed to the final victory of the tobacco control movement. At first, local smoking bans in catering facilities, entertainment locations, private offices, and public sector were dismissed by European observers as US health fanaticism. But the psychological, medical, and financial costs of smoking-related deaths and diseases eventually convinced governments in all advanced industrialized countries to combat smoking. In this sense, the USA was a trend setter because of some unusual cultural characteristics and a popular tradition of holding corporate actors responsible for defective products.

The American example probably exerted both negative and positive influence in that smoking bans were first considered inconsistent with European ideals of consumer sovereignty and individual autonomy. Later, once the mood had shifted, the legal defeats suffered by US tobacco companies may have convinced European health authorities to adopt some of the US strategies to reduce smoking prevalence and to combat secondhand smoke.

Assuming that the developments in US tobacco control inspired European public health officials indirectly, will European hostility towards GMO color American public opinion and shape US food safety policy? The preceding discussion leads me to two answers.

First, it should be noted that smoking measures in Europe are implemented without the vocal and hyperactive backing of a tobacco control movement. It remains an elite project that aims to address a public health scourge. Many consumers or voters continue to be tolerant toward smokers and secondhand smoke, so the debate lacks the intense animosity that peppers US discussions. It would be fair to say that there is a convergence in acceptance of scientific and epidemiological evidence, but there continues to be divergence in how to balance the enjoyment of a legal product against its harmful consequences.

Second, the European aversion to GMO has cultural origins as well. Just as US outrage against cigarette manufacturers has roots in the US collective psyche, European antipathy towards agricultural biotechnology summarizes a mode of thinking and expectations unique to Europe. At some point US consumers may be less acquiescent about the presumed utility of agricultural genetic engineering. Yet it seems highly unlikely that a mass movement will emerge to push GMO products or derivatives off the market. Approximately three-quarters of all food products available in US supermarkets contain some trace elements of GMO. Nonetheless, food safety is not a hot topic in the USA thanks to the perceived vigilance of the FDA and much greater acceptance of processed manufactured foods. GMO do not evoke similar associations of unnatural foods, harm to farmers, destruction of habitat, loss of culinary traditions, and so forth.

However, the commotion in Europe has not left the USA untouched. In addition to the losses recorded by agricultural exporters and seed handling companies, the reluctance of Europeans consumers to accept food products containing GMO has not gone unnoticed by US companies. Because of a possible consumer boycott of GM foods, European food processors and distributors avoided products prepared with soy oil derived from modified soybeans. Large retail stores in Germany, France, UK, Ireland, Italy, and Belgium refused to carry products containing GM soy or corn as of 1998. In addition, food retailers and processors in these countries sought alternative sources of GM-free soybeans (the EU does not grow soybeans) in order to reduce dependence on US imports. As a result, the private sector created a system to detect, trace, and identify the trail of ingredients that go into a final product and found other suppliers (in Canada and Brazil) to meet their demands for GM-free soybeans (Barling 2002; Wales and Mythen 2002; Bernauer 2003).

This has persuaded US companies like Gerber, Heinz, McGain, and Frito Lay that operate in Europe to announce that their products will also be GM-free (Young 2003). In this climate, Monsanto scaled back some of its projects and announced in May 2004 that it was dropping plans to market GM wheat. This decision was taken after farmers themselves avoided planting the new wheat for fear of a potential backlash avoided planting this kind of wheat. Monsanto also shelved plans to bring to the market GM potatoes after McDonald's indicated that it would refuse to use them (Pollack 2004). This means that GM food products in the USA may also find limited outlets as food processors opt for GM-free inputs, which then undermine the incentives to develop such expensive seeds in the first place.

At the same time, the Bush administration continues to lend strong support to the further development of 'designer' crops that go beyond herbicide or insect resistance and include novel compounds to enhance their nutritional value or include pharmaceuticals and thus are targeted to a small segment of the food or feed market. In response, the National Academy of Science cautioned in 2004 that oversight and inspections of genetically modified crops and plants should be tightened, especially as firms are contemplating a new generation of highly specialized genetic engineering (Committee on Biological Confinement 2004). While agro-pharmaceutical companies receive the green light, the federal government has no rules of how to deal with 'inadvertent' contamination of food, feed and seed stocks from experimental sites. A growing number of experts are concerned how to protect conventional crops from contamination from GM seeds or plants. Therefore it is possible that a fresh debate on GMO may emerge. As with the relatively feeble objections seen so far in the USA, it seems unlikely that any such debate would incite a huge wave of protest and controversy.

In short, we can conclude that the glory days of smoking are behind us. Cigarettes will never recover the image of charm, sophistication, and acceptance that they enjoyed in the USA and Europe in the 1950s and 1960s. Likewise, it is unlikely that genetic engineering of crops and plants will disappear but its use may be limited to products not meant for direct human consumption (cotton, soybean, rapeseed oil) or to specifically targeted crops aimed at a small segment of the market. At the same time, substantial differences may persist about how to assess risk, manage harms, regulate biotechnology, and meet consumer expectations for safety, transparency, and security. Though transatlantic differences are real, the EU is hardly a uniform harmonized entity. If the transatlantic differences on salient health issues has been striking in the past few decades, the broader pattern of issues related to safety, risks, and harmful substances stirs plenty of conflicts and controversies inside Europe as well.

References

Albæk, Erik. (2004). 'Holy Smoke, No More? Tobacco Control in Denmark', in R. Bayer and E. Feldman (eds.), *Unfiltered: International Conflict over Tobacco Policy and Public Health*. Cambridge, MA: Harvard University Press, pp. 190–219.

Ansell, C., Maxwell, R., and Sicurelli, D. (forthcoming). 'Protesting Food: NGOs and Political Mobilization in Europe', in C. Ansell and D. Vogel (eds.), *Why the Beef? The Contested Governance of European Food Safety*. Cambridge, MA: Cambridge University Press.

Barling, D. (2002). 'The European Response to GM Foods: Rethinking Food Governance', in B. Bailey and M. Lappe (eds.), *Engineering the Farm*. Washington, DC: Island Press.

Bayer, R. and J. Colgrove (2004). 'Children and Bystanders First: The Ethics and Politics of Tobacco Control in the United States', in R. Bayer and E. Feldman (eds.), *Unfiltered: International Conflict over Tobacco Policy and Public Health*. Cambridge, MA: Harvard University Press, pp. 8–37.

Bernauer, T. (2003). *Genes, Trade, and Regulation: The Seeds of Conflict in Food Biotechnology*. Princeton, NJ: Princeton University Press.

Berridge. V. (1998). 'Science and Policy: The Case of Postwar British Smoking Policy', in S. Lock, L. Reynolds, and E. M. Tansey (eds.), *Ashes to Ashes: The History of Smoking and Health*, Amsterdam: Rodopi, pp. 89–106.

—— (2004). 'Militants, Manufacturers, and Governments: Postwar Smoking Policy in the United Kingdom', in R. Bayer and E. Feldman (eds.), *Unfiltered: International Conflict over Tabocco Policy and Public Health*. Cambridge, MA: Harvard University Press, pp. 114–37.

Bitton, A., Neuman, M. D., and Glantz, S. A. (2002). *Tobacco Industry Attempts to Subvert European Union Tobacco Advertising Legislation*. San Francisco: Center for Tobacco Control Research and Education, available at *<http://www.library.ucsf.edu/tobacco/euad/>*.

Bonny, S. (2003). 'Why Are Most Europeans Opposed to GMOs? Factors Explaining Rejection in France and Europe', *Electronic Journal of Biotechnology*: 6/10, available at *<http://www.ejbiotechnology.info/content/vol6/issue1/ full/4/#27>*.

Bouma, J. (2001). *Het rookgordijn: De macht van de Nederlandse tabaksindutrie*, Amsterdam: L. J. Veen.

Boy, D. and de Cheveigné, S. (2001). 'Biotechnology: A Menace to French Food', in G. Gaskell and M. W. Bauer (eds.), *Biotechnology 1996–2000: The Years of Controversy*, London: Science Museum, pp. 181–90.

Brandt, A. M. (2004). 'Difference and Diffusion: Cross-Cultural Perspectives on the Rise of Antitobacco Policies', in R. Bayer and E. Feldman (eds.), pp. 255–74.

BSE Inquiry (2003). Available at *<http://www.bseinquiry.gov.uk/>*.

Chaloupka, F. J. M., Wakefield, M., and Czart, C. (2001). 'Taxing Tobacco: The Impact of Tobacco Taxes on Cigarette Smoking and Other Tobacco Use', R. Rabin and S. Sugarman (eds.), *Regulating Tobacco*, New York: Oxford University Press.

Clifford Engs, R. (2000). *Clean Living Movements: American Cycles of Health Reform* Westport, CT: Praeger.

Committee on Biological Confinement of Genetically Engineered Organisms/National Academy of Sciences. (2004). *Biological Confinement of Genetically Engineered Organisms*. Washington, DC: National Academies Press.

Cooper, A. and Kurzer, P. (2003). 'Rauch ohne Feuer: Why Germany lags in Tobacco Control', *German Politics and Society*, 21: 24–47.

Cranor, C. F. (1993). *Regulating Toxic Substances*. New York: Oxford University Press.

Craplet, M. (2001). 'Alcohol Problems: Is there a Specifically French view?', *Addiction*, 96: 805–7.

Derthick, M. (2002). *Up in Smoke: From Legislation to Litigation in Tobacco Politics*. Washington, DC: CQ Press.

Doll, R. (1998). 'The First Reports on Smoking and Lung Cancer', S. Lock, L. Reynolds, and E. M. Tansey (eds.), *Ashes to Ashes: The History of Smoking and Health*, Amsterdam: Rodopi, 130–41.

Dubré. D. (2004). *Statistics in Focus: Population and Social Conditions*, Brussels: Eurostat.

Duina, F. and Kurzer, P. (2004). 'Smoke in Your Eyes: The Struggle over Tobacco Control in the European Union', *Journal of European Public Policy*, 11: 57–77.

Echols, M. A. (1998). 'Food Safety Regulation in the European Union and the United States: Different Culture, Different Laws', *Columbia Journal of European Law*, 4: 525–44.

Enriquez, J. and Goldberg, R. (2000). 'Transforming Life, Transforming Business: The Life Science Revolution', *Harvard Business Review*, 78: 94–104.

Eurobarometer (1996). *Biotechnology Survey*. Brussels: Eurobarometer 46.1.

Feldman, E. and Bayer, R. (2004). 'Conclusion: Lessons from the Comparative Study of Tobacco Control', in R. Bayer and E. Feldman (eds.), pp. 292–307.

Fjæstad, B. *et al.* (2001). 'Sweden: The Lid is on, but for how long?', in G. Gaskell and M. Bauer (eds.), *Biotechnology 1996–2000: The Years of Controversy*. London: Science Museum, pp. 267–81.

Gilmore, A. and McKee, M. (2004). 'Tobacco-Control Policy in the European Union: The Legal, Ethical, and Policy Debates', in R. Bayer and E. Feldman (eds.), pp. 219–54.

Glantz, S. (1996). *The Cigarette Papers*. Berkeley: University of California Press.

Grant, W. (1997). 'BSE and the Politics of Food', in P. Dunleavey *et al.* (eds.), *Developments in British Politics*. New York: St Martin's Press, pp. 342–54.

Gusfield, J. R. (1998). 'The Social Symbolism of Smoking and Health', in J. A. Schaler and M. E. Schaler (eds.), *Smoking: Who has the right?* New York: Prometheus Books, pp. 240–66.

Hara, M. (2003). 'Finland: Tobacco Policy Integral to National Health Policy', in K. Hakala and M. Waller (eds.), *Nordic Tobacco Control: Towards Smokefree Societies*. Copenhagen: Nordic Council of Ministers.

Harremoës, P. *et al.* (2002). *The Precautionary Principle in the 20th Century*. London: Earthscan.

Harrison, K. and Hoberg, G. (1994). *Risk, Science, and Politics*. Montreal: McGill-Queen's University Press.

Heller, C. (2001). 'From Risk to Globalization: Discursive Shifts in the French Debate About GMOs', *Medical Anthropology Quarterly*, 5: 25–8.

Hervey, T. K. (2001). 'Up in Smoke? Community (anti)-Tobacco Law and Policy', *European Law Review*, 26: 101–25

Hood, C., Rothstein, H. and Baldwin, R. (2001). *The Government of Risk: Understanding Risk Regulation Regimes*. New York: Oxford University Press.

Hunter, R. (1999). 'European Regulation of Genetically Modified Organisms', in J. Morris and R. Bate (eds.), *Fearing Food: Risk, Health, and Environment*. Boston, MA: Butterworth-Heinemann, pp. 188–232.

Joly, P. and Marris, C. (2003). 'Les Américains ont-ils accepté les OGM? Analyse comparée de la construction des OGM comme problème public en France en aux États-Unis', *Cahiers d'economie et sociologie rurales*, 68–9: 12–45.

Joossens, L. (2004). *Effective Tobacco Control Policies in 28 European Countries*. Brussels: European Network for Smoking Prevention, available at <*http://www.en-sp.org/files/effectivefinal.pdf*>.

Kagan, R. A. and Vogel, D. (1993). 'The Politics of Smoking Regulation: Canada, France and the United States', in R. Rabin and S. Sugarman (eds.), *Smoking Policy: Law, Politics and Culture*. New York: Oxford University Press, pp. 23–48.

Kersh, R. and Morone, J. (2002). 'How the Personal becomes Political: Prohibitions, Public Health, and Obesity', *Studies in American Political Development*, 16: 162–75.

Kurzer, P. and Cooper, A. (2005). 'What's for Dinner? Variations in European Support for Genetically Modified Food'. Paper presented at the 9th Biennial European Union Studies Association conference, Austin, TX, March 31–April 2.

—— (2001). *Markets and Moral Regulation: Cultural Change in Europe*. New York: Cambridge University Press.

LeBesco, K. (2004). *Revolting Bodies: The Struggle to Redefine Fat Identity*. Amherst, MA: University of Massachusetts Press.

Libby, R. (1998). *Eco-Wars: Political Campaigns and Social Movements*. New York: Columbia University Press.

Marouda-Chatjoulis, A., Stathopoulou, A., and Sakellaris, G. (1998). 'Greece', in J. Durant, M. Bauer, and G. Gaskell (eds.), *Biotechnology and the Public Sphere*. London: Science Museum, pp. 77–88.

Meins, E. (2003). *Politics of Public Outrage: Explaining Transatlantic and Intra-European Diversity of Regulation on Food Irradiation and Genetically Modified Food*. Hamburg: Lit Verlag.

Morone, J. (2003). *Hellfire Nation: The Politics of Sin in American History*. New Haven, CT: Yale University Press.

Nathanson, C. (1999). 'Social Movements as Catalysts of Policy Change: The Case of Smoking and Guns', *Journal of Health Politics, Policy and Law*, 24: 421–88.

—— (2004). 'Liberté, Egalité, Fumée: Smoking and Tobacco Control in France', in R. Bayer and E. Feldman (eds.), pp. 138–60.

Parker-Pope, T. (2001). *Cigarettes: Anatomy of an Industry from Seed to Smoke*. New York: New Press.

Patterson, L. A. (2000). 'Biotechnology Policy,' in H. Wallace and W. Wallace (eds.), *Policymaking in the EU*. New York: Oxford University Press, pp. 367–86.

Pertschuk, M. (2001). *Smoke in Their Eyes: Lessons in Movement Leadership from the Tobacco Wars*. Nashville, TN: Vanderbilt University Press.

Petersen, A. and Lupton, D. (1996). *The New Public Health: Health and Self in the Age of Risk*. Thousand Oaks, CA: Sage.

Pollack, A. (2004). 'Monsanto shelves plan for modified wheat', *New York Times*, May 11, 2004.

Poppe, C. and Kjærnes, U. (2003). *Trust in Food in Europe: A Comparative Analysis*. National Institute for Consumer Research, Professional Report No. 5. Available at <*www.trustinfood.org*>.

Proctor, R. (1995). *Cancer Wars: How Politics Shapes What We Know and Don't Know about Cancer*. New York: Basic Books.

Rabin, R. L. (2001). 'The Third Wave of Tobacco Tort Litigation', in R. Rabin and S. Sugarman (eds.), *Regulating Tobacco*. New York: Oxford University Press, pp. 176–206.

Ratzan, S. (ed.) (1998). *The Mad Cow Crisis: Health and the Public Good*. New York: New York University Press.

Roth, A. L., Dunsby, J., and Bero, L. A. (2003). 'Framing Processes in Public Commentary on US Federal Tobacco Control Regulation', *Social Studies of Science*, 33: 7–44.

Rusanen, T. *et al.* (2001). 'Biotechnology in Finland: Transcending Tradition', in Gaskell and Bauer 2001, 172–80.

Sakellaris, G. and Chatjouli, A. (2001). 'Greece: Losing Faith in Biotechnology', in G. Gaskell and M. Bauer (eds.), *Biotechnology 1996–2000: The Years of Controversy*. London: Science Museum, pp. 204–14.

Sassatelli, R. and Scott, A. (2001). 'Novel Food, New Markets, and Trust Regimes', *European Societies*, 3:213–44.

Steffen, M. (1999). 'The Nation's Blood: Medicine, Justice, and the State in France', in E. Feldman and R. Bayer (eds.), *Blood Feuds: AIDS, Blood, and the Politics of Medical Disaster*. New York: Oxford University Press, pp. 95–126.

Studlar, D. (2002). *Tobacco Control: Comparative Politics in the United States and Canada*. Peterborough, Ontario: Broadview Press.

Sweeney, C (2004). 'EU Will not Copy Ireland's Tough Ban on Smoking,' *Irish Independent*, January 13.

Taylor, P. (1984). *Smoke Ring: The Politics of Tobacco*. Toronto: Bodley Head.

Torgersen, H., *et al.* (2000). 'Europe the Spoil-Sport: On the Europeans' Reluctance Towards Genetically Modified Food', *Journal of Biolaw and Business*, 3: 4–10.

—— and Seifert, F. (2000). 'Austria: Precautionary Blockage of Agricultural Biotechnology', *Journal of Risk Research*, 3: 209–17.

Tridimas, G. and Tridimas, T. (2002). 'The European Court of Justice and the Annulment of the Tobacco Advertising Directive: Friend of National Sovereignty or Foe of Public Health', *European Journal of Law and Economics*, 14: 171–83.

Ugland, T. (2003). 'A Case of Strange Bedfellows in the EU: An Institutional Perspective on the French–Swedish Cooperation on Alcohol Control', *Scandinavian Political Studies*, 26: 269–86.

Valverde, M. (1998). *Diseases of the Will: Alcohol and the Dilemmas of Freedom*. New York: Cambridge University Press.

Vogel, D. and Bensedrine, J. (2002). 'Comparing Risk Regulation in the United States and France: Asbestos, AIDS and Genetically Modified Agriculture', *French Politics, Culture and Society*, 20: 13–32.

—— (2003). 'The Hare and the Tortoise Revisited: The New Politics of Consumer and Environmental Regulation in Europe', *British Journal of Political Science*, 33: 557–80.

Wales, C. and Mythen, G. (2002). 'Risky Discourse: The Politics of GM Food', *Environmental Politics*, 11: 121–44.

Watson, R. (2002). 'EU Waters Down its Plan to Restrict Tobacco Advertising', *BMJ.com,* 325: 853–54.

Wolfson, M. (2001). *The Fight Against Big Tobacco: the Movement, the State, and the Public's Health.* New York: Aldine de Gruyter.

Wynne, B. (1995). 'Public Understanding of Science', in S. Jasanoff *et al.* (eds.), *Handbook of Science and Technology Studies.* Thousand Oaks, CA: Sage, pp. 361–88.

Young, A. (2003). 'Political Transfer and Trading Up? Transatlantic Trade in Genetically Modified Food and US Politics', *World Politics*, 55: 457–84.

14

Drawing the EU's Borders: Immigration Policy

VIRGINIE GUIRAUDON

Who decides to allow outsiders to enter and stay in a given territory? Who grants full membership in the community? Across regions and time, the answers to these questions are bound to tell us about the location of authority in a society and to help us draw its boundaries. If the EU that we know today is the embryo of a future European polity, we must analyze the extent to which member states have delegated their prerogatives regarding immigration and citizenship to the EU level. The transfer of competence in areas considered emblematic of national sovereignty should be a litmus test of the 'polity' ambitions of the EU.

This chapter examines the development of an EU immigration policy, bearing in mind the way in which other federal projects such as the USA came to monopolize the control over the movement of people. To understand why member states of the EU decided to cooperate in the immigration policy domain, we need to focus on the actors that prevailed and the interests that they represented. As of the early 1980s, I argue, national officials in charge of migration sought to avoid judicial constraints and conflicting bureaucratic views that that were experiencing at the national level. They consequently moved to relocate some of their decision-making to a secretive intergovernmental forum at the EU level, where they could exclude other ministries and escape judicial monitoring. In other words, the immediate motive for cooperation at the EU level was one of political 'venue shopping,' that is finding a decision-making framework in which the rules and the participants favor one's key objectives. Since these officials were professionally oriented toward viewing migration as a problem of control and policing (as opposed to treating migration in broader sociopolitical perspective), and since the intergovernmental format privileged operational cooperation, 'soft law,' and informal processes, these orientations became characteristics of the EU immigration regime. This kind of policy has in turn been embedded in broader justifications that have evolved over time with the emergence of new frames and changes in the strategic or economic context, connecting at points to the single market, the end of the Cold War, and challenges of terrorism after 9/11.

The chapter is organized in five sections. Section 1 compares EU immigration policy with its US counterpart, asking whether the USA could serve as a model. It also analyzes the ways in which the striking differences between the current policies in the USA and the EU can help us explain the form and content of the emerging EU immigration regime. Section 2 examines the origins of intergovernmental cooperation in immigration, underlining that interior ministry bureaucrats at the national level had an incentive to escape domestic legal constraints and interministerial conflicts by 'going transgovernmental' as of the 1980s. Section 3 analyzes the treaty rules that govern the immigration policy area at the EU level since the coming into force of the Amsterdam Treaty in 1999. The key point that I highlight is that the 'venue shopping' dynamics that led to the development of intergovernmental co-operation account for the enduringly intergovernmental rules of the game. Section 4 focuses on the ways in which the decision-making framework has worked in practice. The evidence suggests that, while the rules favored a 'securitarian' immigration policy, this was reinforced by contextual events such as 9/11 and populist electoral successes. Section 5 explores key trends in the content of European policymaking in this area since 1999: lowest common denominator dynamics when it comes to migrants' rights, the focus on technical police solutions such as databases and biometrics, and the externalization of migration control outside of the EU.

1. EU policy from a US Perspective

Exercising a monopoly over the control of the movement of people became a priority of modern nation-states in the nineteenth century. They wrested this prerogative away from local and private actors like municipalities, states, feudal landowners, or slaveholders. To a great extent this development accompanied the triumph of industrial capitalism, which required the mobility of labor to allow workers to move to new factories. After the French Revolution, the American Civil War, and the unification of Germany and Italy, the attribution of citizenship—the bundle of rights that ties individuals and states and allows them to participate as equals in the polity—also became a national or federal prerogative. Citizenship then became linked to belonging to the national community.

Immigration and citizenship have since become emblematic of national sovereignty in the twentieth century, a development consecrated by international law. Indeed, the postwar human rights regime circumscribes this national prerogative in only a few instances: to call upon states to welcome refugees and prevent foreigners from being sent back to states where their life would be at risk (Geneva Convention of 1951), and to allow foreigners to lead a normal family life and not suffer inhuman and degrading treatment if sent back to their country of origin (European Convention of Human Rights, Arts. 3 and 8).

History suggests that any project seeking to infuse a sense of belonging by creating a common market would authorize and even seek to foster the mobility of people across its internal borders, as did the EEC founding members that signed the Rome Treaty in 1957. One can also comprehend that nation-states would not relinquish easily this hard-won prerogative over immigration and citizenship policies.

Can the USA provide a 'model' for transferring these policies from a lower to a higher level of government? In fact the US case is difficult to 'transplant' to the EU in any broad sense, since its own development is bound up in the history of US slavery. Until the mid-nineteenth century, US states still carried prerogatives including the bestowing of nationality and the rights granted to aliens, stemming from the fact that some states wanted control over their slave populations (Neuman 1998; Schuck 1998). It was in reaction to this past that the US federal government received immense power over migration and citizenship policy after 1865. The Supreme Court and federal judges went so far as to affirm that the federal executive had 'plenary power' over immigration. Today, the US federal bureaucracy in charge of immigration and naturalization directly implements policy at the state and local level, whereas in a federal state such as Germany, the *Länder* apply federal guidelines. If a federal system is 'a means of dividing the power and functions of government between a central government and a specified number of geographically defined regional jurisdictions' (Bowman and Kearney 2005: 5, 24), then the US federal system gives the central government full competence in the area of immigration. In the post-Amsterdam EU, by contrast, power is shared in this area. EU member states retain competence over the bestowing of citizenship: EU citizens are defined since the 1993 Maastricht Treaty as nationals of one of the member states. Even where EU competence have expanded into rules governing immigration, asylum and border controls since the 1997 Amsterdam Treaty, the lower (national) units implement federal-level (EU) rules, as in the German case.

The US and European states have nevertheless borrowed from their respective 'policy toolbox' in the area of immigration control. Most notably, current EU policies to prevent unwanted migrants from leaving their countries of origin emphasize visa policy delivered by consulates abroad and carrier sanctions that force transport companies to check the travel documents of their passengers. Both visas and carrier sanctions were US innovations. The idea that visitors and immigrants should be processed before arriving at port was written into law in the USA in the early twentieth century: the 1902 Passenger Act forced steamship companies to retransport at their own cost inadmissible passengers and the 1924 Immigration Act entrusted US consuls abroad with managing quotas and delivering visas (Zolberg 1997). Transatlantic borrowing has also gone the other way. In 1986 and 1996 the US Congress tried to organize a system of sanctions that require employers to check the legality of the stay of their employees, imitating European measures set up as early as 1926 in France.

The USA and the EU also face broadly similar immigration challenges today. Each year, about a million and a half legal migrants arrive in the EU (374 million inhabitants), proportionally twice as much as in the US (OECD 2003). There are about thirteen million non-EU nationals residing legally in the EU-15, making up about 4 percent of the total EU population (while only 2.8 percent of the world population are international migrants). The eleven and a half million foreign residents in the USA also constitute about 4 percent of the population. Irregular immigration into the EU can only be estimated and figures vary greatly. As an indication, the International Organization for Migration has estimated the upper limit of unauthorized migrants in Europe at three million in 1998 and believes that anywhere between 120,000 and 500,000 foreigners enter Europe illegally every year (IOM 2000). Estimates based on the last census suggest that there may be close to eight million undocumented aliens in the USA, half of which are believed to be Mexicans. Beyond these aggregate numbers and these estimates, national situations differ significantly. Some member states have a long tradition of immigration with significant foreign-born populations, while Southern and Eastern European states have only recently taken it migrants and many only transit through their territory. The numbers admitted vary: flows into Germany have been higher than in France and the UK until the latter became the first recipient of asylum flows in 2002; important numbers of asylum-seekers relative to the total population arrive in smaller countries such as the Netherlands or Denmark. Yet, while immigration levels are high on both sides of the Atlantic, policies differ.

In terms of basic policy orientation, the USA and the EU contrast very sharply. The US *solicits* immigration and sometimes actively recruits high-skilled workers abroad. Every year, the USA delivers large numbers of residence permits to high-skilled workers and to family members of US residents: the US Immigration and Nationality Act sets an annual minimum of 226,000 family-sponsored immigrants and a maximum of 480,000 and 140,000 employment-based preference immigrants. Policies in Europe, in contrast, seek above all to *stem* immigration flows. Countries that had welcomed post colonial migrants and actively sought foreign 'guest workers' after World War II stopped recruiting migrant workers in 1973 at the time of the first oil shock. Immigration continued yet most of the foreigners that came were unsolicited. New legal entrants have either been family members of foreign residents and nationals or persons fleeing zones of conflict and escaping persecution, from the Asian 'boat people' of the 1970s to those fleeing the Balkans or Afghanistan in the 1990s.

The absence of pro-immigration business lobbying and the little weight of the migrant vote in the EU largely account for this stark contrast between stemming and soliciting policies (on interest groups and 'client politics,' see Freeman 2001). During the intense congressional debates of the 1990s, ethnic and business lobbies mobilized in the USA (Tichenor 2002). They convinced enough politicians that reducing migration would be politically costly by invoking the importance of the 'ethnic' (Latino) vote in close elections and their reliance on business support as campaign financers. In Europe, migrant-origin voters are not wooed as they are in the USA. Instead parties seek to contain the anti-immigrant populist vote. Nor do we find business groups actively lobbying for foreign labor in any manner equivalent to the USA. Migrant associations, to the extent that they mobilize, are not focusing on demanding more entries. This means that, in Europe, pro-immigrant organizations are human rights groups including churches and leftist movements engaging in the defense of rights rather than calling for an increase of economic migration. In fact, often these groups do not support the 'brain drain' of third world elites, while this is not the case in the USA.

In brief, the dynamics of policymaking regarding immigration in the EU strongly differ from the USA: the main goal of policy is the restriction of flows and nation-states retain much more input in the decision-making than US states. As we turn to the motives that led European nation-states to cooperate in the area of immigration, it should thus be clear that reinforcing border controls was a key objective.

2. The Origins of EU Immigration Policy: Bureaucratic 'Venue Shopping'

Given the lack of business pressures for more migrant workers and the rise of ethnocentric rhetoric and sentiment in Europe, national policies for the last thirty years have sought to reduce the number of foreigners reaching the territory of member states. After the 1973 halt to the recruitment of foreign 'guest-workers,' authorities in western Europe focused on increasing the return of these workers and stemming further entries by all means possible. Yet they found themselves frustrated by their own constitutional principles on equality before the law and fundamental rights; landmark high court rulings in the late 1970s soon circumscribed administrative discretion and immigration laws (Guiraudon 1997; Joppke 2001). In particular, governments could no longer prevent family reunification. Foreigners enjoyed a more secure residence status and certain categories of foreigners gained protection against expulsion. The end of the 1970s also saw the first major clashes between the ministries of Social Affairs in charge of migrants' integration that argued for a more secure status for settled foreigners and Home Affairs (or Interior) ministries in charge of immigration control.

By the early 1980s, Home Affairs ministries had an incentive to seek new policy venues—and above all European policy venues—to shelter them from domestic legal constraints and conflicting policy goals (Guiraudon 2000, 2003). This is when intergovernmental forums developed, such as the Trevi Group of Interior and Justice ministers, which met regularly after 1975 to exchange and coordinate their actions.

By shifting policymaking away from national venues, migration control agencies gain in the power redistribution by excluding a number of actors that have better access at the national level, where the bargaining process allows almost every ministry and many civil society actors to appeal to head-of-government arbiters. If they can work out a collective agenda at the EU level, home affairs ministries do not need to broker compromises with the ministries that they disagree with. Civil society actors do not have the resources to monitor their secretive activities and mobilize against them beyond the national level. National parliaments can also be largely bypassed, being presented with signed international agreements that they have to ratify without modifications in a few weeks. This was the case with the 1990 Schengen implementation agreement on border controls and the 1990 Dublin Convention on asylum, two multilateral initiatives signed outside the European Community legal order that we briefly describe below.

Schengen, the agreement signed by France, Germany, and the Benelux countries in 1985, was the first opportunity for Interior and Justice officials to set the agenda on intergovernmental cooperation. The aim was to create a 'laboratory': a few countries would create an area with no internal border controls with 'compensating measures' in the form of reinforced external controls. Irregular immigration was included in the set of undesirable phenomena that needed to be fought, alongside organized crime, drugs and arms trafficking. While police officials were monopolizing the negotiation of the follow-up implementation agreement finalized in 1990, the Single European Act set as an EC goal a single market and the freedom of movement of *persons*. The first justification for elaborating a common immigration policy was thus the lifting of internal border checks on persons within the EC, which would also allow for a smoother flow of goods.

Then refugee flows rose dramatically after the fall of the Berlin Wall in 1989. The dismantling of the Yugoslav Republic and the fall of Communist regimes reopened migration routes via the East and Central Europe. A major influx of asylum-seekers into Germany in 1992–3 provided new grounds for cooperation, as did emotional public debates in other core member states covered in the media that prophesized 'tidal waves' of 'bogus refugees.' Military, intelligence and police officials added international migration to the list of transnational threats they thought would replace the Cold War nuclear menace, such as Islamic fundamentalism and global mafias (Huysmans 2000).

Member states facing comparable challenges sought to upgrade their common interests through policy coordination by including immigration and asylum in the 'third pillar' of Justice of Home Affairs created by the 1992 Maastricht Treaty. Germany received an overwhelming majority of the asylum flows (with over 400,000 requests in 1992) and wielded enough power in the EC to convince others to step up cooperation. Germany hoped for a 'burden-sharing' system to distribute asylum-seekers more evenly. Yet the other major member states were in no rush to take Germany's asylum-seekers, and declined. Instead the Dublin Convention was signed in 1990 to establish rules on the state responsible for examining asylum cases and allow for transfers to signatory states where the person had first transited. Other measures were adopted in intergovernmental forums to reduce the numbers of asylum seekers and resend them to another state. Notably, the 1992 London resolutions stated that asylum-seekers could be returned to 'safe third countries,' countries identified as respecting liberal democratic principles. Persons that had gone through these countries could see their asylum claim rejected as 'manifestly unfounded'.

Most of the policy innovations of the pre-Amsterdam Treaty took place outside of the 'third pillar' framework, especially within the Schengen executive committee (which drew in more members). The Schengen model of cooperation had the advantage of allowing the founding members to impose their rules and conditions on incoming states, thereby ensuring that they would not compromise on their interests. Furthermore the secretive bureaucratic decisions became national law without any input from national actors (parliamentarians or NGOs). Yet, the original link between initiatives in the area of border control and freedom of movement within the EEC and the launch of the single market seemed to have been forgotten by the Schengen executive committee. It was up to the EU institutions to remind them—as the Commission and the Dutch Presidency did at Amsterdam in 1997.

3. The Amsterdam Framework of EU Immigration Policy: *À la carte* Cooperation

The Amsterdam Treaty framework integrates immigration and asylum within the EC or 'Community' pillar. But, as this section demonstrates, intergovernmental features still dominate, implying that there is a limited role for supranational institutions and central EU policies. Some member states are even allowed to participate *à la carte* to policy initiatives. This is due to the fact that the ministries in charge of migration control at the national level did not wish to face opposition at the EU level from institutions with oversight powers (such as parliaments and courts) or be outvoted by member states with differing interests.

Practically all participants in the Amsterdam Treaty negotiations agreed that the convoluted intergovernmental 'third pillar' framework needed to be revised for any progress to be made in the coordination of migration control policies. Between 1993 and the coming into force of the Maastricht Treaty and the 1997 Amsterdam Treaty, member states had only agreed on one joint position and five legally binding joint actions on fairly marginal issues (like airport transit and school trips). After much debate, the solution chosen consisted in 'lifting out' of the third pillar the provisions on immigration and asylum and incorporating them into the 'first' or 'Community' (supranational) pillar through a new Title IV of the amended Treaty of the European Communities.

But the surprising element in the last-minute deals brokered in Amsterdam lay elsewhere. The 1990 Schengen agreement and all subsequent measures adopted for its implementation were incorporated into the EC/EU framework. The diplomats negotiating the treaty had been put aside during the Schengen negotiations and avenged themselves at Amsterdam. Foreign affairs ministries were keen to rein in intergovernmental processes dominated by law and order civil servants that had multiplied and run amok. The Schengen *acquis*—three thousand pages with varying legal standing—was published and given a legal character. In spite of many expert meetings, the Treaty came into force before member states had agreed on the detailed content and incorporation method of the Schengen *acquis*.

The Amsterdam Treaty, which came into force on May 1, 1999, marked an important step in making immigration and asylum policy a Community policy—bringing both a greater role of EU institutions in immigration-related decision-making and the use of traditional EC legal instruments such as the adoption of directives and regulations. After a five-year transition period that ended on May 1, 2004 (during which it shared this prerogative with member states), the Commission now has the same exclusive power of initiative that it enjoys in most economic policies. Given that ministers must unanimously approve Commission initiatives, however, the member states knew that the Commission would have a limited margin of maneuver yet could play the role of coordinator of national positions.

Other firewalls against supranational interference were maintained at Amsterdam, however—especially toward the EU institutions for control and review, the EP and the ECJ. The EP, whose opinions and reports have always defended the rights of non-EU nationals, only has a consultative role in these areas. The move to co-decision, whereby the EP could ultimately veto legislation, required a unanimous decision that member states have far deferred until the 2004 Constitutional Treaty. Similarly, while the Amsterdam deal allowed that the ECJ could be asked for a ruling on the interpretation of the new Title IV or measures based on it, this process was limited at French insistence. The past ECJ jurisprudence on third-country nationals had affirmed that certain categories of persons could move within the EU (families of EU nationals, employees of EU firms contracted in another member state, and nationals of countries that had signed association agreements with the EC). The Court was specifically denied jurisdiction over national border-crossing measures aimed at safeguarding internal security. This is significant since the overwhelming majority of administrative measures either barring access to a member state or requiring the expulsion of foreigners are justified by the need to 'maintain public order' and 'safeguard internal security'—so most measures would fall outside of the Court's purview. More importantly, the application of preliminary rulings in areas covered by Title IV is restricted to national courts of last instance (blocking requests for ECJ rulings from lower national courts). This limits the number of cases before the Court and hinders the dynamics of 'integration through law' in this domain.

Interior and Justice officials seeking to escape judicial constraints at the national level do not wish to be faced with similar legal scrutiny at EU level. The result, so far, is that the complaints about weak accountability and democratic oversight often leveled at the EU are particularly acute in immigration and asylum policy. There is a proliferation of committees of national experts whose meetings and minutes are not made public. The most important is the Strategic Committee on Immigration, Frontiers and Asylum (SCIFA), which brings together high-level Home Affairs civil servants. Members of the EP and the couple of nongovernmental organizations that serve as 'watchdogs' such as Statewatch or ECRE (European Council for Refugees and Exiles) regularly denounce the lack of access to documents. European-level policymaking is much harder to supervize than national immigration policy reform or local administrative decisions.

Decision-making rules in the Council of Ministers show that immigration and asylum policies retain an intergovernmental character. The German delegation at Amsterdam obtained unanimous voting in the Council of Ministers because the German regional governments had lobbied against the transfer of decision-making capacity to Brussels on immigration and particularly asylum matters. German *Länder* have been vocal on this issue as they feel that they 'bear the costs' of immigration and some (Conservative) governments have led electoral campaigns on anti-asylum slogans. This attitude can be compared to that of certain US States in the 1990s (California, Texas and Florida) that complained about the fact that they received most migrants and more asylum-seekers than planned who used social services while most migrants' contributions end up in federal coffers. German states that already complained about the federal–local imbalance did not want to further remove decisions on migration to a higher level of governance.

The Nice Treaty of 2000 did not alter the Amsterdam Treaty framework. Significant change would occur if the draft Constitution of the EU is ratified, however: the EP will gain co-decision powers and qualified majority voting would be the rule in the Council of Ministers. Since the process of ratification of the new Treaty is bound to be long and its outcome uncertain, the representatives of member state governments that met in The Hague in the fall of 2004 to agree on a program for the following five years suggested that QMV and co-decision be used informally, yet this is a commitment that is not legally binding. There is still an emphasis on encouraging further interbureaucratic activity. For instance, the draft treaty mentions the need for 'operational cooperation between the competent authorities of the member states.' More importantly, the role of the ECJ remains limited. Thus the key change to watch in the future will be an enhanced involvement of the EP, which has been active in defending civil liberties and may seek to balance security-oriented border control measures and the defense of fundamental rights for all, EU nationals and third country nationals alike.

In addition to preserving much of the intergovernmental character of the EU migration regime, the Amsterdam Treaty strengthened the idea of a *Europe à la carte*. Not all member states take part in Title IV; the UK, Northern Ireland and (as a result) the Republic of Ireland negotiated a selective 'opt-in.' In practice, they ask participating member states permission to take part in cooperation on a case-by-case basis. Denmark, though a member of Schengen, is not bound by the new title and cooperates only on visa policy—a legal nightmare since each new decision has required the signing of a separate Danish–EU Treaty. Norway and Iceland have not joined the EU yet they signed an agreement in 1999 that allows them to participate in the application and development of the Schengen/EU regime (in order to maintain the Nordic Passport Union that includes the Scandinavian EU states).

In brief, immigration and asylum is now governed by a multispeed Europe that extends beyond the EU borders. Moreover, it should be underlined that EU institutions are not the only legitimate set of international institutions to develop common policies, thereby undermining the idea that cooperation in this area was simply a consequence of the creation of the single market. Among the most important parallel processes are the Intergovernmental

Consultations on Asylum, Refugees and Migration Policies, the 'Vienna Club' (Germany, Austria, Switzerland, France and Italy), and the 'Budapest Process' (involving both West and East European countries).

4. The First Five Years After Amsterdam (1999–2004): Immigration Rises to the Fore

How has the Amsterdam institutional framework evolved since it came into force in 1999? Policy practices have been substantially affected by the post-9/11 context, and also by the electoral success of xenophobic populist parties in Europe. These events made immigration and asylum a high priority for member state governments, encouraging them to entrust the Commission bureaucracy with launching a large number of initiatives in this area.

In October 1999 in Tampere, Finland, soon after the Amsterdam Treaty came into effect, European leaders set a more ambitious agenda. For the first time, heads of government committed to making the creation of an 'area of freedom, security and justice' a priority. The summit had long been planned as an act of political communication, signaling that EU leaders wanted to address the increasing preoccupations of European citizens with crime-fighting. Organized and coordinated by the General Secretariat of the Council, the summit had been prepared by preceding Council meetings of the relevant ministers so that heads of government could announce sixty concrete policy initiatives, often with specific deadlines, that covered all aspects of 'area of freedom, security and justice,' including immigration and asylum. The emphasis was on 'freedom' and the rights of European residents, with announcements such as a 'charter of fundamental rights . . . '. The summit conclusions affirmed that a common immigration and asylum policy was necessary to lift internal borders and make freedom of movement a reality. To show that their declarations would be followed by concrete decisions, they demanded that the Commission keep a 'scoreboard' of proposals and track the negotiating process every semester—a sort of 'to-do list' to monitor progress.

In 1999 economic indicators and prospects in Europe were relatively good. This context was propitious to a rebalancing of immigration policy goals. The Commission 2000 'Communication on a common immigration policy,' in fact, underlined that the goal of 'zero immigration' could not be achieved and was not necessarily desirable given labor shortages in certain sectors and the demographic decline of Europe due to low fertility rates (CEC 2000). The External Trade Commissioner suggested that Europe could benefit from lifting immigration controls for the personnel of service companies as part of the world trade negotiations known as GATS (General Agreement on

Trade in services). Individual member states were in fact already recruiting high-skilled workers, with Germany proposing 20,000 'green cards' for Indian computer programmers. Yet the Germans did not propose to adopt similar policies at the EU-level, since the point was to recruit the best for themselves rather than share with other competing EU economies. Still, the beginning of the post-Amsterdam period heralded a less repressive and restrictive policy applauded by NGOs.

This reorientation of immigration policy turned out to be short-lived. The 9/11 attacks in the USA and the economic slowdown that accompanied them marked the return of a more thoroughly security-oriented view of migration control. Official statements emanating from the Council and also the Commission linked terrorism with immigration and asylum. At an extraordinary JHA meeting convened right after the attacks, the German delegation stated that the fight against terrorism required the creation of a EU visa identification system—a common database with biometric data on all visa applicants wishing to travel to the EU. The proposal was deemed a priority at the Laeken summit in December and approved by the Council of Ministers in February 2002, illustrating the remarkable impetus to speedy decision-making following from 9/11. At an October 2001 closed meeting of SCIFA—where a US delegation requested, *inter alia*, detailed personal data on people flying to the USA—the US delegate predicted a complete overhaul of their immigration system 'not targeted specifically at terrorism, but taking the events of 11 September as the trigger for developing a new approach' (Council 2001). For the EU as well, 9/11 served as a trigger. US pressure on the EU in the area of immigration has not subsided and is affecting EU citizens as well. For instance, the Commission prepared legislation in the fall of 2003 so that the passports of EU citizens meet new US document security standards or else all EU citizens travelling to the USA will have to obtain visas at US embassies for $100.

The Commission was under pressure to act more speedily. For instance, the JHA Council of Ministers asked the Commission to examine the relationship between safeguarding internal security and complying with international human rights obligations and the Geneva convention on refugees. The Commission issued a working document on the topic that raised concern among civil liberties groups and refugee organizations, since it seemed to cast suspicion over all asylum-seekers as terrorists in disguise. The JHA Commissioner had to retract part of the contents. After 9/11, member states have asked the Commission more frequently to exercise its power of initiative and the understaffed new Commission Directorate General on Justice and Home Affairs has been operating under time pressures. The work overload has led to some hastily drafted and controversial proposals.

9/11 coincided with the rise of extremist or 'populist' parties that were making electoral breakthroughs on anti-immigration platforms in several member states. Between 2000 and 2002, in a third of the member states (Austria, the Netherlands, Denmark, Italy and Portugal), anti-immigration populist parties joined the ruling coalition. In May 2002, French presidential candidate Jean-Marie Le Pen of the extreme-right wing party National Front came in second with over 17 percent of the first-round votes. Xenophobic parties were also making headway in local and regional elections, most notably in Flanders in Belgium, and Hamburg in Germany. The Spanish Presidency in the first half of 2002 decided to make 'the fight against illegal migration' the focus of the European Council after its Prime Minister Aznar and Tony Blair issued a joint statement on the subject. As head of the right wing *Partido Popular*, Aznar had long advocated (and enacted) tough immigration laws. Blair's adoption of a similar line was newer, as he was confronted by a campaign in the widely read tabloid and regional press against the increasing numbers of asylum-seekers arriving in the South of England via the Eurotunnel under the Channel.

This involvement of national political leaders in making immigration a top EU priority deserves special emphasis, since this policy area had been previously left largely to bureaucrats. It reflects not only the indirect impact of populist parties on the policy agenda but also the state of national electoral competition where issues such as crime and immigration have gained salience over older right/left cleavages regarding the economy. In any case, both before and after Seville, there was a sense of urgency within the JHA Commission Directorate General under pressure from the Council of Ministers.

Since the Amsterdam Treaty came into force, the Commission has more resources to develop proposals. After Maastricht, there was only a taskforce with a dozen bureaucrats. The Justice and Home Affairs Directorate General, set up in 1999 with about 180 civil servants from other DGs, includes over 300 and recruited more 'A level' personnel in 2003. It has been moved to a new building where the Commissioner in charge and his Cabinet are also located. As Emek Uçarer (2002) notes, the Commission has thus been constitutionally but also institutionally empowered after Amsterdam. It is establishing its legitimacy in the field as a broker of compromise among member states, although understaffing and lack of in-house expertise endure.

Over time, member states have also made less use of their right of initiative and instead called upon the Commission to develop ideas that they have put forward. The effective division of labor is that member states control the agenda but delegate policy elaboration to the Commission. One example, mentioned earlier, regards the new visa identification system based on a post-9/11 German demand. The Commission staff first dismissed the suggestion as an exaggerated response to the terrorist attacks. Nevertheless, the German were so adamant to see it through that the Commission's 2002 *Green Paper on a Community Return Policy for Illegal Residents* states that the future visa database of scanned visa and passport pictures will play 'an essential role' in the expulsion of foreigners, as if it had been a Commission priority all along (CEC 2002*a*).

Besides accommodating the member states, Commission proposals also need to show the 'value added' of a common approach. To do so, it benefits from the experience of former staff members of the Internal Market DG. Its recent documents stress economies of scale and the mutual learning of 'best practices.' For example, the Green Paper on return stresses that multinational charter flights to return illegal residents to their country of origin should be encouraged because they are efficient and cost-saving. This is emblematic of the way the Commission argues for 'more Europe' in a number of areas. Ultimately, the Commission has had to bow to member state demands for increasing restrictions on immigration and asylum policies.

In sum, since 1999, domestic electoral developments and international events have brought immigration and asylum to the fore in the EU, along with all Justice and Home Affairs issues. This has meant a greater involvement of the European Council but also of the European Commission as a vehicle and mediator for major member state demands. We now turn to the actual content of the measures adopted from 1999 to 2004.

5. The Content of Policy: Deterring Migrants Before they Reach the EU

This section analyses the decisions taken during the so-called 'transition period' of European immigration and asylum policy to assess the main trends in this area. The key point here is that they reflect the institutional framework in this policy area, in particular the unanimity voting rule in the Council.

In October 1999, at the Tampere summit, EU institutions expressed their will to developing balanced common policies in the area of immigration and asylum. Although they remained committed to fighting illegal migration, they also recognized the need to give a 'fair treatment to third country nationals,' fight racial and ethnic discrimination, respect international obligations with respect to asylum and even consider labor market needs for foreign workers. By the Seville summit of June 2002, 'balance' was no longer an objective. Instead the summit focused solely on fighting illegal migration. By the Thessaloniki summit in June 2003, the British government proposed externalizing asylum requests in 'camps' outside the EU. If European summits are any indication of the orientation of EU policy (as they are meant to be), the examination of their recent agenda and conclusions suggests a clear reinforcement of the EU's anti-immigration and anti-asylum stance.

Decisions in this policy domain are ruled by unanimity in the Council with limited input from any other actor. This leads to a 'lowest common denominator' approach. Negotiations on the harmonization of national legislation that need to take into account the evolving and varied interests of member states are drawn out processes. Watered-down proposals result in vague and flexible texts in the end. One case in point is a directive proposal on family reunification in 1999 that languished on the bargaining table for years. The Commission amended its proposal twice and finally allowed it to be divided into several piecemeal reforms (CEC 2002*b*). A minimal agreement was reached by the Council of Ministers in February 2003 and the directive adopted the following year.

The directives that have been adopted quickly have been those that turn preexisting Schengen rules into EU legislation. Since most member states are Schengen states that had adapted their legislation to comply with the agreement, no additional national reforms are necessary, as is the case for the measures against unwanted immigration. The 2001 regulation on the list of countries whose nationals require a visa to enter the EU, for example, states that 'it follows on the Schengen acquis.' Schengen Article 26 has been replaced by the 2001 directive on sanctions against carriers that transport foreigners without proper documentation. Schengen Article 27 has been replaced by the 2002 directive on the facilitation of unauthorized entry, transit and residence. In other words, most of the binding EU legislation adopted since 1999 is simply updating Schengen.

Unanimity also effectively means the measures that involve coordination, informal cooperation, or technical instruments such as databases have developed much more quickly than have been adopted directives requiring national laws to be changed. One example of such informal cooperation is information exchange among consulates on 'bona fide' and 'migration risk' visa applicants. In November 2002, the Council urged the creation of a network of 'liaison officers' posted at consulates and airports to share operational information on immigrant flows and false documents. Technical instruments mainly include databases. The oldest one is the Schengen Information System (SIS), recently revamped as SIS II to accommodate the data increase from new member states. It includes information on persons and stolen goods that relate to the 'third pillar' of Justice and Home Affairs but also information provided by all participating countries on millions of 'inadmissible aliens' that should be denied entry into the EU. EURODAC is the database that stores the fingerprints of all asylum-seekers in the EU since 2003. When a person applies for asylum, the database is consulted to insure no previous demand has been lodged in another country. Should this be the case, the DUBLIN II Convention rules determine which state should process the asylum request. The official goal is to prevent 'asylum shopping.' A computerized database of visa applicants has been approved at the June 2003 Thessaloniki summit. Finally, the Commission has stated that, as of 2008, the EU global satellite navigation system GALILEO will be used to track people crossing the EU's external borders.

Yet, beyond these technical cooperation examples, the unanimous decision-making rules make the harmonization of legislation difficult to achieve and the use of legal instruments like directives less likely. The difficulty of reaching an agreement on the harmonization of rights for third country nationals and of asylum policy became so evident that alternative methods were suggested in Commission documents and Council minutes. In 2001, the Commission suggested that one should apply an approach used for social policy known as the 'open method of coordination' whereby member states seek to set common reform goals and targets rather than settle on binding EU norms to immigration and asylum (CEC 2001). An alternate solution known as 'enhanced cooperation' suggested that some member states could go further than others in certain areas. In the end, before the end of the five-year transition period after Amsterdam, the Council of Ministers came to an agreement on both directives (family reunification and asylum). Yet the final text makes clear that they consist in making it more difficult for foreign family members of EU residents and for asylum-seekers to reach the territory of the EU.

'Remote control,' making sure that foreigners never reach the EU territory where they may claim rights or receive legal aid for settlement, is now the most consistent and clear goal of EU immigration policy. This has been achieved through a number of policy instruments, such as visa policies that exclude *mala fide* candidates ('bad faith') or applicants in countries with low GDPs, and sanctions against transport companies that do not check the passports and visas of their customers flying to the EU. The next set of instruments consists in delegating control to third states. This includes countries where migrants may transit, effectively turning the new EU entrants and other neighbors into a buffer zone for the Western EU countries. Countries south of the Mediterranean have been threatened with trade sanctions if they do not apply EU norms and accept returned illegal aliens.

Enlargement, trade, and development policy are policy areas in which immigration has become a key issue. During accession negotiations, complying with Schengen standards was an issue of contention between EU and East and Central European countries. Ten percent of PHARE aid funds granted to the applicants were used to reinforce border controls. Immigration control has also been taken into account in EU treaty negotiations, EU programs and operations towards other regions. The interior ministers of the member states insisted that the Cotonou agreement of 2000 (the successor deal to the Lomé Convention between the EU and seventy-one African Caribbean and Pacific countries) include a standard clause whereby countries commit to taking back their nationals deported from an EU member state. In June 2003, the Commission announced €250 million in aid over the next five years for countries that signed readmission agreements. EU programs such as *Med-migrations* that encourage development projects involving North Africans on both sides of the Mediterranean are further strategies to stem migration flows from countries like Morocco.

The 2002 Spanish EU Presidency favored financial or trade sanctions against countries that do not readmit their nationals. The Justice and Home Affairs directorate is cooperating with the UN International Migration Policy Program to monitor the compliance of African countries with the Seville summit conclusions. West African countries are told to adopt a 'common migration regime' based on European norms to then formally cooperate with the EU. Bilateral and multilateral activity is also intense. Italy proposed legal quotas to nationals whose country cooperates in the fight against illegal migration. In October 2003 at La Baule, the interior ministers of the G-5 (The EU's five largest member states) stated that border police from Italy, France and Spain should collaborate with their counterparts in the Maghreb to stop illegal entries.

6. Conclusion

European cooperation in the field of immigration allowed national law and order officials to gain autonomy and devise policies without accommodating judges or conflicting sectoral interests. They successfully defined a policy frame that equated migration with transnational security threats and favored intergovernmental secretive forums. Over time, they were perhaps too successful and, after Amsterdam, they have been forced by other actors to cooperate with EU institutions and publish their decisions. Still, they remain key players. The dominant discourse that pervades both European Council conclusions and Commission documents still emphasize that illegal migration is a form of cross-border crime that must be fought. Thus, in the terms of the editors' introduction, the oft-quoted reason for a European common immigration policy has always been and remains the need to address 'external threats to the European status quo.'

Yet two other mechanisms highlighted in the introduction are also at work here. First, there are sure signs of institutional idiosyncrasies in this policy field. For reasons stated above, EU governments limited the role of most institutions other than the Council when they enacted the rules of the game in this area. Yet unanimity in the Council slowed down the legislative process and greatly impacted on the type of decisions that could be adopted, sometimes in unintended ways.

Second, 'jockeying for national advantage' has influenced the shaping of the immigration policy domain. The high volatility of the immigration issue in domestic politics and changes in the destination of migrants means that over time different member states have been at the forefront in this policy area at EU level. It should be underlined that the member state governments that are most keen to emphasize immigration as a threat requiring a common response are also those that want most to minimize delegations of national sovereignty. There are at least two reasons for this apparent paradox. First, governments want to be able to claim credit for themselves. Second, they generally face pressure to defend national sovereignty in this area either from within their own ranks (e.g. right and center-right parties) or from the larger party system (e.g. in the UK).

This explains why, although there is an incentive for EU-level cooperation, the form of cooperation includes various devices that allow governments to assert that they retain national control in this area. In the early 1990s, Germany wanted to 'share' its large flows of asylum-seekers through EU cooperation yet insisted on unanimity in the Council. In the early 2000s, the UK received the highest numbers of asylum-seekers yet they were adamant to remain able to freely choose when to cooperate with other EU countries (the selective 'opt-in' they have negotiated).

If the degree of supranationality in European immigration policy remains unclear, though, the major story of recent years is that this policy area has moved in major ways to the European level. Immigration is an issue that occupies an ever larger place in the activities of EU institutions. Moreover, immigration and asylum have become integrated into the EU's external policy and also gained prominence in accession negotiations with candidate countries (viewed, in this optic, as 'buffer states'). Transatlantic cooperation in the area of Justice and Home Affairs since 9/11 has also been intense. In January 2005, the US Department of Homeland Security nominated a permanent senior attaché in Brussels to liaise on issues that include border controls, suggesting a potential convergence of views that contrasts with many other areas of transatlantic tension.

Thus a core prerogative of the nation-state is now at the top of the agenda at European meetings with heads of states and governments. While this new EU domain remains largely intergovernmental, hampering the harmonization of national policies, there has nonetheless been an important shift in competence in a policy area that is deeply symbolic of national sovereignty.

References

Bowman, A. and Kearney, R. (2005). *State and Local Government*, 6th edn. New York: Houghton Mifflin.

CEC (Commission of the European Communities) (2000). *Communication of the Commission to the Council and European Parliament on a Community Immigration Policy*. Brussels, November 22, COM (2000) 757 final.

—— (2001). *Communication of the Commission to the Council and European Parliament on an Open Method of Coordination for the Community Immigration Policy*. Brussels, July 11, COM (2001) 387 final.

—— (2002*b*). *Communication of the Commission to the Council and European Parliament on an Open Method of Coordination for the Community Immigration Policy*. Brussels, July 11, 2001, COM (2001) 387 final.

—— (2002*a*). *Green Paper on a Community Return Policy for Illegal Residents*. Brussels, April 10, COM (2002) 175 final.

Council of the European Union (2001). 'Outcome of Proceedings of the Strategic Committee on Immigration, Frontiers and Asylum Meeting with the United States Dated 26 October 2001', Brussels, November 12, doc. 13803/01 ASIM 21 USA 24.

European Council (1999). *Presidency Conclusions*. Tampere European Council, October 15–16, 1999. Brussels: European Council.

Freeman, G. (2001). 'Client Politics or Populism? Immigration Reform in the United States', in V. Guiraudon and C. Joppke (eds.), *Controlling a New Migration World*. London: Routledge, pp. 65–95.

Guiraudon, V. (1997). *Policy Change behind Gilded Doors: Explaining the Evolution of Aliens' Rights in Contemporary Western Europe*. Ph.D. dissertation, Harvard University Department of Government.

—— (2000). 'European Integration and Migration Policy: Vertical Policy-making as Venue Shopping', *Journal of Common Market Studies*, 38/2: 249–69.

—— (2003). 'The Constitution of a European Immigration Policy Domain: A Political Sociology Approach', *Journal of European Public Policy*, 10/2: 263–82.

Huysmans, J. (2000). 'The European Union and the Securitization of Migration', *Journal of Common Market Studies*, 38/5: 751–77.

IOM (International Organization for Migration) (2000). *World Migration Report*. Geneva: IOM.

Joppke, C. (2001). 'The Legal-Domestic Sources of Immigrant Rights', *Comparative Political Studies*, 34/4: 339–66.

Lavenex, S. (2001). *The Europeanization of Refugee Policies: Between Human Rights and Internal Security*. Aldershot: Ashgate.

Lavenex, S. and Uçarer, E. (eds.) (2002). *Migration and the Externalities of European Integration*. Lanham, MD: Lexington Books.

Neuman, G. L. (1998). 'Nationality Law in the United States and Germany: Structure and Current Problems', in P. Schuck and R. Münz (eds.), *Paths to Inclusion: The Integration of Migrants in the United States and Germany*. Providence, RI: Berghahn Books.

OECD (Organization for Economic cooperation and Development) (2003). *Trends in International Migration (Annual Report 2002)*. Paris: OECD.

Schuck, P. (1998). *Citizens, Strangers and In-Betweens. Essays on Immigration and Citizenship*. Boulder, CO: Westview Press.

Tichenor, D. (2002). *Dividing Lines: The Politics of Immigration Control in America*. Princeton, NJ: Princeton University Press.

Uçarer, E. (2002). 'From the Sidelines to Center Stage: Sidekick No More? The European Commission in Justice and Home Affairs', *European Integration online Papers* 5/5.

Zolberg, A. (1997). 'The Great Wall against China: Responses to the first Immigration Crisis, 1885–1925', in J. Lucassen and L. Lucassen (eds.), *Migration, Migration History, History: Old Paradigms and New Perspectives*. New York: Peter Lang, pp. 291–316.

15

The Dynamics of EU Enlargement in American Perspective

JOHN A. SCHERPEREEL

Were we to ask an American schoolchild to give a history of the American flag, she would likely acquit herself quite well. She would tell us the story of Betsy Ross, the Philadelphia widow who, when approached by the country's founding fathers, stitched together the first Stars and Stripes. The flag, she would have us know, initially contained thirteen stars and currently contains fifty. As the union has taken in more states, the flag has taken on more stars.

Our schoolchild would have a hard time interpreting the flag that flies over today's European Union (EU). The blue field with gold stars was formally adopted by the European Community's heads of state and government in 1985. At that point, the flag had twelve stars, and the flag that flies today *still* has twelve stars. Surely, the schoolchild would assure us, there could *not* be more than twelve EU member states!

Of course, the flag is deceiving. On a literal level, today's flag is identical to the one that flew in 1985. The Union for which it stands, though, has taken in fifteen new members since 1985. A Community of ten has become a Union of twenty-five. A population of 280 million has, after the 2004 enlargement, grown to over 455 million. If the Union expands to include all four of the current candidate countries (Bulgaria and Romania are set to join in 2007; Croatian and Turkish membership may also be forthcoming), it will contain twenty-nine states and approximately 560 million citizens. The continuity of the flag notwithstanding, EU enlargement is clearly one of the most visible and consequential developments characterizing contemporary Europe.

This chapter seeks to illuminate the process of EU enlargement and to discuss the forces that drive various dimensions of the enlargement process. It is not, by any means, the first effort to elucidate these processes; literatures on the empirical mechanics and theoretical implications of enlargement are already well-developed. The chapter is novel, however, in two respects. First, it explicitly employs the theoretical framework introduced by the volume's editors. A process as broad and wide-ranging as enlargement is bound to involve multiple mechanisms of change and to stymie metatheoretical grand theorizing. I attempt, though, to identify mechanisms that matter most in the various dimensions of the enlargement process. Second, the chapter engages a preliminary comparison between EU enlargement and the territorial expansion of the United States. I attempt to lay out broad but informative comparisons and contrasts between 'expanding Europe' and 'expanding America.' I stress that incumbents and prospective members on both sides of the Atlantic have faced similarly fundamental questions: Who are 'we'? (When) should we apply for membership? (When) should we admit applicants? What are the normative, institutional, and policy implications of expansion? These fundamental questions have made US and EC/EU expansion similarly consequential developments, and US expansion can throw light on certain dimensions of the EU enlargement process.

The chapter proceeds in three broad sections. Section 1 defines enlargement, discusses the various dimensions of the EU enlargement process, and specifies the variables that play the strongest roles in each dimension. In Section 2, I investigate the extent to which EU enlargement parallels US expansion. There are multiple lenses from which to engage this comparison. In this section, I choose three: pathways to membership, decisions to expand, and power asymmetries. Section 3 offers concluding thoughts on theorizing enlargement and the possible payoffs of EU–US comparisons in doing so.

1. EU Enlargement: Process, Definition, and Mechanisms

The pathway to EU membership is not easily traveled. As Friis has suggested, there are at least seven distinct steps involved in the journey from nonmember to member (Friis 2003). A state aspiring to membership submits a formal application to the Council. If so disposed, the Council passes the application to the European Commission. The Commission drafts and forwards an opinion on the applicant's fitness for membership to the European Council, which decides whether to open formal accession negotiations. Negotiations are generally long and dizzyingly technical affairs. Both sides seek to protect key interests, and applicants seek concessions and provisional derogations. Once all negotiating 'chapters' of the *acquis communautaire* (the accumulated body of EU law, regulations, and decisions) have been closed and a draft accession treaty signed, that treaty is passed for approval to the Commission, the Parliament, and the Council. If each of these hurdles is cleared, a formal signing ceremony takes place, and the accession treaty is referred to incumbent member states and the applicant state for ratification. Ratification procedures vary from one state to the next. In some states, ratification requires parliamentary approval; elsewhere, it requires a referendum. If all states ratify the treaty, the applicant becomes a member on the date specified therein.

The time between application and membership usually exceeds five years. It is not surprising, therefore, that applicant states generally busy themselves adjusting and preparing for enlargement in the interim. This reality—that adaptation begins well before states' formal accession—has been stressed by authors in previous volumes of this series (Friis and Murphy 2000). It has also been captured in Schimmelfennig and Sedelmeier's definition of enlargement as 'a process of gradual and formal horizontal institutionalization of organizational rules and norms,' a process whereby formal and informal rules that govern the behavior of an organization's incumbents come steadily to govern the behavior of actors outside the organization, including (but not limited to) prospective members (Schimmelfennig and Sedelmeier 2002, their emphasis). Though pitched at an abstract level, this definition captures an essential reality: whereas fireworks may be launched, flags hoisted, and bottles uncorked on the day an applicant is welcomed as a full member, the process of enlargement starts well before and continues well beyond the drinking of the champagne. Enlargement, Schimmelfennig and Sedelmeier remind us, is a *process*, not an event.

All the same, a definition that sees enlargement as occurring 'when the group of actors whose actions and relations are governed by the organization's norms becomes larger' is insufficient in one respect (Schimmelfennig and Sedelmeier 2002: 503). Enlargement does not merely involve the extension of norms and institutions. It also involves the renegotiation of extant rules and the recalibration of institutional balances. The 2004 enlargement has certainly required the accession states to adopt and implement thousands of pages of the *acquis*. At the same time, it has required the EU to reconfigure voting weights in the Council, to address the size of the Commission, to reconsider the rules governing the Common Agricultural Policy and the structural funds, etc. Enlargement is, indeed, about institutional adaptation; but adaptation is a two-way street. Bearing this in mind, I propose a slightly amended, rather more 'dialectical' form of Schimmelfennig and Sedelmeier's otherwise-useful definition: enlargement is a process involving *both* the gradual and formal horizontal institutionalization of organizational rules and norms *and* the reconsideration of organizational rules and norms by actors across the enlarging polity.

Enlargement involves thousands of decisions and compromises, many of which 'kick back' to affect the strategies and/or identities of actors involved in later stages of the enlargement process. From an analytical standpoint, this means that there is something in enlargement for almost everyone. Scholars of international relations and foreign policy, for example, analyze the forces that compel prospective member states to apply for membership and to take certain bargaining positions vis-à-vis organizational incumbents. They also focus in on the 'receiving side' of the enlargement process, trying to explain why incumbents favor or combat enlargement and when to expect certain gestures toward applicants from various actors in the Union. They also speculate on the implications of enlargement for the foreign-policy identity of the Union and seek to understand how enlargement affects the Union's standing on the stage of world politics.

Scholars of comparative politics and governance are also attracted to the enlargement process, analyzing the implications of enlargement for the institutional structure, functioning, and identity of the Union and its constituent parts (i.e. EU institutions, member states, subnational actors, and interest groups). They also seek to explain the effects of enlargement on the norms and structures governing domestic politics in prospective member states, tracing the dynamics of Europeanization in locales where this process has traditionally received insufficient attention.

What is more, rationalist and constructivist hypotheses have both found some support in existing studies of enlargement (Schimmelfennig and Sedelmeier 2002). Enlargement involves intense intergovernmental bargains, side-payments, and actions by states to increase their economic well-being and geopolitical strength. Thus, state-centered rationalist theories, which spotlight the strategies of self-interested nation-states, find significant support. But enlargement also involves a strong and direct role for supranational institutions (particularly the Commission) and is frequently justified via reference to a 'common European destiny,' 'common European values,' and historical duties and rights. Thus, neofunctionalist and constructivist theories also receive some confirmation.

At this point, we come to a more circumscribed version of the question asked by this volume's editors in the introduction: is the process of enlargement too large and complex to make clear causal statements? Does it involve too many conflicting logics to yield hypotheses about the future dynamics and implications of enlargement? I suggest that these questions can be answered in the negative. Enlargement is a massive process indeed, and, as Jørgensen has suggested in a discussion of the Union's foreign and security policy, there is no 'master variable' that can explain all dimensions of the process (Jørgensen 2002: 212). I do propose, though, that discrete dimensions of the process can be analyzed and that certain mechanisms of change are disproportionately strong at different moments of the process. While this picture is less than fully parsimonious, it does facilitate hypothesizing. In the paragraphs that follow, I speculate on the relative importance of various mechanisms for the various dimensions of the enlargement process.

1.1. The Dimensions of Enlargement: A Disaggregated Approach

The EU is embedded in a broader international context that conditions opportunities for enlargement. The first steps toward postwar integration, for example, reflected western Europe's position in the global order. West Europeans sought to carve a niche for themselves between the United States and the Soviet Union. Strategic considerations and differing opinions on the objectives of integration meant that only six countries set out on the initial path. As the Cold War progressed, new alliances emerged, and the Community expanded to include the UK, Ireland, and Denmark (1973), Greece (1981), and Spain and Portugal (1986). Cold War divisions, however, made enlargement to certain European countries—including those in central and eastern Europe but also some EFTA independents (i.e. Austria, Finland)—unthinkable. It is not surprising, therefore, that both the EFTA applicants and the central and east European applicants frequently justified their arguments for enlargement by mentioning the new opportunities inherent in the post-Cold War order. A permissive global geopolitical order is, in short, a precondition of enlargement. The arguments, negotiations, imitations, criticisms, adaptations, and posturing that comprise the enlargement process require a geopolitical order that renders enlargement both thinkable and doable.

Geopolitical opportunity, however, is but the tip of the analytical iceberg. Geopolitics cannot fully explain, for example, the UK's initial decisions to hold off on the treaties of Paris (creating the European Coal and Steel Community in 1952) and Rome (creating the European Economic Community in 1958). Nor can it explain the exact timing of EFTA states' applications or the fact that certain post-Soviet republics applied for membership while others did not. The next question, then, might be why, given a favorable geopolitical opportunity structure, non-member states decide to pursue enlargement. Historically, the answer to this question has varied among countries. Some states have favored enlargement as a means of magnifying political strength. Others have viewed enlargement as an opportunity to consolidate democracy or boost economic performance. Still others have pursued enlargement in a quest for recognition of their belonging in Europe. In most applicant states some combination of these motivations has been present, and discernment of which reasons matter most requires close attention to particular cases.

The fact that 'enlargement' is such a broad phenomenon makes the task of explaining the decision to seek enlargement particularly difficult. A formal application to the Council is the most obvious indicator of a country's desire to seek enlargement. This is not the only indicator, however. The conception of enlargement as a process of horizontal institutionalization requires us to recognize that there are ways of pursuing enlargement short of full institutional membership. Intensification of trade with EU states, alignment of foreign policy positions with EU positions, voluntary transposition of the *acquis* into national legal orders—all of these steps reflect a choice for enlargement broadly conceived. Where, then, does this complexity leave the analyst? No systematic study has sought to explain variation in the timing and nature of nonmember states' enlargement demands. It would be a worthy exercise, for example, to try to understand under which conditions countries pursue various species of enlargement: When will they seek preferential trade agreements? When will they submit formal applications? When will they seek voluntarily to fold the *acquis* into national legal orders? And how do the answers to each of these questions impact the answers to the other questions? Though the systematic research is yet to be done, existing single-country accounts suggest that domestic institutional legacies, economic endowments, identities, and integration into other transnational/European networks all play important roles. The demand for enlargement, then, is an especially complex piece of the enlargement puzzle.

A third dimension of enlargement involves EU incumbents—including various institutions and actors within the member states—and their decisions on how and when to offer membership. The theoretical literature on this aspect of enlargement is relatively well developed (Sedelmeier 2000; Schimmelfennig 2001; Sjursen 2002; Moravcsik and Vachudova 2003). Analyses of pre-2004 enlargement rounds tend to explain the decision to offer membership by reference to the economic and geopolitical interests of incumbent member states. With regard to the 2004 enlargement, though, a rather broad agreement (if still not a consensus) has emerged that instrumental security and economic concerns are necessary but not sufficient conditions for the decision to offer membership.[1] States neighboring prospective applicants (most notably Germany, but also Italy, Austria, and Finland) had an obvious economic and security stake in the membership of their neighbors. At the same time, net recipients of EU cohesion and agricultural policies were less enthusiastic, fearing that an influx of relatively poor countries with large agricultural sectors would transfer EU funds away from them. Thus, as numerous authors have noted, the 'Nash optimal' decision for incumbent states to make would be to extend the rules of the internal market to the states in question (thus satisfying 'rich neighbors') without offering full membership and eligibility for regional and agricultural funds (thus satisfying southern and agricultural member states) (Grabbe and Hughes 1997; Sjursen 2002; Schimmelfennig and Sedelmeier 2002).

[1] The authors of the most cogent liberal-intergovernmentalist interpretation of the decision to enlarge, for example, accuse 'scholars who consider EU enlargement as a triumph of supranational entrepreneurship or of norms over interests' of overlooking the primary importance of nation-states' material self-interest. They concede, however, that 'there is no doubt that a measure of idealism played a supporting role in the decision to enlarge' (Moravcsik and Vachudova 2003: 50).

Initially, incumbent member states seemed to act according to this logic. In the early 1990s, politicians in most central and east European states voiced a desire to join the Communities. Responses from Community incumbents were not overwhelming. The Dublin European Council endorsed the idea of opening bilateral trade agreements with central and east European countries in April 1990. When the 'Europe Agreements' were actually negotiated, though, central and east European counterparts left bargaining tables with bitter tastes in their mouths. While reaching some compromises, they had encountered a stubborn partner determined to protect Community markets (particularly in agriculture), and the Community had failed to recognize membership as the ultimate goal of both negotiating sides.[2] As the 1990s progressed, however, central and east European leaders continued to make the case for full membership and were joined by pro-enlargement lobbies within EU institutions, who utilized their central positions to push for enlargement (Sedelmeier 2000). Jockeying for national advantage, while important in determining the eventual decision to expand membership, thus seems ultimately to have been an insufficient cause. Normative phenomena—involving conceptions of who Europeans are and whether it would be just to exclude from full membership European states with whom the Union shares history and values—also shaped the decision. Debate continues about the *ways* that norms and values mattered. Did norms fundamentally constitute the worldviews of actors involved in the decision to increase membership? (Sjursen 2002). Did strategic actors redeploy norms to shame recalcitrant member states into signing on? (Schimmelfennig 2001). Were norms little more than gloss for more fundamental interstate bargains? (Moravcsik and Vachudova 2003). In general, though, the 2004 enlargement suggests that both strategic and normative factors affect the decision to extend EU membership. Compelling economic and geopolitical interests alone cannot explain the decision to expand.

Once EU incumbents have decided to offer membership, accession negotiations commence. The literature has generally interpreted accession negotiations as episodes of hard intergovernmental strategizing and bargaining, and there are no strong reasons to contest this interpretation. As Friis has noted, accession negotiations have a 'dual character' (Friis 2003: 183). On the incumbent side, member states bargain with each other over the positions that the Union, as represented by the Council presidency, should take toward applicants. These 'intra-incumbent' bargains affect dimensions of EU politics that are not directly connected to enlargement. A member

[2] The most comprehensive consideration of the Europe Agreements, and a study that takes the EC's protection of certain strategic markets as a theoretical puzzle, is Papadimitriou 2002.

state that disapproves of an emerging bargaining mandate, for example, might offer to support that mandate in exchange for concessions in some unrelated point of EU business. Once a bargaining mandate has been agreed by incumbents, the Council presidency takes the EU position to the individual applicants, and the second, EU-applicant, stage of bargaining commences. These negotiations are formally bilateral affairs, but the Union has taken advantage of the fact that every enlargement save one (Greece in 1981) has involved more than one applicant. EU negotiators can use the fact that certain chapters have been closed with some applicants to pressure other applicants into accepting bargains to which they are otherwise unlikely to acquiesce.

The dual bargaining process is, therefore, rife with logrolling and quid pro quo, and negotiation results reflect the compromises of strategic state actors. Of course the bargaining position defended by any applicant state is *itself* the product of previous bargains (a) among various state actors and/or interest groups, and, occasionally, (b) among the states negotiating with the Union at a given historical moment (in the case of the most recent negotiations, for example, between Poland and Hungary). A state's position in a given *acquis* chapter will reflect the relative domestic bargaining power of state and societal actors, which *itself* is likely to depend on domestic institutional legacies and economic and demographic structures. The position that a given state takes in negotiations on internal-market matters, for example, will reflect its economic policy style and policymaking structures; we would expect a country with strong corporatist institutions to make different demands than a country with a more pluralistic policy system. Similarly, the demographic and economic profile of an applicant will affect its specific expectations and demands. Agricultural negotiations between the EU side and heavily agricultural Poland, for example, were more heated than those between the EU side and Slovenia, whose agricultural sector is comparatively small.

There is, therefore, no doubt that intergovernmental bargaining, strategic state decisions, and national jockeying play dominant roles at the negotiation stage. The analyst must not overlook, though, that initial bargaining positions have complex histories *and* that the European Commission is also involved in the negotiations process. The Commission drafts initial negotiation mandates, the Enlargement Directorate General possesses significant information-gathering capacities, and the Commission has a daily presence (via its delegations) in applicant-state capitals. The Commission has a direct role in shaping agendas of intra-incumbent negotiations, and it may also indirectly shape applicants' bargaining positions. Its criticisms—publicly aired during the most recent enlargement round in annual *Regular Reports* and informally communicated to national decision-makers on a daily basis—may affect national negotiators' sense of what is reasonable to expect out of the negotiations. In sum, internal demographic and economic factors, domestic institutional legacies, and Commission input all affect bargaining positions during accession negotiations. Once bargaining positions have been constructed, however, national jockeying for advantage is the most salient dynamic. If decisions to pursue enlargement and offer membership are driven by both rational and normative variables, the accession negotiations depend most significantly on intergovernmental bargaining. Theories that focus on two-level dynamics and intergovernmental bargaining (Putnam 1988) are likely to generate the most insight into this dimension of the enlargement process.

In the most recent round of expansion, once accession negotiations had begun, media outlets in accession states focused almost exclusively on events in Brussels. Journalists made much of the great race among candidates. They compared 'their team' with other states to ascertain who had opened and closed the most *acquis* chapters. Their emphasis on the negotiation process was useful, but only to a point. It misleadingly implied (a) that the only real tasks candidates faced was to open and close *acquis* chapters, (b) that the deals reached around negotiating tables would be easy to implement once reached, and (c) that EU actors were concerned exclusively with the formal *acquis*.

In fact, in an important component of the enlargement process, the Commission strongly encouraged candidates to build the administrative capacity to apply the *acquis*. The EU devoted significant sums to institution building in central and eastern Europe. They sought to assure that the deals reached would be put into effect and that new member states would be reliable partners after accession. EU actors were *also* keenly interested in certain non-*acquis* areas, including civil service reform and the establishment of structures of subnational governance; they used a kind of informal, soft conditionality to nudge candidates towards completing reforms and building institutions in areas that lacked a formal *acquis* (Jacoby and Černoch 2002; Scherpereel 2003; Grabbe 2003*a*).

This dimension of the enlargement process is theoretically important for at least two reasons. First, the EU actors most heavily involved in the daily politics of institution-building were not member states but the Commission and private contractors. Second, while the EU's goals were effectively the same for each candidate country—in all cases, EU actors wanted capable and effective state structures—institutional outcomes in candidate countries were mediated by domestic institutional legacies. For example, the Commission's general desire for candidates to have stable systems of territorial relations and regional structures capable of managing structural assistance was transformed, through domestic politics, into quite different systems of territorial relations in Poland, the Czech Republic, and Slovakia (Brusis 2002;

Hughes *et al.* 2001; Marcou 2002; Scherpereel 2003). Explanation of enlargement-related institutional adaptation requires sensitivity to the ways that domestic institutional legacies mediate EU pressure. Emerging studies on Europeanization in central and eastern Europe take up this challenge (Grabbe 2003*b*; Schimmelfennig and Sedelmeier, forthcoming).

The general impression that emerges from this disaggregation of the enlargement process is that state strategies, considerations of economic advantage, and geopolitical considerations matter throughout the process of enlargement. Left to themselves, though, these variables cannot fully explain important dimensions of the process. In the 'early' stages of enlargement, normative considerations about what the EU is and what membership means are also causally significant. In the 'later' stages of enlargement, change is driven not only by state strategies but by an interaction of such strategies with institutional legacies and demographic and economic structures. After accession treaties have been signed, interestingly, citizens across the expanding polity must deliberate on whether to ratify the treaties. This process requires them to revisit many of the same questions with which they began: What does EU membership mean? What rights and obligations does it imply for 'us'? Is enlargement worth it? Enlargement, in short, involves multiple mechanisms of change, but certain mechanisms matter more at different moments of the enlargement process.

2. EU Enlargement in American Perspective

While analysts have made informative comparisons between the enlargement of the EU and the enlargement of other international organizations (i.e. NATO, OSCE, Council of Europe),[3] there have been few efforts to compare 'expanding Europe' with 'expanding America'. In many ways, this analytical gap is understandable. With the exception of Texas, all states that have acceded to the United States have been US territories or territories of particular American states (i.e. Vermont as part of Massachusetts; Kentucky and West Virginia as part of Virginia). This clearly contrasts with the EC/EU, where acceding units have histories as sovereign nation-states. The United States of America, moreover, is a constitutional state, while the EU is a treaty-based, hybridized intergovernmental/supranational organization. The expansion of the US was largely, if not exclusively, a nineteenth-century phenomenon; many states welcomed into the American union have had

[3] See, for example, Stuart Croft *et al.*, *The Enlargement of Europe* (Manchester: Manchester University Press, 1999).

miniscule citizenries, no experience of modern constitutional self-government, and recent histories of quasi-colonial dependence on the US federal center. The expansion of the EC/EU, on the other hand, has been a twentieth- and twenty-first-century phenomenon, involving the incorporation of modern, complex nation-states into an institutional system whose goals, dynamics, and requirements differ markedly from those of the American federation. What is more, US expansion has been driven largely by the concerns of partisan politics and the similarity of party systems in the federal republic and the acceding states. Partisan considerations have played a comparatively weak role in the politics of EC/EU enlargement. For these and other reasons, one might see EU enlargement and US expansion as analytical apples and oranges.

Without discounting these differences, this section nonetheless presents a preliminary comparison of EU enlargement and US expansion that draws on the analysis in the previous section. I do not hope so much to hypothesize about the former via reference to the latter but to show EU specialists that there is insight to be gained from the American experience while convincing US specialists that their subject's history is not as unique as it may at first appear. In fact, many informative comparisons and contrasts can be drawn between EU and US enlargements. While I engage three such comparisons here, other fruitful comparisons could be made as well.

2.1. Pathways to Membership: EU vs. US

As noted above, one major contrast between US and EU expansions concerns the 'pre-union' status of eventually-acceding states. Most states that acceded to the USA after 1789 had previously been American territories—US-owned lands lying outside the boundaries of incumbent states. A longstanding legal and philosophical tradition with roots to Thomas Jefferson has interpreted these US territories as 'states in embryo'. On the Jeffersonian view, the American territorial system was 'a scheme of colonization that would *temporarily* operate in a given area *only until* it had reached a minimum population and after its inhabitants had experienced a brief tutelage in self-government' (Grupo de Investigadores Puertorriqueños 1986: 1111). The Jeffersonian view was legally enshrined in both the Northwest Ordinance of 1787 and subsequent legislation under the American Constitution. It implied a standard of admission that, in European perspective, seems quite lenient. The conditions for admission that inhered in the Jeffersonian view—(a) that a majority of voters living in the prospective state must support statehood, (b) that the state must be committed to republican self-government, and (c) that the prospective state must have at least 60,000 free citizens and be able to support a state government—were relatively lax to begin with and contrast significantly with the EU's Copenhagen conditionality.[4] What is more, the United States has occasionally relaxed the criteria even further, allowing sparsely populated territories (i.e. Ohio, Illinois, Florida, Oregon, Nebraska, and Nevada) into the union. The 'low admission bar' differs considerably from the European case, where accession criteria have been stricter and less malleable.

Still, in light of the widely held idea that territories were destined to become states, it is worth noting that different territories applied at different times and in different ways to be admitted into the American federation. The territories of Tennessee and Wisconsin, for example, were both ceded to the US via treaties with the UK in 1782–83. Tennessee began to push for statehood in the late 1780s. After receiving a chilly response from Congress, Tennessee's statehood movement proceeded largely on its own. It convened a process of drafting a state constitution, held elections for state offices *and* both houses of the US Congress, and sent its 'congressional delegation' to Washington to lobby incumbent members for admission.[5] Wisconsin, on the other hand, did not actively petition Congress for admission until almost forty years after Tennessee. When it did so, it took different strategic and legal paths to membership. Instead of reacting to a state delegation that had drafted a constitution from below, the US Congress passed an Enabling Act that established procedures for drafting and ratifying Wisconsin's state constitution.[6]

These are just two of at least six paths taken toward eventual accession into the American federation.[7] I discuss them for two reasons. First, they suggest

[4] The 'Copenhagen criteria' were promulgated in June 1993, when the heads of state and government (the European Council) recognized eastward enlargement as a mutual goal of central and east European countries and the Union. The Council set three conditions that prospective members would have to meet: (1) stable institutions guaranteeing democracy, the rule of law, human rights, and minority protections, (2) existence of a market economy and the ability to cope with competitive pressures within the Union, and (3) ability to take on the obligations of membership, including adherence to the aims of political, economic, and monetary union. While these conditions remained open to interpretation, they have guided the Union's evaluations of and approach to enlargement since 1993. See the full text of the Copenhagen meeting conclusions at <*http://www.europarl.eu.int/summits/copenhagen/co_en.pdf*>.

[5] Tennessee's pathway to membership became known thereafter (appropriately enough) as 'the Tennessee Plan.' It was subsequently mimicked by other prospective American states, including Michigan, Iowa, California, Oregon, Kansas, and Alaska.

[6] This was the 'enabling way' to membership, used first in Ohio and later in Louisiana, Indiana, Mississippi, Illinois, Alabama, Missouri, Wisconsin, Minnesota, Nevada, Nebraska, Colorado, South Dakota, North Dakota, Montana, Washington, Utah, Oklahoma, Arizona, and New Mexico.

[7] Others, as discussed by the Grupo de Investigadores Puertorriqueños (pp. 1207–29), include the pathway of the original thirteen states (from confederation to federal union), the pathway taken by Texas (joint resolution of annexation between the US federal authority and an independent republic), a pathway involving states carved out from

that the process of US expansion has been much more fluid and less institutionalized than the process of EU enlargement. There has been no single institutional staircase toward accession. In some territories, advocates of statehood have effectively taken the initiative; elsewhere, statehood advocates have been 'enabled' by 'top-down' legislation from the federal center. The flexibility of admission processes and the occasionally active role of central authorities in preparing states for accession distinguish the USA from the European case, where the formal steps involved in accession are tightly institutionalized and the initiative for enlargement comes uniformly 'from below.'

Second, and perhaps more intriguingly, the fact that similarly situated territories in the United States began to campaign for incorporation at different historical moments suggests that the variables presented in the earlier discussion of the decision to pursue EU enlargement may have been operative in the American case as well. Historical investigations of particular statehood campaigns bear this suggestion out: decisions about whether and when to apply for admission to the United States resulted from a combination of political opportunity, geopolitical considerations (i.e. will the accession of our state satisfy the federal desire to counteract British influence in the territories?), economic endowments (i.e. will our state generate sufficient revenue to fund a state edifice?), and identity (i.e. will our state's identity survive incorporation into the Union?). Thus if the US admission process has been institutionally more flexible than the counterpart European process, the variables pushing prospective states toward full union membership have been roughly analogous across the cases.

2.2. The Decision to Expand: EU vs. US

Have similar forces affecting incumbents' decisions to admit new members been at play on both sides of the Atlantic? An answer to this question requires a brief review of American constitutional rules. Article IV, section 3 of the US Constitution gives Congress the power to admit new states. It also limits this power by stipulating that 'no new State shall be formed or erected within the Jurisdiction of any other State; nor any State be formed by the Junction of two or more States, or Parts of States, without the Consent of the Legislatures of the States concerned as well as of the Congress.' Section 4 of Article III places a condition upon prospective states, requiring them to have a 'republican form of government.' These provisions have a number of

other states (Vermont, Maine, Kentucky, West Virginia), and a pathway involving the drafting of a state constitution in the absence of US Congressional enabling legislation and the absence of a pre-statehood US Congressional delegation (Arkansas, Florida, Wyoming, Idaho, Hawaii).

implications. First, because the US Congress possesses the ultimate authority to admit new members, debates about whether a state should be granted admission have been centered in Congress. Second, the process of admitting new states has been formally identical to the process of passing 'normal' (nonconstitutional) American legislation. Enactments admitting states must be signed by the president and can be vetoed by the president. At the same time, a presidential veto can be overridden by a two-thirds supermajority vote in both chambers of Congress. And third, Congress must determine whether an applicant has a 'republican form of government;' in practice, this determination has involved congressional and/or presidential scrutiny of draft state constitutions.

American expansion thus clearly involves fewer institutional veto players than EU expansion. EU accession treaties must survive the scrutiny of the Commission, the Council, the Parliament, and the legislatures of incumbent member states, while admission of a new American State requires 'only' the assent of congressional majorities and the head of state. And note again the contrast between accession conditionality in the American and European cases. Compared to the accession criteria promulgated at the Copenhagen European Council in 1993—stable institutions guaranteeing democracy, the rule of law, human rights, and minority protections; existence of a functioning market economy capable of coping with competitive pressures and market forces within the Union; and ability to take on the obligations of membership and implement the *acquis*—the American stricture that each state possess a 'republican form of government' seems quite tame indeed.

One might suppose, given these contrasts, that the politics of US expansion were smoother, less contentious, and quicker than the politics of EC/EU enlargement. In fact this is not the case. For many central and east European states, for example, the pathway to membership seemed dreadfully long. Most of these states pressed for enlargement in the early 1990s but were not admitted to the club until 2004. Romania and Bulgaria, for their part, will not gain membership until 2007. And poor Turkey! Even the most optimistic prognosticators foresee full Turkish membership in 2015, suggesting an interim between formal application (1987) and full membership of at least twenty-eight years. In American perspective, though, the lag between 'initial accession drive' and welcome into full membership is not unusual. There is significant variation across the thirty-seven states that have joined the USA. Wyoming's 'statehood battle', for example, lasted only two years; Alaska's fourteen, Arizona's forty, and New Mexico's sixty-two![8] It is an

[8] Figures on the length of American 'statehood battles' are taken from the Grupo de Investigadores Puertorriqueños (1986), Table X, 1262–80. See pp. 1252–54 of that volume for a methodological discussion of how to measure the length of an US territory's battle for statehood.

interesting exercise, then, to compare the data in Tables 15.1 and 15.2. Because the American statehood process has been less institutionalized than the EU accession process, the data on the length of each state's 'statehood battle' in Table 15.2 are less precise than those in the right-hand column of Table 15.1. Nonetheless, the rather impressionistic comparison produces an interesting result: the length of the average 'statehood battle' in the USA has been almost four and a half years *longer* than the average lag between formal application and formal membership in the EC-EU.

These data imply that US expansion, despite the formal 'ease' of the process, has, like EC–EU enlargement, occasioned significant debate, deliberation, strategizing, and negotiation. Students of American political development have shown this to be true. US expansion through 1850, they have argued, had a lot to do with the 'peculiar institution' of slavery. Consider events surrounding the 'Missouri Compromise.' Missouri applied for statehood as a slave state in 1817. The state's admission would have tipped the

TABLE 15.1. *Length of interim between formal application and formal accession, European Union*

Country	Applied	Acceded	Months between application and accession	Years between application and accession
UK	August 1961	January 1973	137	11.42
Denmark	August 1961	January 1973	137	11.42
Ireland	July 1961	January 1973	137	11.42
Norway	July 1967	—	—	—
Greece	June 1975	January 1981	67	5.58
Spain	July 1977	January 1986	102	8.50
Portugal	March 1977	January 1986	106	8.83
Austria	July 1989	January 1995	66	5.50
Sweden	July 1991	January 1995	42	3.50
Finland	March 1992	January 1995	34	2.83
Norway	November 1992	—	—	—
Cyprus	July 1990	May 2004	166	13.83
Malta	July 1990	May 2004	166	13.83
Hungary	March 1994	May 2004	122	10.17
Poland	April 1994	May 2004	121	10.08
Slovakia	June 1995	May 2004	107	8.92
Latvia	October 1995	May 2004	103	8.58
Estonia	November 1995	May 2004	102	8.50
Lithuania	December 1995	May 2004	101	8.42
Czech Republic	January 1996	May 2004	100	8.33
Slovenia	June 1996	May 2004	95	7.92
Average			105.84	8.82

TABLE 15.2. *Time between beginning of 'statehood struggle' and formal accession, USA*

State	Acceded	Length of 'statehood battle' (years)
Vermont	March 1791	9
Kentucky	June 1792	8
Tennessee	June 1796	9
Ohio	March 1803	4
Louisiana	April 1812	8
Indiana	December 1816	5
Mississippi	December 1817	7
Illinois	December 1818	0.91
Alabama	December 1819	1.08
Maine	March 1820	35
Missouri	August 1821	4
Arkansas	June 1836	5
Michigan	January 1837	6
Florida	March 1845	23
Texas	February 1846	9
Iowa	December 1846	8
Wisconsin	May 1848	9
California	September 1850	1
Minnesota	May 1858	4
Oregon	February 1859	9
Kansas	January 1861	6
West Virginia	June 1863	2
Nevada	October 1864	2
Nebraska	March 1867	9
Colorado	August 1876	14
North Dakota	November 1889	18
South Dakota	November 1889	18
Montana	November 1889	23
Washington	November 1889	22
Idaho	July 1890	8
Wyoming	July 1890	2
Utah	January 1896	46
Oklahoma	November 1907	17
New Mexico	January 1912	62
Arizona	February 1912	40
Alaska	January 1959	14
Hawaii	August 1959	19
Average		13.16

Source: Grupo de Investigadores Puertorriqueños (1986), pp. 1262–80.

balance of slave and free states in the Senate to twelve versus eleven. To maintain a free state/slave state balance, a compromise was reached in which Maine, which applied in 1819 as a free state, would be admitted at the same time as Missouri, where slavery would be allowed. As additional compensation for the admission of Missouri, northern states received an agreement that slavery would be abolished north of 36°30′ latitude in the remainder of the territory gained via the Louisiana Purchase. After the American Civil War, statehood politics were driven by the Republican Party's desire to shore up support for policies initiated during the war years and the Reconstruction period (Stewart and Weingast 1992; McCarty *et al.* 2002). The Republican-controlled Congress admitted solidly Republican states (i.e. Kansas, West Virginia) while excluding Democratic-leaning states (i.e. Utah), since doing so would allow them to offset Democratic strength in the south and maintain an ambitious federal political agenda.

Thus at different political moments, slavery and partisan politics have figured prominently in Congressional decisions about whether to expand. Never, however, have these issues been the *only* relevant considerations. Debates about admission have also involved the considerations we see playing out in the European milieu—economic matters, strategic concerns, and normative conceptions of 'who belongs' and 'to whom we are obliged.' In Congressional discussions about whether to admit Michigan (1837) and Florida (1845), for example, national opponents argued that these states were too poor to be admitted to the union; their admission would cause incumbent states increased financial hardship and prevent the acceding states from becoming productive members of the union. One heard similar arguments, of course, in the debates preceding the EC-EU's 1981, 1986, and 2004 enlargements and hears such arguments today with regard to Bulgaria, Romania, Croatia, and (especially) Turkey. Admission debates in the USA have also not wanted for considerations of geopolitical strategy. Opponents of Texan admission (gained in 1846), for example, suggested that the republic's admission would exacerbate disputes with Mexico. They were opposed, not surprisingly, by advocates who saw statehood as a means of keeping Mexico at bay and giving the United States an opportunity to expand further to the south. Geostrategic arguments also figured prominently in discussions of West Virginia (1863, where statehood was seen as a bulwark against the Confederacy), California (1850, where statehood was defended for its provision of access to the Pacific), Alaska (1959, which provided a window to the Soviet far east), and Hawaii (1959, which would grant the United States a stronger foothold in the Pacific).[9]

[9] For case studies of the contours of congressional debate for each acceding American state, see Grupo de Investigadores Puertorriqueños (1986), v.1 and the summary tables in Grupo de Investigadores Puertorriqueños (1986), v.2, pp. 1262–80.

Normative arguments have also played major roles in the politics of US expansion. Volumes have been written on the causes and consequences of 'Manifest Destiny'—the notion that the United States possessed a divine vocation to control the expanse of continental territory stretching from the Atlantic to the Pacific (Heidler and Heidler 2003; May 2004; Stephanson 1995). And while there is no logically necessary connection between Manifest Destiny and statehood—one might believe that the US was destined to control continental territory without believing that US-controlled territories were destined to govern themselves as sovereign, incorporated states—the two notions have, nonetheless, been rhetorically conjoined in the arguments of many statehood advocates.

Opponents of American expansion, for their part, have often deployed competing normative claims to justify the exclusion of particular states. In debates over whether Louisiana should be admitted, for example, opponents questioned whether that state's French and Creole cultures were compatible with American identity. Similar arguments—sometimes explicit, often implicit—were deployed in admission debates surrounding Idaho and Utah (is Mormonism compatible with American identity?), Oklahoma (similar questions with regard to Native Americans), New Mexico, and Arizona (regarding individuals of Mexican and Native American descent), and Alaska and Hawaii (individuals of Inuit and Pacific descent). These debates have obvious parallels with current debates in Europe, where questions about the 'cultural preconditions' of membership grab headlines in the newspapers of EU member states and Turkey alike. Nor have these questions been definitively answered in the American case; they continue to be asked in the debates surrounding possible statehood for Puerto Rico.[10]

None of this is to deny that American expansion has been bound up in the unique politics of slavery and Republican entrenchment. It is to suggest, though, that attention to the broader context of American debates facilitates an appreciation for similarities between accession politics in the US and the EC–EU. In both cases, economic and strategic considerations have factored into debates preceding enlargement and have affected the timing of expansion. And one of the most striking points of overlap between American and European experiences of expansion is the increasing salience of 'the normative dimension' and cultural questions over time. As both unions have expanded further beyond their original cores, debates about the 'cultural consistency' between the Union and applicants (i.e. Puerto Rico in the American case, Turkey in the European case) have become exceptionally intense and widespread.

[10] Opponents of US policy toward overseas territories are particularly critical of the so-called 'insular cases' of the early twentieth century, in which the Supreme Court established a legal distinction between 'incorporated' territories (which possessed a right to statehood) and 'non-incorporated' territories (which possessed no such right).

2.3. *The Asymmetries of Accession: EU vs. US*

Observers of EU enlargement have frequently remarked on the existence of power asymmetries between the EU side and the candidate side. This has been particularly clear in the most recent enlargement, where incumbents delayed endorsing expanded membership, required candidates to transpose and implement the *acquis*, and insisted on the construction of new political and administrative institutions. Have similar asymmetries characterized the incumbent-candidate relationship in the United States? In a word, yes. Congress has repeatedly taken advantage of its power to admit by placing states' applications 'on hold.' It has also included restrictive conditions in legislation admitting new states. These conditions have generally been uncontroversial, falling well within the rules of American federalism. In certain acts of admission, for example, Congress has prohibited acceding states from charging tolls, taxes, and fees on navigable waters within state borders, a prohibition that lies within the federal authority's power to regulate interstate commerce. In a number of cases, though, Congress has pushed existing constitutional boundaries to their limits by, for example, requiring a state to locate its capital in a particular city for a particular period of time or requiring English-language competence for applicants to state-level office. There is ample historical precedent, in other words, for the more powerful partner's attempts to 'go beyond the existing rules'—whether the rules of the *acquis* or the rules of US federalism—in accession politics.

Another demonstration of federal-applicant asymmetry in the United States has involved federal authorities' occasional rejection of states' draft constitutions on the grounds that they fail to satisfy accession's political condition (the existence of a 'republican form of government'). In 1911, for example, President William Howard Taft vetoed a joint congressional resolution admitting Arizona to the Union.[11] Taft objected to provisions of Arizona's constitution that gave voters the right to recall judges and declared these provisions incompatible with republican governance. In response to Taft's veto, Congress passed a new resolution requiring Arizona to amend its constitution to protect judges from recall. Arizona's officials prepared such an amendment and submitted it to the state's voters, who dutifully ratified it. Only after Arizona had responded to President Taft's 'command' did Taft (in 1912) sign a proclamation admitting Arizona.

[11] Taft was not the first President to exercise a statehood veto. In 1866, Andrew Johnson vetoed a bill admitting Nebraska to the federation and two acts that would have enabled Colorado to draft a state constitution. The Nebraska veto was quickly overridden by congressional supermajorities, while the consummation of Colorado's statehood push would not occur until 1876.

All of these phenomena—congressional delay tactics, admission-act conditionality, and compelled constitutional redrafting—indicate the asymmetrical nature of the US expansion process. Prospective American states, like EU applicants, are often subject to the whims and fancies of incumbents. It may be equally important to note, though, that new American states have often sought to correct for the 'injustices' of the admission process once they have entered the 'sisterhood of states.' Soon after entering the union, for example, Oklahoma moved its state capital from Guthrie to Oklahoma City, in blatant disregard of its admission conditions. Though the federal government contested its right to do so, the Supreme Court (in Coyle *v.* Oklahoma) sided with Oklahoma. Similarly, in a *new* referendum held shortly after its accession to the union, Arizona's voters 're-amended' the state constitution to allow for the popular recall of judges. The American case suggests that the asymmetries inherent in the accession process are transitory indeed. New member states are no less likely than old member states to pursue their interests within the union. EU actors should not expect new members to be facile or malleable once joining. Acquiescence, the American case suggests, is not so much a habit as an albatross that new members are eager to jettison once 'in.'

3. Conclusions

EU enlargement is a complex and multidimensional process. Many of the critical forces affecting the trajectory of Europe writ large—geopolitical developments, national jockeying, institutional and economic legacies, considerations of who belongs and to whom we are obliged—affect the more limited process of EU enlargement. They do not affect all dimensions of the process equally, though. Normative considerations, for example, have figured prominently in potential applicants' decisions about whether and how to pursue enlargement and in incumbents' decisions about how to approach nonmembers. They have played very minor roles, however, in accession negotiations. Thus, while the question of 'what drives enlargement?' yields an untidy mishmash of variables, the analyst can do more than simply throw up her hands. She can focus on particular dimensions of the process: Which forces compel states to apply for EU membership? Why do incumbents welcome or rebuff certain applications? Why are certain bargains struck in accession negotiations? Why do citizens vote in certain ways in accession referenda? These 'smaller' but illuminating questions are analytically manageable and likely to produce more parsimonious explanations and more testable hypotheses.

EU enlargement has clearly not 'stopped' with the accession of ten new member states. New member states are still adapting to life within the Union.

They are not merely learning the 'ins and outs' of Brussels and becoming experts in 'Euro-speak.' They are developing institutions to maximize their efficacy in the EU's decision-making structures and building structures to draw from EU funds and shore up their ability to implement the *acquis*. Diverse actors from the EU-15, for their part, are still coming to terms with the new opportunities and constraints that inhere in the enlargement process. Adjustment to life within the EU-25 will take years. And it will be complicated by the Union's continued expansion to Romania, Bulgaria, Croatia, and, possibly, Turkey.

Can attention to the experience of the United States yield any insight into how these processes will unfold and whether the Union will continue to expand? This chapter has engaged the second part of that question more than the first. Despite all of the differences between the US and Europe—historical, institutional, ontological—I have proposed that there is some analytical value to be added by engaging the EU-US comparison. One might expect US expansion to have been smoother, less 'political,' and somehow more 'automatic' than EU enlargement. In fact, this has not been the case. Americans have encountered many of the same aspirations, debates, frustrations, and adjustments as Europeans. The questions faced by actors on the European side of the Atlantic—When should we apply? When should we offer membership? What conditions should we place on new member states? How will the changing boundaries of our community affect our strategies, institutions, policies, and identities?—have often been faced in the USA. The American case may be more helpful in understanding some dimensions of EU enlargement than others, and there may be good reason to leave US comparisons out of certain enlargement-related studies. All the same, it would be unwise to neglect American comparisons due only to disciplinary conventions or facile assumptions about American—or European—exceptionalism.

References

Brusis, M. (2002). 'Between EU Requirements, Competitive Politics, and National Traditions: Re-creating Regions in the Accession Countries of Central and Eastern Europe', *Governance*, 15/4: 531–59.

Croft, S. *et al.* (1999). *The Enlargement of Europe*. Manchester: Manchester University Press.

Friis, L. (2003). 'EU Enlargement .... And Then There Were 28?', in E. Bomberg and A. Stubb (eds.), *The European Union: How Does it Work*? Oxford: Oxford University Press, pp. 177–94.

—— and Murphy, A. (2000). 'The Enlargement: A Complex Juggling Act', in M. G. Cowles and M. Smith (eds.), *The State of the European Union: Risks, Reform, Resistance, and Revival*. Oxford: Oxford University Press, pp. 186–204.

Grabbe, H. (2003*a*).'The Implications of EU Enlargement', in S. White, J. Batt, and P. G. Lewis (eds.), *Developments in Central and East European Politics*, Vol 3. Durham, NC: Duke University Press, pp. 253–66.

—— (2003*b*). 'Europeanization Goes East: Power and Uncertainty in the EU Accession Process', in K. Featherstone and C. M. Radaelli (eds.), *The Politics of Europeanization*. Oxford: Oxford University Press.

—— and Hughes, K. (1997). 'Redefining the European Union: Eastward Enlargement', Royal Institute of International Affairs Briefing Paper No. 36.

Grupo de Investigadores Puertorriqueños (1986). *Breakthrough from Colonialism: An Interdisciplinary Study of Statehood.* Rio Piedras: Editorial de la Universidad de Puerto Rico.

Heidler, D. S. and Heidler, J. T. (2003). *Manifest Destiny*. Westport, CT: Greenwood Press.

Hughes, J., Sasse, G., and Gordon, C. (2001). 'The Regional Deficit in Eastward Enlargement of the European Union: Top-Down Policies and Bottom-Up Reactions', ESRC Working Paper 29/01.

Jacoby, W. and Černoch, P. (2002). 'The EU's Pivotal Role in the Creation of Czech Regional Policy', in R. Linden (ed.), *Norms and Nannies: The Impact of International Organizations on the Central and East European States*. Boulder, CO: Rowman & Littlefield.

Jørgensen, K. E. (2002). 'Making the CFSP Work', in J. Peterson and M. Shackleton (eds.), *The Institutions of the European Union*, Oxford: Oxford University Press.

Marcou, G. (2002). 'Regionalization for Development and Accession to the European Union: A Comparative Perspective', in G. Marcou (ed.), *Regionalization for Development and Accession to the European Union: A Comparative Perspective—Hungary, Lithuania, Poland, Slovakia, Ukraine*. Budapest: Open Society Institute/ Local Government and Public Service Reform Initiative, pp. 11–28.

May, R. E. (2004). *Manifest Destiny's Underworld: Filibustering in Antebellum America*. Chapel Hill, NC: University of North Carolina Press.

McCarty, N., Poole, K.T., and Rosenthal, H. (2002). 'Congress and the Territorial Expansion of the United States' in D. W. Brady and M. D. McCubbins (eds.), *Party, Process, and Political Change in Congress: New Perspectives on the History of Congress*. Stanford, CA: Stanford University Press, pp. 392–451.

Moravcsik, A. and Vachudova, M. A. (2003). 'National Interests, State Power and EU Enlargement', *East European Politics and Societies*, 17/1: 42–57.

Papadimitriou, D. (2002). *Negotiating the New Europe: The European Union and Eastern Europe*. Aldershot: Ashgate.

Putnam, R. D. (1988). 'Diplomacy and Domestic Politics: The Logic of Two-Level Games', *International Organization*, 36/3: 427–60.

Scherpereel, J. A. (2003). *Between State Socialism and European Union: Remaking the State in the Czech Republic and Slovakia*. Ph.D. dissertation, University of Wisconsin-Madison, Department of Political Science.

Schimmelfennig, F. (2001). 'The Community Trap: Liberal Norms, Rhetorical Action, and the Eastern Enlargement of the European Union', *International Organization*, 55/1: 47–80.

—— and Sedelmeier, U. (2002). 'Theorizing EU Enlargement: Research Focus, Hypotheses, and the State of the Research', *Journal of European Public Policy*, 9/4.

—— —— (eds.) (forthcoming). *The Europeanization of Central and Eastern Europe*. Ithaca, NY: Cornell University Press.

Sedelmeier, U. (2000). 'Eastern Enlargement: Risk, Rationality, and Role-Compliance,' in M. G. Cowles and M. Smith (eds.), *The State of the European Union: Risks, Reform, Resistance and Renewal*. New York: Oxford University Press, pp. 164–85.

Sjursen, H. (2002). 'Why Expand? The Question of Legitimacy and Justification in the EU's Enlargement Policy', *Journal of Common Market Studies*, 40/3: 491–513.

Stephanson, A. (1995). *Manifest Destiny: American Expansionism and the Empire of Right*. New York: Hill and Wang.

Stewart, C. and Weingast, B. R. (1992). 'Stacking the Senate, Changing the Nation: Republican Rotten Boroughs, Statehood Politics, and American Political Development', *Studies in American Political Development*, 6: 223–71.

V

The Shape of the EU Polity

16

Rights in the European Union: Convergent with the USA?

MARTIN SHAPIRO

Few words in legal discourse are more freighted with multiple meanings than 'rights.' Here I will treat a right as any individual or group interest for which a priority is claimed over other interests. Legislatures may give an interest priority by statute, as for instance in a disability statute that provides direct government payments to the disabled but not to the nondisabled. Such priorities are, of course, politically fragile because what the legislature giveth at one moment it may taketh away at another. Thus the interested are anxious to stabilize their priorities by having them specified in some law higher and more permanent than statutes, such as treaties or constitutions. Often we reserve the word 'rights' for those priorities that have achieved or aspire to such higher priorities. Indeed, often there is political contention about use of the label 'right' or 'rights'. In the USA the simple distinction between statutory right and constitutional right is usually enough. In Europe the European Convention on Human Rights and the European Union Treaties are not, or not quite, constitutions, but generally enjoy legally higher status than member state statutes. In this context it may be convenient to speak of constitutional rights with the understanding that we are including such treaty-based higher law rights.

We may also distinguish between positive and negative rights. A negative right is a claim for priority against government intervention, such as 'Congress shall make no law abridging freedom of speech . . . '. A positive right is a claim for priority in the receipt of government services. A constitutional right to free public education would require the legislature to adequately fund education. In Europe such positive rights are often called social rights.

It is important to note that rights have no necessary logical connection to judicial review. A constitution may specify interest priorities without providing a judicial means for enforcing them, or may specify certain rights but only allow certain parties to pursue them in a judicial forum. The European Convention, for example, provides that individual citizens may seek judicial vindication of convention rights only if their nation states permit them to.

Otherwise only nation-states may appear before the Court of Human Rights. At the opposite extreme, some European national constitutions allow access to constitutional judicial review to any citizen, as opposed to the US system where fairly rigorous standing rules seek to limit access to those citizens whose rights have actually been violated.

Constitutional rights may be derived by judicial constitutional interpretation when they are not evident in the constitutional text. If we are interested in rights convergence between the USA and Europe, one dimension lies in constitutional text and quite another in judicial activism in discovering constitutional rights. The Warren Court may be famous for its boldness in rights creation, but its Bill of Rights was textually evident. The French Constitutional Court inserted a specific bill of rights into its constitution. The European Court of Justice (ECJ) declared its intention to construct one.

The European Union (EU) structure of rights is now being built upon the preexisting rights practices of the member states, which in turn developed in part in the light of US experience. Member states rights development preceded and served as the foundation for EU rights. The EU today presents a rights picture that mixes rights guaranteed by the constitutions of the member states, rights arising from member state subscription to the European Convention on Human Rights and rights derived by judicial interpretation of EU treaties that are in the process of being specified in the EU 'constitution'.

1. Dynamics of Federalism and Judicial Review

Current debate about EU rights is shaped by the immediate post-World War II debate over positive and negative rights and the explosion of judicial review institutions on the continent (Stone Sweet 2000). Most fundamentally, the EU development of constitutional judicial review for rights is conditioned by its quasi-federal structure and the particular nexus between federalism and review.

Before World War II constitutional judicial review was almost exclusively confined to a small number of federal states. Where a federation arises from relatively voluntary association of most or all of the member units, it may be likened to a cartel. Such a cartel was formed by the former British colonies in the USA, in part for security reasons but also with very strong free trade motives. All members agree to free trade with one another while excluding others outside the cartel from free trade privileges. Cartels are notably unstable because for each member the best possible position is that all other members obey the cartel rules while it itself cheats by favoring its own economic interests over those of the others by burdening imports and favoring its own exports. Therefore cartels particularly benefit from surveillance and disciplinary devices. Constitutional judicial review, particularly on the US model of access of private parties to review, is a particularly good surveillance device. Private entrepreneurs pinched by member state cheating will be more alert to the pain than the member state governments themselves. And litigation costs are low enough to encourage this form of private enforcement of cartel, constitutional, free trade provisions. As a disciplinary device judicial review is particularly useful because it often avoids head-to-head conflicts between member states and particularizes complaints of violation rather than agglomerating them into general conflicts.

Most importantly, judicial review avoids alliances of cheating member states, because litigation takes up one particular cheating incident by one state at a time. Thus alliances between a number of states that might wish to cheat do not arise as they would if a central cartel policy sought to enforce a free trade rule, usually against all cheaters at the same time. When a particular state law limiting trade is struck down, other states are not likely to support the cheating state against the central reviewing court. For other states the conflict will not appear to be between state and central interests but between the interest of the cheating state in cheating and of the other states in preventing that cheating. In challenging any one member state on free trade grounds the reviewing court acts for the cartel and thus can expect to receive support from all the rest of its members against the cheating member. In brief, while for each member the best position is that it may cheat while others must obey, that position is unattainable. The second-best position is that it obeys and the others obey. Judicial review benefits every member by aiding in the achievement of the second-best position. The reviewing court, although an organ of the central government, can expect support from all other member states when it brings to book any particular cheating state.

For a quite long period after initiation, constitutional judicial review in the USA, Australia and Canada focused heavily on free trade review. If member states find such review extremely useful, they may accept other judicial interventions as a necessary 'cost' of this free trade review. Constitutional review by central courts in federal states almost inevitably will bring up not only questions of states cheating other states, but also questions of the boundaries between central government and member state government powers. Here judicial review when exercised in favor of central and against member state authority may seem on particularly weak ground. In contrast to cases in which the court prevents one state from cheating on the others, a central court decision that limits the powers of one member state in favor of enhancing the powers of the central government may appear threatening to other member states as well. It is likely to engender an alliance of all states against a central court seen as seeking to favor central government over state governments. Moreover, when deciding questions of state versus central authority, a constitutional court that is part of central government itself is likely to be seen as being a judge in its own case. Yet the member states are likely to see the need for some referee of the constitutionally set boundaries between central and member state authority. That perceived need, plus the general myth of judicial independence, and in the US the 'three great branches' myth, may persuade member states to accept the court of a central government as a neutral referee between themselves and the center even though the court is nominally part of the center.

If constitutional judicial review is especially useful to federalisms, it may follow that all actors in a federal system will accept some non-federalism review as a cost of the federalism review they want. Something similar may occur where such a court seems necessary to make separation of powers work, as in France under the Fifth Republic. Thus judges of constitutional courts in federal systems or separation-of-powers systems may hope for some success in adding rights review to federalism or separation-of-powers review because of the political support for such division-of-powers review that they have built up over time. In fact in the USA, the Supreme Court announced quite early that it could not exercise rights review over the states and in fact initially exercised practically no rights review over the central government. Aside from property rights it undertook practically no rights review over the federal government until World War I, and did not assert much rights review authority over the states until the 1930s (McCloskey 1960). As we shall see, a similar pattern is evident for the ECJ, which did not assert rights review authority until it had demonstrated its usefulness to the member states in federalism matters.

Federalism and rights are interconnected in another way. Those pushing particular interest priorities in particular member states and finding themselves thwarted by particular domestic alliances of opposing political forces may shift their priority to the political arena provided by the central government where the constellation of political forces may be more favorable. A rights battle lost in one arena may be won in the other. Constitutional judicial review will then become the means of enforcing the victory in the central arena on the recalcitrant local arena.

Finally a federal system in which rights are established may be attractive to prospective member states seeking rights. In this process rights come to be defined as an integral feature of the particular federation. This, of course, is clearly one facet of the accession of the eastern European states to the EU.

The basic story we are going to tell in the following pages is one of convergence. In the USA, the Supreme Court and other courts have over time engaged in more and more constitutional judicial review in favor of individual rights. In Europe as well, constitutional judicial review that began in the context of federalism or other constitutional divisions of governmental powers has moved on to more and more rights announcing and protecting review by more and more courts over time. Still, European judicial action favoring rights developed by somewhat different routes and continues to exhibit certain features contrasting with those in the USA as a result of specific European cultural heritages—to which we will now turn.

2. The Postwar Development of European Judicial Review and Rights: National Rights and the Teachings of Hans Kelsen

Immediately following World War II, the three losing Axis powers all introduced written constitutions with rights provisions and judicial review. A strong element of convergence at gunpoint was present, with US occupying forces more or less demanding constitutions and US 'experts' 'assisting' in the drafting. Yet in Germany and Italy there was also considerable domestic support for constitutions and actual drafting was largely in native hands.

Once the choice of federalism was made for Germany, and that choice itself was both dictated from the outside and responsive to historically strong German traditions of regionalism, the choice of judicial review was almost inevitable given previous Anglophone experience. Germany's immediately previous historical experience pointed to constitutional rights provisions just as strongly (Kommers 1976). In US experts' minds bills of rights were intrinsic elements of constitutions and so was judicial review. Thus it would appear that both outside pressures and peculiarly domestic circumstances acted to create convergence.

Yet there were also peculiarly domestic elements that lead to some quite nonconvergent results. The principal one of these was the dominance of the writings of the great interwar jurisprud Hans Kelsen in all European thinking about constitutions and particularly judicial review.

Kelsen taught that written constitutions serve as a higher law against which parliamentary legislation can be checked while parliamentary sovereignty is retained at the lower, statutory level of law. Constitutional judicial review is essential for legally enforcing this hierarchy of law. Yet judicial review inevitably involves a strong component of judicially wielded political discretion. This judicial politics is acceptable because reviewing courts engage only in negative legislative powers. They can strike down statutes but not enact them. Even so the political taint of constitutional judicial review should be further mitigated. Unlike in the Anglophone model, Kelsen held that constitutional judicial review powers should not be assigned to the regular judges of the regular courts but assigned to a single separate court whose members should be selected by some process different from that used to assure the independence and neutrality of the regular judiciary—a process designed to assure some degree of political accountability. These constitutional courts should enforce separation of powers and federalism provisions of constitutions but not their rights provisions because rights review, consisting as it does of deciding which interests shall enjoy priority, is too political to be assigned to any nonrepresentative institution. Given that review is to be confined exclusively to conflicts about the boundaries between various institutions of government, only the official leaders of each of the pieces of government, not ordinary citizens, should have access to the constitutional court. Judicial review preferably should be abstract, that is by challenge to a statute immediately upon its enactment and 'on its face' rather than subsequently as it is applied (Kelsen 1928). For the invasion of separation of powers or federalism boundaries, if it had occurred at all, occurred at the very moment when the challenged legislation was enacted—not later when it was applied to individuals. It was at that moment that the challenged legislation assigned authority to some part of government that the constitution allegedly assigned to another.

Kelsen's logic of exclusive jurisdiction in a special court exercising abstract review powers was intimately tied to the exclusion of rights review. Invasions of the jurisdictions or powers of one part of government by another ought to be discernable immediately after passage of legislation assigning or exercising government powers and before concrete problems arise. If a federal constitution assigns education to member states and the central legislature enacts an education statute, the constitutional breach is evident before anyone does anything to enforce the law. And the state legislatures ought to be alert enough to their own constitutional prerogatives to resort immediately to the constitutional court.

Rights review is intrinsically different. Some statutes may openly and obviously by their very language violate individual rights. But even in such instances individuals are unlikely to be sufficiently vigilant to spot the mere potential violation of their rights that occurs at the moment the legislation is enacted. They are likely to be motivated to litigate only later when the enacted law is actually applied to them. And many laws that do not appear by their language to violate individual constitutional rights, may turn out to do so when applied in particular cases. Moreover, it is the individual whose rights are violated rather than some government official who would appear to be the most appropriate party to challenge the government action. And finally, constitutional rights questions will often arise not separably but inextricably entwined in normal or regular legal proceedings. No league of criminals will seek to mount a general challenge to unconstitutional police search practices. An individual being tried in a regular criminal prosecution for burglary will want to raise the constitutional issue to prevent the introduction of damming evidence in his own case. It is because Kelsen rejects rights review as too political that the rest of his model—immediate, abstract review by a special court open only to government officials—is coherent.

The new German constitution was to be federal, and the Italian contained strong federal features. Judicial review was perceived as an inevitable corollary of this federalism. Given recent history, both constitutions necessarily contained strong negative bills of rights given teeth by judicial review. Given intellectual history, however, both constitutions provided for Kelsenian constitutional courts, separated institutionally and by recruitment from the regular courts and granted a monopoly over constitutional issues. This separation then necessitated a 'reference' procedure in which the regular court's proceedings were suspended, the constitutional issues arising in the regular court transferred for resolution to the constitutional court, and the case then finally decided by the regular court guided by the constitutional finding given it by the constitutional court. This reference procedure was later adopted for the ECJ.

More importantly, the German and Italian conjunctions of Kelsenian courts with rights judicial review disrupted the basic Kelsenian logic which had limited the constitutional court to access only by a few high government officials and to abstract review. To protect individual rights these new constitutions provided for individual access to constitutional courts alongside high official access, and also included concrete review of the application of statutes even long after their enactment alongside abstract review of the language of the statutes. This mix of Kelsenian courts and US-style individual access and concrete review later became a feature of the ECJ.

The tension to be seen between elements of the US and Kelsenian models in the German and Italian constitution will be seen in all subsequent European endeavors as well and constantly complicates any simple story of convergence. It is particularly evident in the EU. Like the US Supreme Court, the ECJ is a court of general jurisdiction hearing both constitutional and nonconstitutional cases arising under EU law. But it also sits as a special, separate court deciding questions of EU law sent to it by 'references' from the national courts of the member states.

The postwar French constitution experience illustrates these dynamics. Unlike Germany and Italy there did not appear to be an overwhelming necessity of new negative constitutional rights as France drew up the plans for its Fourth Republic. As a result a stalemate developed between bourgeois parties interested only in negative rights and socialist parties urging positive or social rights. No bill of rights at all appeared in the new constitution. There was little desire for federalism in France or for a divided central government rather than parliamentary sovereignty. It followed that there was no need of rights, federalism or separation of powers review. As part of its revolutionary heritage, reinforced by specifically acknowledged learning from the US New Deal experience, France earlier had considered and rejected constitutional judicial review, and now did so again.

Then, however, the Algerian war and the peculiar personality of Charles de Gaulle led away from parliamentary sovereignty to a new Fifth Republic constitution that divided powers between legislature and executive. And that alone was sufficient to force the French reluctantly into constitutional judicial review to police the boundaries between the two new great branches—a particularly pressing need because both branches were given lawmaking powers.

Because only separation-of-powers review and not rights review was on the table, the French could and did follow a purely Kelsenian scheme. Constitutional review was vested solely in a Constitutional Council staffed on a political basis entirely separate from the recruitment of regular judges. Access to the Council was limited to a handful of high government officials. Review was at its most abstract. Statutes could only be reviewed in the brief period between passage and promulgation.

Pressures toward more judicial review and particularly more rights review have manifested themselves in France over time. The new constitution was subsequently amended to allow any sixty members of the Assembly to challenge an enacted statute before the Council. Given French party politics, there are always at least sixty members against any significant piece of legislation and challenges have become routine. The Constitutional Council has asserted in its case decisions that the Declaration of the Rights of Man of 1789 is part of the Constitution (Stone 1992). France acquiesced in access to the European Court of Human Rights for individual French citizens bringing rights claims against the French government. French courts also accepted European Union law and the European Convention on Human Rights as enjoying supremacy over French domestic law. Because, as we shall see shortly, the ECJ has proclaimed EU law to contain individual rights guarantees, those rights can now presumably be invoked by French individuals in French and EU courts. Thus against the historical French hostility to constitutional rights (and all other constitutional) judicial review, there is far more rights review available to French citizens now than there once was.

3. Transnational Rights and Review in Europe

While the new German, French and Italian constitutional efforts principally evidenced a concern for state building, or rather rebuilding, each also evidenced a concern for rights (even though in France the initial postwar outcome was silence). In 1950 the Western European states entered into the European Convention on Human Rights. This treaty enumerated quite a long list of negative rights. A few positive rights were included, at least by implications, such as the right of access to justice for the indigent. But a broad array of social rights was not.

In many ways at the time of its signing the Convention was unique rather than converging on anything. It was a treaty falling under international law rather than a constitution generating constitutional law. Like all treaties under international law, it generated legal obligations binding on the signatory states as states rather than endowing individuals with legal rights and obligations directly enforceable in regular courts. Either by constitutional provision or national statute, some of the signatory states incorporated the Convention into domestic law. Others, however, did not. When domesticated, it sometimes generated only statutory entitlements rather than constitutional rights superior to statutes, although through various techniques the courts of some of the signatory states that domesticated managed to treat Convention-specified rights as superior to subsequently enacted statutes. Such results even have occurred in countries like the UK which did not domesticate the Convention.

Although it might be argued that these moves partially 'constitutionalized' the Convention within signatory states, its international treaty status remained very evident in the institutions of enforcement it established. The Commission on Human Rights, which was to receive and investigate complaints of member state convention violations, was to conciliate them if possible. If the Commission found a justified complaint and could not itself achieve a resolution, it—not the complainant—brought a case before the Court of Human Rights. Where the Court found a member state in violation of the Convention, it entered into a negotiation with the member states not for the purpose of remedying the injury done to an individual that had generated the complaint but with the goal of persuading the offending state to modify the statute or administrative practice that had generated the violation. In short, the form of judicial review adopted was designed to keep the sovereignty of the signatory states intact. This international law orientation to state sovereignty was furthered by the provision that only member states, not individuals, were guaranteed the power to bring cases before the Commission and the Court.

Leaving aside its international aspects, the Convention clearly does show elements of convergence with US rights practice. It breaks with the Kelsen model by providing for rights judicial review. Typically the individual articles of the Convention contain a first paragraph stating a right in broad terms and a second enumerating a number of exceptions, qualifications and potential justifications for contrary state action. Unquestionably part of these constructions owe a debt to German thinking about the *Rechtsstatt* which tends toward explicit recognition of public interest limits on private rights. On the other hand the limiting and qualifying second paragraphs of the Convention often read like summaries of the US Supreme Court case law limiting and qualifying the seemingly absolute or open-ended Bill of Rights texts (Frowein, *et al.* 1986). The signing of the Convention, which seeks to transnationalize rights through transnational review, actually foreshadows the campaign of the Warren Court to nationalize the US Bill of Rights.

Indeed the Convention contains yet another decisive move away from Kelsen and toward US practice. Once rights are invoked, the standard Kelsenian contradiction appears in a most dramatic form in the Convention. If the object is the protection of individual rights, even if that protection is vested, as it is by the Convention, in a single, specially selected, separate court, why should access to that court be forbidden to the very parties we are seeking to protect—individuals whose rights have been violated? And more particularly, if only member states may invoke the Court's process, how will the Court of Human Rights protect rights at all? A signatory state hardly will haul itself before the Court for violations of its own citizen's rights. And what incentives are there for Germany to haul Belgium into court for violations of Belgian citizens' rights? Will the Convention only spring to life when one signatory state happens to violate the rights of a citizen of another signatory state influential enough to persuade his government to take up his cause?

In an obvious compromise still bending toward national sovereignty, the Convention provides that member states may individually and voluntarily accede to a Convention provision that allows individuals as well as signatory states access to the Commission-Court process. Eventually all of the signatory states did so. As in Germany and Italy the special separated court remains—with Kelsen here reinforced by the obvious need for a transnational court to enforce a transnational agreement—but access to the special court is 'Americanized.'

The more direct institutional precursors to today's ECJ, in the European Coal and Steel Community and European Economic Community treaties, initially gave no attention to individual rights. The story of how the Community treaties turned into something like a constitution is well known (Craig and de Burca 1995). The treaties did not call themselves a constitution, and if they were merely treaties would neither be supreme over national laws nor have direct effect—and so would not be directly enforceable by member state courts. Yet they did explicitly provide for review. In case decisions rivaling Marbury *v.* Madison in boldness and importance, the ECJ held that the treaties and laws made under their authority were supreme and did have direct effect, thus transforming the treaties into 'constitutional documents.'

Thus the then European Communities and now EU does have constitutional judicial review but, initially at least, it was not rights review. The long association of constitutional review with federalism is demonstrated dramatically by the EU. In issues raised, arguments made, and opinions delivered, many of the decisions of the ECJ were from the beginning startlingly close to the commerce clause federalism decisions of the US Supreme Court. Rights review emerged more slowly and in a sense is just beginning to emerge now.

The early treaties were directed at trade matters. The quasi-federal system established was just the kind of cartel demanding strong surveillance and disciplinary institutions described earlier as leading to judicial review. The central stated purpose of the treaties was to create a free trade market among the member states. One principal means of tearing down the border barriers to trade would be the dismantling of the webs of complex and differing national regulations of private sector economic enterprise. In this sense the move to a common market would be deregulatory. It remained to be seen, however, whether the dismantling of national regulations would lead to laissez-faire or a reregulation at the transnational level to replace national regulations. By hindsight at least it can also be said that the treaties assigned regulation or the absence thereof to the transnational level while leaving welfare state matters and social control matters such as criminal law, family law and so on to the nations. Viewed in this light the EC-EU need not concern itself with either negative or positive rights.

As noted earlier, European socialist parties have generally been very concerned with turning statutory welfare entitlements into 'positive' or 'social' constitutional rights. Socialist parties and socialist politicians were and have remained very active in EC-EU affairs. There is a major echo of the positive versus negative rights debate in the construction of the EC. In parallel to the Council of Ministers which wielded substantially all the legislative power, the Community treaties also established an Economic and Social Council, and there was much talk of the 'social partners.'

The rights agenda of the left, however, touched EC judicial review largely by another route. The drive to a common market was encapsulated in four rights or 'freedoms'; free movement of goods, free movement of persons, free movement of capital and freedom of establishment (the freedom to initiate an economic enterprise in a member state other than ones own). The 'person' in free movement of persons was, given the context, essentially conceived as an economic person. Among the potential barriers to the free movement of labor were member state welfare rules that restricted benefits to citizens or imposed waiting periods on new arrivals before they could begin receiving benefits. In a series of decisions the Court of Justice began to strike down such barriers. In the process the court actually constitutionalized positive welfare rights for those in movement from one member state to another while not constitutionalizing them for stay at homes. And paradoxically this move toward positive rights occurred without an ECJ move toward negative rights, because the court had only the free movement of persons clause and not a constitutional bill of rights to work with.

In this context the construction of positive rights for incomers was more easily accomplished by the Court than would have been the construction of either positive or negative general rights. As we have seen, where a federal court imposes negative rights on any single member state, limiting that state's powers, it threatens all member states and is likely to generate an alliance of all of them against it, unlike the situation where the court catches one state cheating on its free trade commitments. It is noteworthy that the US state Chief Justices Association became the outspoken enemy of the Warren Court when the Warren Court sought to impose nationally uniform negative rights on state governments. Where all a federal court is doing is requiring member states to pay the same benefits to incomers as to stay-at-homes, the member state remains free to decide on whether or not to provide and how much to provide of those benefits. The cost will usually be minimal to the state compared to the cost voluntarily borne by the state in creating the entitlement for insiders. Unlike the situation when a court imposes a positive right for all, the member state retains overall budgetary control because it can always reduce the overall level of payments. The court is not forced into determining a constitutionally mandated minimum payment level or ordering states to raise taxes if necessary to achieve that level.

The same dynamics played out in the USA at roughly the same time. A rather concerted attempt was made by the left to constitutionalize welfare entitlements. This effort was hampered by the absence of explicit positive rights clauses in the Bill of Rights. Ultimately the drive toward positive rights was largely unsuccessful in the Warren Court and largely shut down by the Burger Court. The great exception was Shapiro *v.* Thompson[1] in which the Supreme Court declared unconstitutional a state-imposed waiting period for incoming welfare applicants. It did so by discovering a constitutional right to travel which the state requirement was found to violate. Thus in both the US and the EU equality of incomers and long residents for whatever welfare benefits the state granted was constitutionalized, but not the benefits themselves or any specific level of payments.

In both the USA and Europe ethnic and gender discrimination have been central to rights discourse for the past fifty years. Like ethnicities, women in the Western world have been subject to powerful, long-held stereotypes, but unlike many ethnicities they enjoy strong organizational and communications skills, financial resources and voting strength. In the new Canadian

[1] 394 US 618 (1969).

constitution womens' rights were privileged over nearly all others. In the US, gender antidiscrimination rights have attained somewhat less powerful constitutional status than racial rights, but women have clearly benefited more from affirmative action programs than have African-Americans. The EU treaties have long contained a specific provision against gender pay discrimination.

The picture has been very mixed in the member states of the EU, with women better organized, more politically influential and more successful in achieving statutory entitlements in some countries than others. Women have been very successful at organizing transnational NGOs and networks and welcomed the opportunity to shift their fire to whatever segment or level of government is most receptive. Gender employment discrimination is obviously and easily encompassed within the free movement of workers rights jurisprudence of ECJ. In fact the most fully articulated body of rights case law of the ECJ is in the area of gender employment discrimination and easily linked employments benefits areas such as pensions and disability.

In general then, except in the area of gender discrimination, where relatively specific treaty language could be invoked, and in positive rights to equal welfare entitlements for incoming workers, in its early decades the ECJ had done little about rights compared to what the US Supreme Court was doing in the same time period. Both courts were active in constitutional judicial review, the Supreme Court largely on individual rights matters, the ECJ in knocking down national barriers to the creation of a transnational European market.

In a small number of decisions, not very important in and of themselves, the ECJ then moved on to declare that a full panoply of individual constitutional rights was implicitly contained in the EC-EU treaties and would be rendered explicit in subsequent case law that would be built up by the court from the domestic rights practices of the member states and the European Convention on Human Rights (Weiler and Lockhart 1995). The court did not specify whether positive as well as negative rights would be propounded. Its decisions did mention such negative rights as freedom of speech, religion, and union activity, privacy and nondiscrimination. Nondiscrimination can, of course, also be a positive right if government is required to eliminate private discrimination.

From the materials presented so far it is possible to build up a fairly persuasive historical account of the ECJ's move. We have a court like the US Supreme Court that first acquires such strong legitimacy through its federalism decisions that later it can impose rights limitations on government action. To some degree governments are willing to accept the latter as a cost of maintaining constitutional judicial review for other purposes. We have a court embedded in a global fascination with human rights exemplified by an explosion of constitutional judicial review, including rights review, in a large number of European states individually and collectively in the European Convention. In particularly European terms we have a rights concern so pressing that it transforms the intellectually dominant Kelsenian model of review so drastically as to destroy its coherence. Indeed the ECJ represents the ultimate destruction of the Kelsenian model, for it is constructed as a court of general jurisdiction, rather than a separate court dealing only with constitutional questions. Individuals enjoy access to the ECJ but less access than is enjoyed by individuals to the US Supreme Court.

Moreover, the Court's discovery of a bill of rights in a constitution textually devoid of one had been foreshadowed by decisions of the French Constitutional Court and developed in rough time parallel with the English move toward rights review, which culminated in a UK statutory charter of rights enforced by limited judicial review. In other words, the ECJ movement occurred just as two European national legal cultures historically hostile to constitutional review, the UK and France, also moved toward rights review. In this same period the Netherlands, whose constitution had domesticated the Convention, engaged in a major reform of its administrative courts that facilitated individual claims to judicial rights protections, although without introducing constitutional review as such.

The global fascination with rights and its burgeoning institutional manifestations can hardly be said to have been 'caused' by the constitutional rights successes of the US Supreme Court in general or the Warren Court in particular. Yet the high visibility, apparent rights success of the Warren Court certainly was one of the causes of the global judicial activism in behalf of rights that has been widely noted (Tate and Vallinder 1995). Of course 'converging' can be a matter of common responses to common causes rather than one convergent causing the other. The story of rights review told here is one to some degree of common causes converging with both federalism and rights ideology among the common causes. It also is to some unspecified degree a cause and effect convergence with the US judicial practice serving as model and an encouragement of judicial activism elsewhere.

4. The Competition for Rights Review

To this story a final element must be added that reinforces the federalism factor, while at the same time emphasizing specifically European dynamics. From its inception the ECJ has encountered considerable suspicion from the German and Italian constitutional courts seeking to protect individual rights as guaranteed by their national constitutions (Craig and de Burca 1995: 256–67). Could the EU enact legislation enforcing the treaties and endowed with supremacy and direct effect that violated the rights provisions of member state constitutions? And if the issue of such possible violation arose, which court—the ECJ or the relevant national constitutional court—should decide whether a violation had occurred?

Remember that rights federalism is far riskier for a court than economic federalism. Again, in economic federalism the policing central court is actually disciplining one member state on behalf of the others and can expect their support, while in rights federalism the central court is imposing limitations on one state which do not benefit the others and can be expected soon to be applied to the others. Thus, as we have noted earlier, it could reasonably be expected that a central court's rights limitations on one state would be resisted by the others. Moreover, a central court of a federal system announcing an expansion of the powers of the central government will always find itself in the questionable position of a part of the central government deciding conflicts between its own government and a member state.

The specter raised by the German and Italian constitutional courts was one in which the EU government, unconstrained by EU-level constitutional rights limitations on its power, would enact legislation that violated their national constitutional rights guarantees but would nonetheless be valid because such EU legislation is supreme over national law. Moreover it might well be argued that where an issue of conflict between EU law and national constitutional rights arose, it was the ECJ that had the final say on which should prevail, thus undercutting national constitutional courts' powers to defend national constitutional rights.

For the reasons just indicated, the ECJ was extremely reluctant to directly confront the German Court and simply declare that it itself had the ultimate jurisdiction to decide whether an EU law violated German constitutional rights provisions and what to do about it if such a violation had occurred. The German Court had stressed the rights loophole. If the EU treaties had no rights provisions but EU laws were supreme over member state laws, including member state constitutional rights provisions, then European citizens would find that the very individual rights enshrined in their national constitutions could be violated at will by the new transnational government. In a series of decisions beginning in 1969 (Craig and de Burca 1995: 292–98), the ECJ responded that the German Constitutional Court need not fear because a full panoply of individual rights was implicit in the EU treaties and the ECJ would engage in rights review of EU legislation. The ECJ said that the rights in the EU treaties were the very rights recognized by the member states. Thus the German Constitutional Court could be assured that there was no loophole.

Thus from one perspective the ECJ was responding to global concern for rights and exploiting the rights advantage of a federal constitutional court, or, more briefly, simply doing, what so many other constitutional courts had been doing. From another, however, it was responding to a challenge to its, and the EU's as a whole, supremacy over the member states. Not rights concerns but federalism may have been central to its newly proclaimed rights activism.

If all that was involved was this kind of strategic federalism consideration, we would expect the story to end there or tail off. Having proclaimed rights in order to head off the Germans, the ECJ might then have been quite modest or totally silent about the concrete particularization of rights in subsequent cases, particularly given that the treaties actually contain few rights provisions. That the Court was probably also driven by real rights concerns is evidenced not by the subsequent case law, of which there has been little, but by subsequent developments elsewhere.

5. From Judicial Activism to Treaty Modification: Toward the Charter of Fundamental Rights

However strategic the ECJ's response to the German Court may have been, its declaration that there were rights in the EU and that they would be explicated in future by reference to the rights traditions of the member states was a clear invitation to rights exponents to insist on the explication. In a number of other instances, ideas floated by the Court subsequently have been solidified in revisions of the treaties.

The Amsterdam Treaty of 1997 provided specific textual recognition of 'human rights and fundamental freedoms,' some specific protections for personal privacy and some new procedures for Council monitoring of member state human rights violations.

By the mid 1990s a flurry of EU sponsored and independent efforts, in which NGOs played a major part, called for and then drafted a Charter of Rights. This provoked considerable controversy, particularly over the introduction of positive or social rights. As finally endorsed the Charter contains freedom of speech, privacy, fair trial and nondiscrimination rights but also positive or social rights including housing, environmental and consumer protection, education, employment and disability, old age and unemployment benefits. But the Charter as adopted at Nice in 2000 was not introduced into the treaties. It explicitly stated that it granted no new legislative powers to the Union, and the protocol annexing it to the Nice Treaty explicitly declared it to be judicially unenforceable.

That the member states had been of two minds over rights judicial review had been clear long before Nice. The Maastricht Treaty of 1992 introduced provisions on Justice and Home Affairs. But these provisions were introduced outside of the regular articles of the treaties as a 'third pillar' of the EU. This newly invented pillar status, like the later Nice 'charter' status of rights, was invented in part to prevent the EU from acquiring general lawmaking authority over these matters but also in part so that judicial review by the ECJ could be excluded, which it specially was. The degree of hostility to the Court is indicated by the explicit exclusion of the Court of Justice from enforcement of provisions on justice. Those favoring review, however, achieved a clause that provided that, when member states entered into the cooperation agreements authorized by the Third Pillar, they might, if they wished, include ECJ jurisdiction over the agreements. Moreover, subsequently in the Amsterdam Treaty, much of what had been in the Third Pillar was transformed into regular articles of the treaties (effectively moving into the 'first pillar' of core economic activities), in the process becoming subject to ECJ review. However, those matters transferred from the Third Pillar to the main body of the treaties would be subject to only an especially limited form of judicial review.

In the new Treaty Establishing a Constitution for Europe that now awaits approval by the member states, the Charter of Rights moves from an appendix to a featured place in the primary law of the Union. As in the USA roughly before the 1930's (when the Supreme Court began actively reading the Bill of Rights into the fourteenth Amendment, thus making it applicable to the states), Charter rights are specifically made applicable only to Union laws and to the laws of the member states that implement Union law. By negative implication the Charter does not appear to govern the purely domestic laws of member states, although there have been strong arguments made that if rights are part of the primary law of the treaties, they must be just as supreme over member state domestic law as other parts of the primary law of the Treaties.

The Constitution recognizes the primacy of the European Convention on Human Rights, provides for the Union itself joining the Convention, and echoes the earlier ECJ language of Union rights emanating from member states rights traditions (including member state constitutions), thus leaving a huge need for judicial coordination of many rights sources.

The new Charter also contains a number of sweeping positive or social rights, but makes them subject to 'national laws and practices' rather than prevailing over national laws. Yet it also contains sweeping antidiscrimination rights not limited in this way.

The change in textual position of the Charter would seem to open the door to powerful judicial constitutional rights review, but the Charter itself now contains a murky clause on judicial review that itself will become the subject of much interpretive debate.

6. Conclusion: Mechanisms of Change

The simplest story to be told at this point is one of convergence with some cause and effect elements. Individual rights litigation began in earnest in the USA only at the time of World War I. The great surge of judicial activism in behalf of such rights came with the Warren Court. That Warren Court surge was no doubt partly a cause but surely also was an effect of the global post-World War II surge of rights concerns provoked by totalitarianism. In roughly the same period as the Warren Court, constitutional judicial review came to flourish in a great many Western European states where the intersection of the American model and the European Kelsenian model led to separate constitutional courts exercising rights judicial review.

The ECJ was a move in the US direction in that it was a court of general jurisdiction rather than a separate constitutional court. And, like the US Supreme Court, it gained much of its legitimacy from its position as the high court of a federal system before it moved on to rights. But its 'constitution' did not contain a bill of rights, and it entered the human rights business only hesitantly and sketchily in contrast to the US Supreme Court in the same period. The strong global concerns for human rights that had expressed itself in Europe in new national constitutional rights review and in the European Convention on Human Rights is now pushing Europe toward an EU bill of rights. General European suspicion of US-style judicial activism, and more specific unhappiness with the ECJ, have led to long hesitancy in moving toward ECJ rights judicial activism. The push toward recognition of positive human rights in the new European Charter of Rights moves us beyond convergence because in only rare instances has the US Supreme Court attempted positive rights review. Indeed the big push to move the US Court in that direction largely failed. The next stage of the Charter story in Europe may tell us whether we are experiencing transatlantic convergence of US, EU and other European negative constitutional rights judicial review, or an EU initiative on positive individual rights that carries us beyond convergence—or conceivably predicts a similar future move in the US. Powerful NGO pressures in Europe move the EU in that beyond-convergence direction, but the inherent political problems of positive constitutional rights review suggest that we will get convergence rather than a move beyond it. Moreover, recent US reaction against rights judicial activism and the presence of the European Court of Human Rights are likely to temper any move toward extreme judicial activism by the ECJ or the US Supreme Court, even on negative rights.

Particularly in light of the probable elevation of the Charter of Rights, with its large quantum of positive rights, to the level of primary and, thus, judicially enforceable EU legislation, a number of points may be made about the mechanisms of change in Europe that are the focus of this volume.

First the evolution of rights and rights enforcing judicial review certainly is in part heavily influenced by the globalization of rights ideas and discourse following World War II. European politicians and intellectuals were themselves leaders in this global rights enthusiasm. But US experience, rightly or wrongly comprehended, clearly led the way in Europe and elsewhere in the vision of judicial review as a primary enunciator and protector of rights. Most particularly, the US experience of litigation as an alternative to elections and legislation as a route to policy change, and of various groups and interests depicting themselves as underdogs worthy of judicial protection against discrimination or unequal treatment has been highly instructive to European rights activists and to European judges. Those activists have been successful in part, however, because European political elites, lulled by past European judicial passivity, have consistently underestimated the political potential for generating change of the judicial review to which they acquiesced.

The current European potential for judicially enforced positive rights may also be largely a product of global discourse in a way so far little noticed. The global demise of socialism as an economic theory and political ideology leaves the left scrambling for an alternative. The most obvious alternative is continued and accelerating loyalty to the welfare state. That alternative is, however, severely constrained by limited fiscal resources and the fear that high government costs will undermine global economic competitive positions. Precisely because 'rights' are claims to favorable treatment no matter what the costs, and judges do not have to find the money to pay the costs or worry about the competitive disadvantages of the costs, judicially enforced constitutional welfare or social rights become an attractive route for globally derailed socialism.

The editors note the particular need of the multinational EU to find compromises. Democratic politicians have always found that one route to compromise is a vaguely worded statute providing for deferred and uncertain enforcement. They all get to claim credit for moving forward. They do not have to agree on anything concrete, and there are no immediate costs for which they can be blamed. What they are actually agreeing to is a kind of lottery. The real meaning of the statute will be determined, not by those who voted for it, but by others who later interpret, administer and enforce it. Stating a general positive social right, and assigning it to courts to implement, is the grandest kind of lottery.

Finally, in the context of the Cold War, rights became a major US ideological weapon in the struggle between democracy and communism. The success of the civil rights movement partially is to be attributed to the needs of US foreign policy. Today European expansion eastward, and perhaps even near eastward, clearly is nurtured by the attractions of an EU rights umbrella. There may be grave transatlantic disagreements on tactics, but the USA and Europe remain convergent in the conviction that the more rights are globalized, the safer their own people will be.

References

Craig, P. and de Burca, G. (1995). *EU Law: Text, Cases and Materials*, 2nd edn. Oxford: Oxford University Press.

Frowein, J., Shapiro, M., and Schulhofer, S. (1986). 'The Protection of Human Rights as a Vehicle of Integration,' in M. Cappelletti, M. Seccombe and J. Weiler (eds.), *Integration Through Law*. Berlin: de Gruyter.

Kelsen, H. (1928). 'La Garantie Jurisdictionnel de la Constitution,' *Review of Public Law*, 44: 197–229.

Kommers, D. (1976). *Judicial Politics in West Germany*. London: Sage.

McCloskey, R. (1960). *The American Supreme Court*. Chicago: University of Chicago Press.

Stone, A. (1992). *The Birth of Judicial Politics in France*. Oxford: Oxford University Press.

Stone Sweet, A. (2000). *Governing with Judges: Constitutional Politics in Europe*. Oxford: Oxford University Press.

Tate, C. N. and Vallinder, T. (eds.) (1995). *The Global Expansion of Judicial Power*. New York: New York University Press.

Weiler, J. H. H. and Lockhart, N. (1995). 'Taking Rights Seriously: The European Court and its Fundamental Rights Jurisprudence', *Common Market Law Review*, 32: 51–94.

17

What Lies Beyond a Confederal Europe?

CHRISTOPHER ANSELL AND REBECCA CHEN

In March 1996, the British government announced the discovery of ten cases of a new variant of Creutzfelt-Jakob disease (CJD)—an untreatable brain disease in humans. The announcement appeared to confirm fears that consumption of beef from cattle with Bovine Spongiform Encephalopathy (BSE) or 'mad cow disease' could infect humans. Although a definitive link between CJD and BSE was not yet established, the European Commission, on the advice of its Scientific Veterinary Committee (SVC), imposed a European ban on British beef. The British government was livid and threatened to bring the case to the European Court of Justice (ECJ) and to obstruct the passage of other European Union (EU) legislation in retaliation.

In Britain, however, the issue quickly became a political rout for the Conservative government, which was accused of putting agricultural interests ahead of consumer protection. Despite its apparently prompt action, the European Commission's role in this 'scandal' also became a matter of debate. In response to allegations in the French press that the Commission had earlier been involved in suppressing information about BSE, the European Parliament (EP) set up a special inquiry committee to look into the alleged mishandling of the 'mad cow' crisis by the British government and the Commission from 1989–97. After five months of painstaking investigation, the committee issued a scathing report on February 7, 1997, recommending that the EP table an immediate motion of censure on the Commission. The report submitted by EP representative Manuel Medina Ortega accused the Commission of maladministration and of bowing to British agricultural interests.

In his presentation of the Parliament's findings, Mr. Medina Ortega emphasized that decision-making in the Commission was not only weak but biased towards internal market interests. He explained that 'The Community's citizens are currently alarmed at the development of mysterious institutions which meet in Brussels, and in which there are possible lobbies at work, and they have no assurance that the food they eat, the products they consume, are provided with adequate health safety guarantees.'[1] On February 19, 1997, the EP voted to censure the Commission if it did not implement the report's recommendations. The Commission responded to these criticisms both by claiming that it had lacked the authority to adequately manage the emerging BSE crisis and by initiating some significant internal reforms to give greater priority to consumer protection.[2]

The institutional frictions between the Parliament and the Commission on display during the BSE crisis are emblematic of the dynamic, unfinished nature of the federal project for Europe. Although the Commission has long been seen as the living embodiment of the supranationalist impulse (and it is officially the 'guardian' of the treaties), its executive role and institutional structure betray the EU's origins as an international organization that must respect the prerogatives of the member states. Noted for its dynamic activism in propelling forward the project of European integration, the Commission in this case was being scolded for its recalcitrant protection of member state interests and for non-transparent decision-making. In its threatened censure, the Parliament was breaking with the institutional status quo and asserting its right to speak directly for *European* consumers. In doing so, it was challenging the indirect and state-centered logic of political representation in the EU.

These frictions also vividly illustrate the way the EU is an amalgam of different institutional logics, each one chafing against the others for the upper hand. The EU still retains many of the qualities of an international organization, constructed on the foundation of treaties and characterized by the logic of intergovernmental bargaining. Yet almost miraculously, the EU has developed an institutional structure more like a government than a mere organization. This government is conventionally described as confederal because it is dominated by its individual member states. Yet in several important respects the EU is more federal than confederal. Although still a long way from even the USA of 1789, the EU has distinctly recognizable federal features, as symbolized by the Parliament's assertiveness during the BSE crisis.

This amalgam of intergovernmental, confederal, and federal features gives the EU its distinctive character.[3] As Jabko and Parsons point out in their Introduction, an institutionalist approach revels in the complexity of the European project and is dubious about grand theory that seeks to reduce

[1] Medina Ortega, Manuel. Debates of the European Parliament (on BSE). Sitting of Tuesday, February 18, 1997. Full text available at The European Parliament On-Line, *<http://www.europarl.eu.int>*.

[2] For a fuller account of these events, see Jasanoff (1997), Neyer (2000), and Vos (2000).

[3] Ansell develops the argument about this amalgam of intergovernmental, confederal, and federal features further in Ansell and DiPalma (2004: 225–45).

Europe to its essence. Thus, this chapter is uncomfortable with characterizations of the EU that want to label it fundamentally 'intergovernmental' or 'confederal' or 'federal.' These analytical tags are indeed useful and identify important institutional distinctions, but they are better used in combination to identify political tensions than to provide totalizing descriptions. In the spirit of the 'middle ground approach' developed by Jabko and Parsons, this chapter also points to some of the key causal dynamics that pull and push the European project between intergovernmental, confederal, and federal poles. Rather than insisting upon either the immovable status quo of a state-centered Europe or the inexorable march toward a federalist Europe, these middle ground factors help to demonstrate why European integration is more commonly a process of two steps forward and one step back or one step forward and two steps back.

Each of the six mechanisms Jabko and Parsons describe has the potential to shape the evolving European amalgam of intergovernmental, confederal, and federal features. However, in this chapter, we focus on their last two mechanisms: the impact of institutional legacies, and the defense or extension of democracy. These two mechanisms represent a major institutional dilemma created by European integration. As the scope and importance of EU competences have grown, fears of a 'democratic deficit' have heightened. The fear is that the growth of these powers simultaneously weakens the scope of popular sovereignty within member states while leaving democratic control over European powers weak and indirect. It is this twin concern that creates the horns of a dilemma. One solution is to curtail the growth of European competences and powers in order to prevent the erosion of popular sovereignty at the national level. Of course, the institutional legacy of state sovereignty favors this stance. Yet market integration has advanced a great deal, and this institutional legacy discourages any simple restoration of national sovereignty. The other solution is to more thoroughly democratize the EU itself. However, any serious democratization of the EU would require strengthening European powers and competences, which would at the very least heighten concerns about a further erosion of popular sovereignty at the national level. When the Commission tells British farmers that they cannot export their cattle to Europe, the horns of the dilemma become sharp indeed!

1. The Democratic Deficit in Perspective

We begin by introducing what is at stake in competing descriptions of the EU as intergovernmental, confederal, and federal. As Jabko and Parsons summarize, Andrew Moravcsik has been one of the most cogent and forceful advocates for a grand theory approach to European integration. In his recent work, we can see a strong connection between Moravcsik's claim that the EU is a confederation and his claim that concerns about a democratic deficit are overblown and misplaced. Building on the work of the celebrated federalist scholar Daniel Elazar, Moravcsik succinctly summarizes the case for characterizing the EU as a confederation:

> This analysis confirms Daniel Elazar's conclusion... .that in comparative perspective the EU polity appears more confederal than federal. The EU, we have seen, is a political institution incomparably weaker, narrower, and more decentralized in most respects than any existing national federation. It is substantively limited largely to the tasks of international economic liberalization and stabilization. It lacks the powers to tax, coerce, police, administer, and mandate the uniform application of the law. Its cumbersome decision-making process is constrained by supermajoritarian and unanimous decision-making, as well as direct representation of national and subnational governments. To the extent that these five conditions obtain, the EU should be thought of a polity so much weaker and narrower than any national federation that a difference in quantity becomes a difference in kind. (Nicolaidis and Howse 2001, 176)

In a recent article, Moravcsik (2002) builds on this reasoning to argue that fears of a European superstate are greatly exaggerated because of both the administrative and fiscal weaknesses of the EU and the constitutional checks on its role. Far from being a bureaucratic behemoth, the Commission is a small institution with limited staff and highly circumscribed resources. It is limited mostly to regulatory programs that must be administered through national governments. Building on his analysis of the confederal nature of the EU, Moravcsik argues that the safeguards of democratic accountability are equal to the task. Through the Council, policy decisions are made by elected national officials who are instructed and recalled with relative ease. Though more direct popular accountability via the EP is not negligible, state-centric representation through popularly elected national governments is the central mechanism of democratic control. Moravcsik admits that EU institutions (particularly the Commission and the Courts) often operate in a semiautonomous fashion that is insensitive to popular democratic control. But this, he argues, is consistent with trends to delegate politically sensitive administrative and technical tasks to counter-majoritarian institutions at the national level as well. It is hypocritical to criticize the trend at the European level and ignore it at the national level. Finally, if democrats are still not satisfied, he argues that they should also consider the significant barriers to extending meaningful democratic participation to the European level. The scope of competences and powers at the EU level remain circumscribed and of low salience to voters. High salience political issues like education, healthcare, and law and order remain the prerogatives of national governments. It is highly unlikely, therefore, that citizens will participate significantly at the EU level.

Consequently, Moravcsik argues that the *need* for more direct popular control at the European level is limited, and the current confederal mechanisms for achieving democratic accountability are *adequate* and *appropriate.* His argument is compelling and we mostly agree with his interpretation of the 'facts' of the case. However, we think he is overly sanguine about the lack of a democratic deficit. By contrast, we would make at least four counterarguments:

1. The implications of regulatory action at the European level are more far-reaching than Moravcsik implies despite the circumscribed character of the EU's administrative capacity and resources. A basic feature of a 'regulatory state' like the EU is that its decisions can have far-reaching consequences without extensive administrative capacity or fiscal resources.
2. While the scope of European action may be limited to market integration and related 'spillover' issues, these issues spillover into almost everything and have ramifications that penetrate down to the immediate personal welfare of national citizens. Thus, we would argue that he overestimates the degree to which European integration creates merely low-salience politics that can be bracketed through counter-majoritarian 'technical' institutions.
3. Moravcsik's analogy of semiautonomous European institutions with national level counter-majoritarian institutions underestimates the ways that European institutions alter the relationship to popular sovereignty.
4. Moravcsik provides a mostly static description of European integration. But the debate about the democratic deficit is mostly about the future and is framed by the historical trajectory of the European project.

Each of these points arises, we argue, because Moravcsik ignores significant federal features of the EU. While we broadly agree with him that the EU is predominantly confederal, we argue that these federal features further provoke the dilemma we described above.

Focusing on points (3) and (4), we begin our analysis with a discussion of the historical trajectory of the European project. Although we avoid a federalist teleology, it cannot be ignored that the trajectory of European integration has been an uneven but unmistakable movement from intergovernmentalism toward federalism. This transition is marked by the increasing expansion and integration of specific competences and general powers at the (con)federal level and, simultaneously, the increasing differentiation of federal competences and powers from member state competences and powers. From this broad perspective, European integration has indeed been a march toward federalism.

The half century of European integration is a dramatic example of the expansion of functional competences and the progressive integration and consolidation of these functional competences under general EU powers. This process began with the creation, under the European Coal and Steel Community (ECSC), of a Common Assembly, a Council of Ministers, a High Court, and a High Authority. In 1957, two additional communities—the European Economic Community and Euratom—were created and the three communities were brought together as the European Communities. A single Parliament and a single court—the European Court of Justice (ECJ)—were created for the three communities. Each of the communities, however, retained their own commissions and councils until 1967, when they were merged into a single commission and council. The new Parliamentary Assembly expanded the powers of the Common Assembly, but remained largely consultative. Its members were appointed by national legislatures until 1979. The 1987 Single European Act strengthened the Parliament's power to amend legislation. The Maastricht Treaty, ratified in 1992, further consolidated functional competences under general powers by creating the EU to replace the previous communities and to incorporate the European Councils and Summits. It also further expanded the EP's veto power over legislation.[4] Moreover, the Amsterdam Treaty in 1997 expanded Parliament's legislative powers by requiring *co-decision* with the Council on various policy domains. One of the characteristics of this march toward federalism, however, is its unevenness. In some policy areas (e.g. trade, competition), the EU is strongly federal, while in others (e.g. foreign policy, taxation) it remains predominantly intergovernmental.

Confederations, as Lister (1996) puts it, have a *raison d'être*—a joint interest that binds member states together. However, this interest is conceived of as a *joint or mutual interest* of the respective member states. By contrast, federation implies the definition of a distinctive federal interest that transcends these individual member state interests. The goal of creating a 'Common Market,' as outlined by the Rome Treaty, was a much more ambitious policy of integrating the economies of Europe by comprehensively reducing trade barriers across the board. Integration became a *raison d'être* that bound its members together with a mutual interest. In the mid-1980s, the Delors Commission advanced a more integrated conception of the market—the Single Market Plan. The four freedoms of movement (goods, services, people, capital) upon which the Single Market is built are at least as federalist in conception as the market created by the US Interstate Commerce Clause.

[4] As Kreppel writes of the European Parliament: 'In the nearly thirty years following the first significant increase in its powers (the 1970 Budget Act), the EP has been transformed from a consultative assembly to a true legislative body (Kreppel 2002, 89).

Though still incomplete, monetary integration pushes this single market even further toward being a reality.

To argue that confederal arrangements are an adequate and appropriate match for the existing scope and depth of European integration is to downplay that the trajectory of political and economic integration is toward federal integration. Why would this matter? We argue that it matters for at least three reasons. First, as institutionalists like Fligstein and Stone Sweet (2002) would suggest, market integration has a feedback effect on political integration. Since the consequences of market integration are not yet fully worked out—and are among the most federal features of European integration—we ought to expect these feedback effects to continue into the future. Second, as Weiler (1990–1) argues, the process of integration often proceeds as the outcome of incremental technical adaptation to the details of market integration. It is well known, for instance, that the European Court of Justice established the supremacy of European law over national law through a series of legal decisions scarcely noticed at the time by the public. Third, and less well appreciated, an interesting dynamic relates confederal and federal institutions. Counterintuitively, when member states agree on policy measures, confederation can actually facilitate more centralized policy regimes.[5] The reason is that if states feel themselves to be in political control, and they agree on policy objectives, then little stands in the way of centralization. Yet should member state perspectives change, these centralized policy regimes may be difficult to simply disband or significantly modify. They become powerful institutional legacies. Even if confederal institutions are currently adequate to govern scope and depth of European integration, the historical trajectory and institutional dynamics of integration make it reasonable for citizens to anticipate a growing mismatch in the future. The debate about the democratic deficit is about the future as well as the present.

2. Neither Confederal nor Federal

Our analysis suggests that the EU may be predominantly confederal. But such a discrete assessment fails to recognize the steps that the EU has taken towards federation. After all, the surprise of European integration is not that it is still relatively weak in comparison with US federalism. The surprise is that it has moved in a limited number of areas toward federalism at all. These features are downplayed by Moravscik and lead him, in our opinion, to underestimate a real democratic dilemma. In moving part way toward federalism, the EU has *sharpened* the dilemma of democratic representation.

[5] See Sbragia (in Ansell and Di Palma 2004) for an example in air pollution policy.

We must first clarify the distinctions between confederalism and federalism in the European context. Federalism implies at least two levels of government, with government at both levels organized around a set of general competences and powers.[6] Federalism, however, is not simply a delegation of competences from below, but a division of powers. General competences at both levels are organized under executive, legislative, and judicial powers. The relative autonomy of each level also implies that each level must have its own direct source of popular sovereignty. While a federal state typically retains channels of corporate representation of its member states, the federal level of a federation also establishes a direct relationship with citizens. This relationship provides direct as opposed to indirect legitimation to federal authority, giving the federal government the authority to directly intervene with *federal* citizens.

The confederal model is an intermediate form between intergovernmental and federal systems. Confederal models of governance are similar to federations in that they organize general competences (powers) at two levels of government.[7] In a confederation, however, decisions made at the higher level of government are made through a representative process controlled by its corporate members (e.g. different member states). These decisions may be binding on members and the confederal level may enforce collective decisions by imposing sanctions on recalcitrant members. But two conditions delimit confederal authority. First, its decisions have no form of legitimation independent of the voting procedures of its corporate members; second, although its decisions are binding for individual citizens, it has no authority or capacity to intervene directly to sanction or administer these decisions. The relationship between the confederal level and citizens remains an indirect one, exclusively mediated by the member states.

We distinguish confederalism and federalism further. In both confederations and federations, member states are represented as *corporate actors* in decision-making processes at the confederal and federal levels. In confederations, corporate representation is the *exclusive* mode of representation. In federations, corporate representation becomes one mode of representation alongside individual representation. Typically, this requires a *bicameral* legislative system.

[6] Perhaps the most commonly cited definition of federalism is Riker's: 'A constitution is federal if (1) two levels of government rule the same land and people, (2) each level has at least one area of action in which it is autonomous, and (3) there is some guarantee (even though merely a statement in the constitution) of the autonomy of each government in its own sphere (Riker 1964, 11).

[7] For two good discussions distinguishing confederalism and federalism (with reference to the EU), see Lister (1996) and Kincaid (1999).

In judging the EU by these criteria, we see that it has some features of both a confederation and a federation. For the most part, representation in the EU is dominated by the corporate representation of member states through the Council of Ministers. Although states are represented in the US through the Senate, the corporate basis of that representation has gradually weakened (i.e. senators are no longer appointed by state legislatures). Not only is corporate representation much stronger in the EU, but the powers of the second chamber, the EP, are weaker than those of their US counterpart. Critically, however, members of the EP are now *directly elected*. Thus the EU has a measure of direct legitimation. (However, it is often pointed out that this direct election is constrained by the fact that elections are still 'state-based.') Furthermore, the co-decision requirement that Parliament must agree on legislation with the Council in many issue areas makes the bicameral legislative system a reality. Still, the confederal quality of EU legislation is suggested by the way in which it is enacted in the form of directives that must be transposed into member state laws by national legislatures and in the form of framework directives that give national legislatures discretion in how to write these laws.

By federal standards, however, the integration of general powers and the subordination of functional competences to these general powers remain weak. The EU lacks a full-fledged 'government,' which is the agency of general powers. Parliament's right of censure and oversight over the Commission has recently been expanded, but the Commission retains the right to initiate legislation. In part this reflects the enduringly technocratic nature of EU activities. Although the Commission is a 'collegium' and hence provides some of the general and integrative role of a government, the appointment of Commissioners by the Council accentuates the delegative and technocratic status of their role. The separation of the EU Presidency from the Presidency of the Commission, with the former setting broad European policy priorities (but lacking executive power), and the latter implementing directives and regulations, fragments the government. The functional organization of the Council, the intermittent nature of its meetings, and the rotating six-month basis of the EU Presidency add to this fragmentation.

How does this amalgam of confederal and federal features sharpen the dilemma of democratic representation? In a strictly confederal system, each state has a veto over confederal policy, keeping the sovereignty of member states intact. In such a system, representation through national governments is sufficient to provide for popular control over policy outcomes. With the introduction of a qualified majority voting, however, this tight link between popular sovereignty and policy outcomes is weakened. The move from unanimity voting to majority voting increases the relative autonomy of the federal level and creates the basis for a distinctive 'federal' interest. But it also creates the possibility that a duly elected majority at the national level can be overruled by a qualified majority at the federal level.

Resolving this situation by arguing that it is analogous to the creation of counter-majoritarian institutions at the domestic level, as Moravcsik does, is misleading. At the national level, counter-majoritarian institutions are certainly designed to be less sensitive to democratic pressures. These institutions are typically buffered from the electoral cycle by appointing judges or commissioners for long terms. Nevertheless, when they are appointed, they are appointed by elected officials who represent democratically-established majorities. This is true of central banks and Supreme Court justices and commissioners of regulatory agencies.

Of course, there is a solution to the dilemma created by qualified majority voting: to create a federal majority. This is achieved by creating a representative system at the federal level that represents citizens directly in proportion to population.[8] The EP, in fact, does precisely this and the strengthening of Parliament through the co-decision procedure greatly increases its strength vis-à-vis the Council. However, then we confront the point that many scholars, including Moravcsik, have made about the weakness of political mobilization and representation at the European level. Without strong European parties and lacking a European *demos* and a well-defined European public sphere, how are meaningful majorities to be created at the European level? A similar situation prompted the framers of the US Constitution to create the electoral college—hardly a viable strategy for modern Europe.

The point therefore is that qualified majority voting (a move toward federalism) creates a representational gap that the strengthening of the EP (also a move toward federalism) does not fully plug. It could be resolved by a return to more strictly confederal arrangements or by a further strengthening of federalism. As this analysis suggests, the EU is currently pulled between the logic of confederation and federation. Our expectation is that neither reversion to strictly confederal status nor full federal consolidation is likely in the near future. Instead, we expect European policymaking and institution-building to continue to reflect the hybrid nature of EU institutions.

In the second half of this paper, we return to our opening theme of European food safety regulation in order to evaluate the dynamics of European federalism. This policy area has received great attention in Europe following several food-related controversies, most notably mad cow disease and the introduction of genetically modified organisms (GMOs). European and national regulatory responses to these issues facilitate an understanding of hybrid forms of institutional emergence and interdependence.

[8] Of course, Qualified Majority Voting (QMV) in the Council does take population into account, though QMV remains strongly skewed in favor of small states.

3. Food Safety Regulation and Comparative Federalism

Food safety regulation provides a useful lens into the workings of European governance and into the comparative dynamics of federalism for two reasons. First, recent disputes over food safety in the EU illustrate the tensions within the complex multilevel institutional arrangements in Europe. During the 1990s, the public crisis over mad cow disease and the vociferous debates about genetically modified foods strained the existing governance model and led to significant institutional reform at both the European level and at the national level. Second, our examination of food safety policy sheds significant light on how macro-institutional differences in the multilevel systems of the US and Europe shape policymaking dynamics. The analysis we provide has mostly been elaborated elsewhere, but not in a framework examining its implications for patterns of federalism.[9]

On initial inspection, the types of institutional reform demanded in response to the crisis of mad cow disease fit nicely into a narrative of federalization.[10] Two developments, in particular, can be read as expanding the federal (European) role in the regulation of food safety. The first is the newly assertive role of the EP, which investigated and criticized the Commission for its handling of the mad cow issue. Under the threat of EP censure, the Commission reorganized a variety of its overly compartmentalized Directorates-General (DGs). This assertiveness reflects the increasing power of the Parliament in the EU, a key criteria for federalization, and its ability to hold European-level institutions accountable to the public. Before the expansion of its co-decision powers in 1993, the Parliament had very little legislative influence, as the Commission and Council of Ministers retained all agenda-setting and gatekeeping functions. The co-decision procedure increases face-to-face negotiation between the EP and the Council of Ministers and provides an unconditional power of veto for the Parliament.[11]

The second major shift is the creation of an independent European agency, the European Food Safety Authority (EFSA), which provides more independent scientific advice on food safety matters. From the perspective of the

[9] In our account, we draw heavily on contributions to Ansell and Vogel (forthcoming).

[10] See Keleman (2004) for an account that stresses the federalizing impetus of these reforms. The increasing role of the European institutions in food safety regulation supports Keleman's theory of regulatory federalism in the EU. He argues that the creation of independent regulatory agencies demonstrates the Commission's willingness to delegate competences to 'independent' agencies as a way to expand the EU's regulatory capacity in the food safety domain without eclipsing national regulatory authorities.

[11] For an analysis of the effect of co-decision on the relationship between the Commission and the Parliament in the case of the debate over GMO labeling, see Burns (2004). She argues that co-decision has reduced the power of the Commission relative to the Parliament, but that informal contact between the two institutions mitigates this power discrepancy.

federalization narrative, the EFSA is analogous to the US Food and Drug Administration (FDA). Upon further analysis, it is evident that the EFSA is not the equivalent of the FDA in capacity or authority. We shall return to this point below. Nevertheless, the EFSA represents a step towards creating a system of European agencies with federal competences and a step away from the residual features of intergovernmentalism (e.g. a collegial executive) that characterize the Commission. Most importantly, the EFSA creates the institutional capacity to represent a distinctly European perspective on food safety issues.

4. A Brief History of Food Safety Regulation in Europe (before Mad Cow)

To understand both the Parliament's criticism of the Commission and the meaning of the creation of an independent food safety authority, it is necessary to understand the previous institutional arrangements through which food safety risk analysis were conducted. Food-related disputes have taken a prominent role in European market integration from the outset of the integration project. Trends for both decentralization and centralization have characterized the regulation of foodstuffs in Europe since the 1960s. In the earlier harmonization phase, the European Community tried to create common standards that would eliminate tariff and nontariff barriers to trade. Specifically, the Commission issued numerous directives specifying the composition of all food products. If harmonization was disputed, the ECJ would render a ruling. However, this approach proved to be a difficult and cumbersome way to integrate the market. Citizens wanted to preserve the traditional ingredients of local foods rather than alter their makeup for the purpose of meeting EC labeling standards.

A second phase, stemming from the *Cassis de Dijon* ruling in 1979, ushered in the principle of mutual recognition, a process that facilitated integration without requiring complex negotiations for harmonization. Mutual recognition allowed countries to monitor and regulate only those foods produced within their own borders. In respecting and accepting the norms of their neighbors, many complained that this would result in a downward spiral of food safety standards across Europe. Therefore, even under mutual recognition, the Commission had to play an important role in evaluating different food safety standards. To do this, they used a system of scientific and political committees that epitomized what has come to be called the comitology system (Vos 2000).

Comitology exemplifies the institutional accommodations that reconcile federal level action with intergovernmental power. Committees made up of member state representatives and chaired by the Commission enable a dialogue between the EU and national administrations on matters of policy implementation. It has been described as the 'constitutional fudge' that holds the EU together (Joerges and Neyer 1997). In food safety, the two most important committees were *The Standing Committee on Foodstuffs*—a political committee composed of national representatives—and the *Scientific Committee on Foodstuffs*, which was composed of scientists drawn from different member states. This comitology system was a form of confederalism in that both political and scientific membership on these committees was based on national representation.

5. Reform at the European Level

The Parliamentary inquiry into the BSE scandal in 1996 and the EP's threat of censure pointed to the comitology system as the source of both nontransparent decision-making and of undue British influence. The EP also faulted the Commission for the complexity of its regulatory processes and its underspecified competencies in managing the BSE issue. To reestablish European food safety authority on a sound and legitimate basis, the Commission requested that three well-regarded scientists—Philip James, Fritz Kemper, and Gerard Pascal—make suggestions for institutional reform. They proposed a new EFSA with enhanced powers for both risk assessment and management that would compare favorably in its scope of powers with the US FDA (James *et al.* 1999). Risk assessment is the evaluation of likelihood and severity of potential hazards, whereas risk management is the regulation and enforcement of policies designed to reduce risks. Member states were opposed to giving the new agency risk management capabilities, thus illustrating the limits to the process of federalization.

By contrast, the FDA has broad authority to conduct both risk assessment and management. This more comprehensive authority encourages public confidence in the FDA, because assessing risks and then controlling them are kept under the jurisdiction of one agency.[12] The EFSA is designed only to provide independent scientific risk assessment to a fragmented policymaking system. Risk management responsibilities remain within the Commission and with national governments. Meanwhile, authority within the Commission was reorganized to enhance the capacity and independence of the Commission to engage in risk assessment and management. Consumer protection functions were consolidated in a new DG for Consumer Protection and Health (DG SANCO), an expanded DG XXIV that would be

[12] FDA/USDA *US Food Safety System Country Report*, March 3, 2000. However, we note that food safety authority is also fragmented in the USA For example, meat inspection is the purview of a separate department within the USDA.

responsible for scientific assessment and consultation. With these reforms, the Commission hopes to distance the scientific committees from external political pressures and to streamline the decision-making process.

Thus, the mad cow crisis has led to a more influential Parliament, an independent European agency, and a more autonomous Commission. Each of these steps can be interpreted as steps in a federal direction. Yet they are incremental steps clearly limited by the pull of the confederalism. Although EFSA is designed, in part, to break with the type of confederalism represented by the comitology system and to create a dedicated in-house risk assessment capacity at the European level, the actual effect is rather unclear.[13] The question of 'who' comprises the new EFSA is still a matter of contention. While the agency will have about 150 employees, 70 of whom are scientists, the EFSA will continue to utilize external scientific expertise organized through committees (as does the FDA).[14] But how will these new committees be selected? Will they represent all nations, as one might expect if confederal arrangements were continued? The new rules for committee selection do not say that all nations are required to be represented, only that the EFSA must consult with national ministries. In comparison to the 9,000 employees of the FDA, the EFSA is very much an embryonic organization.[15]

One can argue that institutional reform following the mad cow crisis has moved, in an incremental and highly circumscribed way, in a federal direction. Yet to understand the larger institutional dynamics, it is also important to investigate institutional reforms that occurred at the national level. Similar to demands for better management of the mad cow crisis at the European level, national capacity to respond to public health concerns were also strengthened. In fact, the pattern of reform at the national level was similar to what occurred at the European level. Institutional reforms sought to consolidate food safety authority, to resolve certain perceived conflicts-of-interest between producer and consumer interests, and to increase independence and transparency of food safety.

6. Reform at the National Level

As governance in the EU was restructured to deal more effectively with regulating food, so too were member countries securing domestic institutions

[13] See Majone's (2000) discussion of the credibility crisis of European agencies. He argues that they must maintain the network model of governance that links them to national governments and that US independent regulatory commission model is not appropriate in the context of the EU.

[14] European Food Safety Authority, <*http://www.efsa.eu.int*>.

[15] US Food and Drug Administration, <*http://www.fda.gov/opacom/faqs/faqs.html*>.

against future lapses in food safety regulation. Public trust in foreign standards under the guidelines of mutual recognition also waned as consumers felt that health concerns took a backseat to continuing market integration. At the epicenter of the mad cow crisis, the UK, a new Food Standards Agency (FSA) was created in 2000 to take food safety authority out of the Ministry of Agricultural, Fisheries, and Food. In response to renationalization pressures, the new agency was intended to provide greater capacity for independent risk assessment and management at the national level. In Germany and France, similar reforms were also undertaken. However, the new French and German agencies were intended (like the EFSA) only to provide independent scientific risk assessment (and not management). Therefore, with respect to the federalization thesis, we see that far from relocating authority from the national level to the European level, the hybrid perspective allows us to see that food safety authority at both levels of government has been strengthened.

We must also underscore that the major difference between the American and the European system of food regulation has hardly changed. Most of the scope for risk management (e.g. inspection, enforcement) remains with national governments. In the US case, state level institutions also possess significant competence in risk management. In fact, a form of subsidiarity also exists in the US. County public health agencies are the first line of defense in the US public health system, and they are responsible for many of the risk management functions. State regulators can set more rigorous food safety standards than the FDA. For instance, following an outbreak of E.Coli from lettuce traced back to Fancy Cutt Farms in Hollister, California in 1996, the California State Department of Health Services increased inspections and eventually set the industry standard for field-sanitation regulation.[16] Overall, states play an active role in policy implementation and can impose stricter regulations when they see fit. Nevertheless, the USA has significantly more risk management authority and capacity on the federal level than does the EU.

7. Policy Dynamics: EU Versus US

With the capacity for independent risk assessment increasing at both the national and the European levels, we argue that risk assessment will increasingly be drawn into a relationship of interdependence and de facto shared powers. It is highly likely that the relationship between the EFSA and

[16] Environment, Health and Safety Online, <*http://www.ehso.com/ehshome/FoodSafety/FoodSafetyVegtables.htm*>.

national risk assessment agencies will be partially conflictual. For instance, EFSA can provide alternative assessments of food safety standards that may contradict national assessments. Hence, neither will be able to act authoritatively without considering the position of the other. Our hybrid perspective suggests that the pressures for federal and intergovernmental responses will be simultaneous and not mutually exclusive.

As we described earlier, food regulation has been a core issue in the market integration process. Over the course of regulatory policymaking, a central aspect of 'multilevel dynamics' has been the process of achieving either common standards or mutual recognition. As noted by Vogel, the process of accommodating multiple food safety standards has been a dynamic of 'trading up' to higher standards. In examining this dynamic process in consumer and environmental sector of the EU, Vogel argues that greener or more consumer friendly countries, like Germany and the Netherlands, set stricter regulatory agendas that most member states agree to in an effort to preserve the single market. The end result is a higher minimum standard for all EU countries.

In general, trading up suggests that the dynamic of multilevel market integration leads to a convergence on higher standards. This has contributed to a divergence in the regulatory standards of the EU and the US.[17] In addition to this policy dynamic, there is another mechanism that encourages a divergence between the EU and the USA that relates back to our comparison of the FDA. As Skogstad has argued in her comparison of European and North American food safety regulation, the policy style of North American food safety regulation is technocratic. As an independent regulatory commission, the FDA has resisted attempts to expand its consideration of risks beyond scientific criteria. By contrast, she argues that the EU is more sensitive to 'public opinion,' both by design and inclination. By design, the Commission is more reflective of the political interests of its member states. The Standing Committee on Foodstuffs even institutionalized this political input. But the Commission is also political by inclination in the sense that it is sensitive to its own legitimacy and to claims of a democratic deficit. As Skogstad argues, the Commission focuses strongly on 'output legitimacy' where decisions are seen as acceptable, either in the court of public opinion or by member nations.

Taken together, the trading up dynamic and the greater sensitivity of the Commission to political influence contribute to a divergence in the dynamics of food safety regulation in the Europe and the USA. The trade conflict over beef hormones and GMOs between the EU and the USA illustrates the implications of these different policymaking approaches and institutional

[17] See, for instance, Young's discussion of genetically modified foods (2000).

structures. In order to restore consumer trust in food safety in the EU, European (supranational) regulatory authorities must negotiate with member states to arrive at a comprehensive agenda for risk analysis. Thus policymaking is ultimately more *overtly* political in nature. Among Europeans there is strong political support for banning the import of meat from farm animals treated with natural or synthetic growth hormones. The EU has also enacted severe restrictions against the introduction of genetically modified foods due to the uncertainty of long-term health effects of agricultural biotechnology. On the other hand, the USA embraces agricultural biotechnology and currently has more than fifty genetically engineered crops on the US market.[18] Bernauer refers to the difference between the EU and the USA as 'regulatory polarization,' where differing regulatory styles (cultures) and various interest group pressures contribute to diverging policy responses. The EFSA and national food safety agencies are helping the public to recover from the BSE crisis and are improving institutional transparency. Conversely, Americans have placed relatively more trust in their federal regulatory agencies (at least at this time) and accept that decisions have been weighed against detailed scientific evaluations and risk assessments.

8. Conclusion

The status of the EU as a federation is a contemporary topic of significant dispute for which the USA (and other federal states like Canada, Germany, and Switzerland) provides an important comparative yardstick. While many discuss the type of federalism the EU should acquire (e.g. cooperative or dual),[19] we argue that this federal yardstick is both a useful and a misleading analytical framework for describing the contemporary EU. It is useful to the extent that it calls attention to distinctive institutional logics for organizing power and authority in Europe. It is less useful, and sometimes misleading, when these logics are seen as pure 'ideal types' that neglect an interpretation of political change as a composite of several types that frequently shifts over time. One can look at other Community actions beyond food safety regulation to see that the EU embodies hybrid models of governance unique to this type of ongoing cross-national integration.

The recent signing of a European Constitutional Treaty on October 29, 2004 sheds new light on the debates about Europe's institutional dynamics. The European Constitution marks a milestone in the legitimation of European institutions and EU law, allowing for more transparency and

[18] See the discussion by Bernauer (2003). [19] See Borzel and Hosli (2003).

democracy. Article I-7 of the Constitution establishes the EU as a veritable European state with a legal personality and corporate existence distinct from its member states—just as the USA is a separate state from New York or California. Thus the EU can now enter into treaties in its own right. Furthermore, Article I-6 clarifies that the EU Constitution and laws have primacy over national constitutions and domestic law. If ratified by all twenty-five members, the ECJ would be responsible for interpreting the Constitution and EU laws for many noneconomic policy areas currently under national or intergovernmental jurisdiction, such as civil and criminal law and foreign and security policy. In certain policy areas, such as customs union, competition rules or asylum agreements, the EU would have exclusive competence. Additionally, the Constitution establishes a new voting procedure in the Council that institutionalizes a form of concurrent majorities. In the new system, EU laws would be agreed upon by a 'double majority' of member states and population. A new EU law must have the backing of at least fifteen of twenty-five member states *and* represent at least 65 percent of the population. This new procedure is an important step in more transparently representing a federal majority.

However, as Renaud Dehousse develops strongly in this volume, there are also limits to a truly federal interpretation of the new Constitution. In fact, many say that the current draft only consolidates previous treaties of the EU or institutionalizes rules already in existence without going much further in a federal direction. Its 800 pages delineate the competences of each EU institution and carry over the *acquis communautaire* from the old EU. For example, the EP still operates under co-decision with the Council, without any expansion of power to initiate legislation. The EU Constitution's limited federal capacity suggests that it is not comparable to the Constitution of the USA. According to Justice Stephen Breyer (2004) of the US Supreme Court, the fundamental difference between the two Constitutions is one of differing purposes: 'The US Constitution was drawn up by a rather small number of representatives of thirteen states with little history and a common culture, who were trying to create a single government where none had previously existed. The European document has a completely different purpose. It is the work of 200 delegates from twenty-eight different countries with long histories and more divergent cultures, who set themselves the task, not of creating a new single government where none had previously existed, but rather of making modest changes in existing institutions so as to allow that government to function better.' Ratification of the EU Constitution will be turned over in most member states to its citizens via national referenda. Failing to ratify the Constitution in just one member state would certainly call attention to the tensions that exist between an intergovernmental, a confederal, and a federal Europe.

References

Ansell, C. and Vogel, D. (forthcoming). *Why the Beef? European Food Safety Regulation as Contested Governance*. Cambridge, MA: MIT Press.

—— and DiPalma, G. (2004). *Restructuring Territoriality: Europe and the United States Compared.* Cambridge: Cambridge University Press.

Bernauer, T. (2003). *Genes, Trade and Regulation: The Seeds of Conflict in Food Biotechnology*. Princeton, NJ: Princeton University Press.

Borzel, T. and O Hosli, M. (2003). 'Brussels between Bern and Berlin: Comparative Federalism Meets the European Union', *Governance: An International Journal of Policy, Administration, and Institutions,* 16/2: 179–202.

Breyer, S. G. (2004). 'Europe's Constitution is Welcome, but Very Different from its US Counterpart', Special Report: The Enlarged European Union. *European Affairs: A Publication of the European Institute.*

Burns, C. (2004). 'Co-decision and the European Commission: a Study of Declining Influence?', *Journal of European Public Policy,* 1/1 (February): 1–18.

Fligstein, N. and Stone Sweet, A. (2002). 'Constructing Politics and Markets: An Institutionalist Account of European Integration', *American Journal of Sociology,* 107/5: 1206–43.

Forsyth, M. (1981). *Unions of States*. Leicester: Leicester University Press.

Halberstam, D. (2001). 'Comparative Federalism and the Issue of Commandeering', in Nicolaidis, K. and Howse, R. (eds.), *The Federal Vision: Legitimacy and Levels of Governance in the United States and the European Union*. Oxford: Oxford University Press.

James, P., Kemper, F., and Pascal, G. (1999). *A European Food and Public Health Authority: The Future of Scientific Advice in the EU*. Brussels: DG Health and Consumer Protection, 74 pp.

Jasanoff, S. (1997). 'Civilization and Madness: The Great BSE Scare of 1996', *Public Understanding of Science,* 6: 221–32.

Joerges, C and Neyer, J. (1997). 'Transforming Strategic Interaction into Deliberative Problem-Solving: European Comitology in the Foodstuffs Sector', *Journal of European Public Policy,* 4/4: 609–25.

Keleman, R. D. (2004). *The Rules of Federalism: Institutions and Regulatory Politics in the EU and Beyond.* Cambridge, MA: Harvard University Press.

Kincaid, J. (1999). 'Confederal Federalism and Citizen Representation in the European Union,' in J. Brzinski, T. Lancaster, and C. Tuschhoff (eds.), *Compounded Representation in Western European Federation*. London: Frank Cass.

Kreppel, A. (2002). *The European Parliament and Supranational Party System*. Cambridge: Cambridge University Press.

Lister, F. K. (1996). *The European Union, the United Nations, and the Revival of Confederal Governance*. Westport, CT: Greenwood Press.

Majone, G. (2000). 'The Credibility Crisis of Community Regulation', *Journal of Common Market Studies,* 38/2: 273–302.

Moravcsik, A. (2002). 'In Defence of the 'Democratic Deficit': Reassessing Legitimacy in the European Union', *Journal of Common Market Studies,* 40/4: 603–24.

Nicolaïdis, K. and Howse, R. (eds.) (2001). *The Federal Vision: Legitimacy and Levels of Governance in the United States and the European Union*. Oxford: Oxford University Press.

Neyer, J. (2000). 'The Regulation of Risks and the Power of the People: Lessons from the BSE Crisis', *European Integration Online Papers,* 4/6: 16 pp.

Riker, W. K. (1964). *Federalism: Origin, Operation, Significance*. New York: Little, Brown.

Skogstad, G. (forthcoming). 'Regulating Food Safety Risks in the European Union and North America: Distinctive Policy Styles', in C. Ansell and D. Vogel (eds.), *Why the Beef? The Contested Governance of European Food Safety Regulation.* Cambridge, MA: MIT Press.

Vogel, D. (1995). *Trading Up: Consumer and Environmental Regulation in a Global Economy*. Cambridge, MA: Harvard University Press.

Vos, E. (2000). 'EU Food Safety Regulation in the Aftermath of the BSE Crisis', *Journal of Consumer Policy,* 23: 227–55.

Weiler, J. H. H. (1990–1). 'The Transformation of Europe', *Yale Law Journal*, 100: 2403–484.

Young, A. (2003). 'Political Transfer and 'Trading Up'?: Transatlantic Trade in Genetically Modified Food and US Politics', *World Politics,* 55: 457–84.

18

The EU 'Polity' and the Europeanization of National Polities

VIVIEN A. SCHMIDT

European integration, understood here as the process of building a European polity, has had a tremendous impact on European member states through the process of Europeanization, or European Union (EU) member state adaptation to European integration.[1] Comparisons with the development of United States federalism in this sphere cannot do justice to the major changes experienced by EU member states. This is because, unlike the American states, EU member states before European integration have been highly developed nation-states in their own right, with democracies that evolved differently in terms of institutional structures, policymaking processes, and political representation systems. Europeanization has radically altered its member states' governance practices by shifting the focus of governmental power and authority upward to the EU, by moving the locus of interest access and influence from national capitals to Brussels, and by subordinating the expression of partisan votes and political voice to the EU's consensus-oriented, interest-based politics. Europeanization as discussed in this chapter, in short, has exerted a causal influence along the lines of two of the six mechanisms outlined in the introduction to this volume: on the institutional legacies of European member states and on the defense and extension of democracy.

Europeanization has not affected all of its member states in the same way, however. It has varied depending upon the governance practices of EU member states. These run along a continuum from more 'simple' polities

[1] There are many different ways of defining Europeanization (see Olsen 2002; Radaelli 2003; Radaelli and Featherstone 2002). Sometimes, Europeanization is defined in such a way as to encompass the process of European integration as a whole, with both a bottom up influence of national actors on EU policies and practices and a top down influence on national policies and practices (see Cowles *et al.* 2001). Other times, Europeanization is differentiated from European integration, as largely the top-down influence of the EU on national policies and practices. This is the way I use it here (Schmidt 2002*b*, Chapter 1; see also Ladrech 1994; Radaelli 2003).

such as Britain and France—where power, access, and voice have traditionally been channeled through a single authority as a result of unitary institutional structures, statist policymaking processes, and majoritarian representation systems—to more 'compound' polities such as Germany and Italy—where power, access, and voice have traditionally been more diffused through multiple authorities as a result of federal or regionalized structures, corporatist processes, and proportional representation. The EU, as a highly compound polity, has had a disruptive impact on all national polities, but it has had a somewhat greater disruptive impact on more simple national polities than on more compound national polities, largely as a matter of institutional 'fit.'

The problems for the EU member states, however, are not so much that governance practices have changed in response to Europeanization, and more so in simple than in compound national polities. Rather, it is that national ideas about democracy have largely not changed, as national leaders continue to project traditional visions of democracy to a public which, in consequence, is left in confusion over who is responsible for formulating EU and national policies, who is in control of their implementation, and who can be held accountable for them. The failure of national leaders to engage national publics in discourse and deliberation about the effects of Europeanization on the polity is the source of a national democratic deficit which is arguably more significant than the oft-mentioned deficit at the EU level.

National leaders' failure to communicate fully with regard to Europeanization, in short, has ensured that popular ideas about national democracy have not kept pace with EU-driven changes in national institutions. This is especially problematic for simple polities, where the challenge to traditional democratic practices and ideas is greater than in compound polities. But although national leaders' ability to speak to the issues in simple polities is potentially greater than in compound polities, given that their greater concentration of authority and voice ensures them a stronger communicative discourse to the general public, they have not chosen to do so. And this has meant a greater democratic challenge to more simple polities than to compound ones, where policy issues rather than 'polity' issues may pose the greatest problems.

The chapter begins with an examination of the institutional comparisons between the EU and the USA and the EU and its member states generally, joined by discussions of the EU's differential impact on its member states. The chapter proceeds with a consideration of the differences in the organizing principles of democracy between the EU and the USA, and the EU and its member states, followed by the differential challenges of the EU to its member states' democratic organizing principles. It concludes with a discussion of EU patterns of discourse and their differential effects on national patterns of discourse both in terms of policy actors' 'coordinative' discourse of policy construction and political actors' 'communicative' discourse of legitimization to the general public. Throughout, two matched pairs of cases are used in illustration: Britain and France as simple polities, Germany and Italy as compound polities. At the same time that these serve to demonstrate the general differences resulting from institutional design, they show that countries with similar institutional designs nevertheless differ greatly on the basis of governance practices and ideas, the result of differences in culture, history, and institutional specificities.

1. Governance in the EU

With its great dispersion of activity through multiple authorities at different levels, in different centers, with different forms of governing, the EU's governance system is more highly 'compound' than those of even the most compound of nation-states, such as the USA.[2] Nevertheless, it bears much resemblance to the USA in its quasi-federal institutional structures, its quasi-pluralist policy formulation processes and its regulatory implementation but not in its consensus-oriented, largely indirect political representation system (see Table 18.1).

With such institutional arrangements, the EU has had a major impact upon its member states' governance activities, by 'federalizing' national institutional structures, 'pluralizing' national policymaking processes, and 'depoliticizing' national representative politics. But the EU has also had a differential impact on national polities depending upon where they can be situated along a continuum from 'simple' to 'compound' in terms of their governance practices (see Figure 18.1).

At one end of the spectrum are countries such as Germany, Spain, Belgium, or Italy. These are 'compound' polities which, like the EU, have a high diffusion of power and authority through federal or regionalized institutional structures; a lower but still significant level of interest access and influence through corporatist policymaking processes, in which certain 'privileged' interests—mainly business and labor—are involved in policy formulation and implementation; and also promote consensus or compromise-oriented politics through proportional systems of representation, despite reasonably partisan patterns of voting and exercising voice.

[2] Although it is useful to contrast the EU with the US, the comparison is problematic because the US is a nation-state, the EU is not. The EU is better considered as a 'regional state,' given shared sovereignty, variable boundaries, composite identity, highly differentiated economy on top of its characteristics as a highly compound polity, which are elucidated below. For more on the EU as regional state, see Schmidt 2004a.

Table 18.1. *Institutional comparisons between the USA and EU*

	Federal structures vertical	Federal structures horizontal	Pluralist formulation	Regulatory implementation	Representative Politics
US	Tipped in favor of center	Separation of powers	Open, political, competitive	Rule-making somewhat open, uniform application	Politicized, direct elections for pres., majoritarian electoral system
EU	Tipped in favor of sub-federal units	Dynamic confusion of powers	Less open, more technical, and apolitical, cooperative	Rule-making less transparent, less open, application more delegated, less uniform	Depoliticized, consensus-oriented, no direct elections for president, proportional and indirect

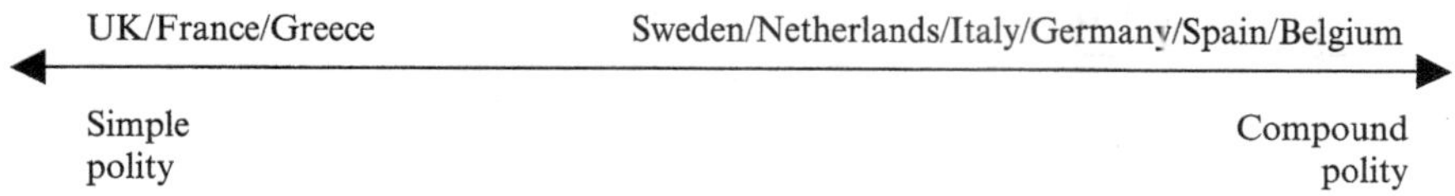

FIGURE 18.1. Countries on a continuum between simple and compound polity.

At the other end are countries such as Britain, France, or Greece. These are more 'simple' polities with a greater concentration of power and authority in unitary institutional structures, a lesser amount of interest access and influence through statist policymaking processes in which the executive has a monopoly on policy formulation but accommodates interests in policy implementation; and a more polarized or conflictual politics in majoritarian representation systems with highly partisan patterns of voting and exercising voice (see Table 18.2).[3]

In between, however, are a range of other countries that often do not fit institutionally as neatly into any one place on the continuum, as one or another institutional element may be more 'simple' even though the polity as a whole functions more in a more compound manner, or vice versa. Thus, for example, while the Netherlands and Sweden are both closer to the compound end of the continuum, given corporatist policymaking processes and consensus-oriented politics, they also exhibit characteristics of more simple polities, since both are unitary states while Sweden also has more majoritarian politics. This enables both countries to act like more simple polities when corporatist processes break down and/or they cannot arrive at consensus, as in the case of the reform of welfare policies in the 1990s (Schmidt 2003). Even in polities that are closer to the simple end of the continuum, however, certain sectors may in fact operate in a more compound manner, as in the case of agricultural policy and certain areas of labor policy in France, or Britain and France in particular aspects of environmental policy. But by the same token, even the most compound of polities act like more simple ones in such sectors as monetary policy and defense and security.

Generally speaking, the EU serves to move all member states' governing practices farther along the continuum toward the compound end. But in doing so, the EU has had a comparatively greater impact on simple polities than on compound ones because of a lack of institutional 'fit.'

[3] The distinctions made here between simple and compound polities are close to those of Lijphart (1984).

TABLE 18.2 *Governance practices in simple and compound polities*

	Institutional structures	Policymaking processes	Representative politics
	Power and authority	Interest access and influence	Orientation and partisanship
Simple Polity (UK, France)	Concentrated	Low	Polarized and politicized
Compound Polity (Germany, Italy)	Diffuse	Moderate	Consensus-oriented and politicized
Supranational Compound Polity (European Union)	Highly diffuse	High	Highly consensus-oriented and nonpoliticized

1.1. Institutional Structures

The institutional structures of the EU bear a certain surface resemblance to the federal structures of the USA, given a vertical division of powers between the EU and its member states and a horizontal separation of powers between EU level institutions (Sbragia 1993; Scharpf 1988). However, the EU's institutional structures are more fully 'multilevel' (Marks *et al.* 1996) and more 'multicentered' (Nicolaides 2001) than those of the USA. The vertical division of powers between EU federal and subfederal levels is more tipped in favor of the subfederal, that is, of the EU member states, than in the USA. The member states in the EU have more independent powers than America's states both in the policy formulation process, to shape as well as to veto legislation, and in the policy implementation process, given their role in transposing EU directives and in administering them (along with the subnational regions). In addition, the horizontal separation of powers in the EU between executive, legislature, and judiciary can be seen as a more 'dynamic confusion of powers' between branches than in the USA, since the directly-elected European Parliament (EP) has a weaker legislative role than the indirectly elected executive in the Council, while the Commission bureaucracy takes on most executive functions and the judiciary overlaps with the executive and legislature in its highly activist role (Schmidt 1999*a*).

The development of the EU's quasi-institutional structures has had a significant impact on all member states' institutional structures, by altering the traditional power and authority of national governments. National executives have become EU level decision-makers in exchange for giving up autonomy in national policymaking. National legislatures have become transposers of EU directives at the same time that they have lost traditional legislative powers of initiative and oversight (Norton 1996). National judiciaries have become interpreters of EU law, and subnational units, implementers of EU regulations, at the same time that both have gained in independence from the national executive (Stone Sweet 2000; Hooghe 1996; Keating and Jones 1995).

For those member states with institutional structures that bear little resemblance to the EU—'simple' polities with great concentration of power in the executive such as traditionally unitary France and Britain—the superimposition of the EU has been disruptive to the traditional distribution of power. In becoming part of the compound EU governance system, the highly autonomous executives in France and Britain have lost a significant amount of power and authority. This is not only because of the shift of decision-making power upward to the EU but also because of the gains in independence by national judiciaries through their empowerment as an enforcement arm of the EU (Conant 2001) and of the regions as a result of their direct relationships with Brussels through the structural and cohesion funds—although such gains in independence are also due to internal dynamics related to increasing judiciary activism and devolutionary reforms (Schmidt 1999*a*). National legislatures, by contrast, have lost even more of their limited powers of initiative and approval, despite the fact that reforms attendant upon the Maastricht Treaty and others subsequently have marginally increased their powers of oversight, particularly in France (Rizzuto 1996).

For those member states with institutional structures that bear greater resemblance to those of the EU—'compound' polities with horizontal and vertical divisions of power such as federal Germany and regionalized Italy—the superimposition of the EU has added another level of governance without as much alteration in the balance of powers among governmental levels and branches. The loss of executive autonomy has not been as significant because the executive has always had to share power and authority with other national and subnational units of government. In a federal state like Germany, the judiciary has always been more independent, while the regions, also represented in the second chamber of the legislature, managed to negotiate a reequilibration of powers at the time of the Maastricht Treaty to make up for the federal executive's EU-related encroachments on the regions' powers (including gaining a place at the table in Brussels on issues of their competence) (Saalfeld 1996). Italy is a more complicated case. Although it is a compound polity with a traditionally powerful but ineffective parliament, highly independent regions as result of devolutionary reforms since the 1970s, and a weak executive, it is technically still a unitary state, with a judiciary traditionally subordinated to the executive. The executive has actually gained in power over other institutional actors even though the regions have also gained in independence as a result of their direct relationship with the EU, while the parliament's EU-related reduction in powers has been balanced out by its greater effectiveness, as the obligation to transpose EU directives has reduced the paralysis and logrolling of the past (Fabbrini 2003). Moreover, the judiciary has gained in independence as a result of its EU-related enforcement powers in addition to internal dynamics related to judiciary activism, much as in France.

1.2. Policymaking Processes

The policymaking processes that infuse these quasi-federal institutional structures also resemble those characteristic of the USA—but again with significant differences from it. The EU's predominant pattern of policymaking , often called the 'community method,' involves a wide range of governmental and nongovernmental actors in a process of joint decision-making akin to the pluralist process of the USA, in which interests are highly involved in policy formulation but largely excluded from policy implementation, which is mainly regulatory, with an arms' length, uniform application of the rules. In the EU, however, the policy formulation process is less open in terms of interest access, given EU civil servants' gatekeeping role; more technical than political in content, given the apolitical status of EU civil servants; and more cooperative than competitive in style, given the EU's consensual culture. In addition, EU regulatory implementation is less transparent in the rule-making process, given the expert-dominated 'comitology' system; more delegated, given the role of member states in transposing and enforcing the rules; and less uniform in application, given national differences in patterns of enforcement.

Here again, EU practices have had a significant impact on its member states. National interests have gained access and influence in an EU policymaking process which involves a much vaster array of actors in a much more complex set of interactions with many more points of entry than that of any member state (Greenwood 2003). This has produced expanding, cross-national networks of interaction among actors who in the past would have had little contact with one another, who are adding to their learning experiences, enhancing their participation at the EU level, and possibly affecting the ways in which they act and interact at the national level. Moreover, national administrations have been pressed into more regulatory and legalistic modes of enforcement—where the rules are applied without exception by independent regulators and judges—from approaches that often relied instead on administrative discretion, joint-regulation, or self-regulation (Majone 1996).

Adaptation to the EU's quasi-pluralist policy formulation process and regulatory implementation has been particularly difficult for simple member state polities, where 'statist' policy formulation traditionally gives little access or influence to organized interests but 'flexible' policy implementation allows for their accommodation, either by making exceptions to the rules as often as not (e.g. France) or limiting the number of rules to allow self-governing arrangements (e.g. Britain). In policy formulation, the learning curve involved in exerting influence at the EU level was arguably the steepest for French interest groups—though they also enjoyed the greatest empowerment in terms of input into such decision-making (Schmidt 1999*b*). British interests, long used to lobbying Parliament but with little direct influence over the executive, needed little additional learning, but also gained in influence (Greenwood 2003). In policy implementation, moreover, both countries had difficulties with the EU regulatory requirements to apply the rules without exception. In France, this was because it denied interests the administrative discretion of the past, leaving those organized interests without access to EU policy formulation little alternative than to engage in confrontation with national authorities, as in the case of truck drivers and public service workers. In Britain, the problem was in the increasing numbers of laws and codified rules which denied organized interests the voluntary rules and self-governing arrangements of the past, leaving them to complain of the increasing rigidity of the public sphere (although this also has national sources) (Schmidt 1999*b*; 2001).

Adaptation to EU policymaking processes has been somewhat easier for more compound member state polities, where corporatist processes have traditionally allowed access and influence in policy formulation and implementation to certain privileged interests, mainly business and labor. The EU's greater openness to interests has simply added even more interests into policy formulation, while policy implementation has not been at issue, since the EU generally allows corporatist implementation to stand. Germany's organized interests have readily adapted to the EU's pluralist policy formulation process, while the country's legalistic patterns of enforcement in areas not covered by corporatism fit well with those of the EU. Italy's organized interests have had more to unlearn rather than to learn, though, given clientelistic patterns of influence-peddling at the national level that are not acceptable at the EU level. In policy implementation, by contrast, its problems are potentially even greater than those of France, given that it has traditionally tended to derogate the rules even more, 90 percent of the time by contrast with France's 50 percent of the time (Schmidt 1999*b*).

1.3. Politics

As the concluding chapter to this volume suggests, the EU is arguably most different from the USA in its system of representative politics. In place of a directly elected presidential system with a strong, directly elected legislature and vigorous political parties in a competitive, majoritarian electoral system, it has the indirect representation afforded by national executives through the Council and the much weaker direct representation of the EP. What is more, unlike the USA, where politics and partisan competition is ever-present, in the EU, partisan differences and political contestion have been submerged by the general quest for interest-based consensus and compromise.

Again, EU practices have had a significant impact on member states. National electoral politics have been complicated by voting in European elections which have often become referenda on national elected officials, especially when they occur in the middle of a government's term in office (Gabel 2001; van der Eijk and Franklin 1996). And national partisan politics remains national since it has little outlet in the EU. Most significantly, national partisan politics have tended to be subordinated, first, to the national interest politics of the Council, as national ministers speak in the Council in the name of the nation rather than as the representative of the governmental majority; second, to the public interest politics of the EP, as members of the EP speak for the general good rather than as representatives of electoral majorities; and, third, to the organized interest politics of the Commission, as citizens exercise voice more effectively when lobbying in Brussels than voting or protesting in national capitals.

Moreover, as with the Europeanization of institutional structures and policymaking processes, so with representative politics: Compound member state polities—where consensus or compromise-oriented politics is the norm, given proportional electoral systems with multiple parties and/or two powerful legislative chambers in which control may be divided between government majority and opposition—are a closer match with the EU's quasi-consensual politics than countries with more simple polities—where more conflictual or polarized politics are the product of majoritarian electoral systems with first-past-the-post elections, two main parties, and only one powerful legislative chamber controlled by the government majority (see Lijphart 1984). In Germany and Italy, the complex negotiations and search for consensus or compromise that go on in the EU are not so different from their own politics, since compromise in negotiated settings is a sine qua non of their proportional representation systems, however partisan the politics. In simple polities such as Britain or France, by contrast, where majoritarian electoral systems generally provide for stronger governments with less need to negotiate or to find consensus, the ambiguity of EU-related compromises is likely to cause greater disaffection in electorates used to more politically demarcated policies and positions.

2. Democracy in the EU

That national governance practices have changed in response to Europeanization, and more in simple national polities than in compound national polities, is not the main problem for EU member state democracies. It is that their ideas about democracy generally have not changed, leaving open questions about the legitimacy of the new practices and confusion over political responsibility, control, and accountability—and more so in simple polities than in compound ones, where the clash is greater between the new practices and traditional ideas about democracy. To see this clearly, however, it is necessary first to consider how democracy in the EU has affected national democracies more generally.

2.1. EU-level Democracy and its General Impact on National Democracy

More ink has been spilt in recent years over the issue of the democratic deficit in the EU than just about any other, so I will not even attempt to lay out the full range of the debates or the literature. Briefly put, increasing numbers of democratic theorists have pointed to a democratic deficit in the EU, mainly because of the lack of 'input democracy' through political participation (Scharpf 2000) and the impossibility of the lack of a collective will and identity (Weiler 1999; Grimm 1995; Habermas 1996) or a common political space (Greven 2000), even though some defend the EU as providing 'output democracy' through effective regulatory governance (Majone 1998) or as no worse than other democracies, given its checks and balances and delegated authorities (Moravcsik 2002).

Most see the main answer to this problem as the development of EU-level institutions that are more participatory and representative, thus the focus on a new Constitutional Treaty intended to strengthen the democratic status of the EU. But this is not so easy.

The central problem for the development of more democratic EU institutions has to do with the fragmented nature of democracy in the EU (see Table 18.3). In national polities, democracy tends to be based on some mix of four main democratic legitimizing mechanisms: government *by* the people through political participation (or 'input democracy'), *of* the people through citizen representation, *for* the people through effective government (or 'output democracy'—including transparency and accountability), and what I call, adding a preposition to the traditional formulation, government *with* the people through interest consultation. In the EU, only two of these four legitimizing mechanisms are very prominent at the supranational level,

TABLE 18.3. *Democratic legitimizing mechanisms in national government and European governance*

	Political participation *by* the people	Citizen representation *of* the people	Effective governing *for* the people	Interest consultation *with* the people
National government	x	x	x	x
European governance				
EU Level			x	x
National Level	x	x		

effective governance *for* the people and interest consultation *with* the people, while government *by* and *of* the people is left largely to the national level (see Schmidt 2004*a*).

Currently, there is no consensus to shift government *by* and *of* the people to the EU level through the direct election of EU leaders with EU-wide parliamentary elections—nor would this necessarily help democratize the EU, given the lack of a collective identity and will. But this means that democratic reforms of the EU still focus mainly on improving governance *for* the people, through greater accountability and transparency, and *with* the people, through more interest-based access and a greater opening to 'civil society'. And such reforms would only increase the fragmentation of EU democracy as a whole.

The deficiencies of this fragmented EU level democracy put tremendous pressure on national politics. This is because in the absence of EU-wide elections for a directly elected EU government, national publics tend to hold national politicians accountable for policies for which they are not fully responsible, over which they may have little control, and to which they may not even be politically committed (Schmidt 2004*a*).

Scholars have elaborated on the resulting problems for national democracy in a wide range of governance areas (see Table 18.4). In areas of supranational governance in which the Commission, the ECB, or the ECJ are the delegated authority responsible for decision-making, the lack of government *by* the people makes this kind of governance *for* the people problematic in cases where rules formerly agreed are no longer accepted, given that rules once made are very difficult to reverse (Scharpf 2000), as in the case of the Stability and Growth Pact (suspended but not amended). In the vast number of policy sectors covered by the Monnet method of joint decision, the problems of consultative democracy *with* the people come from the fact that while Brussels is the center of the public policy sphere in an increasing number of domains, national interest groups (with the exception

TABLE 18.4. *Problems of democracy in a range of governance areas*

Mode of governance	Democratic mechanism	Problem	Examples
Supranational governance through delegated authorities	Governance *for* the people through effective governing	Lack of gov *by* the people problem where rules are no longer accepted	ECB and Stability and Growth Pact
Monnet method of joint decision-making	Governance *with* the people through interest consultation	Although Brussels center of process, national interests mostly still organize, pressure, and protest at national level	Immigration agriculture
Electoral politics	Participatory democracy *by* the people	Mismatch between nat'l elections focused on policy issues that can only be decided by EU and EP elections focused on polity issues that can be decided only by national leaders (in concert)	Elections for national parliaments and European Parliaments
Contentious politics	Consultative democracy *with* the people when the democratic processes of *by* and *with* break down	Protests vs EU policies target nat'l officials who are accountable for implementation but can't change rules while protests vs national policies find more concern but little capacity from EU officials	Truckers' protests or 'euro-strikes' such as Renault

of business) mostly still organize, pressure, and protest primarily at the national level, with relatively little transnational coordination, whether in immigration policy (Guiraudon 2001) or in agricultural policy (Kandermans *et al.* 2001).

Equally problematic are the effects of Europeanization on 'input' democracy '*by* the people' when national governments, elected on a political platform at the national level may have to implement EU-related policies to which they may not be politically committed, as in the case of the French Socialist government's implementation of EU-led deregulation in electricity (Eising and Jabko 2002). The problems of participatory democracy *by* the people also suffers because of a mismatch between national elections which focus on substantive policy issues that increasingly can only be fully addressed at the EU level, such as immigration, food safety, or economic growth, while European Parliamentary elections tend to focus on more general polity issues that can only be resolved by nationally-based actors, such as how to reform EU institutions (Mair 2001).

Finally, contentious politics, which can be understood as a kind of consultative democracy '*with* the people' when the regular consultation process breaks down, confronts similar difficulties (Imig and Tarrow 2001*a*). This is because protests against EU policies tend to target national officials who are accountable for policy implementation but can do little to accommodate the protesters' concerns, as in the case of French and Italian truckers' protests against EU-mandated deregulation, while protests focused on more local issues may find more response from EU officials than national ones, as in the case of the 'euro-strikes' against the closing of French car manufacturer Renault's Belgian plant (Imig and Tarrow 2001*b*).

2.2. *The Differential Impact of the EU on National Democracies*

In addition to these general problems are the differential effects of the EU on simple and compound democracies. The effects are best elucidated in terms of the challenges to the organizing principles of national democracies constituted by the EU-related changes in institutional structures, policymaking processes, and representative politics (see Table 18.5).

To begin with, the EU's 'federalizing' diffusion of power through its multiple authorities largely reinforces the underlying assumptions in compound polities that democracy '*by* the people' is best served by the dispersion of government power and authority, such that citizens' rights are protected from government excess through checks and balances resulting from the vertical and horizontal division of powers. In Germany, this sits well with a centuries-old history of regional power and a postwar constitution written to ensure against any possible return to the excesses of a centralized power. By

TABLE 18.5. *Democratic Ideas in Simple and Compound Polities and the impact of the EU*

	Democratic legitimacy	Ideas about Institutional Structures	Ideas about: Policymaking processes	Ideas about: Representative Politics	EU challenge to Ideas about Democracy
Simple Polity	Legitimacy focused on executive	Power concentrated in executive to govern effectively *for* the people	Policy formulation closed to interests via government *with* the people to safeguard government *by, of,* and *for* the people Policy implementation open to interest consultation *with* the people to govern effectively *for* the people	Politics concentrated in executive elected *by* the people and representative *of* the people to govern effectively *for* the people	EU governance *for* the people undermines nat'l exec's legit. as representative *of* the people and channel for participation *by* the people; EU governance *with* the people introduces interests into process from which excluded as illegitimate

Table 18.5. (*Continued*)

	Democratic legitimacy	Ideas about Institutional Structures	Ideas about: Policymaking processes	Ideas about: Representative Politics	EU challenge to Ideas about Democracy
Compound Polity	Legitimacy focused on system as a whole	Power diffused thru multiple authorities to safeguard vs excesses *by* the people	Policy formulation and implementation open to interests via government *with* the people to govern effectively *for* the people	Politics diffused in multiple authorities representative *of* people to govern effectively *for* the people	EU governance *with* the people may contrib to legit by adding extra interests to process. But EU governance may still undermine system's overall legit thru further dissipation of authority

contrast, the EU challenges the traditional assumptions in more simple polities that democracy is better served by the concentration of governmental power and authority both vertically and horizontally, such that the government has the sole responsibility as well as the capacity to respond to citizens' wants and needs effectively '*for* the people.' For France, the EU challenges the country's Jacobin philosophical foundations that concentrate power and authority in the 'one and indivisible' Republican state. For Britain, it undermines the authority of the executive as the embodiment of parliamentary sovereignty. In Italy, which has a mix of simple and compound structural elements, the EU reinforces the assumptions underlying the increasingly regionalized practices that promote the dispersion of power and authority, even as it challenges what is still in principle a unitary state.

Similarly, the EU's 'pluralizing' of member state policy formulation processes through increasing interest access and influence bolsters the views in compound polities that effective governing *for* the people demands the greatest openness to a multiplicity of inputs from intermediate interests through multiple centers of power via consultation *with* the people. For Germany and Italy, the EU only reinforces legitimacy, since it adds a wider range of interests to those traditionally involved in corporatist or clientelistic processes. By contrast, EU-related institutional changes clash with the assumptions of simple polities that the executive governs most effectively *for all* the people while ensuring against governmental excess by being closed to interest consultation *with* the people. For France, open interest consultation offends ideas prevalent since the Revolution that see direct government relations with any specific slice of the polity (as opposed to broad representatives of the 'general will') as illegitimate; in Britain, it clashes with ideas of executive autonomy—although parliamentary lobbying has been acceptable so long as the government keeps its distance from special interests.

In the implementation process, moreover, the EU's regulatory model clashes with simple polities' commitment to flexibility. For France, the EU's insistence on applying the rules without exceptions reduces the executive's ability to govern effectively *for* the people at the implementation stage, by accommodating minority interests negatively affected by majority decisions at the policy formulation stage. For Britain, the problem is rather with the statutory rules that, by abrogating organized interests' voluntary self-regulatory arrangements, increase the scope and rigidity of the public sphere and thereby encroach on the private sphere which governments see as their duty to protect. By contrast, the EU again tends to reinforce legitimacy in compound polities by promoting governing effectiveness *for* the people through regulatory and legalistic processes that also predominate in Germany, by allowing corporatist processes to continue in both Germany and Italy, or by substituting regulatory enforcement for a discredited clientelism in Italy.

Finally, the EU-related 'depoliticization' of representative politics by way of interest-based, consensus-oriented politics, sustains the assumption in compound polities that political compromise among the plethora of authorities representative *of* the people, elected *by* the people, and open to interest intermediation *with* the people is the best way to express the *will* of *all* the people. In Germany, it matches a consensus-oriented political culture which expects compromise among federal and regional governments, government and opposition (when in control of the upper house), and government, business and labor (on labor-related policies). In Italy, it fits with a conflict-ridden political culture which accepts the need for compromise among myriad parties in coalition governments, with regional governments (on regional issues), and with the social partners (on labor-related policies). By contrast, it clashes with the expectation in simple polities that political leadership by a single executive, representative *of* the people and elected *by* the people requires fulfillment of all political commitments made to the electorate. For France and the UK, it undermines conflict-based political cultures which expect the government to impose its electoral program without compromise, although in France, some accommodation is anticipated in cases of cohabitation between President and Prime Minister of opposing parties, something unknown in the UK's 'elected dictatorship.'

In short, even though EU legitimacy may be increasing with the development of EU institutions, national legitimacy generally suffers from the impact of the evolving EU governance system on national democracies, and more so for simple polities where legitimacy is focused on a single authority than for compound polities, where it rides on the system as a whole. Thus, although national publics generally hold their politicians accountable for decisions for which they may be neither responsible, in control of, or politically committed to, the public of simple polities like Britain and France are likely to hold their politicians more accountable because they see them as more fully responsible for, more fully in control of, and more politically committed to all decisions, whether EU-related or not, than the public of more compound polities, who know that their politicians are never fully responsible for or fully in control of any decisions, even when they are fully politically committed to them. Questions of democratic legitimacy are likely therefore to come up more frequently in simple polities, since they can arise in response to any unpopular policy, than in compound polities, where even when a policy is unpopular, democratic legitimacy is likely to come up only if the people lose trust in the system as a whole—the problem for Italy in the postwar period but less so today, where the EU has contributed to greater governing effectiveness and, thereby, legitimacy. The risk is greater for Germany, where the perception of a dissipation of authority as a result of the greater diffusion of authority through the EU can raise questions of legitimacy.

2.3. *Other Ideas About Democracy*

One caveat, however. The organizing principles of democracy are not the only ideas that affect responses to Europeanization. There are other ideas, grounded in history and culture, that serve to mediate responses to Europeanization. These involve both values and interests. And here, there are no generalizations to make about how simple or compound polities may be affected by Europeanization (see Figure 18.2).

In simple polities, for example, political, social, and economic values lend insight into how countries mediate the clash with their democratic organizing principles. Thus the French—with their ideas about a civilizing cultural mission and the universal rights of man—have embraced Europeanization despite its potential impact on the powers of the 'Republican state,' whereas the British have kept Europe more at arms' length because it threatens ideas about the historically established rights of Englishmen and parliamentary sovereignty. In compound polities, other ideas show how the 'fit' with democratic organizing principles was enhanced by social and political values, with the Germans embracing Europe as a way to submerge national identity in a larger whole, the Italians, as a way to rescue the nation-state, and the Spaniards, as a way to reinforce democracy—the same reason as the Greeks, despite their more 'simple' polity. Moreover, such values shed light on why some Scandinavian countries have resisted the euro—because of concerns about its impact on social justice in the social-democratic welfare state—while Germany has accepted it—because of its fit with notions of economic order and the stability culture of the Deutschmark.

Interests also matter, of course. One cannot understand the general push for European integration without recognizing the economic, political, and social interests that enabled countries to overcome ideational obstacles to change—the French desire to lead politically in Europe; the German interest in serving its economic and social purposes; the British willingness to go with economic interest, despite political reticence; the Italian hope to overcome the economic, political, and social costs of state paralysis; or the need for small states such as Denmark, Sweden, and Austria to be part of a larger political entity in order better to manage economic externalities.

3. The Real Democratic Deficit: The Lack of New Ideas and Discourse about Democracy

That democracy in the EU regional state does not match the democracy of a nation-state such as the US, by emphasizing democracy *for* and *with* the people over and above democracy *by* and *of* the people, is not *the* problem

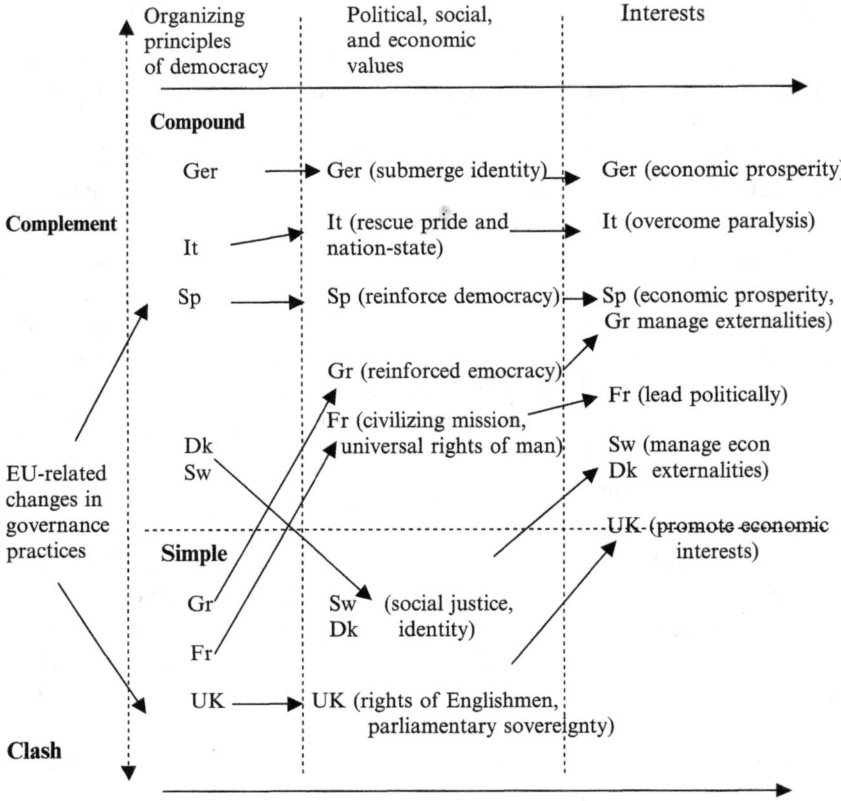

FIGURE 18.2. National responses to EU-related changes in governance practices, depending upon organizing principles of democracy, meditated by other democratic values and interests.

Note: Ger-Germany; It-Italy; Sp-Spain; Dk-Denmark; Sw-Sweden; Gr-Greece; Fr-France; UK-United Kingdom

for democracy in the EU. Moreover, even the fact that EU level democracy has challenged national ideas about democracy is not *the* problem, or that those challenges are greater for simple than compound polities. *the* problem for democracy is that national leaders and publics have failed to come to terms with the changes in the traditional workings of their national democracies.

While national governance practices have changed dramatically in the process of Europeanization, national leaders have not only not generated new ideas to legitimize the new practices, they have generally persisted in speaking about Europeanization as if the old ideas about democracy are still applied, as if little has changed, even though everything has. Although

EU-related policy issues are often at the forefront of national discourse, as national politicians blame the EU for unpopular policies or take credit for the popular ones (often without mentioning the EU's role), polity issues related to the changes in governance practices tend to take a back seat other than in certain 'defining moments,' at times of treaty referenda or accession agreements. Even though this is understandable—politicians, after all, are not likely to use their scarce political resources to speak about changes that are complicated and difficult to 'sell,' and there are no electoral incentives to do so—it adds to the problems of the democratic deficit.

In France, for example, national leaders still speak as if the state were unitary, despite the federalizing trends related not only to the EU but also to internal reforms, as in the case of Corsica. They continue to insist that they remain a leader in Europe, despite the faltering of the Franco-German partnership and, most importantly, the fact that France has followed much more than led in the 1990s, and sometimes quite reluctantly, as in the liberalization of the public services industries, which they loudly opposed (Eising and Jabko 2001), or in the change in immigration policy, which they implemented without any nod to its EU genesis (Geddes and Guiraudon 2004). The problem with ignoring the impact of Europeanization on the policy while emphasizing France's leadership role in the EU is that French leaders risk being held accountable for actions for which they are not fully responsible (Schmidt 2002*b*).

Britain has the opposite problem. National leaders have tended to highlight the impact of the EU on national governance practices: under Margaret Thatcher in highly polemical diatribes against overly ambitious integration plans that challenge national sovereignty and excess regulations that reduce the private sphere while rigidifying the public sphere; under John Major in a quieter, but equally negative discourse. Under Tony Blair, by contrast, there has largely been silence, in particular over possible entry into the eurozone, which has been portrayed as a strictly economic problem—leaving the media barons of Fleet Street to continue the negative polity discourse. The result is that the public has been made maximally aware of the drawbacks of Europeanization and few of the benefits, such that any government that moves toward greater integration risks being seen as responsible for undermining British democracy.

Neither Germany nor Italy has problems as serious as those of France and Britain with regard to the changes in governance practices, given their better fit with the EU as compound democracies. Thus, the discourse of national leaders has been mostly positive in terms of its national impact, with the Italians arguably even more positive, and any potentially negative impact downplayed. For Italy, the problems with regard to governance practices may come when it is forced to implement the rules. For Germany, problems are more likely when EU policies are seen to challenge the practices of its social market economy (of which decision by the Competition Commission against the regional state-owned savings and loan banks was a foretaste), because these are seen as fundamentals with regard to citizens' economic and social rights.[4]

In all countries, however, the lack of polity discourse by mainstream leaders has left the issues wide open to the extremes on both sides of the political spectrum, to exploit for their own electoral purposes—on the extreme right with regard to the impact of immigration and the loss of sovereignty, on the left with regard to the impact of the euro on the welfare state. Indications of the political problems are also found in the surveys, opinion polls, and electoral studies that show that citizens' trust in national governments as well as in EU institutions is down (Reynié and Cautrès 2001: 243–4; Bréchon 2002: 103), while general cynicism about national leaders is rampant and voter apathy, evident in higher rates of abstentionism, is up (Klingemann 1999; Pharr and Putnam 2000).

The democratic deficit, in short, is a significant problem at the national level, whatever one thinks of it in the European arena. And it will remain a problem so long as national leaders and citizens in each and every one of the member states do not start reevaluating what they mean by national democracy today, even before they decide how to democratize the EU for tomorrow. The EU is no longer an elite project supported by a 'permissive consensus'. But it is not yet a peoples' project grounded in a 'democratic consensus'.

But how to build such a democratic consensus? For this, we need to look to the patterns of discourse in European democracy at both EU and national levels, which also differs in simple and compound polities.

4. The Patterns and Problems of Discourse in Europe

The problem with regard to Europeanization is not just that countries hold to old ideas that do not reflect the new practices. It is also that the new EU governance practices have generated new patterns of discourse, and that these have also differentially affected 'simple' and 'compound' polities.

[4] It is important to note here that policy issues with regard to Europeanization that challenge deeply-held national political, economic, and social values can be every bit as problematic for a country as polity issues that challenge the organizing principles of national democracy. With policy issues, however, institutional fit is only one of a number of mediating factors which help explain responses to Europeanization. For more on this, see Schmidt 2002*a*, Chapter 2. For more on the differences between 'policy' and 'polity' issues, see Schmidt 2004*b*. But policy issues, of course, are not our focus here.

In all polities, discourse is an essential element of politics and policymaking , as policy actors seek to generate ideas that are sound and appropriate for the polity through a 'coordinative discourse' of policy construction while political actors seek to communicate those ideas to the public for deliberation through a 'communicative discourse' of political legitimization.[5] But polities differ in their emphasis on the coordinative or communicative discourse, largely as a result of institutional context (see Figure 18.3). In compound polities such as Germany and Italy, the coordinative discourse finds greatest emphasis, given the number of policy actors needed to agree on any new ideas, who then communicate directly with their own constituencies. By contrast, in simple polities such as Britain and France, the communicative discourse finds greater emphasis, given the more restricted access to decision-making and the greater need, therefore, to legitimize any new ideas directly to the more general public (Schmidt 2002*a*: ch. 5).

In the EU, the discursive pattern of compound polities is even more pronounced. While the EU's coordinative discourse involves an extremely wide range of policy actors at both national and EU levels, the EU's communicative discourse has very few EU-level political actors capable of speaking for the EU as a whole and no single European public to whom to speak, given the lack of a common European language, European media, credible EU-level political parties, and European public opinion, let alone European citizenry or directly elected President. In consequence, while the EU benefits from the most elaborate of coordinative discourses, with European policy ideas generated through a complex discursive process with a plethora of actors, it suffers from the thinnest of communicative discourses, with European policy ideas conveyed mostly indirectly, by national political actors in national contexts (Schmidt 2003). As such, it has had a differential impact on countries with simple and compound discursive patterns (see Figure 18.4).

In simple polities, the traditionally strong communicative discourse means that even in the absence of any EU level communicative discourse, national political leaders would be able to speak clearly and in one voice to the changes in national practices and the challenges to traditional ideas about democracy brought about by Europeanization. The problem, however, is that political leaders have not addressed these issues. Instead, we find communicative discourses that, in France, have reiterated the fictions of a unitary state and an all-powerful executive, immune to the pressures of interests or, in Britain, have railed against the EU's incursions on sovereignty (as in the Thatcher years) or fallen totally silent on the EU's impact on the polity (as today). Rather than admitting to EU-related changes that have reduced their

[5] For more extensive discussion of discourse and its application to the policy sphere, see: Schmidt 2002*a*, Chapters 5 and 6; Schmidt and Radaelli 2004.

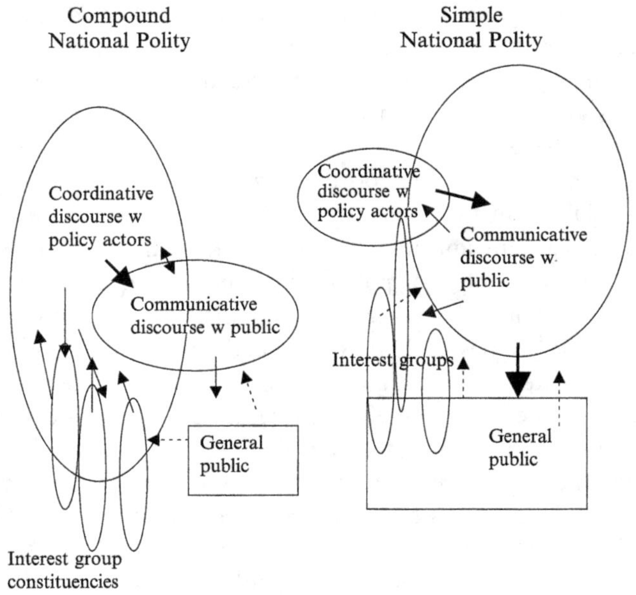

FIGURE 18.3. Discourse interactions in simple and compound national polities.

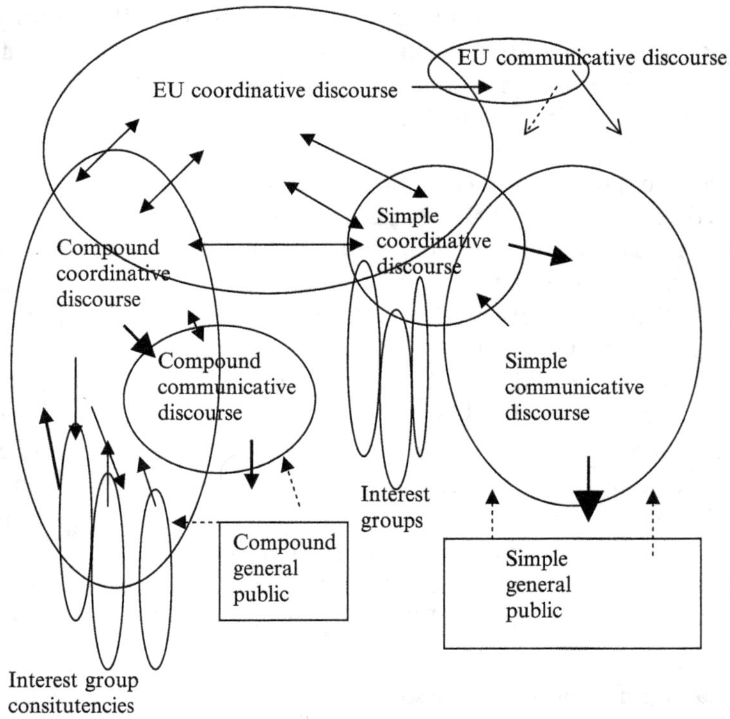

FIGURE 18.4. Discourse interactions in the EU.

autonomy, leaders increasingly focus on purely national issues for which they can be responsible, which they can control, and to which they are politically committed. These are the subject of discourse, whether public services in Blair's second term or the 35 hour work week in Lionel Jospin's prime ministership. This is perhaps politically useful in the short term, but in the long term this absence of substantive discourse and deliberation about the impact of Europeanization on the polity—even as policy change is the focus of an extensive but mixed press—only contributes to public disaffection and depoliticization, while it leaves the issue open to the political extremes to exploit for their own purposes.

'Compound' polities confront a different set of problems since, as in the EU, the communicative discourse is very thin. Political leaders are schooled in communicating only in vague terms on the agreements reached among the wide range of actors involved in 'coordinative' discourse of policy construction. Here, it is a good thing that Europeanization has been less of a challenge to compound polities' organizing principles of democracy. As it is, where Europeanization challenges other nationally specific democratic values—whether political, economic, or social—the general poverty of the communicative discourse may raise major red flags for the public. This was the case with the euro in Germany, and may become increasingly true in areas that challenge the country's economic model; for Italy, it may occur when, as noted earlier, the country is pushed to implement policies thoroughly. Moreover, where the EU challenges national democratic ideas or practices, public discussion and deliberation through the kind of 'deliberative democracy' that Habermas has consistently called for is very difficult, given the range of voices speaking at the same time and seeking to be heard, without any one having any more of an authoritative voice than any others. Reaching a consensus in this context may therefore be quite long and difficult compared to any simple polity.

For both Britain and France, then, the challenge is to change ideas about the polity, but the strong communicative discourse is there to make that a possibility, were leaders willing to engage in the discourse. For Germany and Italy, it is a good thing that the polity issues are not as serious, since they would have a much harder time projecting a successful communicative discourse. Policy issues that challenge deep-seated values, however, do need addressing—and this is where potential problems lie.

5. Conclusion

Although the EU has had a greater impact on simple polities than on compound ones, both kinds of polities have nevertheless had to deal with

EU-related changes in governance practices and challenges to traditional ideas about democracy. Moreover, even though simple polities have an advantage with regard to addressing the issues through the communicative discourse, they have not used such ability to the fullest. Instead, neither simple nor compound polities have sought to generate such new ideas, let alone new national practices to make up for the EU-related changes. The EU itself is no use here. There is no EU-level solution to the democratic deficit at the national level, however 'democratizing' the EU constitutional treaty. Because European integration affects each country differently, given differences in institutions, interests, culture, and history, each country has to find its own way to reevaluate democracy in light of Europeanization.

References

Bréchon, P. (2002). 'Des Valeurs Politiques entre Pérénnité et Changement', *Futuribles,* 277: 92–128.

Conant, L. (2001). 'Contested Legal Boundaries and Institutional Adaptations: The Europeanization of the Law in France, Germany, and the United Kingdom', in M. Cowles, J. Caporaso, and T. Risse (eds.), *Transforming Europe: Europeanization and Domestic Change*. Ithaca, NY: Cornell University Press.

Cowles, M. G., Caporaso, J., and Risse, T. (eds.) (2001). *Transforming Europe: Europeanization and Domestic Change*. Ithaca, NY: Cornell University Press.

Eising, R. and Jabko, N. (2002). 'Moving Targets: Institutional Embeddedness and Domestic Politics in the Liberalization of EU Electricity Markets', *Comparative Political Studies*. 742–67.

Fabbrini, S. (ed.) (2003). *L'Europeizzazione dell'Italia: L'impatto dell'Unione Europea sulle istituzioni e le politiche italiane*. Rome: Laterza.

Gabel, M. (2001). 'European Integration, Voters, and National Politics', in D. Imig and S. Tarrow (eds.), *Contentious European: Protest and Politics in an Emerging Polity*. Lanham, MD: Rowman & Littlefield.

Geddes, A. and Guiraudon, V. (2004). 'Britain, France, and EU Anti-Discrimination Policy: The Emergence of an EU Paradigm', *West European Politics,* 27/2: 152–71.

Greenwood, J. (2003). *Interest Representation in the European Union*. Basingstoke: Palgrave/Macmillan.

Greven, M. (2000). 'Can the European Union Finally Become a Democracy?', in M. Greven and L.W. Pauly (eds.), *Democracy Beyond the State? The European Dilemma and the Emerging Global Order*. Lanham, MD: Rowman & Littlefield.

Grimm, D. (1995). 'Does Europe Need a Constitution?' *European Law Journal*, 1.

Guiraudon, V. (2001). 'Weak Weapons of the Weak? Transnational Mobilization around Migration in the European Union', in D. Imig and S. Tarrow (eds.), *Contentious European*. Lanham, MD: Rowman & Littlefield.

Habermas, J. (1996). *Between Facts and Norms: Contributions to a Discourse Theory*. London: Polity Press.

Hooghe, L. (ed.) (1996). *Cohesion Policy, the European Community and Subnational Government*. Oxford: Oxford University Press.

Imig, D., and Tarrow, S. (2001*b*). 'Political Contention in a Europeanizing Polity', in K. Goetz and S. Hix (eds.), *Europeanized Politics?* London: Frank Cass.

—— —— (eds.) (2001*a*). *Contentious Europeans*. Lanham, MD: Rowman & Littlefield.

Kandermans, B. *et al.* (2001). 'Framing Contention: Dutch and Spanish Farmers Confront the EU', in D. Imig and S. Tarrow (eds.), *Contentious Europeans*. Lanham, MD: Rowman & Littlefield.

Keating, M. and Jones, B. (1995). *The European Union and the Regions*. Oxford: Oxford University Press.

Klingemann, H-D. (1999) 'Mapping Political Support in the 1990s', in P. Norris (ed.), *Critical Citizens*. Oxford: Oxford University Press.

Ladrech, R. (1994). 'The Europeanization of Domestic Politics: The Case of France', *Journal of Common Market Studies*, 32: 69–88.

Lijphart, A. (1984). *Democracies: Patterns of Majoritarian and Consensus Government in Twenty-One Countries*. New Haven, CT: Yale University Press.

Mair, P. (2001). 'The Limited Impact of Europe on National Party Systems', in K. Goetz and S. Hix (eds.), *Europeanized Politics?* London: Frank Cass.

Majone, G. (1998). 'Europe's Democratic Deficit', *European Law Journal,* 4/1: 5–28.

—— (ed.) (1996). *Regulating Europe*. New York: Routledge.

Marks, G., Hooghe, L., and Blank, K. (1996). 'European Integration since the 1980s: State-Centric versus Multi-Level Governance', *Journal of Common Market Studies,* 34/3: 341–78.

Moravcsik, A. (2002). 'Reassessing Legitimacy in the European Union', *Journal of Common Market Studies,* 40/4: 603–24.

Nicolaïdes, K. (2001). 'Conclusion: The Federal Vision Beyond the Nation-State', in K. Nicolaides and R. Howse (eds.), *The Federal Vision*. Oxford: Oxford University Press.

Norton, P. (ed.) (1996). *National Parliaments and the European Union*. London: Frank Cass.

Olsen, J. (2002). 'The Many Faces of Europeanization', ARENA Working Papers WP 02/2.

Pharr, S. and Putnam, R. (eds.) (2000). *Disaffected Democracies*. Princeton, NJ: Princeton University Press.

Radaelli, C. M. (2003). 'The Europeanization of Public Policy', in K. Featherstone and Claudio M. Radaelli (eds.), *The Politics of Europeanization*. Oxford University Press: Oxford, pp. 27–56.

Reynié, D. and Cautrès, B. (2001). *L'Opinion Européenne*. Paris: Presses de Sciences Po.

Rizzuto, F. (1996). 'The French Parliament and the EU: Loosening the Constitutional Straitjacket', in P. Norton (ed.), *National Parliaments and the European Union*. London: Frank Cass.

Saalfeld, T. (1996). 'The German Houses of Parliament and European Legislation', in P. Norton (ed.), *National Parliaments and the European Union*. London: Frank Cass.

Sbragia, A. (1993). 'The European Community: A Balancing Act', Publius, 23.

Scharpf, F. (1988). 'The Joint Decision Trap: Lessons from German Federalism and European Integration', *Public Administration*, 66/3: 239–78.

—— (2000). *Governing in Europe*. Oxford: Oxford University Press.

Schmidt, V. A. (1999*a*). 'European "Federalism" and its Encroachments on National Institutions', *Publius*, 29/1: 19–44.

—— (1999*b*). 'National Patterns of Governance under Siege: The Impact of European Integration', in B. Kohler-Koch and R. Eising (eds.), *The Transformation of Governance in the European Union*. London: Routledge.

—— (2001). 'Federalism and State Governance in the EU and the US: An Institutional Perspective', in K. Nicolaides and R. Howse (eds.), *The Federal Vision*. Oxford: Oxford University Press.

—— (2002*a*). *The Futures of European Capitalism*. Oxford: Oxford University Press.

—— (2002*b*). 'The Effects of European Integration on National Governance: Reconsidering Practices and Reconceptualizing Democracy', in J. Gröte and B. Gbikpi, (eds.), *Participatory Governance*. Opladen: Leske and Budrich.

—— (2003). 'How, Where, and When does Discourse Matter in Small States' Welfare State Adjustment?', *New Political Economy*, 8/1.

—— (2004*a*). 'The European Union: Democratic Legitimacy in a Regional State?' *Journal of Common Market Studies* (forthcoming).

—— (2004*b*). 'Europeanization of National Democracies: The Differential Impact on Simple and Compound Polities', *Politique Européenne*, 13: 113–40.

—— and Radaelli, C. (2004). 'Conceptual and Methodological Issues in Policy Change in Europe', Introduction to Symposium issue of *West European Politics*, 27/4: 1–28.

Stone Sweet, A. (2000). *Governing with Judges: Constitutional Politics in Europe*. Oxford: Oxford University Press.

van der Eijk, C. and Franklin, M. (1996). *Choosing Europe?* Ann Arbor, MI: University of Michigan Press.

Weiler, J. H. H. (1999). *The Constitution of Europe*. Cambridge: Cambridge University Press.

19

The European Union through an American Prism

ROGAN KERSH AND JAMES MORONE

The European Union (EU) has been a work in progress for fifty years. In the shadow of world war, the Rome Treaty (1957) aspired to a lasting peace; by the late 1980s integration promised a commercial power that might match the USA and Japan. And at the start of the twenty-first century, a unified Europe seemed a vital hedge against US economic and diplomatic hegemony. As the EU's structure, spirit, and logic continue to evolve, this volume takes up one especially volatile aspect of integration: the US connection. The United States is deeply implicated in European dreams of a more perfect union, whether as a federal model to emulate, a partner to join with, a rival to compete with, or a threat to defend against.

Thousands of Europeans have trooped to the new world in order to learn, as one commented in 1816, 'what profitably may be learnt here.' What might the US experience—with its complicated, constantly contested union—offer students of contemporary European politics? We take up three aspects of the European-American nexus. First, we focus on the striking gap between politics and administration in contemporary Europe and reflect on the implications for democracy. Second, we examine recent tensions between the USA and European governments, arguing that the source goes far deeper than the bare-knuckles diplomacy of the current Bush Administration. Finally, we examine the early history of US national unity as a model for European efforts. We probe the analogy between 1789 (when the US ratified its constitution) and 2004 (Europe's draft) and speculate that European calendars may be set to a different schedule entirely.

1. The Great Silence

1.1. Missing politics

Back in 1904, a group of Midwestern Progressives invited Max Weber to visit St. Louis. They admired the Prussian model of efficient public administration and were eager to show off their own achievements. Weber's host, former mayor and Missouri Governor David Francis famously expressed the Progressive ideal when he remarked that there was no Democratic or Republican ways to pave a street. Beneficent scientific management—in contrast to USA's raucous party politics—would guide public choices. After his tour, which included the celebrated St Louis World Fair and other Progressive highlights, Weber made a startling declaration. What he admired most about the United States, he is reported to have said, were its political machines. Weber cheering the noxious engines of corruption? His enlightened American hosts could not have been more horrified. But Weber explained: The raw, lively politics of these machines held off the inevitable march of rationalization, of bureaucratization, of modernity's iron cage. Experiencing the US polity, he later remarked, was 'like having your skin peeled off . . . and beginning anew.'[1]

Today, the EU seems to embody the old Progressive dream: administration without politics. Civil servants formulate policies, working across Commission, Council, and Parliament; interest groups, stakeholders, and general publics have little role (and often scant interest) in the process. Decisions are ostensibly technical rather than political, cooperative rather than competitive. Across the papers in this collection, a US observer is struck by a thundering silence where the politics usually appears.

In part, this distinction simply points to an essential difference between systems. The largest European states all feature a long tradition of prestigious, nonpartisan civil service. Despite spasmodic Progressive efforts, the USA never developed a comparable degree of administrative control. In the USA, virtually no realm of governance is separate from politics; all public life is flatly political (Waldo 1948). To be sure, public officials sometimes win independence from political oversight. But it is axiomatic that they act in their own self-interest, usually by cultivating powerful constituencies who will, in turn, offer support when inevitable conflicts arise. While Progressive reformers won many institutional battles, they decisively lost their war against political influence. Instead their ideals became objects of mild derision: they were tagged 'goo goos' (for good government or goody-goody). As one nineteenth-century politician had it, these gentlemen 'forget that [political majorities] are not built by deportment or by ladies' magazines or gush' (Morone 1998: 101).

American politics may seem an overheated, unsavory chaos of swarming interests and narrow partisans. But it does offer comparative grounds for posing one great question to the EU: Where do you hide your politics? After

[1] Weber's sojourn in the USA—which he extended to three months—marked his emergence from a long depression, and is generally credited as sparking his *Protestant Ethic & the Spirit of Capitalism*, completed the year after his US travels. See Coser 1977: 237–9; Gerth and Mills 1958: 16.

all, public officials constantly make judgments that determine winners and losers. In a Union whose integration has largely been driven by 'economic, in particular commercial, interest,' rules forged in Brussels reshape economic competition (Moravcsik 1998: 473). The process requires endless trade-offs. Rigorous food-safety standards, for example, raise the costs of production and drive small farmers out of business or into cooperatives—as when regulations for pasteurizing cheese wiped out almost all the small, independent cheese makers in Brittany. Is this an example of a systematic bias in economic policy making? Do EU regulations routinely favor large concerns (who can afford safety regulations) over small ones (who are being squeezed right out of the business)? Are there, more generally, recurring biases raised by regulation, such as large versus small, regional versus local or development versus environment?

Such questions raise even deeper political matters. Perhaps the popular animosity that occasionally flares up against the Union, as during the spring 2004 EU elections, rises from the fear that the technical, bureaucratic, consensual process represses (or masks) fundamentally political choices about who gets what. EU administrators issue quotidian decisions that slowly add up into major political judgments about the nature of capitalism, the balance between capital and labor, the future of family (and local) enterprise, and, ultimately, the foundations of social solidarity—within nations and across Europe. These are debates that normally animate great political parties. Put differently, every one of these topics hinges on the same underlying issue: class.

Discussions about EU proceed with a peculiar silence regarding social and economic class. When we read the draft papers for this volume not one of them mentioned the term. In part, this may simply reflect today's postmodern, consumer-oriented, media-saturated political discourse. Workers' parties are not what they used to be: *viz.* the Labor parties of Tony Blair, Gerhard Schroeder or Lionel Jospin. But even if European parties no longer organize themselves clearly around class issues, the essential economic dialectics persist. Societies divide into rich and poor, haves and have-nots, and (at the risk of sounding entirely out of style) labor versus capital. It is true that Americans often skirt serious discussion of class, a practice that only submerges the formidable economic consequences (and recently, the audacious class bias) of our public policies. The EU appears to operate even more stealthily: both class and politics itself have slipped from public view.

1.2. The Democratic Deficit

The absence of politics is most vivid in what is widely termed Europe's 'democratic deficit.' The Union might represent government for and perhaps even with the people; as Fritz Scharpf and Vivien Schmidt point out, it is assuredly not by or of them (Schmidt in this volume; Majone 1998; Scharpf 1999). This state of affairs is increasingly acknowledged in Brussels: after constructing their institutional framework, EU officials have increasingly turned their attention to the lack of popular participation. As one scholar notes: 'A substantial part of the European political elite believes that increasing openness and participation in EU policymaking processes . . . will redress the so-called democratic deficit and the presumed distrust in the EU [populations]' (Beyers 2004: 235).

The language of 'deficit' makes a strange metaphor, as if a simple deposit might help balance the political books. Democratic polities do not generally develop in such a formal way, emerging from White Papers and bureaucratic Declarations (like the one hammered out at Laeken in 2001 that called for the European Convention). They normally rise up from below as the people, fired by ideas or grievances or hopes, gather and demand to be heard (Morone 1998). Or a version of democracy is proffered from above, as kings, aristocrats, and powerful leaders use the public to jockey for advantage against one another (back, inevitably, to social classes). In either case, the result is a tribe or people rising up and struggling to select representatives who—and this is the nub of the matter—will effectively articulate their interests. There are countless representational models, of course, but modern electoral politics has generally developed around political parties offering competing visions of the people's interests.

Simply calling elections does not make a representative democracy. This may be in part why EU elections meet with widespread apathy and, in some quarters, derision. What, after all, is at stake in EU elections? Consider a few of the possibilities:

- Perhaps nothing at all. With the technocratic EU process in place, voters are not choosing between alternative values or competing public policies and procedures. They are not adjudicating matters that they care about. This is democracy as window dressing, formal representation without substantive meaning.
- Possibly the effort to forge a link between people and EU leaders simply comes too late to realize a pan-European 'polity.' Even if the elected EU representatives make important policy, it is may be that their putative constituents' history, passions and identity—in short, their political consciousness—are already deeply embedded in twenty-five separate nation-states and cannot easily, if ever, be shifted to another level of governance.
- Alternatively, future elections may represent a real and durable change. Robust electoral institutions are now coming into view. If elections

> affect governance in visible ways, then it may simply be a matter of time before the public makes demands and leaders begin to articulate systematic alternatives. The answer to the democratic deficit, then, is plausibly at hand: Put the institutions in place and await popular political mobilization. (Michael Shackleton's essay on the European Parliament, in this volume, predicts with qualifications that a full-fledged parliamentary system is well along the way to realization.)

Whatever the prospects for a more engaged European electorate, introducing genuine democracy requires at least two additional features: reining in technocracy, and enhancing the transparency of policymaking. On the first score, recent evidence suggests that Europe's bureaucratic experts are governed not only by internalized professional norms, but also do a reasonably good job of accommodating elected officials who answer to the voters. (The most glaring exception: European central bankers.) But much EU policymaking remains out of sight, carried out primarily behind closed Council doors rather than in the more publicly visible Parliament. Resolving the democratic deficit would mean not simply instantiating contested elections, but placing experts in a framework that more visibly answers to the people's representatives. Granting greater access to the public could take place through a more extensive system of interest representation, or encouraging substantive deliberation in Brussels.

2. For US or against US?

The United States often figures into Europeans' calculations. The George W. Bush administration distinctly (at times, it seemed, intentionally) aggravated older international tensions. Indeed, the Bush attitude raises this volume's animating question with particular urgency: for US or against US? At the heart of the inquiry lies a further query: Is the sharp enmity—the 'against US'—largely a consequence of one administration's brash policy? Or does it reflect something deeper? The answer, we argue, is both. The Bush Administration's attitudes and policies towards Europe (and the international realm more generally) reflect an increasingly powerful force in American politics, but it remains a partisan and highly contested perspective even within the United States. However, more important underlying tensions between the USA and the EU stem from deep-seated, enduring differences concerning capitalism and social solidarity, work and leisure. These more profound responses to the 'for/against US' dichotomy speak to clashes over basic social values. And they raise perhaps the most fundamental question about the EU: Will the Union push Europe toward a more US model of government and business? Or will it, somehow, protect Europeans from it?

2.1. Bush Versus Them?

Most European observers in 2000 followed US opinion leaders in viewing president-elect George W. Bush as cast in his father's mold: 'a committed internationalist,' reported the *Wall Street Journal* at the campaign's end.[2] But the new administration quickly jolted European allies with a blunt unilateral style; 'cowboy' became the polite byword in the world press. In short order, the younger Bush scrapped the delicately negotiated Kyoto protocol on global warming, rejected a ballistic missile treaty that had stood for a quarter-century, brusquely spiked international efforts to rein in international money laundering, dismissed a series of inconvenient world court rulings, and attacked family planning efforts as 'antilife.' The terrorist attack in September 2001 heightened growing tensions. A new US policy of preemption departed from longstanding international norms. Gearing up for war in Iraq, the president along with other administration officials warned the United Nations that the only choices were 'for us or against us'; summarily rejected UN Security Council efforts to compromise or delay hostilities; and insulted allies from France to Turkey—a zone that US Defense Secretary Donald Rumsfeld famously derided as 'Old Europe'.[3]

This truculent tone was, for the most part, novel in US-European affairs. During the Cold War Americans and Europeans generally maintained at least a veneer of mutuality. Foreign policy elites in both US political parties, with only a handful of prominent exceptions, were internationalists. Republican Presidents did not change the fundamental predicates of US international diplomacy; indeed, they often evinced considerable daring (Richard Nixon's détente) and a certain dash (George H. W. Bush's alliance building).

As the Cold War drew to a close, however, the USA underwent a dramatic change. The Republican Party transformed itself in the 1980s and early 1990s, moving in a decisively and aggressively conservative direction. Republican leaders and party faithful began voicing a powerful contempt for their rivals. Liberal Democrats were not just the opposition party; they were dangerous, deviant, unmanly, unAmerican. Concerns about declining 'civility' in Washington dominated reports from the early 1990s onward (Carter 1999).

Conservative denunciations of the liberal status quo during this period palpably shifted the discourse of US politics. When a young woman drowned her two sons, US House Speaker Newt Gingrich blamed decadent liberal values. After a murderous rampage by two students at Columbine High

[2] Carla Robbins quoted in Gorin 2000; see also Rice 2000.

[3] Good summaries of these events, and various European responses, appear in Balis and Serfaty 2004.

School, House Majority Leader Tom DeLay blamed secular public schools and savaged the idea of teaching evolution to impressionable students. Even the terrorist attack on the World Trade Center prompted conservative preachers to blame 'the abortionists and the feminists and the gays and the lesbians' for moving God to 'lift his protection over this nation.'[4] Though this comment was roundly rebuked, such religious themes—long a contested trope in US politics—increasingly found favor with conservative US audiences. As one recent *Telegraph* (UK) report summarized, 'in terms of religion, the gulf between the USA and Western Europe is widening. European Christians occupy the political margins. In the USA they are in the thick of it.' Quoting an US Baptist leader, the report concluded that 'The profile of the USA, on a wide range of religious questions, is more like Poland or Nigeria, than Western Europe.'[5]

This combination of sharply confrontational and politico–religious discourse was accompanied by a shift in party control. Beginning with the 1994 midterm election, Republicans swept into power on every level of US government—local, state, and national. 'Liberal' (which in the USA means left-wing) became a term of approbation, leaving leftists to duck and squirm and seek new self-descriptions—most recently 'progressive' (Kersh 2001: 283–4). *New York Times* reporter Elisabeth Bumiller captured the new (and derisive) discourse during a Democratic primary debate when she asked John Kerry: 'Are you a liberal?' and followed up, as time ran out, with the crucial cultural test: 'Really quick, is God on America's side?'[6]

The powerful new US majority does not change its tone for international relations. What shocked many Europeans was precisely the treatment—and jeering, contemptuous tone—that the new right's leaders had been dishing out to the American left. After all, Europeans value the same despised policies: environmentalism, universal health insurance, generous social welfare policies, pacifism, statism, and a complex view of the world order. As the Iraq conflict loomed, Republicans made the term 'French' a synonym for 'liberal'. In fact, the 2004 election season introduced a new derogatory: 'the Latte Liberal', a deft combination of the 'L word' and a taste for things European (i.e. weak, affected, sophisticated, and foreign).

Beneath the American right's reflexive hostility lies a more worrisome indifference to Europe. An old reporter's maxim holds that stories about

[4] Robert Scheer, 'Let's Look at the Real Newt Gingrich,' *Los Angeles Times*, November 27, 1994; Steve Chapman, 'Praise the Lord, Pass the Ammo,' *Slate*, July 1, 1999; John F. Harris, 'God Gave U.S. "What We Deserve," Falwell Says,' *Washington Post*, September 14, 2001.

[5] H. David Rennie, 'Bush's Crusader for Church and State,' *Telegraph* (UK; August 21, 2004). For an extended discussion of this theme through time, see Morone 2003.

[6] As reported in the *American Prospect* (July 2004), p. 33.

the United Nations never get printed west of the Mississippi or in the former Confederate states of the American South. Today, that's where Republican leaders come from. The new majority likes to fashion itself after the first Western president, Andrew Jackson.[7] Contemporary Jacksonians, like their namesake, eschew overly sophisticated political talk and favor what Walter Russell Mead describes as 'an unapologetic flexing of military might' as their basic approach to international relations (Mead 2002). Adam Gopnick captures the perfect antinomy in his fond portrait of French statesmanship: 'Diplomats inside the *Quai d'Orsay* create foreign policy of enormous subtlety and refinement which has absolutely no effect on anyone outside the building' (Gopnick 2000). Contrast that to a foreign policy featuring a minimum of subtlety ('axis of evil', 'for us or against us', 'bring it on') and bearing enormous consequences ('you break it, you own it', as the Secretary of State is said to have told the President before the Iraq conflict) (Woodward 2004: 150). The great debate on the US right is between those who would aggressively promote US values in order to make a better world (as they see it) and those who want to preserve US values by withdrawing from 'entangling alliances,' as George Washington's first inaugural address put it. But traditional striped-pants, Ivy League, Foggy Bottom diplomacy, once a Republican Party hallmark, is not part of the mindset in either camp.

Not all Americans, by any means, buy this perspective; Mead's book reviews three other dominant strains in US foreign policy besides the Bush team's 'Jacksonian' one. Nor is it clear whether a second George W. Bush Administration will hew to its present position or, chastened by difficulties in Iraq, acquiesce to a more traditional and multinational foreign policy. Nevertheless, a powerful new Republican majority rooted in the South and West has established a new tone for US politics—and evinces a distinct skepticism, even xenophobia, about international affairs.

Ultimately, however, the relationship between the USA and the EU does not pivot—and should not be analyzed—only on the tumult of the Bush years. Americans and Europeans genuinely disagree on more important issues than the conduct of foreign policy. Differences over wealth, capitalism, and social justice are all at stake in the great dialectic between the USA and the European Union.

2.2. Markets and (or) Social Solidarity

By the end of the twentieth century every industrial nation found its level of foreign trade rising rapidly. In the USA it rose from 3 percent of GDP in

[7] Dana Milbank, 'Another Ol'Hickory in the White House?' *Washington Post* (September 17, 2002), p. A19; Michael Barone, 'The Jacksonian Persuasion,' *US News & World Report* (September 2, 2004), p. 27.

1970 to 12 percent by the mid-1990s; among all higher-income countries the numbers leapt from 12 percent to 20 percent. The globalized economy sharply exacerbated income inequality within nations; gaps in wealth and income (before taxes and transfer payments) grew substantially in every industrial country. However, different nations reacted in varying ways. Most tried to redress growing income differentials. The single greatest political difference between the USA and Western Europe may lie in their readiness to protect people from the consequences of increasingly open economic markets.[8]

In Western Europe, most governments buffer citizens from the global storm. They offer family and housing allowances, public assistance, generous pensions, and national healthcare programs. As a result, European societies are far more egalitarian than the USA. In the very active welfare states like Sweden, Denmark, Netherlands and France, the poorest households (the lowest decile) earn roughly 60 percent as much income as do median households; in the USA, the poorest manage just 38 percent of the middle. Such discrepancies are even greater for the wealthy. The European outcomes suggest a far greater commitment to social solidarity; US political discourse does not even feature the phrase (Jacobs and Morone 2004; Morone and Jacobs 2005).

Institutional details vary from nation to nation, but wealthy European countries are generally (far) more committed to egalitarian norms. In contrast, Americans tend to defer to economic markets. US social reformers generally emphasize giving everyone an equal chance to compete rather than ensuring a decent outcome. In part this means that vast US inequities stir little public commentary. For example, the USA ranks thirty-first among all nations for male life expectancy at birth—tied with Brunei, and distinctly behind nations like Germany, Holland or Croatia. The dismal US averages mask enormous differences across the population. A male born in Washington, DC, has a life expectancy that is forty years—forty years!—lower than a woman born in wealthy areas.[9] These differences provoke only spasmodic reform efforts. And those efforts are almost inevitably buried under loud protests about creeping 'socialism.'

Superficially, then, the European/American distinction appears self-evident. Americans celebrate markets and begrudge both poor people (for failing the market test) and the state (for meddling with the market). Hence the USA is frequently portrayed in comparative studies as the welfare-state

[8] For figures, and an overview of comparative approaches to inequality, see Richardson 1995; Smeeding 2002; Morone and Jacobs 2005.

[9] For details see APSA Task Force on Inequality and US Democracy, 'Inequality and Public Policy' (American Political Science Association, 2004); forty-year figure from Jacobs and Morone 2004: A20.

laggard of the industrial world. In Denmark, writes John Kingdon, the state pays his niece 80 percent of her salary for a year of maternity leave, after which she is guaranteed a return to her job. In the USA, the Clinton administration had to fight to win twelve weeks of unpaid leave from some companies (Kingdon 1999: 1).

Reality, as usual, is more complex. It is not that the USA flatly rejects welfare policies. Rather, it lodges them in the private sector. Public policies (like substantial tax incentives) push corporations to offer their employees social benefits like health insurance and retirement pensions. The state has organized incentives and filled gaps for people outside the private (mainly corporate) systems. Today, for example, nearly two-thirds of the US population receives health coverage through employment-based plans, compared to less than a quarter covered by government-sponsored insurance (Gottschalk 2000; Hacker 2002; Morone and Jacobs 2005).[10] As for public-sector programs, though these are always fiercely contested in Congress, the programs directed to the middle class have grown large and popular. Social Security and Medicare together account for $789 billion, or 34 percent of the federal budget, and are projected to top $1.5 trillion in 10 years. Most critical commentary reinforces the stingy state image by focusing on programs aimed at the poor; these are indeed meagerly-financed, unpopular, and under constant political fire. The private–public US system, termed the 'shadow welfare state,' worked tolerably well during the industrial era of stable employment in large corporations. And it epitomized a classical liberal ideology, one often described as foundational to the United States: a very rough social justice offered mainly through markets, with the assistance of a highly constrained state which operated largely by offering carrots and brandishing sticks at the private sector.

Today, the new global economy threatens to unravel America's old shadow welfare state. Permanent employment is no longer the norm; capital markets set punishing standards (most notably, meeting shareholders' quarterly expectations); corporations shift health costs to employees; and citizens are urged to invest for their own retirements. Without a culture of solidarity or a tradition of state intervention, there is no popular demand—or state capacity—for buffering individuals from the open economy. Instead, mainstream reaction is limited to a wan economic liberalism (help people compete more effectively) and a reflexive, ineffective, anti-globalism (buy American, reject international trade agreements).

[10] For current figures on Social Security and Medicare from the Congressional Budget Office, see 'The Budget and Economic Outlook: An Update' (September 2004), p. 9 and Table 1–4.

The result is an increasingly bifurcated society, a land of billionaires and homeless children. For example, as private companies reduce their health insurance benefits, upwards of 44 million Americans find themselves with no insurance coverage, and some 30 million more experience significant gaps. Predictably, the uninsured receive less care, they get it later in their illness episodes, and they are roughly three times as likely as insured Americans to have an adverse health outcome. And after the medical trouble there are bills to be paid: half of all US personal bankruptcies arise from health problems and often feature a large hospital suing a family with shaky finances (McLaughlin 2004; Sullivan *et al.* 2000).

Even so, few Americans challenge the logic of wide-open economic markets. Rather, they accord a deep legitimacy to manic capitalism, large corporations and low prices. McDonalds and Disney are popular, and largely uncomplicated, brands. Many Republicans have piled one additional idea onto the triumph of the market model: regardless of the policy problem, it can be solved by lower taxes. Such an outlook tends to further weaken the prospects of state intervention and widen the gap between rich and poor. Ironically, a long, powerful, populist tradition has since the 1980s turned its rage from the greedy rich to the arrogant state (and the latte liberals who support it). Right wing populists gleefully join the state bashing.

Uncontested markets become irresistible. An often proffered solution to US healthcare problems, for example, is to introduce still more market thinking into healthcare delivery—although, to the proclaimed surprise of some policymakers, returning capital to investors undermines efforts to serve poor and chronically ill populations. The solution to budget deficits, to take another example, is to outsource public functions to private firms (private is cast as always more efficient than public). Again, surprise accompanies the discovery that the companies have their own interests and agendas and that paying and overseeing them actually costs more.[11]

From the American perspective, the great question is not whether the EU is for us but whether it will become, willy-nilly, like us; whether the USA's formidable brand of liberal market economics is the irresistible future. Is the EU a vehicle for forcing needed market discipline on a reluctant Europe ('with US')? Or, somehow, a way to protect Europe from the excesses of American capitalism ('against US')? Let us take each view in turn.

2.3. *Irresistible Capitalism?*

The US view is unsentimental: International markets will slowly force reluctant Europeans to accept the triumphant market. Capitalism will roll over

[11] On surprised policymakers, see Lipsky and Rathgeb Smith 1995; on the dubious virtues of privatization, see Savas 1987.

the continent's many forms of social welfare capitalism.[12] Europe will learn to squeeze its labor unions, demand more from workers, lower taxes, and whittle down social welfare benefits (all cheered in currency markets and business journals as 'much-needed efficiencies'). The US business press regularly (and rather jauntily) reports the end of those long, lazy European vacations. The point is always the same: match USA's ruthless efficiency or get left in the economic dust.

How do you transform an entire continent? That, from the US perspective, is the job for the EU. The EU will gradually adjust political-economic practices to the harsh new world of economic liberalism. Low trade barriers, a single currency, unabashedly competitive markets, new financial requirements, and complex international regulations will dismantle nationalist protections for small firms (and farms) and open the door to international capital. Over time, limiting budget deficits (if the limits can be made to stick) will constrain state spending. International competition will do the rest.

Already, a European elite springs free from the narrow bonds of nationalism and social solidarity. It will, in this view, inevitably introduce the winner-take-all logic that dominates US society. The rapid growth of foreign (often Muslim) populations ought to speed the process by injecting a touch of US-style culture wars: a frank hostility towards newcomers who do not seem to share or appreciate 'our' social values helps erode old notions of social solidarity. Slowly, inevitably, multinational corporations will come to dominate each European market sector. Its chieftains—emulating their US cousins—will disdain the old welfare states with their dinosaur-era tax rates and that atavistic urge to share capitalism's bounty by redistributing wealth.

Elliot Posner offers a thoughtful perspective along these lines in his chapter here. Injecting NASDAQ-style institutions into European finance, he argues, will foster a risk-taking spirit among European entrepreneurs. Men and women put their money on the line, expecting to cash in or lose out. Such high-risk financial gambling fits uneasily with the traditional, statist aspiration to protect citizens from the market's extremes. The very idea of social solidarity, and the formidable postwar welfare states it nourished, soon will be a relic of the industrial era. As Posner emphasizes, the European Commission's efforts to advance a common European market hastened the transition.

In short, powerful new forms of capitalism, mediated by the EU and its economic rules, will inevitably challenge traditional practices in European countries, swamping long-standing differences between 'liberal' and 'coord-

[12] On different varieties or 'models' of capitalism, contrasting US and various European economies, see Hall and Soskice 2001.

inated' market economies (for example, Britain and Germany respectively).[13] Citizens in the member states may be put off by the Bush administration or the bluster of the New Jacksonians. But, like it or not, the EU is irresistibly turning Europe into one big, relatively unfettered market economy. Just like the USA.

2.4. *Solidarity Survives?*

Few of the papers in this collection endorse the preceding story about the inexorable triumph of economic liberalism. On the contrary, what might be called the EU distinction runs across these essays. On the one hand, Brussels regulates business and coordinates economies. On the other, individual nations remain responsible for social welfare policies. The EU will rule on what goes into German sausages but not what goes on at the German sickness funds.

The distinction raises urgent questions about the future. After all, social welfare regimes are always embedded in economic systems. Can governments rewrite the rules for one without deep implications for the other? Take the case of healthcare, where the American expectation looks like a primer on basic capitalism. Deregulate international insurance companies and they will sell health policies, competing with sickness funds in Germany, developing a private market in Britain. Savvy underwriters know (or swiftly learn) that, despite state regulators' best efforts to adjust reimbursement rates, poor people and chronic illnesses are bad risks. Capital markets make harsh masters. It is notoriously difficult to sustain universality principles when insurance companies figure out that they can beat market expectations (and raise their stock price) by chasing some risks (healthy, strong, young) and ducking others (poor, chronically sick, older).

In response, those defending the 'EU distinction' point to a nuanced interplay of economics and politics. If Europe can develop enough market power, perhaps European nations can fend off predatory capitalism. Collective power could make it more difficult for international corporations to play off nations against one another. It might carve out a political space that protects domestic politics and social welfare policies. In that case, the EU would be genuinely 'Against the U.S.' Not in the shallow sense of resisting the Bush Administration, but with respect to the arduous task of organizing economies in a way that protects societies and their social welfare arrangements from a global hyper-capitalism.

[13] For a telling recent case study, see Mark Thatcher's (2004) detailed account of how 'overseas reforms and EC regulation' overcame inter-European differences in telecommunications regulation.

Many political scientists shrug off this latest round of crying wolf. Globalization and unvarnished market liberalism are only the latest in a fifty-year string of welfare state 'crises.' The cold war, oil shocks, inflation, stagnation, bureaucratic sclerosis, aging populations, Thatcherism, and a host of other phenomena all promised its inexorable demise. Such constant alarms have only underscored a simple organizational reality: Popular, long-standing social welfare systems are remarkably resilient. They are lodged in great bureaucracies and serve powerful constituencies. That kind of institutional arrangement is built to weather economic and political storms (Pierson 1994).

Other social forces may also help shore up the status quo. Europe's vaunted culture of solidarity may continue to promote ethical norms that render some economic practices unacceptable. Or domestic political forces may set limits that Brussels will never breach: if neither Margaret Thatcher nor Tony Blair could shake up the National Health Service, how is new Commission president Jose Manuel Barroso going to manage the trick? Or perhaps the public (and the political parties) will find their European voices—farewell, democratic deficit—and push the EU to protect, or perhaps even extend, social welfare policies. Bruno Palier and Philippe Pochet's chapter above on social policy at least hints at such a possibility.

European welfare states have prevailed in large part because political institutions are difficult to change. However, US federalism suggests one classic way to get around that barrier: shift state policies to the federal level. Americans destroyed a deeply entrenched Southern racial apartheid, bolstered by a virulently racist majority culture, when they shifted the issue from state to federal policymakers. For their part, Europeans have been constructing an entirely new set of federal institutions. Novel institutional frameworks introduce new biases into political decision-making, a point that James Madison famously emphasized in his tenth *Federalist Paper,* written to persuade Americans that they should ratify the Federal government in 1788.

The crucial point is how the emerging European institutions will respond to the twenty-first-century global economy. Will economists in Brussels push for lower taxes and less redistribution? If so, the quest for efficiency will slowly, surely, encourage the spread of corrosive forms of capitalism across the continent. Or, on the contrary, the EU could generate a collective economic power that buffers member states enough to permit them each their own social welfare arrangements. And there is one final possibility: the EU simply may never develop enough authority to affect (much less reshape) important national issues. To influence long-standing economic and social norms, the EU will need not just to attract grudging allegiance from a handful of elites in member countries, but to win the loyalty and even affection of its variegated Euro-citizenry.

3. Whither the Union?

In his celebrated 1858 'House Divided' speech, Abraham Lincoln remarked, 'If we could first know where we are, and whither we are tending, we could better judge what to do, and how to do it' (cited in Basler 1946: 372). To adapt Lincoln's phrase, whither the EU? How seriously should we take the prospect of a durable union in Europe? Here we might glance again at the USA: this time neither for nor against, but as a simple model of political architecture: a comparative benchmark for judgments of 'where we are' in the development of something like a (in the EU case, supra-) national union.

At first blush, the analogy to the US case is beguiling. Elites representing proud, disunited, constantly quarreling and fiercely independent states, propelled by the imperatives of economics and international politics, deliberately forge a union. The Americans made their confederal arrangement work. Today's Europe may be tracing a similar path, right down to drafting a controversial Constitution.

The analogy, however, is complicated by the issue of time. Americans established an independent political union in short order; what had occurred to few besides Benjamin Franklin and a few worried British leaders in 1763 (at the end of the French and Indian War) became theoretically desirable in 1776 (during the Revolutionary War) and was organized by 1787 (writing of the US constitution). While Americans still wrestle with some of the most basic issues of federal power and jurisdiction, that Constitution ratified in 1789 still stands—and, remarkably, with a scant fifteen formal changes (e.g. constitutional amendments) in the past 200 years. Making the US analogy work means figuring out where in metaphorical time Europeans find themselves. Is it 1789? Not yet? Long—and perhaps irrevocably—past it?

The question has a sharp point because, in seeking to establish political union, eighteenth-century US colonists enjoyed a string of advantages that modern Europeans who strive to fashion a 'more perfect union' lack. British Americans spoke the same language, shared a culture, and professed a common political loyalty.

By the early 1700s, the USA had developed a heterogeneous culture. Immigrants from central and northern Europe mixed with slaves from at least twenty different African tribes. However, all official business and most informal exchanges were conducted in English. The historian J.R. Pole notes that colonists from Maine to Georgia 'used the language in essentially similar ways; there do not even appear to have been marked differences of idiom' (Pole 1977: 74). As for cultural exposure, educated Americans read the same British (and other European) authors, and mostly worship in Protestant churches featuring similar doctrines. Colonial residents also shared a deep loyalty to England, which eventually would complicate the effort for independence but did much to inspire colonists' sense of mutuality into the 1760s (Kersh 2001: 32–7).

In sum, Americans' 'national' spirit was established even before 1776 or 1787–89, and became all the stronger thereafter. European travelers in the USA during the decades after ratification found the country, as France's French ambassador Edmond-Charles Genet observed in 1793, 'in the midst of perpetual fêtes' celebrating the new nation. Genet, like other foreign visitors, found it remarkable that these celebrations were often organized around the Constitution itself. So-called Grand Federal Processions hailed each state's ratification with parades featuring elaborate floats and groups of marchers drawn from all ranks of society, orations, riotous celebratory dinners with numerous toasts, and even public renamings of places: Federal Hill, Constitution Avenue, Union Square. 'All this to honor a legal document!' commented one London observer. 'It is scarcely to be believed, how a few sheets of paper inspire this "many" to boast of being "one"'.[14]

But it was not so much the document that Americans cheered as it was the sense of shared unity that the Constitution represented and affirmed. Nor was it only Federalist gentry that led or participated in these celebrations, but a vast swath of the fast-democratizing country. To these enthusiasts of US national union, which into the nineteenth century remained a dubious certainty—a 'roof without walls,' in one resonant phrase—the Constitution represented a vital source of protection (Murrin 1987). Only later were the institutions of national statehood elaborated: beyond its first century of existence, the USA remained the peculiar combination of a strong nation and weak state.

Europe, as is more typical of past confederations, has erected and burnished the institutions of centralized power without a commensurate sense of nationhood or unity. As a strong state but weak nation, the EU represents the reverse of the USA during its first century-plus of existence. At this juncture it is hard to imagine spontaneous demonstrations on behalf of the EU, much less its recently promulgated constitution, breaking out in Paris and Berlin, or even Luxembourg-Ville and Athens.[15] Efforts during 2003–04 to promulgate a European Constitution have drawn popular apathy and even derision, rather than 'perpetual fetes'; one early book-length recounting is titled 'The Accidental Constitution,' and another recent account dryly

[14] Comment in *London Times*, quoted in *Philadelphia General Advertiser*, September 10, 1788; on celebrations of the Constitution and other national icons, see Waldstreicher 1997; Kammen 1987: 22–3, 36–9.

[15] The highest levels of approval for the EU, in 2004 polls of the EU-15, were logged in Luxembourg and Greece. See Eurobarometer 61 (Spring 2004), pp. 7–8; Lucarelli and Radaelli 2004.

describes the result as 'a fiasco but not a disaster' (Norman 2003; Gilbert 2004).

The possibility of closer integration—of real unity—in Europe appears to remain closely bound by the cautious, often skeptical outlook of the EU's twenty-five member governments and the citizens they represent. As Renaud Dehousse makes clear in his chapter, parallels drawn between the EU Constitution today and US version in the 1780s ultimately are rhetorical constructions; the European enterprise is simply a much less substantive or ambitious undertaking. For today's ardent European unionists, perhaps the most salient historical fact about USA's constitutional founding was its sheer audacity. A 'roof without walls,' a 'machine that would go of itself,' a 'miracle'—these were the terms Americans attached (and historians still apply) to their constitutional project and the ground-clearing institutional change it represented. Arguably, only such a sweeping renovation could draw US hearts and minds away from the separate states in which their political loyalties had long resided. The USA still struggles to equilibrate the balance of national, state, and local powers, but an indisputably decisive moment came when Americans took to the streets after 1787: not to bury their new national union, but to praise it.

As it happens, Europeans recently have taken to the streets in large numbers. Enormous popular demonstrations erupted on February 15, 2003 across the continent in opposition to the American war in Iraq, spurring French political heavyweight Dominique Strauss-Kahn to declare in *Le Monde* that 'a nation was born on the streets . . . the European nation.' Perhaps this prophecy will prove true, but historical experience suggests otherwise. Few enduring national unions have been forged by defining oneself against an Other. As anti-American virulence fades, what is the basis for a unified European nation? As long as the principal source of potential Euro-citizens' identity is their separate nation-states, as long as democratic legitimacy is lodged in their separate governments, so will the 'state of Europe' remain just that: at most a federal state, not a nation.

References

Balis, C. V. and Serfaty, S. (eds.) (2004). *Visions of America and Europe: September 11, Iraq, and Transatlantic Relations*. Washington, DC: Center for Strategic and International Studies Press.

Basler, R. (ed.) (1946). *Abraham Lincoln: His Speeches and Writings*. New York: Da Capo Press.

Beyers, J. (2004). 'Voice and Access', *European Union Politics* 5/2.

Carter, S. L. (1999). *Civility*. New York: Basic Books.

Coser, L. A. (1977). *The Sociology of Max Weber*. New York: Vintage Books.

Gerth, H. and Mills, C. W. (1958). *From Max Weber: Essays in Sociology*. New York: Oxford University Press.

Gilbert, M. (2004). 'A Fiasco but not a Disaster': Europe's Search for a Constitution', *World Policy Journal,* 21/1.

Gorin, S. (2000). 'Presidential Candidates Favor Active Roles in Foreign Policy', *Election 2000 Campaign Spotlight*. Washington, DC: US State Department, June 30, 2000: 2.

Gopnick, A. (2000). *From Paris to the Moon*. New York: Random House.

Gottschalk, M. (2000). *The Shadow Welfare State*. Ithaca, NY: Cornell University Press.

Hacker, J. (2002). *The Divided Welfare State: The Battle over Public and Private Social Benefits in the United States*. New York: Cambridge University Press.

Hall, P. and Soskice, D. (eds.) (2001). *Varieties of Capitalism: The Institutional Foundations of Comparative Advantage*. New York: Oxford University Press.

Jacobs, L. and Morone, J. (2004). 'Health and Wealth', *The American Prospect* (June): A20-1.

Kammen, M. (1987). *A Machine That Would Go of Itself: The Constitution in American Culture*. New York: Vintage.

Kersh, R. (2001). *Dreams of a More Perfect Union*. Ithaca, NY: Cornell University Press.

Kingdon, J. (1999). *America the Unusual*. New York: St Martin/Worth Publishers.

Lipsky, M. and Rathgeb Smith, S. (1995). *Non-Profits for Hire: The Welfare State in the Age of Contracting*. Cambridge: Harvard University Press.

Lucarelli, S. and Radaelli, C. M. (2004). 'The European Convention: A Process of Mobilization?' *South European Society & Politics*. 9/1: 16–9.

Majone, G. (1998). 'Europe's Democratic Deficit', *European Law Journal,* 4/1.

McLaughlin, C. G. (ed.) (2004). *Health Policy and the Uninsured*. Washington, DC: Urban Institute Press.

Mead, W. R. (2002). *Special Providence: American Foreign Policy and How it Changed the World*. New York: Routledge.

Moravcsik, A. (1998). *The Choice for Europe: Social Purpose and State Power from Messina to Maastricht*. Ithaca, NY: Cornell University Press.

Morone, J. (1998). *The Democratic Wish: Popular Participation and the Limits of American Government*. New Haven, CT: Yale University Press.

—— (2003). *Hellfire Nation: The Politics of Sin in American History*. New Haven, CT: Yale University Press.

—— and Jacobs, L. (eds.) (2005). *Healthy, Wealthy and Fair: Health Care for a Good Society*. New York: Oxford University Press.

Murrin, J. (1987). 'A Roof without Walls: The Dilemma of American National Identity', in R. Beeman et al. (eds.), *Beyond Confederation*. Chapel Hill, NC: University of North Carolina Press.

Norman, P. (2003). *The Accidental Constitution: The Story of the European Convention*. Brussels: EuroComment.

Pierson, Paul. (1994). *Dismantling the Welfare State?* New York: Cambridge University Press.

Pole, J. R. (1977). *The Idea of Union*. Alexandria, VA.: Bicentennial Council.

Rice, C. (2000). 'Campaign 2000: Promoting the National Interest', *Foreign Affairs*, 79.

Richardson, J. D. (1995). 'Income Inequality and Trade: How to Think, What to Conclude', *Journal of Economic Perspectives*, 9: 33–55;

Savas, E. S. (1987). *Privatization: The Key to Better Government*. Chatham, NJ: Chatham House.

Scharpf, F. (1999). *Governance in Europe*. Oxford: Oxford University Press.

Smeeding, T. (2002). 'Globalization, Inequality and the Rich Countries of the G-20: Evidence from the Luxembourg Study', Luxembourg Income Study Working Paper No. 320.

Sullivan, T. A., Warren, E. and Westbrook, J. L. (2000). *The Fragile Middle Class: Americans in Debt*. New Haven, CT: Yale University Press.

Thatcher, M. (2004). 'Varieties of Capitalism in an Internationalized World: Domestic Institutional Change in European Telecommunications', *Comparative Political Studies*, 37.

Waldo, D. (1948). *The Administrative State: A Study of the Political Theory of American Public Administration*. New York: The Ronald Press.

Waldstreicher, D. (1997). *In the Midst of Perpetual Fetes: The Making of American Nationalism, 1776–1820*. Chapel Hill, NC: University of North Carolina Press.

Woodward, B. (2004). *Plan of Attack*. New York: Simon & Schuster.

INDEX

The manufacturer's authorised representative in the EU for product safety is Oxford University Press España S.A. of el Parque Empresarial San Fernando de Henares, Avenida de Castilla, 2 – 28830 Madrid (www.oup.es/en or product.safety@oup.com). OUP España S.A. also acts as importer into Spain of products made by the manufacturer.

www.ingramcontent.com/pod-product-compliance
Lightning Source LLC
LaVergne TN
LVHW011859200926
848484LV00002B/486
9780199283958